D0652022

ULTIMATE POCKET BOOK OF THE WORLD ATLAS

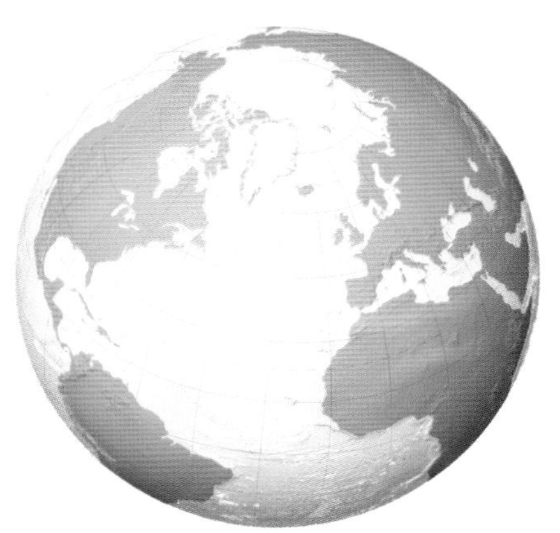

A DORLING KINDERSLEY BOOK

Project Cartography and Design
Julia Lunn, Peter Winfield

Cartographic Research Michael Martin

Project Editor and Index-Gazetteer
Jayne Parsons

Digital base maps produced on DK Cartopia by
Simon Lewis, Rob Stokes, Thomas Robertshaw

Production Controller Hilary Stephens

Editorial Director Andrew Heritage

Art Director Chez Picthall

First published in Great Britain in 1996
by Dorling Kindersley Limited,
9 Henrietta Street, London, WC2E 8PS
First published in this version 1998

Visit us on the World Wide Web at http://www.dk.com

A CIP catalogue record for this book is available from the British Library.

ISBN: 0-7513-0603-7

Film output in England, by Euroscan
Printed and bound in Italy, by L.E.G.O.

Ultimate Pocket Book of The World

Atlas

DORLING KINDERSLEY
LONDON • NEW YORK • STUTTGART • MOSCOW

Key

International border
Disputed border
Claimed border
International border along river
State border
State border along river
River
Lake
Canal
Seasonal river
Seasonal lake
Waterfall
Road
Railway
Capital city
Major town
Minor town
Major port
Minor port
International airport
Spot height – metres
Spot depth – metres

Contents

The Physical World 6-7
The Political World 8-9
Time Zones 10-11
The Arctic Ocean 12-13

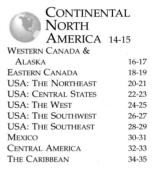

Continental North America 14-15
Western Canada & Alaska 16-17
Eastern Canada 18-19
USA: The Northeast 20-21
USA: Central States 22-23
USA: The West 24-25
USA: The Southwest 26-27
USA: The Southeast 28-29
Mexico 30-31
Central America 32-33
The Caribbean 34-35

Continental South America 36-37
Northern South America 38-39
Peru, Bolivia & North Brazil 40-41
Paraguay, Uruguay & South Brazil 42-43
Chile & Argentina 44-45
The Atlantic Ocean 46-47

Continental Africa 48-49

Northwest Africa 50-51
West Africa 52-53
Northeast Africa 54-55
Central Africa 56-57
Southern Africa 58-59

Continental Europe 60-61

The North Atlantic 62-63
Scandinavia & Finland 64-65
The Low Countries 66-67
The British Isles 68-69
France & Andorra 70-71
Spain & Portugal 72-73
Germany, Switzerland & Austria 74-75
Italy & Malta 76-77
Central Europe 78-79
The Western Balkans 80-81
The Mediterranean 82-83
Bulgaria & Greece 84-85
The Baltic States & Belorussia 86-87
Ukraine, Moldavia & Romania 88-89
European Russia 90-91

North & West Asia 92-93

Russia & Kazakhstan 94-95
Turkey, Cyprus & The Caucasus 96-97
The Near East 98-99
The Middle East 100-101
Central Asia 102-103

East & South Asia 104-105

Western China & Mongolia 106-107
Eastern China & Korea 108-109
Japan 110-111
The Indian Ocean 112-113
North India, Pakistan & Bangladesh 114-115
Southern India 116-117
Mainland Southeast Asia 118-119
Maritime Southeast Asia 120-121
The Pacific Ocean 122-123

Australasia & Oceania 124-125

The Southwest Pacific 126-127
Western Australia 128-129
Southeast Australia 130
New Zealand 131
Antarctica 132-133

Glossary of abbreviations 134
Index 135

THE PHYSICAL WORLD

A
B
C
D
1
2
3
4
5
ARCTIC OCEAN
Franz Josef Land
Severnaya Zemlya
Svalbard
New Siberian Is
Greenland Sea
Novaya Zemlya
Laptev Sea
North Cape
Barents Sea
Kara Sea
Denmark Strait
Lapland
Scandinavia
Central Siberian Plateau
Lena
Khrebet Cherskogo
Norwegian Sea
Yenisey
Iceland
Ural Mts.
Ob'
Siberia
Kamchatka
Volga
North Sea
Baltic Sea
Sea of Okhotsk
British Isles
EUROPE
L. Baikal
ASIA
Sakhalin
Danube
Alps
Aral Sea
Bay of Biscay
Black Sea
L. Balkhash
Altai Mts.
Manchurian Plain
Kurile Is
Tien Shan
Gobi
Caspian Sea
Sea of Japan
Hokkaidō
Iberia
Anatolia
Hindu Kush
Plateau of Tibet
Yellow R.
Yellow Sea
Honshū
Mediterranean Sea
Zagros Mts.
Iranian Plateau
Madeira
Atlas Mts.
Himalayas
Yangtze
East China Sea
Kyūshū
Canary Is.
Ganges
Thar Desert
Taiwan
Sahara
Arabian Peninsula
Cape Verde Is.
AFRICA
Red Sea
Deccan
Philippine Sea
Mekong
Arabian Sea
Bay of Bengal
South China Sea
Sahel
L. Chad
Ethiopian Highlands
Horn of Africa
Niger
Philippine Islands
Great Rift Valley
Nile
Sri Lanka
Borneo
Melanesia
Somali Basin
Gulf of Guinea
East Indies
New Guinea
Congo
L. Victoria
Congo Basin
Sumatra
Java Sea
Timor
Mid-Atlantic Ridge
L. Tanganyika
Seychelles
Angola Basin
Java
Timor Sea
L. Nyasa
Mozambique Channel
INDIAN
Great Barrier Reef
Zambezi
Arnhem Land
Namib Desert
Mauritius
Réunion
Kalahari Desert
AUSTRALIA
Madagascar
Great Victoria Desert
Cape Basin
OCEAN
Darling
Drakensberg
Cape of Good Hope
Southwest Indian Ridge
Bass Strait
Tasmania
Kerguelen
South Sandwich Is.
Dronning Maud Land
ANTARCTICA
Wilkes Land

E
F
G
H
ARCTIC OCEAN
Ellesmere I.
Limit of permanent pack ice
Queen Elizabeth Islands
Greenland
Baffin Bay
Chukchi Sea
Beaufort Sea
Baffin I.
Bering Strait
Brooks Range
Great Bear Lake
Davis Strait
Arctic Circle
Yukon
Mackenzie
Great Slave Lake
Iceland
Rocky Mountains
Hudson Bay
Labrador Sea
Bering Sea
Gulf of Alaska
Mid-Atlantic Ridge
Aleutian Islands
Labrador
Vancouver I.
NORTH AMERICA
Missouri
Great Lakes
Grand Banks
St Lawrence
Emperor Seamounts
North American Basin
Mississippi
Baja California
Sierra Madre
Gulf of Mexico
ATLANTIC
Tropic of Cancer
Hawaiian Is.
West Indies
PACIFIC
Caribbean Sea
OCEAN
Polynesia
OCEAN
Guiana Highlands
Equator
Micronesia
Amazon
Galapagos Is.
Amazon Basin
Andes
SOUTH AMERICA
Brazil Basin
Fiji
Tahiti
Mato Grosso
New Caledonia
Kermadec Trench
Peru Basin
Tropic of Capricorn
Paraná
Pampas
North I.
Southwest Pacific Basin
Argentine Basin
New Zealand
Patagonia
South I.
Falkland Is.
Tierra del Fuego
South Georgia
Cape Horn
Southeast Pacific Basin
Drake Passage
Antarctic Peninsula
Antarctic Circle
Ross Sea
ANTARCTICA
Weddell Sea
1
2
3
4
5

THE POLITICAL WORLD

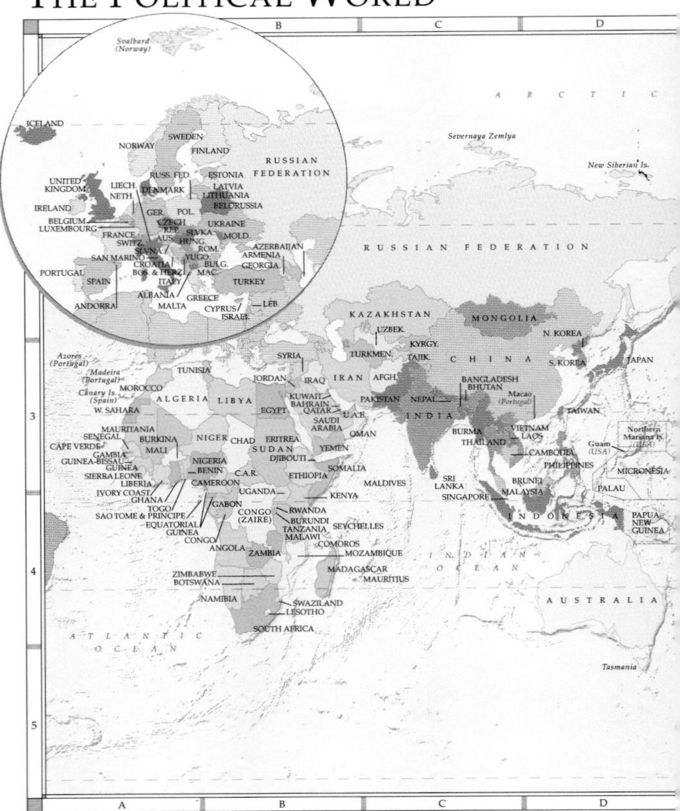

A
B
C
D
Svalbard (Norway)
ICELAND
NORWAY
SWEDEN
FINLAND
RUSSIAN FEDERATION
UNITED KINGDOM
IRELAND
RUSS. FED.
ESTONIA
LATVIA
LITHUANIA
BELORUSSIA
LIECH.
DENMARK
NETH.
GER.
POL.
BELGIUM
LUXEMBOURG
CZECH REP.
UKRAINE
FRANCE
SLVKA.
MOLD.
SWITZ.
AUS.
HUNG.
ROM.
SLVNA.
SAN MARINO
CROATIA
YUGO.
AZERBAIJAN
ARMENIA
GEORGIA
PORTUGAL
BOS. & HERZ.
BULG.
MAC.
SPAIN
ITALY
TURKEY
ALBANIA
GREECE
ANDORRA
MALTA
CYPRUS
ISRAEL
LEB.
A R C T I C
Severnaya Zemlya
New Siberian Is.
RUSSIAN FEDERATION
KAZAKHSTAN
MONGOLIA
UZBEK.
N. KOREA
KYRGY.
TURKMEN.
TAJIK.
CHINA
S. KOREA
JAPAN
Azores (Portugal)
Madeira (Portugal)
Canary Is. (Spain)
TUNISIA
SYRIA
JORDAN
IRAQ
IRAN
AFGH.
BANGLADESH
BHUTAN
MOROCCO
ALGERIA
LIBYA
KUWAIT
BAHRAIN
QATAR
PAKISTAN
NEPAL
Macao (Portugal)
W. SAHARA
EGYPT
U.A.E.
INDIA
TAIWAN
3
MAURITANIA
SAUDI ARABIA
BURMA
VIETNAM
Northern Mariana Is.
SENEGAL
OMAN
LAOS
CAPE VERDE
BURKINA
NIGER
CHAD
ERITREA
THAILAND
Guam (USA)
GAMBIA
MALI
SUDAN
YEMEN
CAMBODIA
GUINEA-BISSAU
NIGERIA
DJIBOUTI
PHILIPPINES
GUINEA
BENIN
C.A.R.
SOMALIA
MICRONESIA
SIERRA LEONE
ETHIOPIA
LIBERIA
CAMEROON
MALDIVES
SRI LANKA
BRUNEI
IVORY COAST
UGANDA
MALAYSIA
PALAU
GHANA
KENYA
SINGAPORE
TOGO
GABON
SAO TOME & PRINCIPE
CONGO (ZAIRE)
RWANDA
INDONESIA
PAPUA NEW GUINEA
EQUATORIAL GUINEA
BURUNDI
TANZANIA
SEYCHELLES
MALAWI
CONGO
COMOROS
ANGOLA
ZAMBIA
MOZAMBIQUE
INDIAN OCEAN
4
MADAGASCAR
ZIMBABWE
MAURITIUS
BOTSWANA
NAMIBIA
AUSTRALIA
SWAZILAND
LESOTHO
SOUTH AFRICA
ATLANTIC OCEAN
Tasmania
5

For full list of abbreviations see page 134.

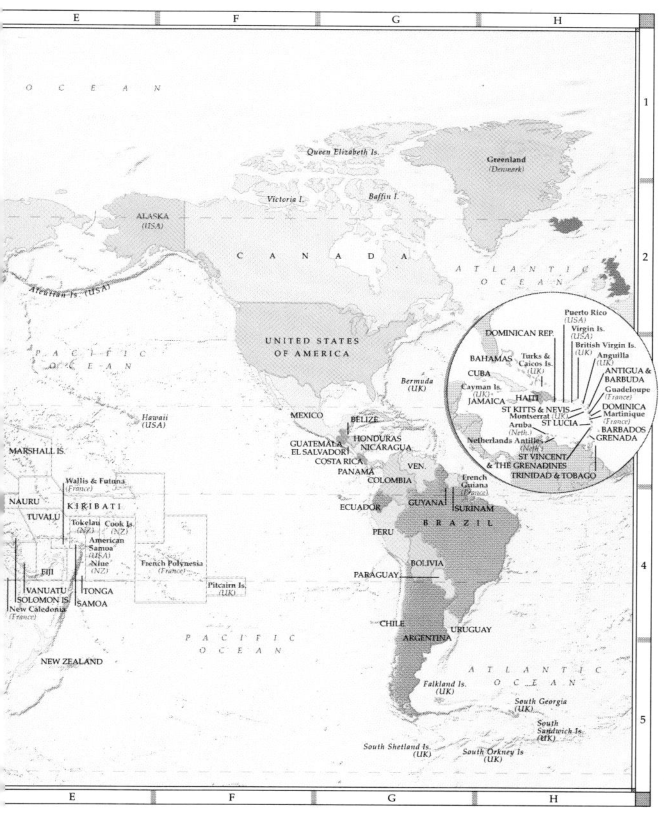
E
F
G
H
1
2
4
5
O C E A N
Queen Elizabeth Is.
Greenland
(Denmark)
Victoria I.
Baffin I.
ALASKA
(USA)
C A N A D A
A T L A N T I C
O C E A N
Aleutian Is. (USA)
UNITED STATES
OF AMERICA
P A C I F I C
O C E A N
Bermuda
(UK)
Hawaii
(USA)
MEXICO
BELIZE
GUATEMALA
EL SALVADOR
HONDURAS
NICARAGUA
COSTA RICA
PANAMA
VEN.
COLOMBIA
French
Guiana
(France)
GUYANA
SURINAM
ECUADOR
B R A Z I L
PERU
BOLIVIA
PARAGUAY
CHILE
ARGENTINA
URUGUAY
Puerto Rico
(USA)
Virgin Is.
(USA)
British Virgin Is.
(UK)
Anguilla
(UK)
DOMINICAN REP.
BAHAMAS
Turks &
Caicos Is.
(UK)
CUBA
ANTIGUA &
BARBUDA
Guadeloupe
(France)
Cayman Is.
(UK)
JAMAICA
HAITI
DOMINICA
Martinique
(France)
ST KITTS & NEVIS
Montserrat (UK)
Aruba
(Neth.)
ST LUCIA
BARBADOS
GRENADA
Netherlands Antilles
(Neth.)
ST VINCENT
& THE GRENADINES
TRINIDAD & TOBAGO
MARSHALL IS.
Wallis & Futuna
(France)
NAURU
KIRIBATI
TUVALU
Tokelau
(NZ)
Cook Is.
(NZ)
American
Samoa
(USA)
Niue
(NZ)
FIJI
French Polynesia
(France)
Pitcairn Is.
(UK)
VANUATU
TONGA
SOLOMON IS.
SAMOA
New Caledonia
(France)
P A C I F I C
O C E A N
NEW ZEALAND
A T L A N T I C
O C E A N
Falkland Is.
(UK)
South Georgia
(UK)
South
Sandwich Is.
(UK)
South Shetland Is.
(UK)
South Orkney Is
(UK)

TIME ZONES

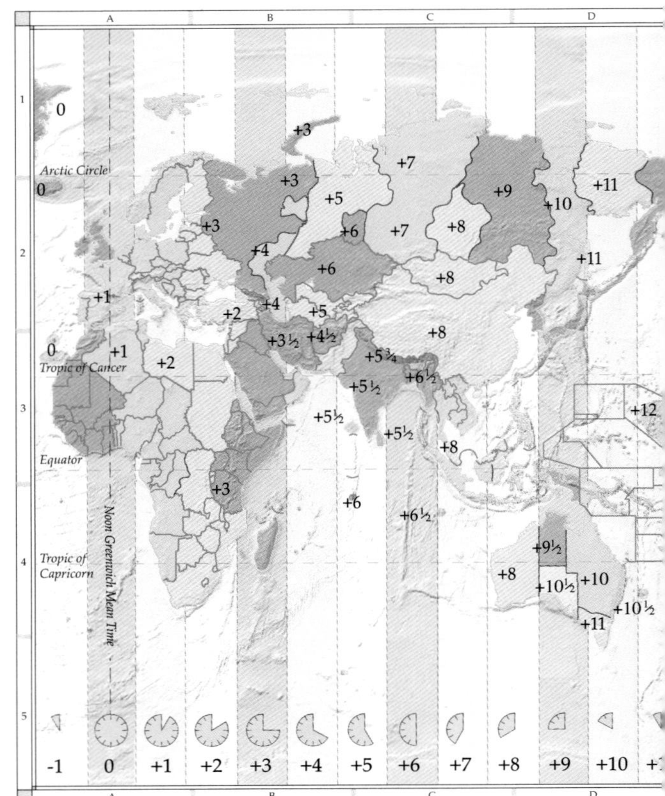

A
B
C
D
1
2
3
4
5
0
+3
+7
Arctic Circle
0
+3
+5
+9
+11
+10
+3
+6
+7
+8
+4
+11
+6
+8
+1
+4
+5
+2
+8
0
+3½
+4½
+1
+5¾
Tropic of Cancer
+2
+6½
+5½
+12
+5½
+5½
+8
Equator
+3
+6
+6½
Noon Greenwich Mean Time
+9½
Tropic of Capricorn
+8
+10
+10½
+10½
+11
-1
0
+1
+2
+3
+4
+5
+6
+7
+8
+9
+10

Numbers on the map show the number of hours ahead of, or behind, GMT.

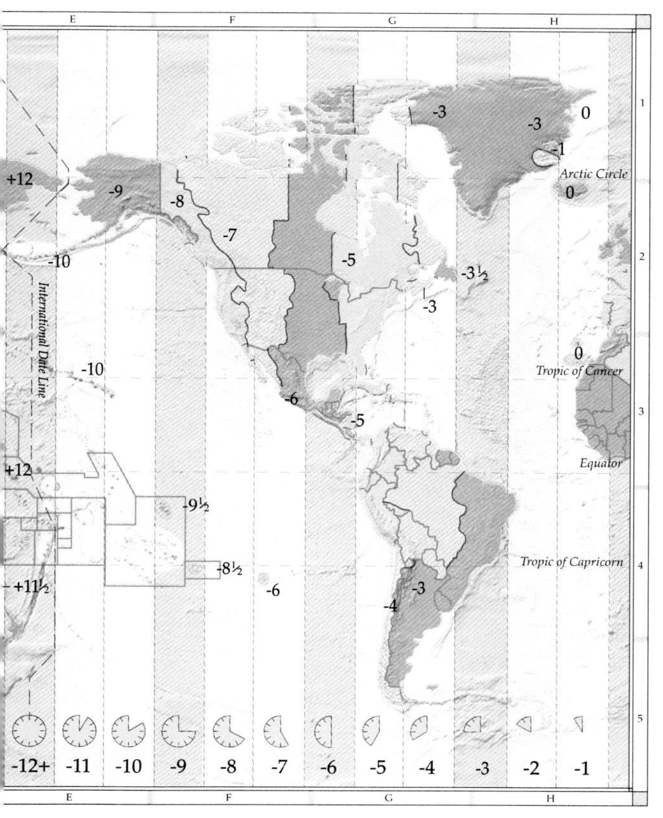
E
F
G
H
1
2
3
4
5
-3
-3
0
-1
Arctic Circle
0
+12
-9
-8
-7
-5
-10
-3½
-3
International Date Line
0
-10
Tropic of Cancer
-6
-5
Equator
+12
-9½
Tropic of Capricorn
-8½
+11½
-6
-3
-4
-12+
-11
-10
-9
-8
-7
-6
-5
-4
-3
-2
-1

THE ARCTIC OCEAN

ASIA
Lena
Tiksi
Laptev Sea
92
East Siberian Sea
New Siberian Is. (Russ. Fed.)
Severnaya Zemlya (Russ. Fed.)
Lomonosov (Harris) Ridge
ARCTIC OCEAN
Pevek
Wrangel I. (Russ. Fed.)
Arctic Circle
122
Chukchi Sea
Bering Strait
Limit of permanent pack ice
Fram (Angara) Basin
North Pole
Canada (Laurentian) Basin
NORTH AMERICA
14
Beaufort Sea
Prince Patrick I. (Canada)
Axel Heiberg I. (Canada)
Melville I. (Canada)
Bathurst I. (Canada)
Queen Elizabeth Is. (Canada)
Banks I. (Canada)
Tuktoyaktuk
Mackenzie

0 km 500

0 miles 500

Devon I.
(Canada)
Ellesmere I.
(Canada)
Nares Strait
Lincoln
Sea
Knud Rasmussen Land
Baffin
Bay
Wandel
Sea
Franz Josef Land
(Russ. Fed.)
Novaya Zemlya
(Russ. Fed.)
Kara
Sea
Greenland
(Denmark)
Svalbard
(Norway)
Spitsbergen
Longyearbyen
Greenland
Sea
Limit of temporary pack ice
Barents
Sea
Greenland
Basin
North Cape
Murmansk
Hammerfest
Tromsø
Arctic Circle
Ittoqqortoormiit
Jan Mayen
(Norway)
Denmark Strait
Narvik
EUROPE
ICELAND
Reykjavik
Norwegian
Sea
Gulf of Bothnia
60
ATLANTIC
OCEAN
46
5
6
7
8
A
B
C
D
E

CONTINENTAL NORTH AMERICA

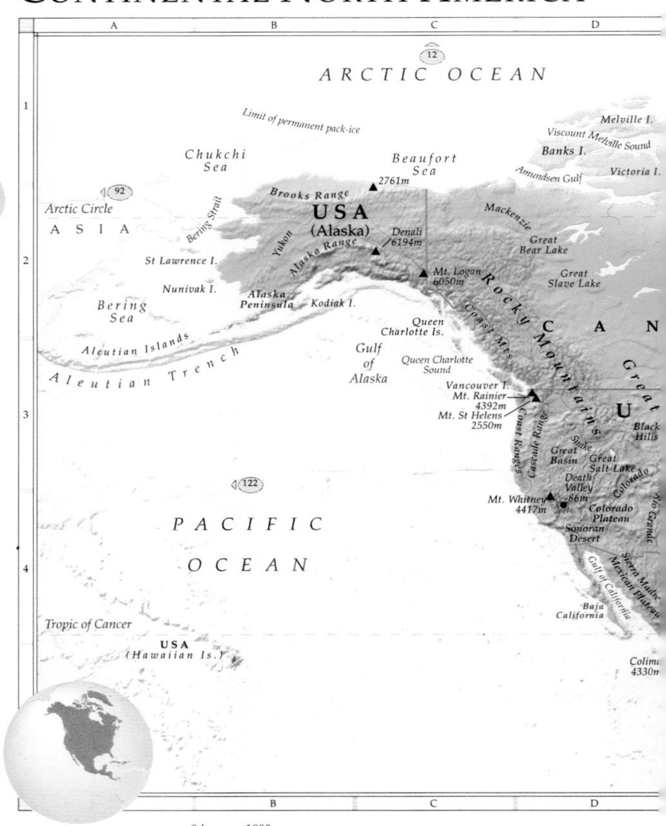
A
B
C
D
1
2
3
4
12
ARCTIC OCEAN
Limit of permanent pack-ice
Melville I.
Viscount Melville Sound
Banks I.
Chukchi Sea
Beaufort Sea
Amundsen Gulf
Victoria I.
2761m
92
Brooks Range
Arctic Circle
USA (Alaska)
Mackenzie
ASIA
Bering Strait
Yukon
Denali 6194m
Great Bear Lake
Alaska Range
St Lawrence I.
Mt. Logan 6050m
Great Slave Lake
Nunivak I.
Alaska Peninsula
Kodiak I.
Bering Sea
Queen Charlotte Is.
Coast Mts
Rocky Mountains
CAN
Aleutian Islands
Gulf of Alaska
Queen Charlotte Sound
Aleutian Trench
Vancouver I.
Mt. Rainier 4392m
Mt. St Helens 2550m
U
Black Hills
Coast Ranges
Cascade Range
Snake
Great Basin
Great Salt Lake
Death Valley -86m
Colorado
Rio Grande
122
Mt. Whitney 4417m
Colorado Plateau
Sonoran Desert
PACIFIC OCEAN
Sierra Madre
Mexican Plateau
Gulf of California
Baja California
Tropic of Cancer
USA (Hawaiian Is.)
Colima 4330m
0 km 1000
0 miles 1000

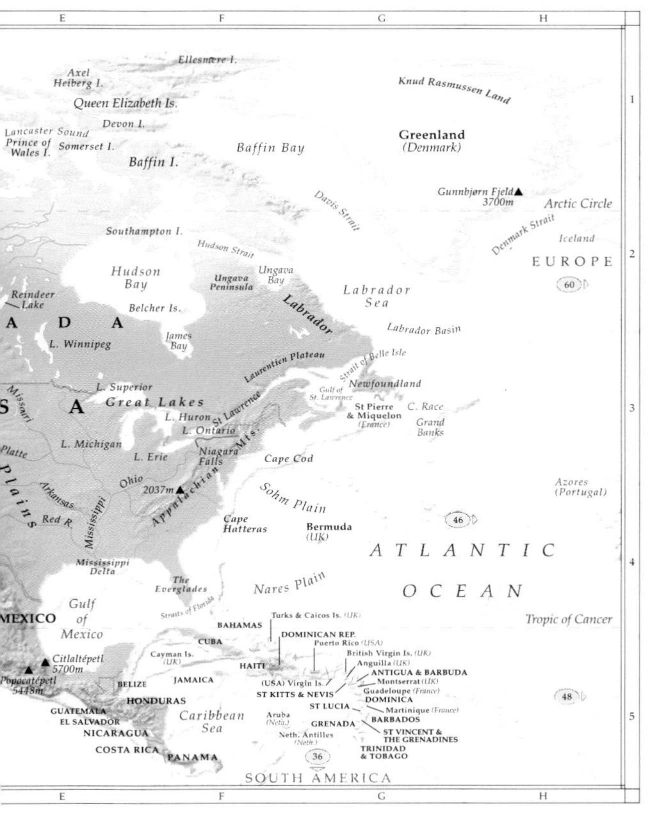
E
F
G
H
1
2
3
4
5
Ellesmere I.
Axel Heiberg I.
Queen Elizabeth Is.
Knud Rasmussen Land
Devon I.
Lancaster Sound
Prince of Wales I.
Somerset I.
Baffin I.
Baffin Bay
Greenland (Denmark)
Davis Strait
Gunnbjørn Fjeld 3700m
Arctic Circle
Denmark Strait
Iceland
Southampton I.
Hudson Strait
EUROPE
Hudson Bay
Ungava Peninsula
Ungava Bay
60
Reindeer Lake
Labrador
Labrador Sea
Belcher Is.
A D A
Labrador Basin
James Bay
L. Winnipeg
Laurentien Plateau
Strait of Belle Isle
Newfoundland
L. Superior
Missouri
Gulf of St. Lawrence
S A
Great Lakes
St Lawrence
St Pierre & Miquelon (France)
C. Race
Grand Banks
L. Huron
L. Ontario
Platte
L. Michigan
L. Erie
Niagara Falls
Cape Cod
Plains
Ohio
2037m
Appalachian Mts.
Arkansas
Sohm Plain
Azores (Portugal)
Red R.
Mississippi
Cape Hatteras
Bermuda (UK)
46
ATLANTIC
OCEAN
Mississippi Delta
The Everglades
Nares Plain
Gulf of Mexico
MEXICO
Straits of Florida
Turks & Caicos Is. (UK)
BAHAMAS
Tropic of Cancer
DOMINICAN REP.
CUBA
Puerto Rico (USA)
Citlaltépetl 5700m
Cayman Is. (UK)
British Virgin Is. (UK)
Anguilla (UK)
HAITI
Popocatépetl 5448m
ANTIGUA & BARBUDA
BELIZE
JAMAICA
(USA) Virgin Is.
Montserrat (UK)
Guadeloupe (France)
ST KITTS & NEVIS
DOMINICA
HONDURAS
48
ST LUCIA
Martinique (France)
GUATEMALA
Caribbean Sea
Aruba (Neth.)
BARBADOS
EL SALVADOR
GRENADA
NICARAGUA
ST VINCENT & THE GRENADINES
Neth. Antilles (Neth.)
COSTA RICA
TRINIDAD & TOBAGO
PANAMA
36
SOUTH AMERICA

WESTERN CANADA & ALASKA

A
B
C
D
1
2
3
4
60°
180°
94
RUSSIAN FEDERATION
Wrangel I.
Arctic Circle
12
Attu I.
Bering Sea
Bering Strait
Kiska I.
St. Lawrence I.
Prudho Bay
Brooks Range
Aleutian Islands
180°
Nunivak I.
Yukon
ALASKA (USA)
Fairbanks
Alaska Range
Umnak I.
Dutch Harbor
Unalaska I.
Anchorage
Dawsor
Valdez
Kodiak I.
Kodiak
Cordova
Aleutian Trench
YUKON TERRITORY
WHITEHORSE
Gulf of Alaska
JUNEAU
Ketchikan
PACIFIC OCEAN
Prince Rupert
Queen Charlotte Is.
Queen Charlotte Sound
122
Port Alice
Vancouver I.
140°
VICTORI

0 km 400
0 miles 400

E
F
G
H
160°
140°
120°
100°
80°
60°
80°
40°
Ellesmere I.
Greenland
(Denmark)
1
I C
Axel Heiberg I.
40°
N
Queen Elizabeth Is.
Bathurst I.
Devon I.
Baffin Bay
Melville I.
Parry Is.
Lancaster Sound
Resolute
Davis Strait
2
Viscount Melville Sound
Somerset I.
Beaufort Sea
Banks I.
Prince of Wales I.
Baffin I.
60°
Amundsen Gulf
Victoria I.
King William I.
Arctic Circle
Inuvik
Iqaluit
Coppermine
Hudson Strait
60°
3
Great Bear L.
Southampton I.
NORTHWEST TERRITORIES
Mackenzie
YELLOWKNIFE
Dubawnt
Rankin Inlet
QUÉBEC
Hudson Bay
Great Slave L.
Watson Lake
Hay River
Fort Smith
Churchill
4
ALBERTA
L. Athabasca
MANITOBA
Fort St. John
Fort McMurray
CANADA
Flin Flon
Thompson
Grande Prairie
SASKATCHEWAN
18
80°
EDMONTON
Saskatchewan
L. Winnipeg
Prince George
ONTARIO
Leduc
Prince Albert
L. Winnipegosis
Red Deer
Saskatoon
5
Kamloops
Yorkton
Vancouver
Calgary
REGINA
WINNIPEG
Kelowna
Brandon
20
Lethbridge
Estevan
120°
100°
USA

EASTERN CANADA

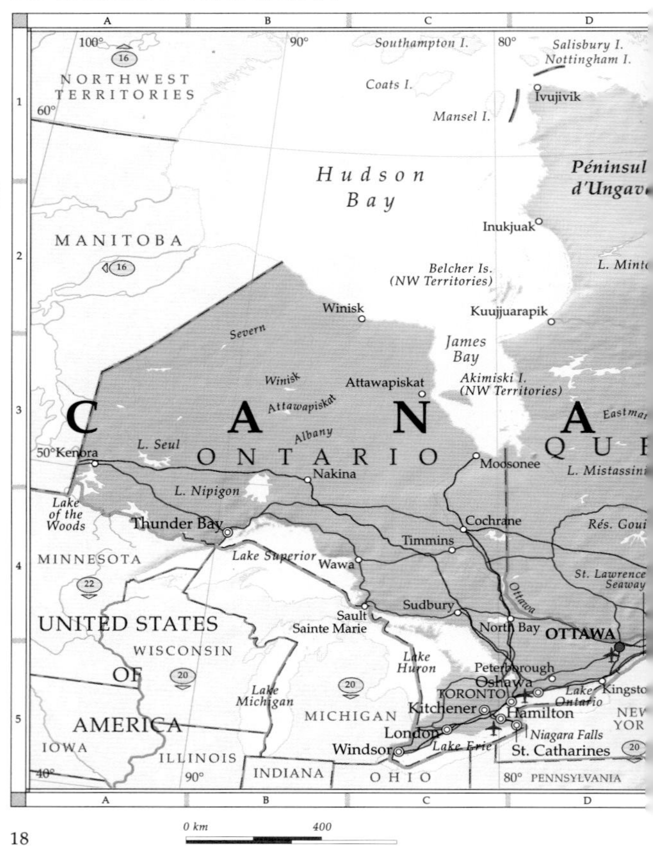
A
B
C
D
1
2
3
4
5
100°
90°
80°
60°
50°
40°
Southampton I.
Salisbury I.
Nottingham I.
NORTHWEST TERRITORIES
Coats I.
Ivujivik
Mansel I.
Hudson Bay
Péninsul
d'Ungav
Inukjuak
MANITOBA
L. Mint
Belcher Is. (NW Territories)
Winisk
Kuujjuarapik
Severn
James Bay
Winisk
Attawapiskat
Akimiski I. (NW Territories)
Attawapiskat
Eastma
CANADA
Albany
L. Seul
Kenora
ONTARIO
QU
Moosonee
Nakina
L. Mistassini
L. Nipigon
Lake of the Woods
Thunder Bay
Cochrane
Rés. Gou
Timmins
MINNESOTA
Lake Superior
Wawa
St. Lawrence Seaway
Ottawa
Sudbury
Sault Sainte Marie
UNITED STATES OF AMERICA
North Bay
OTTAWA
WISCONSIN
Lake Huron
Peterborough
Oshawa
TORONTO
Lake Ontario
Kingsto
Lake Michigan
MICHIGAN
Kitchener
Hamilton
NEW YOR
London
Niagara Falls
IOWA
Windsor
Lake Erie
St. Catharines
ILLINOIS
INDIANA
OHIO
PENNSYLVANIA
16
22
20
0 km 400
0 miles 400

E
F
G
H
70°
60°
50°
Baffin I.
Labrador Sea
Hudson Strait
C. Chidley
Akpatok I. (NW Territories)
Labrador Basin
Ungava Bay
ATLANTIC OCEAN
Kuujjuaq
Nain
Caniapiscau
Hopedale
Makkovik
NEWFOUNDLAND
Cartwright
Schefferville
Labrador
Port Hope Simpson
Smallwood Reservoir
Happy Valley-Goose Bay
Réservoir Caniapiscau
Churchill Falls
Strait of Belle Isle
Labrador City
Newfoundland
Havre-Saint-Pierre
Gander
Réservoir Manicouagan
Grand Falls
Clarenville
ST JOHN'S
Sept-Îles
Île d'Anticosti
Corner Brook
St. Lawrence
Gulf of St.Lawrence
L. Saint-Jean
Gaspé
Channel-Port-aux-Basques
C. Race
Jonquière
Cabot Strait
St Pierre
Chicoutimi
PRINCE EDWARD ISLAND
St Pierre & Miquelon (France)
Bathurst
Grand Banks
NEW BRUNSWICK
Sydney
QUÉBEC
CHARLOTTETOWN
FREDERICTON
Moncton
NOVA SCOTIA
Trois-Rivières
MAINE
Sherbrooke
Saint John
Dartmouth
HALIFAX
Montréal
Sohm Plain
Yarmouth
NEW HAMPSHIRE
C. Sable
VERMONT
MASSACHUSETTS
RHODE ISLAND
CONNECTICUT
1
2
3
4

USA: THE NORTHEAST

A
B
C
D
1
2
3
4
5
90°
80°
40°
CA
MINNESOTA
ONTARIO
Lake Superior
Superior
Marquette
Sault Ste Marie
Cheboygan
Lake Huron
WISCONSIN
MICHIGAN
Eau Claire
Traverse City
Green Bay
La Crosse
Mississippi
Lake Michigan
Oshkosh
Bay City
Saginaw
Flint
MADISON
Milwaukee
Grand Rapids
LANSING
IOWA
Rockford
Detroit
Ann Arbor
Chicago
Lake Erie
Aurora
Joliet
Gary
South Bend
Toledo
Rock Island
Galesburg
Peoria
Fort Wayne
Akron
Youngstown
Canton
Lima
Wheeling
ILLINOIS
INDIANA
OHIO
Muncie
SPRINGFIELD
COLUMBUS
Decatur
INDIANAPOLIS
Dayton
UNITED STATES OF AME
Cincinnati
Missouri
East St Louis
Bloomington
Wabash
Ohio
Huntington
Louisville
Mt. Vernon
CHARLESTON
MISSOURI
Evansville
FRANKFORT
Lexington
WEST VIRGINIA
Carbondale
KENTUCKY
Paducah
Bowling Green
Cumberland
Hopkinsville
ARKANSAS
TENNESSEE
22
18
28
0 km
200
0 miles
200

E
F
G
H
70°
CANADA
QUÉBEC
18
NEW BRUNSWICK
18
Presque Isle
MAINE
Calais
Bay of Fundy
Bangor
NOVA SCOTIA
Ottawa
St Lawrence
AUGUSTA
Lewiston
Ogdensburg
Burlington
MONTPELIER
VERMONT
NEW HAMPSHIRE
Portland
Watertown
Rutland
CONCORD
Georges Bank
Lake Ontario
Utica
Manchester
Syracuse
BOSTON
Buffalo
Rochester
ALBANY
Worcester
Cape Cod
Niagara Falls
NEW YORK
Springfield
MASSACHUSETTS
Elmira
Binghamton
PROVIDENCE
HARTFORD
RHODE ISLAND
Hudson
Scranton
Appalachian Mts
CONNECTICUT
Williamsport
New Haven
PENNSYLVANIA
Newark
New York
Long Island
40°
Allentown
HARRISBURG
TRENTON
Philadelphia
NEW JERSEY
Gettysburg
Wilmington
Atlantic City
Cumberland
Baltimore
DOVER
DELAWARE
ATLANTIC OCEAN
WASHINGTON D.C.
ANNAPOLIS
Delaware Bay
MARYLAND
Appalachian Mts
Charlottesville
46
RICHMOND
Chesapeake Bay
VIRGINIA
Newport News
Roanoke
Norfolk
Danville
NORTH CAROLINA
70°
1
2
3
4

USA: Central States

A
B
C
D
1
2
3
4
5
120°
110°
40°
BRITISH COLUMBIA
ALBERTA
CANADA
SASKATCHEWAN
16
WASHINGTON
Kalispell
Havre
Malta
Glasgow
Fort Peck L.
Missouri
Williston
Great Falls
Missoula
MONTANA
Glendive
L. Sakakawea
HELENA
OREGON
Butte
Bozeman
Yellowstone
Dickinson
Miles City
Billings
Snake
Powder
Bighorn Mts.
Sheridan
SOUTH
24
IDAHO
Gillette
Black Hills
Rapid City
WYOMING
UNITED STATES
Rocky Mountains
Casper
Torrington
Scottsbluff
Great Salt Lake
Rock Springs
Ogden
N. Platte
SALT LAKE CITY
Laramie
CHEYENNE
Ogallala
Orem
Fort Collins
Provo
NEVADA
UTAH
Boulder
DENVER
Grand Junction
Lakewood
Aurora
Salina
Colorado Springs
Colorado
COLORADO
Arkansas
L. Powell
Durango
L. Mead
ARIZONA
NEW MEXICO
26
Canadian
0 km 200
0 miles 200

CANADA
MANITOBA
Lake of the Woods
ONTARIO
MINNESOTA
Lake Superior
MICHIGAN
Grand Forks
Virginia
DAKOTA
Duluth
Moorhead
Fargo
BISMARCK
Brainerd
WISCONSIN
Aberdeen
St Cloud
Minneapolis
ST PAUL
DAKOTA
Watertown
Lake Michigan
PIERRE
Rochester
Mitchell
Sioux Falls
Mason City
OF AMERICA
Missouri
Dubuque
Valentine
Sioux City
IOWA
Cedar Rapids
RASKA
DES MOINES
Davenport
INDIANA
North Platte
Columbus
Omaha
Council Bluffs
Burlington
Platte
LINCOLN
Hastings
Mississippi
ILLINOIS
Kirksville
St Joseph
Kansas City
Independence
Oakley
Hays
TOPEKA
Missouri
ST LOUIS
Kansas City
Jefferson City
Ohio
KANSAS
MISSOURI
KENTUCKY
Pratt
Dodge City
Wichita
Springfield
Arkansas
Ozark Plateau
OKLAHOMA
ARKANSAS
100°
90°
50°
80°
40°
18
20
26
28
E
F
G
H
1
2
3
4

USA: The West

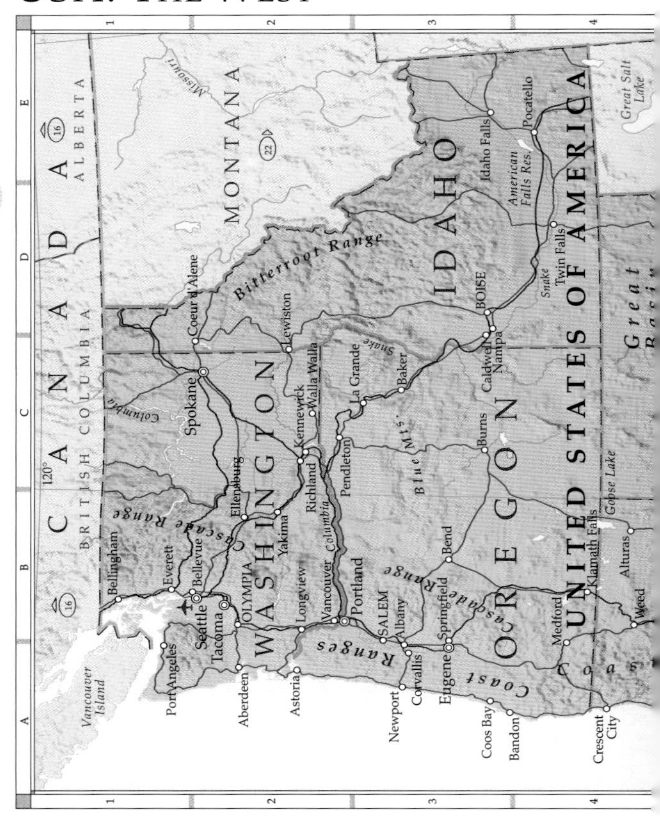
CANADA
ALBERTA
BRITISH COLUMBIA
MONTANA
IDAHO
WASHINGTON
OREGON
UNITED STATES OF AMERICA
Vancouver Island
Missouri
Columbia
Snake
Bitterroot Range
Cascade Range
Coast Ranges
Blue Mts
Great Salt Lake
American Falls Res.
Goose Lake
Great Basin
Bellingham
Everett
Bellevue
Seattle
Tacoma
OLYMPIA
Port Angeles
Aberdeen
Astoria
Longview
Vancouver
Portland
SALEM
Albany
Corvallis
Newport
Eugene
Springfield
Coos Bay
Bandon
Bend
Medford
Klamath Falls
Crescent City
Weed
Alturas
Yakima
Ellensburg
Richland
Kennewick
Walla Walla
Pendleton
La Grande
Baker
Burns
Spokane
Coeur d'Alene
Lewiston
BOISE
Nampa
Caldwell
Twin Falls
Idaho Falls
Pocatello
120°
16
22

0 km 200
0 miles 200

Redding
Susanville
Elko
NEVADA
UTAH
Humboldt
Pyramid Lake
Chico
Reno
Sparks
Fallon
Yuba City
Lake Tahoe
CARSON CITY
Ely
22
SACRAMENTO
Auburn
Santa Rosa
Hawthorne
Sierra Nevada
Concord
Stockton
San Francisco
Oakland
Tonopah
Modesto
San Jose
Bishop
Merced
Santa Cruz
Salinas
Monterey
Coast Ranges
San Joaquin
Fresno
Death Valley
Visalia
North Las Vegas
Lake Mead
Colorado
CALIFORNIA
Las Vegas
122
Bakersfield
Mojave Desert
PACIFIC
OCEAN
Mojave
Barstow
ARIZONA
Lancaster
26
Santa Barbara
Pasadena
Oxnard
San Bernardino
Los Angeles
Riverside
Santa Rosa I.
Long Beach
Santa Ana
Palm Springs
Channel Islands
Santa Catalina I.
Oceanside
San Nicolas I.
Salton Sea
San Clemente I.
San Diego
30
MEXICO
40°
120°
5
6
7
8
B
C
D
E

USA: The Southwest

A
B
C
D
1
2
3
4
110°
24
NEVADA
UTAH
COLORADO
L. Powell
Monument Valley
L. Mead
Grand Canyon
Painted Desert
Colorado Plateau
Farmington
Taos
Rio Grande
Los Alamos
Gallup
SANTA FE
24
CALIFORNIA
Flagstaff
Albuquerque
Pecos
UNITED STATES
Prescott
ARIZONA
NEW MEXICO
Colorado
Glendale
Scottsdale
Mesa
PHOENIX
Sonoran Desert
Yuma
Roswell
Alamogordo
Artesia
Casa Grande
Tucson
Las Cruces
Carlsbad
El Paso
Douglas
Rio Grande
30°
Baja California
Golfo de California
122
PACIFIC OCEAN
MEXICO
30
110°
B
C
D
0 km
200
0 miles
200

E
F
G
H
1
2
3
4
5
100°
22
KANSAS
MISSOURI
OKLAHOMA
OKLAHOMA CITY
Ponca City
Enid
Tulsa
Broken Arrow
Shawnee
Norman
Lawton
Borger
Pampa
Amarillo
OF AMERICA
Arkansas
ARKANSAS
28
Clovis
Portales
Red River
Vernon
Paris
Wichita Falls
Denton
Lubbock
Brownfield
Hobbs
Fort Worth
Dallas
Tyler
Longview
LOUISIANA
Abilene
Sweetwater
Big Spring
Jacksonville
Toledo Bend Res.
Odessa
Midland
San Angelo
Pecos
Colorado
Brazos
Waco
Neches
L. Livingston
TEXAS
Bryan
L. Travis
AUSTIN
30°
Beaumont
Port Arthur
Edwards Plateau
Houston
Pasadena
Texas City
Galveston
Freeport
San Antonio
Del Rio
Victoria
Eagle Pass
Corpus Christi
Kingsville
Laredo
CO
Gulf of Mexico
Padre Island
Rio Grande
Brownsville
100°

USA: The Southeast

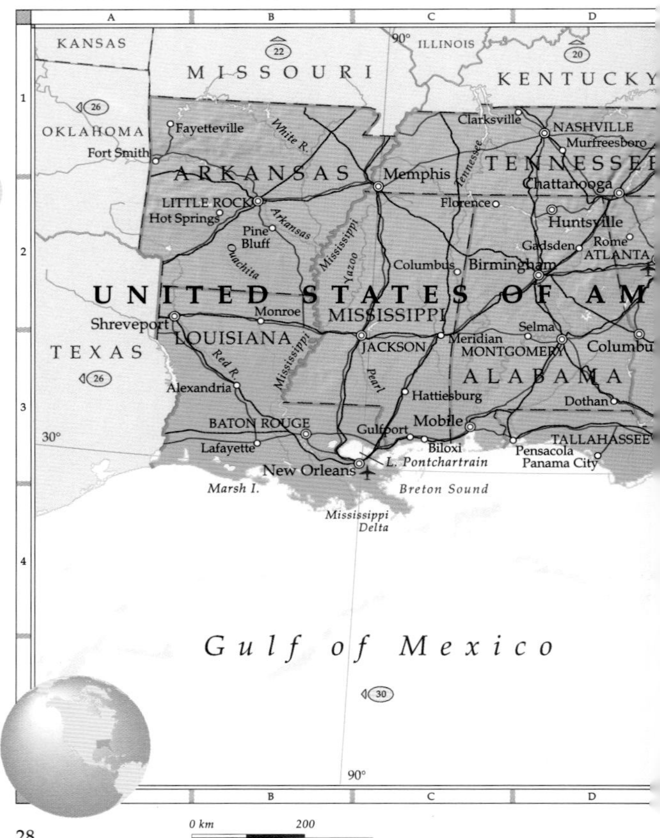
KANSAS
MISSOURI
ILLINOIS
KENTUCKY
OKLAHOMA
Fayetteville
White R.
Fort Smith
ARKANSAS
Memphis
Clarksville
NASHVILLE
Murfreesboro
TENNESSEE
Tennessee
Chattanooga
LITTLE ROCK
Hot Springs
Arkansas
Pine Bluff
Florence
Huntsville
Gadsden
Rome
ATLANTA
Ouachita
Mississippi
Yazoo
Columbus
Birmingham
UNITED STATES OF AM
Shreveport
Monroe
MISSISSIPPI
LOUISIANA
JACKSON
Meridian
Selma
MONTGOMERY
Columbu
TEXAS
Red R.
Pearl
ALABAMA
Alexandria
Hattiesburg
Dothan
BATON ROUGE
Gulfport
Mobile
TALLAHASSEE
30°
Lafayette
Biloxi
Pensacola
Panama City
New Orleans
L. Pontchartrain
Marsh I.
Breton Sound
Mississippi Delta
Gulf of Mexico
90°
A
B
C
D
1
2
3
4
22
20
26
30
0 km
200
0 miles
200

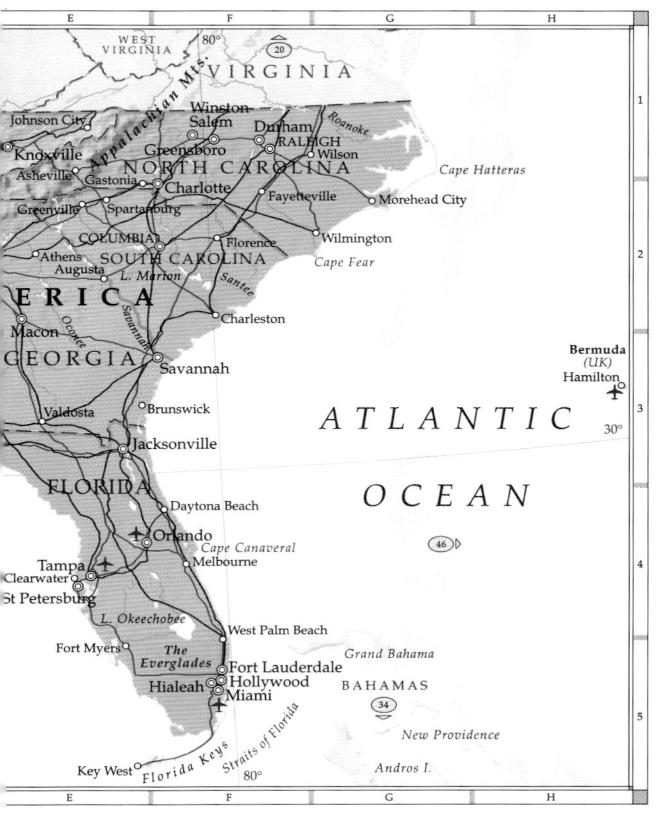

E
F
G
H
WEST VIRGINIA
80°
20
VIRGINIA
Appalachian Mts.
Winston-Salem
Johnson City
Durham
Roanoke
RALEIGH
Knoxville
Greensboro
Wilson
NORTH CAROLINA
Cape Hatteras
Asheville
Gastonia
Charlotte
Fayetteville
Morehead City
Greenville
Spartanburg
COLUMBIA
Wilmington
Florence
Athens
SOUTH CAROLINA
Cape Fear
Augusta
L. Marion
Santee
ERICA
Charleston
Macon
Oconee
Savannah
GEORGIA
Savannah
Bermuda
(UK)
Hamilton
Brunswick
ATLANTIC
Valdosta
30°
Jacksonville
FLORIDA
OCEAN
Daytona Beach
Orlando
46
Cape Canaveral
Melbourne
Tampa
Clearwater
St Petersburg
L. Okeechobee
West Palm Beach
Fort Myers
The Everglades
Grand Bahama
Fort Lauderdale
Hollywood
Hialeah
Miami
BAHAMAS
34
New Providence
Straits of Florida
Florida Keys
Key West
80°
Andros I.
1
2
3
4
5

MEXICO

A
B
C
D
1
2
3
4
Mexicali
Tijuana
Ensenada
ARIZONA
NEW MEXICO
UNITED
110°
30°
20°
Ciudad Juárez
Rio Grande
I. Ángel de la Guarda
I. Cedros
Baja California
Golfo de California
Hermosillo
Yaqui
Chihuahua
Sierra Madre Occidental
Sierra Madre
Conchos
Ciudad Obregón
Los Mochis
Gómez Palacio
Torreón
Culiacán
Durango
La Paz
Tropic of Cancer
Mazatlán
Aguascalientes
Islas Marías
Tepic
Guadalajara
Puerto Vallarta
L. de Chapala
PACIFIC OCEAN
Islas Revillagigedo (Mexico)
Middle
MEX
0 km 200
0 miles 200

E
F
G
H
100°
90°
STATES OF AMERICA
LOUISIANA
Mississippi
TEXAS
Rio Grande
Nuevo Laredo
Monclova
Reynosa
Matamoros
Monterrey
Saltillo
Gulf of Mexico
Tropic of Cancer
34
Ciudad Victoria
Oriental
Tampico
San Luis Potosí
Pánuco
Cancún
Mérida
20°
I. de Cozumel
Yucatan Peninsula
Campeche
León
Irapuato
Querétaro
Poza Rica
Bahía de Campeche
Pachuca
Jalapa
MEXICO CITY
Veracruz
Morelia
Cuernavaca
Puebla
Coatzacoalcos
Minatitlán
Villahermosa
Uruapan
BELIZE
32
Balsas
Sierra Madre del Sur
Oaxaca
Tuxtla Gutiérrez
GUATEMALA
Acapulco
Golfo de Tehuantepec
Tapachula
America Trench
1
2
3
4
5

Central America

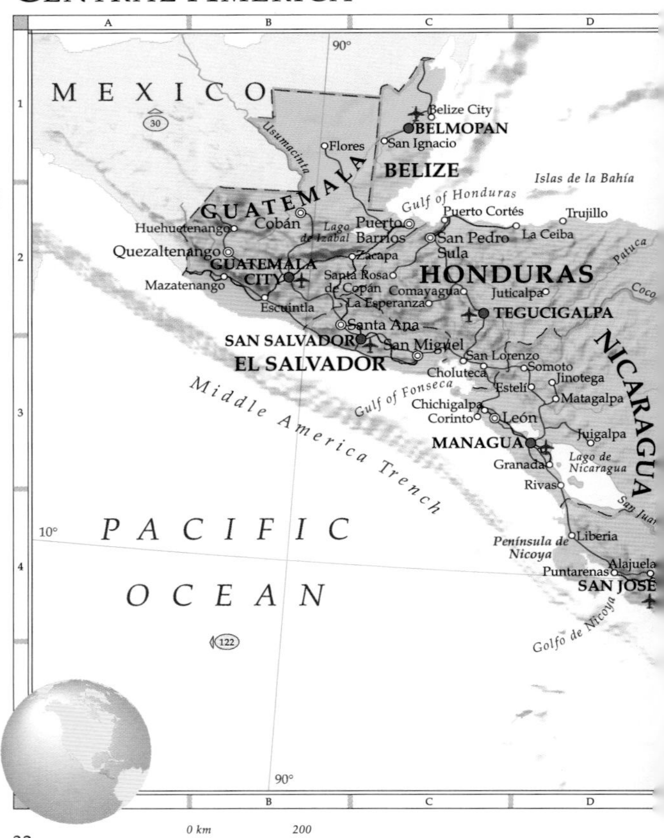
A
B
C
D
1
2
3
4
90°
MEXICO
30
Usumacinta
Belize City
BELMOPAN
Flores
San Ignacio
BELIZE
GUATEMALA
Islas de la Bahía
Gulf of Honduras
Puerto Cortés
Trujillo
Huehuetenango
Cobán
Lago de Izabal
Puerto Barrios
San Pedro Sula
La Ceiba
Quezaltenango
GUATEMALA CITY
Zacapa
Patuca
Mazatenango
Santa Rosa de Copán
HONDURAS
Coco
Escuintla
Comayagua
La Esperanza
Juticalpa
TEGUCIGALPA
Santa Ana
SAN SALVADOR
San Miguel
EL SALVADOR
NICARAGUA
San Lorenzo
Choluteca
Somoto
Middle America Trench
Gulf of Fonseca
Estelí
Jinotega
Matagalpa
Chichigalpa
Corinto
León
Juigalpa
MANAGUA
Lago de Nicaragua
Granada
Rivas
10°
PACIFIC
OCEAN
Península de Nicoya
Liberia
Alajuela
Puntarenas
SAN JOSÉ
Golfo de Nicoya
122
0 km
200
0 miles
200

E
F
G
H
80°
Cayman Trench
Greater Antilles
HAITI
JAMAICA
Islas Santanilla (Honduras)
Bajo Nuevo (Colombia)
34
Caribbean Sea
Mosquito Coast
Cayos Miskitos (Nicaragua)
I. de Providencia (Colombia)
I. de San Andrés (Colombia)
Islas del Maiz (Nicaragua)
Bluefields
COSTA RICA
Limón
Cartago
Cord. de Talamanca
PANAMA
Colón
PANAMA CITY
Gulf of Darien
Penonomé
Panama Canal
Isla del Rey
David
Santiago
Chitré
Las Tablas
Golfo de Chiriquí
Golfo de Panamá
COLOMBIA
38
10°
1
2
3
4
5

THE CARIBBEAN

A
B
C
D
1
2
3
4
USA
(FLORIDA)
80°
28
Gulf of Mexico
Grand Bahama
Freeport
Great Abaco
Straits of Florida
NASSAU
New Providence
Eleuthera
BAHAMAS
Andros I.
Cat I.
Tropic of Cancer
HAVANA
Matanzas
Great Exuma
Long I.
Great Bahama Bank
Pinar del Río
Santa Clara
Mayaguana
Acklins I.
Yucatan Channel
Cienfuegos
CUBA
Isla de la Juventud
Great Inagua
Camagüey
Holguín
Greater Antilles
Bayamo
Guantánamo
20°
Cayman Islands
(UK)
Santiago de Cuba
Port-de-Paix
Cap-Haïtien
Guantánamo Bay
(USA)
Gonaïves
30
George Town
Cayman Trench
Navassa Island
(USA)
HAITI
PORT-AU-PRINCE
Montego Bay
Jérémie
Jacmel
KINGSTON
JAMAICA
Yucatan Basin
HONDURAS
Caribbean Sea
Cayos Miskitos
(Nicaragua)
32
NICARAGUA
I. de Providencia
(Columbia)
I. de San Andrés
(Columbia)
Colombian Basin
Islas del Maíz
(Nicaragua)
COLOMBIA
80°
0 km
200
0 miles
200

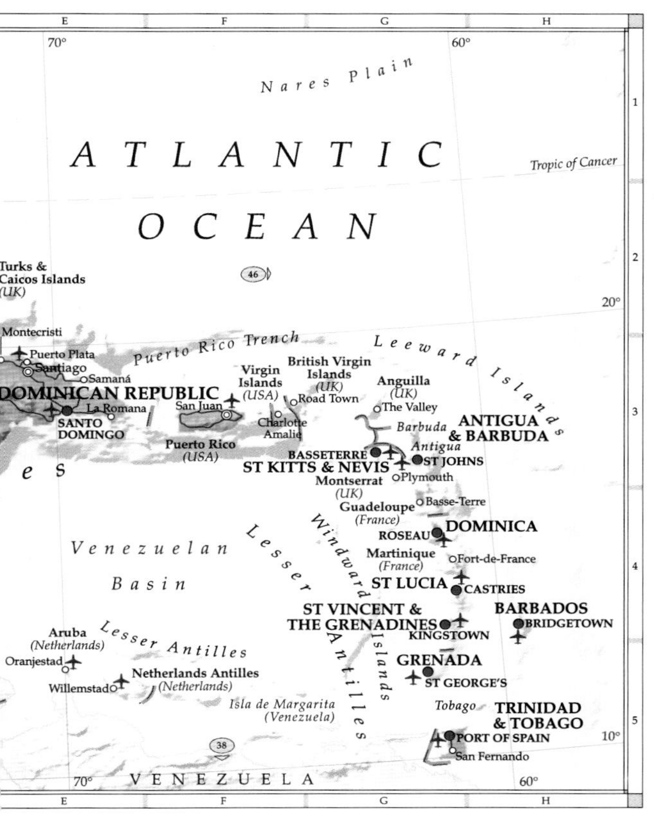

E
F
G
H
70°
60°
Nares Plain
ATLANTIC
OCEAN
Tropic of Cancer
Turks & Caicos Islands (UK)
46
20°
Montecristi
Puerto Plata
Santiago
Samaná
DOMINICAN REPUBLIC
La Romana
SANTO DOMINGO
Puerto Rico Trench
Virgin Islands (USA)
British Virgin Islands (UK)
Road Town
San Juan
Charlotte Amalie
Puerto Rico (USA)
Anguilla (UK)
The Valley
Leeward Islands
Barbuda
Antigua
ANTIGUA & BARBUDA
BASSETERRE
ST KITTS & NEVIS
ST JOHNS
Montserrat (UK)
Plymouth
Guadeloupe (France)
Basse-Terre
DOMINICA
ROSEAU
Martinique (France)
Fort-de-France
ST LUCIA
CASTRIES
ST VINCENT & THE GRENADINES
KINGSTOWN
BARBADOS
BRIDGETOWN
GRENADA
ST GEORGE'S
Windward Islands
Lesser Antilles
Venezuelan Basin
Aruba (Netherlands)
Oranjestad
Netherlands Antilles (Netherlands)
Willemstad
Isla de Margarita (Venezuela)
Tobago
TRINIDAD & TOBAGO
PORT OF SPAIN
San Fernando
10°
38
VENEZUELA
1
2
3
4
5

CONTINENTAL SOUTH AMERICA

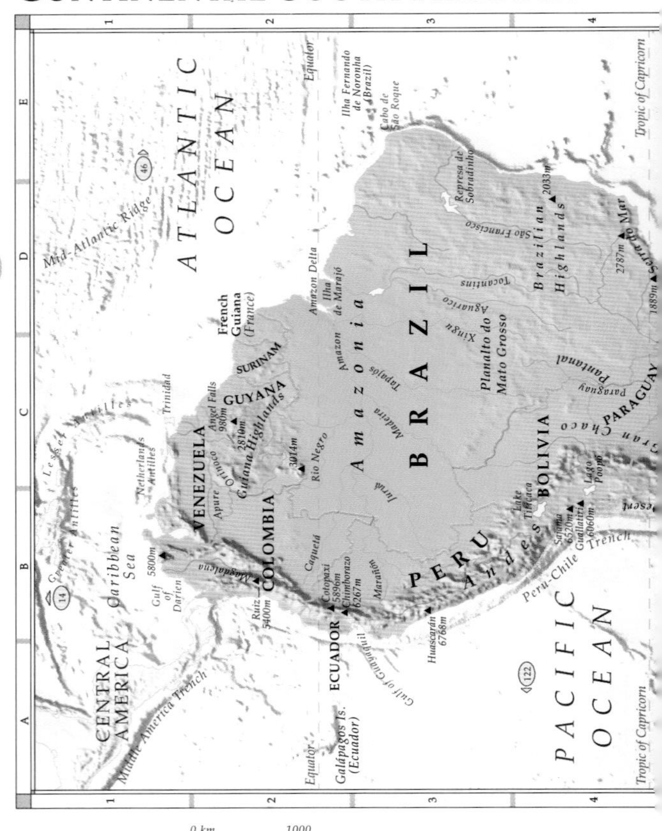
ATLANTIC
OCEAN
PACIFIC
OCEAN
Mid-Atlantic Ridge
Equator
Ilha Fernando de Noronha (Brazil)
Cabo de São Roque
Represa de Sobradinho
São Francisco
Brazilian Highlands
2033m
2787m
Serra do Mar
1889m
Tropic of Capricorn
Amazon Delta
Ilha de Marajó
French Guiana (France)
SURINAM
GUYANA
Guiana Highlands
Angel Falls 980m
2810m
3014m
Rio Negro
Amazon
Amazonia
BRAZIL
Tocantins
Araguaia
Xingu
Tapajós
Madeira
Juruá
Planalto do Mato Grosso
Pantanal
Paraguay
PARAGUAY
Gran Chaco
BOLIVIA
Lake Titicaca
Lago Poopó
Sajama 6520m
Guallatiri 6060m
Peru-Chile Trench
PERU
Andes
Huascarán 6768m
Marañón
Caquetá
COLOMBIA
VENEZUELA
Orinoco
Apure
Trinidad
Netherlands Antilles
Lesser Antilles
Greater Antilles
Caribbean Sea
5800m
Gulf of Darien
Magdalena
Ruiz 5400m
Cotopaxi 5896m
Chimborazo 6267m
ECUADOR
Gulf of Guayaquil
Galápagos Is. (Ecuador)
CENTRAL AMERICA
Middle America Trench
14
46
122
0 km
1000
0 miles
1000

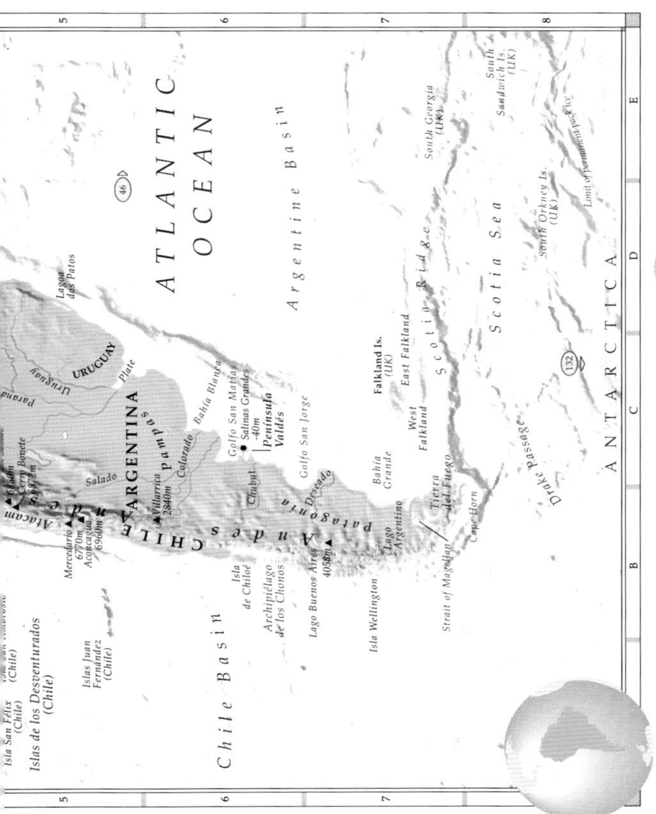
ATLANTIC OCEAN
Argentine Basin
Chile Basin
Scotia Ridge
Scotia Sea
ANTARCTICA
Drake Passage
South Georgia (UK)
South Sandwich Is. (UK)
South Orkney Is. (UK)
Limit of permanent pack ice
Falkland Is. (UK)
East Falkland
West Falkland
Bahía Grande
Tierra del Fuego
Cape Horn
Strait of Magellan
Lago Argentino
Isla Wellington
Lago Buenos Aires
4058m
Archipiélago de los Chonos
Isla de Chiloé
Patagonia
Andes
CHILE
ARGENTINA
Pampas
URUGUAY
Uruguay
Paraná
Plate
Lagoa dos Patos
Bahía Blanca
Golfo San Matías
Salinas Grandes -40m
Península Valdés
Golfo San Jorge
Deseado
Chubut
Colorado
Salado
Villarrica 2840m
Mercedario 6770m
Aconcagua 6960m
Cerro Bonete
Islas Juan Fernández (Chile)
Isla San Félix (Chile)
Islas de los Desventurados (Chile)
46
132
5
6
7
8
B
C
D
E

NORTHERN SOUTH AMERICA

A
B
C
D
80°
70°
Caribbean Sea
Gulf of Venezuela
Lesser
Santa Marta
Barranquilla
Cartagena
Valledupar
Maicao
Coro
Maracaibo
Cabimas
CARACAS
Maracay
Valencia
Ciudad Ojeda
Barquisimeto
Lago de Maracaibo
Guanare
Acarigua
Valera
San Juan de los Morros
Mérida
Barinas
Guanare
Sincelejo
Montería
PANAMA
Cauca
Magdalena
Cúcuta
San Cristóbal
Apure
San Fernando
Arauca
Bucaramanga
Floridablanca
VENE
Bello
Medellín
Itagüí
Quibdó
Tunja
Yopal
Puerto Carreño
PACIFIC OCEAN
Manizales
Pereira
Armenia
BOGOTÁ
Ibagué
Meta
Orinoco
Guaviare
Buenaventura
Cali
Villavicencio
COLOMBIA
Andes
Neiva
Popayán
San José del Guaviare
Florencia
Pasto
Mocoa
Esmeraldas
Tulcán
Ibarra
0° Equator
QUITO
Aguarico
Santo Domingo de los Colorados
Manta
Portoviejo
Ambato
Riobamba
Guayaquil
Milagro
ECUADOR
Caquetá
Putumayo
Cuenca
Gulf of Guayaquil
Machala
Loja
PERU
10°
34
32
122
40
1
2
3
4
5
0 km
200
0 miles
200

E
F
G
H
GRENADA
60°
ntilles
46
Isla de Margarita
Carúpano
TRINIDAD & TOBAGO
aiquetía
Cumaná
ATLANTIC
10°
Barcelona
The Serpent's Mouth
Maturín
Tucupita
OCEAN
El Tigre
Orinoco
Ciudad Guayana
Morawhanna
Ciudad Bolívar
Embalse de Guri
ZUELA
Cuyuni
GEORGETOWN
Nieuw Amsterdam
New Amsterdam
Bartica
St.-Laurent-du-Maroni
Rockstone
Linden
PARAMARIBO
Sinnamary
GUYANA
Kourou
Caura
Caroni
W.J. van Blommesteinmeer
Paragua
Guiana Highlands
Cayenne
Kabalebo Reservoir
Essequibo
Marowijne
SURINAM
French Guiana
(France)
rinoco
Courantyne
Corantijn
Acarai Mts.
Equator 0°
BRAZIL
40
Amazon
60°
1
2
3
4

PERU, BOLIVIA & NORTH BRAZIL

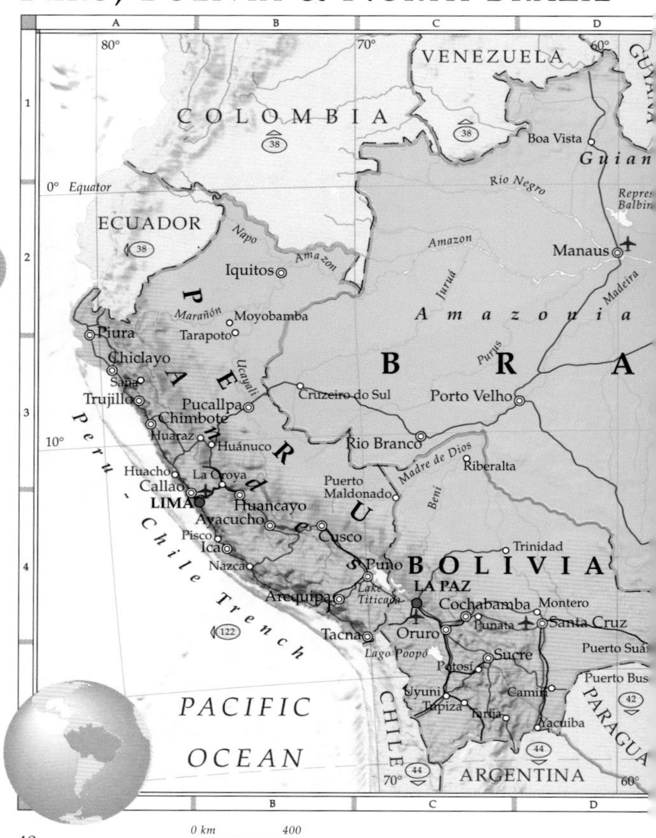
A
B
C
D
1
2
3
4
80°
70°
60°
10°
0° Equator
VENEZUELA
GUYANA
COLOMBIA
38
Boa Vista
Guian
Rio Negro
Repres
Balbin
ECUADOR
Napo
Amazon
Manaus
Iquitos
Juruá
Madeira
PERU
Marañón
Moyobamba
Tarapoto
Amazonia
Piura
Chiclayo
Saña
Trujillo
Ucayali
BRAZIL
Purus
Pucallpa
Cruzeiro do Sul
Porto Velho
Chimbote
Huaraz
Huánuco
Rio Branco
Madre de Dios
Riberalta
Peru - Chile Trench
Huacho
La Oroya
Callao
LIMA
Huancayo
Puerto Maldonado
Beni
Ayacucho
Cusco
Pisco
Ica
Trinidad
Nazca
Puno
BOLIVIA
LA PAZ
Lake Titicaca
Arequipa
Cochabamba
Montero
Punata
Santa Cruz
122
Tacna
Oruro
Lago Poopó
Sucre
Puerto Suá
Potosí
Puerto Bus
Uyuni
Camiri
PACIFIC
Tupiza
Tarija
PARAGUAY
Yacuiba
42
OCEAN
CHILE
44
ARGENTINA
0 km
400
0 miles
400

E
F
G
H
1
2
3
4
5
50°
40°
10°
20°
SURINAM
French Guiana (France)
38
46
ATLANTIC
OCEAN
Highlands
Macapá
Ilha Caviana
Ilha de Marajó
Equator 0°
Amazon
Belém
Santarém
São Luís
Paranaíba
Ilha Fernando de Noronha
Represa de Tucuruí
Fortaleza
Xingu
Imperatriz
Teresina
Mossoró
Natal
Carolina
João Pessoa
Z
I
L
Juàzeiro do Norte
Campina Grande
Tocantins
São Francisco
Recife
Represa de Sobradinho
Juàzeiro
Maceió
Araguaia
Palmas
Aracaju
Planalto de Mato Grosso
Taguatinga
Feira de Santana
Salvador
Brazilian
Highlands
Cuiabá
Itabuna
Anápolis
BRASÍLIA
Vitória da Conquista
Goiânia
Montes Claros
Governador Valadares
Uberlândia
Hotspur Seamount
Abrolhos Bank
Uberaba
Belo Horizonte
Divinópolis
Campo Grande
Paraná
Ribeirão Preto
Vitória
Marília
Campos
Nova Iguaçu
Juiz de Fora
Campinas
Londrina
Sorocaba
Taubaté
Rio de Janeiro
42
São Paulo
Tropic of Capricorn

PARAGUAY, URUGUAY & SOUTH BRAZIL

A
B
C
D
1
2
3
4
5
60°
50°
20°
30°
BOLIVIA
40
BRA
São José do Rio Preto
Campo Grande
General Eugenio A. Garay
Gran
Chaco
Puerto Bahía Negra
Mariscal Estigarribia
Dourados
Presidente Prudente
Marília
Bauru
Paraná
Ourinhos
Londrina
Maringá
PARAGUAY
Tropic of Capricorn
Pozo Colorado
Concepción
Paraguay
Pilcomayo
Caaguazú
Ciudad del Este
Ponta Grossa
ASUNCIÓN
Coronel Oviedo
Fernando de la Mora
Lambaré
Guarapuava
Curitiba
Joinville
San Ignacio
Pilar
Encarnación
Blumenau
Salado
Erechim
Florianópolis
Lajes
Pelotas
Passo Fundo
Carazinho
44
Uruguay
São Borja
Caxias do Sul
ARGENTINA
Serra do Mar
Uruguaiana
Santa Maria
Canoas
Porto Alegre
Bella Unión
Artigas
Rivera
Bagé
Lagoa dos Patos
Salto
Tacuarembó
Pelotas
Rio Grande
URUGUAY
Paysandú
Melo
Young
Embalse del Río Negro
Lake Mirim
Fray Bentos
Mercedes
Durazno
Chuí
Trinidad
Las Piedras
San Carlos
MONTEVIDEO
Plate
0 km
200
0 miles
200

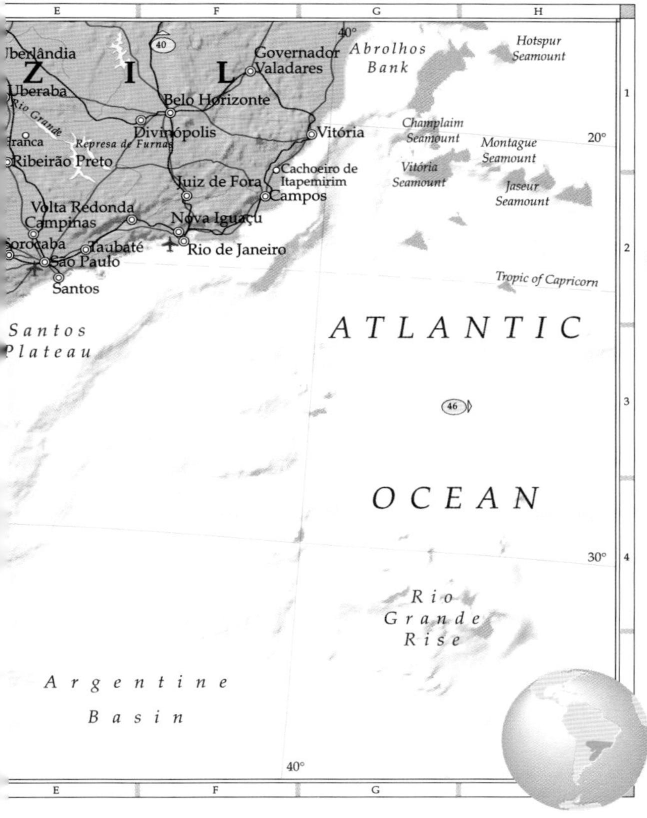

E
F
G
H
Uberlândia
Governador Valadares
Abrolhos Bank
Hotspur Seamount
Uberaba
Rio Grande
Belo Horizonte
Divinópolis
Vitória
Champlaim Seamount
Montague Seamount
20°
Franca
Represa de Furnas
Ribeirão Preto
Cachoeiro de Itapemirim
Vitória Seamount
Juiz de Fora
Campos
Jaseur Seamount
Volta Redonda
Campinas
Nova Iguaçu
Sorocaba
Taubaté
Rio de Janeiro
São Paulo
Santos
Tropic of Capricorn
Santos Plateau
ATLANTIC
OCEAN
30°
Rio Grande Rise
Argentine Basin
40°
1
2
3
4

CHILE & ARGENTINA

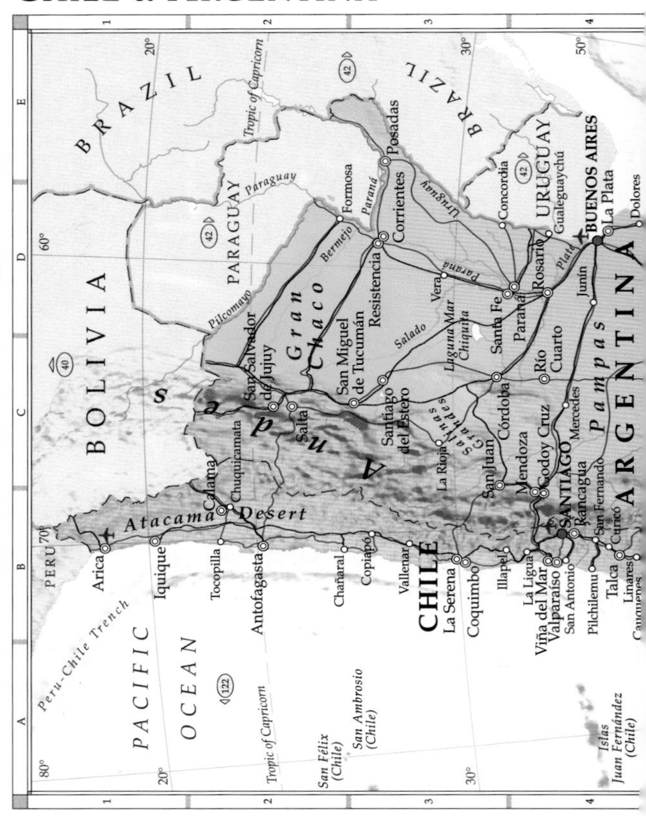
BRAZIL
BOLIVIA
PARAGUAY
URUGUAY
ARGENTINA
CHILE
PERU
PACIFIC OCEAN
Tropic of Capricorn
Peru-Chile Trench
Atacama Desert
Gran Chaco
Pampas
Andes
Salinas Grandes
Laguna Mar Chiquita
Paraguay
Paraná
Uruguay
Pilcomayo
Bermejo
Salado
Plata
Posadas
Corrientes
Resistencia
Formosa
Concordia
Gualeguaychú
BUENOS AIRES
La Plata
Dolores
Junín
Rosario
Paraná
Santa Fe
Vera
Río Cuarto
Córdoba
Mercedes
San Miguel de Tucumán
Santiago del Estero
San Salvador de Jujuy
Salta
La Rioja
San Juan
Mendoza
Godoy Cruz
SANTIAGO
Rancagua
San Fernando
Curicó
Talca
Linares
Arica
Iquique
Tocopilla
Antofagasta
Calama
Chuquicamata
Chañaral
Copiapó
Vallenar
La Serena
Coquimbo
Illapel
La Ligua
Viña del Mar
Valparaíso
San Antonio
Pilchilemu
San Félix (Chile)
San Ambrosio (Chile)
Islas Juan Fernández (Chile)
1
2
3
4
A
B
C
D
E
20°
30°
50°
60°
70°
80°
40
42
122

0 km 200
0 miles 200

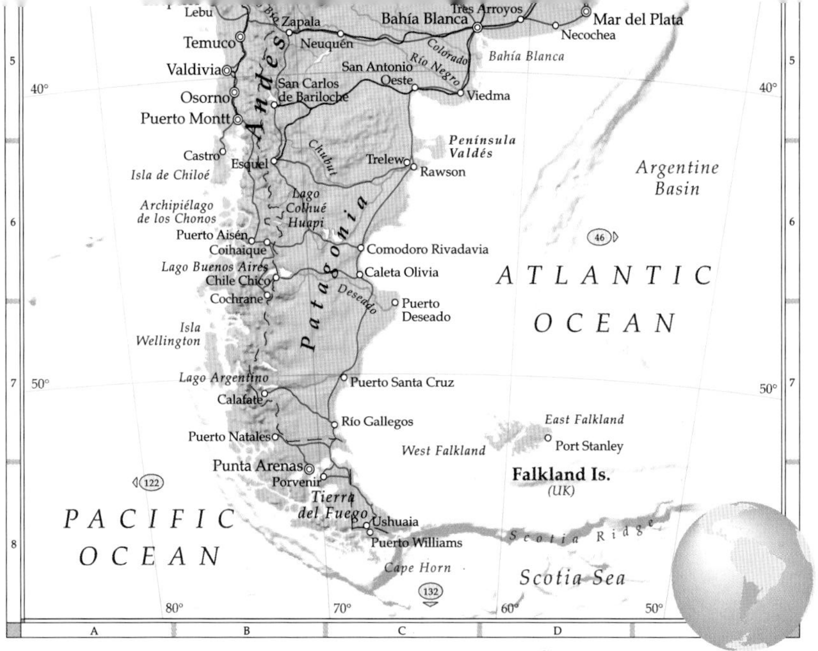
Lebu
Zapala
Bahía Blanca
Tres Arroyos
Mar del Plata
Necochea
Temuco
Neuquén
Colorado
Bahía Blanca
Valdivia
San Antonio Oeste
Río Negro
San Carlos de Bariloche
Viedma
Osorno
Puerto Montt
Andes
Península Valdés
Castro
Esquel
Chubut
Trelew
Rawson
Argentine Basin
Isla de Chiloé
Lago Colhué Huapi
Archipiélago de los Chonos
Patagonia
46
Puerto Aisén
Coihaique
Comodoro Rivadavia
Lago Buenos Aires
Chile Chico
Caleta Olivia
ATLANTIC OCEAN
Cochrane
Deseado
Puerto Deseado
Isla Wellington
Lago Argentino
Puerto Santa Cruz
Calafate
Río Gallegos
East Falkland
Puerto Natales
Port Stanley
West Falkland
Punta Arenas
Falkland Is.
(UK)
122
Porvenir
Tierra del Fuego
PACIFIC OCEAN
Ushuaia
Puerto Williams
Scotia Ridge
Cape Horn
Scotia Sea
132
40°
50°
80°
70°
60°
A
B
C
D
5
6
7
8

THE ATLANTIC OCEAN

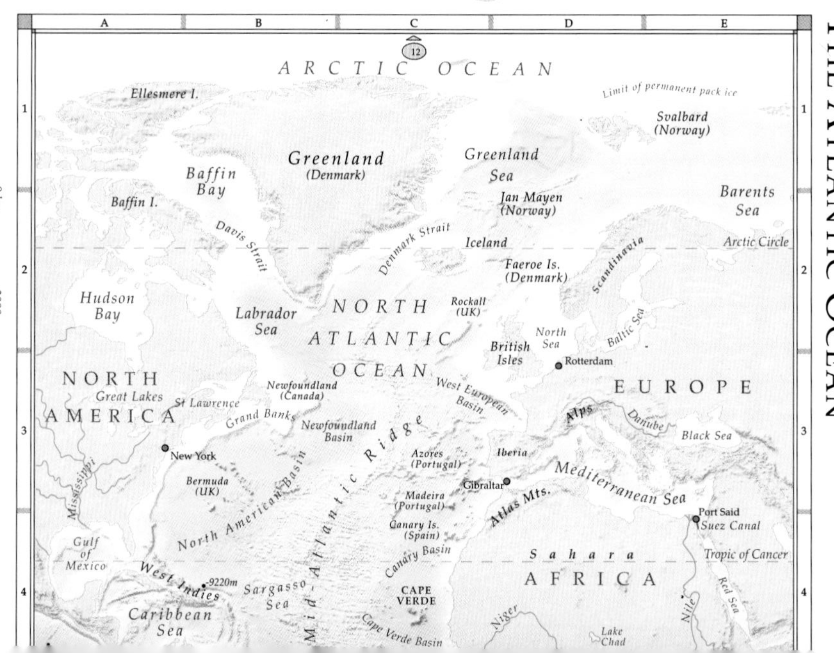
ARCTIC OCEAN
Limit of permanent pack ice
Svalbard (Norway)
Barents Sea
Arctic Circle
Greenland Sea
Jan Mayen (Norway)
Greenland (Denmark)
Ellesmere I.
Baffin Bay
Baffin I.
Davis Strait
Denmark Strait
Iceland
Faeroe Is. (Denmark)
Scandinavia
Baltic Sea
North Sea
British Isles
Rotterdam
EUROPE
Black Sea
Danube
Alps
Port Said
Suez Canal
Tropic of Cancer
Red Sea
Nile
Mediterranean Sea
Iberia
Gibraltar
Atlas Mts.
Sahara
AFRICA
Niger
Lake Chad
Rockall (UK)
NORTH ATLANTIC OCEAN
West European Basin
Azores (Portugal)
Madeira (Portugal)
Canary Is. (Spain)
Canary Basin
CAPE VERDE
Cape Verde Basin
Mid-Atlantic Ridge
Newfoundland Basin
Newfoundland (Canada)
Grand Banks
Labrador Sea
Hudson Bay
St Lawrence
Great Lakes
NORTH AMERICA
New York
Bermuda (UK)
North American Basin
Sargasso Sea
9220m
West Indies
Caribbean Sea
Gulf of Mexico
Mississippi
12
0 km 2000
0 miles 2000

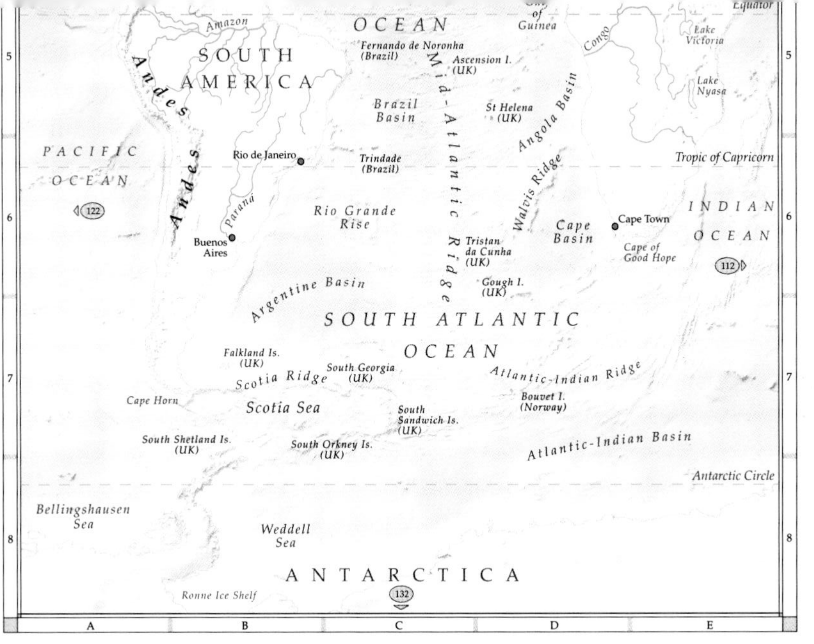
Equator
of Guinea
OCEAN
Amazon
SOUTH AMERICA
Andes
Fernando de Noronha (Brazil)
Ascension I. (UK)
Congo
Lake Victoria
Lake Nyasa
Brazil Basin
St Helena (UK)
Angola Basin
Mid-Atlantic Ridge
PACIFIC OCEAN
Rio de Janeiro
Trindade (Brazil)
Walvis Ridge
Tropic of Capricorn
122
Paraná
Rio Grande Rise
Buenos Aires
Cape Basin
Cape Town
Cape of Good Hope
INDIAN OCEAN
112
Tristan da Cunha (UK)
Gough I. (UK)
Argentine Basin
SOUTH ATLANTIC OCEAN
Falkland Is. (UK)
Scotia Ridge
South Georgia (UK)
Atlantic-Indian Ridge
Cape Horn
Scotia Sea
Bouvet I. (Norway)
South Sandwich Is. (UK)
South Shetland Is. (UK)
South Orkney Is. (UK)
Atlantic-Indian Basin
Antarctic Circle
Bellingshausen Sea
Weddell Sea
ANTARCTICA
Ronne Ice Shelf
132
5
6
7
8
A
B
C
D
E

CONTINENTAL AFRICA

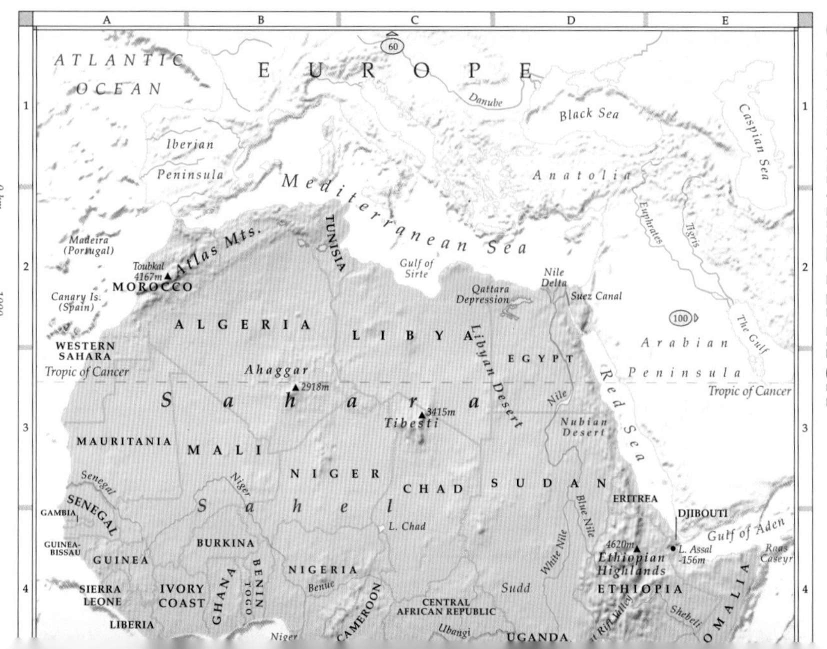
A
B
C
D
E
1
2
3
4
60
ATLANTIC OCEAN
EUROPE
Danube
Black Sea
Caspian Sea
Iberian Peninsula
Anatolia
Mediterranean Sea
Euphrates
Tigris
Madeira (Portugal)
Atlas Mts.
Toubkal 4167m
MOROCCO
TUNISIA
Gulf of Sirte
Nile Delta
Qattara Depression
Suez Canal
100
The Gulf
Canary Is. (Spain)
ALGERIA
LIBYA
Libyan Desert
EGYPT
Arabian Peninsula
WESTERN SAHARA
Tropic of Cancer
Ahaggar
2918m
Sahara
3415m
Tibesti
Nile
Red Sea
Tropic of Cancer
Nubian Desert
MAURITANIA
MALI
NIGER
CHAD
SUDAN
Senegal
Niger
Sahel
SENEGAL
GAMBIA
L. Chad
Blue Nile
ERITREA
DJIBOUTI
Gulf of Aden
GUINEA-BISSAU
BURKINA
White Nile
4620m
Ethiopian Highlands
L. Assal -156m
Raas Caseyr
GUINEA
NIGERIA
Benue
SIERRA LEONE
IVORY COAST
GHANA
BENIN
TOGO
CAMEROON
CENTRAL AFRICAN REPUBLIC
Sudd
ETHIOPIA
Rift Valley
Shebeli
SOMALIA
LIBERIA
Niger
Ubangi
UGANDA

0 km 1000
0 miles 1000

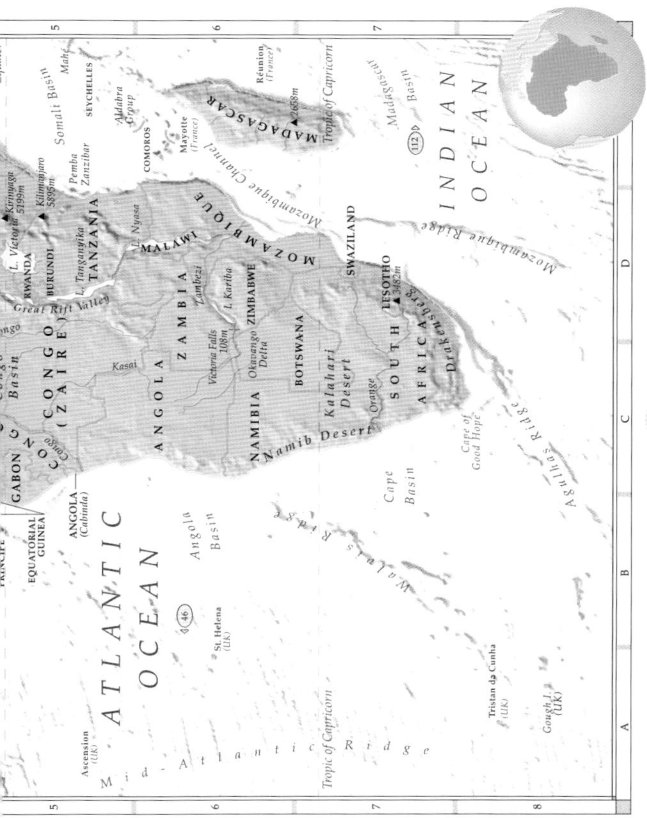
ATLANTIC
OCEAN
INDIAN
OCEAN
Mid-Atlantic Ridge
Ascension
(UK)
St. Helena
(UK)
Tristan da Cunha
(UK)
Gough I.
(UK)
Angola
Basin
Cape
Basin
Walvis Ridge
Agulhas Ridge
Cape of
Good Hope
Tropic of Capricorn
EQUATORIAL
GUINEA
GABON
ANGOLA
(Cabinda)
CONGO
CONGO
(ZAIRE)
ANGOLA
NAMIBIA
Namib Desert
BOTSWANA
Kalahari
Desert
Okavango
Delta
Orange
SOUTH
AFRICA
Drakensberg
LESOTHO
3482m
SWAZILAND
ZIMBABWE
L. Kariba
Victoria Falls
108m
ZAMBIA
Zambezi
Kasai
MALAWI
L. Nyasa
MOZAMBIQUE
Mozambique Channel
Mozambique Ridge
TANZANIA
L. Tanganyika
BURUNDI
RWANDA
L. Victoria
Kirinyaga
5199m
Kilimanjaro
5895m
Great Rift Valley
Pemba
Zanzibar
COMOROS
Mayotte
(France)
MADAGASCAR
2658m
Aldabra
Group
SEYCHELLES
Mahé
Somali Basin
Réunion
(France)
Madagascar
Basin
Tropic of Capricorn
46
112
A
B
C
D
5
6
7
8

Northwest Africa

A
B
C
D
1
2
3
4
5
20°
10°
0°
30°
SPAIN
72
ATLANTIC
OCEAN
46
ALGIERS
Blida
Ceuta (Spain)
Mostaganem
Tanger
Oran
Tétouan
Melilla (Spain)
Tiaret
Kénitra
Tlemcen
Sidi Bel Abbès
Madeira (Portugal)
RABAT
Fès
Oujda
Casablanca
Meknès
Atlas Mountains
Laghouat
Khouribga
Safi
Beni Mellal
Figuig
Ghardaïa
Essaouira
Er Rachidia
Marrakech
Béchar
Canary Islands (Spain)
Agadir
MOROCCO
Grand Erg Occidental
La Palma
Tenerife
Lanzarote
Fuerteventura
Gran Canaria
Tan-Tan
LAÂYOUNE
ALGERIA
Tindouf
In Salah
Semara
WESTERN SAHARA (occupied by Morocco)
Reggane
Ad Dakhla
Tropic of Cancer
Sah
Guerguerat
20°
52
52
MAURITANIA
MALI
10°
0°

0 km 400
0 miles 400

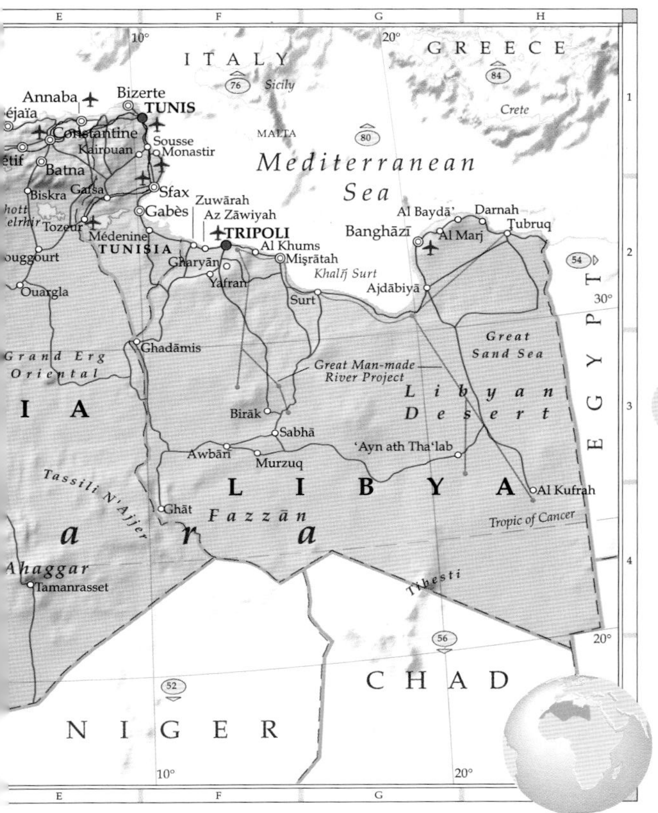

E
F
G
H
10°
20°
ITALY
GREECE
Sicily
76
84
Crete
MALTA
80
Mediterranean Sea
Annaba
Bizerte
TUNIS
Constantine
Sousse
Monastir
Kairouan
Batna
Sfax
Gafsa
Biskra
Gabès
Zuwārah
Az Zāwiyah
TRIPOLI
Tozeur
Médenine
TUNISIA
Al Khums
Miṣrātah
Gharyān
Yafran
Ouargla
Khalīj Surt
Surt
Al Bayḍā'
Darnah
Ţubruq
Banghāzī
Al Marj
Ajdābiyā
54
30°
Ghadāmis
Grand Erg Oriental
Great Sand Sea
Great Man-made River Project
Libyan Desert
EGYPT
Birāk
Sabhā
Awbārī
Murzuq
'Ayn ath Tha'lab
Tassili N'Ajjer
LIBYA
Al Kufrah
Ghāt
Fazzān
Tropic of Cancer
Ahaggar
Tamanrasset
Tibesti
56
20°
CHAD
52
NIGER
1
2
3
4

West Africa

A
B
C
D
1
2
3
4
20°
10°
Tropic of Cancer
WESTERN SAHARA
(occupied by Morocco)
ATLANTIC OCEAN
Zouérat
Nouâdhibou
Râs Nouâdhibou
Atâr
MAURITANIA
NOUAKCHOTT
L. Rkîz
Rosso
Aleg
Kiffa
Saint-Louis
Senegal
Kaédi
CAPE VERDE
PRAIA
DAKAR
Thiès
Diourbel
Nioro
Kaolack
SENEGAL
Kayes
GAMBIA
BANJUL
Georgetown
Kolda
Ségou
Ziguinchor
BAMAKO
BISSAU
Bafatá
GUINEA-BISSAU
Labé
Siguiri
Bougouni
GUINEA
Kindia
Kankan
CONAKRY
Odienné
Korhogo
Makeni
FREETOWN
Bo
SIERRA LEONE
Nzérékoré
Kenema
Man
Daloa
Bouaké
Tubmanburg
MONROVIA
YAMOUSSOUKRO
Buchanan
Zwedru
Gagnoa
LIBERIA
Harper
46
0 km 250
0 miles 250

E
F
G
H
1
2
3
4
5
0°
10°
20°
50
56
ALGERIA
LIBYA
Tropic of Cancer
Plateau du Manguéni
h a r a
Adrar des Ifôghas
Aïr
MALI
Tombouctou
L. Faguibine
L. Niangay
Gao
Agadez
NIGER
Sahel
Mopti
Tillabéri
Niger
NIAMEY
Birni-Nkonni
Zinder
N'Guigmi
Diffa
CHAD
L. Chad
Ouahigouya
BURKINA
OUAGADOUGOU
Sokoto
Dosso
Maradi
Katsina
Hadejia
Kano
Maiduguri
Gusau
Fada-Ngourma
Zaria
Bobo-Dioulasso
Kandi
NIGERIA
BENIN
Natitingou
Kainji Res.
Kaduna
Jos
Bauchi
Yola
Black Volta
White Volta
Wa
Tamale
Parakou
ABUJA
GHANA
TOGO
Ouémé
Ilorin
Sokodé
L. Volta
Oyo
Ogbomosho
Benue
Makurdi
Sunyani
Atakpamé
Abeokuta
Ede
Kumasi
Ibadan
Ijebu-Ode
Abengourou
LOMÉ
Lagos
Enugu
Asamankese
Benin City
Onitsha
Abidjan
ACCRA
PORTO-NOVO
Aba
Uyo
CAMEROON
Cape Coast
Calabar
Sekondi-Takoradi
Cotonou
Niger Delta
Port Harcourt
Bight of Benin

NORTHEAST AFRICA

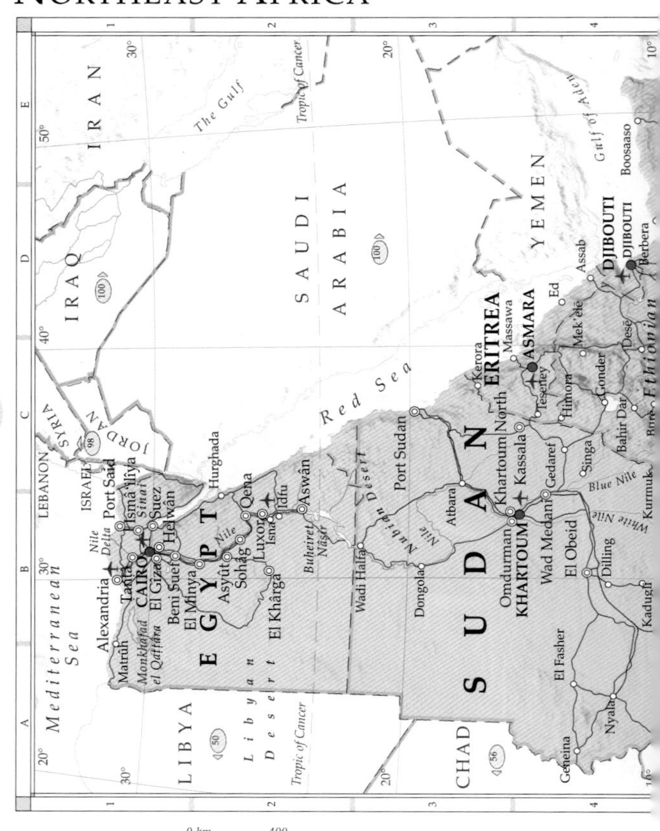

Mediterranean Sea
LIBYA
EGYPT
SUDAN
CHAD
SAUDI ARABIA
IRAQ
IRAN
SYRIA
JORDAN
LEBANON
ISRAEL
YEMEN
ERITREA
DJIBOUTI
Red Sea
The Gulf
Gulf of Aden
Libyan Desert
Nubian Desert
Tropic of Cancer
Nile Delta
Sinai
Nile
Blue Nile
White Nile
Buheiret Nâsir
Monkhafad el Qattâra
Alexandria
Matrûh
Tanta
CAIRO
El Gîza
Port Said
Ismâ'ilîya
Suez
Helwân
Beni Suef
El Minya
Asyût
Sohâg
Qena
Luxor
Isna
Idfu
Aswân
Hurghada
El Khârga
Wadi Halfa
Dongola
Port Sudan
Atbara
Omdurman
KHARTOUM
Khartoum North
Kassala
Gedaref
Wad Medani
El Obeid
Dilling
Kadugli
Kurmuk
Singa
El Fasher
Nyala
Geneina
Kerora
Massawa
ASMARA
Teseney
Himora
Gonder
Bahir Dar
Mek'ele
Desē
Ed
Assab
Berbera
Boosaaso

0 km 400

0 miles 400

CENTRAL AFRICAN REPUBLIC
ETHIOPIA
SOMALIA
KENYA
UGANDA
TANZANIA
RWANDA
BURUNDI
CONGO (ZAIRE)
ZAMBIA
MALAWI
MOZAMBIQUE
COMOROS
SEYCHELLES
MADAGASCAR
INDIAN OCEAN
MOGADISHU
NAIROBI
KAMPALA
KIGALI
BUJUMBURA
DODOMA
Sudd
White Nile
Highlands
Ogaden
Shebeli
Equator
Great Rift Valley
Lake Rudolph
Lake Victoria
Lake Albert
Lake Edward
Lake Kivu
Lake Tanganyika
Lake Nyasa
Ruvuma
Ubangi
Congo
Wau
Rumbek
Yambio
Juba
Gore
Jima
Debre Zeyit
Nazrēt
Dila
Negēlē
Dawa
Garoowe
Gaalkacyo
Beledweyne
Baydhabo
Wanlaweyn
Buurhakaba
Marka
Jamaame
Kismaayo
Lokitaung
Moyale
Garissa
Meru
Nyeri
Machakos
Eldoret
Nakuru
Kisumu
Mbale
Lira
Gulu
Arua
Masindi
Entebbe
Kabale
Mwanza
Shinyanga
Arusha
Moshi
Malindi
Mombasa
Tanga
Zanzibar
Dar es Salaam
Tabora
Kigoma
Morogoro
Iringa
Mbeya
Sumbawanga
Songea
Lindi
Mtwara
Aldabra Group
Cosmolédo Atoll
Grande Comore
Anjouan
Mohéli
Mayotte (France)
56
58
112
0°
10°
30°
40°
50°
5
6
7
8
B
C
D
E

CENTRAL AFRICA

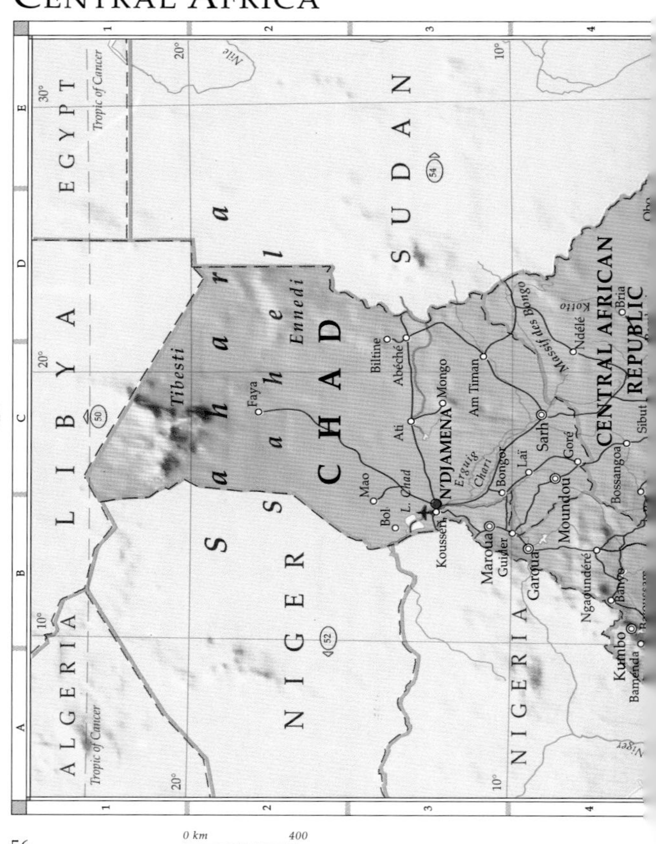
EGYPT
LIBYA
ALGERIA
NIGER
CHAD
SUDAN
NIGERIA
CENTRAL AFRICAN REPUBLIC
Sahara
Tibesti
Ennedi
Tropic of Cancer
Nile
Niger
Faya
Biltine
Abéché
Ati
Mongo
N'DJAMENA
Mao
Bol
L. Chad
Am Timan
Erguig
Chari
Bongor
Laï
Sarh
Moundou
Goré
Bossangoa
Sibut
Ndélé
Bria
Kotto
Massif des Bongo
Maroua
Guider
Garoua
Ngaoundéré
Banyo
Kumbo
Bamenda
50
52
54

0 km 400
0 miles 400

CONGO (ZAIRE)
CONGO
GABON
CAMEROON
EQUATORIAL GUINEA
SAO TOME & PRINCIPE
ANGOLA
ANGOLA (Cabinda)
ZAMBIA
UGANDA
RWANDA
BURUNDI
TANZANIA
ATLANTIC OCEAN
KINSHASA
BRAZZAVILLE
LIBREVILLE
YAOUNDÉ
BANGUI
MALABO
SÃO TOMÉ
Douala
Kribio
Bertoua
Berbérati
Ebolowa
Bata
Oyem
Ouésso
Impfondo
Owando
Djambala
Mossendjo
Lambaréné
Massoukou
Port-Gentil
Loubomo
Pointe-Noire
Boma
Matadi
Kikwit
Bandundu
Mbandaka
Gemena
Bumba
Kisangani
Isiro
Bunia
Butembo
Goma
Bukavu
Kindu
Kasongo
Lodja
Ilebo
Kananga
Tshikapa
Mbuji-Mayi
Kabinda
Mwene-Ditu
Kamina
Kalemie
Manono
Kolwezi
Likasi
Lubumbashi
Dilolo
Príncipe
São Tomé
Equator
Congo
Ubangi
Uele
Bomu
Kasai
Kwango
L. Albert
L. Edward
L. Kivu
L. Tanganyika
L. Mweru
0°
10°
20°
30°
46
54
58
B
C
D
E
5
6
7
8

SOUTHERN AFRICA

A
B
C
D
1
2
3
4
5
10°
20°
30°
0°
Cabinda
(Angola)
Cabinda
Congo
CONGO
(ZAIRE)
Lake
Tanganyika
Uíge
Ambriz
Lucapa
LUANDA
N'Dalatando
Saurimo
Malanje
Cuanza
Ndola
Mufulira
Sumbe
ANGOLA
Lobito
Benguela
Chingola
Kitwe
Luanshya
Kuito
Huambo
Zambezi
Menongue
ZAMBIA
Lubango
Namibe
Tombua
LUSAKA
Choma
Lake
Kariba
N'Giva
Okavango
Cuito
Cunene
Zambezi
Ondangwa
Rundu
Livingstone
Chitungwiza
Etosha
Pan
Tsumeb
Okavango Delta
Skeleton Coast
Grootfontein
Maun
Makgadikgadi
NAMIBIA
Bulawayo
Francistown
Ghanzi
Okahandja
Swakopmund
Walvis Bay
WINDHOEK
BOTSWANA
Kalahari
Mahalapye
Limpopo
Tropic of Capricorn
Rehoboth
GABORONE
Lobatse
PRETORIA
Desert
Fish
Mmabatho
Soweto
Keetmanshoop
Johannesburg
Lüderitz
Kroonstad
46
Karasburg
Vaal
Orange R.
Kimberley
MASERU
ATLANTIC
Bloemfontein
SOUTH
LESOTHO
AFRICA
Middelburg
OCEAN
Beaufort West
Drakensberg
Bellville
Oudtshoorn
East
Cape Town
Port
Elizabeth
Cape of Good Hope
Cape Basin
56
0 km 400
0 miles 400

E
F
G
H
40°
50°
54
TANZANIA
SEYCHELLES
Inner Islands
VICTORIA
Mahé
Amirante Islands
Mbala
Aldabra Group
Farquhar Group
Outer Islands
MALAWI
Kasama
Mzuzu
Lake Nyasa
Rovuma
COMOROS
Grande Comore
MORONI
Mpika
Nkhotakota
Mocímboa da Praia
Mohéli
Anjouan
10°
LILONGWE
Salima
Mamoudzou
Antsirañana
Zomba
Nacala
Mayotte
(France)
Ambanja
Antalaha
Blantyre
Tete
Moçambique
Antsohihy
Nampula
MOZAMBIQUE
Nsanje
Mahajanga
HARARE
Mocuba
MADAGASCAR
Quelimane
Fenoarivo Atsinanana
Chimoio
Mozambique Channel
ANTANANARIVO
Toamasina
Beira
Morondava
Ambositra
MAURITIUS
Fianarantsoa
Mananjary
Réunion
(France)
PORT LOUIS
Ihosy
Saint-Denis
20°
Limpopo
Toliara
Farafangana
Inhambane
Vangaindrano
Mascarene Is.
Xai-Xai
Tropic of Capricorn
MAPUTO
MBABANE
SWAZILAND
Amboasary
Madagascar Basin
Pietermaritzburg
Durban
112
INDIAN OCEAN
1
2
3
4

Continental Europe

A
B
C
D
1
2
3
4
ARCTIC OCEAN
12
Norwegian Basin
Arctic Circle
Norwegian Sea
ICELAND
Kjølen Mts.
Faeroe-Iceland Ridge
Faeroe Islands (Denmark)
2469m
Shetland Is.
NORWAY
Orkney Is.
Outer Hebrides
SWEDEN
46
North Sea
UNITED KINGDOM
DENMARK
ATLANTIC OCEAN
IRELAND
Elbe
NETHERLANDS
Thames
English Channel
GERMANY
BELGIUM
Rhine
LUX.
Seine
Meuse
Danube
FRANCE
Loire
Alps
AUSTRI
Biscay Plain
SWITZ.
LIECH.
SLOVENI
Bay of Biscay
1886m
Massif Central
Mont Blanc 4807m
Po
ITALY
SAN MARINO
Garonne
Rhône
C. Finisterre
3404m
MONACO
Apennines
Pyrenees
ANDORRA
Corsica
VATICAN CITY
PORTUGAL
SPAIN
Balearic Is.
Sardinia
Tyrrhenian Sea
Guadalquivir
Mulhacen 3478m
Mediterranean Sea
Etna 3369m
C. St Vincent
Sicily
Gibraltar (UK)
48
MALTA
AFRICA
0 km
600
0 miles
600

E
F
G
H
North Cape
Barents Sea
Lapland
2117m
Kola Peninsula
White Sea
Arctic Circle
Ural Mountains
Gulf of Bothnia
FINLAND
N. Dvina
Gulf of Finland
Baltic Sea
ESTONIA
RUSSIAN FEDERATION
92
LATVIA
Dvina
Volga
LITHUANIA
RUSSIAN FED. (Kaliningrad)
European Plain
BELORUSSIA
Vistula
Pripet Marshes
POLAND
UKRAINE
Carpathians
Dnieper
Don
SLOVAKIA
Volga
HUNGARY
MOLDAVIA
ROMANIA
Sea of Azov
Volga Delta -28m
Aral Sea
CROATIA
BOS. & HERZ.
YUGO.
Danube
Balkan Mts.
Black Sea
Caucasus Mts.
El'brus 5642m
Caspian Sea
BULGARIA
MAC.
ALBANIA
Pindus Mts.
Aegean Sea
Ionian Sea
GREECE
Tigris
Euphrates
ASIA
92
Crete
1
2
3
4
5

THE NORTH ATLANTIC

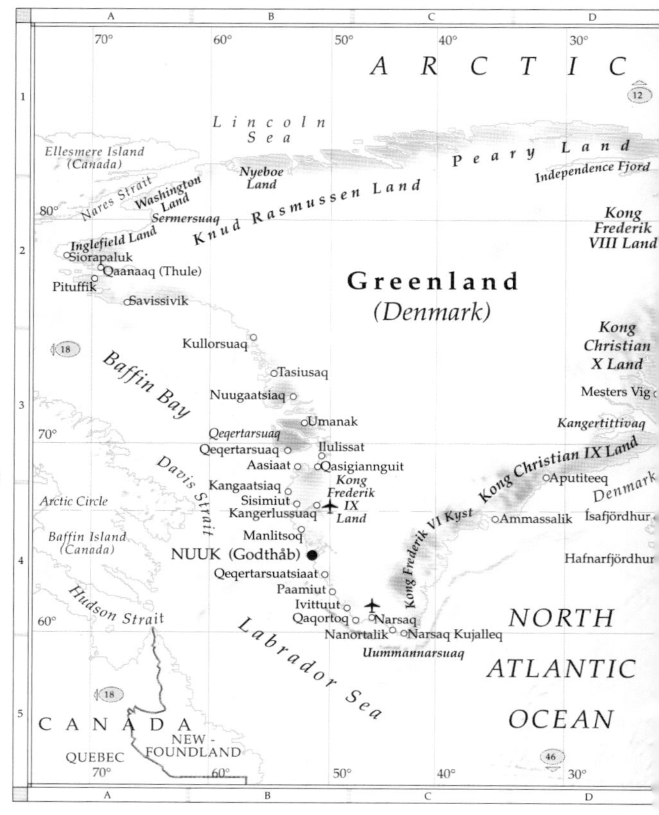
ARCTIC
Lincoln Sea
Ellesmere Island (Canada)
Nares Strait
Washington Land
Nyeboe Land
Peary Land
Independence Fjord
Knud Rasmussen Land
Sermersuaq
Inglefield Land
Siorapaluk
Qaanaaq (Thule)
Pituffik
Savissivik
Kong Frederik VIII Land
Greenland (Denmark)
Kullorsuaq
Baffin Bay
Tasiusaq
Nuugaatsiaq
Kong Christian X Land
Mesters Vig
Umanak
Qeqertarsuaq
Qeqertarsuaq
Kangertittivaq
Ilulissat
Aasiaat
Qasigiannguit
Davis Strait
Kangaatsiaq
Kong Frederik IX Land
Sisimiut
Kangerlussuaq
Kong Christian IX Land
Aputiteeq
Denmark
Arctic Circle
Ammassalik
Ísafjördhur
Kong Frederik VI Kyst
Baffin Island (Canada)
Manlitsoq
NUUK (Godthåb)
Hafnarfjördhur
Qeqertarsuatsiaat
Paamiut
Hudson Strait
Ivittuut
Qaqortoq
Narsaq
Nanortalik
Narsaq Kujalleq
Uummannarsuaq
Labrador Sea
NORTH ATLANTIC OCEAN
CANADA
QUEBEC
NEW-FOUNDLAND
0 km 500
0 miles 500

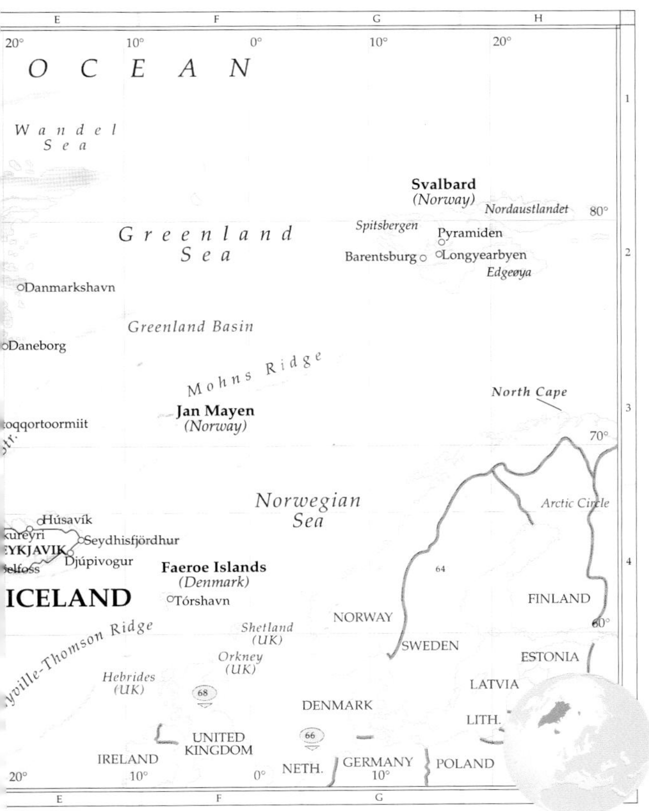
E
F
G
H
20°
10°
0°
10°
20°
OCEAN
Wandel Sea
Svalbard
(Norway)
Nordaustlandet
80°
Spitsbergen
Pyramiden
Greenland Sea
Barentsburg
Longyearbyen
Edgeøya
Danmarkshavn
Greenland Basin
Daneborg
Mohns Ridge
North Cape
Jan Mayen
(Norway)
70°
Norwegian Sea
Arctic Circle
Húsavík
Seydhisfjördhur
Djúpivogur
Faeroe Islands
(Denmark)
64
ICELAND
Tórshavn
FINLAND
NORWAY
60°
Shetland
(UK)
SWEDEN
ESTONIA
Orkney
(UK)
Hebrides
(UK)
68
LATVIA
DENMARK
LITH.
UNITED
KINGDOM
66
IRELAND
GERMANY
POLAND
NETH.
20°
10°
0°
10°
1
2
3
4

SCANDINAVIA & FINLAND

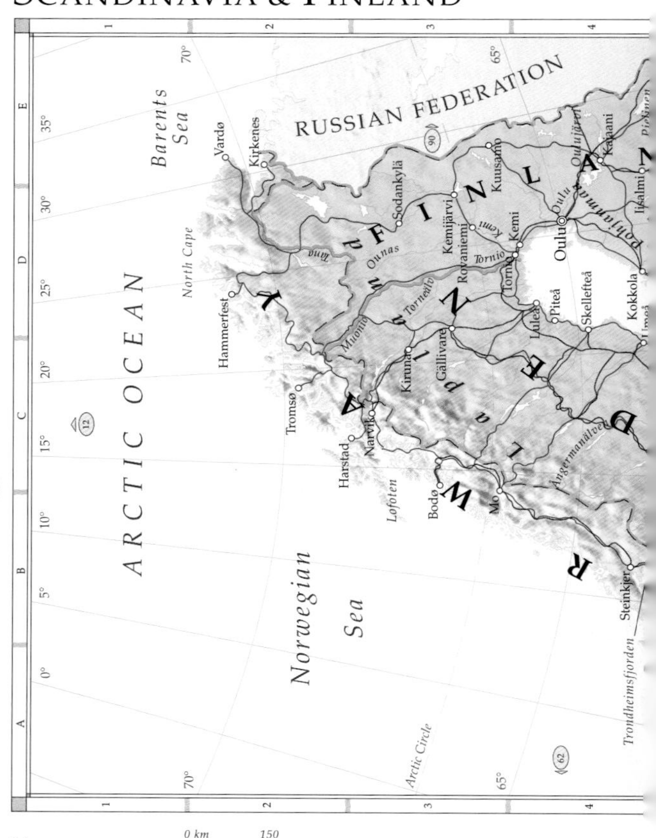
ARCTIC OCEAN
Barents Sea
Norwegian Sea
RUSSIAN FEDERATION
FINLAND
SWEDEN
NORWAY
Lapland
North Cape
Lofoten
Arctic Circle
Trondheimsfjorden
Vardø
Kirkenes
Hammerfest
Tromsø
Harstad
Narvik
Bodø
Mo
Steinkjer
Kiruna
Gällivare
Luleå
Piteå
Skellefteå
Tornio
Kemi
Oulu
Kokkola
Rovaniemi
Kemijärvi
Sodankylä
Kuusamo
Kajaani
Iisalmi
Ounas
Tana
Muonio
Torneälv
Kemi
Oulu
Oulujärvi
Ångermanälven
Pohjanmaa
70°
65°
35°
30°
25°
20°
15°
10°
5°
0°
A
B
C
D
E
1
2
3
4
12
62
90
0 km
150
0 miles
150

Ålesund
Ljusnan
Örnsköldsvik
Sundsvall
Gulf of Bothnia
Seinäjoki
Jyväskylä
Varkaus
Savonlinna
Saimaa
Mikkeli
Imatra
Tampere
Lappeenranta
Hämeenlinna
Pori
Rauma
Kouvola
Kotka
Riihimäki
Vantaa
Järvenpää
Turku
Åland
Espoo
HELSINKI
Mariehamn
Gulf of Finland
Hermansverk
Sognefjorden
Lågen
Lillehammer
Bergen
Gjøvik
Hamar
Mjøsa
Falun
Gävle
Borlänge
Hønefoss
Kongsvinger
OSLO
Uppsala
Haugesund
Drammen
Moss
Karlstad
Västerås
Stavanger
Fredrikstad
Örebro
STOCKHOLM
Porsgrunn
Halden
ESTONIA
Otra
Vänern
Nyköping
Arendal
Skövde
Norrköping
Kristiansand
Trollhättan
Vättern
Linköping
Skagerrak
Göteborg
Borås
Västervik
Jönköping
Visby
Hjørring
Frederikshavn
Gotland
Jylland
Ålborg
LATVIA
DENMARK
Randers
Halmstad
Växjö
Öland
Herning
Århus
Kalmar
Silkeborg
Helsingør
Helsingborg
Karlskrona
Vejle
Horsens
Kristianstad
Esbjerg
COPENHAGEN
Malmö
Baltic Sea
LITHUANIA
Odense
Næstved
Sjælland
Bornholm
Åbenrå
Rønne
Nakskov
Nykøbing-Falster
RUSS. FED.
(Kaliningrad)
GERMANY
POLAND
74
78
86
10°
15°
20°
55°
60°
A
B
C
D
5
6
7
8

THE LOW COUNTRIES

Waddeneilanden
Schiermonnikoog
Ameland
Terschelling
Waddenzee
Vlieland
Texel
Leeuwarden
Groningen
Delfzijl
Ems
Assen
Heerenveen
Den Helder
NETHERLANDS
Emmen
Meppel
Alkmaar
Hoorn
IJsselmeer
Lelystad
IJssel
Zwolle
Purmerend
Haarlem
AMSTERDAM
Almelo
Hilversum
Deventer
Hengelo
Enschede
Apeldoorn
Leiden
's-Gravenhage
(The Hague)
Amersfoort
Zoetermeer
Utrecht
Ede
Delft
Arnhem
Hoek van Holland
Gouda
Lek
Waal
Rotterdam
Overflakkee
Nijmegen
Dordrecht
Oss
Oosterschelde
's-Hertogenbosch
Breda
Tilburg
North Sea
4°
6°
52°

0 km 50
0 miles 50

Zeebrugge
Westerschelde
Terneuzen
Turnhout
Venlo
Oostende
Brugge
Scheldt
Antwerpen
Rhine
Sint-Niklaas
Flanders
Mechelen
Gent
GERMANY
Roeselare
Aalst
Genk
Heerlen
74
Ieper
Hasselt
Leuven
Maastricht
Kortrijk
BRUSSELS
Tienen
Mouscron
BELGIUM
Liège
Tournai
Seraing
Verviers
La Louvière
Meuse
Namur
Ourthe
Mons
Charleroi
Sambre
Dinant
Ardennes
50°
Bastogne
Vianden
Sûre
Our
FRANCE
Diekirch
LUXEMBOURG
70
Arlon
LUXEMBOURG
Meuse
Moselle
Esch-sur-Alzette
4°
6°
5
6
7
8
B
C
D
E

THE BRITISH ISLES

North Sea
ATLANTIC OCEAN
Shetland
Lerwick
Orkney
Kirkwall
Thurso
Moray Firth
Elgin
Inverness
Aberdeen
SCOTLAND
Grampian Mts.
Dundee
Perth
Firth of Forth
EDINBURGH
Stirling
Forth
Tweed
Southern Uplands
Glasgow
Greenock
Ayr
Arran
Dumfries
Loch Lomond
Oban
Fort William
Loch Ness
Ullapool
North Minch
Little Minch
Skye
Mull
Jura
Islay
Lewis
Stornoway
Outer Hebrides
North Uist
South Uist
Barra
Rosemary Bank
Newcastle upon Tyne
UNITED KINGDOM
Pennines
NORTHERN
66
62
0 km 100
0 miles 100

IRELAND
ENGLAND
WALES
FRANCE
ATLANTIC
OCEAN
Irish
Sea
English Channel
DUBLIN
LONDON
CARDIFF
Sligo
Athlone
Galway
Shannon
Tralee
Killarney
Limerick
Cork
Waterford
Wexford
Dundalk
Newry
Lough Ree
Lough Derg
Lough Corrib
Shannon
Blackwater
Barrow
Liffey
Wicklow Mts
Dingle Bay
Bantry Bay
Douglas
Man (UK)
Lancaster
Blackpool
Preston
Liverpool
Bradford
Bolton
Manchester
Leeds
York
Kingston upon Hull
Grimsby
Sheffield
Lincoln
The Wash
Norwich
Nottingham
Derby
Leicester
Peterborough
The Fens
Cambridge
Ipswich
Colchester
Southend-on-Sea
Dover
Canterbury
Channel Tunnel
Chester
Stoke-on-Trent
Shrewsbury
Birmingham
Coventry
Stratford-upon-Avon
Worcester
Gloucester
Oxford
Swindon
Reading
Thames
Severn
Bristol
Bath
Salisbury
Southampton
Portsmouth
Brighton
Isle of Wight
Bournemouth
Taunton
Exeter
Exmoor
Dartmoor
Plymouth
Barnstaple
Penzance
Land's End
Isles of Scilly
Swansea
Rhondda
Brecon Beacons
Milford Haven
Fishguard
Aberystwyth
Cardigan Bay
Snowdonia
Caernarfon
Holyhead
Anglesey
Channel Is. (UK)
St. Peter Port
Guernsey
St. Helier
Jersey
52°
50°
5°
0°
46
70
5
6
7
8
B
C
D
E

Administrative border

FRANCE & ANDORRA

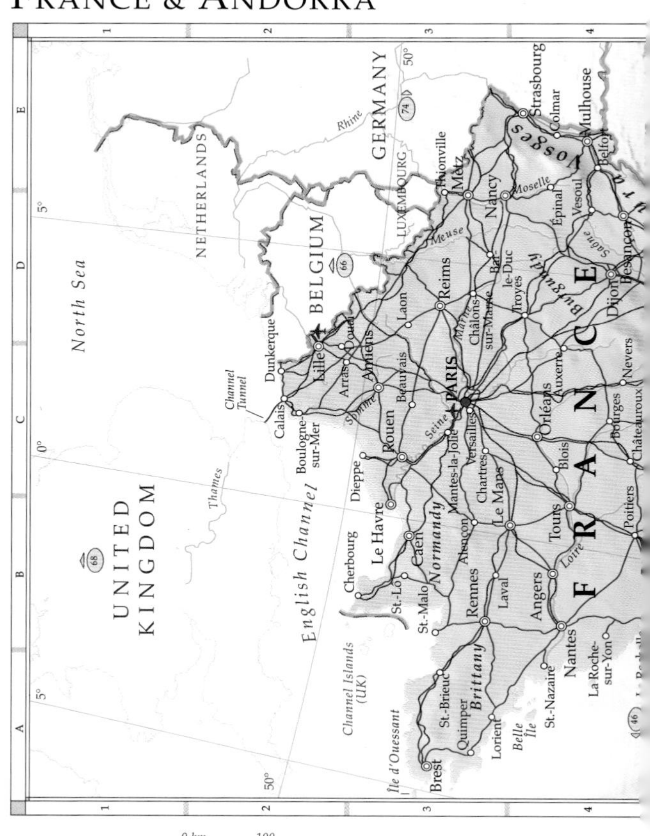
North Sea
NETHERLANDS
BELGIUM
GERMANY
LUXEMBOURG
UNITED KINGDOM
English Channel
Channel Tunnel
Thames
Rhine
Meuse
Moselle
Somme
Seine
Marne
Saône
Loire
Dunkerque
Calais
Boulogne-sur-Mer
Lille
Arras
Douai
Amiens
Dieppe
Rouen
Le Havre
Cherbourg
Caen
St.-Lô
Normandy
St.-Malo
Channel Islands (UK)
Île d'Ouessant
Brest
St.-Brieuc
Quimper
Brittany
Lorient
Belle Île
Rennes
Laval
Angers
Nantes
St.-Nazaire
La Roche-sur-Yon
Le Mans
Alençon
Mantes-la-Jolie
Chartres
Versailles
PARIS
Beauvais
Laon
Reims
Châlons-sur-Marne
Thionville
Metz
Nancy
Bar-le-Duc
Troyes
Épinal
Vesoul
Vosges
Strasbourg
Colmar
Mulhouse
Belfort
Besançon
Dijon
Burgundy
Auxerre
Orléans
Blois
Tours
Poitiers
Bourges
Châteauroux
Nevers
FRANCE
5°
0°
50°
68
66
74
46
A
B
C
D
E
1
2
3
4
0 km 100
0 miles 100

Bay of Biscay
Angoulême
Roanne
Lake Geneva
Clermont-Ferrand
Périgueux
Lyon
St.-Chamond
Annecy
Chambéry
Bordeaux
St.-Étienne
Massif Central
Dordogne
Aurillac
Le Puy
Alps
ITALY
Lot
Grenoble
Valence
Cahors
Rodez
Mende
Rhône
Mont-de-Marsan
Agen
Garonne
Bayonne
Montauban
Tarn
Auch
Albi
Cévennes
Avignon
Provence
Pau
Toulouse
Nîmes
Aix-en-Provence
MONACO
MONTE CARLO
Pyrenees
Tarbes
Montpellier
Arles
Cannes
Nice
Carcassonne
Béziers
Narbonne
Marseille
Côte d'Azur
Ligurian Sea
Perpignan
Golfe du Lion
Toulon
Îles d'Hyères
ANDORRA
ANDORRA LA VELLA
Ebro
Bastia
Corse
Ajaccio
SPAIN
Mediterranean Sea
Balearic Is. (Spain)
Sardinia (Italy)
45°
40°
0°
5°
72
74
76
B
C
D
E
5
6
7
8

SPAIN & PORTUGAL

A
B
C
D
1
2
3
4
15°
10°
40°
5°
ATLANTIC
OCEAN
Ferrol
A Coruña
Avilés
Gijón
Oviedo
Cabo Finisterre
Galicia
Lugo
Santiago
Cordillera Cantábrica
León
Miño
Pontevedra
Vigo
Ourense
Minho
Emb. de Esla
Viana do Castelo
Póvoa de Varzim
Chaves
Braga
Bragança
Valladolid
Palenc
Guimarães
Duero
Matosinhos
Vila Real
Zamora
Porto
Vila Nova de Gaia
Douro
S
P
Aveiro
Viseu
Salamanca
Coimbra
Covilhã
Figueira da Foz
Sierra de Gredo
PORTUGAL
Plasencia
Castelo Branco
Tagus
Caldas da Rainha
46
Cáceres
Santarém
Portalegre
Sintra
Cascais
Mérida
Guadiana
LISBON
Badajoz
Setúbal
Alcácer do Sal
Sierra Morena
Beja
Sines
Córdoba
Guadiana
Guadalquivir
Sevilla
Algarve
Lagos
Huelva
Andalucía
Cabo de São Vicente
Faro
Olhão
Jerez de la Frontera
Málaga
Cádiz
Marbe
Algeciras
Gibralt
(UK)
Strait of Gibraltar
50
Ceuta
(Spain)
MOROCCO
0 km
100
0 miles
100

E
F
G
H
Bay of Biscay
FRANCE
Santander
Bilbao
San Sebastián
Basque Provinces
Vitoria
Pamplona
Pyrenees
Miranda de Ebro
Logroño
Burgos
ANDORRA
Golfe du Lion
Huesca
Girona
Figueres
Catalonia
Costa Brava
Ebro
Soria
Terrassa
Lleida
Mataró
Zaragoza
Sabadell
Badalona
Barcelona
Reus
Tarragona
Tortosa
MADRID
Alcalá de Henares
Getafe
Teruel
Cuenca
Menorca
Castellón de la Plana
Palma
Mallorca
Júcar
Valencia
Islas Baleares
Albacete
Gandía
Eivissa
Formentera
Elda
Benidorm
Segura
Cieza
Alicante
Elche
Linares
Murcia
Costa Blanca
Lorca
Mediterranean Sea
Cartagena
Almería
Motril
ALGERIA
0°
5°
40°
35°
70
76
50
1
2
3
4
5

GERMANY, SWITZERLAND & AUSTRIA

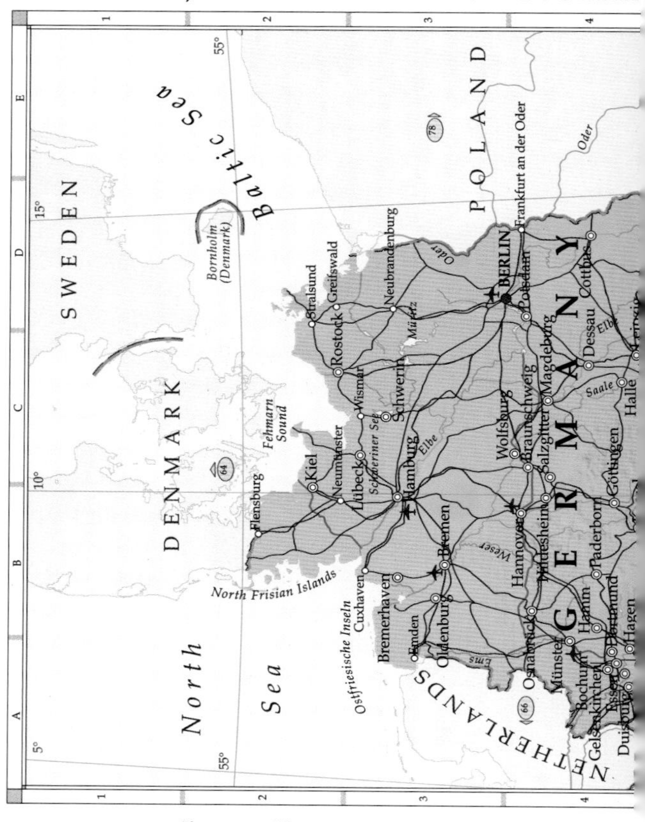
SWEDEN
DENMARK
North Sea
Baltic Sea
POLAND
GERMANY
NETHERLANDS
Bornholm (Denmark)
Fehmarn Sound
North Frisian Islands
Ostfriesische Inseln
Schweriner See
Müritz
Oder
Elbe
Weser
Ems
Saale
Flensburg
Kiel
Neumünster
Lübeck
Wismar
Rostock
Stralsund
Greifswald
Neubrandenburg
Schwerin
Hamburg
Cuxhaven
Bremerhaven
Bremen
Emden
Oldenburg
Osnabrück
Münster
Hamm
Dortmund
Bochum
Gelsenkirchen
Essen
Hagen
Paderborn
Hannover
Hildesheim
Wolfsburg
Braunschweig
Salzgitter
Magdeburg
Göttingen
Halle
Dessau
Potsdam
BERLIN
Frankfurt an der Oder
Cottbus
55°
15°
10°
5°
78
64
66
A
B
C
D
E
1
2
3
4

0 km 100
0 miles 100

CZECH REPUBLIC
AUSTRIA
SWITZERLAND
LIECHTENSTEIN
ITALY
FRANCE
SLOVENIA
BELG.
LUX.
VIENNA
BERN
VADUZ
Adriatic Sea
Lake Constance
Lake Maggiore
Bohemian Forest
Schwarzwald
Schwäbische Alb
Fränkische Alb
Thüringer Wald
Bavarian Alps
Alps
Tirol
Danube
Donau
Rhine
Inn
Mosel
Neckar
Drau
Mur
Enns
Po
Rhône
Aare
Chiemsee
Attersee
Traunsee
Neusiedler See
Lac de Neuchâtel
Lake Geneva
Aachen
Bonn
Koblenz
Trier
Wiesbaden
Mainz
Frankfurt am Main
Offenbach
Darmstadt
Fulda
Würzburg
Mannheim
Heidelberg
Saarbrücken
Karlsruhe
Heilbronn
Pforzheim
Stuttgart
Nürnberg
Erlangen
Zwickau
Jena
Regensburg
Ingolstadt
Augsburg
Ulm
München
Freiburg im Breisgau
Schaffhausen
Winterthur
Zürich
Basel
Delémont
Olten
Biel
Zug
Luzern
Interlaken
Thun
Fribourg
Yverdon
Lausanne
Montreux
Genève
Sion
Brig
Locarno
Lugano
Chur
Sankt Gallen
Bregenz
Dornbirn
Innsbruck
Lienz
Villach
Klagenfurt
Judenburg
Knittelfeld
Graz
Kapfenberg
Wiener Neustadt
Eisenstadt
Baden
Mödling
Stockerau
Krems an der Donau
Sankt Pölten
Amstetten
Linz
Traun
Wels
Braunau am Inn
Salzburg
Hallein
A
B
C
D
5
6
7
8
50°
10°
15°
70
76
78
80

ITALY & MALTA

GERMANY
AUSTRIA
HUNGARY
SWITZERLAND
LIECHTENSTEIN
FRANCE
SLOVENIA
CROATIA
BOSNIA & HERZEGOVINA
SAN MARINO
VATICAN CITY
ROME
ITALY
Alps
Dolomiti
Appennino
Adriatic Sea
Ligurian Sea
Gulf of Venice
Golfo di Genova
Po Delta
Corsica (France)
Isola d'Elba
Arcipelago Toscano
Palagruza (Croatia)
Pianosa
Isole Tremiti
Lake Geneva
Lake Maggiore
Lago di Como
Lago di Garda
Lago Trasimeno
Rhône
Po
Adige
Piave
Arno
Tevere
Toscana
Aosta
Torino
Novara
Alessandria
Monza
Milano
Bergamo
Brescia
Cremona
Piacenza
Genova
Savona
San Remo
Bolzano
Trento
Verona
Vicenza
Padova
Mantova
Treviso
Mestre
Venezia
Belluno
Udine
Trieste
Parma
Reggio nell'Emilia
Modena
Ferrara
Bologna
Ravenna
Forlì
Rimini
La Spezia
Viareggio
Pisa
Livorno
Prato
Firenze
Siena
Arezzo
Grosseto
Perugia
Assisi
Terni
Viterbo
Ancona
Ascoli Piceno
Pescara
L'Aquila
10°
15°
45°
70
74
80

0 km 100
0 miles 100

Alghero
Tirso
Nuoro
40°
Sardegna
Oristano
Mannu
Arbatax
Iglesias
Cagliari
Golfo di Gaeta
Napoli
Isola d'Ischia
Sorrento
Isola di Capri
Benevento
Ofanto
Salerno
Golfo di Salerno
Potenza
Bari
Strait of Otranto
Altamura
Brindisi
Taranto
Lecce
Golfo di Taranto
Otranto
Gallipoli
40°
Tyrrhenian
Sea
72
Cosenza
Calabria
Crotone
Catanzaro
Mediterranean Sea
Ustica
Isole Eolie
Salina
Lipari
Stromboli
Vulcano
Ionian Sea
Trapani
Palermo
Messina
Cefalù
Isole Egadi
Marsala
Sicilia
Reggio di Calabria
84
Stretto di Messina
Sicilian Channel
Caltanissetta
Salso
Agrigento
Catania
Caltagirone
Augusta
Siracusa
Pantelleria
Ragusa
Malta Channel
Mediterranean
Sea
Isole Pelagie (Italy)
Linosa
Gozo
VALLETTA
50
Lampione
Lampedusa
TUNISIA
MALTA
35°
10°
15°
50
A
B
C
D
5
6
7
8

CENTRAL EUROPE

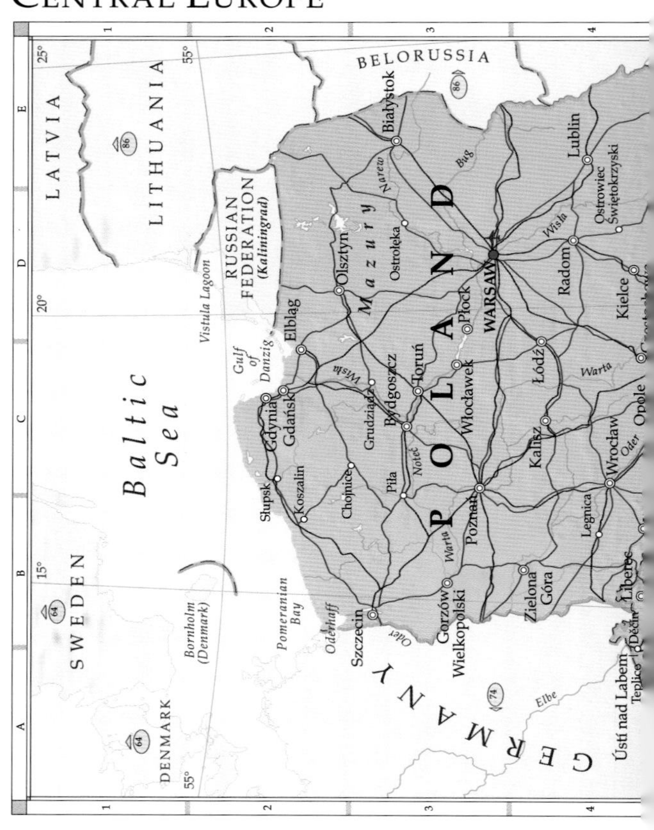
LATVIA
LITHUANIA
BELORUSSIA
RUSSIAN FEDERATION (Kaliningrad)
Baltic Sea
SWEDEN
DENMARK
Bornholm (Denmark)
Pomeranian Bay
Oderhaff
Gulf of Danzig
Vistula Lagoon
POLAND
GERMANY
Mazury
Białystok
Narew
Bug
Lublin
Ostrowiec Świętokrzyski
Wisła
Ostrołęka
Olsztyn
Elbląg
WARSAW
Płock
Radom
Kielce
Toruń
Włocławek
Łódź
Warta
Bydgoszcz
Grudziądz
Gdańsk
Gdynia
Słupsk
Koszalin
Chojnice
Piła
Noteć
Poznań
Kalisz
Wrocław
Oder
Opole
Legnica
Zielona Góra
Gorzów Wielkopolski
Szczecin
Liberec
Děčín
Teplice
Ústí nad Labem
Elbe
20°
15°
25°
55°
86
64
74

0 km 100

0 miles 100

CZECH REPUBLIC
SLOVAKIA
HUNGARY
AUSTRIA
SLOVENIA
CROATIA
BOSNIA - HERZEGOVINA
YUGOSLAVIA (Serbia)
ROMANIA
UKRAINE
ITALY
Adriatic Sea
Carpathian Mts.
Sudeten
PRAGUE
BRATISLAVA
BUDAPEST
Karlovy Vary
Kladno
Plzeň
Tábor
Jihlava
Strakonice
České Budějovice
Pardubice
Brno
Olomouc
Prostějov
Ostrava
Wodzisław Śląski
Rybnik
Gliwice
Bytom
Sosnowiec
Kraków
Tarnów
Rzeszów
Bielsko-Biała
Žilina
Martin
Trenčín
Piešťany
Trnava
Nitra
Nové Zámky
Komárno
Banská Bystrica
Lučenec
Poprad
Prešov
Košice
Rožňava
Ózd
Miskolc
Nyíregyháza
Debrecen
Szolnok
Kecskemét
Békéscsaba
Szeged
Baja
Szekszárd
Pécs
Kaposvár
Nagykanizsa
Zalaegerszeg
Szombathely
Sopron
Győr
Tatabánya
Székesfehérvár
Veszprém
Balaton
Danube
Morava
Váh
Tisza
Körös
Mures
Drava
Rába
Laborec
San
Dnestr
Elbe
88
80
74
5
6
7
8
A
B
C
D
50°
45°
15°
20°

THE WESTERN BALKANS

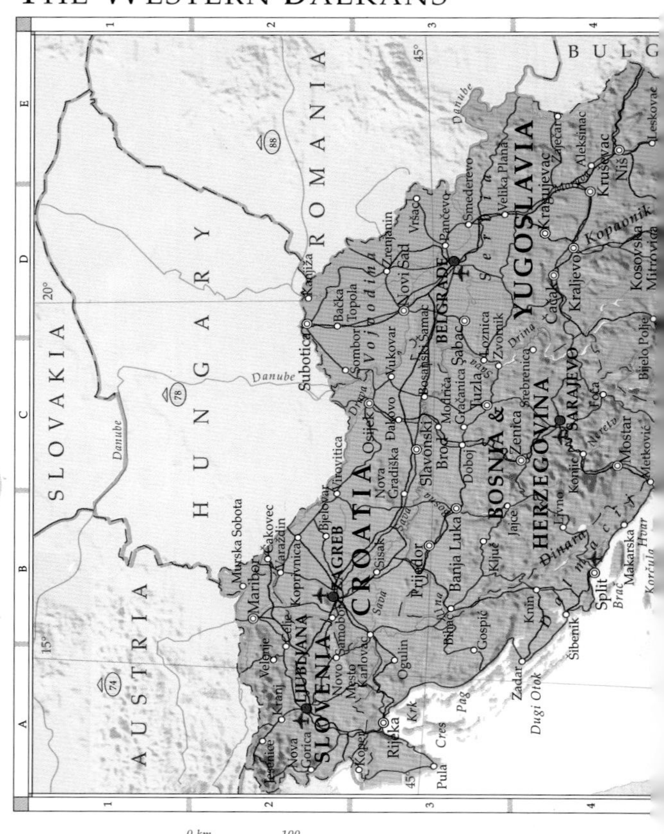
AUSTRIA
SLOVAKIA
HUNGARY
ROMANIA
BULG
SLOVENIA
CROATIA
BOSNIA & HERZEGOVINA
YUGOSLAVIA
LJUBLJANA
ZAGREB
BELGRADE
SARAJEVO
Danube
Sava
Drava
Drina
Neretva
Vojvodina
Serbia
Dinara
Kopaonik
Dalmacija
Jesenice
Nova Gorica
Kranj
Velenje
Celje
Maribor
Murska Sobota
Čakovec
Varaždin
Koprivnica
Bjelovar
Virovitica
Novo Mesto
Samobor
Karlovac
Sisak
Ogulin
Koper
Rijeka
Pula
Krk
Cres
Pag
Dugi Otok
Zadar
Gospić
Bihać
Knin
Šibenik
Split
Brač
Hvar
Korčula
Makarska
Metković
Mostar
Konjic
Livno
Jajce
Ključ
Banja Luka
Prijedor
Nova Gradiška
Slavonski Brod
Doboj
Zenica
Tuzla
Gračanica
Modriča
Bosanski Šamac
Đakovo
Osijek
Vukovar
Sombor
Subotica
Bačka Topola
Kanjiža
Novi Sad
Zrenjanin
Vršac
Pančevo
Smederevo
Šabac
Loznica
Zvornik
Srebrenica
Foča
Bijelo Polje
Čačak
Kraljevo
Kragujevac
Velika Plana
Zaječar
Aleksinac
Kruševac
Niš
Leskovac
Kosovska Mitrovica
Sava
Danube
Drava
45°
20°
15°
74
78
88
A
B
C
D
E
1
2
3
4

0 km 100
0 miles 100

Adriatic Sea
Ionian Sea
ITALY
GREECE
ALBANIA
MACEDONIA
Kosovo
TIRANA
SKOPJE
Strait of Otranto
Ionian Islands
Palagruza
(Croatia)
Dubrovnik
Podgorica
Lake Scutari
Shkodër
Lezhë
Durrës
Lushnjë
Kuçovë
Fier
Vlorë
Berat
Tepelenë
Gjirokastër
Sarandë
Konispol
Elbasan
Korçë
Lake Ohrid
Lake Prespa
Ohrid
Bitola
Prilep
Kavadarci
Gevgelija
Strumica
Štip
Kočani
Kumanovo
Titov Veles
Kičevo
Gostivar
Tetovo
Prizren
Uroševac
Priština
Peć
Black Drin
Vardar
North Albanian Alps
Lumi i Devollit
Lumi i Vjosës
40°
20°
84
76

THE MEDITERRANEAN

A
B
C
D
1
2
3
4
5
Thames
English Channel
Seine
Rhine
E U
Danube
46
ATLANTIC
OCEAN
Loire
L. Geneva
Mt. Blanc
4807m
Alps
Alps
Bay of Biscay
Massif Central
Dordogne
Rhône
Po
Apennines
Garonne
Genoa
Marseille
Livorno
C. Finisterre
Pyrenees
3404m
Golfe du Lion
2914
Ebro
Corsica
Barcelona
Iberian
Naples
Tagus
Sardinia
Valencia
Tyrrhenian Sea
Peninsula
Balearic Is.
Guadalquivir
Medite
C. St Vincent
3478m
Algiers
Tunis
Gibraltar
Oran
Tell Atlas
Malt
Strait of Gibraltar
2328m
Rif
Atlas Mountains
Sfax
Chott el Jerid
Tripoli
46
4165m
Grand Erg Occidental
Canary Is. (Spain)
Grand Erg Oriental
A F R I
48
S a h a r

0 km 400
0 miles 400

E
F
G
H
60
R O P E
2653m
Carpathians
2303m
Hungarian Plain
2543m
Dnieper
Don
Sea of Azov
Danube Delta
Crimea
Danube
Dinaric Alps
2693m
Balkan Mts.
2376m
2925m
Rhodope Mts.
Black Sea
Bosporus
El'brus 5642m
Caucasus Mts.
Adriatic Sea
Pindus Mts.
Mt. Ararat 5122m
Lesbos
Aegean Sea
Izmir
Anatolia
Lake Van
Ionian Sea
Piraeus
3917m
Taurus Mts.
cily
Peloponnese
Kos
Rhodes
Euphrates
Tigris
Crete
Cyprus
3088m
Anti-Lebanon
ranean Sea
Haifa
878m
Syrian Desert
Gulf of Sirte
Nile Delta
Port Said
Dead Sea -400m
92
Suez Canal
Qattara Depression -133m
ASIA
Nile
C A
Red Sea
Arabian Peninsula
Libyan Desert
a
1
2
3
4
5

BULGARIA & GREECE

ROMANIA
BULGARIA
YUGOSLAVIA
(Serbia)
MACEDONIA
ALBANIA
GREECE
TURKEY
Black Sea
Thracian Sea
Marmara Denizi
Danube
Olt
Iskŭr
Morava
Struma
Vardar
Maritsa
Tundzha
Arda
Kamchiya
Pineios
Balkan Mountains
Rhodope Mountains
Pindos
Vidin
Ruse
Pleven
Lovech
Vratsa
Botevgrad
SOFIA
Pernik
Razgrad
Dobrich
Varna
Shumen
Gabrovo
Kazanlŭk
Sliven
Yambol
Stara Zagora
Burgas
Pomorie
Plovdiv
Pazardzhik
Velingrad
Khaskovo
Yazovir Iskŭr
Blagoevgrad
Petrich
Orestiáda
Alexandroúpoli
Komotiní
Xánthi
Kavála
Dráma
Sérres
Kilkís
Thessaloníki
Kalamariá
Kateríni
Véroia
Kozáni
Flórina
Lárisa
Kardítsa
Tríkala
Vólos
Ioánnina
Kérkyra
Lake Ohrid
Lake Prespa
Thásos
Samothráki
Límnos
Lésvos
Thermaïkós Kólpos
Ákra Kanestron
Ákra Dhrepanon
Ákra Pínnes
Voreioi Sporades
20°
25°
40°
88
80
96
A
B
C
D
E
1
2
3
4

0 km 100

0 miles 100

TURKEY
LIBYA
Aegean Sea
Ionian Sea
Mediterranean Sea
Sea of Crete
Mirtóo Pelagos
Kykládes
Dodekánisos
Pelopónnisos
ónioi Nísoi
Evvoia
Chalkida
Acharnes
Chalandri
ATHENS
Peiraias
Dioriga Korinthou
Korinthiakós Kólpos
Kórinthos
Trípoli
Spárti
Kalamata
Pátra
Agrinio
Leivádia
Lefkáda
Kefallinía
Zákynthos
Kýthira
Kéa
Mílos
Páros
Thíra
Íos
Náxos
Amorgós
Astypálaia
Míkonos
Tínos
Ándros
Ikaría
Sámos
Chíos
Chíos
Kos
Ródos
Ródos
Kárpathos
Kríti
Chaniá
Irákleio
96
76
50
54
20°
25°
35°
35°
A
B
C
D
5
6
7
8

THE BALTIC STATES & BELORUSSIA

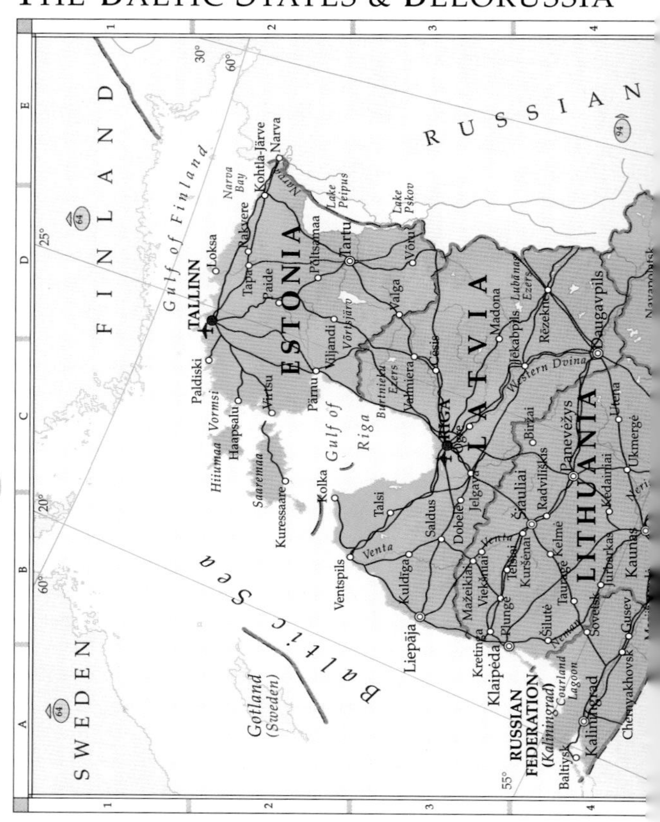
FINLAND
SWEDEN
RUSSIAN
RUSSIAN FEDERATION (Kaliningrad)
ESTONIA
LATVIA
LITHUANIA
Gulf of Finland
Gulf of Riga
Baltic Sea
Gotland (Sweden)
Hiiumaa
Saaremaa
Vormsi
Narva Bay
Lake Peipus
Lake Pskov
Võrtsjärv
Burtnieku Ezers
Lubānas Ezers
Western Dvina
Venta
Neman
Courland Lagoon
TALLINN
RIGA
Paldiski
Loksa
Rakvere
Kohtla-Järve
Narva
Tapa
Paide
Põltsamaa
Tartu
Võru
Valga
Viljandi
Pärnu
Virtsu
Haapsalu
Kuressaare
Kolka
Talsi
Ventspils
Valmiera
Cēsis
Madona
Rēzekne
Jēkabpils
Daugavpils
Ogre
Jelgava
Dobele
Saldus
Kuldīga
Liepāja
Birżai
Panevėžys
Utena
Ukmergė
Kėdainiai
Šiauliai
Radviliškis
Kaunas
Jurbarkas
Tauragė
Kelmė
Telšiai
Kuršėnai
Mažeikiai
Viekšniai
Plungė
Kretinga
Klaipėda
Šilutė
Sovetsk
Gusev
Chernyakhovsk
Kaliningrad
Baltiysk
Navapolatsk
64
94
1
2
3
4
A
B
C
D
E
20°
25°
30°
55°
60°

0 km 100

0 miles 100

FEDERATION
BELORUSSIA
UKRAINE
POLAND
Hlybokaye
Druskininkai
Lyepyel'
Western Dvina
Vitsyebsk
Hrodna
Maladzyechna
Orsha
Barysaw
Dnieper
Neman
MINSK
Zhodzina
Bug
Vawkavysk
Horki
Byerazino
Slonim
Baranavichy
Mahilyow
Bykhaw
Krychaw
Brest
Slutsk
Kobryn
Salihorsk
Babruysk
Pinsk
Luninyets
Ptsich
Zhlobin
Pripet
Pripet Marshes
Svyetlahorsk
Rechytsa
Homyel'
Mazyr
Kalinkavichy
Kyyivs'ke Vdskh.
78
88
40°
50°
25°
30°
5
6
7
8
B
C
D
E

UKRAINE, MOLDAVIA & ROMANIA

BELORUSSIA
POLAND
SLOVAKIA
HUNGARY
YUGOSLAVIA
(Serbia)
BULGARIA
ROMANIA
MOLDAVIA
U K R
Pripet
Pripet Marshes
Bug
Vistula
Kovel'
Luts'k
Korosten'
Rivne
Zhytomyr
L'viv
Ternopil'
Khmel'-nyts'kyy
Vinnytsy
Uzhhorod
Mukacheve
Ivano-Frankivs'k
Kam"yanets'-Podil's'kyy
Carpathian Mountains
Chernivtsi
Dniester
Satu Mare
Baia Mare
Dej
Suceava
Botoşani
Rîbniţa
Bălţi
Oradea
Transylvania
Dubăsari
Iaşi
CHIŞINĂU
Cluj-Napoca
Piatra-Neamţ
Tiraspol
Arad
Târgu Mureş
Bacău
Tighina
Alba Iulia
Siret
Timişoara
Deva
Basarabeasca
Danube
Sibiu
Focşani
Reşiţa
Carpaţii Meridionali
Braşov
Galaţi
Râmnicu Vâlcea
Reni
Târgovişte
Buzău
Tulcea
Piteşti
Brăila
Drobeta-Turnu Severin
Ploieşti
Danube Delta
Craiova
BUCHAREST
Danube
Olt
Constanţa
Corabia
Giurgiu
Eforie-Nord
Mangalia
78
86
80
84
20°
50°
30°
A
B
C
D
1
2
3
4
5
0 km 100
0 miles 100

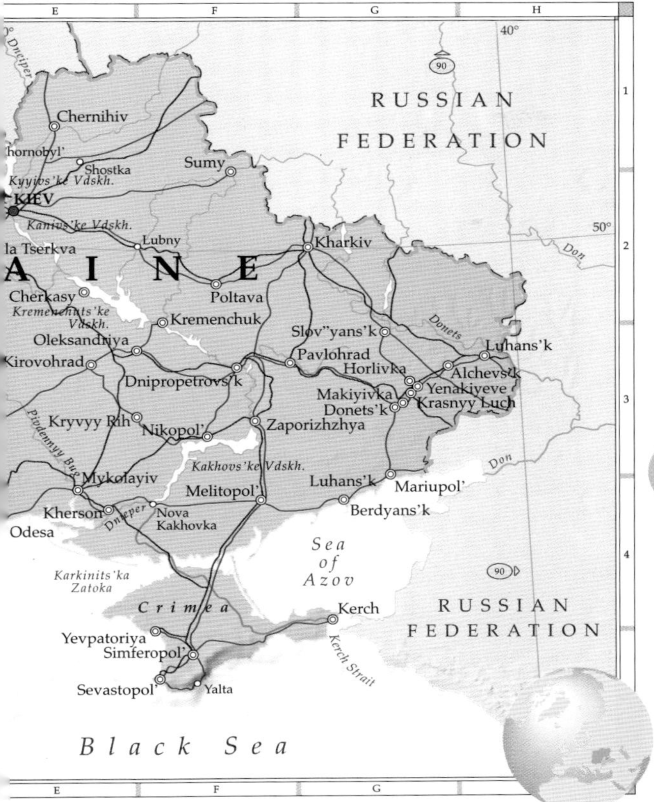
E
F
G
H
1
2
3
4
40°
50°
90
RUSSIAN FEDERATION
Chernihiv
Shostka
Sumy
Kyyivs'ke Vdskh.
KIEV
Kanivs'ke Vdskh.
Lubny
Kharkiv
Don
Poltava
Cherkasy
Kremenchuts'ke Vdskh.
Kremenchuk
Oleksandriya
Slov"yans'k
Donets
Luhans'k
Kirovohrad
Pavlohrad
Horlivka
Alchevs'k
Dnipropetrovs'k
Makiyivka
Yenakiyeve
Donets'k
Krasnyy Luch
Pivdennyy Buh
Kryvyy Rih
Nikopol'
Zaporizhzhya
Kakhovs'ke Vdskh.
Mykolayiv
Melitopol'
Luhans'k
Mariupol'
Kherson
Dnieper
Nova Kakhovka
Berdyans'k
Odesa
Sea of Azov
Karkinits'ka Zatoka
Crimea
Kerch
RUSSIAN FEDERATION
Yevpatoriya
Simferopol'
Kerch Strait
Sevastopol'
Yalta
Black Sea

European Russia

ARCTIC OCEAN
Norwegian Sea
Arctic Circle
Barents Sea
Novaya Zemlya
Karskoye More
Ostrov Kolguyev
Ostrov Vaygach
NORWAY
SWEDEN
FINLAND
Murmansk
Kol'skiy Poluostrov
Beloye More
Baltic Sea
Gulf of Finland
ESTONIA
St Petersburg
LATVIA
LITHUANIA
BELORUSSIA
Pskov
Nevel'
Smolensk
Tver'
Yaroslavl'
Novgorod
Ladozhskoye Ozero
Petrozavodsk
Onezhskoye Ozero
Onega
Cherepovets
Rybinskoye Vdkhr.
Vologda
Kotlas
Syktyvkar
Arkhangel'sk
Severnaya Dvina
Pinega
Mezen'
Pechora
Arctic Circle
Usa
Vorkuta
Ural Mountains
RUSSIAN FEDERATION
0 km 400
0 miles 400

Ural Mountains
KAZAKHSTAN
UZBEKISTAN
UKRAINE
GEORGIA
ARMENIA
AZERBAIJAN
AZ
TURKEY
IRAN
IRAQ
Caspian Sea
Black Sea
Sea of Azov
Aral Sea
Caucasus
Volga
Don
Donets
Ural
Kuma
Vyatka
Syr Darya
Perm'
Izhevsk
Naberezhnyye Chelny
Ufa
Orenburg
Orsk
Nizhniy Novgorod
Cheboksary
Kazan
Ul'yanovsk
Tol'yatti
Samara
Balakovo
Saransk
Penza
Saratov
Mikhaylovka
Volgograd
Astrakhan'
Elista
Stavropol'
Nal'chik
Vladikavkaz
Groznyy
Makhachkala
Rostov-na-Donu
Krasnodar
Cherkessk
Sochi
Vladimir
Ryazan
Tambov
Tula
Orël
Bryansk
Belgorod
Voronezh
50°
60°
40°
A
B
C
D
5
6
7
8
94
88
96
100

CONTINENTAL NORTH & WEST ASIA

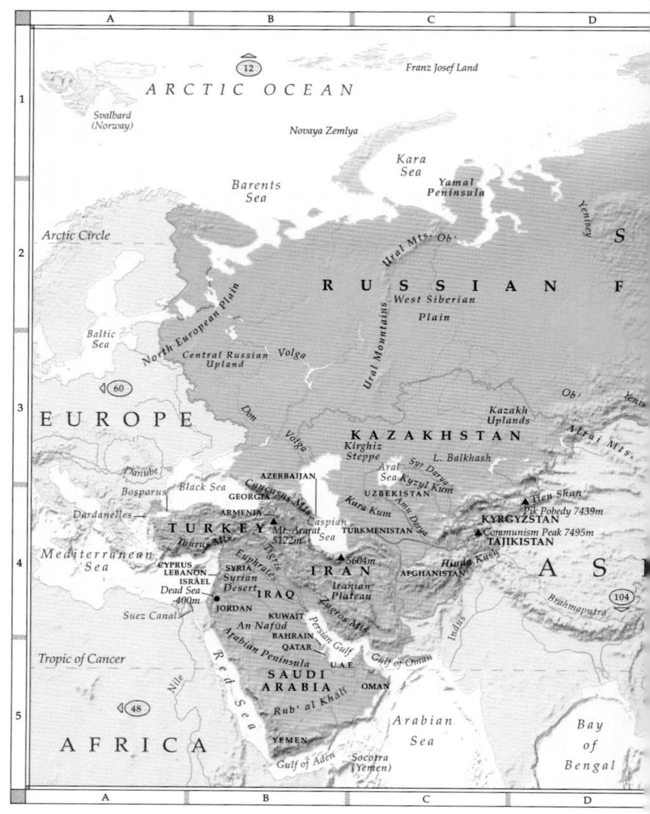
A
B
C
D
1
2
3
4
5
12
ARCTIC OCEAN
Franz Josef Land
Svalbard (Norway)
Novaya Zemlya
Kara Sea
Yamal Peninsula
Barents Sea
Yenisey
Arctic Circle
Ural Mts.
Ob'
S
RUSSIAN F
West Siberian Plain
North European Plain
Baltic Sea
Central Russian Upland
Volga
Ural Mountains
60
Ob'
Yenis
Kazakh Uplands
EUROPE
Don
Volga
Altai Mts.
KAZAKHSTAN
Kirghiz Steppe
L. Balkhash
Aral Sea
Syr Darya
Danube
AZERBAIJAN
Kyzyl Kum
Bosporus
Black Sea
Caucasus Mts.
UZBEKISTAN
Tien Shan
GEORGIA
Kara Kum
Amu Darya
Pik Pobedy 7439m
Dardanelles
ARMENIA
KYRGYZSTAN
Caspian Sea
TURKEY
Mt. Ararat 5122m
TURKMENISTAN
Communism Peak 7495m
TAJIKISTAN
Taurus Mts.
Mediterranean Sea
Euphrates
Tigris
5604m
Hindu Kush
CYPRUS
LEBANON
SYRIA
IRAN
AFGHANISTAN
ASI
ISRAEL
Syrian Desert
Iranian Plateau
Dead Sea -400m
IRAQ
104
Brahmaputra
JORDAN
Suez Canal
KUWAIT
Zagros Mts.
Indus
An Nafūd
Persian Gulf
BAHRAIN
Arabian Peninsula
QATAR
Tropic of Cancer
U.A.E.
Gulf of Oman
SAUDI ARABIA
Red Sea
Nile
OMAN
48
Rub' al Khali
Arabian Sea
Bay of Bengal
AFRICA
YEMEN
Gulf of Aden
Socotra (Yemen)
0 km
1000
0 miles
1000

E
F
G
H
12
ARCTIC OCEAN
New Siberian Islands
Limit of permanent pack-ice
Laptev Sea
East Siberian Sea
Wrangel I.
Chukchi Sea
Arctic Circle
Bering Strait
Verkhoyansk Range
Lena
Cherskiy Range
Kolyma Range
ERATION
Lena
Dzhugdzhur Range
Stanovoy Range
Amur
Angara
L. Baikal
Sea of Okhotsk
Kamchatka
4750m
Bering Sea
Sakhalin
Sikhote-Alin Range
Hokkaidō
Sea of Japan
Honshū
122
PACIFIC OCEAN
Yangtze
Kyūshū
Taiwan
Tropic of Cancer
Northern Marianas (USA)
Mariana Trench
Hainan Dao
Mekong
South China Sea
Luzon
Guam (USA)
1
2
3
4

RUSSIA & KAZAKHSTAN

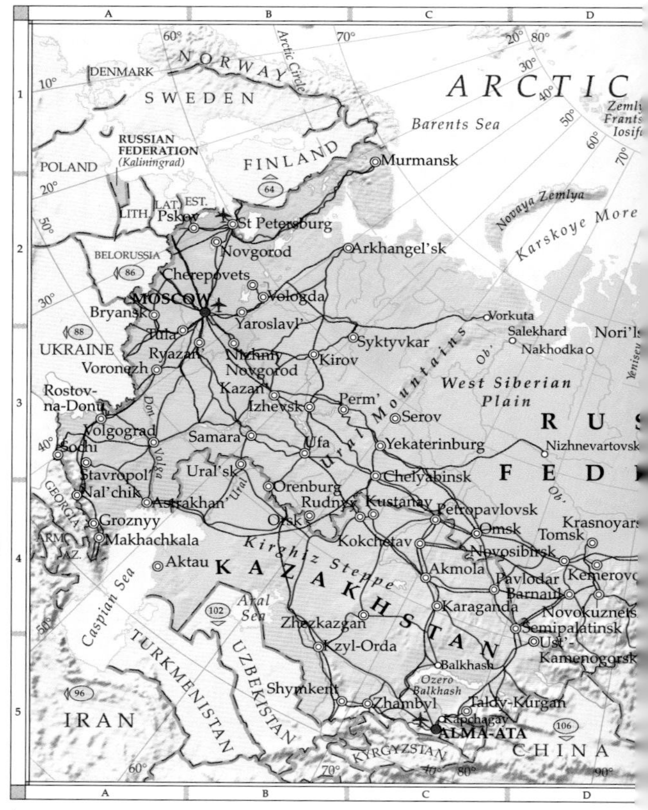

ARCTIC
Barents Sea
NORWAY
SWEDEN
DENMARK
FINLAND
RUSSIAN FEDERATION (Kaliningrad)
POLAND
LAT.
EST.
LITH.
BELORUSSIA
UKRAINE
GEORGIA
ARM.
AZ.
Murmansk
St Petersburg
Pskov
Novgorod
Arkhangel'sk
Cherepovets
Vologda
MOSCOW
Bryansk
Yaroslavl'
Tula
Ryazan'
Nizhniy Novgorod
Kirov
Syktyvkar
Vorkuta
Salekhard
Nakhodka
Nori'l'sk
Voronezh
Rostov-na-Donu
Kazan'
Perm'
Izhevsk
Serov
Volgograd
Samara
Ufa
Yekaterinburg
Nizhnevartovsk
Sochi
Stavropol'
Nal'chik
Ural'sk
Orenburg
Chelyabinsk
Astrakhan'
Rudnyy
Kustanay
Petropavlovsk
Orsk
Omsk
Tomsk
Krasnoyarsk
Groznyy
Makhachkala
Kokchetav
Novosibirsk
Aktau
Akmola
Pavlodar
Kemerovo
Barnaul
Karaganda
Novokuznetsk
Semipalatinsk
Zhezkazgan
Kzyl-Orda
Ust'-Kamenogorsk
Balkhash
Ozero Balkhash
Shymkent
Zhambyl
Taldy-Kurgan
Kapchagay
ALMA-ATA
Novaya Zemlya
Karskoye More
Zemlya Frantsa Iosifa
Ural Mountains
West Siberian Plain
RUSSIAN FEDERATION
Kirghiz Steppe
KAZAKHSTAN
Caspian Sea
Aral Sea
TURKMENISTAN
UZBEKISTAN
KYRGYZSTAN
CHINA
IRAN
Ob'
Yenisey
Don
Volga
Ural
Arctic Circle
64
86
88
96
102
106
0 km 500
0 miles 500

OCEAN
Ostrov Vrangel'ya
Vostochno-Sibirskoye More
Arctic Circle
Pevek
Ust' Chaun
Anadyr'
Ambarchik
Bering Sea
Severnaya Zemlya
Novosibirskiye Ostrova
More Laptevykh
Ozero Taymyr
Tiksi
Ossora
Ust'-Kamchatsk
Kamchatka
Magadan
Petropavlovsk-Kamchatskiy
Verkhoyanskiy Khrebet
Lena
Olenëk
Central Siberian Plateau
Okhotsk
Yakutsk
Suntar
Siberia
Sea of Okhotsk
Sakhalin
Kurile Islands
Komsomol'sk-na-Amure
Skovorodno
Bratsk
Ozero Baykal
Romanovka
Blagoveshchensk
Khabarovsk
Yuzhhno-Sakhalinsk
JAPAN
Chita
Amur
Oka
Irkutsk
Ulan-Ude
Vladivostok
CHINA
MONGOLIA

TURKEY, CYPRUS & THE CAUCASUS

ROMANIA
Danube
BULGARIA
Black Sea
Edirne
Kırklareli
GREECE
Bosporus
Tekirdağ
Kâgıthane
İstanbul
Zonguldak
Dardanelles
Marmara Denizi
İzmit
Karabük
Kastamonu
Sinop
Samsun
Çanakkale
Bursa
Adapazarı
Çankırı
Kızıl Irmak
Çorum
Tokat
ANKARA
Balıkesir
Eskişehir
Yozgat
Ayvalık
Kütahya
Lesbos (Greece)
Manisa
Uşak
Afyon
Chios
İzmir
Nevşehir
Kayseri
Samos
Aydın
Tuz Gölü
Niğde
Denizli
Konya
Muğla
İsparta
Ereğli
Bodrum
Antalya
Osmaniye
Adana
Tarsus
Gaziantep
Dalaman
Toros Dağları
Mersin
İskenderun
Antalya Körfezi
Antakya
Rhodes (Greece)
Girne (Kyrenia)
TURKISH REPUBLIC OF NORTHERN CYPRUS
Gazimağusa (Famagusta)
Kárpathos (Greece)
NICOSIA
Larnaca
Paphos
Limassol
Mediterranean Sea
CYPRUS
Crete (Greece)
LEBANON
0 km 200
0 miles 200

RUSSIAN FEDERATION
Caucasus
Caspian Sea
GEORGIA
TBILISI
Rust'avi
K'ut'aisi
Gagra
Sokhumi
Och'amch'ire
P'ot'i
Bat'umi
Hopa
Rize
Trabzon
Gyumri
Kars
Vanadzor
ARMENIA
YEREVAN
Sevana Lich
AZERBAIJAN
Gäncä
Mingäçevir
Quba
Sumqayıt
BAKU
Nagorno Karabakh
Xankändi
Naxçıvan
AZERBAIJAN
Länkäran
Erzincan
Erzurum
Muş
Van Gölü
Van
Elâzığ
Malatya
Diyarbakır
Siirt
Batman
Adıyaman
Mardin
Şanlıurfa
IRAN
IRAQ
SYRIA
Euphrates
Tigris
Aras
Kura
Enguri
Alazani

THE NEAR EAST

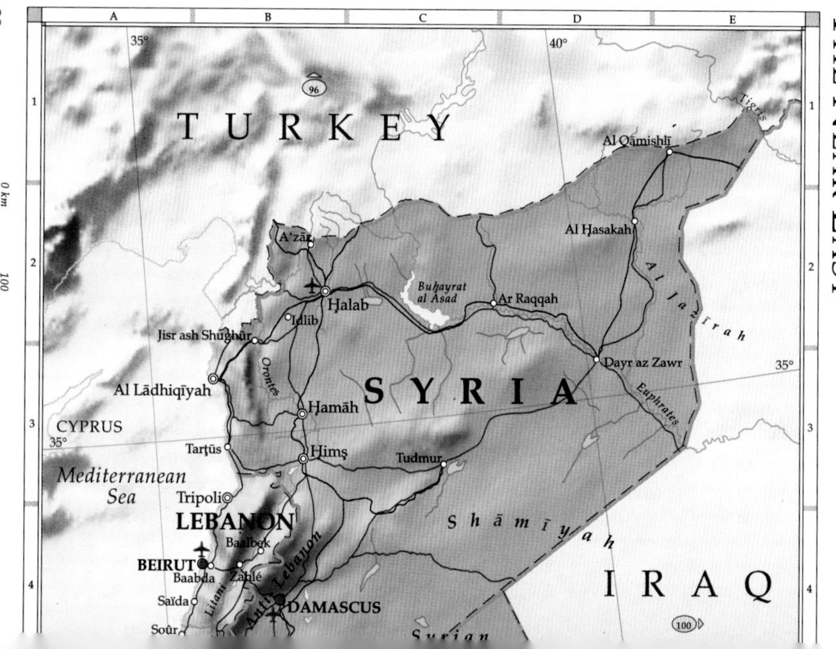
TURKEY
SYRIA
IRAQ
LEBANON
CYPRUS
Mediterranean Sea
Tigris
Euphrates
Orontes
Litani
Al Jazīrah
Shāmīyah
Anti-Lebanon
Buḥayrat al Asad
Al Qāmishlī
Al Ḥasakah
Dayr az Zawr
Ar Raqqah
Tudmur
Ḥalab
A'zāz
Idlib
Jisr ash Shughūr
Al Lādhiqīyah
Ḥamāh
Ḥimṣ
Ṭarṭūs
Tripoli
Baalbek
Zahlé
DAMASCUS
BEIRUT
Baabda
Saïda
Soûr
96
100
35°
40°

0 km 100
0 miles 100

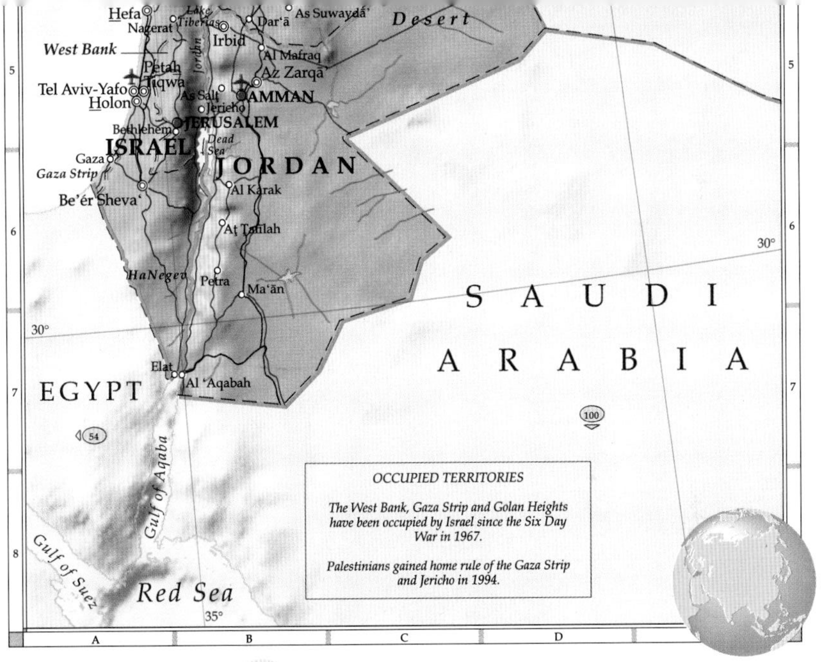
Hefa
Lake Tiberias
As Suwaydā'
Nazerat
Dar'ā
Desert
Irbid
West Bank
Jordan
Al Mafraq
Petah Tiqwa
Az Zarqā
Tel Aviv-Yafo
As Salt
AMMAN
Holon
Jericho
JERUSALEM
Bethlehem
ISRAEL
Dead Sea
Gaza
JORDAN
Gaza Strip
Al Karak
Be'ér Sheva'
Aṭ Ṭafīlah
30°
HaNegev
Petra
Ma'ān
SAUDI
30°
ARABIA
Elat
Al 'Aqabah
EGYPT
100
54
OCCUPIED TERRITORIES
The West Bank, Gaza Strip and Golan Heights have been occupied by Israel since the Six Day War in 1967.
Palestinians gained home rule of the Gaza Strip and Jericho in 1994.
Gulf of Aqaba
Gulf of Suez
Red Sea
35°
A
B
C
D
5
6
7
8

THE MIDDLE EAST

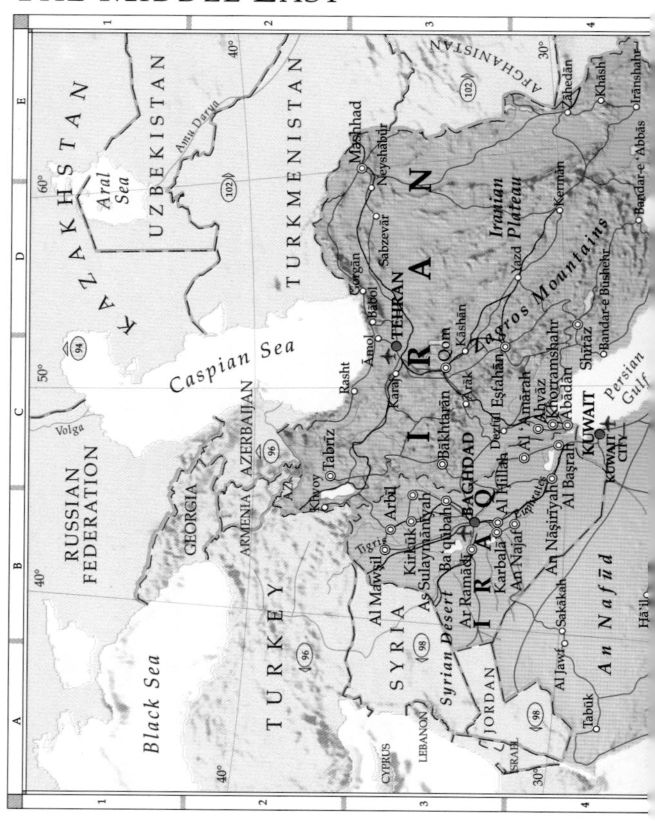
KAZAKHSTAN
UZBEKISTAN
TURKMENISTAN
AFGHANISTAN
RUSSIAN FEDERATION
GEORGIA
ARMENIA
AZERBAIJAN
TURKEY
SYRIA
IRAQ
IRAN
KUWAIT
JORDAN
LEBANON
ISRAEL
CYPRUS
Aral Sea
Caspian Sea
Black Sea
Persian Gulf
Amu Darya
Volga
Tigris
Euphrates
Iranian Plateau
Zagros Mountains
Syrian Desert
An Nafūd
Mashhad
Neyshābūr
Sabzevār
Gorgān
Bābol
Āmol
TEHRAN
Karaj
Rasht
Qom
Kāshān
Arāk
Eşfahān
Yazd
Kermān
Zāhedān
Khāsh
Īrānshahr
Bandar-e 'Abbās
Bandar-e Būshehr
Shīrāz
Bākhtarān
Dezfūl
Ahvāz
Khorramshahr
Ābādān
Al 'Amārah
Tabrīz
Khvoy
Arbīl
Kirkūk
As Sulaymānīyah
Al Mawşil
Ba'qūbah
BAGHDAD
Ar Ramādī
Karbalā
An Najaf
Al Hillah
An Nāşirīyah
Al Başrah
KUWAIT CITY
Sakākah
Al Jawf
Tabūk
Hā'il
1
2
3
4
A
B
C
D
E
30°
40°
50°
60°
94
96
98
102

0 km 400
0 miles 400

SAUDI ARABIA
QATAR
DOHA
UNITED ARAB EMIRATES
ABU DHABI
MUSCAT
OMAN
YEMEN
SANA
ERITREA
DJIBOUTI
SOMALIA
ETHIOPIA
SUDAN
EGYPT
RIYADH
Red Sea
Gulf of Oman
Arabian Sea
Gulf of Aden
Bab el Mandeb
INDIAN OCEAN
Rub' al Khālī
Tropic of Cancer
Suquţrá (Yemen)
Al Madīnah
Buraydah
Shaqrā'
Al Hufūf
Ḥaraḍ
Laylá
As Sulayyil
Makkah
Jiddah
Yanbu' al Baḥr
Aṭ Ṭā'if
Abhā
Najrān
Jīzān
Ṣa'dah
Al Ḥudaydah
Zabīd
Ta'izz
'Adan
Al Mukallā
Say'ūn
Sanāw
Sayḥūt
Ṣalālah
Şawqirah
Duqm
Nazwá
Ar Rustāq
Şuḥār
Şūr
Dubai
Sharjah
5
6
7
8
A
B
C
D
20°
10°
40°
50°
54
112

CENTRAL ASIA

A
B
C
D
1
2
3
4
5
50°
60°
40°
30°
KAZAKHSTAN
Aral Sea
Syr Darya
Ustyurt Plateau
UZBEKISTAN
Nukus
Këneurgench
Tel'mansk
Dashkhovuz
Urgench
Turtkul'
Uchkuduk
Zarafshan
Ozero Aydarku
Caspian Sea
Zaliv Kara-Bogaz-Gol
TURKMENISTAN
Turkmenbashy
Cheleken
Nebitdag
Gazandzhyk
Gyzylarbat
Turan Lowland
Karakumy
Bukhara
Seydi
Samarkand
Chardzhev
Komsomol'sk
Karshi
Sayat
Amu Darya
Bakherden
Gëkdepe
Byuzmeyin
ASHGABAT
Karakumskiy Kanal
Kaka
Tedzhen
Mary
Bayramaly
Yëloten
Kerki
Murgab
Āqchah
Sheberghān
Mazār-e Sharif
Meymaneh
Bālā Morghāb
Gushgy
Qal'eh-ye Now
Band-e Torkestān
Morghāb
Herāt
Harīrūd
100
I R A N
AFGHANISTAN
Farāh
Gereshk
Kalāt
Kandahār
Zaranj
Dasht-e-Mārgow
Helmand
60°

0 km 200
0 miles 200

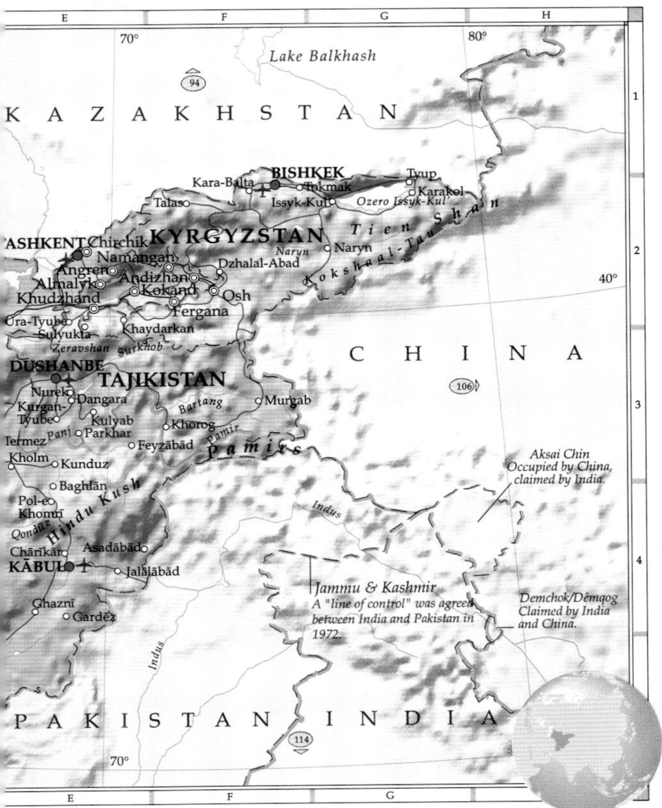

Lake Balkhash
KAZAKHSTAN
BISHKEK
Kara-Balta
Tokmak
Tyup
Karakol
Talas
Issyk-Kul
Ozero Issyk-Kul'
KYRGYZSTAN
Tien Shan
TASHKENT
Chirchik
Namangan
Naryn
Dzhalal-Abad
Kokshaal-Tau
Angren
Andizhan
Almalyk
Kokand
Osh
Khudzhand
Fergana
Ura-Tyube
Sulyukta
Khaydarkan
Zeravshan
Surkhob
DUSHANBE
TAJIKISTAN
CHINA
Nurek
Dangara
Kurgan-Tyube
Kulyab
Bartang
Murgab
Khorog
Panj
Parkhar
Termez
Feyzābād
Pamir
Pamirs
Kholm
Kunduz
Baghlān
Hindu Kush
Pol-e-Khomrī
Qondūz
Chārīkār
Asadābād
KĀBUL
Jalālābād
Ghaznī
Gardēz
Indus
Aksai Chin
Occupied by China, claimed by India.
Jammu & Kashmir
A "line of control" was agreed between India and Pakistan in 1972.
Demchok/Dêmqog
Claimed by India and China.
PAKISTAN
INDIA
70°
80°
40°
94
106
114

EAST & SOUTH ASIA

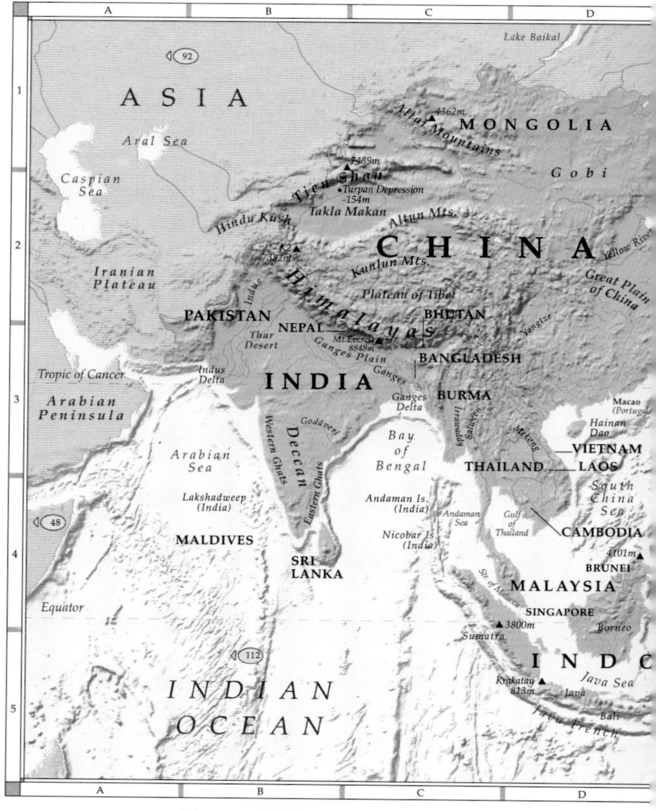

A
B
C
D
1
2
3
4
5
Lake Baikal
92
ASIA
Altai Mountains
4362m
MONGOLIA
Aral Sea
7439m
Gobi
Caspian Sea
Tien Shan
Turpan Depression -154m
Takla Makan
Hindu Kush
Altun Mts.
K2 7382m
CHINA
Yellow River
Kunlun Mts.
Iranian Plateau
Great Plain of China
Himalayas
Plateau of Tibet
Indus
PAKISTAN
BHUTAN
NEPAL
Yangtze
Thar Desert
Mt.Everest 8848m
Ganges Plain
BANGLADESH
Tropic of Cancer
Indus Delta
Ganges
INDIA
Ganges Delta
BURMA
Macao
Arabian Peninsula
Hainan Dao
Godavari
Irrawaddy
Salween
Mekong
Western Ghats
Deccan
Bay of Bengal
VIETNAM
Arabian Sea
THAILAND
LAOS
Eastern Ghats
South China Sea
Lakshadweep (India)
Andaman Is. (India)
Andaman Sea
Gulf of Thailand
48
CAMBODIA
MALDIVES
Nicobar Is. (India)
4101m
SRI LANKA
BRUNEI
MALAYSIA
Equator
SINGAPORE
3800m
Borneo
Sumatra
112
Krakatau 813m
Java Sea
Java
INDIAN OCEAN
Bali
Java Trench
0 km
1000
0 miles
1000

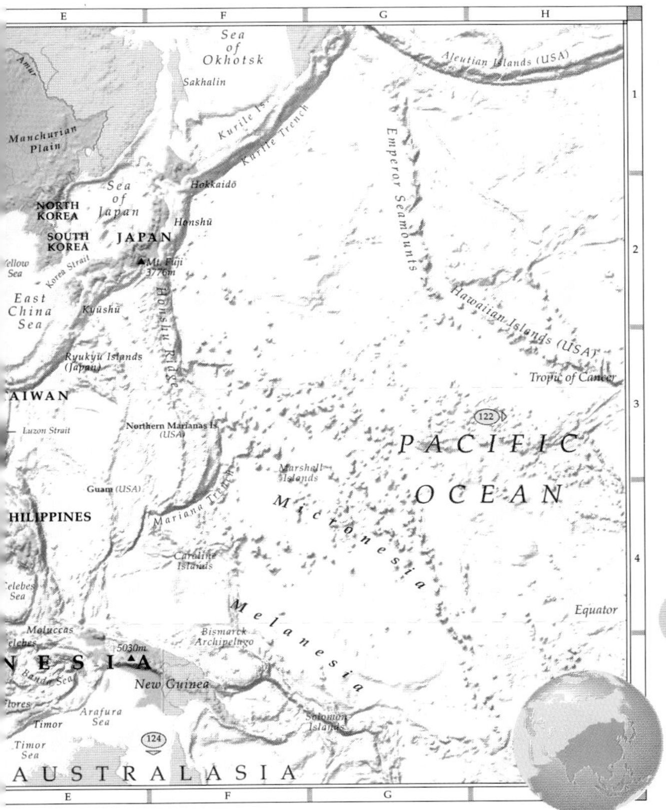
E
F
G
H
1
2
3
4
Sea of Okhotsk
Sakhalin
Aleutian Islands (USA)
Amur
Manchurian Plain
Kurile Is.
Kurile Trench
Emperor Seamounts
Sea of Japan
Hokkaidō
NORTH KOREA
SOUTH KOREA
Honshū
JAPAN
Yellow Sea
Korea Strait
Mt. Fuji 3776m
East China Sea
Kyūshū
Honshu Ridge
Hawaiian Islands (USA)
Ryukyu Islands (Japan)
Tropic of Cancer
TAIWAN
122
Luzon Strait
Northern Marianas Is (USA)
PACIFIC OCEAN
Marshall Islands
Guam (USA)
Mariana Trench
Micronesia
PHILIPPINES
Caroline Islands
Celebes Sea
Melanesia
Equator
Moluccas
Bismarck Archipelago
5030m
INDONESIA
Banda Sea
New Guinea
Flores
Arafura Sea
Solomon Islands
Timor
124
Timor Sea
AUSTRALASIA

WESTERN CHINA & MONGOLIA

RUSSIAN FE
KAZAKHSTAN
Lake Balkhash
KYRGYZSTAN
TAJIKISTAN
PAKISTAN
Aksai Chin Occupied by China, claimed by India.
Demchok/Dêmqog Claimed by India and China
INDIA
NEPAL
BHUTAN
BURMA
XINJIANG
Tarim Pendi
Taklimakan Shamo
Dzungaria
Tien Shan
Altun Shan
Kunlun Shan
Qing-Zang Gaoyuan
TIBET
Tanggula Shan
Himalayas
Altai Mountains
Hangayn Nuruu
Qilian Shan
CHI
MON
G
Hövsgöl Nuur
Uvs Nuur
Hyargas Nuur
Ulaangom
Hovd
Altay
Tsetserleg
Karamay
Irtysh
Yining
Kuytun
ÜRÜMQI
Hami
Korla
Tarim He
Kashi
Lop Nur
Hotan
Golmud
Qinghai Hu
Tongtian He
Yushu
Mekong
Qamdo
Salween
Nagqu
LHASA
Siling Co
Tangra Yumco
Gar
Indus
Xigazê
Brahmaputra
Yamuna
A
B
C
D
1
2
3
4
5
70°
80°
90°
100°
50°
40°
30°
94
102
114

0 km 400

0 miles 400

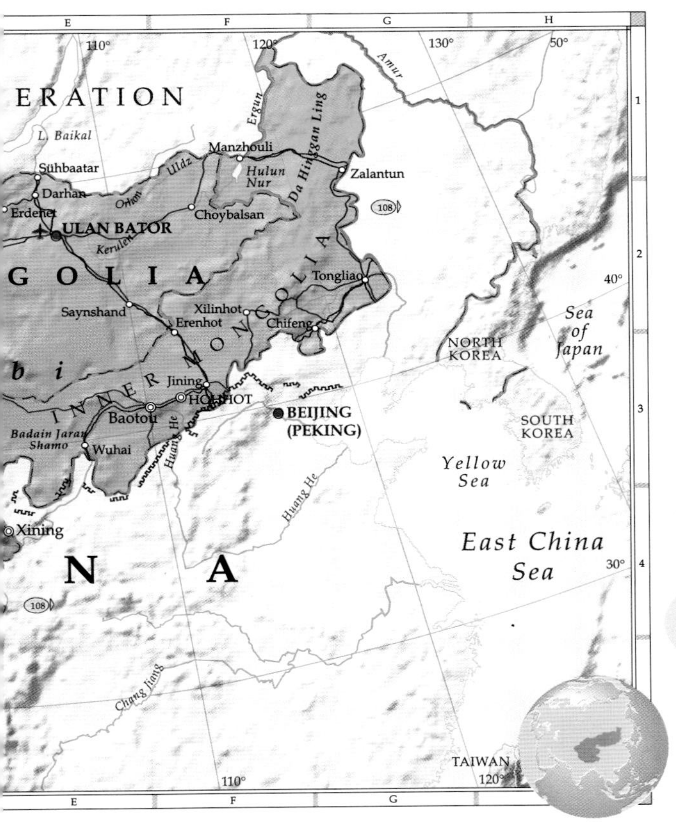
E
F
G
H
110°
120°
130°
50°
Amur
ERATION
L. Baikal
Ergun
Da Hinggan Ling
Manzhouli
Sühbaatar
Uldz
Hulun Nur
Zalantun
Darhan
Orhon
Erdenet
Choybalsan
108
ULAN BATOR
Kerulen
GOLIA
MONGOLIA
Tongliao
40°
Saynshand
Xilinhot
Erenhot
Chifeng
Sea of Japan
NORTH KOREA
b i
INNER
Jining
HOHHOT
Baotou
Huang He
BEIJING (PEKING)
SOUTH KOREA
Badain Jaran Shamo
Wuhai
Yellow Sea
Huang He
Xining
East China Sea
N
A
30°
108
Chang Jiang
TAIWAN
110°
120°
1
2
3
4

EASTERN CHINA & KOREA

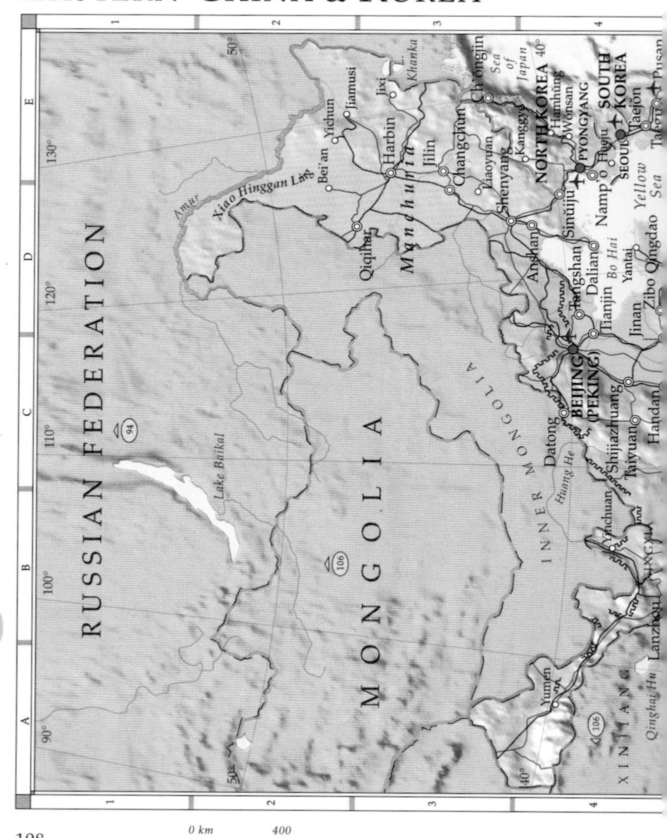
RUSSIAN FEDERATION
MONGOLIA
INNER MONGOLIA
NORTH KOREA
SOUTH KOREA
Manchuria
Lake Baikal
Amur
Xiao Hinggan Ling
L. Khanka
Sea of Japan
Yellow Sea
Bo Hai
Huang He
Qinghai Hu
XINJIANG
NINGXIA
BEIJING (PEKING)
PYONGYANG
SEOUL
Harbin
Qiqihar
Bei'an
Yichun
Jiamusi
Jixi
Jilin
Changchun
Liaoyuan
Shenyang
Anshan
Ch'ŏngjin
Hamhŭng
Wŏnsan
Kanggye
Sinŭiju
Namp'o
Haeju
Taejŏn
Taegu
Pusan
Dalian
Yantai
Qingdao
Zibo
Jinan
Tangshan
Tianjin
Shijiazhuang
Handan
Datong
Taiyuan
Yinchuan
Lanzhou
Yumen
94
106
50°
40°
90°
100°
110°
120°
130°
A
B
C
D
E
1
2
3
4
0 km 400
0 miles 400

CHINA
TIBET
Qin Ling
GUANGXI
Chang Jiang
Yalong Jiang
Jinsha Jiang
Salween
Mekong
Tropic of Cancer
Baoji
Xi'an
Zhengzhou
Zaozhuang
Liangyungang
Xuzhou
Hongze Hu
Huainan
Xinyang
Nanjing
Wuxi
Shanghai
Ningbo
Shaoxing
Hangzhou
Hefei
Wuhan
Poyang Hu
Jingdezhen
Nanchang
Changsha
Yueyang
Dongting Hu
Yichang
Chongqing
Chengdu
Zigong
Litang
Panzhihua
Dali
Kunming
Guiyang
Liuzhou
Nanning
Wuzhou
Pingxiang
Ganzhou
Shaoguan
Guangzhou
Hong Kong
Macao
(Portuguese until 1999)
Zhanjiang
Haikou
Leizhou Bandao
Hainan Dao
Sanya
Gulf of Tongking
Fuzhou
Xiamen
Shantou
Taiwan Strait
TAIPEI
TAIWAN
Kao-hsiung
Tropic of Cancer
East China Sea
Nansei-shotō (Japan)
Cheju Strait
Cheju-do
Korea Strait
JAPAN
PACIFIC OCEAN
PHILIPPINES
Luzon
South China Sea
BURMA
VIETNAM
LAOS
THAILAND
110
122
118
120
30°
20°
100°
110°
120°
A
B
C
D
5
6
7
8

JAPAN

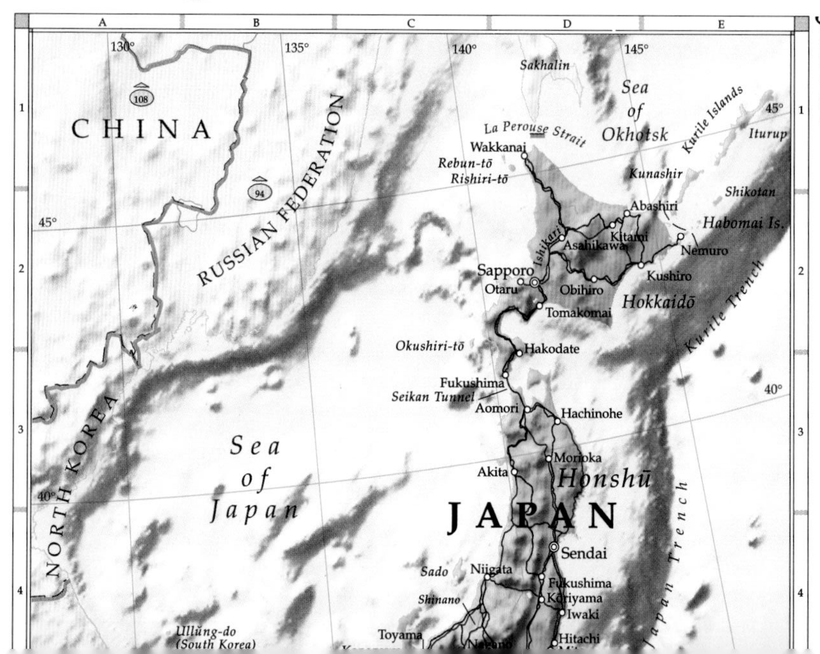
CHINA
108
RUSSIAN FEDERATION
94
NORTH KOREA
Sea of Japan
Ullŭng-do (South Korea)
Sakhalin
Sea of Okhotsk
La Perouse Strait
Kurile Islands
Iturup
Wakkanai
Rebun-tō
Rishiri-tō
Kunashir
Shikotan
Abashiri
Habomai Is.
Kitami
Asahikawa
Ishikari
Nemuro
Sapporo
Otaru
Obihiro
Kushiro
Hokkaidō
Tomakomai
Kurile Trench
Okushiri-tō
Hakodate
Fukushima
Seikan Tunnel
Aomori
Hachinohe
Morioka
Akita
Honshū
JAPAN
Sendai
Japan Trench
Sado
Niigata
Fukushima
Shinano
Koriyama
Iwaki
Toyama
Hitachi

0 km 200

0 miles 200

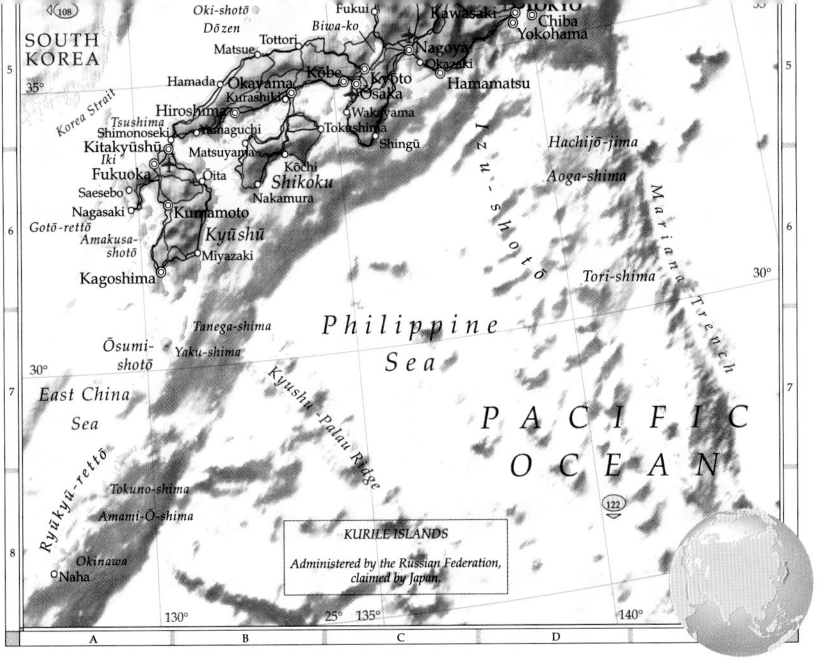
SOUTH KOREA
Korea Strait
Tsushima
Iki
Gotō-rettō
Amakusa-shotō
Oki-shotō
Dōzen
Matsue
Tottori
Hamada
Hiroshima
Okayama
Kurashiki
Shimonoseki
Kitakyūshū
Fukuoka
Saesebo
Nagasaki
Kumamoto
Kyūshū
Miyazaki
Kagoshima
Ōita
Matsuyama
Shikoku
Kōchi
Nakamura
Kōbe
Ōsaka
Wakayama
Shingū
Biwa-ko
Fukui
Nagoya
Okazaki
Hamamatsu
Kawasaki
Yokohama
Chiba
Izu-shotō
Hachijō-jima
Aoga-shima
Tori-shima
Mariana Trench
PACIFIC OCEAN
Philippine Sea
Kyushu-Palau Ridge
Tanega-shima
Yaku-shima
Ōsumi-shotō
East China Sea
Tokuno-shima
Amami-Ō-shima
Ryūkyū-rettō
Okinawa
Naha
KURILE ISLANDS
Administered by the Russian Federation, claimed by Japan.
108
122
35°
30°
25°
130°
135°
140°
A
B
C
D
5
6
7
8

THE INDIAN OCEAN

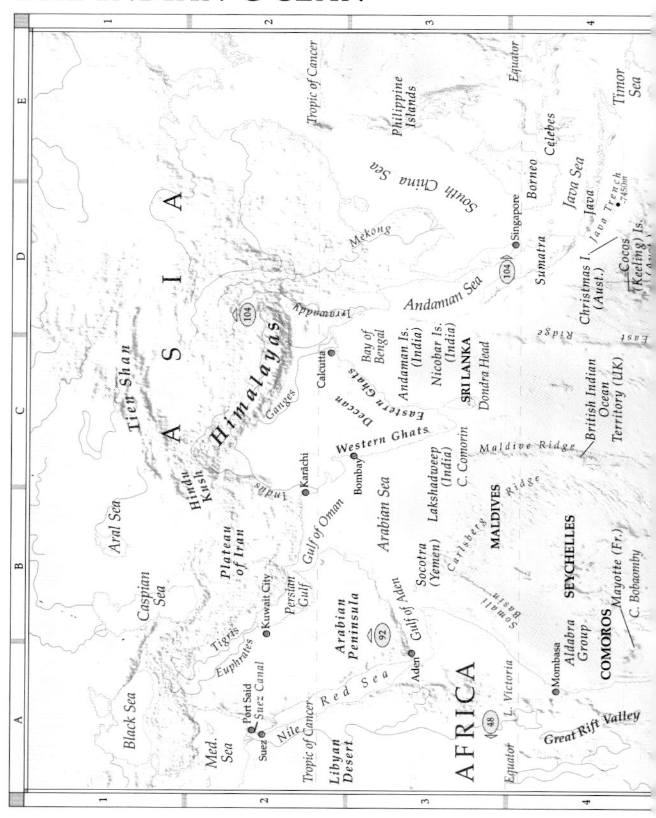
ASIA
Black Sea
Med. Sea
Caspian Sea
Aral Sea
Tien Shan
Himalayas
Hindu Kush
Plateau of Iran
Tigris
Euphrates
Port Said
Suez Canal
Suez
Nile
Kuwait City
Persian Gulf
Gulf of Oman
Karāchi
Indus
Ganges
Calcutta
Irrawaddy
Mekong
South China Sea
Philippine Islands
Tropic of Cancer
Equator
Timor Sea
Celebes
Borneo
Java Sea
Java
Java Trench
7450m
Singapore
Sumatra
Andaman Sea
Christmas I. (Aust.)
Cocos (Keeling) Is.
Ridge
East
Bay of Bengal
Andaman Is. (India)
Nicobar Is. (India)
SRI LANKA
Dondra Head
Eastern Ghats
Deccan
Western Ghats
Bombay
Arabian Sea
Lakshadweep (India)
C. Comorin
Maldive Ridge
British Indian Ocean Territory (UK)
MALDIVES
Carlsberg Ridge
Socotra (Yemen)
Gulf of Aden
Arabian Peninsula
Red Sea
Aden
Tropic of Cancer
Libyan Desert
AFRICA
L. Victoria
Equator
Mombasa
Aldabra Group
COMOROS
SEYCHELLES
Mayotte (Fr.)
C. Bobaomby
Somali Basin
Great Rift Valley
104
92
48

0 km 1000
0 miles 1000

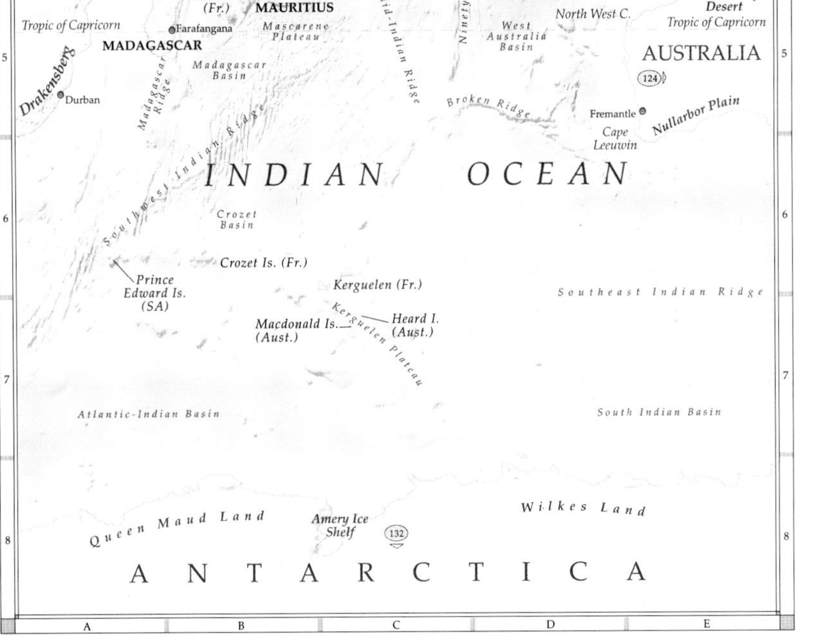
(Fr.)
MAURITIUS
Tropic of Capricorn
Farafangana
Mascarene Plateau
Mid-Indian Ridge
Ninety
West Australia Basin
North West C.
Desert
Tropic of Capricorn
MADAGASCAR
AUSTRALIA
124
Drakensberg
Durban
Madagascar Ridge
Madagascar Basin
Broken Ridge
Fremantle
Nullarbor Plain
Cape Leeuwin
Southwest Indian Ridge
INDIAN OCEAN
Crozet Basin
Crozet Is. (Fr.)
Prince Edward Is. (SA)
Kerguelen (Fr.)
Southeast Indian Ridge
Kerguelen Plateau
Macdonald Is. (Aust.)
Heard I. (Aust.)
Atlantic-Indian Basin
South Indian Basin
Wilkes Land
Queen Maud Land
Amery Ice Shelf
132
ANTARCTICA
A
B
C
D
E
5
6
7
8

NORTH INDIA, PAKISTAN & BANGLADESH

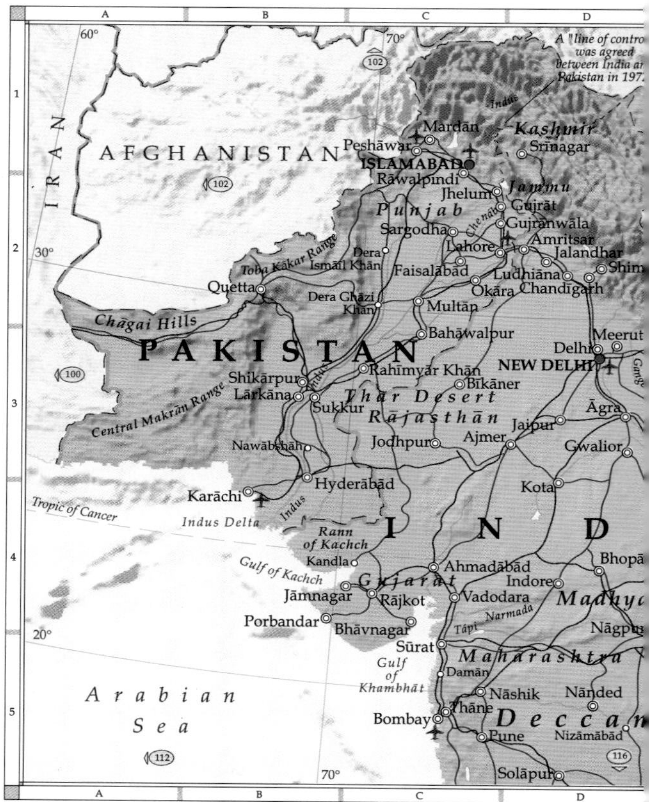
A "line of control" was agreed between India and Pakistan in 1972
AFGHANISTAN
IRAN
PAKISTAN
INDIA
Kashmir
Jammu
Punjab
Rajasthan
Thar Desert
Gujarat
Madhya
Maharashtra
Deccan
Toba Kakar Range
Chagai Hills
Central Makran Range
Indus
Chenab
Narmada
Tapi
Ganga
Indus Delta
Rann of Kachch
Gulf of Kachch
Gulf of Khambhat
Tropic of Cancer
Arabian Sea
Peshawar
Mardan
ISLAMABAD
Rawalpindi
Srinagar
Jhelum
Gujrat
Gujranwala
Sargodha
Lahore
Amritsar
Jalandhar
Ludhiana
Chandigarh
Shimla
Dera Ismail Khan
Faisalabad
Okara
Quetta
Dera Ghazi Khan
Multan
Bahawalpur
Meerut
Delhi
NEW DELHI
Shikarpur
Larkana
Sukkur
Rahimyar Khan
Bikaner
Agra
Jaipur
Nawabshah
Jodhpur
Ajmer
Gwalior
Hyderabad
Karachi
Kota
Kandla
Ahmadabad
Bhopal
Indore
Jamnagar
Rajkot
Vadodara
Porbandar
Bhavnagar
Nagpur
Surat
Daman
Nashik
Nanded
Thane
Bombay
Pune
Nizamabad
Solapur
60°
70°
30°
20°
A
B
C
D
1
2
3
4
5
102
100
112
116
0 km 200
0 miles 200

XINJIANG
QINGHAI
CHINA
TIBET
Himalayas
NEPAL
KATHMANDU
Punakha
THIMPHU
BHUTAN
Gangtok
Biratnagar
Birganj
Bareilly
Nepalganj
Uttar Pradesh
Lucknow
Kānpur
Vārānasi
Allahābād
Patna
Bihar
Gaya
Saidpur
Jamālpur
BANGLADESH
Rājshāhi
DHAKA
West Bengal
Dhanbād
Rānchi
Calcutta
Khulna
Ganges Delta
Guwāhāti
Dispur
Shillong
Sylhet
Kohima
Imphāl
Agartala
Āizawl
Comilla
Chittagong
BURMA
Tropic of Cancer
Brahmaputra
Ganges
Jabalpur
Pradesh
Bhātāpāra
Raipur
Mahānadi
Cuttack
Orissa
Eastern Ghats
Godāveri
Warangal
Visākhapatnam
Bay of Bengal
106
118

SOUTHERN INDIA

A
B
C
D
1
2
3
4
70°
10°
Arabian
Sea
Arabian Basin
Thāne
Nānded
Bombay
Nizāmābād
114
Pune
Deccan
Western Ghats
Solāpur
Krishna
Hyderābād
INDIA
Belgaum
Karnātaka
Hubli
Pānāji
Goa
Dāvangere
Kurnool
Andhra Pradesh
Bangalore
Vellore
Mangalore
Mysore
Tamil Nadu
Salem
Amīndīvi Is.
Lakshadweep
(India)
Calicut
Coimbatore
Tiruchchirāppalli
Kavaratti I.
Ernākulam
Kalpeni I.
Cochin
Kerala
Madurai
Dhanushkodi
112
Minicoy I.
Trivandrum
Gulf of Mannar
Nāgercoil
Thiladhunmathi Atoll
MALDIVES
MALE'
Maldive Ridge
Kolhumadulu Atoll
INDIAN
Equator
Huvadhu Atoll
0 km
300
0 miles
300

E
F
G
H
90°
118
BURMA
Irrawaddy Delta
Eastern Ghats
Visākhapatnam
Rajahmundry
Vijayawāda
Bay of Bengal
Andaman Is.
(India)
North Andaman
Middle Andaman
Andaman-Nicobar Ridge
Madras
Māmallapuram
Port Blair
South Andaman
Little Andaman
10°
Palk Strait
Andaman Sea
SRI LANKA
Trincomalee
Batticaloa
Nicobar Is.
(India)
Kandy
COLOMBO
Great Nicobar
Galle
Matara
120
Sumatra
Ceylon Plain
Ninetyeast Ridge
0°
Equator
AN OCEAN
112
90°
1
2
3
4
5

MAINLAND SOUTHEAST ASIA

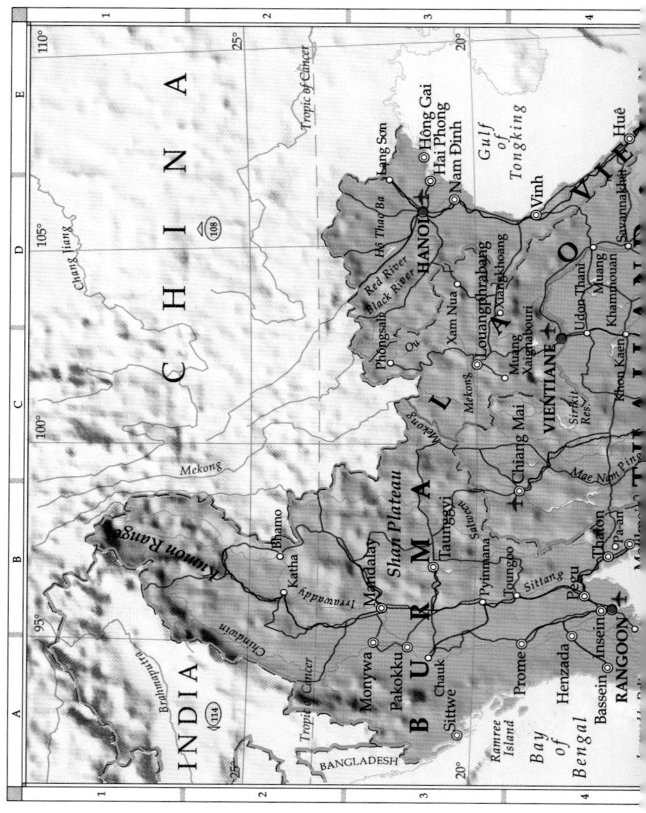
CHINA
INDIA
BURMA
LAOS
BANGLADESH
Bay of Bengal
Gulf of Tongking
Tropic of Cancer
Shan Plateau
Kumon Range
Mekong
Irrawaddy
Chindwin
Brahmaputra
Salween
Sittang
Red River
Black River
Chang Jiang
Mae Nam Ping
HANOI
VIENTIANE
RANGOON
Hông Gai
Hai Phong
Nam Dinh
Lang Son
Vinh
Huê
Louangphrabang
Xiangkhoang
Xam Nua
Phôngsali
Chiang Mai
Udon Thani
Khon Kaen
Mandalay
Taunggyi
Pyinmana
Toungoo
Pegu
Thaton
Pa-an
Bhamo
Katha
Monywa
Pakokku
Chauk
Sittwe
Prome
Henzada
Bassein
Insein
Ramree Island
Sirikit Res.

0 km 200
0 miles 200

CAMBODIA
PHNOM PENH
BANGKOK
Gulf of Thailand
South China Sea
Andaman Sea
Strait of Malacca
Malay Peninsula
MALAYSIA
INDONESIA
INDIAN OCEAN
Sumatra
Andaman Islands (India)
Nicobar Islands (India)
Mergui Archipelago
Isthmus of Kra
Mekong Delta
Mekong
Tônlé Sap
Hô Chi Minh
Cân Thơ
Rach Gia
Kâmpôt
Kâmpóng Saôm
Kâmpóng Chhnăng
Bătdâmbâng
Kâmpóng Cham
Svay Riĕng
Đa Lat
Nha Trang
Qui Nhơn
Phumĭ Sâmraông
Muang Không
Ko Chang
Ko Phangan
Ko Samui
Ko Phuket
Phuket
Chumphon
Surat Thani
Nakhon Si Thammarat
Songkhla
Pattani
Hat Yai
Trang
Yala
Tavoy
Mergui
Ratchaburi
Thon Buri
Ayutthaya
Chon Buri
Pattaya
Nakhon Ratchasima
Ratchathani
Srinagarind Res.

MARITIME SOUTHEAST ASIA

BURMA
LAOS
VIETNAM
THAILAND
CAMBODIA
Gulf of Tongking
Hainan Dao
Andaman Sea
South China Sea
Gulf of Thailand
Spratly Is. (Disputed)
Nicobar Is. (India)
Balabac Str
Banda Aceh
George Town
P. Pinang
Taiping
Ipoh
Medan
Pematangsiantar
Danau Toba
Kota Bharu
Kuala Terengganu
Kuantan
Kelang
KUALA LUMPUR
Seremban
Melaka
Johor Bharau
SINGAPORE
MALAYSIA
Kep. Natuna (Indonesia)
Kota Kinabalu
BANDAR SERI BEGAWAN
BRUNEI
Sibu
Kuching
Sarawak
Borneo
Peg. Muller
Kapuas
Pontianak
Samarinda
Balikpapan
Banjarmasin
Equator
Kep. Banyak
Sumatra
Pakambaru
Kep. Lingga
Padang
Kep. Mentawai
Peg. Barisan
Jambi
P. Bangka
Pangkalpinang
P. Belitung
Bengkulu
Palembang
Tanjungkarang
Java Sea
JAKARTA
Bogor
Cirebon
Semarang
Bandung
Yogyakarta
Malang
Surabaya
Jember
Java
Bali
Lombo
Denpasa
INDIAN OCEAN
Java Trench
INDONESIA
0 km 400
0 miles 400

Luzon Strait
Luzon
Tuguegarao
Ilagan
Baguio
Dagupan
Cabanatuan
MANILA
PHILIPPINES
Lucena
Batangas
Naga
Legaspi
Mindoro
Mindoro Strait
Panay
Leyte
Calbayog
Samar
Cadiz
Tacloban
Palawan
Iloilo
Cebu
Bacolod
Surigao
Puerto Princesa
Negros
Bohol
Butuan
Iligan
Cagayan de Oro
Sulu Sea
Mindanao
Zamboanga
Davao
General Santos
Sulu Archipelago
Philippine Sea
Philippine Trench
Philippine Basin
Kyushu - Palau Ridge
Mariana Trench
Yap
MICRONESIA
PALAU
122
PACIFIC OCEAN
Equator
Kep. Talaud
Celebes Sea
P. Morotai
Manado
Gorontalo
Teluk Tomini
Laut Maluku
Halmahera
P. Waigeo
P. Biak
P. Bacan
128
Palu
Kep. Banggai
P. Yapen
Jayapura
Mamberamo
Sulawesi
Maluku
Kep. Sula
Seram
Danau Towuti
Pegunungan Maoke
Kendari
Buru
Ambon
Irian Jaya
Parepare
Banda Sea
Kep. Kai
Kep. Aru
P. Muna
Digul
Ujungpandang
Kep. Tanimbar
PAPUA NEW GUINEA
INDONESIA
P. Yamdena
Flores Sea
Flores
Kep. Alor
P. Wetar
Kep. Leti
Dili
Timor
Timor Sea
Arafura Sea
Sumba
Kupang
126
20°
10°
0°
120°
130°
140°
E
F
G
H
2
3
4
5

THE PACIFIC OCEAN

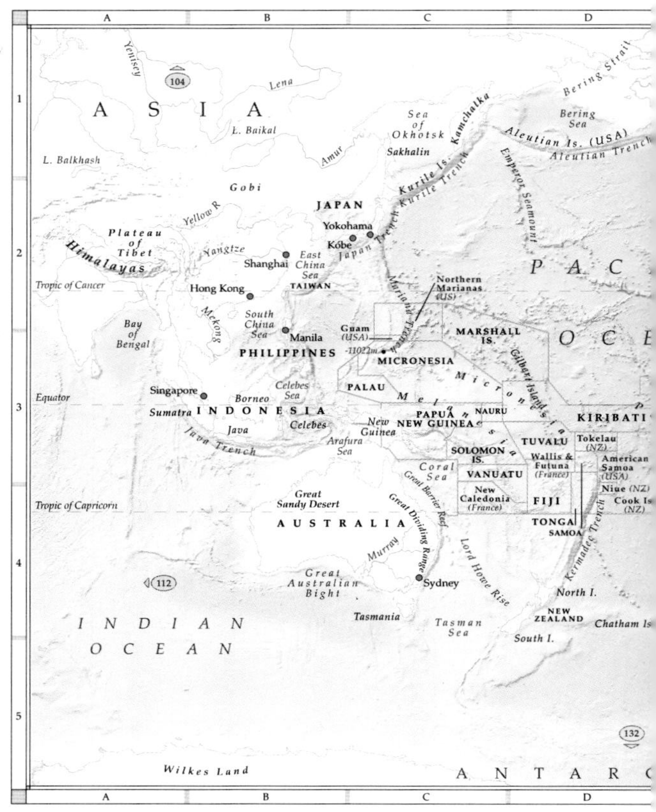

A B C D
1 2 3 4 5
ASIA
L. Baikal
L. Balkhash
Yenisey
Lena
Amur
Gobi
Yellow R.
Plateau of Tibet
Himalayas
Yangtze
Mekong
Tropic of Cancer
Bay of Bengal
JAPAN
Yokohama
Kóbe
Shanghai
East China Sea
TAIWAN
Hong Kong
South China Sea
Manila
PHILIPPINES
Sea of Okhotsk
Sakhalin
Kamchatka
Kurile Is.
Kurile Trench
Japan Trench
Mariana Trench
Northern Marianas (US)
Guam (USA)
-11022m
MICRONESIA
MARSHALL IS.
Bering Strait
Bering Sea
Aleutian Is. (USA)
Aleutian Trench
Emperor Seamount
PAC
OCE
Gilbert Islands
Micronesia
Melanesia
KIRIBATI
NAURU
PALAU
Equator
Singapore
Sumatra
INDONESIA
Borneo
Celebes Sea
Celebes
Java
Java Trench
New Guinea
PAPUA NEW GUINEA
Arafura Sea
SOLOMON IS.
TUVALU
Tokelau (NZ)
Wallis & Futuna (France)
American Samoa (USA)
Coral Sea
VANUATU
Niue (NZ)
Cook Is (NZ)
New Caledonia (France)
FIJI
TONGA
SAMOA
Great Barrier Reef
Great Dividing Range
Kermadec Trench
Tropic of Capricorn
Great Sandy Desert
AUSTRALIA
Murray
Great Australian Bight
Sydney
Lord Howe Rise
North I.
NEW ZEALAND
Chatham Is
South I.
Tasmania
Tasman Sea
INDIAN OCEAN
104
112
132
Wilkes Land
ANTARC
0 km 2000
0 miles 2000

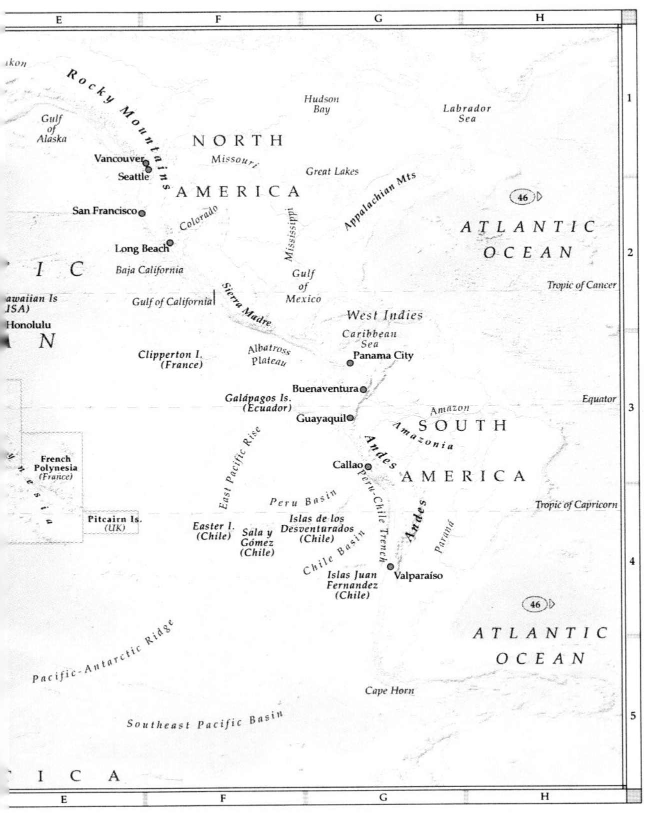
E
F
G
H
1
2
3
4
5
Rocky Mountains
Gulf of Alaska
Hudson Bay
Labrador Sea
NORTH AMERICA
Missouri
Vancouver
Seattle
Great Lakes
Appalachian Mts
46
San Francisco
Colorado
Mississippi
ATLANTIC OCEAN
Long Beach
Baja California
Gulf of Mexico
Tropic of Cancer
Gulf of California
Sierra Madre
Honolulu
West Indies
Caribbean Sea
Clipperton I. (France)
Albatross Plateau
Panama City
Buenaventura
Galápagos Is. (Ecuador)
Equator
Amazon
Guayaquil
SOUTH AMERICA
Amazonia
Andes
French Polynesia (France)
East Pacific Rise
Callao
Peru-Chile Trench
Peru Basin
Tropic of Capricorn
Pitcairn Is. (UK)
Easter I. (Chile)
Sala y Gómez (Chile)
Islas de los Desventurados (Chile)
Paraná
Chile Basin
Islas Juan Fernandez (Chile)
Valparaíso
Pacific-Antarctic Ridge
Cape Horn
Southeast Pacific Basin

AUSTRALASIA & OCEANIA

A
B
C
D
1
2
3
4
5
Borneo
Celebes Sea
104
Equator
ASIA
PALAU
MICRONESIA
Melanesia
PAPUA NEW GUINEA
Bismarck Archipelago
New Britain
Celebes
Irian Jaya
New Guinea
Mt. Wilhelm 4509m
Java Sea
Banda Sea
Java
Flores
Arafura Sea
Solomon Sea
Java Trench
Sumba
Timor
Torres Strait
Bathurst I.
Melville I.
SOLOMON
Timor Sea
Arnhem Land
C. Londonderry
Gulf of Carpentaria
Coral Sea Islands (Australia)
North Australian Basin
Victoria
Cape York Peninsula
Great Barrier Reef
Coral Sea
Fitzroy
New Caledonia
Great Sandy Desert
Tropic of Capricorn
Macdonnell Ranges
L. Disappointment
L. Mackay
Gibson Desert
Uluru 868m (Ayer's Rock)
Dirk Hartog I.
L. Carnegie
Fraser I.
AUSTRALIA
Great Dividing Range
Great Victoria Desert
Lake Eyre -16m
L. Barlee
Perth Basin
Nullarbor Plain
L. Torrens
Flinders Range
Darling
L. Gairdner
C. Leeuwin
Great Australian Bight
Murray
Mt. Kosciusko 2228m
Kangaroo I.
Cape Howe
Bass Strait
112
King I.
Flinders I.
Tasman Sea
INDIAN OCEAN
Tasmania
South East Cape
Tasman Plateau
South Australian Basin
132
0 km
1000
0 miles
1000

MARSHALL IS.
Kingman Reef (USA)
Palmyra Atoll (USA)
Baker & Howland Is. (USA)
Jarvis Island (USA)
104
Equator
NAURU
Gilbert Is.
KIRIBATI
Phoenix Is.
Line Islands
PACIFIC OCEAN
Polynesia
Marquesas Is.
TUVALU
Tokelau (New Zealand)
Northern Cook Is.
Wallis & Futuna (France)
SAMOA
American Samoa (USA)
Cook Islands (New Zealand)
French Polynesia (France)
VANUATU
Vanua Levu
Viti Levu
Niue (New Zealand)
Tahiti
TONGA
Îles Loyauté
FIJI
Southern Cook Is.
Society Islands
Tropic of Capricorn
South Fiji Basin
Norfolk I. (Australia)
Kermadec Islands (NZ)
Keramadec Trench
122
North Cape
Bay of Plenty
North I.
East Cape
PACIFIC OCEAN
NEW ZEALAND
South I.
Cook Strait
Mt. Cook 3764m
Chatham I. (NZ)
Canterbury Bight
Foveaux Strait
Stewart I.
Southwest Pacific Basin
Auckland I. (NZ)
E
F
G
H
1
2
3
4

THE SOUTHWEST PACIFIC

Guam
(USA)
Agaña
MARSHALL ISLANDS
Marianas Trench
Micronesia
Yap
Caroline Islands
Chuuk Is.
Pohnpei I.
PALIKIR
Kosrae
Ratak Chain
Ralik Chain
Majuro
KOROR
PALAU
MICRONESIA
Equator
PAPUA NEW GUINEA
NAURU
Bismarck Archipelago
New Ireland
INDONESIA
New Guinea
Madang
Mendi
Lae
New Britain
Bougainville I.
New Georgia
Melanesia
PORT MORESBY
Solomon Sea
HONIARA
Santa Cruz Is.
Arafura Sea
Torres Strait
SOLOMON ISLANDS
VANUATU
Banks Is
Arnhem Land
Gulf of Carpentaria
Coral Sea
Cooktown
Cairns
NORTHERN TERRITORY
Normanton
Great Barrier Reef
Coral Sea Islands
(Australia)
PORT-VILA
Tennant Creek
Townsville
New Caledonia
(France)
Mount Isa
Cloncurry
Great Dividing Range
Mackay
Nouméa
Îles Loyauté
AUSTRALIA
Rockhampton
Longreach
Alice Springs
QUEENSLAND
Bundaberg
0 km 400
0 miles 400

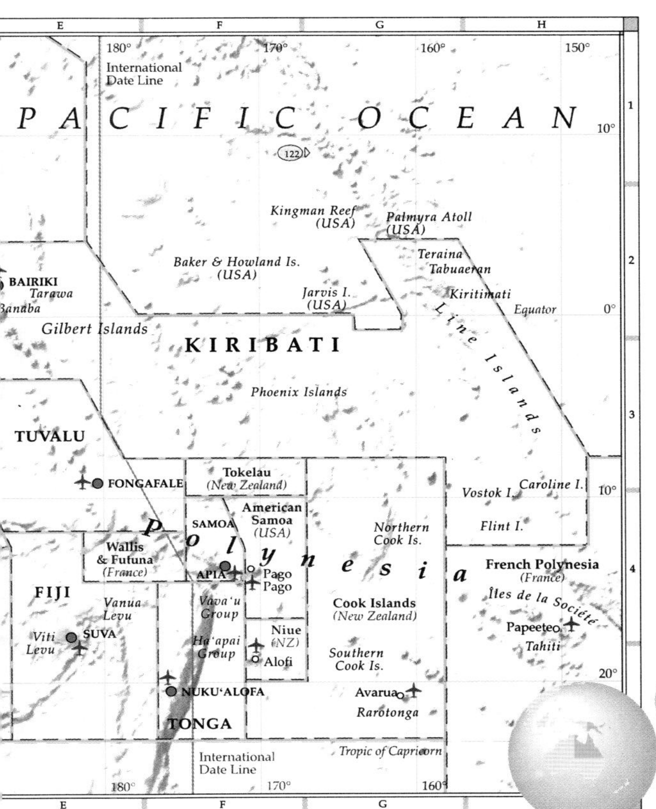

E
F
G
H
180°
170°
160°
150°
International Date Line
PACIFIC OCEAN
10°
1
122
Kingman Reef (USA)
Palmyra Atoll (USA)
Teraina
Tabuaeran
2
Baker & Howland Is. (USA)
BAIRIKI
Tarawa
Banaba
Jarvis I. (USA)
Kiritimati
Equator
0°
Gilbert Islands
KIRIBATI
Line Islands
Phoenix Islands
3
TUVALU
FONGAFALE
Tokelau (New Zealand)
Vostok I.
Caroline I.
10°
SAMOA
American Samoa (USA)
Northern Cook Is.
Flint I.
Wallis & Futuna (France)
Polynesia
French Polynesia (France)
4
APIA
Pago Pago
FIJI
Vanua Levu
Vava'u Group
Cook Islands (New Zealand)
Îles de la Société
Papeete
Tahiti
Viti Levu
SUVA
Ha'apai Group
Niue (NZ)
Alofi
Southern Cook Is.
20°
NUKU'ALOFA
Avarua
Rarotonga
TONGA
International Date Line
Tropic of Capricorn
180°
170°
160°
E
F
G

WESTERN AUSTRALIA

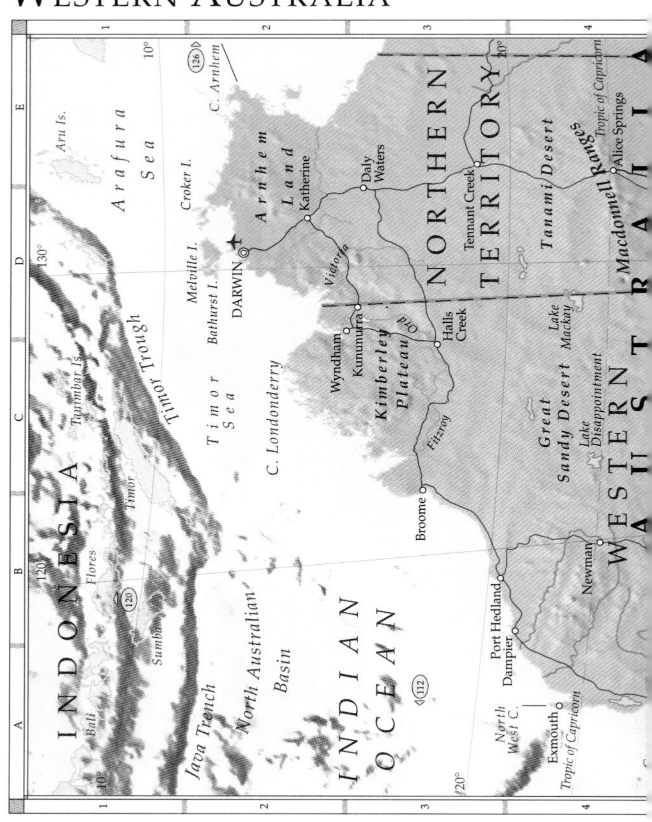
INDONESIA
Aru Is.
Arafura Sea
Croker I.
C. Arnhem
126
Melville I.
Bathurst I.
DARWIN
Arnhem Land
Katherine
Daly Waters
NORTHERN TERRITORY
Tennant Creek
Tanami Desert
Macdonnell Ranges
Alice Springs
Tropic of Capricorn
Victoria
Wyndham
Kununurra
Kimberley Plateau
Ord
Halls Creek
Lake Mackay
Great Sandy Desert
Lake Disappointment
Fitzroy
Broome
Newman
Port Hedland
Dampier
North West C.
Exmouth
Tropic of Capricorn
WESTERN AUSTRALIA
Tanimbar Is.
Timor Trough
Timor Sea
C. Londonderry
Timor
Flores
Sumba
Bali
120
Java Trench
North Australian Basin
INDIAN OCEAN
112

0 km 400
0 miles 400

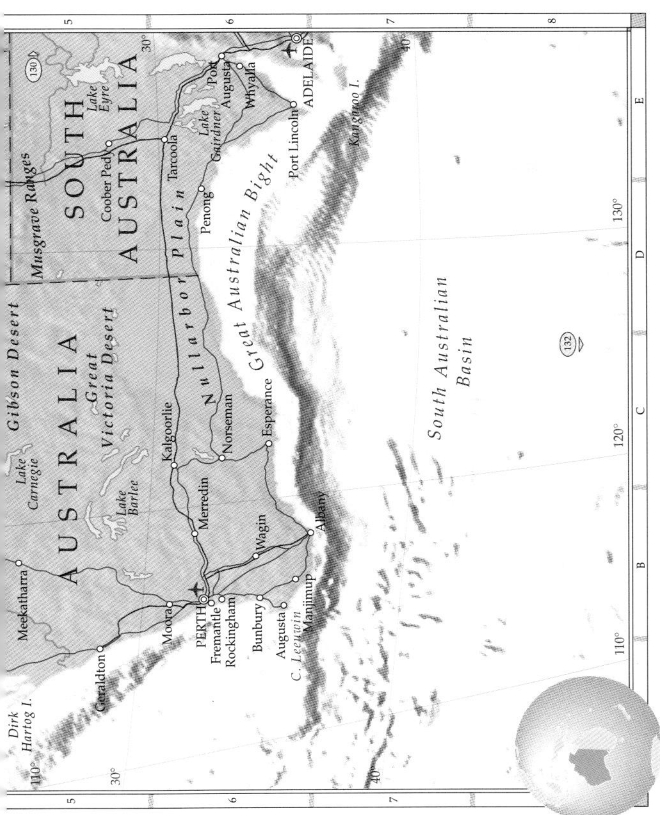
SOUTH AUSTRALIA
AUSTRALIA
Gibson Desert
Great Victoria Desert
Musgrave Ranges
Lake Carnegie
Lake Barlee
Lake Eyre
Lake Gairdner
Nullarbor Plain
Great Australian Bight
South Australian Basin
Dirk Hartog I.
Geraldton
Meekatharra
Moora
PERTH
Fremantle
Rockingham
Bunbury
Augusta
C. Leeuwin
Manjimup
Wagin
Merredin
Albany
Kalgoorlie
Norseman
Esperance
Coober Pedy
Tarcoola
Penong
Port Augusta
Whyalla
Port Lincoln
ADELAIDE
Kangaroo I.
130
132
110°
120°
130°
30°
40°
B
C
D
E
5
6
7
8

Southeast Australia

A
B
C
D
1
2
3
4
140°
150°
160°
30°
40°
Mount Isa
Cloncurry
Hughenden
Mackay
Great Dividing Range
126
Diamantina
Tropic of Capricorn
Longreach
Rockhampton
Bundaberg
Fraser I.
128
QUEENSLAND
Charleville
Roma
Miles
AUSTRALIA
Toowoomba
BRISBANE
Ipswich
Gold Coast
SOUTH AUSTRALIA
Cunnamulla
Goondiwindi
Grafton
L. Eyre
Milparinka
Moree
Bourke
L. Torrens
Flinders Ranges
L. Frome
Darling
Armidale
Coffs Harbour
Broken Hill
Wilcannia
NEW SOUTH WALES
Tamworth
Port Augusta
Dubbo
Whyalla
Ivanhoe
Orange
Newcastle
Murray
Bathurst
SYDNEY
Mildura
Murrumbidgee
Wollongong
Port Lincoln
ADELAIDE
Wagga Wagga
Albury
CANBERRA
(AUSTRALIAN CAPITAL TERRITORY)
Keith
Kangaroo I.
Bendigo
Shepparton
VICTORIA
Mount Gambier
Ballarat
MELBOURNE
Cape Howe
Geelong
Sale
Bass Strait
King I.
Flinders I.
Tasman Sea
Burnie
Devonport
Launceston
TASMANIA
HOBART
South East Cape
131
132
0 km
400
0 miles
400

NEW ZEALAND

E
F
G
H
170°
North Cape
126
122
Kaitaia
PACIFIC OCEAN
Whangarei
180°
Tasman Sea
Auckland
Coromandel
Bay of Plenty
Hamilton
Tauranga
East Cape
Rotorua
North Island
Taupo
Raukumara Range
Gisborne
New Plymouth
L. Taupo
Napier
40°
NEW ZEALAND
Wanganui
Hastings
130
Cook Strait
Palmerston North
Masterton
Nelson
WELLINGTON
Westport
Blenheim
Greymouth
Kaikoura
Campbell Plateau
Southern Alps
Christchurch
South Island
Canterbury Plains
Ashburton
Canterbury Bight
Timaru
122
Milford Sound
Queenstown
Hampden
PACIFIC OCEAN
Lumsden
Dunedin
Invercargill
Foveaux Strait
Stewart I.
132
1
2
3
4

0 km 200

0 miles 200

ANTARCTICA

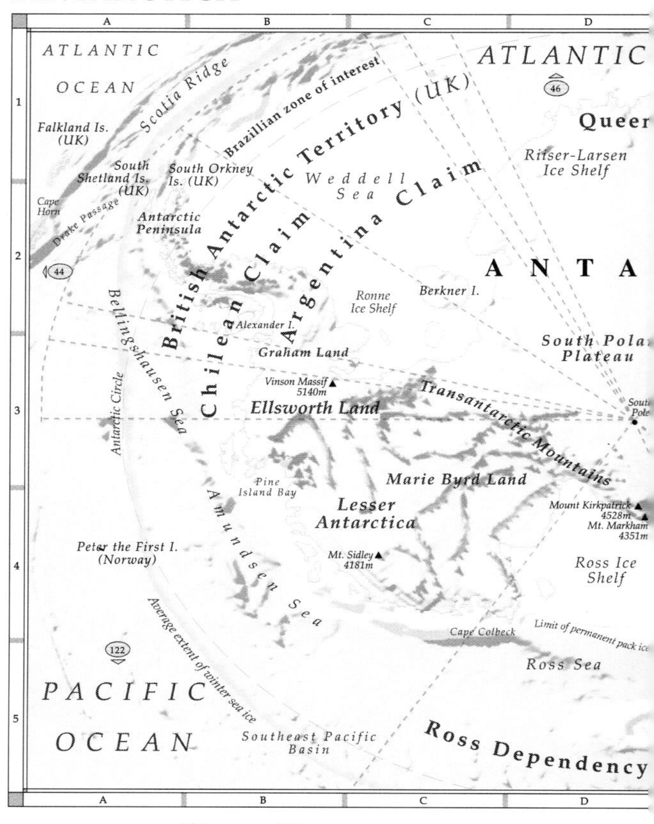
A
B
C
D
1
2
3
4
5
ATLANTIC
OCEAN
Scotia Ridge
Brazilian zone of interest
British Antarctic Territory (UK)
ATLANTIC
46
Queen
Falkland Is.
(UK)
South
Shetland Is.
(UK)
South Orkney
Is. (UK)
Weddell
Sea
Argentina Claim
Riiser-Larsen
Ice Shelf
Cape
Horn
Drake Passage
Antarctic
Peninsula
Chilean Claim
44
ANTA
Bellingshausen Sea
Ronne
Ice Shelf
Berkner I.
Alexander I.
Graham Land
South Pola
Plateau
Vinson Massif
5140m
Antarctic Circle
Ellsworth Land
Transantarctic Mountains
South
Pole
Pine
Island Bay
Marie Byrd Land
Amundsen Sea
Lesser
Antarctica
Mount Kirkpatrick
4528m
Mt. Markham
4351m
Peter the First I.
(Norway)
Mt. Sidley
4181m
Ross Ice
Shelf
Average extent of winter sea ice
Cape Colbeck
Limit of permanent pack ice
122
Ross Sea
PACIFIC
OCEAN
Southeast Pacific
Basin
Ross Dependency
0 km
750
0 miles
750

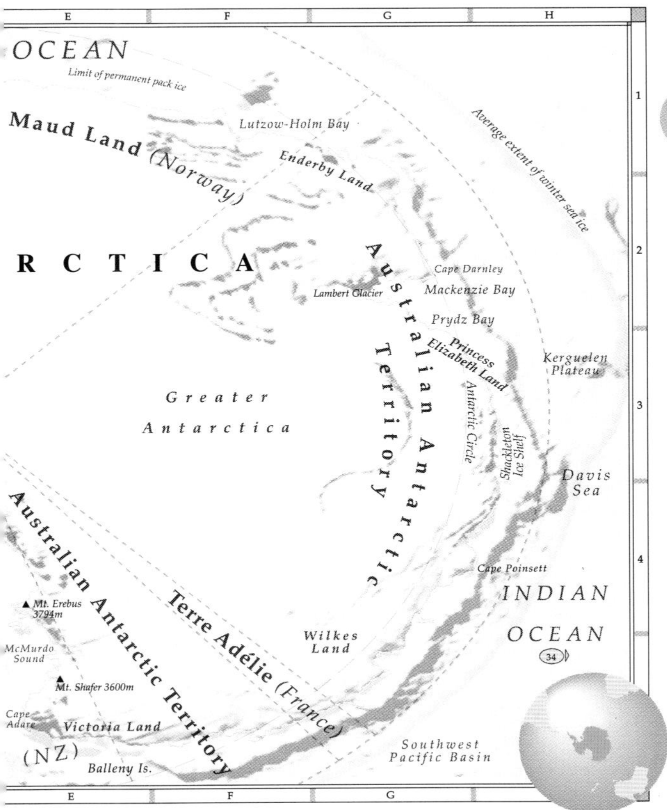
E
F
G
H
1
2
3
4
OCEAN
Limit of permanent pack ice
Maud Land (Norway)
Lutzow-Holm Bay
Enderby Land
Average extent of winter sea ice
RCTICA
Australian Antarctic Territory
Cape Darnley
Mackenzie Bay
Lambert Glacier
Prydz Bay
Princess Elizabeth Land
Kerguelen Plateau
Greater Antarctica
Antarctic Circle
Shackleton Ice Shelf
Davis Sea
Australian Antarctic Territory
Cape Poinsett
INDIAN OCEAN
34
Mt. Erebus 3794m
Terre Adélie (France)
Wilkes Land
McMurdo Sound
Mt. Shafer 3600m
Cape Adare
Victoria Land
(NZ)
Balleny Is.
Southwest Pacific Basin
E
F
G

GLOSSARY OF ABBREVIATIONS

This glossary provides a comprehensive guide to the abbreviations used in this Atlas.

abbrev. abbreviation
Afgh. Afghanistan
Amh. Amharic
anc. ancient
Ar. Arabic
Arm. Armenia / Armenian
Aus. Austria
Aust. Australia
Az. Azerbaijan / Azerbaijani

Bas. Basque
Bel. Belorussian
Belg. Belgium
Bos. & Herz. Bosnia & Herzegovina
Bul. Bulgarian
Bulg. Bulgaria
Bur. Burmese

C Central
C. Cape
Cam. Cambodian
Cast. Castilian
Chin. Chinese
Cord. Cordillera (Spanish for mountain range)
Cz. Czech
Czech Rep. Czech Republic

D.C. District of Columbia
Dan. Danish
Dominican Rep. Dominican Republic

E East
Emb. Embalse
Eng. English
Est. Estonia / Estonian

Faer. Faeroese
Fin. Finnish
Flem. Flemish
Fr. France / French

Geo. Georgia
Geor. Georgian
Ger. Germany / German
Gk. Greek

Heb. Hebrew
Hung. Hungary / Hungarian

I. Island
Ind. Indonesian
Is. Islands
It. Italian

Kaz. Kazakh
Kep. Kepulauan (Indonesian / Malay for island group)
Kir. Kirghiz
Kor. Korean
Kurd. Kurdish
Kyrgy. Kyrgyzstan

L. Lake, Lago
Lat. Latvia
Latv. Latvian
Leb. Lebanon
Liech. Liechtenstein
Lith. Lithuania / Lithuanian
Lux. Luxembourg

m metres
Mac. Macedonia
Med. Sea Mediterranean Sea
Mold. Moldavia
Mt. Mount / Mountain
Mts. Mountains

N North
N. Korea North Korea
Neth. Netherlands
NW Northwest
NZ New Zealand

P. Pulau (Indonesian / Malay for island)
Peg. Pegunungan (Indonesian / Malay for mountain range)
Per. Persian
Pol. Poland / Polish
Port. Portuguese
prev. previously

R. River, Rio, Río
Res. Reservoir
Rom. Romania / Romanian
Rus. Russian
Russ. Fed. Russian Federation

S South
S. Korea South Korea
SA South Africa
SCr. Serbo-Croatian
Slvka. Slovakia
Slvna. Slovenia
Som. Somali
Sp. Spanish

St, St. Saint
Str. Strait
Swed. Swedish
Switz. Switzerland

Tajik. Tajikistan
Th. Thai
Turk. Turkish
Turkm. Turkmen
Turkmen. Turkmenistan

U.A.E. United Arab Emirates
UK United Kingdom
Ukr. Ukrainian
USA United States of America
Uzb. Uzbek
Uzbek. Uzbekistan

var. variant
Vdkhr. Vodokhranilishche (Russian for reservoir)
Vdskh. Vodoskhovyshche (Ukrainian for reservoir)
Ven. Venezuela

W West
W. Sahara Western Sahara
Wel. Welsh

Yugo. Yugoslavia

Dorling Kindersley Cartography would like to thank the following for their assistance in producing this Atlas:

James Anderson, Laura Porter, Margaret Hynes, Ruth Duxbury, Roger Bullen, Julie Phillis, Robin Giddings and Tony Chambers.

INDEX

A

Aachen Germany 75 D7
Aalst Belgium 67 B6
Aare *River* Switzerland 75 A7
Aasiaat Greenland 62 B3
Aba Nigeria 53 G5
Ābādān Iran 100 C4
Abashiri Japan 110 D2
Abéché Chad 56 D3
Abengourou Ivory Coast 53 E5
Åbenrå Denmark 65 A8
Abeokuta Nigeria 53 F5
Aberdeen Scotland, UK 68 D3
Aberdeen South Dakota, USA 23 E2
Aberdeen Washington, USA 24 A2
Aberystwyth Wales, UK 69 C6
Abhā Saudi Arabia 101 B6
Abidjan Ivory Coast 53 E5
Abilene Texas, USA 27 F3
Abrolhos Bank *Undersea feature* Atlantic Ocean 41 G5 43 G1
Abu Dhabi *Capital of* United Arab Emirates *var.* Abū Ẓaby 101 D5
Abuja *Capital of* Nigeria 53 G4
Abū Ẓaby *see* Abu Dhabi
Acapulco Mexico 31 E5
Acarai Mountains *Mountain range* Brazil/Guyana 39 F3
Acarigua Venezuela 38 D1
Accra *Capital of* Ghana 53 E5
Acharnés Greece 85 C5
Acklins Island *Island* Bahamas 43 D2
Aconcagua *Peak* Argentina 37 B5
A Coruña Spain *Cast.* La Coruña 72 C1
ACT *see* Australian Capital Territory
Adalia *see* Antalya
Adalia, Gulf of *see* Antalya Körfezi
'Adan Yemen *Eng.* Aden 101 B7 112 A3
Adana Turkey *var.* Seyhan 96 D4
Adapazarı Turkey *var.* Sakarya 96 B2
Adare, Cape *Coastal feature* Antarctica 133 E5
Ad Dakhla Western Sahara 50 A4
Ad Dawḩah *see* Doha
Addis Ababa *Capital of* Ethiopia *Amh.* Ādīs Ābeba 55 C5
Adelaide Australia 129 E6 130 A3
Adélie, Terre d' *Territory* Antarctica 132-133
Aden *see* 'Adan
Aden, Gulf of *Sea feature* Indian Ocean 112 B3
Adige *River* Italy 76 C2
Ādīs Ābeba *see* Addis Ababa
Adıyaman Turkey 97 E4
Adriatic Sea Mediterranean Sea 76 D3
Aegean Sea Mediterranean Sea *Gk.* Aigaío Pélagos, *Turk.* Ege Denizi 85 D5
Aeolian Islands *see* Isole Eolie
Afghanistan *Country* C Asia 102-103
Africa 82-83
Afyon Turkey *prev.* Afyonkarahisar 96 B3
Afyonkarahisar *see* Afyon
Agadez Niger 53 G3
Agadir Morocco 50 B2
Agaña Guam 126 B1
Agartala India 115 G4
Agen France 71 B6
Āgra India 114 D3
Agrigento Italy 77 C7
Agrínio Greece 85 A5
Aguarico *River* Ecuador/Peru 38 B4
Aguascalientes Mexico 30 D4
Agulhas Ridge *Undersea feature* Indian Ocean 49 C8
Ahaggar *Mountains* Algeria *var.* Hoggar 51 E4
Ahmadābād India 114 C4
Ahvāz Iran 100 C4
Ahvenanmaa see Åland
Aigaío Pélagos *see* Aegean Sea
Aintab *see* Gaziantep
Aïr *Region* Niger 53 G2
Aix-en-Provence France 71 D6
Āīzawl India 115 G4
Ajaccio Corse, France 71 E7
Ajdābiyā Libya 51 G2
Ajmer India 114 D3
Akaba *see* Al 'Aqabah
Akimiski Island *Island* Canada 18 C3
Akita Japan 110 D3
Akmola Kazakhstan *prev.* Akmolinsk, Tselinograd 94 C4
Akmolinsk *see* Akmola
Akpatok Island *Island* Canada 19 E1
Akron Ohio, USA 20 D3
Aksai Chin *Disputed region* China/India 106 A4 114-115
Aktau Kazakhstan *prev.* Shevchenko 94 A4
Akureyri Iceland 63 E4
Akyab *see* Sittwe
Alabama *State* USA 28 D3
Alajuela Costa Rica 32 D4
Al 'Amārah Iraq *var.* Amara 100 C4
Alamogordo New Mexico, USA 26 D3
Åland *Island group* Finland *Fin.* Ahvenanmaa 65 D6
Al 'Aqabah Jordan *var.* Akaba 99 B7
Alaska *State* USA 16
Alaska, Gulf of *Sea feature* Pacific Ocean 14 C3
Alaska Peninsula *Peninsula* Alaska, USA 14 B2
Alaska Range *Mountain range* Alaska, USA 16 C3
Alazani *River* Azerbaijan/Georgia 97 G2
Albacete Spain 73 E4
Alba Iulia Romania 88 B4
Albania *Country* SE Europe 81
Albany Australia 129 B6
Albany New York, USA 21 F3
Albany Oregon, USA 24 A3
Albany *River* Canada 18 B3
Al Başrah Iraq *var.* Basra 100 C4
Albatross Plateau *Undersea feature* Pacific Ocean 122 F3
Al Bayḑā' Libya 51 G2
Albert, Lake *Lake* Uganda/Congo (Zaire) 55 B6 57 E5
Alberta *Province* Canada 17 E4
Albi France 71 C6
Ålborg Denmark 65 A5
Albuquerque New Mexico, USA 26 D2

Albury Australia 130 B3
Alcácer do Sal Portugal 72 C4
Alcalá de Henares Spain 73 E3
Alchevs'k Ukraine 89 G3
Aldabra Group *Island group* Seychelles 59 G1
Aleg Mauritania 52 C3
Aleksandriya *see* Oleksandriya
Aleksandropol' *see* Gyumri
Aleksinac Yugoslavia 80 E4
Alençon France 70 B3
Alessandria Italy 76 A2
Ålesund Norway 65 A5
Aleutian Islands *Islands* Alaska, USA 16 A3
Aleutian Trench *Undersea feature* Pacific Ocean 122 D1
Alexander Island *Island* Antarctica 132 B2
Alexandretta *see* İskenderun
Alexandria Egypt 54 B1
Alexandria Louisiana, USA 28 B3
Alexandroúpoli Greece 84 D3
Al Fāshir *see* El Fasher
Alföld *Plain* Hungary 79 D7
Algarve *Region* Portugal 72 C4
Algeciras Spain 72 D5
Algeria *Country* N Africa 50-51
Alghero Italy 77 A5
Algiers *Capital of* Algeria 50 D1
Al Ḩasakah Syria 98 D2
Al Ḩillah Iraq *var.* Hilla 100 B3
Al Ḩudaydah Yemen 101 B7
Al Hufūf Saudi Arabia 101 C5
Alicante Spain 73 F4
Alice Springs Australia 126 A5 128 E4
Al Jawf Saudi Arabia 100 B4
Al Jazīrah *Region* Iraq/Syria 98 E2
Al Jīzah *see* El Gîza
Al Karak Jordan 99 B6
Al Khārijah *see* El Khârga
Al Khums Libya 51 F2
Al Khurţūm *see* Khartoum
Alkmaar Netherlands 66 C2
Al Kufrah Libya 51 H4
Al Lādhiqīyah Syria *Eng.* Latakia 98 B3
Allahābād India 114 C4
Allenstein *see* Olsztyn
Allentown Pennsylvania, USA 21 F4
Alma-Ata *Capital of* Kazakhstan *Rus./Kaz.* Almaty 95 C5
Al Madīnah Saudi Arabia *Eng.* Medina 100 A5
Al Mafraq Jordan 99 B5
Almalyk Uzbekistan *Uzb.* Olmaliq 103 E2
Al Manāmah *see* Manama
Al Marj Libya 51 G2
Almaty *see* Alma-Ata
Al Mawşil Iraq *Eng.* Mosul 100 B3
Almelo Netherlands 66 E3
Almería Spain 73 E5
Al Mukallā Yemen 101 C7
Alofi *Capital of* Niue 127 F5
Alor, Kepulauan *Island group* Indonesia 121 E5
Alps *Mountain range* C Europe 60 D4
Al Qāhirah *see* Cairo
Al Qāmishlī Syria *var.* Kamishli 98 E1
Al Qunayţirah Syria 98 B4
Altai Mountains *Mountain Range* C Asia 106 C2
Altamura Italy 77 E5
Altay China 106 C2
Altay Mongolia 106 D2
Altun Shan *Mountain Range* China 106 B4
Alturas California, USA 24 B4
Al Wajh Saudi Arabia 100 A5
Alytus Lithuania *Pol.* Olita 87 B5
Amakusa-shotō *Island group* Japan 111 A6
Amami-Ō-shima *Island* Japan 111 A8
Amara *see* Al 'Amārah
Amarillo Texas, USA 27 E2
Amazon *River* South America 36 C2
Amazon Delta *Wetland* Brazil 36 D2
Amazonia *Region* C South America 40 C2
Ambanja Madagascar 59 G2
Ambarchik Russian Federation 95 G2
Ambato Ecuador 38 A4
Amboasary Madagascar 59 F4
Ambon Indonesia 121 F4
Ambositra Madagascar 59 G3
Ambriz Angola 58 B1
Ameland *Island* Netherlands 66 D1
American Falls Reservoir *Reservoir* Idaho, USA 24 E4
American Samoa *External territory* USA, Pacific Ocean 122 D3
Amersfoort Netherlands 66 D3
Amiens France 70 C3
Amīndīvi Islands *Island group* India 116 C2
Amirante Islands *Island group* Seychelles 59 H1
Amman *Capital of* Jordan 99 B5
Ammassalik Greenland *var.* Angmagssalik 62 C4
Ammochostos *see* Gazimağusa
Āmol Iran 100 C3
Amorgós *Island* Greece 85 D6
Amritsar India 114 D2
Amsterdam *Capital of* Netherlands 66 C3
Amstetten Austria 75 D6
Am Timan Chad 56 C3
Amu Darya *River* C Asia 102 D3
Amundsen Gulf *Sea feature* Canada 17 E2
Amundsen Sea Antarctica 132 B4
Amur *River* E Asia 93 F3 105 E1
Anadolu Dağları *see* Doğu Karadeniz Dağlarıı
Anadyr' Russian Federation 95 H1
Anápolis Brazil 41 F4
Anatolia *Region* SE Europe 83 G3
Anchorage Alaska, USA 16 C3
Ancona Italy 76 C3
Andalucía *Region* Spain 72 D4
Andaman Islands *Island group* India 117 H2 119 A5
Andaman Sea Indian Ocean 112 D3
Andaman-Nicobar Ridge *Undersea feature* Indian Ocean 117 H3
Andes *Mountain range* South America 37 B6

Andijon *see* Andizhan
Andizhan Uzbekistan *Uzb.* Andijon 103 F2
Andorra *Country* SW Europe 71 B6
Andorra la Vella *Capital of* Andorra 71 B6
Ándros *Island* Greece 85 C5
Andros Island *Island* Bahamas 34 C1
Angara *River* C Asia 93 E2
Angara Basin *see* Fram Basin
Ángel de la Guarda, Isla *Island* Mexico 30 B2
Angel Falls *Waterfall* Venezuela 36 C2
Angeles Philippines 121 E1
Ångermanälven *River* Sweden 64 C4
Angers France 70 B4
Anglesey *Island* Wales, UK 69 C5
Angmagssalik *see* Ammassalik
Angola *Country* C Africa 58
Angola Basin *Undersea feature* Atlantic Ocean 47 D5
Angora *see* Ankara
Angoulême France 71 B5
Angren Uzbekistan 103 E2
Anguilla *External territory* UK, West Indies 35
Anjouan *Island* Comoros 59 G2
Ankara *Capital of* Turkey *prev.* Angora 96 C3
Annaba Algeria 51 E1
An Nafūd *Desert region* Saudi Arabia 100 B4
An Najaf Iraq *var.* Najaf 100 B4
Annapolis Maryland, USA 21 F4
Ann Arbor Michigan, USA 20 C3
An Nāşirīyah Iraq *var.* Nasiriya 100 C4
Annecy France 71 D5
Anshan China 108 D4
Antakya Turkey *var.* Hatay 96 D4
Antalaha Madagascar 59 G2
Antalya Turkey *prev.* Adalia 96 B4
Antalya, Gulf of *see* Antalya Körfezi
Antalya Körfezi *Sea feature* Mediterranean Sea *Eng.* Gulf of Antalya, *var.* Gulf of Adalia 96 B4
Antananarivo *Capital of* Madagascar *prev.* Tananarive 59 G3
Antarctica 132-133
Antarctic Peninsula *Peninsula* Antarctica 132 A2
Antequera Spain 72 D5
Anticosti, Île d' *Island* Canada 19 E3
Antigua *Island* Antigua & Barbuda 34 D2
Antigua & Barbuda *Country* West Indies 35
Anti-Lebanon *Mountains* Lebanon/Syria 98 B4
Antofagasta Chile 44 B2
Antsirañana Madagascar 59 G2
Antsohihy Madagascar 59 G2
Antwerp *see* Antwerpen
Antwerpen Belgium *Eng.* Antwerp 67 C5
Aoga-shima *Island* Japan 111 D6
Aomori Japan 110 D3
Aorangi *see* Cook, Mount
Aosta Italy 76 A2
Apeldoorn Netherlands 66 D3
Apennines *see* Appennino
Apia *Capital of* Samoa 127 F4
Appalachian Mountains *Mountain range* E USA 15 F4
Appennino *Mountain range* Italy *Eng.* Apennines 60 D5 76 C4
Apure *River* Venezuela 36 B2
Aputiteeq Greenland 62 D3
Aqaba *see* Al 'Aqabah
Aqaba, Gulf of *Sea feature* Red Sea *Ar.* Khalīj al 'Aqabah 99 A8
'Aqabah, Khalīj al *see* Red Sea
Āqchah Afghanistan *var.* Āqcheh 102 D3
Āqcheh *see* Āqchah
Arabian Basin *Undersea feature* Indian Ocean 116 B2
Arabian Peninsula *Peninsula* Asia 83 H5 92 B5
Arabian Sea Indian Ocean 112 B3
Aracaju Brazil 41 H3
Arad Romania 88 A4
Arafura Sea Asia/Australasia 122 B3
Araguaia *River* Brazil 41 E3
Arāk Iran 100 C3
Araks *see* Aras
Arak's *see* Aras
Aral Sea *Inland sea* Kazakhstan/Uzbekistan 92 C3
Ararat, Mount *Peak* Turkey *var.* Great Ararat, *Turk.* Büyükağrı Dağı 92 B4
Aras *River* SW Asia *Arm.* Arak's, *Per.* Rūd-e Aras, *Rus.* Araks, *Turk.* Aras Nehri 97 G3
Aras Nehri *see* Aras
Arauca Colombia 38 C2
Arauca *River* Colombia/Venezuela 38 C2
Arbatax Italy 77 A5
Arbīl Iraq *Kurd.* Hawlēr 100 B3
Arctic Ocean 16-17
Arda *River* Bulgaria/Greece 84 C3
Ardennes *Region* W Europe 67 D7
Arendal Norway 65 A6
Arensburg *see* Kuressaare
Arequipa Peru 40 B4
Arezzo Italy 76 C3
Argentina *Country* S South America 44-45
Argentine Basin *Undersea feature* Atlantic Ocean 47 B6
Argentine claim in Antarctica 132 C2
Argentino, Lago *Lake* Argentina 45 B7
Århus Denmark 65 A7
Arica Chile 44 B1
Arizona *State* USA 26 B2
Arkansas *State* USA 28 B1
Arkansas *River* C USA 15 E4
Arkhangel'sk Russian Federation 90 C3 94 C2
Arles France 71 D6
Arlon Belgium 67 D8
Armenia *Country* SW Asia 97 G2
Armenia Colombia 38 B3
Armidale Australia 130 C2
Arnhem Netherlands 66 D4
Arnhem, Cape *Coastal feature* Australia 128 E2

Arnhem Land *Region* Australia 128 E2
Arno *River* Italy 76 B3
Ar Ramādī Iraq 100 B3
Arran *Island* Scotland, UK 68 C4
Ar Raqqah Syria 98 C2
Arras France 70 C2
Ar Riyāḍ *see* Riyadh
Ar Rustāq Oman *var.* Rostak 101 D5
Artesia New Mexico, USA 26 D3
Artigas Uruguay 42 B4
Aru, Kepulauan *Island group* Indonesia 121 G5
Arua Uganda 55 B6
Aruba *External territory* Netherlands, West Indies 35 E5
Arun *River* India/Nepal 115 F3
Arusha Tanzania 55 C7
Asad, Buḩayrat al *Reservoir* Syria 98 C2
Asadābād Afghanistan 103 E4
Asahikawa Japan 110 D2
Asamankese Ghana 53 E5
Ascension *Island* Atlantic Ocean 47 C5
Ascoli Piceno Italy 76 C4
Ashburton New Zealand 131 F4
Asheville North Carolina, USA 29 E1
Ashgabat *Capital of* Turkmenistan *prev.* Ashkhabad, Poltoratsk 102 B3
Ashkhabad *see* Ashgabat
Ash Shāriqah *see* Sharjah
Asia 92-93 104-105
Asmara *Capital of* Eritrea *Amh.* Asmera 54 C4
Asmera *see* Asmara
Assab Eritrea 54 D4
'Assal, Lac *see* Lake Assal
Assal, Lake *Lake* Djibouti *var.* Lac 'Assal 48 E4
As Salţ Jordan *var.* Salt 99 B5
Assen Netherlands 66 E2
Assisi Italy 76 C4
As Sulaymānīyah Iraq 100 B3
As Sulayyil Saudi Arabia 101 B6
As Suwaydā' Syria 99 B5
Astoria Oregon, USA 24 A2
Astrakhan' Russian Federation 91 B7 95 A4
Astypálaia *Island* Greece 85 D6
Asunción *Capital of* Paraguay 42 B3
Aswân Egypt 54 B2
Asyût Egypt 54 B2
Atacama Desert *Desert* Chile 44 B2
Atakpamé Togo 53 F4
Aţâr Mauritania 52 C2
Atbara Sudan 54 C3
Athabasca, Lake *Lake* Canada 17 F4
Athens *Capital of* Greece *Gk.* Athína, *prev.* Athínai 85 C5
Athens Georgia, USA 29 E2
Athína *see* Athens
Athínai *see* Athens
Athlone Ireland 69 B5
Ati Chad 56 C3
Atlanta Georgia, USA 28 D2
Atlantic City New Jersey, USA 21 F4
Atlantic Ocean 46-47
Atlantic-Indian Basin *Undersea feature* Indian Ocean 113 A7
Atlantic-Indian Ridge *Undersea feature* Atlantic Ocean 47 D7
Atlas Mountains *Mountain range* Morocco 50 C2
Aţ Ţafīlah Jordan 99 B6
Aţ Ţā'if Saudi Arabia 100 B6
Attapu Laos 119 E5
Attawapiskat Canada 18 C3
Attawapiskat *River* Canada 18 B3
Attersee *Lake* Austria 75 D7
Attu Island *Island* Alaska, USA 16 A2
Auburn California, USA 25 B5
Auch France 71 B6
Auckland New Zealand 131 G2
Augsburg Germany 75 C6
Augusta Italy 77 D7
Augusta Georgia, USA 29 E2
Augusta Maine, USA 20 G2
Aurillac France 71 C5
Aurora Colorado, USA 22 D4
Aurora Illinois, USA 20 B3
Aussig *see* Ústí nad Labem
Austin Texas, USA 27 G4
Australasia 124-125
Australia *Country* Pacific Ocean 126-130
Australian Antarctic Territory *Territory* Antarctica 132-133
Australian Capital Territory *Territory* Australia *abbrev.* A.C.T. 130 C3
Austria *Country* C Europe 75
Auxerre France 70 C4
Avarua *Capital of* Cook Islands 127 G5
Aveiro Portugal 72 C3
Avignon France 71 D6
Ávila Spain 72 D3
Avilés Spain 72 D1
Awbārī Libya 51 F3
Axel Heiberg Island *Island* Canada 17 F1
Axios *see* Vardar
Ayacucho Peru 40 B4
Aydarkul', Ozero *Lake* Uzbekistan 102 D2
Aydın Turkey 96 A3
Ayer's Rock *see* Uluru
'Ayn ath Tha'lab Libya 51 G3
Ayr Scotland, UK 68 C4
Ayutthaya Thailand 119 C5
Ayvalık Turkey 96 A3
A'zāz Syria 98 B2
Azerbaijan *Country* SW Asia 97 G2
Azores *Islands* Portugal, Atlantic Ocean 46 C3
Azov, Sea of Black Sea *Ukr.* Azovs'ke More, *Rus.* Azovskoye More 91 A6
Azovs'ke More *see* Azov, Sea of
Azovskoye More *see* Azov, Sea of
Azul Argentina 44 D4
Azur, Côte d' *Coastal region* France 71 E6
Az Zarqā' Jordan 99 B5
Az Zāwiyah Libya 51 F2

B

Baabda Lebanon 98 B4
Baalbek Lebanon *var.* Ba'labakk 98 B4
Bab el Mandeb *Sea feature* Djibouti/Yemen 101 B7

Bābol Iran 100 D3
Babruysk Belorussia *Rus.* Bobruysk 87 D6
Bacan, Pulau *Island* Indonesia 121 F4
Bačka Topola Yugoslavia 80 D2
Bacolod Philippines 121 E2
Bacău Romania 88 C4
Badain Jaran Shamo *Desert region* China 107 E3
Badajoz Spain 72 C4
Badalona Spain 73 G2
Baden Switzerland 75 E6
Bādiyat ash Shām *see* Syrian Desert
Bafatá Guinea-Bissau 52 C4
Baffin Bay *Sea feature* Atlantic Ocean 46 B1
Baffin Island *Island* Canada 15 F1
Bafoussam Cameroon 56 B4
Bagdad *see* Baghdad
Bagé Brazil 42 C4
Baghdad *Capital of* Iraq *var.* Bagdad, *Ar.* Baghdād 100 B3
Baghdād *see* Baghdad
Baghlān Afghanistan 103 E4
Baguio Philippines 121 E1
Bahamas *Country* West Indies, Atlantic Ocean 34
Baharden *see* Bakherden
Bahāwalpur Pakistan 114 C3
Bäherden *see* Bakherden
Bahía, Islas de la *Islands* Honduras 32 D2
Bahir Dar Ethiopia 54 C4
Bahrain *Country* SW Asia 101 C5
Baia Mare Romania 88 B3
Bai'an China 108 D2
Baikal, Lake *see* Baykal, Ozero
Bairiki *Capital of* Kiribati 127 E2
Baja Hungary 79 C7
Baja California *Peninsula* Mexico *Eng.* Lower California 30 B2
Bajo Nuevo *Island* Colombia 33 F2
Baker Oregon, USA 24 C3
Baker & Howland Islands *External territory* USA, Pacific Ocean 127 F2
Bakersfield California, USA 25 C7
Bakharden *see* Bakherden
Bakherden Turkmenistan *prev.* Bakharden, *var.* Baharden, *Turkm.* Bäherden 102 B3
Bākhtarān Iran *prev.* Kermānshāh 100 C3
Bakı *see* Baku
Baku *Capital of* Azerbaijan *Az.* Bakı, *var.* Baky 96 A3
Baky *see* Baku
Balabac Strait *Sea feature* South China Sea / Sulu Sea 120 D2
Ba'labakk *see* Baalbek
Balakovo Russian Federation 91 C6
Bālā Morghāb Afghanistan 102 D4
Balaton *Lake* Hungary *var.* Lake Balaton, *Ger.* Plattensee 79 C7
Balaton, Lake *see* Balaton
Balbina, Represa *Reservoir* Brazil 40 D2
Baleares, Islas *Island group* Spain *Eng.* Balearic Islands 73 H3 82 C3
Balearic Islands *see* Baleares, Islas
Bali *Island* Indonesia 120 D5
Balıkesir Turkey 96 A3
Balikpapan Indonesia 120 D4
Balkan Mountains *Mountain range* Bulgaria *Bul.* Stara Planina 84 C2
Balkhash Kazakhstan 94 C5
Balkhash, Lake *see* Balkhash, Ozero
Balkhash, Ozero *Lake* Kazakhstan *Eng.* Lake Balkhash 92 C3 94 C5
Ballarat Australia 130 B4
Balleny Islands *Island group* Antarctica 133 E5
Balsas *River* Mexico 31 E5
Bălţi Moldavia 88 D3
Baltic Port *see* Paldiski
Baltic Sea Atlantic Ocean 65 C7
Baltimore Maryland, USA 21 F4
Baltischport *see* Paldiski
Baltiski *see* Paldiski
Baltiysk Kaliningrad, Russian Federation *prev.* Pillau 86 A4
Bamako *Capital of* Mali 52 D4
Bambari Central African Republic 56 C4
Bamenda Cameroon 56 B4
Banaba *Island* Kiribati *prev.* Ocean Island 127 E2
Banda, Laut *see* Banda Sea
Banda Aceh Indonesia 120 A3
Banda Sea *Sea feature* Pacific Ocean *Ind.* Laut Banda 105 E5 121 F4
Bandar-e 'Abbās Iran 100 D4
Bandar-e Būshehr Iran 100 C4
Bandar Seri Begawan *Capital of* Brunei 120 D3
Bandon Oregon, USA 24 A3
Bandundu Congo (Zaire) 57 C6
Bandung Indonesia 120 C5
Bangalore India 116 D2
Banggai, Kepulauan *Island group* Indonesia 121 E4
Banghāzī Libya *Eng.* Benghazi 51 G2
Bangka, Pulau *Island* Indonesia 120 C4
Bangkok *Capital of* Thailand *Th.* Krung Thep 119 C5
Bangladesh *Country* S Asia 115
Bangor Northern Ireland, UK 69 B5
Bangor Maine, USA 21 G2
Bangui *Capital of* Central African Republic 57 C5
Bani *River* Mali 52 D3
Banī Suwayf *see* Beni Suef
Banja Luka Bosnia & Herzegovina 80 B3
Banjarmasin Indonesia 120 D4
Banjul *Capital of* Gambia 52 B3
Banks Island *Island* Canada 17 E2
Banks Island *Island* Vanuatu, Pacific Ocean 126 D4
Banská Bystrica Slovakia *Ger.* Neusohl, *Hung.* Besztercebánya 79 C6
Bantry Bay *Sea feature* Ireland 69 A6
Banyak, Kepulauan *Island group* Indonesia 120 A3
Banyo Cameroon 56 B4
Baoji China 109 B5
Baotou China 107 E3
Ba'qūbah C Iraq 100 B3

Baracaldo Spain 73 E1
Baranavichy Belorussia *Rus.* Baranovichi, *Pol.* Baranowicze 87 C6
Baranovichi *see* Baranavichy
Baranowicze *see* Baranavichy
Barbados *Country* West Indies 35 E4
Barbuda *Island* Antigua & Barbuda 35 G3
Barcelona Spain 73 G2
Barcelona Venezuela 39 E1
Bareilly India 115 E3
Barentsburg Svalbard 63 G2
Barents Sea Arctic Ocean 64 E1
Bari Italy 77 E5
Barinas Venezuela 38 D2
Barisan, Pegunungan *Mountains* Indonesia 120 B4
Bar-le-Duc France 70 D3
Barito *River* Indonesia 120 D4
Barlee, Lake *Lake* Australia 124 B3 129 B 5
Barnaul Russian Federation 94 D4
Barnstaple England, UK 69 C7
Barquisimeto Venezuela 38 D1
Barra *Island* Scotland, UK 68 B3
Barranquilla Colombia 38 B1
Barrow *River* Ireland 69 B6
Barstow California, USA 25 C7
Bartang *River* Tajikistan 103 F3
Bartica Guyana 39 G2
Barysaw Belorussia *Rus.* Borisov 87 D5
Basarabeasca Moldavia 88 D4
Basel Switzerland 75 A7
Basque Provinces *Region* Spain *Sp.* País Vasco 73 E1
Basra *see* Al Başrah
Bassein Burma 118 A4
Basse-Terre *Capital of* Guadeloupe 35 G4
Basseterre *Capital of* St Kitts & Nevis 35 G3
Bass Strait *Sea feature* Australia 130 B4
Bastia Corse, France 71 E7
Bastogne Belgium 67 D7
Bata Equatorial Guinea 56 A5
Batangas Philippines 121 E1
Bătdâmbâng Cambodia 119 D5
Bath England, UK 69 D7
Bathurst Australia 130 C3
Bathurst Canada 19 F4
Bathurst Island *Island* Australia 128 D2
Bathurst Island *Island* Canada 17 F2
Batman Turkey *var.* İluh 97 F2
Batna Algeria 51 E1
Baton Rouge Louisiana, USA 28 B3
Batticaloa Sri Lanka 117 E3
Bat'umi Georgia 97 F2
Bauchi Nigeria 53 G4
Bauru Brazil 42 D2
Bavarian Alps *Mountains* Austria/Germany 75 C7
Bayamo Cuba 34 C2
Bay City Michigan, USA 20 C3
Baydhabo Somalia 55 D6
Baykal, Ozero *Lake* Russian Federation *Eng.* Lake Baikal 93 E3 95 F4
Bayonne France 71 A6
Bayramaly Turkmenistan 102 C3
Bayrūt *see* Beirut
Beaufort Sea Arctic Ocean 17 E2
Beaufort West South Africa 58 C5
Beaumont Texas, USA 27 H4
Beauvais France 70 C3
Béchar Algeria 50 C2
Be'ér Sheva' Israel 99 A6
Beijing *Capital of* China *var.* Peking 108 C4
Beira Mozambique 59 E3
Beirut *Capital of* Lebanon *var.* Beyrouth, Bayrūt 98 B4
Beja Portugal 72 C4
Béjaïa Algeria 51 E1
Bek-Budi *see* Karshi
Békéscsaba Hungary 79 D7
Belarus *see* Belorussia
Belau see Palau
Belcher Islands *Islands* Canada 18 C2
Beledweyne Somalia 55 D5
Belém Brazil 41 F2
Belfast Northern Ireland, UK 69 B5
Belfort France 70 E4
Belgaum India 116 C1
Belgium *Country* W Europe 67
Belgorod Russian Federation 91 A5
Belgrade *Capital of* Yugoslavia *SCr.* Beograd 80 D3
Belitung, Pulau *Island* Indonesia 120 C4
Belize *Country* Central America 32
Belize City Belize 32 C1
Bella Unión Uruguay 42 B4
Belle Île *Island* France 70 A4
Belle Isle, Strait of *Sea feature* Canada 15 G3 19 H3
Bellevue Washington, USA 24 B2
Bellingham Washington, USA 24 B1
Bellingshausen Sea Antarctica 47 A8 132 A3
Bello Colombia 38 B2
Belluno Italy 76 C2
Bellville South Africa 58 C5
Belmopan *Capital of* Belize 32 C1
Belo Horizonte Brazil 41 G5 43 F1
Belorussia *Country* E Europe *var.* Belarus 87
Belostok *see* Białystok
Beloye More Arctic Ocean *Eng.* White Sea 61 F1 90 C3
Bend Oregon, USA 24 B3
Bendery *see* Tighina
Bendigo Australia 130 B4
Benevento Italy 77 D5
Bengal, Bay of *Sea feature* Indian Ocean 112 C3
Benghazi *see* Banghāzī
Bengkulu Indonesia 120 B4
Benguela Angola 58 B2
Beni *River* Bolivia 40 C4
Benidorm Spain 73 F4
Beni Mellal Morocco 50 C2
Benin *Country* N Africa *prev.* Dahomey 53
Benin, Bight of *Sea feature* W Africa 53 F5
Benin City Nigeria 53 F5
Beni Suef Egypt *var.* Banī Suwayf 54 B1
Benue *River* Cameroon/Nigeria 53 G4
Beograd *see* Belgrade

Berat Albania 81 B3
Berbera Somalia 54 D4
Berbérati Central African Republic 56 C5
Berdyans'k Ukraine 88 G4
Berezina *see* Byerazino
Bergamo Italy 76 B2
Bergen Norway 65 A5
Bering Sea Pacific Ocean 122 D1
Bering Strait *Sea feature* Bering Sea / Chukchi Sea 122 D1
Berkner Island *Island* Antarctica 132 C2
Berlin *Capital of* Germany 74 D3
Bermejo *River* Argentina 44 D2
Bermuda *External territory* UK, Atlantic Ocean 46 B3
Bern *Capital of* Switzerland *Fr.* Berne 75 A7
Berne *see* Bern
Bertoua Cameroon 57 B5
Besançon France 70 D4
Besztercebánya *see* Banská Bystrica
Bethlehem West Bank 99 B5
Beuthen *see* Bytom
Beyrouth *see* Beirut
Béziers France 71 C6
Bezmein *see* Byuzmeyin
Bhamo Burma 118 B2
Bhātāpāra India 114 C4
Bhāvnagar India 114 C4
Bhōpal India 114 D4
Bhutan *Country* S Asia 115
Biak, Pulau *Island* Indonesia 121 G4
Białystok Poland *Rus.* Belostok 78 E3
Biel Switzerland 75 A7
Bielitz-Biala *see* Bielsko-Biała
Bielsko-Biała Poland *Ger.* Bielitz-Biala 79 C5
Bighorn Mountains *Mountains* C USA 22 C2
Big Spring Texas, USA 27 E3
Bihać Bosnia & Herzegovina 80 B3
Bihār *State* India 115 F3
Bijelo Polje Yugoslavia 80 D4
Bikāner India 114 C3
Bila Tserkva Ukraine 89 E2
Bilbao Spain 73 E1
Billings Montana, USA 22 C2
Biloxi Mississippi, USA 28 C3
Biltine Chad 56 D3
Binghamton New York, USA 21 F3
Bío Bío *River* Chile 45 B5
Birāk Libya 51 F3
Biratnagar Nepal 115 F3
Birganj Nepal 115 F3
Birmingham England, UK 69 D6
Birmingham Alabama, USA 28 D2
Birni-Nkonni Niger 53 F3
Birsen *see* Biržai
Biržai Lithuania *Ger.* Birsen 86 C4
Biscay, Bay of *Sea feature* Atlantic Ocean 71 A5 73 E1
Biscay Plain *Undersea feature* Atlantic Ocean 60 B4
Bishkek *Capital of* Kyrgyzstan *prev.* Frunze, Pishpek 103 F2
Bishop California, USA 25 C6
Biskra Algeria 51 E2
Bismarck North Dakota, USA 23 E2
Bismarck Archipelago *Island group* Papua New Guinea 126 B3
Bissau *Capital of* Guinea-Bissau 52 B4
Bitola Macedonia 81 D6
Bitterroot Range *Mountains* NW USA 24 D2
Biwa-ko *Lake* Japan 111 C5
Bizerte Tunisia 51 E1
Bjelovar Croatia 80 B2
Black Drin *River* Albania / Macedonia 81 D5
Black Forest *see* Schwarzwald
Black Hills *Mountains* C USA 22 D3
Blackpool England, UK 69 C5
Black River *River* China / Vietnam 118 D3
Black Sea Asia / Europe 61 F1 82 B4
Black Volta *River* Ghana / Ivory Coast 53 E4
Blackwater *River* Ireland 69 A6
Blagoevgrad Bulgaria 84 B3
Blagoveshchensk Russian Federation 95 G4
Blanca, Bahía *Sea feature* Argentina 37 C6
Blantyre Malawi 59 E2
Blenheim New Zealand 131 G3
Blida Algeria 50 D1
Bloemfontein South Africa 58 D4
Blois France 70 C4
Bloomington Indiana, USA 20 C4
Bluefields Nicaragua 33 E3
Blue Mountains *Mountains* W USA 24 C3
Blue Nile *River* Ethiopia / Sudan 55 C4
Blumenau Brazil 42 D3
Bo Sierra Leone 52 C4
Boa Vista Brazil 40 D1
Bobo-Dioulasso Burkina 53 E4
Bobruysk *see* Babruysk
Boca de la Serpiente *see* Serpent's Mouth, The
Bochum Germany 74 A4
Bodø Norway 64 C3
Bodrum Turkey 96 A4
Bogor Indonesia 120 C5
Bogotá *Capital of* Colombia 38 B3
Bo Hai *Sea feature* Yellow Sea 108 D4
Bohemian Forest *Region* Czech Rep 75 D6
Bohol *Island* Philippines 121 E2
Boise Idaho, USA 24 D3
Bokhara *see* Bukhara
Bol Chad 56 B3
Bolivia *Country* C South America 40-41
Bologna Italy 76 C3
Bolton England, UK 69 D5
Bolzano Italy *Ger.* Bozen 76 C1
Boma Congo (Zaire) 57 B7
Bombay India *var.* Mumbai 115 C5 116 C1
Bomu *River* Central African Republic / Congo (Zaire) 57 D5
Bonete, Cerro *Peak* Chile 37 B5
Bongo, Massif des *Upland* Central African Republic 56 D4
Bongor Chad 56 C3
Bonn Germany 75 A5
Boosaaso Somalia 54 E4

Borås Sweden 65 B7
Bordeaux France 71 B5
Borger Texas, USA 27 E2
Borisov *see* Barysaw
Borlänge Sweden 65 C6
Borneo *Island* SE Asia 120-121
Bornholm *Island* Denmark 65 C8
Bosanski Šamac Bosnia & Herzegovina 80 C3
Bosna *River* Bosnia & Herzegovina 80 B3
Bosnia & Herzegovina *Country* SE Europe 80-81
Bosporus *Sea feature* Turkey *Turk.* İstanbul Boğazi 96 B2
Bossangoa Central African Republic 56 C4
Boston Massachusetts, USA 21 G3
Botevgrad Bulgaria 84 C2
Bothnia, Gulf of *Sea feature* Baltic Sea 65 C5
Botoşani Romania 88 C3
Botswana *Country* southern Africa 58
Bouaké Ivory Coast 52 D4
Bouar Central African Republic 56 C4
Bougainville Island *Island* Papua New Guinea 126 C3
Bougouni Mali 52 D4
Boulder Colorado, USA 22 C4
Boulogne-sur-Mer France 70 C2
Bourges France 70 C4
Bourgogne *Region* France *Eng.* Burgundy 70 D4
Bourke Australia 130 B2
Bournemouth England, UK 69 D7
Bouvet Island *External territory* Norway, Atlantic Ocean 47 D7
Bowling Green Kentucky, USA 20 C5
Bozeman Montana, USA 22 B2
Bozen *see* Bolzano
Brač *Island* Croatia 80 B4
Bradford England, UK 69 D5
Braga Portugal 72 C2
Bragança Portugal 72 C2
Brahmaputra *River* S Asia 106 B5 115 G3
Brăila Romania 88 D4
Brainerd Minnesota, USA 23 F2
Brandon Canada 17 G5
Brasília *Capital of* Brazil 41 F4
Braşov Romania 88 C4
Bratislava *Capital of* Slovakia *Ger.* Pressburg, *Hung.* Pozsony 79 C6
Bratsk Russian Federation 95 E4
Braunau am Inn Austria 75 D6
Braunschweig Germany *Eng.* Brunswick 74 C4
Brazil *Country* South America 40-43
Brazil Basin *Undersea feature* Atlantic Ocean 47 C5
Brazilian Highlands *Upland* Brazil 41 G4
Brazos *River* SW USA 27 G3
Brazzaville *Capital of* Congo 57 B6
Brecon Beacons *Hills* Wales, UK 69 E7
Breda Netherlands 66 D4
Bregenz Austria 75 B7
Bremen Germany 74 B3
Bremerhaven Germany 74 B3
Brescia Italy 76 B2
Breslau *see* Wrocław
Brest Belorussia *Pol.* Brześć nad Bugiem, *prev.* Brześć Litewski, *Rus.* Brest-Litovsk 87 B6
Brest France 70 A3
Brest-Litovsk *see* Brest
Bretagne *Region* France *Eng.* Brittany 70 A3
Breton Sound *Inlet* Louisiana, USA 28 C4
Brezhnev *see* Naberezhnyye Chelny
Bria Central African Republic 56 D4
Bridgetown *Capital of* Barbados 35 H5
Brig Switzerland 75 D5
Brighton England, UK 69 E7
Brindisi Italy 77 E5
Brisbane Australia 130 D2
Bristol England, UK 69 D7
British Antarctic Territory *Territory* Antarctica 132 B2
British Columbia *Province* Canada 16-17
British Indian Ocean Territory *External territory* UK, Indian Ocean 112 C4
British Isles *Islands* W Europe 68-69
British Virgin Islands *External territory* UK, West Indies 35
Brittany *see* Bretagne
Brno Czech Republic *Ger.* Brünn 79 B5
Broken Arrow Oklahoma, USA 27 G1
Broken Hill Australia 130 B3
Broken Ridge *Undersea feature* Indian Ocean 113 D5
Bromberg *see* Bydgoszcz
Brooks Range *Mountains* Alaska, USA 17 F2
Broome Australia 128 C3
Brownfield Texas, USA 27 E3
Brownsville Texas, USA 27 G5
Bruges *see* Brugge
Brugge Belgium *Fr.* Bruges 67 A5
Brunei *Country* E Asia 120 D3
Brünn *see* Brno
Brunswick Georgia, USA 29 E3
Brunswick *see* Braunschweig
Brusa *see* Bursa
Brussel *see* Brussels
Brussels *Capital of* Belgium *Fr.* Bruxelles, *Flem.* Brussel 67 C6
Brüx *see* Most
Bruxelles *see* Brussels
Bryan Texas, USA 27 G3
Bryansk Russian Federation 91 A5 94 A2
Brześć Litewski *see* Brest
Brześć nad Bugiem *see* Brest
Bucaramanga Colombia 38 C2
Buchanan Liberia 52 C5
Bucharest *Capital of* Romania 88 C5
Budapest *Capital of* Hungary 79 C6
Budweis *see* České Budějovice
Buenaventura Colombia 38 B3
Buenos Aires *Capital of* Argentina 44 D4
Buenos Aires, Lago *Lake* Argentina/Chile 45 B6
Buffalo New York, USA 21 E3
Bug *River* E Europe 78 E3 88 C1

Bujumbura *Capital of* Burundi *prev.* Usumbura 55 B7
Bukavu Congo (Zaire) 57 E6
Bukhara Uzbekistan *var.* Bokhara, *Uzb.* Bukhoro 102 D2
Bukhoro *see* Bukhara
Bulawayo Zimbabwe 58 D3
Bulgaria *Country* E Europe 84
Bumba Congo (Zaire) 57 D5
Bunbury Australia 129 B6
Bundaberg Australia 126 C5 130 C1
Bunia Congo (Zaire) 57 E5
Buraydah Saudi Arabia 101 B5
Burē Ethiopia 54 C4
Burgas Bulgaria 84 E2
Burgos Spain 73 E2
Burgundy *see* Bourgogne
Burkina *Country* W Africa 53
Burlington Iowa, USA 23 G4
Burlington Vermont, USA 21 F2
Burma *Country* SE Asia *var.* Myanmar 118-119
Burnie Tasmania 130 B4
Burns Oregon, USA 24 C3
Bursa Turkey *prev.* Brusa 96 B3
Burtnieku Ezers *Lake* Latvia 86 C3
Buru *Island* Indonesia 121 F4
Burundi *Country* C Africa 55
Butembo Congo (Zaire) 57 E5
Butte Montana, USA 22 B2
Butuan Philippines 121 F2
Buurhakaba Somalia 55 D6
Buyo Reservoir *Reservoir* Ivory Coast 52 D5
Büyükağrı Dağı *see* Ararat, Mount
Buzău Romania 88 C4
Bydgoszcz Poland *Ger.* Bromberg 78 C3
Byerazino *River* Belorussia *Rus.* Berezina 87 D6
Bykhaw Belorussia *Rus.* Bykhov 87 D6
Bykhov *see* Bykhaw
Bytom Poland *Ger.* Beuthen 79 C5
Byuzmeyin Turkmenistan *prev.* Bezmein 102 B3
Byzantium *see* İstanbul

C

Caaguazú Paraguay 42 C2
Cabanatuan Philippines 121 E1
Cabimas Venezuela 38 C1
Cabinda *Exclave* Angola 57 B7 58 B1
Cabot Strait *Sea feature* Atlantic Ocean 19 G4
Čačak Yugoslavia 80 D4
Cáceres Spain 72 D3
Cachoeiro de Itapemirim Brazil 43 F1
Cadiz Philippines 121 E2
Cádiz Spain 72 D5
Caen France 70 B3
Caernarfon Wales, UK 69 C5
Cagayan de Oro Philippines 121 F2
Cagliari Italy 77 A6
Cahors France 71 B5
Cairns Australia 126 B4
Cairo *Capital of* Egypt *Ar.* Al Qāhirah, *var.* El Qâhira 54 B1
Čakovec Croatia 80 B2
Calabar Nigeria 53 G5
Calabria *Region* Italy 77 D6
Calafate Argentina 45 B7
Calais France 70 C2
Calais Maine, USA 21 H1
Calama Chile 44 B2
Calbayog Philippines 121 F2
Calcutta India 115 F4
Caldas da Rainha Portugal 72 B3
Caldwell Idaho, USA 25 C3
Caleta Olivia Argentina 45 C6
Calgary Canada 17 E5
Cali Colombia 38 B3
Calicut India *var.* Kozhikode 116 D2
California *State* USA 24-25
California, Golfo de *Sea feature* Pacific Ocean *Eng.* California, Gulf of 30 B2 123 F2
Callao Peru 40 A4
Caltagirone Italy 77 D7
Caltanissetta Italy 77 C7
Camagüey Cuba 34 C2
Cambodia *Country* SE Asia *Cam.* Kampuchea 118-119
Cambridge England, UK 69 E6
Cameroon *Country* W Africa 56-57
Camiri Bolivia 40 D5
Campbell Plateau *Undersea feature* Pacific Ocean 131 H4
Campeche Mexico 31 H4
Campeche, Bahía de *Sea feature* Mexico *Eng.* Gulf of Campeche 31G4
Campina Grande Brazil 41 H3
Campinas Brazil 41 F5 43 E2
Campo Grande Brazil 41 E5 42 C1
Campos Brazil 41 G5 43 F2
Canada *Country* North America 16-17 18-19
Canada Basin *Undersea feature* Arctic Ocean *var.* Laurentian Basin 12 B4
Canadian River *River* SW USA 27 E2
Çanakkale Turkey 96 A2
Çanakkale Boğazı *see* Dardanelles
Canarias, Islas *Islands* Spain *Eng.* Canary Islands 46 C4 50 A2
Canary Basin *Undersea feature* Atlantic Ocean 46 C4
Canary Islands *see* Canarias, Islas
Canaveral, Cape *Coastal feature* Florida, USA 29 F4
Canberra *Capital of* Australia 130 C3
Cancún Mexico 31 H3
Caniapiscau *River* Canada 19 E2
Caniapiscau, Réservoir *Reservoir* Canada 19 E3
Canik Dağları *Mountains* Turkey 96 D2
Çankırı Turkey 96 C2
Cannes France 71 D6
Canoas Brazil 42 D4
Canterbury England, UK 69 E7
Canterbury Bight *Sea feature* Pacific Ocean 131 G4
Canterbury Plains *Plain* New Zealand 131 G4
Cân Thơ Vietnam 119 D6
Canton Ohio, USA 20 D4
Canton *see* Guangzhou
Cape Basin *Undersea feature* Atlantic Ocean 49 C7 58 B5

Cape Coast Ghana 53 E5
Cape Town South Africa 58 C5
Cape Verde *Country* Atlantic Ocean 52 A3
Cape Verde Basin *Undersea feature* Atlantic Ocean 46 C4
Cape York Peninsula *Peninsula* Australia 124 C2
Cap-Haïtien Haiti 34 D3
Capri, Isola di *Island* Italy 77 C5
Caquetá *River* Colombia 38 C4
CAR *see* Central African Republic
Caracas *Capital of* Venezuela 38 D1
Carazinho Brazil 42 C3
Carbondale Illinois, USA 20 B5
Carcassonne France 71 C6
Cardiff Wales, UK 69 C7
Cardigan Bay *Sea feature* Wales, UK 69 C6
Caribbean Sea Atlantic Ocean 34-35
Carlisle England, UK 68 D4
Carlsbad New Mexico, USA 26 D3
Carlsberg Ridge *Undersea feature* Indian Ocean 112 B3
Carnavon Australia 128 A4
Carnegie, Lake *Lake* Australia 129 C5
Carolina Brazil 41 F3
Caroline Island *Island* Kiribati 127 H3
Caroline Islands *Island group* Micronesia 126 B1
Caroní *River* Venezuela 39 F2
Carpathian Mountains *Mountain range* E Europe *var.* Carpathians 61 E4
Carpathians *see* Carpathian Mountains
Carpaţii Meridionali *Mountain range* Romania *Eng.* South Carpathians, Transylvanian Alps 88 B4
Carpentaria, Gulf of *Sea feature* Australia 126 A4
Carson City Nevada, USA 25 C5
Cartagena Colombia 38 B1
Cartagena Spain 73 F4
Cartago Costa Rica 33 E4
Cartwright Canada 19 G2
Carúpano Venezuela 39 E1
Casablanca Morocco 50 C2
Casa Grande Arizona, USA 26 3
Cascade Range *Mountain range* Canada/USA 24 B3
Cascais Portugal 72 B4
Caseyr, Raas *Coastal feature* Somalia 48 E4
Casper Wyoming, USA 22 C3
Caspian Sea *Inland sea* Asia/Europe 94 A4
Castellón de la Plana Spain 73 F3
Castelo Branco Portugal 72 C3
Castries *Capital of* St Lucia 35 G4
Castro Chile 45 B6
Cat Island *Island* Bahamas 34 D1
Catania Italy 77 D7
Catanzaro Italy 77 D6
Cauca *River* Colombia 38 B2
Caucasus *Mountains* Asia/Europe 61 G4 92 B2
Cauquenes Chile 44 B4
Caura *River* Venezuela 39 E2
Caviana, Ilha *Island* Brazil 41 F1
Cawnpore *see* Kānpur
Caxias do Sul Brazil 42 D4
Cayenne *Capital of* French Guiana 39 H3
Cayman Islands *External territory* UK, West Indies 34
Cayman Trench *Undersea feature* Caribbean Sea 34 B3
Cebu Philippines 121 E2
Cedar Rapids Iowa, USA 23 G3
Cedros, Isla *Island* Mexico 30 A2
Cefalù Italy 77 C7
Celebes *see* Sulawesi
Celebes Sea Pacific Ocean *Ind.* Laut Sulawesi 122 B3
Celje Slovenia 80 A2
Central African Republic *Country* C Africa *abbrev.* CAR 56-57
Central Makrān Range *Mountains* Pakistan 114 A3
Central Russian Upland *Upland* Russian Federation 92 B3
Central Siberian Plateau *Plateau* Russian Federation 95 E3
Cephalonia *see* Kefallonía
Cernăuţi *see* Chernivtsi
Cēsis Latvia *Ger.* Wenden 86 C3
České Budějovice Czech Republic *Ger.* Budweis 79 B5
Ceuta *External territory* Spain, N Africa 50 C1
Cévennes *Mountains* France 71 C6
Ceylon *see* Sri Lanka
Ceylon Plain *Undersea feature* Indian Ocean 117 F4
Chad *Country* C Africa 56
Chad, Lake *Lake* C Africa 48 C4
Chāgai Hills *Mountains* Pakistan 114 A2
Chalándri Greece 85 C5
Chalkída Greece 85 C5
Châlons-sur-Marne France 70 D3
Chambéry France 71 D5
Champlaim Seamount *Undersea feature* Atlantic Ocean 43 G1
Chañaral Chile 44 B2
Chandīgarh India 114 D2
Chang, Ko *Island* Thailand 119 C5
Changchun China 108 D3
Chang Jiang *River* China *var.* Yangtze 104 D4 109 B5
Changsha China 109 C6
Changzhi China 109 C5
Chaniá Greece 85 C7
Channel Islands *Islands* UK 69 D8
Channel-Port-aux-Basques Canada 19 G4
Channel Tunnel France/UK 69 E7
Chapala, Lago de *Lake* Mexico 30 D4
Chardzhev Turkmenistan *prev.* Chardzhou, *prev.* Leninsk, *Turkm.* Chärjew 102 D3
Chardzhou *see* Chardzhev
Chari *River* C Africa 56 C3
Chārīkār Afghanistan 103 E4
Chärjew *see* Chardzhev
Charleroi Belgium 67 C7
Charleston South Carolina, USA 29 F2
Charleston West Virginia, USA 20 D5

Charleville Australia 130 B2
Charlotte North Carolina, USA 29 F2
Charlotte Amalie *Capital of* Virgin Islands 35 F3
Charlottesville Virginia, USA 21 E5
Charlottetown Canada 19 G4
Chartres France 70 C3
Châteauroux France 70 C4
Chatham Islands *Islands* New Zealand 122 D4
Chattanooga Tennessee, USA 28 D2
Chauk Burma 118 A3
Chaves Portugal 72 C2
Cheboksary Russian Federation 91 C5
Cheboygan Michigan, USA 20 C2
Cheju-do *Island* South Korea 109 E5
Cheju Strait *Sea feature* South Korea 109 E5
Cheleken Turkmenistan 102 E2
Chelyabinsk Russian Federation 94 C3
Chemnitz Germany *prev.* Karl-Marx-Stadt 75 D5
Chenāb *River* Pakistan 114 C2
Chengdu China 109 B5
Cherbourg France 70 B3
Cherepovets Russian Federation 90 B4
Cherkasy Ukraine 89 E2
Cherkessk Russian Federation 91 A7
Chernigov see Chernihiv
Chernihiv Ukraine *Rus.* Chernigov 89 E1
Chernivtsi Ukraine *Rus.* Chernovtsy, *Rom.* Cernăuţi 88 C3
Chernobyl' *see* Chornobyl'
Chernovtsy *see* Chernivtsi
Chernyakhovsk Kaliningrad, Russian Federation 86 A4
Cherskiy Range *Mountains* Russian Federation 93 G2
Chesapeake Bay *Sea feature* USA 21 F5
Chester England, UK 69 D5
Cheyenne Wyoming, USA 22 D4
Chiang Mai Thailand 118 B4
Chiba Japan 111 D5
Chicago Illinois, USA 20 B3
Chichigalpa Nicaragua 32 C3
Chiclayo Peru 40 A3
Chico California, USA 25 B5
Chicoutimi Canada 19 E4
Chidley, Cape *Coastal feature* Canada 19 E1
Chiemsee *Lake* Germany 75 C7
Chifeng China 107 G2
Chihuahua Mexico 30 C2
Chile *Country* S South America 44-45
Chilean Claim in Antarctica 132 B2
Chile Basin *Undersea feature* Pacific Ocean 123 G4
Chile Chico Chile 45 B6
Chillán Chile 44 B4
Chiloé, Isla de *Island* Chile 45 B6
Chimborazo *Peak* Ecuador 36 B2
Chimbote Peru 40 A3
Chimkent *see* Shymkent
Chimoio Mozambique 59 E3
China *Country* E Asia 106-107 108-109
Chindwin *River* Burma 118 A2
Chingola Zambia 58 D2
Chíos Greece 85 D5
Chíos *Island* Greece *prev.* Khíos 85 D5
Chirchik Uzbekistan *Uzb.* Chirchiq 103 E2
Chirchiq *see* Chirchik
Chiriquí, Golfo de *Sea feature* Panama 33 E5
Chişinău *Capital of* Moldavia, *var.* Kishinev 88 D3
Chita Russian Federation 95 F4
Chitré Panama 33 F5
Chittagong Bangladesh 115 G4
Chitungwiza Zimbabwe 58 D3
Chojnice Poland 78 C3
Choluteca Honduras 32 C3
Choma Zambia 58 D2
Chomutov Czech Republic *Ger.* Komotau 78 A4
Chon Buri Thailand 119 C5
Ch'ŏngjin North Korea 108 E3
Chongqing China *var.* Chungking 109 B6
Chonos, Archipiélago de los *Island group* Chile 45 B6
Chornobyl' Ukraine *Rus.* Chernobyl' 89 E1
Choybalsan Mongolia 107 F2
Christchurch New Zealand 131 G4
Christmas Island *External territory* Australia, Indian Ocean 112 D4
Christmas Island *see* Kiritimati
Chubut *River* Argentina 45 B6
Chudskoye Ozero *see* Peipus, Lake
Chuí Brazil *var.* Chuy 42 C5
Chukchi Sea Arctic Ocean *Rus.* Chukotskoye More 12 C1
Chukotskoye More *see* Chukchi Sea
Chumphon Thailand 119 C6
Chungking *see* Chongqing
Chuquicamata Chile 44 B2
Chur Switzerland 75 B7
Churchill Canada 17 G4
Churchill Falls Canada 19 F3
Chuuk Islands *Island group* Micronesia 126 B1
Chuy *see* Chuí
Cienfuegos Cuba 34 B2
Cieza Spain 73 F4
Cincinnati Ohio, USA 20 C4
Cirebon Indonesia 120 C5
Citlaltépetl *Peak* Mexico *var.* Pico de Orizaba 15 E5
Ciudad Bolívar Venezuela 39 E2
Ciudad del Este Paraguay 42 C3
Ciudad de México *see* Mexico City
Ciudad Guayana Venezuela 39 E2
Ciudad Juárez Mexico 30 C1
Ciudad Obregón Mexico 30 B2
Ciudad Ojeda Venezuela 38 C1
Ciudad Real Spain 73 E4
Ciudad Victoria Mexico 31 E3
Clarenville Canada 19 H3
Clarksville Tennessee, USA 28 D1
Clearwater Florida, USA 29 E4

Clermont-Ferrand France 71 C5
Cleveland Ohio, USA 20 D3
Clipperton Island *External territory* France, Pacific Ocean 123 F3
Cloncurry Australia 126 B5 130 A1
Clovis New Mexico, USA 27 E2
Cluj-Napoca Romania 88 B3
Coast Mountains *Mountain range* Canada 14 C2
Coast Ranges *Mountain range* W USA 24 A3
Coats Island *Island* Canada 18 C1
Coatzacoalcos Mexico 31 G4
Cobán Guatemala 32 B2
Cochabamba Bolivia 40 C4
Cochin India 116 D3
Cochrane Canada 18 C4
Cochrane Chile 45 B6
Coco *River* Honduras / Nicaragua 32 D2
Cocos (Keeling) Islands *External territory* Australia, Indian Ocean 112 D4
Cod, Cape *Coastal feature* NE USA 15 F3 21 G3
Coeur d'Alene Idaho, USA 24 C2
Coffs Harbour Australia 130 C2
Coihaique Chile 45 B6
Coimbatore India 116 D3
Coimbra Portugal 72 C3
Colbeck, Cape *Coastal feature* Antarctica 132 C4
Colchester England, UK 69 E6
Colhué Huapi, Lago *Lake* Argentina 45 B6
Colima *Peak* Mexico 15 E5
Colmar France 70 E4
Cologne *see* Köln
Colombia *Country* N South America 38-39
Colombian Basin *Undersea feature* Caribbean Sea 34 D5
Colombo *Capital of* Sri Lanka 117 E3
Colón, Archipiélago de *see* Galapagos Islands
Colorado *State* USA 22 C5
Colorado *River* USA 14 D3
Colorado *River* Argentina 45 C5
Colorado Plateau *Upland region* S USA 26 B1
Colorado Springs Colorado, USA 22 D4
Columbia South Carolina, USA 29 F2
Columbia *River* NW USA 24 C1
Columbus Georgia, USA 28 D3
Columbus Mississippi, USA 28 C2
Columbus Nebraska, USA 23 E4
Columbus Ohio, USA 20 D4
Comayagua Honduras 32 C2
Comilla Bangladesh 115 G4
Communism Peak *Peak* Tajikistan *Rus.* Pik Kommunizma, *prev.* Stalin Peak, Garmo Peak 92 C4
Como, Lago di *Lake* Italy 76 B2
Comodoro Rivadavia Argentina 45 C6
Comoros *Country* Indian Ocean 59
Conakry *Capital of* Guinea 52 C4
Concepción Chile 45 B5
Concepción Paraguay 42 B2
Conchos *River* Mexico 30 C2
Concord California, USA 25 B6
Concord New Hampshire, USA 20 G2
Concordia E Argentina 44 D3
Congo *Country* C Africa 57
Congo *River* C Africa *var.* Zaire 49 C5
Congo Basin *Drainage basin* C Africa 49 C5
Congo (Zaire) *Country* C Africa 57
Connecticut *State* USA 21 G3
Constance, Lake *River* C Europe 75 B7
Constantine Algeria 51 E1
Constantinople *see* İstanbul
Constanţa Romania 88 D5
Coober Pedy Australia 129 E5
Cook, Mount *Peak* New Zealand *prev.* Aorangi 125 E5
Cook Islands *External territory* New Zealand, Pacific Ocean 122 D4
Cook Strait *Sea feature* New Zealand 131 G3
Cooktown Australia 126 B4
Coos Bay Oregon, USA 24 A3
Copenhagen *Capital of* Denmark 65 B7
Copiapó Chile 44 B3
Coppermine Canada 17 E3
Coquimbo Chile 44 B3
Corabia Romania 88 B5
Coral Sea Pacific Ocean 122 C3
Coral Sea Islands *External territory* Australia, Coral Sea 126 C4
Corantijn *River* Guyana / Surinam *var.* Courantyne 39 C3
Cordillera Cantábrica *Mountain range* Spain 72 D1
Córdoba Argentina 44 C3
Córdoba Spain 72 D4
Cordova Alaska, USA 16 D3
Corfu *see* Kérkyra
Corinth *see* Kórinthos
Corinth, Gulf of *see* Korinthiakós Kólpos
Corinto Nicaragua 32 C3
Cork Ireland 69 A6
Corner Brook Canada 19 G3
Coro Venezuela 38 D1
Coromandel New Zealand 131 G2
Coronel Oviedo Paraguay 42 C2
Corpus Christi Texas, USA 27 G4
Corrib, Lough *Lake* Ireland 69 A5
Corrientes Argentina 44 D3
Corse *Island* France *Eng.* Corsica 71 E7 82 D2
Corsica *see* Corse
Çorum Turkey 96 D2
Corvallis Oregon, USA 24 A3
Cosenza Italy 77 D6
Costa Blanca *Coastal region* Spain 73 F4
Costa Brava *Coastal region* Spain 73 H2
Costa Rica *Country* Central America 32-33
Côte d'Ivoire *see* Ivory Coast
Cotonou Benin 53 F5
Cotopaxi *Peak* Ecuador 36 B2
Cottbus Germany 74 D4
Council Bluffs Iowa, USA 23 F4

Courantyne *River* Guyana/Surinam *var.* Corantijn 39 G3
Courland Lagoon *Sea feature* Baltic Sea 86 A4
Coventry England, UK 69 D6
Covilhã Portugal 72 C3
Cozumel, Isla de *Island* Mexico 31 H3
Cracow *see* Kraków
Craiova Romania 88 B5
Cremona Italy 76 B2
Cres *Island* Croatia 80 A3
Crescent City California, USA 24 A4
Crete Greece *see* Kríti 83 F4
Crete, Sea of Mediterranean Sea *Gk.* Kritikó Pélagos 85 D5
Crimea *Peninsula* Ukraine *var.* Krym 88 F4
Croatia *Country* SE Europe 80
Croker Island *Island* Australia 128 D2
Crotone Italy 77 E6
Crozet Basin *Undersea feature* Indian Ocean 113 B6
Crozet Islands *Island group* Indian Ocean 113 B6
Cruzeiro do Sul Brazil 40 B3
Cuanza *River* Angola 58 B1
Cuba *Country* West Indies 34
Cubango *see* Okavango
Cúcuta Colombia 38 C2
Cuenca Ecuador 38 A5
Cuenca Spain 73 E3
Cuernavaca Mexico 31 E4
Cuiabá Brazil 41 E4
Cuito *River* Angola 58 C2
Culiacán Mexico 30 C3
Cumaná Venezuela 39 E1
Cumberland Maryland, USA 21 E4
Cumberland *River* C USA 20 C5
Cunene *River* Angola/Namibia 58 B2
Cunnamulla Australia 130 B2
Curicó Chile 44 B4
Curitiba Brazil 42 D3
Cusco Peru *prev.* Cuzco 40 B4
Cuttack India 115 F5
Cuxhaven Germany 74 B3
Cuyuni *River* Guyana/Venezuela 39 F2
Cuzco *see* Cusco
Cyclades *see* Kykládes
Cymru *see* Wales
Cyprus *Country* Mediterranean Sea 96 C5
Czechoslovakia *see* Czech Republic *or* Slovakia
Czech Republic *Country* C Europe 78-79
Częstochowa Poland *Ger.* Tschenstochau 78 C4

D

Dacca *see* Dhaka
Dagden *see* Hiiumaa
Dagö *see* Hiiumaa
Dagupan Philippines 121 E1
Da Hinggan Ling *Mountain range* China *Eng.* Great Khingan Range 107 G1
Dahomey *see* Benin
Dakar *Capital of* Senegal 52 B3
Đakovo Croatia 80 C3
Dalaman Turkey 96 B4
Đa Lat Vietnam 119 E5
Dali China 109 A6
Dalian China 108 D4
Dallas Texas, USA 27 G3
Dalmacija *Region* Croatia 80 B4
Daloa Ivory Coast 52 D5
Daly Waters Australia 128 E3
Damān India 114 C5
Damas *see* Damascus
Damascus Syria *var.* Esh Sham, *Fr.* Damas, *Ar.* Dimashq 98 B4
Dampier Australia 128 B4
Đa Nâng Vietnam 119 E4
Daneborg Greenland 63 E3
Dangara Tajikistan 103 E3
Danmarkshavn Greenland 63 E2
Danmarksstraedet *see* Denmark Strait
Danube *River* C Europe 60 D4
Danube Delta *Wetland* Romania/Ukraine 88 D5
Danville Virginia, USA 21 E5
Danzig *see* Gdańsk
Dar'ā Syria 99 B5
Dardanelles *Sea feature* Turkey *Turk.* Çanakkale Boğazı 96 A2
Dar es Salaam Tanzania 55 C8
Darhan Mongolia 107 E2
Darien, Gulf of *Sea feature* Caribbean Sea 33 G5
Darling *River* Australia 130 B2
Darmstadt Germany 75 B5
Darnah Libya 51 H2
Darnley, Cape *Coastal feature* Antarctica 133 G2
Dartmoor *Region* England, UK 69 C7
Dartmouth Canada 19 G4
Darwin Australia 128 D2
Dashhowuz *see* Dashkhovuz
Dashkhovuz Turkmenistan *prev.* Tashauz, *Turkm.* Dashhowuz 102 C2
Datong China 108 C4
Daugava *see* Western Dvina
Daugavpils Latvia *Ger.* Dünaburg, *Rus.* Dvinsk 86 C4
Dāvangere India 116 D2
Davao Philippines 121 F2
Davenport Iowa, USA 23 G3
David Panama 33 E5
Davis Sea Indian Ocean 133 H3
Davis Strait *Sea feature* Atlantic Ocean 17 H2 62 B4
Dawson Canada 16 D3
Dayr az Zawr Syria 98 D3
Dayton Ohio, USA 20 C4
Daytona Beach Florida, USA 29 F4
Dead Sea *Salt Lake* SW Asia *Ar.* Al Baḩr al Mayyit, Baḩrat Lūt, *Heb.* Yam HaMelah̲ 99 B5
Death Valley *Valley* W USA 14 D4 25 D6
Debre Zeyit Ethiopia 55 C5
Debrecen Hungary *prev.* Debreczen, *Ger.* Debreczin 79 D6
Debreczen *see* Debrecen
Debreczin *see* Debrecen
Decatur Illinois, USA 20 B4
Deccan *Plateau* India 104 B3
Děčín Czech Republic *Ger.* Tetschen 78 B4
Dej Romania 88 B3
Delaware *State* USA 21 F4
Delaware Bay *Sea feature* USA 21 F4
Delémont Switzerland 75 A7

Delft Netherlands 66 B4
Delfzijl Netherlands 66 E1
Delhi India 114 D3
Del Rio Texas, USA 27 F4
Demchok *Disputed region* China / India *var.* Dêmqog 106 A4 115 E2
Dêmqog *see* Demchok
Denali *Peak* Alaska, USA *prev.* Mount McKinley 14 C2
Den Helder Netherlands 66 C2
Denizli Turkey 96 B4
Denmark *Country* NW Europe 65
Denmark Strait *Sea feature* Greenland / Iceland *var.* Danmarksstraedet 63 D3
Denpasar Indonesia 120 D5
Denton Texas, USA 27 G2
Denver Colorado, USA 22 D4
Dera Ghāzi Khān Pakistan 114 C2
Dera Ismāīl Khān Pakistan 114 C2
Derby England, UK 69 D6
Derg, Lough *Lake* Ireland 69 B6
Desē Ethiopia 54 C4
Deseado *River* Argentina 45 C6
Des Moines Iowa, USA 23 F3
Despoto Planina *see* Rhodope Mountains
Dessau Germany 74 C4
Desventurados, Islas de los *Islands* Chile 37 A5 123 G4
Detroit Michigan, USA 20 D3
Deutschendorf *see* Poprad
Deva Romania 88 B4
Deventer Netherlands 66 D3
Devollit, Lumi i *River* Albania 81 D6
Devon Island *Island* Canada 17 G2
Devonport Tasmania, Australia 130 B5
Dezfūl Iran 100 C3
Dhaka *Capital of* Bangladesh *var.* Dacca 115 G4
Dhanbād India 115 F4
Dhanushkodi India 116 D3
Dhrepanon, Ákra *Coastal feature* Greece 84 C4
Diamantina *River* Australia 130 B1
Dickinson North Dakota, USA 22 D2
Diekirch Luxembourg 67 D7
Dieppe France 70 C3
Diffa Niger 53 H3
Digul *River* Indonesia 121 H5
Dijon France 70 D4
Dīla Ethiopia 55 C5
Dili Indonesia 121 F5
Dilling Sudan 54 B4
Dilolo Congo (Zaire) 57 D8
Dimashq *see* Damascus
Dimitrovo *see* Pernik
Dinant Belgium 67 C7
Dinara *Mountains* Bosnia & Herzegovina / Croatia 80 B4
Dingle Bay *Sea feature* Ireland 69 A5
Diourbel Senegal 52 B3
Dirē Dawa Ethiopia 55 D5
Dirk Hartog Island *Island* Australia 129 A5
Disappointment, Lake *Salt lake* Australia 118 C4
Dispur India 115 G3
Divinópolis Brazil 43 F1
Diyarbakır Turkey 97 E4
Djambala Congo 57 B6
Djibouti *Country* E Africa 54
Djibouti *Capital of* Djibouti *var.* Jibuti 54 D4
Djúpivogur Iceland 63 E4
Dnieper *River* E Europe 51 F4
Dniester *River* Moldavia / Ukraine 88 D3
Dnipropetrovs'k Ukraine 89 F3
Dobele Latvia *Ger.* Doblen 86 B3
Doblen *see* Dobele
Doboj Bosnia & Herzegovina 80 C3
Dobrich Bulgaria 84 E1
Dodecanese *see* Dodekánisos
Dodekánisos *Islands* Greece *Eng.* Dodecanese 85 E6
Dodge City Kansas, USA 23 E5
Dodoma *Capital of* Tanzania 55 C7
Doğu Karadeniz Dağlarıı *Mountains* Turkey *var.* Anadolu Dağları 97 E2
Doha *Capital of* Qatar *Ar.* Ad Dawḩah 101 C5
Dolomites *see* Dolomiti
Dolomiti *Mountains* Italy *Eng.* Dolomites 76 C2
Dolores Argentina 44 D4
Dominica *Country* West Indies 35
Dominican Republic *Country* West Indies 35
Don *River* Russian Federation 94 A3
Donegal Bay *Sea feature* Ireland 69 A5
Donets *River* Russian Federation / Ukraine 88 G3 91 A6
Donets'k Ukraine 89 G3
Dongola Sudan 54 B3
Dongting Hu *Lake* China 109 C6
Donostia *see* San Sebastián
Dordogne *River* France 71 B5
Dordrecht Netherlands 66 C4
Dornbirn Austria 75 B7
Dorpat *see* Tartu
Dortmund Germany 74 A4
Dosso Niger 53 F3
Dothan Alabama, USA 28 D3
Douai France 70 C2
Douala Cameroon 57 A5
Douglas UK 69 C5
Douglas Arizona, USA 26 C3
Dourados Brazil 42 C2
Douro *River* Portugal / Spain *Sp.* Duero 72 C2
Dover England, UK 69 E7
Dover Delaware, USA 21 F4
Dōzen *Island* Japan 111 B5
Drakensberg *Mountain range* Lesotho / South Africa 58 D5
Drake Passage *Sea feature* Atlantic Ocean / Pacific Ocean 37 C8
Dráma Greece 84 C3
Drammen Norway 65 B6
Drau *River* C Europe *var.* Drava 75 D7 80 C3
Drava *River* C Europe *var.* Drau 79 C7
Dresden Germany 74 D4
Drina *River* Bosnia & Herzegovina / Yugoslavia 80 D4

Drobeta-Turnu Severin Romania *prev.* Turnu Severin 88 B4
Druskieniki *see* Druskininkai
Druskininkai Lithuania *Pol.* Druskieniki 87 B5
Dubai United Arab Emirates 101 D5
Dubăsari Moldavia 88 D3
Dubawnt *River* Canada 17 F4
Dubbo Australia 130 C3
Dublin *Capital of* Ireland 69 B5
Dubrovnik Croatia 81 C5
Dubuque Iowa, USA 23 G3
Duero *River* Portugal/Spain *Port.* Douro 72 D2
Dugi Otok *Island* Croatia 80 A4
Duisburg Germany 74 A4
Duluth Minnesota, USA 23 F2
Dumfries Scotland, UK 68 C4
Düna *see* Western Dvina
Dünaburg *see* Daugavpils
Dundalk Ireland 69 B5
Dundee Scotland, UK 68 C3
Dunedin New Zealand 131 F5
Dunkerque France *Eng.* Dunkirk 70 C2
Dunkirk *see* Dunkerque
Duqm Oman 101 E6
Durango Mexico 30 D3
Durango Colorado, USA 22 C5
Durazno Uruguay 42 C5
Durban South Africa 58 E4
Durham North Carolina, USA 29 F1
Durrës Albania 81 C6
Dushanbe *Capital of* Tajikistan *var.* Dyushambe, *prev.* Stalinabad 103 E3
Düsseldorf Germany 74 A4
Dutch Harbor Alaska, USA 16 B3
Dutch West Indies *see* Netherland Antilles
Dvina *River* E Europe 61 E3
Dvinsk *see* Daugavpils
Dyushambe *see* Dushanbe
Dzaudzhikau *see* Vladikavkaz
Dzhalal-Abad Kyrgyzstan *Kir.* Jalal-Abad 103 F2
Dzhambul *see* Zhambyl
Dzhezkazgan see Zhezkazgan
Dzhugdzhur Range *Mountain range* Russian Federation 93 F3
Dzvina *see* Western Dvina

E

Eagle Pass Texas, USA 27 F4
East Cape *Coastal feature* New Zealand 131 H2
East China Sea Pacific Ocean 122 B2
Easter Island *Island* Pacific Ocean 123 F4
Eastern Ghats *Mountain range* India 104 B4
Eastern Sierra Madre *see* Sierra Madre Oriental
East Falkland *Island* Falkland Islands 45 D7
East Frisian Islands *see* Ostfriesische Inseln
East London South Africa 58 D5
Eastmain *River* Canada 18 D3
East Pacific Rise *Undersea feature* Pacific Ocean 123 F3
East Siberian Sea *see* Vostochno-Sibirskoye More
East St Louis Illinois, USA 20 B4
Eau Claire Wisconsin, USA 20 A2
Ebolowa Cameroon 57 B5
Ebro *River* Spain 73 F2
Ecuador *Country* NW South America 38
Ed Eritrea 54 D4
Ede Netherlands 66 D3
Ede Nigeria 53 F4
Edgeøya *Island* Svalbard 63 H2
Edinburgh Scotland, UK 68 C4
Edirne Turkey 96 A2
Edmonton Canada 17 E5
Edward, Lake *Lake* Uganda/Congo (Zaire) 57 E6
Edwards Plateau *Upland* S USA 27 F4
Eforie-Nord Romania 88 D5
Egadi, Isole *Island group* Italy 77 B7
Ege Denizi *see* Aegean Sea
Eger *see* Ohře
Egiyn Gol *River* Mongolia 106 D2
Egypt *Country* NE Africa 54
Eindhoven Netherlands 67 D5
Eisenstadt Austria 75 E7
Eivissa *Island* Spain *Cast.* Ibiza 73 G4
Elat Israel 99 B7
Elâzığ Turkey 97 E3
Elba, Isola d' *Island* Italy 76 B4
Elbasan Albania 81 D6
Elbe *River* Czech Republic/Germany 79 B5
Elbing *see* Elbląg
Elbląg Poland *Ger.* Elbing 78 C2
El'brus *Peak* Russian Federation 61 G4 83 H2
Elche Spain 73 F4
Elda Spain 73 F4
Eldoret Kenya 55 C6
Eleuthera *Island* Bahamas 34 C1
El Fasher Sudan *var.* Al Fāshir 54 A4
Elgin Scotland, UK 68 C3
El Gîza Egypt *var.* Al Jīzah 54 B1
Elista Russian Federation 91 B7
El Khârga Egypt *var.* Al Khārijah 54 B2
Elko Nevada, USA 25 D5
Ellensburg Washington, USA 24 B2
Ellesmere Island *Island* Canada 17 F1
Ellsworth Land *Region* Antarctica 132 B3
El Minya Egypt 54 B2
Elmira New York, USA 21 E3
El Obeid Sudan 54 B4
El Paso Texas, USA 26 D3
El Qâhira *see* Cairo
El Salvador *Country* Central America 32
El Tigre Venezuela 39 E2
Ely NV USA 25 D5
Emden Germany 74 A3
Emmen Netherlands 66 E2
Emperor Seamount *Undersea feature* Pacific Ocean 122 D2
Empty Quarter *see* Rub' al Khali
Ems *River* Germany/Netherlands 74 A3
Encarnación Paraguay 42 C3

Enderby Land *Region* Antarctica 133 G2
England *National region* UK 68-69
English Channel *Sea feature* Atlantic Ocean 60 C4
Enguri *River* Georgia *Rus.* Inguri 97 F1
Enid Oklahoma, USA 27 F1
Ennedi *Plateau* Chad 56 D2
Enns *River* Austria 75 D7
Enschede Netherlands 66 E3
Ensenada Mexico 30 A1
Entebbe Uganda 55 B6
Enugu Nigeria 53 G5
Eolie, Isole *Island group* Italy *Eng.* Lipari Islands, *var.* Aeolian Islands 77 D6
Eperies *see* Prešov
Eperjes *see* Prešov
Épinal France 70 E4
Equatorial Guinea *Country* W Africa 57
Erdenet Mongolia 107 E2
Erebus, Mount *Peak* Antarctica 133 E4
Erechim Brazil 42 D3
Erevan *see* Yerevan
Ereğli Turkey 96 C4
Erfurt Germany 75 C5
Erguig *River* Chad 56 C3
Erie Pennsylvania, USA 20 D3
Erie, Lake *Lake* Canada/USA 18 C5 20 D3
Eritrea *Country* E Africa 54
Erivan *see* Yerevan
Erlangen Germany 75 C5
Ernākulam India 116 D3
Er Rachidia Morocco 50 C2
Érsekújvár *see* Nové Zámky
Erzerum *see* Erzurum
Erzincan Turkey 97 E3
Erzurum Turkey *prev.* Erzerum 97 F3
Esbjerg Denmark 65 A7
Esch-sur-Alzette Luxembourg 67 D8
Escuintla Guatemala 32 B2
Eşfahān Iran 100 C3
Esh Sham *see* Damascus
Eskişehir Turkey 96 B3
Esla, Embalse de *Reservoir* Spain 72 D2
Esmeraldas Ecuador 38 A4
Esperance Australia 129 C6
Espoo Finland 65 D6
Esquel Argentina 45 B6
Essaouira Morocco 50 B2
Essen Germany 74 A4
Essequibo *River* Guyana 39 G3
Estelí Nicaragua 32 D3
Estevan Canada 17 F5
Estonia *Country* E Europe 86 D2
Ethiopia *Country* E Africa 54-55
Ethiopian Highlands *Upland* E Africa 48 D4
Etna, Mount *Peak* Sicily, Italy 60 D5
Etosha Pan *Salt basin* Namibia 58 B3
Eugene Oregon, USA 24 A3
Eugene Washington, USA 24 B1
Euphrates *River* SW Asia 92 B4
Europe 82-83
Evansville Indiana, USA 20 B5
Everest, Mount *Peak* China/Nepal 106 B5
Everett Washington, USA 24 B1
Everglades, The *Wetlands* Florida, USA 29 G5
Évvoia *Island* Greece 85 C5
Exeter England, UK 69 C7
Exmoor *Region* England, UK 69 C7
Exmouth Australia 128 A4
Eyre, Lake *Lake* Australia 124 C3

F

Fada-N'gourma Burkina 53 E4
Faeroe-Iceland Rise *Undersea feature* Atlantic Ocean 60 B2
Faeroe Islands *External territory* Denmark, Atlantic Ocean *Faer.* Fóroyar, *Dan.* Færøerne 63 F4
Færøerne *see* Faeroe Islands
Faguibine, Lac *Lake* Mali 53 E3
Fairbanks Alaska, USA 16 D3
Faisalābād Pakistan 114 C2
Faizabad *see* Feyzābād
Falkland Islands *External territory* UK, Atlantic Ocean 45 D7
Fallon Nevada, USA 25 C5
Falun Sweden 65 C6
Famagusta *see* Gazimağusa
Farafangana Madagascar 59 G3
Farāh Afghanistan 102 C5
Farewell, Cape *see* Uummannarsuaq
Farghona *see* Fergana
Fargo North Dakota, USA 23 E2
Farmington New Mexico, USA 26 C1
Faro Portugal 72 C5
Farquhar Group *Island group* Seychelles 59 G1
Farvel, Cap *see* Uummannarsuaq
Faya Chad 56 C2
Fayetteville Arkansas, USA 28 A1
Fayetteville North Carolina, USA 29 F2
Fazzān *Region* Libya 51 F4
Fear, Cape *Coastal feature* North Carolina, USA 29 G2
Fehmarn Sound *Sea feature* Germany 74 C2
Feira de Santana Brazil 41 G4
Fellin *see* Viljandi
Fénérive *see* Fenoarivo Atsinanana
Fenoarivo Atsinanana Madagascar *prev.* Fénérive 59 G3
Fens, The *Wetland* England, UK 69 E6
Fergana Uzbekistan *prev.* Novyy Margilan, *Uzb.* Farghona 103 F2
Fernando de la Mora Paraguay 42 B3
Fernando de Noronha, Ilha *Island* Brazil 41 H2
Ferrara Italy 76 C2
Ferrol Spain 72 C1
Fès Morocco *Eng.* Fez 50 C2
Feyzābād Afghanistan *var.* Faizabad 103 E3
Fez *see* Fès
Fianarantsoa Madagascar 59 G3
Fier Albania 81 D6
Figueira da Foz Portugal 72 C3
Figueres Spain 73 G2
Figuig Morocco 50 D2
Fiji *Country* Pacific Ocean 122

Finisterre, Cape *Coastal feature* Spain 72 B1
Finland *Country* N Europe 64-65
Finland, Gulf of *Sea feature* Baltic Sea 65 E6
Firenze Italy *Eng.* Florence 76 B3
Fish *River* Namibia 58 C4
Fishguard Wales, UK 69 C6
Fitzroy *River* Australia 124 B2 128 C3
Fiume see Rijeka
Flagstaff Arizona, USA 26 B2
Flanders *Region* Belgium 67 A5
Flensburg Germany 74 B2
Flinders Island *Island* Australia 130 B4
Flinders Ranges *Mountain range* Australia 130 A2
Flin Flon Canada 17 F5
Flint Michigan, USA 20 C3
Flint Island *Island* Kiribati 127 H4
Florence Alabama, USA 28 C2
Florence South Carolina, USA 29 F2
Florence *see* Firenze
Florencia Colombia 38 B3
Flores Guatemala 32 B1
Flores *Island* Indonesia 121 E5
Flores, Laut *see* Flores Sea
Flores Sea Pacific Ocean *Ind.* Laut Flores 121 E5
Florianópolis Brazil 42 D3
Florida *State* USA 29 E4
Florida, Straits of *Sea feature* Bahamas/USA 29 F5 34 B1
Floridablanca Colombia 38 C2
Florida Keys *Island chain* Florida, USA 29 F5
Flórina Greece 84 A3
Flushing *see* Vlissingen
Foča Bosnia & Herzegovina 80 C4
Focşani Romania 88 C4
Foggia Italy 77 D5
Fongafale *Capital of* Tuvalu 127 E3
Fonseca, Gulf of *Sea feature* El Salvador/Honduras 32 C3
Forlì Italy 76 C3
Formentera *Island* Spain 73 G4
Former Yugoslav Republic of Macedonia *see* Macedonia
Formosa Argentina 44 D2
Formosa *see* Taiwan
Formosa Strait *see* Taiwan Strait
Fóroyar *see* Faeroe Islands
Fortaleza Brazil 41 H2
Fort Collins Colorado, USA 22 D4
Fort-de-France *Capital of* Martinique 35 G4
Forth *River* Scotland, UK 68 C4
Forth, Firth of *Inlet* Scotland, UK 68 D4
Fort Lauderdale Florida, USA 29 F5
Fort McMurray Canada 17 F4
Fort Myers Florida, USA 29 E5
Fort Peck Lake *Lake* Montana, USA 22 C1
Fort Saint John Canada 17 E4
Fort Smith Canada 17 F4
Fort Smith Arkansas, USA 28 A1
Fort Wayne Indiana, USA 20 C4
Fort William Scotland, UK 68 C3
Fort Worth Texas, USA 27 G3
Foveaux Strait *Sea feature* New Zealand 131 E5
Fram Basin *Undersea feature* Arctic Ocean *var.* Angara Basin 12 C4
Franca Brazil 43 E1
France *Country* W Europe 70-71
Francistown Botswana 58 D3
Frankfort Kentucky, USA 20 C5
Frankfurt *see* Frankfurt am Main
Frankfurt am Main Germany *Eng.* Frankfurt 75 B5
Frankfurt an der Oder Germany 74 D4
Fränkische Alb *Mountains* Germany 75 C6
Frantsa-Iosifa, Zemlya *Islands* Russian Federation *Eng.* Franz Josef Land 13 D6 94 D1
Franz Josef Land *see* Frantsa-Iosifa, Zemlya
Fraser Island *Island* Australia 130 D1
Frauenburg *see* Saldus
Fray Bentos Uruguay 42 B5
Fredericton Canada 19 F4
Frederikshavn Denmark 65 B7
Fredrikstad Norway 65 B6
Freeport Bahamas 34 C1
Freeport Texas, USA 27 G4
Freetown *Capital of* Sierra Leone 52 C4
Freiburg im Breisgau Germany 75 B7
Fremantle Australia 129 B6
French Guiana *External territory* France, N South America 39
French Polynesia *External territory* France, Pacific Ocean 123 E3
Fresno California, USA 25 B6
Fribourg Switzerland 75 A7
Frome, Lake *Salt lake* Australia 130 A2
Frosinone Italy 76 C4
Frunze *see* Bishkek
Fuerteventura *Island* Spain 50 A3
Fuji, Mount *Peak* Japan 105 E2
Fukui Japan 111 C5
Fukuoka Japan 111 A6
Fukushima Japan 110 D3
Fulda Germany 75 B5
Fünfkirchen *see* Pécs
Furnas, Represa de *Reservoir* Brazil 43 E1
Fuzhou China 109 D6
FYR Macedonia *see* Macedonia

G

Gaalkacyo Somalia 55 E5
Gabès Tunisia 51 E2
Gabon *Country* W Africa 57
Gaborone *Capital of* Botswana 58 D4
Gabrovo Bulgaria 84 D2
Gadsden Alabama, USA 28 D2
Gaeta, Golfo di *Sea feature* Italy 77 C5
Gafsa Tunisia 51 E2
Gagnoa Ivory Coast 52 D5
Gagra Georgia 97 E1
Gairdner, Lake *Lake* Australia 129 E6

Galapagos Islands *Islands* Ecuador, Pacific Ocean *var.* Tortoise Islands, *Sp.* Archipiélago de Colón 36 A2
Galaţi Romania 88 D4
Galesburg Illinois, USA 20 B4
Galicia Spain 72 C1
Galilee, Sea of *see* Tiberias, Lake
Galle Sri Lanka 117 E4
Gallipoli Italy 77 E5
Gällivare Sweden 64 D3
Gallup New Mexico, USA 26 C2
Galveston Texas, USA 27 G4
Galway Ireland 69 A5
Gambia *Country* W Africa 52
Gäncä Azerbaijan *Rus.* Gyandzha, *prev.* Kirovabad, Yelisavetpol 97 G2
Gand see Gent
Gander Canada 19 H3
Gandía Spain 73 F3
Ganges *River* S Asia 114 D3
Ganges Delta *Wetlands* Bangladesh / India 115 G4
Ganges Plain *Region* S Asia 104 C3
Gangtok India 115 G3
Ganzhou China 109 C6
Gao Mali 53 E3
Gar China 106 A4
Garagum *see* Karakumy
Garagum Kanaly *see* Karakumskiy Kanal
Garda, Lago di *Lake* Italy 76 C2
Gardēz Afghanistan 103 E4
Garissa Kenya 55 C6
Garmo Peak *see* Communism Peak
Garonne *River* France 71 B5
Garoowe Somalia 55 E5
Garoua Cameroon 56 B4
Gary Indiana, USA 20 B3
Gaspé Canada 19 F4
Gastonia North Carolina, USA 29 E2
Gävle Sweden 65 C6
Gaya India 115 F4
Gaza Gaza Strip 99 A6
Gazandzhyk Turkmenistan *var.* Kazandzhik, *Turkm.* Gazanjyk 102 B2
Gazanjyk *see* Gazandzhyk
Gaza Strip *Disputed territory* SW Asia 99 A6
Gaziantep Turkey *prev.* Aintab 96 D4
Gazimağusa Cyprus *var.* Famagusta *Gk.* Ammochostos 96 C5
Gdańsk Poland *Ger.* Danzig 78 C2
Gdingen *see* Gdynia
Gdynia Poland *Ger.* Gdingen 78 C2
Gedaref Sudan 54 C4
Geelong Australia 130 B4
Gëkdepe Turkmenistan *prev.* Geok-Tepe, *Turkm.* Gökdepe 102 B3
Gelsenkirchen Germany 74 A4
Gemena Congo (Zaire) 57 C5
Geneina Sudan 54 A4
General Eugenio A. Garay Paraguay 42 A1
General Santos Philippines 121 F3
Geneva *see* Genève
Geneva, Lake *Lake* France / Switzerland *Fr.* Lac Léman, *var.* Le Léman, *Ger.* Genfer See 71 D5 75 A8
Genève Switzerland *Eng.* Geneva 75 A5
Genfer See *see* Geneva, Lake
Genk Belgium 67 D6
Genoa *see* Genova
Genova Italy *see* Genoa 76 B3
Genova, Golfo di *Sea feature* Italy 76 B3
Gent Belgium *Fr.* Gand, *Eng.* Ghent 67 B5
Geok-Tepe *see* Gëkdepe
Georgenburg *see* Jurbarkas
Georges Bank *Undersea feature* Atlantic Ocean 21 H2
George Town *Capital of* Cayman Islands 34 B3
Georgetown Gambia 52 B3
Georgetown *Capital of* Guyana 39 G2
George Town Malaysia 120 B3
Georgia *Country* SW Asia 97 F2
Georgia *State* USA 29 E3
Gera Germany 75 C5
Geraldton Australia 129 A5
Gereshk Afghanistan 102 D5
Germany *Country* W Europe 74-75
Getafe Spain 73 E3
Gettysburg Pennsylvania, USA 21 E4
Gevgelija Macedonia 81 E6
Ghadāmis Libya 51 E3
Ghana *Country* W Africa 53
Ghanzi Botswana 58 C3
Ghardaïa Algeria 50 D2
Gharyān Libya 51 F2
Ghāt Libya 51 F4
Ghaznī Afghanistan 103 E4
Ghent *see* Gent
Gibraltar *External territory* UK, SW Europe 72 D5
Gibraltar, Strait of *Sea feature* Atlantic Ocean / Mediterranean Sea 72 D5
Gibson Desert *Desert region* Australia 129 C5
Gijón Spain 72 D1
Gilbert Islands *Islands* Kiribati 127 E2
Gillette Wyoming, USA 22 C3
Girne Cyprus *var.* Kyrenia 96 C5
Girona Spain 73 G2
Gisborne New Zealand 131 H2
Giurgiu Romania 88 C5
Gjirokastër Albania 81 D6
Gjøvik Norway 65 B5
Glasgow Scotland, UK 68 C4
Glasgow Montana, USA 22 C1
Gleiwitz *see* Gliwice
Glendale Arizona, USA 26 B2
Glendive Montana, USA 22 D2
Gliwice Poland *Ger.* Gleiwitz 79 C5
Gloucester England, UK 69 D6
Glubokoye *see* Hlybokaye
Goa *State* India 116 C2
Gobi *Desert* China / Mongolia 106 D3
Godāveri *River* India 104 B3
Godoy Cruz Argentina 44 B4
Godthåb *see* Nuuk
Godwin Austin, Mount *see* K2
Goiânia Brazil 41 F4
Gökdepe *see* Gëkdepe
Golan Heights *Disputed territory* SW Asia 98 B4

Gold Coast *Coastal region* Australia 130 D2
Goldingen *see* Kuldīga
Golmud China 106 D4
Goma Congo (Zaire) 57 E6
Gomel' *see* Homyel'
Gómez Palacio Mexico 30 D2
Gonaïves Haiti 34 D3
Gonder Ethiopia 54 C4
Good Hope, Cape of *Coastal feature* South Africa 58 C5
Goondiwindi Australia 130 C2
Goose Lake *Lake* W USA 24 B4
Goré Chad 56 C4
Gorē Ethiopia 55 C5
Gorgān Iran 100 D3
Gorki *see* Horki
Gor'kiy *see* Nizhniy Novgorod
Gorlovka *see* Horlivka
Gorontalo Indonesia 121 E4
Gorzów Wielkopolski Poland *Ger.* Landsberg 78 B3
Gospić Croatia 80 A3
Gostivar Macedonia 81 D5
Göteborg Sweden 65 B7
Gotland *Island* Sweden 65 C7
Gotō-rettō *Island group* Japan 111 A6
Göttingen Germany 74 B4
Gouda Netherlands 66 C4
Gough Island *External territory* UK, Atlantic Ocean 47 D6
Gouin, Réservoir *Reservoir* Canada 18 D4
Governador Valadares Brazil 41 G4 43 F1
Gozo *Island* Malta 77 C8
Gračanica Bosnia & Herzegovina 80 C3
Grafton Australia 130 D2
Graham Land *Region* Antarctica 132 B3
Grampian Mountains *Mountains* Scotland, UK 68 C3
Granada Nicaragua 32 D3
Granada Spain 73 E4
Gran Canaria *Island* Spain 50 A3
Gran Chaco *Region* C South America 36 C4
Grand Bahama *Island* Bahamas 34 C1
Grand Banks *Undersea feature* Atlantic Ocean 46 B3
Grand Canyon *Valley* SW USA 26 B1
Grande, Bahía *Sea feature* Argentina 37 C7
Grande, Rio *River* Brazil 42 D4 43 E1
Grande Comore *Island* Comoros 59 F2
Grande Prairie Canada 17 E5
Grand Erg Occidental *Desert region* Algeria 50 D2
Grand Erg Oriental *Desert region* Algeria/Tunisia 51 E3
Grand Falls Canada 19 H3
Grand Forks North Dakota, USA 23 E1
Grand Junction Colorado, USA 22 C4
Grand Rapids Michigan, USA 20 C3
Graudenz *see* Grudziądz
Graz Austria 75 E7
Great Abaco *Island* Bahamas 34 C1
Great Ararat *see* Ararat, Mount
Great Australian Bight *Sea feature* Australia 122 B4 129 D6
Great Bahama Bank *Undersea feature* Atlantic Ocean 34 C2
Great Barrier Reef *Coral reef* Coral Sea 122 C4
Great Basin *Region* USA 24 D4
Great Bear Lake *Lake* Canada 17 E3
Great Dividing Range *Mountain range* Australia 124 D3
Greater Antarctica *Region* Antarctica 133 F3
Greater Antilles *Island group* West Indies 34 C3
Great Exuma Island *Island* Bahamas 34 C2
Great Falls Montana, USA 22 B1
Great Inagua *Island* Bahamas 34 D2
Great Khingan Range *see* Da Hinggan Ling
Great Lakes, The *Lakes* N America *see* Erie, Huron, Michigan, Ontario, Superior 15 F3
Great Nicobar *Island* India 117 H3
Great Plain of China *Region* China 104 D2
Great Plains *Region* N America 14 D3
Great Rift Valley *Valley* E Africa/SW Asia 55 C6
Great Salt Lake *Salt lake* Utah, USA 22 B3
Great Sand Sea *Desert region* Egypt/Libya 51 H3
Great Sandy Desert *Desert* Australia 128 C4
Great Sandy Desert *see* Rub' al Khali
Great Slave Lake *Lake* Canada 17 F4
Great Victoria Desert *Desert* Australia 129 C5
Gredos, Sierra de *Mountains* Spain 72 D3
Greece *Country* SE Europe 84-85
Green Bay Wisconsin, USA 20 B2
Greenland *External territory* Denmark, Atlantic Ocean *var.* Grønland 62
Greenland Basin *Undersea feature* Atlantic Ocean 63 F2
Greenland Sea Atlantic Ocean 63 F2
Greenock Scotland, UK 68 C4
Greensboro North Carolina, USA 29 F1
Greenville South Carolina, USA 29 E2
Greifswald Germany 74 D2
Grenada *Country* West Indies 35 G5
Grenoble France 71 D5
Greymouth New Zealand 131 F3
Grimsby England, UK 69 E5
Grodno *see* Hrodna
Groningen Netherlands 66 E1
Grønland *see* Greenland
Grootfontein Namibia 58 C3
Grosseto Italy 76 B4
Grosskanizsa *see* Nagykanizsa
Groznyy Russian Federation 91 B7 94 A4
Grudziądz Poland *Ger.* Graudenz 78 C3
Grünberg in Schlesien *see* Zielona Góra
Guadalajara Mexico 30 D4

Guadalquivir *River* Spain 72 D4
Guadeloupe *External territory* France, West Indies 35 G4
Guadiana *River* Portugal/Spain 72 C4
Gualeguaychú Argentina 44 D4
Guallatiri *Peak* Chile 36 B4
Guam *External territory* USA, Pacific Ocean 122 C3
Guanare Venezuela 38 D1
Guanare *River* Venezuela 38 D2
Guangxi *Autonomous region* China *var.* Kwangsi 109 B6
Guangzhou China *Eng.* Canton 109 C7
Guantánamo Cuba 34 D3
Guantanamo Bay *External territory* USA, Cuba 34 D3
Guatemala *Country* Central America 32
Guatemala City *Capital of* Guatemala 32 B2
Guaviare *River* Colombia 38 D3
Guayaquil Ecuador 38 A4
Guayaquil, Gulf of *Sea feature* Ecuador/Peru 38 A5
Guerguerat Western Sahara 50 A4
Guernsey *Island* Channel Islands 69 D8
Guiana Basin *Undersea feature* Atlantic Ocean 47 B4
Guiana Highlands *Upland* N South America 36 C2
Guider Cameroon 56 B4
Guimarães Portugal 72 C2
Guinea *Country* W Africa 52
Guinea, Gulf of *Sea feature* Atlantic Ocean 47 D5
Guinea-Bissau *Country* W Africa 52
Guiyang China 109 B6
Gujarāt *State* India 114 C4
Gujrānwāla Pakistan 114 C2
Gujrāt Pakistan 114 C2
Gulf, The *see* Persian Gulf
Gulfport Mississippi, USA 28 C3
Gulu Uganda 55 B6
Gumbinnen *see* Gusev
Guri, Embalse de *Reservoir* Venezuela 39 E2
Gusau Nigeria 53 G4
Gusev Kaliningrad, Russian Federation *prev.* Gumbinnen 86 B4
Gushgy Turkmenistan *prev.* Kushka 102 C4
Guwāhāti India 115 G3
Guyana *Country* NE South America 39
Gwalior India 114 D3
Gyandzha *see* Gäncä
Győr Hungary *Ger.* Raab 79 C6
Gyumri Armenia *Rus.* Kumayri, *prev.* Leninakan, Aleksandropol' 97 F2
Gyzylarbat Turkmenistan *prev.* Kizyl-Arvat 102 B2

H

Ha'apai Group *Islands* Tonga 127 F5
Haapsalu Estonia *Ger.* Hapsal 86 C2
Haarlem Netherlands 66 C3
Habomai Islands *Islands* Japan/Russian Federation (disputed) 110 E2
Hachijō-jima *Island* Japan 111 D5
Hachinohe Japan 110 D3
Hadejia *River* Nigeria 53 G3
Haeju North Korea 108 E4
Hafnarfjördhur Iceland 62 D4
Hagen Germany 74 A4
Hague, The *see* 's-Gravenhage
Haifa Israel *Heb.* Hefa 83 G4
Haikou China 109 C7
Ḩā'il Saudi Arabia 100 B4
Hainan *Island* China *var.* Hainan Dao 104 D3 109 C8
Hainan Dao *see* Hainan Dao
Hai Phong Vietnam 118 D3
Haiti *Country* West Indies 34
Hajdarken *see* Khaydarkan
Hakodate Japan 110 D3
Ḩalab Syria 98 B2
Halden Norway 65 B6
Halifax Canada 19 F4
Halle Germany 74 C4
Hallein Austria 75 D7
Halls Creek Australia 128 C3
Halmahera *Island* Indonesia 121 F3
Halmstad Sweden 65 B7
Hamada Japan 111 B5
Ḩamāh Syria 98 B3
Hamamatsu Japan 111 C5
Hamar Norway 65 B5
Hamburg Germany 74 B3
Hämeenlinna Finland 65 D5
HaMelah, Yam *see* Dead Sea
Hamhŭng North Korea 108 E4
Hami China 106 C3
Hamilton Canada 18 D5
Hamilton New Zealand 131 G2
Hamm Germany 74 B4
Hammerfest Norway 64 D2
Hampden New Zealand 131 F4
Handan China 108 C4
HaNegev *Desert region* Israel *Eng.* Negev 99 A6
Hangayn Nuruu *Mountain range* Mongolia 106 D2
Hangzhou China 109 D5
Hannover Germany *Eng.* Hanover 74 B4
Hanoi Vietnam 118 D3
Hanover *see* Hannover
Happy Valley-Goose Bay Canada 19 F2
Hapsal *see* Haapsalu
Ḩaraḑ Yemen 101 C5
Harare *Capital of* Zimbabwe 59 E3
Harbin China 108 E3
Hargeysa Somalia 55 D5
Hari *River* Indonesia 120 B4
Harīrūd *River* C Asia 102 D4
Harper Liberia 52 D5
Harrisburg Pennsylvania, USA 21 E4
Harris Ridge *see* Lomonosov Ridge
Harstad Norway 64 C3
Hartford Connecticut, USA 21 G3
Hasselt Belgium 67 C6
Hastings New Zealand 131 H3
Hastings Nebraska, USA 22 E4
Hatay *see* Antakya
Hatteras, Cape *Coastal feature* North Carolina, USA 29 G1

Hattiesburg Mississippi, USA 28 C3
Hat Yai Thailand 119 C7
Haugesund Norway 65 A6
Havana *Capital of* Cuba *Sp.* La Habana 34 B2
Havre Montana, USA 22 C1
Havre-Saint-Pierre Canada 19 F3
Hawaii *State* USA 123 E2
Hawaiian Islands *Islands* USA 93 H4
Hawlēr *see* Arbīl
Hawthorne Nevada, USA 25 C6
Hay River Canada 17 E4
Hays Kansas, USA 23 E4
Heard Island *Island* Indian Ocean 113 C7
Heerenveen Netherlands 66 D2
Heerlen Netherlands 67 D6
Hefa Israel *prev.* Haifa 99 A5
Hefei China 109 D5
Heidelberg Germany 75 B6
Heilbronn Germany 75 B6
Helena Montana, USA 22 B2
Helmand *River* Afghanistan 102 C5
Helmond Netherlands 67 D5
Helsingborg Sweden 65 B7
Helsingør Denmark 65 B7
Helsinki *Capital of* Finland 65 D6
Ḥelwân Egypt 54 B1
Hengelo Netherlands 66 E3
Henzada Burma 118 A4
Herāt Afghanistan 102 C4
Hermansverk Norway 65 A5
Hermosillo Mexico 30 B2
Herning Denmark 65 A7
Hialeah Florida, USA 29 F5
Hiiumaa *Island* Estonia *Ger.* Dagden, *Swed.* Dagö 86 C2
Hildesheim Germany 74 B4
Hilla *see* Al Ḥillah
Hilversum Netherlands 66 C3
Himalayas *Mountain range* S Asia 104 B2
Himora Ethiopia 54 C4
Ḥimş Syria 98 B3
Hindu Kush *Mountain range* C Asia 103 E4
Hiroshima Japan 111 B5
Hitachi Japan 110 D4
Hjørring Denmark 65 A7
Hlybokaye Belorussia *Rus.* Glubokoye 87 D5
Hobart Tasmania 130 B5
Hobbs New Mexico, USA 5627 E3
Hô Chi Minh Vietnam *var.* Ho Chi Minh City, *prev.* Saigon 119 E6
Ho Chi Minh City *see* Hô Chi Minh
Hodeida *see* Al Ḥudaydah
Hoek van Holland Netherlands 66 B4
Hoggar *see* Ahaggar
Hohhot China 107 F3
Hokkaidō *Island* Japan 110 D2
Holguín Cuba 34 C2
Hollywood Florida, USA 29 F5
Holland *see* Netherlands
Holon Israel 99 A5
Holyhead Wales, UK 69 C5
Homyel' Belorussia *Rus.* Gomel' 87 D7
Honduras *Country* Central America 32-33
Honduras, Gulf of *Sea feature* Caribbean Sea 32 C2
Hønefoss Norway 65 B6
Hông Gai Vietnam 118 E3
Hong Kong China *var* Xianggang 109 C7
Hongze Hu *Lake* China 109 D5
Honiara *Capital of* Solomon Islands 126 C3
Honolulu Hawaii, USA 123 E2
Honshū *Island* Japan 110 D3
Honshu Ridge *Undersea feature* Pacific Ocean 105 F2
Hoorn Netherlands 66 C2
Hopa Turkey 97 F2
Hopedale Canada 19 F2
Hopkinsville Kentucky, USA 20 B5
Horki Belorussia *Rus.* Gorki 87 E6
Horlivka Ukraine *Rus.* Gorlovka 88 G3
Horn, Cape *Coastal feature* Chile 45 C8
Horog *see* Khorog
Horsens Denmark 65 A7
Hotan China 106 B4
Hot Springs Arkansas, USA 28 B2
Hotspur Seamount *Undersea feature* Atlantic Ocean 41 H5 43 H1
Hô Thac Ba *Lake* Vietnam 118 D3
Houston Texas, USA 27 G4
Hovd Mongolia 106 C2
Hövsgöl Nuur *Lake* Mongolia 106 D1
Howe, Cape *Coastal feature* Australia 124 D4 130 C4
Hradec Králové Czech Republic *Ger.* Königgrätz 79 B5
Hrodna Belorussia *Rus.* Grodno 87 B5
Huacho Peru 40 A3
Huainan China 109 D5
Huambo Angola 58 B2
Huancayo Peru 40 B4
Huang He *River* China *Eng.* Yellow River 104 D2 107 F4 108 C4
Huánuco Peru 40 B4
Huaraz Peru 40 B3
Huascarán *Peak* Peru 36 B3
Hubli India 116 C2
Hudson *River* NE USA 21 F3
Hudson Bay *Sea feature* Canada 15 E2
Hudson Strait *Sea feature* Canada 15 F2
Huê Vietnam 118 E4
Huehuetenango Guatemala 32 B2
Huelva Spain 72 C4
Huesca Spain 73 F2
Hughenden Australia 130 B1
Hull *see* Kingston upon Hull
Hulun Nur *Lake* China 107 F1
Humboldt *River* W USA 25 C5
Hungarian Plain *Plain* C Europe 83 E1
Hungary *Country* C Europe 79
Huntington West Virginia, USA 20 D5
Huntsville Alabama, USA 28 D2
Hurghada Egypt 54 B2
Huron, Lake *Lake* Canada/USA 15 F3

Húsavík Iceland 63 E4
Huvadhu Atoll *Island* Maldives 116 C5
Hvar *Island* Croatia 80 B4
Hyargas Nuur *Lake* Mongolia 106 C2
Hyderābād India 114 B3 116 D1
Hyères, Îles d' *Islands* France 71 D6

I

Iaşi Romania 88 D3
Ibadan Nigeria 53 F5
Ibagué Colombia 38 B3
Ibarra Ecuador 38 A4
Iberian Peninsula *Peninsula* SW Europe 46 D3 82 D3
Ibiza *see* Eivissa
Ica Peru 40 B4
İçel *see* Mersin
Iceland *Country* Atlantic Ocean 63 E4
Idaho *State* USA 24
Idaho Falls Idaho, USA 24 E3
Idfu Egypt 54 B2
Idlib Syria 98 B2
Ieper Belgium *Fr.* Ypres 67 A6
Ifôghas, Adrar des *Upland* Mali *var.* Adrar des Iforas 53 F2
Iforas, Adrar des *see* Ifôghas, Adrar des
Iglau *see* Jihlava
Iglesias Italy 77 A5
Ihosy Madagascar 59 G3
Iisalmi Finland 64 E4
Ijebu-Ode Nigeria 53 F5
IJssel *River* Netherlands 66 D3
IJsselmeer *Lake* Netherlands *prev.* Zuider Zee 66 D2
Ikaría *Island* Greece 85 D5
Iki *Island* Japan 111 A6
Ilagan Philippines 121 E1
Ilebo Congo (Zaire) 57 C6
Iligan Philippines 121 E2
Illapel Chile 44 B3
Illinois *State* USA 20 B4
Iloilo Philippines 121 E2
Ilorin Nigeria 53 F4
İluh *see* Batman
Ilulissat Greenland 62 B3
Imatra Finland 65 E5
Imperatriz Brazil 41 F2
Impfondo Congo 57 C5
Imphāl India 115 H4
Independence Missouri, USA 23 F4
Independence Fjord *Inlet* Greenland 62 D1
India *Country* S Asia 114-115 116-117
Indian Ocean 112-113
Indiana *State* USA 20 C4
Indianapolis Indiana, USA 20 C4
Indonesia *Country* SE Asia 120-121
Indore India 114 D4
Indus *River* S Asia 114 C1
Indus Delta *Wetlands* Pakistan 114 B4
Inglefield Land *Region* Greenland 62 A2
Ingolstadt Germany 75 E6
Inguri *see* Enguri
Inhambane Mozambique 59 E3
Inn *River* C Europe 75 D6
Inner Islands *Islands* Seychelles 59 H1
Inner Mongolia *Autonomous region* China 107 F3
Innsbruck Austria 75 C7
In Salah Algeria 50 D3
Insein Burma 118 B4
Interlaken Switzerland 75 B7
Inukjuak Canada 18 D2
Inuvik Canada 17 E3
Invercargill New Zealand 131 F5
Inverness Scotland, UK 68 C3
Ioánnina Greece 84 A4
Ionian Islands *see* Iónioi Nísoi
Ionian Sea Mediterranean Sea 83 E3
Iónioi Nísoi *Island group* Greece *Eng.* Ionian Islands 85 A5
Íos *Island* Greece 85 D6
Iowa *State* USA 23 F3
Ipoh Malaysia 120 B3
Ipswich Australia 130 C2
Ipswich England, UK 69 E6
Iqaluit Canada 17 H3
Iquique Chile 44 B1
Iquitos Peru 40 B2
Irákleio Greece 85 D7
Iran *Country* SW Asia 100-101
Iranian Plateau *Upland* Iran 100 D3
Irānshahr Iran 100 E4
Irapuato Mexico 31 E4
Iraq *Country* SW Asia 100 B3
Irbid Jordan 99 B5
Ireland *Country* W Europe 68-69
Irian Jaya *Province* Indonesia 121 H4
Iringa Tanzania 55 C7
Irish Sea British Isles 69 C5
Irkutsk Russian Federation 95 E4
Irrawaddy *River* Burma 118 B2
Irrawaddy Delta *Wetlands* Burma 118 A4
Ísafjördhur Iceland 62 D4
Ischia, Isola d' *Island* Italy 77 C5
Ishikari *River* Japan 110 D2
Isiro Congo (Zaire) 57 E5
İskenderun Turkey *Eng.* Alexandretta 96 D4
Iskŭr *River* Bulgaria 84 C1
Iskŭr, Yazovir *Reservoir* Bulgaria 84 C2
Islay *Island* Scotland, UK 68 B4
Islāmābād *Capital of* Pakistan 114 C1
Ismailia *see* Ismâ'ilîya
Ismâ'ilîya Egypt *Eng.* Ismailia 54 B1
Isna Egypt 54 B2
İsparta Turkey 96 B4
Israel *Country* SW Asia 98-99
Issyk-Kul' Kyrgyzstan *prev.* Rybach'ye, *Kir.* Ysyk-Köl 103 G2
Issyk-Kul, Ozero *Lake* Kyrgyzstan 103 G2
İstanbul Turkey *var.* Stambul, *prev.* Constantinople, Byzantium, *Bul.* Tsarigrad 96 B2
İstanbul Boğazi *see* Bosporus
Itabuna Brazil 41 G4
Itagüí Colombia 38 B2
Italy *Country* S Europe 76-77

Ittoqqortoormiit Greenland 13 B7 63 B3
Iturup *Island* Japan/Russian Federation (disputed) 110 E1
Ivanhoe Australia 130 B3
Ivano-Frankivs'k Ukraine 88 C2
Ivanovo Russian Federation 90 B4
Ivittuut Greenland 62 B4
Ivory Coast *Country* W Africa *Fr.* Côte d'Ivoire 52
Ivujivik Canada 18 D1
Iwaki Japan 110 D4
Izabal, Lago de *Lake* Guatemala 32 C2
Izhevsk Russian Federation 91 C5 94 B3
İzmir Turkey *prev.* Smyrna 96 A3
İzmit Turkey *var.* Kocaeli 96 B2
Izu-shotō *Island group* Japan 111 D6

J

Jabalpur India 114 E4
Jackson Mississippi, USA 28 C3
Jacksonville Florida, USA 29 E3
Jacksonville Texas, USA 27 G3
Jacmel Haiti 34 D3
Jaén Spain 73 E4
Jaffna Sri Lanka 117 E3
Jaipur India 114 D3
Jajce Bosnia & Herzegovina 80 B3
Jakarta *Capital of* Indonesia 120 C5
Jakobstad Finland 64 D4
Jakobstadt *see* Jēkabpils
Jalālābād Afghanistan 103 E4
Jalal-Abad *see* Dzhalal-Abad
Jalandhar India 114 D2
Jalapa Mexico 31 F4
Jamaame Somalia 55 D6
Jamaica *Country* West Indies 34
Jamāpur Bangladesh 115 G4
Jambi Indonesia 120 B4
James Bay *Sea feature* Canada 18 C3
Jammu *Disputed region* India/Pakistan 114 D2
Jāmnagar India 114 B4
Jan Mayen *External territory* Norway, Arctic Ocean 46 A2 63 F3
Japan *Country* E Asia 110-111
Japan, Sea of Pacific Ocean 93 F4 110 B3
Japan Trench *Undersea feature* Pacific Ocean 122 C2
Järvenpää Finland 65 D5
Jarvis Island *External territory* USA, Pacific Ocean 127 G2
Jaseur Seamount *Undersea feature* Atlantic Ocean 43 H2
Java *Island* Indonesia 120 D5
Java Sea Pacific Ocean *var.* Laut Jawa 112 D4
Java Trench *Undersea feature* Indian Ocean 112 D4
Jawa, Laut *see* Java Sea
Jayapura Indonesia 121 H4
Jedda *see* Jiddah
Jefferson City Missouri, USA 23 G4
Jēkabpils Latvia *Ger.* Jakobstadt 86 C4
Jelgava Latvia *Ger.* Mitau 86 C3
Jember Indonesia 120 D5
Jena Germany 75 C5
Jérémie Haiti 34 D3
Jerevan *see* Yerevan
Jerez de la Frontera Spain 72 D5
Jericho West Bank 99 B5
Jerid, Chott el *Salt lake* Africa 82 D4
Jersey *Island* Channel Islands 69 D8
Jerusalem *Capital of* Israel 99 B5
Jesenice Slovenia 80 A2
Jhelum Pakistan 114 C2
Jiamusi China 108 E2
Jibuti *see* Djibouti
Jiddah Saudi Arabia *Eng.* Jedda 101 A6
Jihlava Czech Republic *Ger.* Iglau 79 B5
Jilin China 108 E3
Jīma Ethiopia 55 C5
Jinan China 109 C4
Jingdezhen China 109 D6
Jining China 107 F2
Jinotega Nicaragua 32 D3
Jinsha Jiang *River* China 109 A6
Jisr ash Shughūr Syria 98 B2
Jixi China 108 E3
Jīzān Saudi Arabia 101 B6
João Pessoa Brazil 41 H3
Jodhpur India 114 C3
Joensuu Finland 65 E5
Johannesburg South Africa 58 D4
Johnson City Tennessee, USA 29 E1
Johor Bahru Malaysia 120 B3
Joinville Brazil 42 D3
Joliet Illinois, USA 20 B3
Jönköping Sweden 65 B7
Jonquière Canada 19 E4
Jordan *Country* SW Asia 98-99
Jordan *River* SW Asia 99 B5
Jos Nigeria 53 G4
Juan Fernandez, Islas *Islands* Chile 123 G4
Juàzeiro Brazil 41 G3
Juàzeiro do Norte Brazil 41 G3
Juba Sudan 55 B5
Júcar *River* Spain 73 E3
Judenburg Austria 75 D7
Juigalpa Nicaragua 32 D3
Juiz de Fora Brazil 41 G5 43 F2
Juneau Alaska, USA 16 D4
Junín Argentina 44 D4
Jura *Mountains* France/Switzerland 70 D4 75 A7
Jura *Island* Scotland, UK 68 B4
Jurbarkas Lithuania *Ger.* Jurburg, *var.* Georgenburg 86 B4
Jurburg *see* Jurbarkas
Juruá *River* Brazil/Peru 40 C2
Juticalpa Honduras 32 D2
Jutland see Jylland
Juventud, Isla de la *Island* Cuba 34 B2
Jylland *Peninsula* Denmark *Eng.* Jutland 65 A7
Jyväskylä Finland 65 D5

K

K2 *Peak* China/Pakistan *Eng.* Mount Godwin Austen 104 C2
Kaachka *see* Kaka
Kaakhka *see* Kaka
Kabale Uganda 55 B6

Kabalebo Reservoir *Reservoir* Surinam 39 G3
Kabinda Congo (Zaire) 57 D7
Kābol *see* Kābul
Kābul *Capital of* Afghanistan *Per.* Kābol 103 E4
Kachch, Gulf of *Sea feature* Arabian Sea 114 B4
Kachch, Rann of *Wetland* India/Pakistan *var.* Rann of Kutch 114 B4
Kadugli Sudan 54 B4
Kaduna Nigeria 53 G4
Kaédi Mauritania 52 C3
Kâgıthane Turkey 96 B2
Kagoshima Japan 111 A6
Kahramanmaraş Turkey *var.* Marash, Maraş 96 D4
Kai, Kepulauan *Island group* Indonesia 120 A3
Kaikoura New Zealand 131 G3
Kainji Reservoir *Reservoir* Nigeria 53 F4
Kairouan Tunisia 51 E1
Kaitaia New Zealand 131 G1
Kajaani Finland 64 E4
Kaka Turkmenistan *prev.* Kaakhka, *var.* Kaachka 102 C3
Kakhovs'ke Vodoskhovyshche *Reservoir* Ukraine 89 F3
Kalahari Desert *Desert* southern Africa 58 C3
Kalamariá Greece 84 B3
Kalámata Greece 85 B6
Kalāt Afghanistan 102 D5
Kalemie Congo (Zaire) 57 E7
Kalgoorlie Australia 129 C6
Kaliningrad *External territory* Russian Federation 86 A4 94 A2
Kaliningrad Kaliningrad, Russian Federation *prev.* Königsberg 86 A4
Kalinkavichy Belorussia *Rus.* Kalinkovichi 87 D7
Kalinkovichi *see* Kalinkavichy
Kalisch *see* Kalisz
Kalispell Montana, USA 22 B1
Kalisz Poland *Ger.* Kalisch 78 C4
Kalmar Sweden 65 C7
Kalpeni Island *Island* India 116 C3
Kama *River* Russian Federation 90 D4
Kamchatka *Peninsula* Russian Federation 95 A3
Kamchiya *River* Bulgaria 84 E2
Kamina Congo (Zaire) 57 D7
Kamishli *see* Al Qāmishlī
Kamloops Canada 17 E5
Kampala *Capital of* Uganda 55 B6
Kâmpóng Cham Cambodia 119 D6
Kâmpóng Chhnăng Cambodia 119 D5
Kâmpóng Saôm Cambodia 119 D6
Kâmpôt Cambodia 119 D6
Kampuchea *see* Cambodia
Kam"yanets'-Podil's'kyy Ukraine 88 C3
Kananga Congo (Zaire) 57 D7
Kanazawa Japan 110 C4
Kandahār Afghanistan *var.* Qandahār 102 D5
Kandi Benin 53 F4
Kandla India 114 C4
Kandy Sri Lanka 117 E3
Kanestron, Ákra *Coastal feature* Greece 84 C4
Kangaatsiaq Greenland 62 B4
Kangaroo Island *Island* Australia 124 C4
Kangerlussuaq Greenland 62 B4
Kangertittivaq *Region* Greenland 62 D3
Kanggye North Korea 108 E4
Kanjiža Yugoslavia 80 D2
Kankan Guinea 52 D4
Kano Nigeria 53 G4
Kānpur India *prev.* Cawnpore 115 E3
Kansas *State* USA 22-23
Kansas City Kansas, USA 23 F4
Kansas City Missouri, USA 23 F4
Kansk Russian Federation 95 E4
Kao-hsiung Taiwan 109 D7
Kaolack Senegal 52 B3
Kapchagay Kazakhstan 94 C5
Kapfenberg Austria 75 E7
Kaposvár Hungary 79 C7
Kapsukas *see* Marijampolė
Kapuas *River* Indonesia 120 C4
Kara-Balta Kyrgyzstan 103 F2
Kara-Bogaz-Gol, Zaliv *Sea feature* Caspian Sea 102 A2
Karabük Turkey 96 C2
Karāchi Pakistan 114 B4
Karaganda Kazakhstan 94 C4
Karaj Iran 100 C3
Karakol Kyrgyzstan *prev.* Przheval'sk 103 G2
Kara Kum *Desert* Turkmenistan *see* Karakumy 92 C4
Karakumskiy Kanal *Canal* Turkmenistan *Turkm.* Garagum Kanaly 102 C3
Karakumy *Desert* Turkmenistan *Turkm.* Garagum, *var.* Qara Qum *Eng.* Kara Kum 102 C2
Karamay China 106 B2
Karasburg Namibia 58 C4
Kara Sea *see* Karskoye More
Karbalā' Iraq *var.* Kerbala 100 B3
Kardítsa Greece 84 B4
Kariba, Lake *Lake* Zambia/Zimbabwe 58 D2
Karkinits'ka Zatoka *Sea feature* Black Sea 89 E4
Karl-Marx-Stadt *see* Chemnitz
Karlovac Croatia 80 B3
Karlovy Vary Czech Republic *Ger.* Karlsbad 79 A5
Karlsbad *see* Karlovy Vary
Karlskrona Sweden 65 C7
Karlsruhe Germany 75 B6
Karlstad Sweden 65 B6
Karnātaka *State* India 116 D1
Kárpathos *Island* Greece 85 E7
Kars Turkey 97 F2
Karshi Uzbekistan *prev.* Bek-Budi, *Uzb.* Qarshi 102 D3
Karskoye More Arctic Ocean *Eng.* Kara Sea 13 E6 90 E2 94 D2
Kasai *River* Congo (Zaire) 57 C6
Kasama Zambia 59 E1
Kaschau *see* Košice
Kāshān Iran 100 C3
Kashi China 106 A3
Kashmir *Disputed region* India/Pakistan 114 D1
Kasongo Congo (Zaire) 57 E6
Kassa *see* Košice
Kassala Sudan 54 C4

Kassel Germany 74 B4
Kastamonu Turkey 96 C2
Kateríni Greece 84 B4
Katha Burma 118 B2
Katherine Australia 128 D2
Kathmandu *Capital of* Nepal 115 F3
Katsina Nigeria 53 G3
Kauen *see* Kaunas
Kaunas Lithuania *Ger.* Kauen, *Pol.* Kowno, *Rus.* Kovno 86 B4
Kavadarci Macedonia 80 E5
Kavála Greece 84 C3
Kavaratti Island *Island* India 116 C3
Kawasaki Japan 111 D5
Kayan *River* Indonesia 120 D3
Kayes Mali 52 C3
Kayseri Turkey 96 D3
Kazakhskiy Melkosopochnik *see* Kazakh Upland
Kazakhstan *Country* C Asia 94
Kazakh Upland *Upland* Kazakhstan *var.* Kazakhskiy Melkosopochnik 92 D3
Kazan' Russian Federation 91 C5 94 B3
Kazandzhik *see* Gazandzhyk
Kazanlŭk Bulgaria 84 D2
Kéa *Island* Greece 85 C6
Kecskemét Hungary 79 D7
Kėdainiai Lithuania 86 B4
Keetmanshoop Namibia 58 C4
Kefallonía *Island* Greece *Eng.* Cephalonia 85 A5
Keith Australia 130 B4
Kelang Malaysia 120 B3
Kelmė Lithuania 86 B4
Kelowna Canada 17 E5
Kemerovo Russian Federation 94 D4
Kemi Finland 64 D4
Kemi *River* Finland 64 D3
Kemijärvi Finland 64 D3
Kendari Indonesia 121 E4
Kenema Sierra Leone 52 C4
Këneurgench Turkmenistan *prev.* Kunya-Urgench, *Turkm.* Köneürgench 102 C2
Kénitra Morocco 50 C2
Kennewick Washington, USA 24 C2
Kenora Canada 18 A3
Kentucky *State* USA 20 C5
Kenya *Country* E Africa 55
Kenya, Mount *see* Kirinyaga
Kerala *State* India 116 D3
Kerbala *see* Karbalā'
Kerch Ukraine 89 G4
Kerguelen Islands *Island group* Indian Ocean 113 C6
Kerguelen Plateau *Undersea feature* Indian Ocean 113 C7
Kerki Turkmenistan 102 D3
Kérkira *see* Kérkyra
Kérkyra Greece 84 A4
Kérkyra *Island* Greece *prev.* Kérkira, *Eng.* Corfu 84 A4
Kermadec Islands *Island group* Pacific Ocean 125 F3
Kermadec Trench *Undersea feature* Pacific Ocean 122 D4
Kermān Iran *var.* Kirman 100 D4
Kermānshāh *see* Bākhtarān
Kerora Eritrea 54 C3
Kerulen *River* China/Mongolia 107 E2
Ketchikan Alaska, USA 16 D4
Key West Florida, USA 29 E5
Khabarovsk Russian Federation 95 G4
Khanka, Lake *Lake* China/Russian Federation 108 E3
Khankendy *see* Xankändi
Kharkiv Ukraine *Rus.* Khar'kov 89 G2
Khartoum *Capital of* Sudan *var.* Al Khurṭūm 54 B4
Khartoum North Sudan 54 B4
Khāsh Iran 100 E4
Khaskovo Bulgaria 84 D2
Khaydarkan Kyrgyzstan *var.* Khaydarken, Hajdarken 103 E2
Khaydarken *see* Khaydarkan
Kherson Ukraine 89 E4
Khíos *see* Chíos
Khmel 'nyts'kyy Ukraine 88 C2
Khodzhent *see* Khudzhand
Khojend *see* Khudzhand
Khokand *see* Kokand
Kholm Afghanistan 103 E3
Khon Kaen Thailand 118 C4
Khorog Tajikistan *var.* Horog 103 F3
Khorramshahr Iran *var.* Khūnīnshahr 100 C4
Khouribga Morocco 50 C2
Khudzhand Tajikistan *prev.* Leninabad, Khodzhent, Khojend 103 E2
Khulna Bangladesh 115 G4
Khūnīnshahr *see* Khorramshahr
Khvoy Iran 100 B2
Kičevo Macedonia 81 D5
Kiel Germany 74 B2
Kielce Poland 78 D4
Kiev *Capital of* Ukraine *Ukr.* Kyyiv 89 E2
Kiffa Mauritania 52 C3
Kigali *Capital of* Rwanda 55 B6
Kigoma Tanzania 55 B7
Kikládhes *see* Kyklades
Kikwit Congo (Zaire) 57 C7
Kilimanjaro *Peak* Tanzania 49 D5
Kilkís Greece 84 B3
Killarney Ireland 69 A6
Kimberley South Africa 58 D4
Kimberley Plateau *Upland* Australia 128 C3
Kindia Guinea 52 C4
Kindu Congo (Zaire) 57 D6
King Island *Island* Australia 130 B4
Kingissepp *see* Kuressaare
Kingman Reef *External territory* USA, Pacific Ocean 127 G2
Kingston Canada 18 C5
Kingston *Capital of* Jamaica 34 C3
Kingston upon Hull England, UK *var.* Hull 69 D5
Kingstown St Vincent & The Grenadines 34 G4
King William Island *Island* Canada 17 F3
Kinneret, Yam *see* Tiberius, Lake
Kinshasa *Capital of* Congo (Zaire) *prev.* Léopoldville 57 B6
Kirghizia *see* Kyrgyzstan
Kirghiz Steppe *Plain* Kazakhstan 95 B4
Kiribati *Country* Pacific Ocean 122

Kirinyaga *Peak* Kenya *var.* Mount Kenya 49 D5
Kiritimati *Island* Kiribati *var.* Christmas Island 127 G2
Kirkenes Norway 64 E2
Kirklareli Turkey 96 A2
Kirkpatrick, Mount *Peak* Antarctica 132 D4
Kirksville Missouri, USA 23 G4
Kirkūk Iraq 100 B3
Kirkwall Scotland, UK 68 C2
Kirman *see* Kermān
Kirov Russian Federation 90 C4 94 B3
Kirovabad *see* Gäncä
Kirovakan *see* Vanadzor
Kirovohrad Ukraine 89 E8
Kiruna Sweden 64 C3
Kisangani Congo (Zaire) *prev.* Stanleyville 57 D5
Kishinev *see* Chişinău
Kiska Island *Island* Alaska, USA 16 A2
Kismaayo Somalia 55 D6
Kisumu Kenya 55 C6
Kitakyūshū Japan 111 A5
Kitami Japan 110 D2
Kitchener Canada 18 C5
Kitwe Zambia 58 D2
Kivu, Lake *Lake* Rwanda/Congo (Zaire) 55 B6 57 E6
Kızıl Irmak *River* Turkey 96 C2
Kizil Kum *see* Kyzyl Kum
Kizyl-Arvat *see* Gyzylarbat
Kjølen Mountains *Mountain range* Sweden *see* Kölen 60 D2
Kladno Czech Republic 79 A5
Klagenfurt Austria 75 D7
Klaipėda Lithuania *Ger.* Memel 86 B4
Klamath Falls Oregon, USA 24 B4
Ključ Bosnia & Herzegovina 80 B3
Knin Croatia 80 B4
Knittelfeld Austria 75 D7
Knoxville Tennessee, USA 29 E1
Knud Rasmussen Land *Region* Greenland 62 B2
Kōbe Japan 111 C5
Koblenz Germany 75 A5
Kobryn Belorussia 87 B6
Kocaeli *see* İzmit
Kočani Macedonia 81 E5
Kōchi Japan 111 B6
Kodiak Alaska, USA 16 C3
Kodiak Island *Island* Alaska, USA 16 C3
Kohīma India 115 H3
Kohtla-Järve Estonia 86 D2
Kokand Uzbekistan *var.* Khokand, *Uzb.* Qŭqon 103 E2
Kokchetav Kazakhstan 94 C4
Kokkola Finland 64 D4
Koko Nor *see* Qinghai Hu
Kokshaal-Tau *Mountain range* Kyrgyzstan 103 G2
Kola Peninsula *see* Kol'skiy Poluostrov
Kolda Senegal 52 B3
Kölen *see* Kjølen Mountains
Kolguyev, Ostrov *Island* Russian Federation 90 D2
Kolhumadulu Atoll *Island* Maldives 116 C5
Kolka Latvia 86 B2
Köln Germany *Eng.* Cologne 75 A5
Kol'skiy Poluostrov *Peninsula* Russian Federation *Eng.* Kola Peninsula 61 F1 90 C2
Kolwezi Congo (Zaire) 57 D8
Kolyma Range *Mountain range* Russian Federation 93 G2
Komárno Slovakia *Ger.* Komorn, *Hung.* Komárom 79 C6
Komárom *see* Komárno
Kommunizma, Pik *see* Communism Peak
Komoé *River* Ivory Coast 53 E4
Komorn *see* Komárno
Komotau *see* Chomutov
Komotiní Greece 84 D3
Komsomol'sk Turkmenistan 102 D3
Komsomol'sk-na-Amure Russian Federation 95 G4
Kondoz *see* Kunduz
Kondūz *see* Kunduz
Köneürgench *see* Këneurgench
Kong Christian IX Land *Region* Greenland 62 D3
Kong Christian X Land *Region* Greenland 62 D3
Kong Frederik VI Kyst *Region* Greenland 62 C4
Kong Frederik VIII Land *Region* Greenland 62 D2
Kong Frederik IX Land *Region* Greenland 62 C4
Kongsvinger Norway 65 B6
Konia *see* Konya
Königgrätz *see* Hradec Králové
Königsberg *see* Kaliningrad
Konispol Albania 81 D7
Konjic Bosnia & Herzegovina 80 C4
Konya Turkey *prev.* Konia 96 C4
Kopaonik *Mountains* Yugoslavia 81 D4
Koper Slovenia 80 A3
Koprivnica Croatia 80 B2
Korçë Albania 81 D6
Korčula *Island* Croatia 80 B4
Korea Strait *Sea feature* Japan/South Korea 108-109 E5
Korhogo Ivory Coast 52 D4
Korinthiakós Kólpos *Sea feature* Greece *Eng.* Gulf of Corinth 85 B5
Kórinthos Greece *Eng.* Corinth 85 B5
Kōriyama Japan 111 D4
Korla China 106 B3
Koror *Capital of* Palau 126 A1
Körös *River* Hungary 79 D7
Korosten' Ukraine 88 D1
Kortrijk Belgium 67 A6
Kos *Island* Greece 85 E6
Kosciusko, Mount *Peak* Australia 124 C4
Košice Slovakia *Ger.* Kaschau, *Hung.* Kassa 79 D6
Köslin *see* Koszalin
Kosovo *Province* Yugoslavia 81 D5
Kosovska Mitrovica Yugoslavia 80 D4
Kosrae *Island* Micronesia 126 C2
Koszalin Poland *Ger.* Köslin 78 B2
Kota India 114 D4
Kota Bharu Malaysia 120 B3
Kota Kinabalu Malaysia 120 D3
Kotka Finland 65 E5
Kotlas NW Russia 90 C4

Kotto *River* C Africa 56 D4
Koudougou Burkina 53 E4
Kourou French Guiana 39 H2
Kousséri Cameroon 56 B3
Kouvola Finland 65 E5
Kovel' Ukraine 88 C1
Kovno *see* Kaunas
Kowno *see* Kaunas
Kozáni Greece 84 B4
Kozhikode *see* Calicut
Kra, Isthmus of *Coastal feature* Burma/Thailand 119 B6
Kragujevac Yugoslavia 80 D4
Krakatau *Peak* Indonesia 104 D5
Krakau *see* Kraków
Kraków Poland *Eng.* Cracow, *Ger.* Krakau 79 D5
Kraljevo Yugoslavia 80 D4
Kranj Slovenia 80 A2
Krasnodar Russian Federation 91 A6
Krasnovodsk *see* Turkmenbashy
Krasnoyarsk Russian Federation 94 D4
Krasnyy Luch Ukraine 89 G5
Kremenchuk Ukraine 89 F2
Kremenchuts'ke Vodoskhovyshche *Reservoir* Ukraine 89 E2
Krems an der Donau Austria 75 E6
Kretinga Lithuania *Ger.* Krottingen 86 B3
Kribi Cameroon 57 B5
Krichev *see* Krychaw
Krishna *River* India 116 C1
Kristiansand Norway 65 A6
Kristianstad Sweden 65 B7
Kríti *Island* Greece *Eng.* Crete 85 C7
Kritikó Pélagos *see* Crete, Sea of
Krivoy Rog *see* Kryvyy Rih
Krk *Island* Croatia 80 A3
Kroonstad South Africa 58 D4
Krottingen *see* Kretinga
Krung Thep *see* Bangkok
Kruševac Yugoslavia 81 D4
Krychaw Belorussia *Rus.* Krichev 87 E6
Krym *see* Crimea
Kryvyy Rih Ukraine *Rus.* Krivoy Rog 89 E3
Kuala Lumpur *Capital of* Malaysia 120 B3
Kuala Terengganu Malaysia 120 B3
Kuantan Malaysia 120 B3
Kuba *see* Quba
Kuching Malaysia 120 C3
Kuçovë Albania *prev.* Qyteti Stalin 81 D6
Kuito Angola 58 C2
Kuldīga Latvia *Ger.* Goldingen 86 B3
Kullorsuaq Greenland 62 B3
Kulyab SW Tajikistan 103 E3
Kum *see* Qom
Kuma *River* Russian Federation 91 B7
Kumamoto Japan 111 A6
Kumanovo Macedonia 81 E5
Kumasi Ghana 53 E5
Kumayri *see* Gyumri 97 F2
Kumbo Cameroon 56 B4
Kumon Range *Mountain range* Burma 118 B1
Kunashir *Island* Japan/Russian Federation (disputed) 110 E1
Kunduz Afghanistan *var.* Kondūz, Qondūz, Kondoz 103 E3
Kunja-Urgenč *see* Këneurgench
Kunlun Mountains *see* Kunlun Shan
Kunlun Shan *Mountain range* China *Eng.* Kunlun Mountains 104 C2 106 B4
Kunming China 109 A6
Kununurra Australia 128 D3
Kupang Indonesia 120 E5
Kür *see* Kura
Kura *River* Azerbaijan/Georgia *Az.* Kür 96 G2
Kurashiki Japan 111 B5
Küre Dağları *Mountains* Turkey 96 C2
Kuressaare Estonia *prev.* Kingissepp, *Ger.* Arensburg 86 C2
Kurgan-Tyube Tajikistan 103 E3
Kurile Islands *Islands* Pacific Ocean 105 F1
Kurile Trench *Undersea feature* Pacific Ocean 122 C2
Kurmuk Sudan 54 C4
Kurnool India 116 D2
Kuršėnai Lithuania 86 B4
Kushiro Japan 110 E2
Kushka *see* Gushgy
Kustanay Kazakhstan 94 C4
Kütahya Turkey *prev.* Kutaiah 96 B3
Kutaiah *see* Kütahya
K'ut'aisi Georgia 97 F2
Kutch, Rann of *see* Kachch, Rann of
Kuujjuaq Canada 19 E2
Kuujjuarapik Canada 18 D2
Kuusamo Finland 64 E3
Kuwait *Country* SW Asia 100 C4
Kuwait City *Capital of* Kuwait 100 C4
Kuytun China 106 B3
Kwangju South Korea 109 E5
Kwango *River* Congo (Zaire) 57 C7
Kykládes *Island group* Greece *prev.* Kikládhes, *Eng.* Cyclades 85 D6
Kyrenia *see* Girne
Kyrgyzstan *Country* C Asia *var.* Kirghizia 103
Kýthira *Island* Greece 85 B6
Kyushu-Palau Ridge *Undersea feature* Pacific Ocean 111 B7 121 G1
Kyyiv *see* Kiev
Kyzyl Kum *Desert* Kazakhstan/Uzbekistan *var.* Kizil Kum, *Uzb.* Qizilqum 92 C3
Kyōto Japan 111 C5
Kyūshū *Island* Japan 111 B6
Kzyl-Orda Kazakhstan 94 B5

L

Laâyoune Western Sahara 50 B3
Labé Guinea 52 C4
Laborca *see* Laborec
Laborec *River* Slovakia *Hung.* Laborca 79 E5
Labrador *Region* Canada 19 F2
Labrador Basin *Undersea feature* Atlantic Ocean 15 G2 19 G1
Labrador City Canada 19 E3
Labrador Sea Atlantic Ocean 62 B5

Laccadive Islands *see* Lakshadweep
La Ceiba Honduras 32 D2
La Coruña *see* A Coruña
La Crosse Wisconsin, USA 20 A2
Ladoga, Lake *see* Ladozhskoye Ozero
Ladozhskoye Ozero *Lake* Russian Federation *Eng.* Lake Ladoga 90 B3
Lae Papua New Guinea 126 B3
La Esperanza Honduras 32 C2
Lafayette Louisiana, USA 28 B3
Lågen *River* Norway 65 B5
Laghouat Algeria 50 D2
Lagos Nigeria 53 F5
Lagos Portugal 72 C4
La Grande Oregon, USA 24 C3
La Habana *see* Havana
Lahore Pakistan 114 C2
Laï Chad 56 C4
Laila *see* Laylá
Lajes Brazil 42 D3
Lake District *Region* England, UK 69 C5
Lakewood Colorado, USA 22 D4
Lakshadweep *Island group* India *Eng.* Laccadive Islands 116 B2
La Ligua Chile 44 B4
La Louvière Belgium 67 B6
Lambaré Paraguay 42 B3
Lambaréné Gabon 57 B6
Lambert Glacier *Ice feature* Antarctica 133 G2
Lamía Greece 85 B5
Lampedusa *Island* Italy 77 B8
Lampione *Island* Italy 77 B8
Lancaster England, UK 69 D5
Lancaster California, USA 25 C7
Lancaster Sound *Sea feature* Canada 17 G2
Landsberg *see* Gorzów Wielkopolski
Land's End *Coastal feature* England, UK 69 B7
Lang Sơn Vietnam 118 D3
Länkäran Azerbaijan *Rus.* Lenkoran' 97 H3
Lansing Michigan, USA 20 C3
Lanzarote *Island* Spain 50 B3
Lanzhou China 108 B4
Laon France 70 D3
La Oroya Peru 40 B3
Laos *Country* SE Asia 118
La Palma *Island* Spain 50 A3
La Paz *Capital of* Bolivia 40 C4
La Paz Mexico 30 B3
La Pérouse Strait *Sea feature* Japan 110 D1
Lapland *Region* N Europe 64 C3
La Plata Argentina 44 D4
Lappeenranta Finland 65 E5
Laptev Sea *see* Laptevykh, More
Laptevykh, More Arctic Ocean *Eng.* Laptev Sea 12 E3 95 F2
L'Aquila Italy 76 C4
Laramie Wyoming, USA 22 C4
Laredo Texas, USA 27 F5
La Rioja Argentina 44 C3
Lárisa Greece 84 B4
Lārkāna Pakistan 114 B3
Larnaca Cyprus *var.* Larnaka, Larnax 96 C5
Larnaka *see* Larnaca
Larnax *see* Larnaca
La Rochelle France 70 B4
La Roche-sur-Yon France 70 B4
La Romana Dominican Republic 34 E3
Las Cruces New Mexico, USA 26 D3
La Serena Chile 44 B3
La Spezia Italy 76 B3
Las Piedras Uruguay 42 C5
Las Tablas Panama 33 F5
Las Vegas Nevada, USA 25 D7
Latakia *see* Al Lādhiqīyah
Latvia *Country* NE Europe 86
Launceston Tasmania 130 B5
Laurentian Basin *see* Canada Basin
Laurentian Plateau *Upland* Canada 15 F3
Lausanne Switzerland 75 A7
Laval France 70 B3
Lawton Oklahoma, USA 27 F2
Laylá Saudi Arabia 101 C5
Lebanon *Country* SW Asia 98-99
Lebu Chile 45 B5
Lecce Italy 77 E5
Leduc Canada 17 E5
Leeds England, UK 69 D5
Leeuwarden Netherlands 66 D1
Leeuwin, Cape *Coastal feature* Australia 129 B6
Leeward Islands *Island group* West Indies 35 G3
Lefkáda *Island* Greece *prev.* Levkás 85 A5
Lefkoşa *see* Nicosia
Lefkosia *see* Nicosia
Legaspi Philippines 120 E2
Legnica Poland *Ger.* Liegnitz 78 B4
Le Havre France 70 B3
Leicester England, UK 69 D6
Leiden Netherlands 66 C3
Leipzig Germany 74 C4
Leivádia Greece 85 B5
Leizhou Bandao *Peninsula* China 109 C7
Lek *River* Netherlands 66 C4
Le Léman *see* Geneva, Lake
Lelystad Netherlands 66 D3
Léman, Lac *see* Geneva, Lake
Le Mans France 70 B3
Lemesos *see* Limassol
Lemnos *see* Límnos
Lena *River* Russian Federation 95 F3
Leninabad *see* Khudzhand
Leninakan *see* Gyumri
Leningrad *see* St Petersburg
Leninsk *see* Chardzhev
Lenkoran' *see* Länkäran
León Mexico 31 E4
León Nicaragua 32 C3
León Spain 72 D2
Léopoldville *see* Kinshasa
Lepel' *see* Lyepyel'
Le Puy France 71 C5
Lérida *see* Lleida
Lerwick Scotland, UK 68 D1
Lesbos *see* Lésvos
Leskovac Yugoslavia 80 E4
Lesotho *Country* southern Africa 58
Lesser Antarctica *Region* Antarctica 134 C2
Lesser Antilles *Island group* West Indies 35 G4
Lésvos *Island* Greece *Eng.* Lesbos 83 F3 85 D4

Lethbridge Canada 17 F5
Leti, Kepulauan *Island group* Indonesia 121 F5
Leuven Belgium 67 C6
Leverkusen Germany 75 A5
Levkás *see* Lefkáda
Lewis *Island* Scotland, UK 68 B2
Lewiston Idaho, USA 24 C2
Lewiston Maine, USA 21 G2
Lexington Kentucky, USA 20 C5
Leyte *Island* Philippines 121 E2
Lezhë Albania 81 D5
Lhasa China 106 C5
Liangyungang China 109 D5
Liaoyuan China 108 D3
Libau *see* Liepāja
Liberec Czech Republic *Ger.* Reichenberg 78 B4
Liberia *Country* W Africa 52
Liberia Costa Rica 32 D4
Libreville *Capital of* Gabon 57 A5
Libya *Country* N Africa 51
Libyan Desert *Desert* N Africa 48 C3
Liechtenstein *Country* C Europe 75 B7
Liège Belgium 67 D6
Liegnitz *see* Legnica
Lienz Austria 75 D7
Liepāja Latvia *Ger.* Libau 86 B3
Liffey *River* Ireland 69 B5
Ligurian Sea Mediterranean Sea 71 E6
Likasi Congo (Zaire) 57 E8
Lille France 70 C2
Lillehammer Norway 65 B5
Lilongwe *Capital of* Malawi 59 E2
Lima *Capital of* Peru 40 B4
Lima Ohio, USA 20 C4
Limassol Cyprus *var.* Lemesos 96 C5
Limerick Ireland 69 A6
Límnos *Island* Greece *var.* Lemnos 84 C4
Limoges France 70 C5
Limón Costa Rica 33 E4
Limpopo *River* southern Africa 58 D3
Linares Chile 44 B4
Linares Spain 73 E4
Lincoln England, UK 69 D5
Lincoln Nebraska, USA 23 F4
Lincoln Sea Arctic Ocean 62 B1
Linden Guyana 39 G2
Lindi *River* Congo (Zaire) 55 C8
Line Islands *Island group* Kiribati 127 H3
Lingga, Kepulauan *Island group* Indonesia 120 B4
Linköping Sweden 65 C6
Linosa *Island* Italy 77 C8
Linz Austria 75 D6
Lion, Golfe du *Sea feature* Mediterranean Sea 82 C2
Lipari *Island* Italy 77 D6
Lipari Islands *see* Isole Eolie
Lira Uganda 55 B6
Lisbon *Capital of* Portugal *Port.* Lisboa 72 B4
Litang China 109 A5
Litani *River* SW Asia 89 B4
Lithuania *Country* E Europe 86-87
Little Andaman *Island* India 117 G2
Little Minch *Sea feature* Scotland, UK 68 B3
Little Rock Arkansas, USA 28 B2
Liuzhou China 109 B7
Liverpool England, UK 69 D5
Livingston, Lake *Lake* Texas, USA 27 H3
Livingstone Zambia 58 D3
Livno Bosnia & Herzegovina 80 B4
Livorno Italy 76 B3
Ljubljana *Capital of* Slovenia 80 A2
Ljusnan *River* Sweden 65 B5
Llanos *Region* Colombia/Venezuela 39 E2
Lleida Spain *Cast.* Lérida 73 F2
Lobatse Botswana 58 D4
Lobito Angola 58 B2
Locarno Switzerland 75 B8
Lodja Congo (Zaire) 57 D6
Łódź Poland *Rus.* Lodz 78 D4
Lofoten *Island group* Norway 64 B3
Logan, Mount *Peak* Canada 14 C2
Logroño Spain 73 E2
Loire *River* France 70 B4
Loja Ecuador 38 A5
Lokitaung Kenya 55 C5
Loksa Estonia *Ger.* Loxa 86 D2
Lombok *Island* Indonesia 120 D5
Lomé *Capital of* Togo 53 F5
Lomond, Loch *Lake* Scotland, UK 68 C4
Lomonosov Ridge *Undersea feature* Arctic Ocean *var.* Harris Ridge 12 D4
London Canada 18 C5
London *Capital of* UK 69 E6
Londonderry Northern Ireland, UK 68 B4
Londonderry, Cape *Coastal feature* Australia 124 B2 128 C2
Londrina Brazil 42 D2
Long Beach California, USA 25 C8
Long Island *Island* Bahamas 34 D2
Long Island *Island* NE USA 21 G3
Longreach Australia 126 B5
Longview Texas, USA 27 G3
Longview Washington, USA 24 B2
Longyearbyen Svalbard 63 G2
Lop Nur *Lake* China 106 C3
Lorca Spain 73 F4
Lord Howe Rise *Undersea feature* Pacific Ocean 122 C4
Lorient France 70 A3
Los Alamos New Mexico, USA 26 D2
Los Angeles California, USA 25 C8
Loslau *see* Wodzisław Śląski
Los Mochis Mexico 30 C3
Losonc *see* Lučenec
Losontz *see* Lučenec
Lot *River* France 71 B5
Louangphrabang Laos 118 C3
Loubomo Congo 57 B6
Louisiana *State* USA 28 B3
Louisville Kentucky, USA 20 C5
Lovech Bulgaria 84 C2
Lower California *see* Baja California

Loxa *see* Loksa
Loyauté, Îles *Island group* New Caledonia 126 D5
Loznica Yugoslavia 80 C3
Luanda *Capital of* Angola 58 B1
Luanshya Zambia 58 D2
Lubānas Ezers *Lake* Latvia 86 D4
Lubango Angola 58 B2
Lubbock Texas, USA 27 E2
Lübeck Germany 74 C3
Lublin Poland *Rus.* Lyublin 78 E4
Lubny Ukraine 89 F2
Lubumbashi Congo (Zaire) 57 E8
Lucapa Angola 58 C1
Lucena Philippines 120 E1
Lučenec Slovakia *Hung.* Losonc, *Ger.* Losontz 79 D6
Lucerne *see* Luzern
Lucknow India 115 E3
Lüderitz Namibia 58 B4
Ludhiāna India 114 D2
Lugano Switzerland 75 B8
Lugo Spain 72 C1
Luhans'k Ukraine 89 H3
Luleå Sweden 64 D4
Lumsden New Zealand 131 F5
Luninyets Belorussia 97 C6
Lusaka *Capital of* Zambia 58 D2
Lushnjë Albania 81 D6
Lūt, Baḩrat *see* Dead Sea
Luts'k Ukraine 88 C1
Lutzow-Holm Bay *Sea feature* Antarctica 133 F1
Luxembourg *Country* W Europe 67 D8
Luxembourg *Capital of* Luxembourg 67 D8
Luxor Egypt 54 B2
Luzern Switzerland *Fr.* Lucerne 75 B7
Luzon *Island* Philippines 121 E1
Luzon Strait *Sea feature* Philippines/Taiwan 105 E3
L'viv Ukraine *Rus.* L'vov 88 B2
L'vov see L'viv
Lyepyel' Belorussia *Rus.* Lepel' 87 D5
Lyon France 71 D5
Lyublin *see* Lublin

M

Ma'ān Jordan 99 B6
Maas *River* W Europe *var.* Meuse 66 D4
Maastricht Netherlands 67 D6
Macao *External territory* Portugal, E Asia *var.* Macau 109 C7
Macapá Brazil 41 F1
Macau *see* Macao
Macdonald Islands *Islands* Indian Ocean 113 B7
Macdonnell Ranges *Mountains* Australia 128 D4
Macedonia *Country* SE Europe officially Former Yugoslav Republic of Macedonia, *abbrev.* FYR Macedonia 81
Maceió Brazil 41 H3
Machakos Kenya 55 C6
Machala Ecuador 38 A5
Mackay Australia 126 B5 130 C1
Mackay, Lake *Lake* Australia 128 D4
Mackenzie *River* Canada 17 E4
Mackenzie Bay *Sea feature* Atlantic Ocean 133 G2
Mâcon France 70 D5
Macon Georgia, USA 29 E2
Madagascar *Country* Indian Ocean 59
Madagascar Basin *Undersea feature* Indian Ocean 113 B5
Madagascar Ridge *Undersea feature* Indian Ocean 113 A5
Madang Papua New Guinea 126 B3
Madeira *River* Bolivia/Brazil 40 D2
Madeira *Island group* Portugal 50 A2
Madhya Pradesh *State* India 115 E4
Madison Wisconsin, USA 20 B3
Madona Latvia *Ger.* Modohn 86 D3
Madras India 117 E2
Madre de Dios *River* Bolivia/Peru 40 C3
Madrid *Capital of* Spain 73 E3
Madurai India 116 D3
Magadan Russian Federation 95 G3
Magallanes *see* Punta Arenas
Magallanes, Estrecho de *see* Magellan, Strait of
Magdalena *River* Colombia 38 B2
Magdeburg Germany 74 C4
Magellan, Strait of *Sea feature* S South America *Sp.* Estrecho de Magallanes 37 B7
Maggiore, Lake *Lake* Italy/Switzerland 75 B8
Mahajanga Madagascar 59 G2
Mahalapye Botswana 58 D3
Mahanādi *River* India 115 F5
Mahārashtra *State* India 114 D5
Mahé *Island* Seychelles 59 H1
Mahilyow Belorussia *Rus.* Mogilëv 87 E6
Mährisch-Ostrau *see* Ostrava
Maicao Colombia 38 C1
Maiduguri Nigeria 53 H4
Maimana *see* Meymaneh
Maine *State* USA 21 G1
Mainz Germany 75 B5
Maiquetía Venezuela 38 D1
Maíz, Islas del *Islands* Nicaragua 33 E3 34 B5
Majorca *see* Mallorca
Majuro *Island* Marshall Islands 126 D1
Makarska Croatia 80 B4
Makeni Sierra Leone 52 C4
Makeyevka *see* Makiyivka
Makgadikgadi *Salt pan* Botswana 58 D3
Makhachkala Russian Federation 91 B7 94 A4
Makiyivka Ukraine *Rus.* Makeyevka 89 G5
Makkah Saudi Arabia *Eng.* Mecca 101 A5
Makkovik Canada 19 G2
Makurdi Nigeria 53 G4
Malabo *Capital of* Equatorial Guinea 57 A5
Malacca *see* Melaka
Malacca, Strait of *Sea feature* Indonesia/ Malaysia 104 C4 119 C8

Maladzyechna Belorussia *Rus.* Molodechno, *Pol.* Molodeczno 87 C5
Málaga Spain 72 D5
Malakal Sudan 55 B5
Malang Indonesia 120 D5
Malanje Angola 58 B1
Malatya Turkey 97 E3
Malawi *Country* southern Africa 59
Malay Peninsula *Peninsula* Malaysia/Thailand 119 D8
Malaysia *Country* Asia 120
Maldive Ridge *Undersea feature* Indian Ocean 112 C4
Maldives *Country* Indian Ocean 116
Male' *Capital of* Maldives 116 C4
Mali *Country* W Africa 53
Malindi Kenya 55 C7
Mallorca *Island* Spain *Eng.* Majorca 73 H3
Malmö Sweden 65 B5
Malta *Country* Mediterranean Sea 77 C8
Malta Montana, USA 22 C1
Malta Channel *Sea feature* Mediterranean Sea 77 C7
Maluku *Island group* Indonesia *var.* Moluccas 105 E4 121 F4
Maluku, Laut Pacific Ocean *Eng.* Molucca Sea 121 F4
Māmallapuram India 117 E2
Mamberamo *River* Indonesia 121 H4
Mamoudzou *Capital of* Mayotte 59 G2
Man Ivory Coast 52 D4
Man, Isle of *Island* UK 69 C5
Manado Indonesia 120 F3
Managua *Capital of* Nicaragua 32 D3
Manama *Capital of* Bahrain *Ar.* Al Manāmah 101 C5
Mananjary Madagascar 59 G3
Manaus Brazil 40 D2
Manchester England, UK 69 D5
Manchester New Hampshire, USA 21 G2
Manchuria *Region* China 108 D3
Manchurian Plain *Plain* E Asia 105 E1
Mandalay Burma 118 B3
Mangalia Romania 88 D5
Mangalore India 116 C2
Manguéni, Plateau du *Upland* Niger 53 H2
Manicouagan, Réservoir *Reservoir* Canada 19 E3
Manila *Capital of* Philippines 120 E1
Manisa Turkey *prev.* Saruhan 96 A3
Manitoba *Province* Canada 17 G4
Manizales Colombia 38 B3
Manjimup Australia 129 B6
Manlitsoq Greenland 62 B4
Mannar Sri Lanka 117 E3
Mannar, Gulf of *Sea feature* Indian Ocean 116 D3
Mannheim Germany 75 B5
Mannu *River* Italy 77 A5
Manono Congo (Zaire) 57 E7
Mansel Island *Island* Canada 18 C1
Manta Ecuador 38 A4
Mantes-la-Jolie France 70 C3
Mantova Italy *Eng.* Mantua 76 B2
Mantua *see* Mantova
Manzhouli China 107 F1
Mao Chad 56 B3
Maoke, Pegunungan *Mountains* Indonesia 121 H4
Maputo *Capital of* Mozambique 59 E4
Mar, Serra do *Mountains* Brazil 36 D4
Maracaibo Venezuela 38 C1
Maracaibo, Lago de *Inlet* Venezuela 38 C1
Maracay Venezuela 38 D1
Maradi Niger 53 G3
Marajó, Ilha de *Island* Brazil 41 F2
Marañón *River* Peru 40 B2
Maraş *see* Kahramanmaraş
Marash *see* Kahramanmaraş
Marbella Spain 72 D5
Mar Chiquita, Laguna *Salt lake* Argentina 44 D3
Mardān Pakistan 114 C1
Mar del Plata Argentina 45 D5
Mardin Turkey 97 E4
Margarita, Isla de *Island* Venezuela 35 F3 39 E1
Mārgow, Dasht-e- *Desert* Afghanistan 102 C5
Mariana Trench *Undersea feature* Pacific Ocean 122 C2
Marías, Islas *Islands* Mexico 30 C4
Maribor Slovenia 80 B2
Marie Byrd Land *Region* Antarctica 132 C3
Mariehamn Finland 65 D6
Marijampolė Lithuania *prev.* Kapsukas 86 B4
Marília Brazil 41 F5 42 D2
Maringá Brazil 42 D2
Marion, Lake *Lake* South Carolina, USA 29 F2
Mariscal Estigarribia Paraguay 42 B2
Maritsa *River* SE Europe 84 D3
Mariupol' Ukraine *prev.* Shdanov 89 G4
Marka Somalia 55 D6
Markham, Mount *Peak* Antarctica 132 D4
Marmara, Sea of *see* Marmara Denizi
Marmara Denizi Turkey *Eng.* Sea of Marmara 96 B2
Marne *River* France 70 D3
Maroua Cameroon 56 B3
Marowijne *River* French Guiana/Surinam 39 H3
Marqueses Islands *Island group* French Polynesia *Fr.* Îles Marquises 125 H2
Marquette Michigan, USA 20 B1
Marquisas, Îles *see* Marquesas Islands
Marrakech Morocco *Eng.* Marrakesh 50 B2
Marsala Italy 77 C7
Marseille France 71 D6
Marshall Islands *Country* Pacific Ocean 126-127
Marsh Island *Island* Louisiana, USA 29 B4
Martin Slovakia *prev.* Turčianský Svätý Martin, *Ger.* Sankt Martin, *Hung.* Turócszentmárton 79 C5
Martinique *External territory* France, West Indies 35

Mary Turkmenistan *prev.* Merv 102 C3
Maryland *State* USA 21 F4
Mascarene Islands *Island group* Indian Ocean 59 H3
Mascarene Plateau *Undersea feature* Indian Ocean 113 B5
Maseru *Capital of* Lesotho 58 D4
Mashhad Iran *var.* Meshed 100 E3
Masindi Uganda 55 B6
Mason City Iowa, USA 23 F3
Masqaţ *see* Muscat
Massachusetts *State* USA 21 G3
Massawa Eritrea 54 C4
Massif Central *Upland* France 71 C5
Massoukou Gabon 57 B6
Masterton New Zealand 131 G3
Matadi Congo (Zaire) 57 B7
Matagalpa Nicaragua 32 D3
Matamoros Mexico 31 E2
Matanzas Cuba 34 B2
Matara Sri Lanka 117 E4
Mataró Spain 73 G2
Mato Grosso, Planalto de *Upland* Brazil 41 E3
Matosinhos Portugal 72 C2
Matrûh Egypt 54 B1
Matsue Japan 111 B5
Matsuyama Japan 111 B5
Maturín Venezuela 39 E1
Maun Botswana 58 D3
Mauritania *Country* W Africa 52
Mauritius *Country* Indian Ocean 59 H3
Mayaguana *Island* Bahamas 34 D2
Mayotte *External territory* France, Indian Ocean 59 G2
Mayyit, Al Baḩr al *see* Dead Sea
Mazār-e Sharīf Afghanistan 102 D3
Mazatenango Guatemala 32 B2
Mazatlán Mexico 30 C3
Mažeikiai Lithuania 86 B3
Mazury *Region* Poland 78 D3
Mazyr Belorussia *Rus.* Mozyr' 87 D7
Mbabane *Capital of* Swaziland 59 E4
Mbala Zambia 59 E1
Mbale Uganda 55 C6
Mbandaka Congo (Zaire) 57 C5
Mbeya Tanzania 55 B8
Mbuji-Mayi Congo (Zaire) 57 D7
McKinley, Mount *see* Denali
McMurdo Sound *Sea feature* Antarctica 133 E5
Mead, Lake *Lake* SW USA 25 D7 26 A1
Mecca *see* Makkah
Mechelen Belgium 67 C5
Medan Indonesia 120 A3
Medellín Colombia 38 B2
Médenine Tunisia 51 F2
Medford Oregon, USA 24 B4
Medina *see* Al Madīnah
Mediterranean Sea Atlantic Ocean 82-83
Meekatharra Australia 129 B5
Meerut India 114 D3
Mek'elē Ethiopia 54 C4
Meknès Morocco 50 C2
Mekong *River* SE Asia 104 D3
Mekong Delta *Wetlands* Vietnam 119 E6
Melaka Malaysia *prev.* Malacca 120 B3
Melanesia *Region* Pacific Ocean 124-125 126-127
Melbourne Australia 130 B4
Melbourne Florida, USA 29 F4
Melilla *External territory* Spain, N Africa 50 C1
Melitopol' Ukraine 89 F4
Melo Uruguay 42 C4
Melville Island *Island* Australia 128 D2
Melville Island *Island* Canada 17 E2
Memel *see* Klaipėda
Memel *see* Neman
Memphis Tennessee, USA 28 C2
Mende France 71 C6
Mendi Papua New Guinea 126 B3
Mendoza Argentina 44 B4
Menongue Angola 58 C2
Menorca *Island* Spain *Eng.* Minorca 73 H3
Mentawai, Kepulauan *Island group* Indonesia 120 A4
Meppel Netherlands 66 D2
Merced California, USA 25 B6
Mercedario *Peak* Argentina 37 B5
Mercedes Argentina 44 C4
Mercedes Uruguay 42 B5
Mergui Burma 119 B5
Mergui Archipelago *Island chain* Burma 119 B6
Mérida Mexico 31 H3
Mérida Spain 72 D4
Mérida Venezuela 38 C2
Meridian Mississippi, USA 28 C3
Merredin Australia 129 B6
Mersin Turkey *var.* İçel 96 C4
Meru Kenya 55 C5
Merv *see* Mary
Mesa Arizona, USA 26 B2
Meshed *see* Mashhad
Messina Italy 77 D6
Messina, Stretto di *Sea feature* Ionian Sea/Tyrrhenian Sea 77 D7
Mesters Vig Greenland 62 D3
Mestre Italy 76 C2
Meta *River* Colombia/Venezuela 38 C2
Metković Croatia 80 C4
Metz France 70 D3
Meuse *River* W Europe *var.* Maas 70 D3
Mexicali Mexico 30 A1
Mexicana, Altiplanicie *see* Mexico, Plateau of
Mexico *Country* North America 30-31
México, Golfo de *see* Mexico, Gulf of
Mexico, Gulf of *Sea feature* Atlantic Ocean/Caribbean Sea 46 A4
Mexico, Plateau of *Upland* Mexico *Sp.* Altiplanicie Mexicana 14 D4
Mexico City *Capital of* Mexico *Sp.* Ciudad de México 31 E4
Meymaneh Afghanistan *var.* Maimana 102 D4
Mezen' *River* Russian Federation 90 D3
Miami Florida, USA 29 F5
Michigan *State* USA 20 C2

Michigan, Lake *Lake* USA 20 C2
Micronesia *Country* Pacific Ocean 126
Micronesia *Region* Pacific Ocean 126-127
Mid Atlantic Ridge *Undersea feature* Atlantic Ocean 46 B4
Middelburg South Africa 58 D5
Middle America Trench *Undersea feature* Pacific Ocean 36 A1
Middle Andaman *Island* India 117 G2
Middlesbrough England, UK 69 D5
Mid-Indian Ridge *Undersea feature* Indian Ocean 113 C5
Midland Texas, USA 27 E2
Mikhaylovka Russian Federation 91 B6
Mikkeli Finland 65 E5
Míkonos *Island* Greece 85 D6
Milagro Ecuador 38 A4
Milan *see* Milano
Milano Italy *Eng.* Milan 76 B2
Mildura Australia 130 B3
Miles Australia 130 C2
Miles City Montana, USA 22 C2
Milford Haven Wales, UK 69 C6
Milford Sound New Zealand 131 E4
Mílos *Island* Greece 85 C6
Milparinka Australia 130 B2
Milwaukee Wisconsin, USA 20 B3
Minatitlán Mexico 31 G4
Mindanao *Island* Philippines 121 F2
Mindoro *Island* Philippines 121 E2
Mindoro Strait *Sea feature* South China Sea/Sulu Sea 121 E2
Mingäçevir Azerbaijan *Rus.* Mingechaur 97 G2
Mingechaur *see* Mingäçevir
Minho *River* Portugal/Spain *Sp.* Miño 72 C2
Minicoy Island *Island* India 116 C3
Minneapolis Minnesota, USA 23 F2
Minnesota *State* USA 23 F1
Miño *River* Portugal/Spain *Port.* Minho 72 C1
Minorca *see* Menorca
Minot North Dakota, USA 22 D1
Minsk *Capital of* Belorussia 87 C5
Minto, Lake *Lake* Canada 18 D2
Miranda de Ebro Spain 73 E2
Mirim, Lake *Lagoon* Brazil/Uruguay *var.* Mirim Lagoon 42 C5
Mirtóo Pelagos *Sea feature* Mediterranean Sea 85 C6
Miskitos Cayos *Islands* Nicaragua 33 E2
Miskolc Hungary 79 D6
Mişrātah Libya 51 F2
Mississippi *State* USA 28 C2
Mississippi *River* USA 15 E4
Mississippi Delta *Wetlands* USA 15 E4
Missoula Montana, USA 22 B2
Missouri *State* USA 23 G5
Missouri *River* USA 23 G4
Mistassini, Lake *Lake* Canada 18 D3
Mitau *see* Jelgava
Mitchell South Dakota, USA 23 E3
Mitilíni Greece 84 D4
Mito Japan 110 D4
Miyazaki Japan 111 B6
Mjøsa *Lake* Norway 65 B5
Mljet *Island* Croatia 81 C5
Mmabatho South Africa 58 D4
Mo Norway 64 C3
Mobile Alabama, USA 28 C3
Moçambique Mozambique 59 F2
Mocímboa da Praia Mozambique 59 F2
Mocoa Colombia 38 B4
Mocuba Mozambique 59 F2
Modena Italy 76 B3
Modesto California, USA 25 B6
Mödling Austria 75 E6
Modohn *see* Madona
Modriča Bosnia & Herzegovina 80 C3
Mogadiscio *see* Mogadishu
Mogadishu *Capital of* Somalia *Som.* Muqdisho, *It.* Mogadiscio 55 D6
Mogilëv *see* Mahilyow
Mohéli *Island* Comoros 59 F2
Mohns Ridge *Undersea feature* Greenland Sea 63 F3
Mojave California, USA 25 C7
Mojave Desert *Desert* W USA 25 D7
Moldavia *Country* E Europe *var.* Moldova 88
Molde Norway 65 A5
Moldova *see* Moldavia
Molodechno *see* Maladzyechna
Molodeczno *see* Maladzyechna
Molotov *see* Perm'
Moluccas *see* Maluku
Molucca Sea *see* Maluku, Laut
Mombasa Kenya 55 C7
Monaco *Country* W Europe 71 E6
Monastir Tunisia 51 F1
Monclova Mexico 31 E2
Moncton Canada 19 F4
Mongo Chad 56 C3
Mongolia *Country* NE Asia 106-107
Monroe Louisiana, USA 28 B2
Monrovia *Capital of* Liberia 52 C5
Mons Belgium 67 B6
Montague Seamount *Undersea feature* Atlantic Ocean 43 H1
Montana *State* USA 22 C2
Montauban France 71 B6
Mont Blanc *Peak* France/Italy 60 D4
Mont-de-Marsan France 70 B6
Monte-Carlo Monaco 71 E6
Montecristi Dominican Republic 35 E3
Montego Bay Jamaica 34 C3
Montenegro *Republic* Yugoslavia 81 D5
Monterey California, USA 25 B6
Montería Colombia 38 B2
Montero Bolivia 40 D4
Monterrey Mexico 31 E2
Montes Claros Brazil 41 G4
Montevideo *Capital of* Uruguay 42 C5
Montgomery Alabama, USA 28 D3
Montpelier Vermont, USA 21 F2
Montpellier France 71 C6

Montréal Canada 19 E4
Montreux Switzerland 75 A5
Montserrat *External territory* UK, West Indies 35
Monument Valley *Valley* SW USA 26 C1
Monywa Burma 118 A3
Monza Italy 76 B2
Moora Australia 129 B6
Moorhead Minnesota, USA 23 E2
Moosonee Canada 18 C3
Mopti Mali 53 E3
Morava *River* C Europe 79 B6 80 E4
Moravská Ostrava *see* Ostrava
Morawhanna Guyana 39 F2
Moray Firth *Inlet* Scotland, UK 68 C3
Moree Australia 130 C2
Morehead City North Carolina, USA 29 G2
Morelia Mexico 31 E4
Morena, Sierra *Mountain range* Spain 72 D4
Morghāb *River* Afghanistan / Turkmenistan 102 D4
Morioka Japan 110 D3
Morocco *Country* N Africa 50
Morogoro Tanzania 55 C7
Morondava Madagascar 59 F3
Moroni *Capital of* Comoros 59 F2
Morotai, Pulau *Island* Indonesia 121 F3
Moscow *Capital of* Russian Federation *Rus.* Moskva 90 B4 94 B2
Mosel *River* W Europe *Fr.* Moselle 75 A5
Moselle *River* W Europe *Ger.* Mosel 67 E8 70 E4
Moshi Tanzania 55 C7
Moskva *see* Moscow
Mosquito Coast *Coastal region* Nicaragua 33 E3
Moss Norway 65 B6
Mossendjo Congo 57 B6
Mossoró Brazil 41 H2
Most Czech Republic *Ger.* Brüx 78 A4
Mostaganem Algeria 50 D1
Mostar Bosnia & Herzegovina 80 C4
Mosul *see* Al Mawşil
Motril Spain 73 E5
Moulins France 70 C4
Moulmein Burma 118 B4
Moundou Chad 56 C4
Mount Gambier Australia 130 A4
Mount Isa Australia 126 A5 130 A1
Mount Vernon Illinois, USA 20 B5
Mouscron Belgium 67 A6
Moyale Kenya 55 C5
Moyobamba Peru 40 B2
Mozambique *Country* SE Africa 59
Mozambique Channel *Sea Feature* Indian Ocean 59 F3
Mozambique Ridge *Undersea feature* Indian Ocean 49 D8
Mozyr' *see* Mazyr
Mpika Zambia 59 E2
Mtwara Tanzania 55 C8
Muang Khammouan Laos 118 D4
Muang Không Laos 119 D5
Muang Xaignabouri Laos 118 C3
Mufulira Zambia 58 D2
Mugla Turkey 96 A4
Mukacheve Ukraine 88 B2
Mulhacen *Peak* Spain 60 C5
Mulhouse France 70 E4
Mull *Island* Scotland, UK 68 B3
Muller, Pegunungan *Mountains* Indonesia 120 D4
Multān Pakistan 114 C2
Mumbai *see* Bombay
Muna, Pulau *Island* Indonesia 121 E4
München Germany *Eng.* Munich 75 C6
Muncie Indiana, USA 20 C4
Munich *see* München
Münster Germany 74 A4
Muonio *River* Finland / Sweden 64 D3
Muqdisho *see* Mogadishu
Mur *River* C Europe 75 D7
Murcia *Region* Spain 73 F4
Mures *River* Hungary / Romania 79 D7
Murfreesboro Tennessee, USA 28 D1
Murgab Tajikistan 103 F3
Murgab *River* Turkmenistan *var.* Murghab 102 C3
Murghab *see* Murgab
Müritz *Lake* Germany 74 D3
Murmansk Russian Federation 90 C2 94 C1
Murray *River* Australia 130 A3
Murrumbidgee *River* Australia 130 B3
Murska Sobota Slovenia 80 B2
Murzuq Libya 51 F3
Muş Turkey 97 F3
Muscat *Capital of* Oman *Ar.* Masqaţ 101 E5
Musgrave Ranges *Mountain range* Australia 129 D5
Mwanza Tanzania 55 B6
Mwene-Ditu Congo (Zaire) 57 D7
Mweru, Lake *Lake* Congo (Zaire) / Zambia 57 D7
Myanmar *see* Burma
Mykolayiv Ukraine *Rus.* Nikolayev 89 E4
Mysore India 116 D2
Mzuzu Malawi 59 E2

N

Naberezhnyye Chelny Russian Federation *prev.* Brezhnev 91 C5
Nacala Mozambique 59 F2
Næstved Denmark 65 D8
Naga Philippines 120 E1
Nagano Japan 110 C4
Nagasaki Japan 111 A6
Nāgercoil India 116 D3
Nagorno-Karabakh *Region* Azerbaijan 97 G2
Nagoya Japan 111 C5
Nāgpur India 114 D4
Nagqu China 106 C5
Nagykanizsa Hungary *Ger.* Grosskanizsa 79 C7
Nagyszombat *see* Trnava
Naha Japan 111 A8
Nain Canada 19 N2

Nairobi *Capital of* Kenya 55 C6
Najaf *see* An Najaf
Najrān Saudi Arabia 101 B6
Nakamura Japan 111 B6
Nakhichevan' *see* Naxçıvan
Nakhodka Russian Federation 94 C3
Nakhon Ratchasima Thailand 119 C5
Nakhon Sawan Thailand 119 C5
Nakhon Si Thammarat Thailand 119 C6
Nakina Canada 18 B3
Nakskov Denmark 65 D8
Nakuru Kenya 55 C6
Nal'chik Russian Federation 91 A7 94 A4
Namangan Uzbekistan 103 E2
Nam Đinh Vietnam 118 D3
Namib Desert *Desert* Namibia 58 B3
Namibe Angola 58 B2
Namibia *Country* southern Africa 58
Nampa Idaho, USA 24 D3
Namp'o North Korea 108 E4
Nampula Mozambique 59 F2
Namur Belgium 67 C6
Nanchang China 109 C6
Nancy France 70 D3
Nāndad India 114 D5 116 D1
Nanjing China 109 D5
Nanning China 109 B7
Nanortalik Greenland 62 C4
Nantes France 70 B4
Napier New Zealand 131 H2
Naples *see* Napoli
Napo *River* Ecuador/Peru 40 B2
Napoli Italy *Eng.* Naples 77 D5
Narbonne France 71 C6
Nares Plain *Undersea feature* Atlantic Ocean 15 F4
Nares Strait *Sea feature* Canada/Greenland 62 A2
Narew *River* Poland 78 E3
Narmada *River* India 114 D4
Narsaq Greenland 62 C4
Narsaq Kujalleq Greenland 62 C4
Narva Estonia 86 E2
Narva *River* Estonia/Russian Federation 86 E2
Narva Bay *Sea feature* Gulf of Finland *Est.* Narva Laht, *Rus.* Narvskiy Zaliv 86 E2
Narva Laht *see* Narva Bay
Narvik Norway 64 C3
Narvskiy Zaliv *see* Narva Bay
Naryn Kyrgyzstan 103 G2
Naryn *River* Kyrgyzstan/Uzbekistan 103 F2
Nāshik India 114 C5
Nashville Tennessee, USA 28 D1
Nâṣir, Buḥeiret *Reservoir* Egypt 55 B2
Nasiriya *see* An Nāṣirīyah
Nassau *Capital of* Bahamas 34 C1
Natal Brazil 41 H3
Natitingou Benin 53 F4
Natuna, Kepulauan *Island group* Indonesia 120 C3
Nauru *Country* Pacific Ocean 126 D3
Navapolatsk Belorussia *Rus.* Novopolotsk 87 D5
Navassa Island *External territory* USA, West Indies 34 D3
Navoi Uzbekistan *Uzb.* Nawoly 102 D2
Nawābshāh Pakistan 114 B3
Nawoly *see* Navoi
Naxçıvan Azerbaijan *Rus.* Nakhichevan' 97 G3
Náxos *Island* Greece 85 D6
Nazareth *see* Nazerat
Nazca Peru 40 B4
Nazerat Israel *Eng.* Nazareth 99 A5
Nazrēt Ethiopia 55 C5
Nazwá Oman 101 E5
N'Dalatando Angola 58 B1
Ndélé Central African Republic 56 C4
N'Djamena *Capital of* Chad 56 B3
Ndola Zambia 58 D2
Nebitdag Turkmenistan 102 B2
Nebraska *State* USA 22-23 E3
Neches *River* S USA 27 H3
Neckar *River* Germany 75 B6
Necochea Argentina 45 D5
Neftezavodsk *see* Seydi
Negēlē Ethiopia 55 C5
Negev *see* HaNegev
Negro, Río *River* Argentina 45 C5
Negro, Rio *River* Brazil/Uruguay 40 D2
Negro, Rio *River* N South America 38 D3
Negros *Island* Philippines 121 E2
Neiva Colombia 38 B3
Nellore India 117 E2
Nelson New Zealand 131 G3
Neman *River* NE Europe *Bel.* Nyoman, *Lith.* Nemunas, *Ger.* Memel, *Pol.* Niemen 86 B4
Nemunas *see* Neman
Nemuro Japan 110 E2
Nepal *Country* S Asia 115
Nepalganj Nepal 115 E3
Neretva *River* Bosnia & Herzegovina 80 C4
Neris *River* Belorussia/Lithuania *Bel.* Viliya, *Pol.* Wilja 86 C4
Ness, Loch *Lake* Scotland, UK 68 C3
Netherlands *Country* W Europe *var.* Holland 66-67
Netherlands Antilles *External territory* Netherlands, West Indies *prev.* Dutch West Indies 36 C1
Netze *see* Noteć
Neubrandenburg Germany 74 D3
Neuchâtel, Lac de *Lake* Switzerland 75 A7
Neuhäusl *see* Nové Zámky
Neumünster Germany 74 B2
Neuquén Argentina 45 C5
Neusiedler See *Lake* Austria/Hungary 75 E7
Neusohl *see* Banská Bystrica
Neutra *see* Nitra
Nevada *State* USA 24-25
Nevel' Russian Federation 90 A4
Nevers France 70 C4
Nevşehir Turkey 96 D3
New Amsterdam Guyana 39 G2
Newark New Jersey, USA 21 F3
New Britain *Island* Papua New Guinea 126 C3

New Brunswick *Province* Canada 19 F4
New Caledonia *External territory* France, Pacific Ocean 122 C4
Newcastle Australia 130 C3
Newcastle upon Tyne England, UK 68 D4
New Delhi *Capital of* India 114 D3
Newfoundland *Province* Canada 19 G2
Newfoundland *Island* Canada 19 H3
Newfoundland Basin *Undersea feature* Atlantic Ocean 46 B3
New Georgia *Island* Solomon Is 126 C3
New Guinea *Island* Pacific Ocean 126 B3
New Hampshire *State* USA 21 G2
New Haven Connecticut, USA 21 G3
New Ireland *Island* Papua New Guinea 126 C3
New Jersey *State* USA 21 F4
Newman Australia 128 B4
New Mexico *State* USA 26-27 D2
New Orleans Louisiana, USA 28 C3
New Plymouth New Zealand 131 G2
Newport Oregon, USA 24 A3
Newport News Virginia, USA 21 F5
New Providence *Island* Bahamas 34 C1
Newry Northern Ireland, UK 69 B5
New Siberian Islands *see* Novosibirskiye Ostrova
New Wales *State* Australia 130 B3
New York *State* USA 21 F3
New York New York, USA 21 F3
New Zealand *Country* Pacific Ocean 131
Neyshābūr Iran 100 D3
Ngaoundéré Cameroon 56 B4
N'Giva Angola 58 B2
N'Guigmi Niger 53 H3
Nha Trang Vietnam 119 E5
Niagara Falls *Waterfall* Canada/USA 18 D5 21 E3
Niamey *Capital of* Niger 53 F3
Niangay, Lac *Lake* Mali 52 E3
Nicaragua *Country* Central America 32-33
Nicaragua, Lago de *Lake* Nicaragua 32 D3
Nice France 71 E6
Nicobar Islands *Island group* India 117 H3
Nicosia *Capital of* Cyprus *var.* Lefkosia, *Turk.* Lefkoşa 96 C5
Nicoya, Golfo de *Sea feature* Costa Rica 32 D4
Nicoya, Península de *Peninsula* Costa Rica 32 D4
Niemen *see* Neman
Nieuw Amsterdam Surinam 39 H2
Niğde Turkey 96 D4
Niger *Country* W Africa 53
Niger *River* W Africa 52-53 D3
Niger Delta *Wetlands* Nigeria 48 B4
Nigeria *Country* W Africa 53
Niigata Japan 110 C4
Nijmegen Netherlands 66 D4
Nikolayev *see* Mykolayiv
Nikopol' Ukraine 89 F3
Nile *River* N Africa 54 B3
Nile Delta *Wetlands* Egypt 48 D2
Nîmes France 71 C6
Ninetyeast Ridge *Undersea feature* Indian Ocean 112 C4 117 G5
Ningbo China 109 D6
Ningxia *Autonomous region* China 108-109 B4
Nioro Mali 52 D3
Nipigon, Lake *Lake* Canada 18 B4
Niš Yugoslavia 80 E4
Nitra Slovakia *Ger.* Neutra, *Hung.* Nyitra 79 C6
Nitra *River* Slovakia *Ger.* Neutra, *Hung.* Nyitra 79 C6
Niue *External territory* New Zealand, Pacific Ocean 122 D4 127 F4
Nizāmābād India 114 D5 116 D1
Nizhnevartovsk Russian Federation 94 D3
Nizhniy Novgorod Russian Federation *prev.* Gor'kiy 91 C5 94 B3
Nkhotakota Malawi 59 E2
Nkongsamba Cameroon 56 B4
Nordaustlandet *Island* Svalbard 63 H2
Norfolk Virginia, USA 21 F5
Norfolk Island *External territory* Australia, Pacific Ocean 125 E3
Nori'lsk Russian Federation 94 D3
Norman Oklahoma, USA 26 F2
Normandie *Region* France *Eng.* Normandy 70 B3
Normandy *see* Normandie
Normantown Australia 126 B4
Norrköping Sweden 65 C6
Norseman Australia 129 C6
North Albanian Alps *Mountains* Albania/Yugoslavia 81 D5
North America 14-15
North American Basin *Undersea feature* Atlantic Ocean 46 B4
North Andaman *Island* India 117 G2
North Atlantic Ocean 62-63
North Australian Basin *Undersea feature* Indian Ocean 124 A2 128 A2
North Bay Canada 18 D4
North Cape *Coastal feature* New Zealand 131 F1
North Cape *Coastal feature* Norway 64 D2
North Carolina *State* USA 29 F1
North Dakota *State* USA 22-23 D2
Northern Cook Islands *Islands* Cook Islands 127 G4
Northern Cyprus, Turkish Republic of *Disputed region* Cyprus 96 C5
Northern Dvina *River* Russian Federation *see* Severnaya Dvina 61 G2
Northern Ireland *Province* UK 68-69
Northern Marianas *External territory* USA, Pacific Ocean 122 C2

Northern Sporades *see* Voreioi Sporades
Northern Territory *Territory* Australia 126 A4 128 E3
North European Plain *Region* N Europe 60-61 E3 92 B2
North Frisian Islands *Islands* Denmark / Germany 74 B2
North Island *Island* New Zealand 131 G2
North Korea *Country* E Asia 108
North Las Vegas Nevada, USA 25 D7
North Minch *Sea feature* Scotland, UK 68 C2
North Platte Nebraska, USA 23 E4
North Platte *River* C USA 22 D3
North Pole *Ice feature* Arctic Ocean 12 C4
North Sea Atlantic Ocean 68 E2
North Uist *Island* Scotland, UK 68 B3
North West Cape *Coastal feature* Australia 128 A4
Northwest Territories *Territory* Canada 17 F3
Norway *Country* N Europe 64-65
Norwegian Basin *Undersea feature* Atlantic Ocean 60 C1
Norwegian Sea Arctic Ocean 13 C8
Norwich England, UK 69 E6
Noteć *River* Poland *Ger.* Netze 78 C3
Nottingham England, UK 69 D6
Nottingham Island *Island* Hudson Strait 18 D1
Nouâdhibou Mauritania 52 B2
Nouâdhibou, Râs *Coastal feature* Mauritania 52 B2
Nouakchott *Capital of* Mauritania 52 B2
Nouméa *Capital of* New Caledonia 126 D5
Nova Gorica Slovenia 80 A2
Nova Gradiška Croatia 80 B3
Nova Iguaçu Brazil 41 F5 43 F2
Nova Kakhovka Ukraine 89 F4
Novara Italy 76 A2
Nova Scotia *Province* Canada 19 G4
Novaya Zemlya *Islands* Russian Federation 90 E2 94 D2
Nové Zámky Slovakia *Ger.* Neuhäusl, *Hung.* Érsekújvár 79 C6
Novgorod Russian Federation 90 B4 94 B2
Novi Sad Yugoslavia 80 D3
Novokuznetsk Russian Federation *prev.* Stalinsk 94 D4
Novo Mesto Slovenia 80 A2
Novopolotsk *see* Navapolatsk
Novosibirsk Russian Federation 94 D4
Novosibirskiye Ostrova *Islands* Russian Federation *Eng.* New Siberian Islands 12 D2 93 F1 95 F2
Novo Urgench *see* Urgench
Novyy Margilan *see* Fergana
Nsanje Malawi 59 E2
Nubian Desert *Desert* Sudan 54 B3
Nuevo Laredo Mexico 31 E2
Nuku'alofa *Capital of* Tonga 127 F5
Nukus Uzbekistan 102 C1
Nullarbor Plain *Region* Australia 129 D6
Nunivak Island *Island* Alaska, USA 16 B2
Nuoro Italy 77 A5
Nurek Tajikistan 103 E3
Nuremberg *see* Nürnberg
Nürnberg Germany *Eng.* Nuremberg 75 C6
Nuugaatsiaq Greenland 62 B3
Nuuk Greenland *var.* Godthåb 62 B4
Nyala Sudan 54 A4
Nyasa, Lake *Lake* E Africa 49 D5
Nyeboe Land *Region* Greenland 62 B2
Nyeri Kenya 55 C6
Nyíregyháza Hungary 79 E6
Nyitra *see* Nitra
Nykøbing-Falster Denmark 65 D8
Nyköping Sweden 65 C6
Nyoman *see* Neman
Nzérékoré Guinea 52 D4

O

Oakland California, USA 25 B6
Oakley Kansas, USA 23 E4
Oaxaca Mexico 31 F5
Ob' *River* Russian Federation 94 C3
Oban Scotland, UK 68 D3
Oberpahlen *see* Põltsamaa
Obihiro Japan 110 D2
Obo Central African Republic 56 D4
Oceania 124-125
Ocean Island *see* Banaba
Oceanside California, USA 25 C8
Ochamchira *see* Och'amch'ire
Och'amch'ire Georgia *Rus.* Ochamchira 97 E1
Oconee *River* SE USA 29 E3
Ödenburg *see* Sopron
Odense Denmark 65 D7
Oder *River* C Europe 74 E4 78 C4
Odesa Ukraine *Rus.* Odessa 89 E4
Odessa see Odesa
Odessa Texas, USA 27 E3
Odienné Ivory Coast 52 D4
Oesel *see* Saaremaa
Ofanto *River* Italy 77 D5
Offenbach Germany 75 B5
Ogaden *Plateau* Ethiopia 55 D5
Ogallala Nebraska, USA 22 D4
Ogbomosho Nigeria 53 F4
Ogden Utah, USA 22 B3
Ogdensburg New York, USA 21 F2
Oger *see* Ogre
Ogre Latvia *Ger.* Oger 86 C3
Ogulin Croatia 80 A3
Ohio *State* USA 20 D4
Ohio *River* N USA 20 B5
Ohrid Macedonia 81 D6
Ohrid, Lake *Lake* Albania / Macedonia 81 D6
Ohře *River* Czech Republic / Germany *Ger.* Eger 79 A5
Oil City Pennsylvania, USA 21 E3
Ōita Japan 111 B6

Oka *River* Russian Federation 95 E4
Okahandja Namibia 58 C3
Okavango *River var.* Cubango southern Africa 58 C2
Okavango Delta *Wetland* Botswana 58 C3
Okayama Japan 111 B5
Okazaki Japan 111 C5
Okeechobee, Lake *Lake* Florida, USA 29 F4
Okhotsk Russian Federation 95 G3
Okhotsk, Sea of Pacific Ocean 122 C1
Okinawa *Island* Japan 111 A8
Oki-shotō *Island group* Japan 111 B5
Oklahoma *State* USA 27 F1
Oklahoma City Oklahoma, USA 27 F2
Okushiri-tō *Island* Japan 110 C2
Okāra Pakistan 114 C2
Öland *Island* Sweden 65 C7
Olavarría Argentina 44 D4
Olbia Italy 77 A5
Oldenburg Germany 74 B3
Oleksandriya Ukraine *Rus.* Aleksandriya 89 E3
Olenëk Russian Federation 95 E3
Olhão Portugal 72 C5
Olita *see* Alytus
Olmaliq *see* Almalyk
Olmütz *see* Olomouc
Olomouc Czech Republic *Ger.* Olmütz 79 C5
Olsztyn Poland *Ger.* Allenstein 78 D2
Olt *River* Romania 88 B5
Olten Switzerland 75 B7
Olympia Washington, USA 24 B2
Omaha Nebraska, USA 23 F4
Oman *Country* SW Asia 101 D6
Oman, Gulf of *Sea feature* Indian Ocean 112 B2
Omdurman Sudan 54 B4
Omsk Russian Federation 94 C4
Ondangwa Namibia 58 C3
Onega *River* Russian Federation 90 B4
Onega, Lake *see* Onezhskoye Ozero
Onezhskoye Ozero *Lake* Russian Federation *Eng.* Lake Onega 90 B3
Ongole India 117 E2
Onitsha Nigeria 53 G5
Ontario *Province* Canada 18 B3
Ontario, Lake *Lake* Canada / USA 15 F3
Oostende Belgium *Eng.* Ostend 67 A5
Oosterschelde *Inlet* Netherlands 66 B4
Opole Poland *Ger.* Oppeln 78 C4
Oporto *see* Porto
Oppeln *see* Opole
Oradea Romania 88 B3
Oran Algeria 50 D1
Orange Australia 130 C3
Orange River *River* southern Africa 58 C4
Oranjestad Netherlands Antilles 35 E5
Ord *River* Australia 128 D3
Ordu Turkey 96 D2
Ordzhonikidze *see* Vladikavkaz
Örebro Sweden 65 C6
Oregon *State* USA 24
Orël Russian Federation 81 A5
Orem Utah, USA 22 B4
Orenburg Russian Federation 91 C6 94 B4
Orense *see* Ourense
Orestiáda Greece 84 D3
Orhon *River* Mongolia 107 E2
Orinoco *River* Colombia / Venezuela 39 E3
Orissa *State* India 115 E5
Oristano Italy 77 A5
Orizaba, Pico de *see* Citlaltépetl
Orkney *Islands* Scotland, UK 68 C2
Orlando Florida, USA 29 E4
Orléans France 70 C4
Ormsö *see* Vormsi
Örnsköldsvik Sweden 65 C5
Orontes *River* SW Asia 98 B3
Orosirá Rodópis *see* Rhodope Mountains
Orsha Belorussia 87 E5
Orsk Russian Federation 91 D6 94 B4
Oruro Bolivia 40 C4
Ōsaka Japan 111 C5
Ösel *see* Saaremaa
Osh Kyrgyzstan 103 F2
Oshawa Canada 18 D5
Oshkosh Wisconsin, USA 20 B2
Osijek Croatia 80 C3
Oslo *Capital of* Norway 65 B6
Osmaniye Turkey 96 D4
Osnabrück Germany 74 B4
Osorno Chile 45 B5
Oss Netherlands 66 D4
Ossora Russian Federation 95 H2
Ostend *see* Oostende
Östersund Sweden 65 C5
Ostfriesische Inseln *Islands* Germany *Eng.* East Frisian Islands 74 A3
Ostrava Czech Republic *Ger.* Mährisch-Ostrau, *prev.* Moravská Ostrava 79 C5
Ostrołęka Poland 78 D3
Ostrowiec Świętokrzyski Poland 78 D4
Ōsumi-shotō *Island group* Japan 111 A7
Otaru Japan 110 D2
Otra *River* Norway 65 A6
Otranto Italy 77 E5
Otranto, Strait of *Sea feature* Albania / Italy 81 C6
Ottawa *Capital of* Canada 18 D5
Ottawa *River* Canada 18 D4
Ou *River* Laos 118 C3
Ouachita *River* SE USA 28 B2
Ouagadougou *Capital of* Burkina 53 E4
Ouahigouya Burkina 53 E3
Ouargla Algeria 51 E2
Oudtshoorn South Africa 58 C5
Ouémé *River* Benin 53 F4
Ouessant, Île d' *Island* France 70 A3
Ouésso Congo 57 C5
Oujda Morocco 50 D2
Oulu Finland 64 D4
Oulu *River* Finland 64 D4
Oulujärvi *Lake* Finland 64 E4
Ounas *River* Finland 64 D3

Our *River* W Europe 67 E7
Ourense Spain *Cast.* Orense 72 C2
Ourinhos Brazil 42 D2
Ourthe *River* Belgium 67 D6
Outer Hebrides *Island group* UK *var.* Western Isles 68 B2
Outer Islands *Island group* Seychelles 59 H1
Overflakkee *Island* Netherlands 66 B4
Oviedo Spain 72 D1
Owando Congo 57 C6
Oxford England, UK 69 D6
Oxnard California, USA 27 C7
Oyem Gabon 57 B5
Oyo Nigeria 53 F4
Ózd Hungary 79 D6

P

Paamiut Greenland 62 B4
Pa-an Burma 118 B4
Pachuca Mexico 31 E4
Pacific-Antarctic Ridge *Undersea feature* Pacific Ocean 123 E5
Pacific Ocean 122-123
Padang Indonesia 120 B4
Paderborn Germany 74 B4
Padova Italy *Eng.* Padua 76 C2
Padre Island *Island* Texas, USA 27 G5
Padua *see* Padova
Paducah Kentucky, USA 20 B5
Pafos *see* Paphos
Pag *Island* Croatia 80 A3
Pago Pago *Capital of* American Samoa 126 F4
Paide Estonia *Ger.* Weissenstein 86 D2
Painted Desert *Desert* SW USA 26 C1
País Vasco *see* Basque Provinces
Pakambaru Indonesia 120 B4
Pakistan *Country* S Asia 114
Pakokku Burma 118 A3
Palagruza *Island* Croatia 76 E4
Palau *Country* Pacific Ocean *var.* Belau 122
Palawan *Island* Philippines 121 E2
Paldiski Estonia *prev.* Baltiski, *Eng.* Baltic Port, *Ger.* Baltischport 86 C2
Palembang Indonesia 120 B4
Palencia Spain 72 D2
Palermo Italy 77 C6
Palikir *Capital of* Micronesia 126 C2
Palk Strait *Sea feature* India/Sri Lanka 117 E3
Palm Springs California, USA 25 D8
Palma Spain 73 G3
Palmas Brazil 41 F3
Palmerston North New Zealand 131 G3
Palmyra *see* Tudmur
Palmyra Atoll *External territory* USA, Pacific Ocean 127 G2
Palu Indonesia 120 E4
Pamir *River* Afghanistan/Tajikistan 103 F3
Pamirs *Mountains* Tajikistan 103 F3
Pampa Texas, USA 27 E2
Pampas *Region* South America 37 C6
Pamplona Spain 73 F1
Pānāji India 116 C2
Panama *Country* Central America 33
Panamá, Golfo de *Sea feature* Panama 33 F5
Panama Canal *Canal* Panama 46 A4
Panama City *Capital of* Panama 33 F5
Panama City Florida, USA 28 D3
Panay *Island* Philippines 121 E2
Panćevo Yugoslavia 80 D3
Panevėžys Lithuania 86 C4
Pangkalpinang Indonesia 120 C4
Panj *River* Afghanistan/Tajikistan *Rus.* Pyandzh 103 E3
Pantanal *Region* Brazil 36 C4
Pantelleria *Island* Italy 77 B7
Pánuco *River* Mexico 30 E4
Panzhihua China 109 A6
Papeete *Capital of* French Polynesia 127 H4
Paphos Cyprus *var.* Pafos 96 B5
Papua New Guinea *Country* Pacific Ocean 122
Paragua *River* Bolivia/Venezuela 39 E3
Paraguay *Country* South America 42
Paraguay *River* C South America 36 C4
Parakou Benin 53 F4
Paramaribo *Capital of* Surinam 39 H2
Paraná Argentina 44 D4
Paraná *River* C South America 37 C5
Paranaíba Brazil 41 G2
Pardubice Czech Republic *Ger.* Pardubitz 79 B5
Pardubitz *see* Pardubice
Parepare Indonesia 120 E4
Paris *Capital of* France 70 C3
Paris Texas, USA 27 G2
Parkhar Tajikistan 103 E3
Parma Italy 76 B2
Pärnu Estonia *Rus.* Pyarnu, *prev.* Pernov, *Ger.* Pernau 86 C2
Páros *Island* Greece 85 C6
Parry Islands *Islands* Canada 17 F2
Pasadena California, USA 25 C7
Pasadena Texas, USA 27 G4
Passo Fundo Brazil 42 D3
Pasto Colombia 38 B4
Patagonia *Region* S South America 45 C6
Patna India 115 F3
Patos, Lagoa dos *Lagoon* Brazil 42 D4
Pátra Greece 85 B5
Pattani Thailand 119 C7
Pattaya Thailand 119 C5
Patuca *River* Honduras 32 D2
Pau France 71 B6
Pavlodar Kazakhstan 94 C4
Pavlohrad Ukraine *Rus.* Pavlograd 89 F3
Paysandú Uruguay 42 B4
Pazardzhik Bulgaria *prev.* Tatar Pazardzhik 84 C2
Pearl *River* SE USA 28 C3
Peary Land *Region* Greenland 62 D1
Peć Yugoslavia 81 D5

Pechora *River* Russian Federation 90 D3
Pecos Texas, USA 27 E3
Pecos *River* SW USA 26 D2
Pécs Hungary *Ger.* Fünfkirchen 79 C7
Pegu Burma 118 B4
Peipsi Järv *see* Peipus, Lake
Peipus, Lake *Lake* Estonia/Russian Federation *Est.* Peipsi Järv, *Rus.* Chudskoye Ozero 86 D2
Peiraías Greece *var.* Piraiévs, *Eng.* Piraeus 83 F3 85 C5
Peking *see* Beijing
Pelagie, Isola *Island* Italy 77 B8
Peloponnese *see* Pelopónnisos
Pelopónnisos *Peninsula* Greece *Eng.* Peloponnese 85 B6
Pelotas Brazil 42 C4
Pelotas *River* Brazil 42 D3
Pematangsiantar Indonesia 120 A3
Pemba *Island* Tanzania 49 E5
Pendleton Oregon, USA 24 C2
Pennines *Hills* England, UK 68 D4
Pennsylvania *State* USA 20-21
Penong Australia 129 D6
Penonomé Panama 33 F5
Pensacola Florida, USA 28 D3
Penza Russian Federation 91 B5
Penzance England, UK 69 C7
Peoria Illinois, USA 20 B4
Pereira Colombia 38 B3
Périgueux France 71 B5
Perm' Russian Federation *prev.* Molotov 91 D5 94 B3
Pernau *see* Pärnu
Pernik Bulgaria *prev.* Dimitrovo 84 B2
Pernov *see* Pärnu
Perpignan France 71 C6
Persian Gulf *Sea feature* Arabian Sea *var.* The Gulf 112 B2
Perth Australia 129 B6
Perth Scotland, UK 68 C3
Perth Basin *Undersea feature* Indian Ocean 124 A3
Peru C South America 40
Peru Basin *Undersea feature* Pacific Ocean 123 G4
Peru-Chile Trench *Undersea feature* Pacific Ocean 123 G4
Perugia Italy 76 C4
Pescara Italy 76 D4
Peshāwar Pakistan 114 C1
Petah Tiqwa Israel 99 A5
Peterborough England, UK 69 E6
Peterborough Canada 18 D5
Peter the First Island *Island* Antarctica 132 A4
Petra Jordan 99 B6
Petrich Bulgaria 84 B3
Petroaleksandrovsk *see* Turtkul'
Petrograd *see* St Petersburg
Petropavlovsk Russian Federation 94 C4
Petropavlovsk-Kamchatskiy Russian Federation 95 H3
Petrozavodsk Russian Federation 90 B3
Pevek Russian Federation 95 G1
Pforzheim Germany 75 B6
Phangan, Ko *Island* Thailand 119 C6
Philadelphia Pennsylvania, USA 21 F4
Philippines *Country* Asia 121
Philippine Sea Pacific Ocean 121 F1
Philippopolis *see* Plovdiv
Phnom Penh *Capital of* Cambodia 119 D6
Phoenix Arizona, USA 26 B2
Phoenix Islands *Island group* Kiribati 127 F3
Phôngsali Laos 118 C3
Phuket Thailand 119 B7
Phuket, Ko *Island* Thailand 119 B7
Phumĭ Sâmraông Cambodia 119 D5
Piacenza Italy 76 B2
Pianosa *Island* Italy 76 D4
Piatra-Neamţ Romania 88 C3
Piave *River* Italy 76 C2
Pielinen *Lake* Finland 64 E4
Pierre South Dakota, USA 23 E3
Piešťany Slovakia *Ger.* Pistyan, *Hung.* Pöstyén 79 C6
Pietermaritzburg South Africa 58 D4
Pihkva Järv *see* Pskov, Lake
Piła Poland *Ger.* Schneidemühl 78 C3
Pilar Paraguay 42 B3
Pilchilemu Chile 44 B4
Pilcomayo *River* C South America 42 B2 44 D2
Pillau *see* Baltiysk
Pilsen *see* Plzeň
Pinang, Pulau *Island* Malaysia 120 B3
Pinar del Río Cuba 34 A2
Píndos *Mountain range* Greece *Eng.* Pindus Mountains 61 E5 84 A4
Pindus Mountains *see* Pindos
Pine Bluff Arkansas, USA 28 B2
Pinega *River* Russian Federation 90 C3
Pineiós *River* Greece 84 B4
Pine Island Bay *Sea feature* Antarctica 132 B3
Ping, Mae Nam *River* Thailand 118 C4
Pingxiang China 109 B7
Pínnes, Ákra *Coastal feature* Greece 84 C4
Pinsk Belorussia *Pol.* Pińsk 87 B4
Piraeus *see* Peiraías
Piraiévs *see* Peiraías
Pisa Italy 76 B3
Pisco Peru 40 B4
Pishpek *see* Bishkek
Pistyan *see* Piešťany
Pitcairn Islands *External territory* UK, Pacific Ocean 123 E4
Piteå Sweden 64 D4
Piteşti Romania 88 C4
Pittsburgh Pennsylvania, USA 21 E4
Pituffik Greenland 62 A2
Piura Peru 40 A2
Pivdennyy Bug *River* Ukraine 89 E3
Plasencia Spain 72 D3
Plate *River* Argentina/Uruguay 42 B5 44 D4
Platte *River* C USA 23 E4
Plattensee *see* Balaton
Plenty, Bay of *Sea feature* New Zealand 131 H2
Pleven Bulgaria 84 C1
Płock Poland 78 D3

Ploieşti Romania 88 C4
Plovdiv Bulgaria *Gk.* Philippopolis 84 C2
Plungė Lithuania 86 B3
Plymouth *Capital of* Montserrat 35 G3
Plymouth England, UK 69 C7
Plzeň Czech Republic *Ger.* Pilsen 79 A5
Po *River* Italy 76 C2
Pobeda Peak *see* Pobedy
Pobedy *Peak* China/Kyrgzstan *var.* Pobeda Peak, *Chin.* Tomur Feng 92 D4
Pocatello Idaho, USA 24 E4
Po Delta *Wetland* Italy 76 C3
Podgorica Yugoslavia 81 C5
Pohjanmaa *Region* Finland 64 D4
Pohnpei Island *Island* Micronesia 126 C2
Poinsett, Cape *Coastal feature* Antarctica 133 H5
Pointe-Noire Congo 57 B6
Poitiers France 70 B4
Poland *Country* E Europe 78-79
Polatsk Belorussia 87 D5
Pol-e Khomrī Afghanistan 103 E4
Poltava Ukraine 89 F2
Poltoratsk *see* Ashgabat
Põltsamaa Estonia *Ger.* Oberpahlen 86 D2
Polynesia *Region* Pacific Ocean 125 G2 127 F4
Pomorie Bulgaria 84 E2
Ponca City Oklahoma, USA 27 G1
Pondicherry India 117 E2
Ponta Grossa Brazil 42 D2
Pontchartrain, Lake *Inlet* Louisiana, USA 28 C3
Pontevedra Spain 72 C2
Pontianak Indonesia 120 C4
Poona *see* Pune
Poopó, Lake *Lake* Bolivia 40 C5
Popayán Colombia 38 B3
Popocatépetl *Peak* Mexico 15 E5
Poprad Slovakia *Ger.* Deutschendorf 79 D5
Porbandar India 114 B4
Pori Finland 65 D5
Porsgrunn Norway 65 B6
Portalegre Portugal 72 C3
Portales New Mexico, USA 27 E2
Port Alice Canada 16 D5
Port Angeles Washington, USA 24 A1
Port Arthur Texas, USA 27 H4
Port Augusta Australia 129 E6 130 A3
Port-au-Prince *Capital of* Haiti 34 D3
Port Blair India 117 G2
Port-de-Paix Haiti 34 D3
Port Elizabeth South Africa 58 D5
Port-Gentil Gabon 57 A6
Port Harcourt Nigeria 53 G5
Port Hedland Australia 128 B3
Port Hope Simpson Canada 19 G3
Portland Maine, USA 21 G2
Portland Oregon, USA 24 B2
Port Lincoln Australia 129 E6 130 A3
Port Louis *Capital of* Mauritius 59 H3
Port Moresby *Capital of* Papua New Guinea 126 B3
Porto Portugal *Eng.* Oporto 72 C2
Port-of-Spain *Capital of* Trinidad & Tobago 35 G5
Porto-Novo *Capital of* Benin 53 F5
Porto Velho Brazil 40 D3
Portoviejo Ecuador 38 A4
Port Said Egypt 54 B1
Portsmouth England, UK 69 D7
Port Stanley *Capital of* Falkland Islands 45 D7
Port Sudan Sudan 54 C3
Portugal *Country* SW Europe 72
Port-Vila *Capital of* Vanuatu 126 D5
Porvenir Chile 45 B8
Posadas Argentina 44 E3
Posen *see* Poznań
Pöstyén *see* Piešťany
Potenza S Italy 77 D5
P'ot'i Georgia 97 F2
Potosí Bolivia 40 C5
Potsdam Germany 74 D4
Póvoa de Varzim Portugal 72 C2
Powder *River* N USA 22 C2
Powell, Lake *Lake* SW USA 22 B5 26 B1
Poyang Hu *Lake* China 109 C6
Poza Rica Mexico 31 F4
Poznań Poland *Ger.* Posen 78 C3
Pozo Colorado Paraguay 42 B2
Pozsony *see* Bratislava
Prag *see* Prague
Prague *Capital of* Czech Republic *Cz.* Praha, *Ger.* Prag 79 B5
Praha *see* Prague
Praia *Capital of* Cape Verde 52 A3
Prato Italy 76 B3
Pratt Kansas, USA 23 E5
Preschau *see* Prešov
Prescott Arizona, USA 26 B2
Presidente Prudente Brazil 42 D2
Prešov Slovakia *Ger.* Eperies, *var.* Preschau, *Hung.* Eperjes 79 D5
Prespa, Lake *Lake* SE Europe 81 D6 84 A3
Presque Isle Maine, USA 21 H1
Pressburg *see* Bratislava
Preston England, UK 69 D5
Pretoria *Capital of* South Africa 58 D4
Préveza Greece 84 A4
Prijedor Bosnia & Herzegovina 80 B3
Prilep Macedonia 81 E6
Prince Albert Canada 17 F5
Prince Edward Island *Province* Canada 19 F4
Prince George Canada 17 E5
Prince of Wales Island *Island* Canada 17 F2
Prince Patrick Island *Island* Canada 12 A3
Prince Rupert Canada 16 D4
Princess Elizabeth Land *Region* Antarctica 133 G3
Príncipe *Island* Sao Tome & Principe 57 A5
Pripet *River* Belorussia/Ukraine 87 B6 88 C1
Pripet Marshes *Wetlands* Belorussia/Ukraine 88 C1
Priština Yugoslavia 81 D5
Prizren Yugoslavia 81 D5

Prome Burma 118 A4
Prossnitz *see* Prostějov
Prostějov Czech Republic *Ger.* Prossnitz 79 C5
Provence *Region* France 71 D6
Providence Rhode Island, USA 21 G3
Providencia, Isla de *Island* Colombia 33 E3 34 B4
Provo Utah, USA 22 B4
Prudhoe Bay Alaska, USA 16 D2
Prydz Bay *Sea feature* Antarctica 133 G2
Przheval'sk *see* Karakol
Pskov Russian Federation 90 A4
Pskov, Lake *Lake* Estonia / Russian Federation *Est.* Pihkva Järv, *Rus.* Pskovskoye Ozero 86 D3
Pskovskoye Ozero *see* Pskov, Lake
Ptich' *see* Ptsich
Ptsich *River* Belorussia *Rus.* Ptich' 87 D6
Pucallpa Peru 40 B3
Puebla Mexico 31 F4
Puerto Aisén Chile 45 B6
Puerto Bahía Negra Paraguay 42 B1
Puerto Barrios Guatemala 32 C2
Puerto Busch Bolivia 40 D5
Puerto Carreño Colombia 38 D2
Puerto Cortés Honduras 32 C2
Puerto Deseado Argentina 45 C7
Puerto Maldonado Peru 40 C4
Puerto Montt Chile 45 B5
Puerto Natales Chile 45 B7
Puerto Plata Dominican Republic 35 E3
Puerto Princesa Philippines 120 E2
Puerto Rico *External territory* USA, West Indies 35 F3
Puerto Rico Trench *Undersea feature* Caribbean Sea 35 F3
Puerto Santa Cruz Argentina 45 C7
Puerto Suárez Bolivia 40 D5
Puerto Vallarta Mexico 30 D4
Puerto Williams Chile 45 C8
Pula Croatia 80 B2
Punakha Bhutan 115 G3
Punata Bolivia 40 C4
Pune India *prev.* Poona 114 C5 116 C1
Punjab *State* India 114 C2
Puno Peru 40 C4
Punta Arenas Chile *prev.* Magallanes 45 B8
Puntarenas Costa Rica 32 D4
Purmerend Netherlands 66 C3
Purus *River* Brazil / Peru 40 C3
Pusan South Korea 108 E4
Putumayo *River* NW South America 38 C4
Pyandzh *see* Panj
Pyapon Burma 118 B4
Pyarnu *see* Pärnu
Pyinmana Burma 118 B3
Pyongyang *Capital of* North Korea 108 E4
Pyramiden Svalbard 63 G2
Pyramid Lake *Lake* Nevada, USA 25 C5
Pyrenees *Mountain range* SW Europe 60 C5

Q

Qaanaaq Greenland *var.* Thule 62 A2
Qal'eh-ye Now Afghanistan 102 D4
Qamdo China 106 D5
Qandahār *see* Kandahār
Qaqortoq Greenland 62 C4
Qara Qum *see* Karakumy
Qarshi *see* Karshi
Qasigiannguit Greenland 62 B3
Qatar *Country* SW Asia 101 D5
Qattara Depression *see* Qaṭṭâra, Monkhafad el
Qaṭṭâra, Monkhafad el *Desert basin* Egypt *Eng.* Qattara Depression 48 C2 54 A1
Qena Egypt 54 B2
Qeqertarsuaq Greenland 62 B3
Qeqertarsuaq *Island* Greenland 62 B3
Qeqertarsuatsiaat Greenland 62 B4
Qilian Shan *Mountain range* China 106 D4
Qingdao China 108 D4
Qinghai Hu *Lake* China *var.* Koko Nor 106 D4
Qing-Zang Gaoyuan *Plateau* China *Eng.* Plateau of Tibet 104 C2 106 B4
Qin Ling *Mountains* China 109 B5
Qiqihar China 108 D3
Qizilqum *see* Kyzyl Kum
Qom Iran *var.* Kum 100 C3
Qondūz *River* Afghanistan 103 E4
Qondūz *see* Kunduz
Quba Azerbaijan *Rus.* Kuba 97 H2
Québec Canada 19 E4
Québec *Province* Canada 18 D3
Queen Charlotte Islands *Islands* Canada 16 D5
Queen Charlotte Sound *Sea feature* Canada 16 D5
Queen Elizabeth Islands *Islands* Canada 17 F1
Queen Maud Land *Region* Antarctica 133 E1
Queensland *State* Australia 126 B5 130 B1
Queenstown New Zealand 131 F4
Quelimane Mozambique 59 E3
Querétaro Mexico 31 E4
Quetta Pakistan 114 B2
Quezaltenango Guatemala 32 B2
Quibdó Colombia 38 B2
Quimper France 70 A3
Qui Nhơn Vietnam 119 E5
Quito *Capital of* Ecuador 38 A4
Qŭqon *see* Kokand
Qyteti Stalin *see* Kuçovë

R

Raab *see* Győr
Raab *see* Rába
Rába *River* Austria / Hungary *Ger.* Raab 79 C7
Rabat *Capital of* Morocco 50 C2
Race, Cape *Coastal feature* Canada 15 G3 19 H4
Rach Gia Vietnam 119 D6

Radom Poland 78 D4
Radviliškis Lithuania 86 B4
Ragusa Italy 77 D7
Rahīmyār Khān Pakistan 114 C3
Rainier, Mount *Peak* USA 14 D3
Raipur India 115 E5
Rājahmundry India 117 E1
Rajang *River* Malaysia 120 D3
Rājasthān *State* India 114 C3
Rājkot India 114 C4
Rājshāhi Bangladesh 115 G4
Rakvere Estonia *Ger.* Wesenberg 86 D2
Raleigh North Carolina, USA 29 F1
Ralik Chain *Islands* Marshall Islands 126 D1
Râmnicu Vâlcea Romania *prev.* Rîmnicu Vîlcea 88 B4
Ramree Island *Island* Burma 118 A3
Rancagua Chile 44 B4
Rānchi India 115 F4
Randers Denmark 65 A7
Rangoon *Capital of* Burma *Bur.* Yangon 118 B4
Rankin Inlet Canada 17 G3
Rankumara Range *Mountain range* New Zealand 131 H2
Rapid City South Dakota, USA 22 D3
Rarotonga *Island* Cook Islands 127 G5
Rasht Iran 100 C3
Ratak Chain *Islands* Marshall Islands 126 D1
Ratchaburi Thailand 119 C5
Rauma Finland 65 D5
Ravenna Italy 76 C3
Rāwalpindi Pakistan 114 C1
Rawson Argentina 45 C6
Razgrad Bulgaria 84 D1
Reading England, UK 69 D7
Rebun-tō *Island* Japan 110 C1
Rechytsa Belorussia 87 D7
Recife Brazil 41 H3
Red Deer Canada 17 E5
Redding California, USA 25 B5
Red River *River* S USA 27 G2 28 B3
Red River *River* China / Vietnam 118
Red Sea Indian Ocean 112 A3
Regensburg Germany 75 C6
Reggane Algeria 50 D3
Reggio di Calabria Italy 77 D7
Reggio nell' Emilia Italy 76 B3
Regina Canada 17 F5
Rehoboth Namibia 58 C3
Reichenberg *see* Liberec
Reims France *Eng.* Rheims 70 D3
Reindeer Lake *Lake* Canada 15 E2
Reni Ukraine 88 D4
Rennes France 70 B3
Reno Nevada, USA 25 B5
Resistencia Argentina 44 D3
Reşiţa Romania 88 B4
Resolute Canada 17 F2
Réunion *External territory* France, Indian Ocean 113 B5
Reus Spain 73 G2
Reval *see* Tallinn
Revel *see* Tallinn
Revillagigedo, Islas *Island* Mexico 30 C4
Rey, Isla del *Island* Panama 33 F5
Reykjavík *Capital of* Iceland 63 E4
Reynosa Mexico 31 E2
Rēzekne Latvia *Ger.* Rositten, *Rus.* Rezhitsa 86 D4
Rezhitsa *see* Rēzekne
Rheims *see* Reims
Rhine *River* W Europe 60 D4
Rhode Island *State* USA 21 G3
Rhodes *see* Ródos
Rhodope Mountains *Mountain range* Bulgaria / Greece *Gk.* Orosirá Rodópis, *Bul.* Despoto Planina 84 C3
Rhondda Wales, UK 69 C6
Rhône *River* France / Switzerland 60 C4
Ribeirão Preto Brazil 41 F5 43 E1
Riberalta Bolivia 40 C3
Rîbniţa Moldavia 88 D3
Richland Washington, USA 24 C2
Richmond Virginia, USA 21 E5
Riga *Capital of* Latvia *Latv.* Rīga 86 C3
Riga, Gulf of *Sea feature* Baltic Sea 86 C3
Riihimäki Finland 65 D5
Riiser-Larsen Ice Shelf *Ice feature* Antarctica 132 D1
Rijeka Croatia *It.* Fiume 80 A3
Rimini Italy 76 C3
Rîmnicu Vîlcea *see* Râmnicu Vâlcea
Riobamba Ecuador 38 A4
Rio Branco Brazil 40 C3
Río Cuarto Argentina 44 C4
Rio de Janeiro Brazil 41 G5 43 F2
Río Gallegos Argentina 45 C7
Rio Grande *River* N America 14 D4
Rio Grande Rise *Undersea feature* Atlantic Ocean 47 C6
Río Negro, Embalse del *Reservoir* Uruguay 42 C5
Rishiri-tō *Island* Japan 110 C1
Rivas Nicaragua 32 D3
Rivera Uruguay 42 C4
Riverside California, USA 25 C8
Rivne Ukraine *Rus.* Rovno 88 C2
Riyadh *Capital of* Saudi Arabia *Ar.* Ar Riyāḑ 101 C5
Rize Turkey 97 E2
Rkîz, Lac *Lake* Mauritania 52 B3
Road Town *Capital of* British Virgin Islands 35 F3
Roanne France 71 D5
Roanoke Virginia, USA 21 E5
Roanoke *River* SE USA 29 G1
Rochester Minnesota, USA 23 F3
Rochester New York, USA 21 E3
Rockall *Island* UK 46 C2
Rockhampton Australia 126 B5 130 C1
Rockingham Australia 129 B6
Rock Island Illinois, USA 20 A3
Rock Springs Wyoming, USA 22 C3
Rockstone Guyana 39 G2
Rocky Mountains *Mountain range* Canada / USA 16-17 22
Rodez France 71 C6
Ródhos *see* Ródos
Ródos *Island* Greece *var.* Ródhos, *Eng.* Rhodes 83 F3 85 E6

Ródos Greece *Eng.* Rhodes 85 E6
Rodosto *see* Tekirdağ
Roeselare Belgium 67 A6
Roma Australia 130 C2
Roma *see* Rome
Romania *Country* SE Europe 88
Romanovka Russian Federation 95 F4
Rome *Capital of* Italy *It.* Roma 76 C4
Rome Georgia, USA 28 D2
Rønne Denmark 65 D8
Ronne Ice Shelf *Ice feature* Antarctica 132 C2
Roosendaal Netherlands 66 C4
Rosario Argentina 44 D4
Roseau *Capital of* Dominica 35 G4
Rosenau *see* Rožňava
Rositten *see* Rēzekne
Ross Dependency *Territory* New Zealand, Antarctica 132-133
Ross Ice Shelf *Ice feature* Antarctica 132 D4
Rosso Mauritania 52 B3
Ross Sea Antarctica 132 D5
Rostak *see* Ar Rustāq
Rostock Germany 74 C2
Rostov-na-Donu Russian Federation 91 A6 94 A3
Roswell New Mexico, USA 26 D2
Rotorua New Zealand 131 G2
Rotterdam Netherlands 66 C4
Rouen France 70 C3
Rovaniemi Finland 64 D3
Rovno *see* Rivne
Rovuma *River* Mozambique/ Tanzania 55 B7 59 F2
Rožňava Slovakia *Ger.* Rosenau, *Hung.* Rozsnyó 79 D6
Rozsnyó *see* Rožňava
Rub' al Khali *Desert* SW Asia *Eng.* Great Sandy Desert, Empty Quarter 101 D6
Rudnyy Kazakhstan 94 B4
Rudolf, Lake *Lake* Ethiopia/ Kenya *var.* Lake Turkana 48 D4 55 C5
Ruiz *Peak* Colombia 36 B2
Rumbek Sudan 55 B5
Rundu Namibia 58 C3
Ruse Bulgaria 84 D1
Russian Federation *Country* Europe/Asia 90-91 94-95
Rust'avi Georgia 97 G2
Rutland Vermont, USA 21 F2
Rwanda *Country* C Africa 55
Ryazan' Russian Federation 91 B5 94 B3
Rybach'ye *see* Issyk-Kul'
Rybinskoye Vodokhranilishche *Reservoir* Russian Federation *Eng.* Rybinsk Reservoir 90 B4
Rybnik Poland 79 C5
Ryūkyū-rettō *Island group* Japan 111 A8
Rzeszów Poland 79 E5

S

Saale *River* Germany 74 C4
Saarbrücken Germany 75 A6
Saare *see* Saaremaa
Saaremaa *Island* Estonia *var.* Saare, Sarema, *Ger.* Ösel, *var.* Oesel 86 C2
Sabadell Spain 73 G2
Sabhā Libya 51 F3
Sable, Cape *Coastal feature* Canada 19 F5
Sabzevār Iran 100 D3
Sacramento California, USA 25 B6
Şa'dah Yemen 101 B6
Sado *Island* Japan 110 C4
Safi Morocco 50 B2
Saginaw Michigan, USA 20 C3
Sahara *Desert* N Africa 48 B3
Sahel *Region* W Africa 48 B3 53 F3
Saïda Lebanon *anc.* Sidon 98 B4
Saidpur Bangladesh 115 G3
Saigon *see* Hô Chi Minh
Saimaa *Lake* Finland 65 E5
Saint-Brieuc France 70 A3
Saint Catherines Canada 18 D5
Saint-Chamond France 71 D5
St Christopher & Nevis *see* St Kitts & Nevis
St Cloud Minnesota, USA 23 F2
St-Denis *Capital of* Réunion 59 H3
Saintes France 70 B5
Saint-Étienne France 71 D5
St. George's *Capital of* Grenada 35 G5
St Helena *External territory* UK, Atlantic Ocean 47 D5
St Helens, Mount *Peak* USA 14 D3
St Helier *Capital* Jersey 69 D8
Saint-Jean, Lake *Lake* Canada 19 E4
Saint John Canada 19 F4
Saint John's Canada 19 H3
St Joseph Missouri, USA 23 F4
St Kitts & Nevis *Country* West Indies *var.* St Christopher & Nevis 35
St.-Laurent-du-Maroni French Guiana 39 H2
Saint Lawrence *River* Canada 19 E4
Saint Lawrence, Gulf of *Sea feature* Canada 19 G4
St. Lawrence Island *Island* Alaska, USA 16 B2
Saint-Lô France 71 B3
Saint-Louis Senegal 52 B3
St Louis Missouri, USA 23 G4
St Lucia *Country* West Indies 35
Saint-Malo France 70 B3
Saint-Nazaire France 70 A4
St Paul Minnesota, USA 23 F2
St Peter Port *Capital of* Guernsey 69 D8
St Petersburg Russian Federation *Rus.* Sankt-Peterburg, *prev.* Leningrad, Petrograd 90 B3 94 B2
St Petersburg Florida, USA 29 E4
St Pierre Canada 19 H4
Saint Pierre Saint Pierre & Miquelon 19 H4
Saint Pierre & Miquelon *External territory* France, Atlantic Ocean 19 H4
St Vincent, Cape *see* São Vicente, Cabo de
St Vincent & The Grenadines *Country* West Indies 35
Sajama *Peak* Bolivia 36 B4
Sakākah Saudi Arabia 100 B4
Sakakawea, Lake *Lake* North Dakota, USA 22 D2

Sakarya *see* Adapazarı
Sakhalin *Island* Russian Federation 95 H4
Salado *River* Argentina 44 C3
Şalālah Oman 101 D6
Salamanca Spain 72 D2
Sala y Gómez *Island* Chile, Pacific Ocean 123 F4
Saldus Latvia *Ger.* Frauenburg 86 B3
Sale Australia 130 B4
Salekhard Russian Federation 94 D3
Salem India 116 D2
Salem Oregon, USA 24 B3
Salerno Italy 77 D5
Salerno, Golfo di *Sea feature* Italy 77 D5
Salihorsk Belorussia *Rus.* Soligorsk 87 C6
Salima Malawi 59 E2
Salina *Island* Italy 77 D6
Salina Utah, USA 22 B4
Salinas California, USA 25 B6
Salinas Grandes *Lowpoint* Argentina 44 C3
Salisbury England, UK 69 D7
Salisbury Island *Island* Canada 18 D1
Salonica *see* Thessaloníki
Salso *River* Italy 77 C7
Salt *see* As Salţ
Salta Argentina 44 C2
Saltillo Mexico 31 E2
Salt Lake City Utah, USA 22 B2
Salto Uruguay 42 B4
Salton Sea *Lake* California, USA 25 D8
Salvador Brazil 41 H4
Salween *River* SE Asia 104 C3
Salzburg Austria 75 D7
Salzgitter Germany 74 C4
Samaná Dominican Republic 35 E3
Samar *Island* Philippines 121 F2
Samara Russian Federation 91 C6 94 B3
Samarinda Indonesia 120 D4
Samarkand Uzbekistan 102 D2
Sambre *River* Belgium 67 B7
Samoa *Country* Pacific Ocean 127 F4
Samobor Croatia 80 B2
Sámos *Island* Greece 85 D5
Samothrace *see* Samothráki
Samothráki *Island* Greece *Eng.* Samothrace 84 D3
Samsun Turkey 96 D2
Samui, Ko *Island group* Thailand 119 C6
San *River* Cambodia / Vietnam 118-119
San *River* Poland 79 E5
Saña Peru 40 A3
Sana *Capital of* Yemen *var.* Şan'ā' 101 B7
San Ambrosio, Isla *Island* Chile 44 A3
San Andrés, Isla de *Island* Colombia 33 E3 34 B5
San Angelo Texas, USA 27 F3
San Antonio Chile 44 B4
San Antonio Texas, USA 27 F4
San Antonio *River* S USA 27 G4
San Antonio Oeste Argentina 45 C5
Sanāw Yemen 101 C6
San Bernardino California, USA 25 C7
San Carlos Uruguay 42 C5
San Carlos de Bariloche Argentina 45 B5
San Clemente Island *Island* W USA 25 C8
San Cristóbal Venezuela 38 C2
San Diego California, USA 25 C8
San Félix, Isla *Island* Chile 44 A2
San Fernando Chile 44 B4
San Fernando Trinidad & Tobago 35 G5
San Fernando Venezuela 38 D2
San Francisco California, USA 25 B6
San Ignacio Belize 32 C1
San Ignacio Paraguay 42 B3
San Joaquin *River* W USA 25 B6
San Jorge, Golfo *Sea feature* Argentina 37 C6
San José *Capital of* Costa Rica 32 D4
San Jose California, USA 25 B6
San José del Guaviare Colombia 38 C3
San Juan Argentina 44 B3
San Juan *River* Costa Rica / Nicaragua 32 D4
San Juan *Capital of* Puerto Rico 35 F3
San Juan de los Morros Venezuela 38 D1
Sankt Gallen Switzerland 75 B7
Sankt Martin *see* Martin
Sankt-Peterburg *see* St Petersburg
Sankt Pölten Austria 75 E6
Şanlıurfa Turkey *prev.* Urfa 96 E4
San Lorenzo Honduras 32 C3
San Luis Potosí Mexico 31 E3
San Marino *Country* S Europe 76 C3
San Matías, Golfo *Sea feature* Argentina 37 C6
San Miguel El Salvador 32 C3
San Miguel de Tucumán Argentina 44 C3
San Nicolas Island *Island* W USA 25 C8
San Pedro Sula Honduras 32 C2
San Remo Italy 76 A3
San Salvador *Capital of* El Salvador 32 C3
San Salvador de Jujuy Argentina 44 C2
San Sebastián Spain *Bas.* Donostia 73 E1
Santa Ana El Salvador 32 B2
Santa Ana California, USA 25 C8
Santa Barbara California, USA 25 B7
Santa Catalina Island *Island* W USA 25 C8
Santa Clara Cuba 34 B2
Santa Cruz Bolivia 40 D4
Santa Cruz California, USA 25 B6
Santa Cruz Islands *Island group* Solomon Islands 126 D3
Santa Fe Argentina 44 D3
Santa Fe New Mexico, USA 26 D2
Santa Maria Brazil 42 C4
Santa Marta Colombia 38 C1
Santander Spain 73 E1
Santanilla, Islas *Islands* Honduras 33 E1
Santarém Brazil 41 E2
Santarém Portugal 72 C3

Santa Rosa Argentina 45 C4
Santa Rosa California, USA 25 A6
Santa Rosa de Copán Honduras 32 C2
Santa Rosa Island *Island* W USA 25 B8
Santee *River* SE USA 29 F2
Santiago *Capital of* Chile 44 B4
Santiago Dominican Republic 35 E3
Santiago Panama 33 F5
Santiago Spain 72 C1
Santiago de Cuba Cuba 34 C3
Santiago del Estero Argentina 44 C3
Santo Domingo *Capital of* Dominican Republic 35 E3
Santo Domingo de los Colorados Ecuador 38 A4
Santos Brazil 43 E2
Santos Plateau *Undersea feature* Atlantic Ocean 43 E3
Sanya China 109 B8
São Borja Brazil 42 C3
São Francisco *River* Brazil 41 G3
São José do Rio Preto Brazil 42 D1
São Luís Brazil 41 G2
Saône *River* France 70 D4
São Paulo Brazil 41 F5 43 E2
São Roque, Cabo de *Coastal feature* Brazil 36 E3
São Tomé *Capital of* Sao Tome & Principe 57 A5
São Tomé *Island* Sao Tome & Principe 57 A6
Sao Tome & Principe *Country* W Africa 57
São Vicente, Cabo de *Coastal feature* Portugal *Eng.* Cape St Vincent 60 B5 72 B5
Sapporo Japan 110 D2
Saragossa *see* Zaragoza
Sarajevo *Capital of* Bosnia & Herzegovina 80 C4
Sarandë Albania 81 D7
Saransk Russian Federation 91 B5
Saratov Russian Federation 91 B6
Sarawak *State* Malaysia 120 D3
Sardegna *Island* Italy *Eng.* Sardinia 77 B5 83 D3
Sardinia *see* Sardegna
Sarema *see* Saaremaa
Sargasso Sea Atlantic Ocean 46 B4
Sargodha Pakistan 114 C2
Sarh Chad 56 C4
Saruhan *see* Manisa
Sasebo Japan 111 A6
Saskatchewan *Province* Canada 17 F5
Saskatchewan *River* Canada 17 F5
Saskatoon Canada 17 F5
Sassari Italy 77 A5
Satu Mare Romania 88 B3
Saudi Arabia *Country* SW Asia 100-101
Sault Sainte Marie Canada 18 C4
Sault Sainte Marie Michigan, USA 20 C1
Saurimo Angola 58 C1
Sava *River* SE Europe 80 C3
Savannah Georgia, USA 29 F3
Savannah *River* SE USA 29 E2
Savannakhét Laos 118 D4
Savissivik Greenland 62 A2
Savona Italy 76 A3
Savonlinna Finland 65 E5
Şawqirah Oman 101 D6
Sayat Turkmenistan 102 D3
Sayhūt Yemen 101 D7
Saynshand Mongolia 107 E2
Say 'ūn Yemen 101 C6
Schaffhausen Switzerland 75 B7
Schaulen *see* Šiauliai
Schefferville Canada 19 E2
Scheldt *River* W Europe 67 B5
Schiermonnikoog *Island* Netherlands 66 D1
Schneidemühl *see* Piła
Schwäbische Alb *Mountains* Germany 75 B6
Schwarzwald *Forested mountain region* Germany *Eng.* Black Forest 75 B6
Schwerin Germany 74 C3
Schweriner See *Lake* Germany 74 C3
Scilly, Isles of *Islands* UK 69 B8
Scotia Ridge *Undersea feature* Atlantic Ocean 47 B7
Scotia Sea Atlantic Ocean 47 B7
Scotland *National region* UK 68
Scottsbluff Nebraska, USA 22 D3
Scottsdale Arizona, USA 26 B2
Scranton Pennsylvania, USA 21 F3
Scutari, Lake *Lake* Albania / Yugoslavia 81 C5
Seattle Washington, USA 24 B2
Ségou Mali 52 D3
Segovia Spain 73 E2
Segura *River* Spain 73 E4
Seikan Tunnel *Tunnel* Japan 110 D3
Seinäjoki Finland 65 D5
Seine *River* France 70 C3
Sekondi-Takoradi Ghana 53 E5
Selfoss Iceland 63 E4
Selma Alabama, USA 28 D3
Semara Western Sahara 50 B3
Semarang Indonesia 120 C5
Semipalatinsk Kazakhstan 94 D4
Sên *River* Cambodia 118-119 D5
Sendai Japan 110 D4
Senegal *Country* W Africa 52
Senegal *River* Africa 52 B3
Seoul *Capital of* South Korea *Kor.* Sŏul 108 E4
Sept-Iles Canada 19 F3
Seraing Belgium 67 D6
Seram *Island* Indonesia 121 F4
Serbia *Republic* Yugoslavia 80 D3
Seremban Malaysia 120 B3
Sermersuaq *Region* Greenland 62 B2
Serov Russian Federation 94 C3
Serpent's Mouth, The *Sea feature* Trinidad & Tobago / Venezuela *Sp.* Boca de la Serpiente 39 F1
Serra do Mar *Mountains* Brazil 42 D3
Sérres Greece 84 C3
Sétif Algeria 51 E1
Setúbal Portugal 72 C4
Seul, Lake *Lake* Canada 18 A3
Sevana Lich *Lake* Armenia 97 G2
Sevastopol' Ukraine 89 C5

Severn *River* Canada 18 B3
Severn *River* England/Wales, UK 69 D6
Severnaya Dvina *River* Russian Federation *Eng.* Northern Dvina 90 C3
Severnaya Zemlya *Island group* Russian Federation 95 E1
Sevilla Spain *Eng.* Seville 72 D4
Seville *see* Sevilla
Seychelles *Country* Indian Ocean 59
Seydi Turkmenistan *prev.* Neftezavodsk 102 D2
Seyhan *see* Adana
Sfax Tunisia 51 F2
's-Gravenhage *Capital of* Netherlands *Eng.* The Hague 66 B3
Shackleton Ice Shelf *Ice feature* Antarctica 133 H3
Shafer, Mount *Peak* Antarctica 133 E5
Shāmīyah *Desert* Iraq/Syria 98 D4
Shanghai China 109 D5
Shannon Ireland 69 A6
Shannon *River* Ireland 69 A5
Shan Plateau *Upland* Burma 118 B3
Shantou China 109 D7
Shaoguan China 109 C7
Shaqrā' Saudi Arabia 101 B5
Sharjah United Arab Emirates *Ar.* Ash Shāriqah 101 D5
Shawnee Oklahoma, USA 27 G2
Shebeli *River* Ethiopia/Somalia 55 D5
Sheberghān Afghanistan 102 D3
Sheffield England, UK 69 D5
Shenyang China 108 D3
Shepparton Australia 130 B4
Sherbrooke Canada 19 E4
Sheridan Wyoming, USA 22 C2
's-Hertogenbosch Netherlands 66 C4
Shetland *Islands* Scotland, UK 68 D1
Shevchenko *see* Aktau
Shigatse *see* Xigazê
Shijiazhuang China 108 C4
Shikoku *Island* Japan 111 B6
Shikotan *Island* Japan/Russian Federation (disputed) 110 E1
Shikārpur Pakistan 114 B3
Shillong India 115 G3
Shimla India *prev.* Simla 114 D2
Shimonoseki Japan 111 A5
Shinano *River* Japan 110 C4
Shingū Japan 111 C5
Shinyanga Tanzania 55 B7
Shīrāz Iran 100 D4
Shkodër Albania 81 D5
Shostka Ukraine 89 E1
Shreveport Louisiana, USA 28 A2
Shrewsbury England, UK 69 D6
Shumen Bulgaria 84 D1
Shymkent Kazakhstan *prev.* Chimkent 94 B5
Šiauliai Lithuania *Ger.* Schaulen 86 B4
Šibenik Croatia 80 B4
Siberia *Region* Russian Federation 93 E2 95 E3
Sibiu Romania 88 B4
Sibu Malaysia 120 C3
Sibut Central African Republic 56 C4
Sicilia *Island* Italy *Eng.* Sicily 77 C7
Sicilian Channel *Sea feature* Mediterranean Sea 77 B7 83 E3
Sicily *see* Sicilia
Sidi Bel Abbès Algeria 50 D1
Sidley, Mount *Peak* Antarctica 132 C4
Sidon *see* Saïda
Sidra *see* Surt
Sidra, Gulf of *see* Surt, Khalīj
Siegen Germany 75 B5
Siena Italy 76 B3
Sierra Leone *Country* W Africa 52
Sierra Madre *Mountain range* Guatemala/Mexico 14 D4
Sierra Madre del Sur *Mountain range* Mexico 31 E5
Sierra Madre Occidental *Mountain range* Mexico *var.* Western Sierra Madre 30 C3
Sierra Madre Oriental *Mountain range* Mexico *var.* Eastern Sierra Madre 30 D3
Sierra Nevada *Mountain range* Spain 73 E5
Sierra Nevada *Mountain range* W USA 25 C6
Siguiri Guinea 52 D4
Siirt Turkey 97 F3
Sikasso Mali 52 D4
Sikhote-Alin Range *Mountain range* Russian Federation 93 F3
Siling Co *Lake* China 106 D5
Silkeborg Denmark 65 A7
Sillein *see* Žilina
Šilutė Lithuania 86 B4
Simferopol Ukraine 89 C5
Simla *see* Shimla
Sinai *Desert* Egypt 54 B1
Sincelejo Colombia 38 B1
Sines Portugal 72 C4
Singa Sudan 54 C4
Singapore *Country* SE Asia 120
Singapore *Capital of* Singapore 120 B3
Sinkiang *see* Xinjiang
Sinnamary French Guiana 39 H2
Sinop Turkey 96 D2
Sint-Niklaas Belgium 67 B5
Sintra Portugal 72 B3
Sinŭiju North Korea 108 D4
Sion Switzerland 75 A5
Siorapaluk Greenland 62 A2
Sioux City Iowa, USA 23 F3
Sioux Falls South Dakota, USA 23 E3
Siracusa Italy *Eng.* Syracuse 77 D7
Siret *River* Romania/Ukraine 88 C4
Sirikit Reservoir *Reservoir* Thailand 118 C4
Sirte, Gulf of *see* Surt, Khalīj
Sisak Croatia 80 B3
Sisimiut Greenland 62 B4
Sittang *River* Burma 118 B4
Sittwe Burma *prev.* Akyab 118 A3
Sivas Turkey 96 D3
Sjælland *Island* Denmark 65 B8
Skagerrak *Sea feature* Denmark/Norway 65 A7
Skeleton Coast *Coastal feature* Namibia 58 B3

Skellefteå Sweden 64 D4
Skopje *Capital of* Macedonia 81 E5
Skövde Sweden 65 B6
Skovorodino Russian Federation 95 F4
Skye *Island* Scotland, UK 68 B3
Slavonski Brod Croatia 80 C3
Sligo Ireland 69 A5
Sliven Bulgaria 84 D2
Slonim Belorussia 87 B6
Slovakia *Country* C Europe 79
Slovenia *Country* SE Europe 80
Slov'yans'k Ukraine 89 G5
Słupsk Poland *Ger.* Stolp 78 C2
Slutsk Belorussia 87 C6
Smallwood Reservoir *Lake* Canada 19 E3
Smederevo Yugoslavia 80 D3
Smolensk Russian Federation 90 A4
Smyrna *see* İzmir
Snake *River* NW USA 24 D4
Snowdonia *Mountains* Wales, UK 69 C6
Sobradinho, Represa de *Reservoir* Brazil 41 G3
Sochi Russian Federation 91 A7 94 A3
Société, Îles de la *Islands* French Polynesia *Eng.* Society Islands 125 H3 127 H4
Society Islands *see* Société, Îles de la
Socotra *see* Suquṭrá
Sodankylä Finland 64 D3
Sofia *Capital of* Bulgaria *var.* Sofija, *Bul.* Sofiya 84 C2
Sofija *see* Sofia
Sofiya *see* Sofia
Sognefjorden *Inlet* Norway 65 A5
Sohâg Egypt 54 B2
Sohm Plain *Undersea feature* Atlantic Ocean 15 F4 19 H5
Sokhumi Georgia *Rus.* Sukhumi 97 E1
Sokodé Togo 53 F4
Sokoto Nigeria 53 F3
Sokoto *River* Nigeria 53 G3
Solāpur India 114 D5 116 D1
Soligorsk *see* Salihorsk
Solomon Islands *Country* Pacific Ocean 126
Solomon Sea Pacific Ocean 126 C3
Somalia *Country* E Africa 54-55
Somali Basin *Undersea feature* Indian Ocean 112 B3
Sombor Yugoslavia 80 C2
Somerset Island *Island* Canada 17 F2
Somme *River* France 70 C3
Somoto Nicaragua 32 D3
Songea Tanzania 55 C8
Songkhla Thailand 119 C7
Sonoran Desert *Desert* Mexico/USA 26 A2
Sopron Hungary *Ger.* Ödenburg 79 B6
Soria Spain 73 E2
Sorocaba Brazil 41 F5 43 E2
Sorrento Italy 77 D5
Sosnowiec Poland *Ger.* Sosnowitz 79 C5
Sosnowitz *see* Sosnowiec
Soûr Lebanon *anc.* Tyre 98 A4
Sousse Tunisia 51 F1
South Africa *Country* southern Africa 58-59
South America 36-37
Southampton England, UK 69 D7
Southampton Island *Island* Canada 15 F2
South Andaman *Island* India 117 G2
South Atlantic Ocean 47 C7
South Australia *State* Australia 129 E5 130 A2
South Australian Basin *Undersea feature* Southern Ocean 124 B5 129 C7
South Bend Indiana, USA 20 C3
South Carolina *State* USA 29 F2
South Carpathians *see* Carpaţii Meridionali
South China Sea Pacific Ocean 122 B2
South Dakota *State* USA 22-23 D2
South East Cape *Coastal feature* Australia 130 B5
Southeast Indian Ridge *Undersea feature* Indian Ocean 113 E6
Southeast Pacific Basin *Undersea feature* Pacific Ocean 123 F5
Southend-on-Sea England, UK 69 E6
Southern Alps *Mountain range* New Zealand 131 E4
Southern Cook Islands *Islands* Cook Islands 127 G5
Southern Upland *Mountain range* Scotland, UK 68 C4
South Fiji Basin *Undersea feature* Pacific Ocean 125 E3
South Georgia *External territory* UK, Atlantic Ocean 37 E7
South Indian Basin *Undersea feature* Indian Ocean 113 E7
South Island *Island* New Zealand 131 F4
South Korea *Country* E Asia 108-109
South Orkney Islands *Islands* Antarctica 37 D8
South Polar Plateau *Upland* Antarctica 132 D3
South Pole *Ice feature* Antarctica 132 D3
South Sandwich Islands *External territory* UK, Atlantic Ocean 37 E8
South Shetland Islands *Islands* Antarctica 47 B7
South Uist *Island* UK 68 B3
Southwest Indian Ridge *Undersea feature* Indian Ocean 113 B6
Southwest Pacific Basin *Undersea feature* Pacific Ocean 133 G5
Sovetsk Kaliningrad, Russian Federation *prev.* Tilsit 86 B4
Soweto South Africa 58 D4
Spain *Country* SW Europe 72-73
Sparks Nevada, USA 25 C5
Sparta *see* Spárti
Spartanburg South Carolina, USA 29 E2
Spárti Greece *Eng.* Sparta 85 B6
Spitsbergen *Island* Svalbard 63 G2
Split Croatia 80 B4
Spokane Washington, USA 24 C2
Spratly Islands *Islands* South China Sea 120 D2

Springfield Illinois, USA 20 B4
Springfield Massachusetts, USA 21 G3
Springfield Missouri, USA 23 F5
Springfield Oregon, USA 24 B3
Srebrenica Bosnia & Herzegovina 80 C4
Sri Lanka *Country* S Asia *prev.* Ceylon 117
Srīnagar India 114 D1
Srinagarind Reservoir *Reservoir* Thailand 119 C5
Stalinabad *see* Dushanbe
Stalingrad *see* Volgograd
Stalin Peak *see* Communism Peak
Stalinsk *see* Novokuznetsk
Stambul *see* İstanbul
Stanleyville *see* Kisangani
Stanovoy Range *Mountain range* Russian Federation 93 F3
Stara Planina *see* Balkan Mountains
Stara Zagora Bulgaria 84 D2
Stavanger Norway 65 A6
Stavropol' Russian Federation 91 A7 94 A3
Steinamanger *see* Szombathely
Steinkjer Norway 64 B4
Stepanakert *see* Xankändi
Stettin *see* Szczecin
Stewart Island *Island* New Zealand 131 F5
Štip Macedonia 81 E5
Stirling Scotland, UK 68 C4
Stockerau Austria 75 E6
Stockholm *Capital of* Sweden 65 C6
Stockton California, USA 25 B6
Stœng Treng Cambodia 119 D5
Stoke-on-Trent England, UK 69 D6
Stolp *see* Słupsk
Stornoway Scotland, UK 68 B2
Stralsund Germany 74 D2
Stranraer Scotland, UK 68 C4
Strasbourg France *Ger.* Strassburg 70 E4
Stratford-upon-Avon England, UK 69 D6
Stratonice Czech Republic 79 A5
Strimon *see* Struma
Stromboli *Island* Italy 77 D6
Struma *prev.* Ceylon Bulgaria/Greece *Gk.* Strimon, *var.* Strymon 84 C3
Strumica Macedonia 81 E5
Strymon *see* Struma
Stuhlweissenburg *see* Székesfehérvár
Stuttgart Germany 75 B6
Subotica Yugoslavia 80 D2
Suceava Romania 88 C3
Sucre *Capital of* Bolivia 40 C5
Sudan *Country* NE Africa 54-55
Sudbury Canada 18 C4
Sudd *Region* Sudan 55 B5
Sudeten *Mountains* Central Europe *var.* Sudetes, Sudetic Mountains, *Cz./Pol.* Sudety 79 B5
Sudetes *see* Sudeten
Sudetic Mountains *see* Sudeten
Sudety *see* Sudeten
Suez Egypt 54 B1
Suez, Gulf of *Sea feature* Red Sea 99 A8
Suez Canal *Canal* Egypt *Ar.* Qanāt as Suways 48 D2
Şuḩār Oman 101 D5
Sühbaatar Mongolia 107 E1
Sukhumi *see* Sokhumi
Sukkur Pakistan 114 B3
Sula, Kepulauan *Island group* Indonesia 121 F4
Sulawesi *Island* Indonesia *Eng.* Celebes 121 E4
Sulu Archipelago *Island group* Philippines 121 E3
Sülüktü *see* Sulyukta
Sulu Sea Pacific Ocean 121 E2
Sulyukta Kyrgyzstan *Kir.* Sülüktü 103 E2
Sumatra *Island* Indonesia 121 B4
Sumba *Island* Indonesia 121 E5
Sumbawanga Tanzania 55 B7
Sumbe Angola 58 B2
Sumgait *see* Sumqayıt
Sumqayıt Azerbaijan *Rus.* Sumgait 97 H2
Sumy Ukraine 89 F2
Sunderland England, UK 68 D4
Sundsvall Sweden 65 C5
Suntar Russian Federation 94 F3
Sunyani Ghana 53 E4
Superior Wisconsin, USA 20 A1
Superior, Lake *Lake* Canada/USA 15 E3
Suquṭrá *Island* Yemen *var.* Socotra 101 D7 112 B3
Şūr Oman 101 E5
Surabaya Indonesia 120 D5
Sūrat India 114 C5
Surat Thani Thailand 119 C6
Sûre *River* W Europe 67 D7
Surigao Philippines 120 F2
Surinam *Country* NE South America *var.* Suriname 39
Suriname *see* Surinam
Surkhob *River* Tajikistan 103 E3
Surt Libya *var.* Sidra 51 G2
Surt, Khalīj *Sea feature* Mediterranean Sea *Eng.* Gulf of Sirte, Gulf of Sidra 51 G2 83 E4
Susanville California, USA 25 B5
Suways, Qanāt as *see* Suez Canal
Suva *Capital of* Fiji 127 E4
Svalbard *External territory* Norway, Arctic Ocean 63 G2
Svay Riĕng Cambodia 119 D6
Sverdlovsk *see* Yekaterinburg
Svetlogorsk *see* Svyetlahorsk
Svyetlahorsk Belorussia *Rus.* Svetlogorsk 87 D7
Swakopmund Namibia 58 B3
Swansea Wales, UK 69 C6
Swaziland *Country* southern Africa 58-59
Sweden *Country* N Europe 64-65
Sweetwater Texas, USA 27 F3
Swindon England, UK 69 D6
Switzerland *Country* C Europe 75
Sydney Australia 130 C3
Sydney Canada 19 G4
Syktyvkar Russian Federation 90 D4 94 C3
Sylhet Bangladesh 115 G4
Syracuse *see* Siracusa
Syracuse New York, USA 21 F3
Syr Darya *River* C Asia 92 C3
Syria *Country* SW Asia 98-99
Syrian Desert *Desert* SW Asia *Ar.* Bādiyat ash Shām 100 A3

Szczecin Poland *Ger.* Stettin 78 B3
Szeged Hungary *Ger.* Szegedin 79 D7
Szegedin *see* Szeged
Székesfehérvár Hungary *Ger.* Stuhlweissenburg 79 C7
Szekszárd Hungary 79 C7
Szolnok Hungary 79 D7
Szombathely Hungary *Ger.* Steinamanger 79 B7

T

Tabariya, Bahrat *see* Tiberius, Lake
Tábor Czech Republic 79 B5
Tabora Tanzania 55 B7
Tabrīz Iran 100 C2
Tabuaeran *Island* Kiribati 127 G2
Tabūk Saudi Arabia 100 A4
Tacloban Philippines 120 F2
Tacna Peru 40 C4
Tacoma Washington, USA 24 B2
Tacuarembó Uruguay 42 C4
Tadmur *see* Tudmur
Taegu South Korea 108 E4
Taejŏn South Korea 108 E4
Taguatinga Brazil 41 F4
Tagus *River* Portugal / Spain *Port.* Tejo, *Sp.* Tajo 72 C3
Tahiti *Island* French Polynesia 12 7H4
Tahoe, Lake *Lake* W USA 25 B5
Taipei *Capital of* Taiwan 109 D6
Taiping Malaysia 120 B3
Taiwan *Country* E Asia *prev.* Formosa 109
Taiwan Strait *Sea feature* East China Sea / South China Sea *var.* Formosa Strait 109 D7
Taiyuan China 108 C4
Ta'izz Yemen 101 B7
Tajikistan *Country* C Asia 103
Tajo *see* Tagus
Takla Makan *see* Taklimakan Shamo
Taklimakan Shamo *Desert region* China *var.* Takla Makan 104 B2 106 B3
Talamanca, Cordillera de *Mountains* Costa Rica 33 E4
Talas Kyrgyzstan 103 F2
Talaud, Kepulauan *Island group* Indonesia 121 F3
Talca Chile 44 B4
Talcahuano Chile 44 B4
Taldy-Kurgan Kazakhstan 94 C5
Tallahassee Florida, USA 28 D3
Tallinn *Capital of* Estonia *prev.* Revel, *Ger.* Reval, *Rus.* Tallin 86 D2
Talsen *see* Talsi
Talsi Latvia *Ger.* Talsen 86 B3
Tamale Ghana 53 E4
Tamanrasset Algeria 51 E4
Tambov Russian Federation 91 B5
Tamil Nādu *State* India 116 D2
Tampa Florida, USA 29 E4
Tampere Finland 65 D5
Tampico Mexico 31 F3
Tamworth Australia 130 C3
Tana *River* Finland / Norway 64 D2
Tanami Desert *Desert* Australia 128 D4
Tananarive *see* Antananarivo
Tanega-shima *Island* Japan 111 B7
Tanga Tanzania 55 C7
Tanganyika, Lake *Lake* E Africa 49 D5
Tanger Morocco *var.* Tangiers 50 C1
Tanggula Shan *Mountain range* China 106 C4
Tangiers *see* Tanger
Tangra Yumco *Lake* China 106 B5
Tangshan China 108 D4
Tanimbar Islands *see* Tanimbar, Kepulauan
Tanimbar, Kepulauan *Island group* Indonesia *Eng.* Tanimbar Islands 121 G5
Tanjungkarang Indonesia 120 B5
Ṭanṭâ Egypt 54 B1
Tan-Tan Morocco 50 B3
Tanzania *Country* E Africa 55
Taos New Mexico, USA 26 D1
Tapa Estonia *Ger.* Taps 86 D2
Tapachula Mexico 31 G5
Tapajós *River* Brazil 41 E2
Tāpi *River* India 114 C4
Taps *see* Tapa
Ṭarābulus *see* Tripoli, Lebanon
Ṭarābulus al-Gharb *see* Tripoli, Libya
Taranto Italy 77 E5
Taranto, Golfo di *Sea feature* Mediterranean Sea 77 E5
Tarapoto Peru 40 B2
Tarawa *Island* Kiribati 127 E2
Tarbes France 71 B6
Tarcoola Australia 129 E6
Târgovişte Romania *prev.* Tîrgovişte 88 C4
Târgu Mureş Romania *prev.* Tîrgu Mureş 88 C4
Tarija Bolivia 40 C5
Tarim He *River* China 106 B3
Tarn *River* France 71 C6
Tarnów Poland 79 D5
Tarragona Spain 73 G2
Tarsus Turkey 96 D4
Tartu Estonia *prev.* Yur'yev, *var.* Yurev, *Ger.* Dorpat 86 D3
Ṭarṭus Syria 98 B3
Tashauz *see* Dashkhovuz
Tashkent *Capital of* Uzbekistan *var.* Taškent, *Uzb.* Toshkent 103 E2
Tasiusaq Greenland 62 B3
Tasmania *State* Australia 130 B5
Tasman Plateau *Undersea feature* Pacific Ocean 124 D5
Tasman Sea Pacific Ocean 122 C4
Tassili N'Ajjer *Desert plateau* Algeria 51 E4
Tatabánya Hungary 79 C6
Tatar Pazardzhik *see* Pazardzhik
Taubaté Brazil 41 F5 43 E2
Taunggyi Burma 118 B3
Taunton England, UK 69 C7
Taupo New Zealand 131 G2
Taupo, Lake *Lake* New Zealand 131 G2
Tauragė Lithuania 86 B4
Tauranga New Zealand 131 H2
Taurus Mountains *Mountain range* Turkey *see* Toros Dağları 92 D4
Tavoy Burma 119 B5
Tawau Malaysia 120 D3

Taymyr, Ozero *Lake* Russian Federation 95 E2
Taymyr, Poluostrov *Peninsula* Russian Federation *Eng.* Taymyr Peninsula 93 E1 95 E2
Taymyr Peninsula *see* Taymyr, Poluostrov
Tbilisi *Capital of* Georgia *Geor.* T'bilisi, *prev.* Tiflis 97 F2
Tedzhen Turkmenistan *Turkm.* Tejen 102 C3
Tegucigalpa *Capital of* Honduras 32 C2
Teheran *see* Tehrān
Tehrān *Capital of* Iran *prev.* Teheran 100 C3
Tehuantepec, Golfo de *Sea feature* Mexico 31 G5
Tejen *see* Tedzhen
Tejo *see* Tagus
Tekirdağ Turkey *It.* Rodosto 96 A2
Tel Aviv-Yafo Israel 99 A5
Teles Piras *River* Brazil 41 E3
Tell Atlas *Plateau* Africa 82 C3
Tel'man *see* Tel'mansk
Tel'mansk Turkmenistan *Turkm.* Tel'man 102 C2
Telschen *see* Telšiai
Telšiai Lithuania *Ger.* Telschen 86 B3
Temuco Chile 45 B5
Tenerife *Island* Spain 50 A3
Tennant Creek Australia 126 A5 128 E3
Tennessee *State* USA 28 D1
Tennessee *River* SE USA 29 C1
Tepelenë Albania 81 D6
Tepic Mexico 30 D4
Teplice Czech Republic *Ger.* Teplitz, *prev.* Teplice-Šanov, *Ger.* Teplitz-Schönau 78 A4
Teplice-Šanov *see* Teplice
Teplitz *see* Teplice
Teplitz-Schönau *see* Teplice
Teraina *Island* Kiribati 127 G2
Teresina Brazil 41 G2
Termez Uzbekistan 103 E3
Terneuzen Netherlands 67 B5
Terni Italy 76 C4
Ternopil' Ukraine *Rus.* Ternopol' 88 C2
Terrassa Spain 73 G2
Terschelling *Island* Netherlands 66 C1
Teruel Spain 73 F3
Teseney Eritrea 54 C4
Tete Mozambique 59 E2
Tétouan Morocco 50 C1
Tetovo Macedonia 81 D5
Tetschen *see* Děčín
Tevere *River* Italy 76 C4
Texas *State* USA 26-27
Texas City Texas, USA 27 G4
Texel *Island* Netherlands 66 C2
Thailand *Country* SE Asia 118-119
Thailand, Gulf of *Sea feature* South China Sea 119 C6
Thames *River* England, UK 69 D6
Thāne India 115 C5 116 C1
Thar Desert *Desert* India / Pakistan 114 C3
Thásos *Island* Greece 84 C3
Thaton Burma 118 B4
Theiss *see* Tisza
Thermaic Gulf *see* Thermaïkós Kólpos
Thermaïkós Kólpos *Sea feature* Greece *Eng.* Thermaic Gulf 84 B4
Thessaloníki Greece *var.* Salonica 84 B3
Thiès Senegal 52 B3
Thiladunmathi Atoll *Island* Maldives 116 C4
Thimphu *Capital of* Bhutan 115 G3
Thionville France 70 D3
Thíra *Island* Greece 85 D6
Thompson Canada 17 G4
Thon Buri Thailand 119 C5
Thorn *see* Toruń
Thorshavn *see* Tórshavn
Thracian Sea Greece *Gk.* Thrakikó Pélagos 84 D3
Thrakikó Pélagos *see* Thracian Sea
Thule *see* Qaanaaq
Thun Switzerland 75 A7
Thunder Bay Canada 18 B4
Thüringer Wald *Forested mountains* Germany 75 C5
Thurso Scotland, UK 68 C2
Tianjin China *var.* Tientsin 108 D4
Tiaret Algeria 50 D1
Tiberias, Lake *Lake* Israel *var.* Sea of Galilee, *Heb.* Yam Kinneret, *Ar.* Bahrat Tabariya 99 B5
Tibesti *Mountains* Chad / Libya 48 C3
Tibet *Autonomous region* China *Chin.* Xizang 106 C5
Tibet, Plateau of *see* Qing-Zang Gaoyuan
Tienen Belgium 67 C6
Tien Shan *Mountain range* C Asia 92 D4
Tientsin see Tianjin
Tierra del Fuego *Island* Argentina / Chile 45 C8
Tiflis *see* Tbilisi
Tighina Moldavia *prev.* Bendery 88 D4
Tigris *River* SW Asia 92 B4
Tijuana Mexico 30 A1
Tiksi Russian Federation 95 F2
Tilburg Netherlands 66 C4
Tillabéri Niger 53 F3
Tilsit *see* Sovetsk
Timaru New Zealand 131 F4
Timişoara Romania 88 A4
Timmins Canada 18 C4
Timor *Island* Indonesia 121 F5
Timor Sea Indian Ocean 112 E4
Timor Trough *Undersea feature* Indian Ocean 128 C1
Tindouf Algeria 50 B3
Tínos *Island* Greece 85 D5
Tirana *Capital of* Albania 81 D6
Tiraspol Moldavia 88 A4
Tîrgovişte *see* Târgovişte
Tîrgu Mureş *see* Târgu Mureş
Tirol *Region* Austria *var.* Tyrol 75 C7
Tirso *River* Italy 77 A5
Tiruchchirāppalli India 116 D3
Tisa *see* Tisza
Tisza *River* E Europe *Ger.* Theiss, *Cz. / Rom. / SCr.* Tisa 79 D6
Titicaca, Lake *Lake* Bolivia / Peru 40 C4
Titov Veles Macedonia 81 E5
Tlemcen Algeria 50 D2
Toamasina Madagascar 59 G3

Toba, Danau *Lake* Indonesia 120 A3
Toba Kākar Range *Mountains* Pakistan 114 B2
Tobruk *see* Ţubruq
Tocantins *River* Brazil 41 E3
Tocopilla Chile 44 B2
Togo *Country* W Africa 53 F4
Tokat Turkey 96 D3
Tokelau *External territory* New Zealand, Pacific Ocean 122 D3
Tokmak Kyrgyzstan 103 F2
Tokuno-shima *Island* Japan 111 A8
Tokushima Japan 111 B5
Tokyo *Capital of* Japan 111 D5
Toledo Spain 73 E3
Toledo Ohio, USA 20 D3
Toledo Bend Reservoir *Reservoir* S USA 27 H3
Toliara Madagascar 59 F3
Tol'yatti *prev.* Stavropol' Russian Federation 91 C5
Tomakomai Japan 110 D2
Tombouctou Mali 53 E3
Tombua Angola 58 B2
Tomini, Teluk *Sea feature* Indonesia 121 E4
Tomsk Russian Federation 94 D4
Tomur Feng *see* Pobedy
Tonga *Country* Pacific Ocean 122
Tongking, Gulf of *Sea feature* South China Sea *var.* Gulf of Tonkin 109 B7 118 E3
Tongliao China 107 G2
Tongtian He *River* China 106 C4
Tonkin, Gulf of *see* Tongking, Gulf of
Tônlé Sap *Lake* Cambodia 119 D5
Tonopah Nevada, USA 25 C6
Toowoomba Australia 130 C2
Topeka Kansas, USA 23 F4
Torino Italy *Eng.* Turin 76 A2
Tori-shima *Island* Japan 111 D6
Torkestān, Band-e *Mountain range* Afghanistan 102 D4
Torneälv *River* Sweden 64 D3
Tornio Finland 64 D4
Tornio *River* Finland/Sweden 64 D3
Toronto Canada 18 D5
Toros Dağları *Mountain range* Turkey *Eng.* Taurus Mountains 96 C4
Torrens, Lake *Lake* Australia 130 A2
Torreón Mexico 30 D2
Torres Strait *Sea feature* Arafura Sea/Coral Sea 126 B4
Torrington Wyoming, USA 22 D3
Tórshavn *Capital of* Faeroe Islands *Dan.* Thorshavn 63 F4
Tortoise Islands *see* Galapagos Islands
Tortosa Spain 73 F3
Toruń Poland *Ger.* Thorn 78 C3
Toscana *Region* Italy *Eng.* Tuscany 76 B3
Toscano, Archipelago *Island group* Italy 76 B4
Toshkent *see* Tashkent
Tottori Japan 111 B5
Toubkal *Peak* Morocco 48 A2
Touggourt Algeria 51 E2
Toulon France 71 D6
Toulouse France 71 B6
Toungoo Burma 118 B4
Tournai Belgium 67 B6
Tours France 70 B4
Townsville Australia 126 B5
Towuti, Danau *Lake* Indonesia 121 E4
Toyama Japan 110 C4
Tozeur Tunisia 51 E2
Trâblous *see* Tripoli, Lebanon
Trabzon Turkey *Eng.* Trebizond 97 E2
Tralee Ireland 69 A6
Trang Thailand 119 C7
Transantarctic Mountains *Mountain range* Antarctica 132 D3
Transylvania *Region* Romania 88 B3
Transylvanian Alps *see* Carpaţii Meridionali
Trapani Italy 77 C6
Traun Austria 75 D6
Traunsee *Lake* Austria 75 D7
Traverse City Michigan, USA 20 C2
Travis, Lake *Lake* Texas, USA 27 F3
Trebinje Bosnia & Herzegovina 81 C5
Trebizond *see* Trabzon
Trelew Argentina 45 C6
Tremiti, Isole *Island group* Italy 76 D4
Trenčín Slovakia *Ger.* Trentschin *Hung.* Trencsén 79 C6
Trencsén *see* Trenčín
Trento Italy *Ger.* Trient 76 C2
Trenton New Jersey, USA 21 F4
Trentschin *see* Trenčín
Tres Arroyos Argentina 45 D5
Treviso Italy 76 C2
Trient *see* Trento
Trier Germany 75 A5
Trieste Italy 76 D2
Tríkala Greece 84 B4
Trincomalee Sri Lanka 117 E3
Trindade *External territory* Brazil, Atlantic Ocean 47 C6
Trinidad Bolivia 40 C4
Trinidad Uruguay 42 B5
Trinidad *Island* Trinidad & Tobago 36 C1
Trinidad & Tobago *Country* West Indies 35 H5
Trípoli Greece 85 B6
Tripoli Lebanon *var.* Trâblous, Ţarābulus 98 B3
Tripoli *Capital of* Libya *Ar.* Ţarābulus al-Gharb 51 F2
Tristan da Cunha *External territory* UK, Atlantic Ocean 47 D6
Trivandrum India 116 D3
Trnava Slovakia *Ger.* Tyrnau, *Hung.* Nagyszombat 79 C6
Trois-Rivières Canada 19 E4
Trollhättan Sweden 65 B6
Tromsø Norway 64 C2
Trondheim Norway 64 B4
Trondheimsfjorden *Inlet* Norway 64 A4
Troyes France 70 D4
Trujillo Honduras 32 D2
Trujillo Peru 40 A3
Tsarigrad *see* İstanbul
Tschenstochau *see* Częstochowa
Tselinograd *see* Akmola
Tsetserleg Mongolia 106 D2

Tshikapa Congo (Zaire) 57 C7
Tsumeb Namibia 58 C3
Tsushima *Island* Japan 111 A5
Tubmanburg Liberia 52 C5
Ţubruq Libya *Eng.* Tobruk 51 H2
Tucson Arizona, USA 26 B3
Tucupita Venezuela 39 F1
Tucuruí, Represa de *Reservoir* Brazil 41 F2
Tudmur Syria *var.* Tadmur, *Eng.* Palmyra 98 C3
Tuguegarao Philippines 120 E1
Tuktoyaktuk Canada 12 A2
Tula Russian Federation 91 B5 94 A3
Tulcán Ecuador 38 A4
Tulcea Romania 88 D4
Tulsa Oklahoma, USA 27 G1
Tundzha *River* Bulgaria 84 D2
Tunis *Capital of* Tunisia 51 F1
Tunisia *Country* N Africa 51
Tunja Colombia 38 C2
Tupiza Bolivia 40 C5
Turan Lowland *Lowland* Turkmenistan/Uzbekistan *var.* Turan Plain, *Rus.* Turanskaya Nizmennost' 102 C2
Turan Plain *see* Turan Lowland
Turanskaya Nizmennost' *see* Turan Lowland
Turčianský Svätý Martin *see* Martin
Turin *see* Torino
Turkana, Lake *see* Rudolf, Lake
Turkey *Country* SW Asia 96-97
Turkmenbashy Turkmenistan *prev.* Krasnovodsk 102 A2
Turkmenistan *Country* C Asia 102
Turks & Caicos Islands *External territory* UK, West Indies 35
Turku Finland 65 D6
Turnhout Belgium 67 C5
Turnu Severin *see* Drobeta-Turnu Severin
Turócszentmárton *see* Martin
Turpan Depression *Lowland* China 104 B2
Turtkul' Uzbekistan *prev.* Petroaleksandrovsk, *Uzb.* Tŭrtkŭl 102 C3
Tŭrtkŭl *see* Turtkul'
Tuscany *see* Toscana
Tuvalu *Country* Pacific Ocean 122
Tuxtla Gutiérrez Mexico 31 G5
Tuz Gölü *Lake* Turkey 96 C3
Tuzla Bosnia & Herzegovina 80 C3
Tver' Russian Federation 90 B4
Tweed *River* Scotland, UK 68 D4
Twin Falls Idaho, USA 24 D4
Tyler Texas, USA 27 G3
Tyre *see* Soûr
Tyrnau *see* Trnava
Tyrol *see* Tirol
Tyrrhenian Sea Mediterranean Sea 77 C6
Tyup Kyrgyzstan 103 G2

U

Ubangi *River* C Africa 57 C5
Uberaba Brazil 41 F5 43 E1
Uberlândia Brazil 41 F5 43 E1
Ubon Ratchathani Thailand 119 D5
Ucayali *River* Peru 40 B3
Uchkuduk Uzbekistan *Uzb.* Uchquduq 102 D2
Uchquduq *see* Uchkuduk
Udine Italy 76 C2
Udon Thani Thailand 118 C4
Uele *River* Congo (Zaire) 56 D5
Ufa Russian Federation 91 D6 94 B3
Uganda *Country* E Africa 55
Uíge Angola 58 B1
Ujungpandang Indonesia 120 E5
Ukmergė Lithuania 86 C4
Ukraine *Country* E Europe 88-89
Ulaanbaatar *see* Ulan Bator
Ulaangom Mongolia 106 C2
Ulan Bator *Capital of* Mongolia *var.* Ulaanbaatar 107 E2
Ulan-Ude Russian Federation 95 E4
Uldz *River* Mongolia 107 F1
Ullapool Scotland, UK 68 C3
Ullŭng-do *Island* South Korea 110 B4
Ulm Germany 75 B6
Ulster *Region* Ireland/UK 69 B5
Uluru *Peak* Australia *var.* Ayers Rock 124 B3
Ul'yanovsk Russian Federation 91 C5
Umanak Greenland 62 B3
Umeå Sweden 64 C4
Umnak Island *Island* Alaska, USA 16 A3
Una *River* Bosnia & Herzegovina/Croatia 80 B3
Unalaska Island *Island* Alaska, USA 16 B3
Ungava, Péninsule d' *Peninsula* Canada 18 D1
Ungava Bay *Sea feature* Canada 19 E1
United Arab Emirates *Country* SW Asia 101 D5
United Kingdom *Country* NW Europe 68-69
United States of America *Country* North America 20-29
Uppsala Sweden 65 C6
Ural *River* Kazakhstan/Russian Federation 91 C7 94 B4
Ural Mountains *Mountain range* Russian Federation *var.* Ural'skiy Khrebet, Ural'skiye Gory 94 C3
Ural'sk Kazakhstan 94 B3
Ural'skiy Khrebet *see* Ural Mountains
Ural'skiye Gory *see* Ural Mountains
Ura-Tyube Tajikistan 103 E2
Urfa *see* Şanlıurfa
Urganch *see* Urgench
Urgench Uzbekistan *prev.* Novo Urgench, *Uzb.* Urganch 102 C2
Uroševac Yugoslavia 81 D5
Uruapan Mexico 31 E4
Uruguaiana Brazil 42 B4
Uruguay *Country* SE South America 42
Uruguay *River* S South America 37 C5
Urumchi *see* Ürümqi
Ürümqi China *prev.* Urumchi 106 C3
Usa *River* Russian Federation 90 D3
Uşak Turkey *prev.* Ushak 96 B3

Ushak *see* Uşak
Ushuaia Argentina 45 C8
Ust'-Chaun Russian Federation 95 G1
Ustica, Isola de *Island* Italy 77 C6
Ústí nad Labem Czech Republic *Ger.* Aussig 78 A4
Ust'-Kamchatsk Russian Federation 95 H2
Ust'-Kamenogorsk Kazakhstan 94 D5
Ustyurt Plateau *Upland* Kazakhstan / Uzbekistan 102 B1
Usumacinta *River* Guatemala / Mexico 32 B1
Usumbura *see* Bujumbura
Utah *State* USA 22 B4
Utena Lithuania 86 C4
Utica New York, USA 21 F2
Utrecht Netherlands 66 C3
Uttar Pradesh *State* India 115 E3
Uummannarsuaq *Coastal feature* Greenland *Dan.* Cap Farvel, *Eng.* Cape Farewell 62 C5
Uvs Nuur *Lake* Mongolia 106 C2
Uyo Nigeria 53 G5
Uyuni Bolivia 41 C5
Uzbekistan *Country* C Asia 102-103
Uzhhorod Ukraine *Rus.* Uzhgorod 88 B2

V

Vaal *River* South Africa 58 D4
Vaasa Finland 65 D5
Vadodara India 114 C4
Vaduz *Capital of* Liechtenstein 75 B7
Vág *see* Váh
Váh *River* Slovakia *Ger.* Waag, *Hung.* Vág 79 C6
Valdés, Península *Peninsula* Argentina 45 C6
Valdez Alaska, USA 16 D3
Valdivia Chile 45 B5
Valdosta Georgia, USA 29 E3
Valence France 71 D5
Valencia Spain 73 F3
Valencia Venezuela 38 D1
Valencia *Region* Spain 73 F3
Valentine Nebraska, USA 23 E3
Valera Venezuela 38 C1
Valga Estonia *Ger.* Walk 86 D3
Valladolid Spain 72 D2
Valledupar Colombia 38 C1
Vallenar Chile 44 B3
Valletta *Capital of* Malta 77 C8
Valley, The *Capital of* Anguilla 35 G3
Valmiera Latvia *Ger.* Wolmar 86 C3
Valparaíso Chile 44 B4
Van Turkey 97 F3
Van, Lake *see* Van Gölü
Vanadzor Armenia *prev.* Kirovakan 97 F2
Vancouver Canada 17 E5
Vancouver Washington, USA 24 B2
Vancouver Island *Island* Canada 16 D5
Vänern *Lake* Sweden 65 B6
Vangaindrano Madagascar 59 G4
Van Gölü *Lake* Turkey *Eng.* Lake Van 97 F3
Vantaa Finland 65 D5
Vanua Levu *Island* Fiji 127 E4
Vanuatu *Country* Pacific Ocean 122
Vārānasi India 115 E3
Varaždin Croatia 80 B2
Vardar *River* Greece / Macedonia *prev.* Axios 81 E6 84 B3
Vardø Norway 64 E2
Varkaus Finland 65 E5
Varna Bulgaria 84 E1
Västerås Sweden 65 C6
Västervik Sweden 65 C7
Vatican City *Country* S Europe 76 C4
Vättern *Lake* Sweden 65 B6
Vava'u Group *Island group* Tonga 127 F4
Vawkavysk Belorussia *Rus.* Volkovysk, *Pol.* Wołkowysk 87 B6
Växjö Sweden 65 B7
Vaygach, Ostrov *Island* Russian Federation 90 E3
Vejle Denmark 65 A7
Velenje Slovenia 80 A2
Velika Plana Yugoslavia 80 D3
Velingrad Bulgaria 84 C2
Vellore India 116 D2
Venezia Italy *Eng.* Venice 76 C2
Venezuela *Country* N South America 38-39
Venezuela, Gulf of *Sea feature* Caribbean Sea 38 C1
Venezuelan Basin *Undersea feature* Caribbean Sea 35 F4
Venice *see* Venezia
Venice, Gulf of *Sea feature* Adriatic Sea 76 C2
Venlo Netherlands 67 D5
Venta *River* Latvia / Lithuania 86 B3
Ventspils Latvia *Ger.* Windau 86 B3
Vera Argentina 44 D3
Veracruz Mexico 31 F4
Verkhoyanskiy Khrebet *Mountain range* Russian Federation *Eng.* Verkhoyansk Range 93 F2 95 F3
Verkhoyansk Range *see* Verkhoyanskiy Khrebet
Vermont *State* USA 21 G2
Vernon Texas, USA 27 F2
Véroia Greece 84 B3
Verona Italy 76 B2
Versailles France 70 C3
Verviers Belgium 67 D6
Vesoul France 70 D4
Veszprém Hungary *Ger.* Veszprim 79 C7
Veszprim *see* Veszprém
Viana do Castelo Portugal 72 C2
Vianden Luxembourg 67 D7
Viareggio Italy 76 B3
Vicenza Italy 76 B2
Vichy France 71 C5
Victoria *State* Australia 128 D2 130 B4
Victoria Canada 16 D5
Victoria *Capital of* Seychelles 59 H1
Victoria Texas, USA 27 G4
Victoria *River* Australia 124 B2
Victoria, Lake *Lake* E Africa *var.* Victoria Nyanza 55 B6
Victoria Falls *Waterfall* Zambia / Zimbabwe 49 C6

Victoria Island *Island* Canada 17 F2
Victoria Land *Region* Antarctica 133 E5
Victoria Nyanza *see* Victoria, Lake
Vidin Bulgaria 84 B1
Viedma Argentina 45 C5
Viekšniai Lithuania 86 B3
Vienna *Capital of* Austria *Ger.* Wien 75 E6
Vientiane *Capital of* Laos 118 C4
Vietnam *Country* SE Asia 118-119
Vigo Spain 72 C2
Vijayawāda India 117 E1
Vila Nova de Gaia Portugal 72 C2
Vila Real Portugal 72 C2
Viliya *see* Neris
Viljandi Estonia *Ger.* Fellin 86 D2
Villach Austria 75 D7
Villahermosa Mexico 31 G4
Villarrica *Peak* Chile 37 B6
Villavicencio Colombia 38 C3
Vilna *see* Vilnius
Vilnius *Capital of* Lithuania *Pol.* Wilno, *Ger.* Wilna, *Rus.* Vilna 87 C5
Viña del Mar Chile 44 B4
Vinh Vietnam 118 D4
Vinnitsa *see* Vinnytsya
Vinnytsya Ukraine *Rus.* Vinnitsa 88 D2
Vinson Massif *Peak* Antarctica 132 B3
Virgin Islands *External territory* USA, West Indies 35 F3
Virginia Minnesota, USA 23 F2
Virginia *State* USA 20-21
Virovitica Croatia 80 B2
Virtsu Estonia *Ger.* Werder 86 C2
Visākhapatnam India 115 E5 117 E1
Visalia California, USA 25 C7
Visby Sweden 65 C7
Viscount Melville Sound *Sea feature* Arctic Ocean 17 F2
Viseu Portugal 72 C3
Vistula *see* Wisła
Vitebsk *see* Vitsyebsk
Viterbo Italy 76 C4
Viti Levu *Island* Fiji 125 F2 127 E4
Vitória Brazil 41 G5 43 G1
Vitoria Spain 73 E1
Vitória da Conquista Brazil 41 G4
Vitória Seamount *Undersea feature* Atlantic Ocean 43 G1
Vitsyebsk Belorussia *Rus.* Vitebsk 86 E5
Vjosës, Lumi i *River* Albania 81 D6
Vladikavkaz Russian Federation *prev.* Ordzhonikidze, Dzaudzhikau 91 A7
Vladimir Russian Federation 91 B5
Vladimirovka *see* Yuzhno-Sakhalinsk
Vladivostok Russian Federation 95 G5
Vlieland *Island* Netherlands 66 C1
Vlissingen Netherlands *Eng.* Flushing 67 B5
Vlorë Albania 81 D6
Vojvodina *Region* Yugoslavia 80 D3
Volga *River* Russian Federation 94 A3
Volga Delta *Wetland* Russian Federation 61 G4
Volgograd Russian Federation *prev.* Stalingrad 91 B6 94 A3
Volkovysk *see* Vawkavysk
Vologda Russian Federation 90 B4 94 B2
Vólos Greece 84 B4
Volta, Lake *Lake* Ghana 53 E4
Volta Redonda Brazil 43 E2
Voreioi Sporades *Island group* Greece *Eng.* Northern Sporades 84 C4
Vorkuta Russian Federation 90 E3 94 C2
Vormsi *Island* Estonia *Ger.* Worms, *Swed.* Ormsö 86 C2
Voronezh Russian Federation 91 B5
Võrtsjärv *Lake* Estonia 86 D3
Võru Estonia *Ger.* Werro 86 D3
Vosges *Mountain range* France 70 E4
Vostochno-Sibirskoye More Arctic Ocean *Eng.* East Siberian Sea 12 D2 95 G1
Vostok Island *Island* Kiribati 127 H3
Vrangel'ya, Ostrov *Island* Russian Federation *Eng.* Wrangel Island 12 C1 95 G1
Vratsa Bulgaria 84 C2
Vršac Yugoslavia 80 D3
Vukovar Croatia 80 C3
Vulcano *Island* Italy 77 D6
Vyatka *River* Russian Federation 91 C5

W

Wa Ghana 53 E4
Waag *see* Váh
Waal *River* Netherlands 66 D4
Wabash *River* C USA 20 B4
Waco Texas, USA 27 G3
Waddeneilanden *Island group* Netherlands *Eng.* West Frisian Islands 66 C1
Waddenzee *Sea feature* Netherlands 66 D1
Wadi Halfa Sudan 54 B3
Wad Medani Sudan 54 B4
Wagga Wagga Australia 130 B3
Wagin Australia 129 B6
Waigeo, Pulau *Island* Indonesia 121 G4
Wakayama Japan 111 C5
Wakkanai Japan 110 D1
Wałbrzych Poland *Ger.* Waldenburg 78 B4
Waldenburg *see* Wałbrzych
Wales *National region* UK *Wel.* Cymru 69
Walk *see* Valga
Walla Walla Washington, USA 24 C2
Wallis & Futuna *External territory* France, Pacific Ocean 122 D3
Walvis Bay Namibia 58 B3
Walvis Ridge *Undersea feature* Atlantic Ocean 47 D6
Wandel Sea Arctic Ocean 63 E1
Wanganui New Zealand 131 G3
Wanlaweyn Somalia 55 B6

Warangal India 115 E5 117 E1
Warsaw *Capital of* Poland *Pol.* Warszawa, *Ger.* Warschau 78 D3
Warschau *see* Warsaw
Warszawa *see* Warsaw
Warta *River* Poland *Ger.* Warthe 78 C4
Warthe *see* Warta
Wash, The *Inlet* England, UK 69 E5
Washington *State* USA 24
Washington DC *Capital of* USA 21 E4
Washington Land *Region* Greenland 62 A2
Waterford Ireland 69 B6
Watertown New York, USA 21 F2
Watertown South Dakota, USA 23 E2
Watson Lake Canada 17 E4
Wau Sudan 55 B5
Wawa Canada 18 C4
Weddell Sea Antarctica 132 C2
Weed California, USA 24 B4
Weichsel *see* Wisła
Weissenstein *see* Paide
Wellington *Capital of* New Zealand 131 G3
Wellington, Isla *Island* Chile 45 B7
Wels Austria 75 D6
Wenden *see* Cēsis
Werder *see* Virtsu
Werro *see* Võru
Wesenberg *see* Rakvere
Weser *River* Germany 74 B3
West Australian Basin *Undersea feature* Indian Ocean 113 D5
West Bank *Disputed territory* SW Asia 99 A5
West Bengal *State* India 115 F4
Western Australia *State* Australia 128 C4
Western Dvina *River* E Europe *Bel.* Dzvina, *Ger.* Düna, *Latv.* Daugava, *Rus.* Zapadnaya Dvina 86 C4
Western Ghats *Mountain range* India 104 B3
Western Isles *see* Outer Hebrides
Western Sahara *Region occupied by Morocco* N Africa 50 A3
Western Sierra Madre *see* Sierra Madre Occidental
Westerschelde *Inlet* Netherlands 67 B5
West European Basin *Undersea feature* Atlantic Ocean 46 C3
West Falkland *Island* Falkland Islands 45 C7
West Frisian Islands *see* Waddeneilanden
West Indies *Island group* North America 46 A4
West Palm Beach Florida, USA 29 F5
Westport New Zealand 131 F3
West Siberian Plain *Region* Russian Federation 92 C2 94 D3
West Virginia *State* USA 20-21 D5
Wetar, Pulau *Island* Indonesia 121 F5
Wexford Ireland 69 B6
Whangarei New Zealand 131 G1
Wheeling Ohio, USA 20 D4
Whitehorse Canada 16 D4
White Nile *River* Sudan 55 B5
White River *River* S USA 28 B1
White Sea *see* Beloye More
White Volta *River* Burkina/Ghana 53 E4
Whitney, Mount *Peak* W USA 14 D4
Whyalla Australia 129 E6 130 A3
Wichita Kansas, USA 23 E5
Wichita Falls Texas, USA 27 F2
Wicklow Mountains *Mountains* Ireland 69 B6
Wien *see* Vienna
Wiener Neustadt Austria 75 E7
Wiesbaden Germany 75 B5
Wight, Isle of *Island* England, UK 69 D7
Wilcannia Australia 130 B3
Wilhelm, Mount *Peak* Papua New Guinea 124 C1
Wilja *see* Neris
Wilkes Land *Region* Antarctica 133 G5
Willemstad Netherlands Antilles 35 E5
Williamsport Pennsylvania, USA 21 E3
Williston North Dakota, USA 22 D1
Wilmington Delaware, USA 21 F4
Wilmington North Carolina, USA 29 G2
Wilna *see* Vilnius
Wilno *see* Vilnius
Wilson North Carolina, USA 29 F1
Windau *see* Ventspils
Windhoek *Capital of* Namibia 58 C3
Windsor Canada 18 C5
Windward Islands *Islands* West Indies 35 G4
Winisk Canada 18 C2
Winisk *River* Canada 18 B3
Winnemucca Nevada, USA 25 C5
Winnipeg Canada 17 G5
Winnipeg, Lake *Lake* Canada 17 G5
Winnipegosis, Lake *Lake* Canada 17 G5
Winston-Salem North Carolina, USA 29 F1
Winterthur Switzerland 75 B7
Wisconsin *State* USA 20 B2
Wismar Germany 74 C3
Wisła *River* Poland *Ger.* Weichsel, *Eng.* Vistula 61 E3 78 D4
W.J. van Blommesteinmeer *Reservoir* Surinam 39 H3
Włocławek Poland 78 C3
Wodzisław Śląski Poland *Ger.* Loslau 79 C5
Wolfsburg Germany 74 C4
Wollongong Australia 130 C3
Wolmar *see* Valmiera
Wŏnsan North Korea 108 E4
Woods, Lake of the *Lake* Canada/USA 18 A4
Worcester England, UK 69 D6
Worcester Massachusetts, USA 21 G3
Worms *see* Vormsi
Wołkowysk *see* Vawkavysk

Wrangel Island *see* Vrangel'ya, Ostrov
Wrocław Poland *Ger.* Breslau 78 C4
Wuhai China 107 E3
Wuhan China 109 C5
Wuppertal Germany 74 A4
Würzburg Germany 75 B5
Wuxi China 109 D5
Wuzhou China 109 C7
Wyndham Australia 128 D3
Wyoming *State* USA 22 C3
Wyville-Thomson Ridge *Undersea feature* Atlantic Ocean 63 E5

Xai-Xai Mozambique 59 E4
Xam Nua Laos 118 D3
Xankändi Azerbaijan *Rus.* Khankendy, *prev.* Stepanakert 97 G2
Xánthi Greece 84 C3
Xiamen China 109 D7
Xi'an China 109 B5
Xianggang *see* Hong Kong
Xigazê China *prev.* Shigatse 106 C5
Xilinhot China 107 F2
Xingu *River* Brazil 41 E2
Xining China 107 E4
Xinjiang *Autonomous region* China *var.* Sinkiang 106 B3
Xinyang China 109 C5
Xizang *see* Tibet
Xuzhou China 109 D5

Yacuiba Bolivia 40 D5
Yafran Libya 51 F2
Yakima Washington, USA 24 B2
Yaku-shima *Island* Japan 111 B7
Yakutsk Russian Federation 95 F3
Yala Thailand 119 C7
Yalong Jiang *River* China 109 A5
Yalta Ukraine 89 C5
Yamaguchi Japan 111 B5
Yamal, Poluostrov *Peninsula* Russian Federation *var.* Yamal Peninsula 92 C2
Yambio Sudan 55 B5
Yambol Bulgaria 84 D2
Yamdena, Pulau *Island* Indonesia 121 G5
Yamoussoukro *Capital of* Ivory Coast 52 D5
Yamuna *River* India 115 E3
Yanbu' al Baḩr Saudi Arabia 101 A5
Yangon *see* Rangoon
Yangtze *see* Chang Jiang
Yantai China 108 D4
Yaoundé *Capital of* Cameroon 57 B5
Yap *Island* Micronesia 126 A1
Yapen, Pulau *Island* Indonesia 121 G4
Yaqui *River* Mexico 30 B2
Yarmouth Canada 19 F5
Yaroslavl' Russian Federation 90 B4 94 B2
Yazd Iran 100 D4
Yazoo *River* SE USA 28 C2
Yekaterinburg Russian Federation *prev.* Sverdlovsk 94 C3
Yelisavetpol *see* Gäncä
Yellowknife Canada 17 E4
Yellow River *see* Huang He
Yellow Sea Pacific Ocean 108-109
Yellowstone *River* NW USA 22 C2
Yëloten Turkmenistan 102 C3
Yemen *Country* SW Asia 101 C7
Yenakiyeve Ukraine 89 G3
Yenisey *River* Russian Federation 94 D3
Yerevan *Capital of* Armenia *var.* Erevan, Jerevan, *Eng.* Erivan 97 F2
Yevpatoriya Ukraine 89 C5
Yichang China 109 C5
Yichun China 108 E2
Yinchuan China 108 B4
Yining China 106 B3
Yogyakarta Indonesia 120 C5
Yokohama Japan 111 D5
Yola Nigeria 53 H4
Yopal Colombia 38 C2
York England, UK 69 D5
Yorkton Canada 17 F5
Young Uruguay 42 B5
Yozgat Turkey 96 D3
Ypres *see* Ieper
Ysyk-Köl *see* Issyk-Kul'
Yuba City California, USA 25 B5
Yucatan Basin *Undersea feature* Caribbean Sea 34 B4
Yucatan Peninsula *Peninsula* Mexico 31 H4
Yueyang China 109 C6
Yugoslavia *Country* SE Europe 80-81
Yukon *River* Canada/USA 16 C2
Yukon Territory *Territory* Canada 16 D3
Yuma Arizona, USA 26 A3
Yumen China 108 A4
Yurev *see* Tartu
Yur'yev *see* Tartu
Yushu China 106 D4
Yuzhno-Sakhalinsk Russian Federation *var.* Vladimirovka 95 H4
Yverdon Switzerland 75 A7

Z

Zabīd Yemen 101 B7
Zacapa Guatemala 32 C2
Zadar Croatia 80 A4
Zagreb *Capital of* Croatia 80 B2
Zagros Mountains *Mountain range* Iran/Iraq 100 D4
Zāhedān Iran 100 E4
Zahlé Lebanon 98 B4
Zaire *Country see* Congo (Zaire)
Zaire *River see* Congo
Zaječar Yugoslavia 80 E4
Zákinthos *see* Zákynthos
Zákynthos *Island* Greece *prev.* Zákinthos 85 A5
Zalaegerszeg Hungary 79 B7
Zalantun China 107 G1
Zambezi Zambia 58 C2
Zambezi *River* southern Africa 58 C2

Zambia *Country* southern Africa 58-59
Zamboanga Philippines 120 E3
Zamora Spain 72 D2
Zanzibar Tanzania 55 C7
Zanzibar *Island* Tanzania 49 E5
Zaozhuang China 109 D5
Zapadnaya Dvina *see* Western Dvina
Zapala Argentina 45 B5
Zaporizhzhya Ukraine *Rus.* Zaporozh'ye 89 F3
Zaporozh'ye *see* Zaporizhzhya
Zarafshan Uzbekistan 102 D2
Zaragoza Spain *Eng.* Saragossa 73 F2
Zaranj Afghanistan 102 C5
Zaria Nigeria 53 G4
Zeebrugge Belgium 67 A5
Zenica Bosnia & Herzegovina 80 C4
Zeravshan *River* C Asia 103 E3
Zhambyl Kazakhstan *prev.* Dzhambul 94 C5
Zhanjiang China 109 C7
Zhdanov *see* Mariupol'
Zhengzhou China 109 C5
Zhezkazgan Kazakhstan *prev.* Zdhezkazgan 94 C4
Zhitomir *see* Zhytomyr
Zhlobin Belorussia 87 D6
Zhodzina Belorussia 87 D5
Zhytomyr Ukraine *Rus.* Zhitomir 88 D2
Zibo China 108 D4
Zielona Góra Poland *Ger.* Grünberg in Schlesien 78 B4
Zigong China 109 B6
Ziguinchor Senegal 52 B3
Žilina Slovakia *Hung.* Zsolna, *Ger.* Sillein 79 C5
Zimbabwe *Country* southern Africa 58-59
Zinder Niger 53 G3
Zoetermeer Netherlands 66 C4
Zomba Malawi 59 E2
Zonguldak Turkey 96 C2
Zouérat Mauritania 52 C1
Zrenjanin Yugoslavia 80 D3
Zsolna *see* Žilina
Zug Switzerland 75 B7
Zuider Zee *see* IJsselmeer
Zürich Switzerland *Eng.* Zurich 75 B7
Zurich *see* Zürich
Zuwārah Libya 51 F2
Zvornik Bosnia & Herzegovina 80 C3
Zwedru Liberia 52 D5
Zwickau Germany 75 C5
Zwolle Netherlands 66 D3

ULTIMATE POCKET BOOK OF THE WORLD

FACTFILE

A DORLING KINDERSLEY BOOK

Project Editor Debra Clapson
Project Cartographer Julia Lunn
Project Art Editor Yahya El-Droubie

Designer Katy Wall
Cartographic Research Michael Martin
Database Editor Ruth Duxbury

Art Director Chez Picthall
Editorial Direction Andrew Heritage, Louise Cavanagh
Production Controller David Proffit

Editorial Contributors
Kevin McRae, Melanie McRae, Louisa Somerville, Sean Connolly

Dorling Kindersley would like to thank
The Flag Institute, Chester for providing the national flags

Produced by Dorling Kindersley Cartography

First published in Great Britain in 1996
by Dorling Kindersley Limited
9 Henrietta Street, London WC2E 8PS
First published in this version 1998

Visit us on the World Wide Web at http://www.dk.com

A CIP catalogue record for this book is available from the British Library

ISBN 0-7513-0603-7

Film output in England by Euroscan
Printed and bound in Italy by L.E.G.O

ULTIMATE POCKET BOOK OF THE WORLD

FACTFILE

DORLING KINDERSLEY

LONDON • NEW YORK • STUTTGART • MOSCOW

CONTENTS

The Physical World..............................8-9
The Political World 10-11
World Time Zones 12-13

NORTH & CENTRAL AMERICA 14-15

Canada 16-17
United States of America...............18-19
Mexico 20-21
Guatemala / Belize............................22-23
El Salvador / Honduras...................24-25
Nicaragua / Costa Rica....................26-27
Panama / Jamaica.............................28-29
Cuba / Bahamas................................30-31
Haiti / Dominican Republic............32-33
St Kitts & Nevis 34
Antigua & Barbuda 35
Dominica / St Lucia 36-37
St Vincent & the Grenadines 38
Barbados 39
Grenada / Trinidad & Tobago.........40-41

SOUTH AMERICA 42-43

Colombia / Venezuela 44-45
Guyana / Surinam............................46-47
Ecuador / Peru..................................48-49
Brazil...50-51
Chile / Bolivia 52-53
Paraguay / Uruguay 54-55
Argentina 56-57

AFRICA 58-59

Morocco / Algeria 60-61
Tunisia / Libya 62-63
Egypt / Sudan 64-65
Eritrea / Djibouti...............................66-67
Ethiopia / Somalia........................... 68-69
Uganda / Kenya 70-71
Rwanda / Burundi 72-73
Central African Republic / Congo (Zaire)..74-75
Niger / Chad 76-77
Mauritania / Mali 78-79
Senegal / Gambia 80-81
Cape Verde / Guinea Bissau 82-83
Guinea / Sierra Leone 84-85
Liberia / Ivory Coast.........................86-87
Burkina / Ghana 88-89
Togo / Benin 90-91
Nigeria / Cameroon 92-93
Equatorial Guinea 94
Sao Tome & Principe............................95
Gabon / Congo 96-97
Angola / Zambia 98-99
Tanzania / Malawi 100-101
Zimbabwe / Mozambique...........102-103
Namibia / Botswana 104-105
Lesotho / Swaziland 106-107
South Africa.................................108-109
Seychelles / Comoros 110-111
Madagascar / Mauritius...............112-113

EUROPE 114-115

Iceland / Norway..........................116-117
Denmark / Sweden.......................118-119

Finland / Estonia 120-121
Latvia / Lithuania 122-123
Poland / Germany 124-125
Netherlands / Belgium 126-127
Ireland / United Kingdom 128-129
France / Luxembourg 130-131
Monaco / Andorra 132-133
Portugal / Spain 134-135
Italy / Malta 136-137
Vatican City / San Marino 138-139
Switzerland / Liechtenstein 140-141
Austria / Hungary 142-143
Czech Republic / Slovakia 144-145
Slovenia / Croatia 146-147
Bosnia & Herzegovina 148
Yugoslavia
(Serbia & Montenegro) 149
Albania / Macedonia 150-151
Bulgaria / Greece 152-153
Romania 154
Moldavia (Moldova) 155
Belorussia (Belarus) / Ukraine 156-157
Russian Federation 158-159

ASIA 160-161

Azerbaijan / Armenia 162-163
Turkey / Georgia 164-165
Lebanon / Syria 166-167
Cyprus / Israel 168-169
Jordan / Saudi Arabia 170-171
Yemen / Oman 172-173
United Arab Emirates / Qatar 174-175
Bahrain / Kuwait 176-177
Iraq / Iran 178-179
Turkmenistan / Uzbekistan 180-181
Kazakhstan / Mongolia 182-183
Kyrgyzstan / Tajikistan 184-185
Afghanistan / Pakistan 186-187
Nepal / Bhutan 188-189
India 190-191
Maldives / Sri Lanka 192-193
Bangladesh 194
Burma (Myanmar) 195
Thailand / Laos 196-197
Cambodia / Vietnam 198-199
Malaysia / Indonesia 200-201
Singapore / Brunei 202-203
Philippines / Taiwan 204-205
China 206-207
North Korea / South Korea 208-209
Japan 210-211

AUSTRALASIA & OCEANIA 212-213

Australia 214-215
Vanuatu / Fiji 216-217
Papua New Guinea 218
Solomon Islands 219
Palau / Micronesia 220-221
Marshall Islands / Nauru 222-223
Kiribati / Tuvalu 224-225
Samoa / Tonga 226-227
New Zealand 228
Antarctica 229

Overseas Territories 230-236
International Organizations 237

Key/Abbreviations 238
Index 239-240

PHYSICAL WORLD

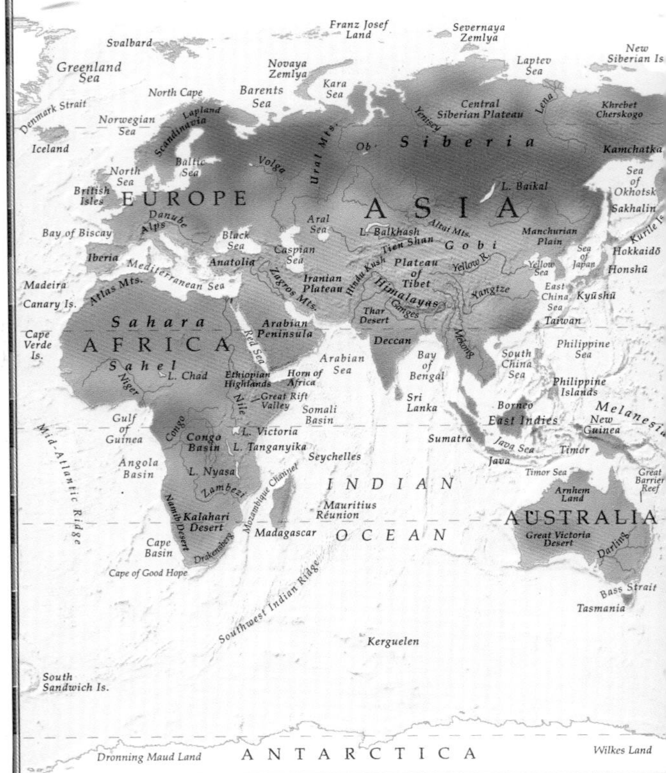

Franz Josef Land
Severnaya Zemlya
Svalbard
New Siberian Is
Greenland Sea
Novaya Zemlya
Laptev Sea
Kara Sea
North Cape
Barents Sea
Denmark Strait
Lapland
Central Siberian Plateau
Lena
Khrebet Cherskogo
Norwegian Sea
Scandinavia
Yenisey
Iceland
Ob
Siberia
Kamchatka
Baltic Sea
Volga
Ural Mts.
North Sea
Sea of Okhotsk
British Isles
EUROPE
L. Baikal
ASIA
Sakhalin
Danube
Alps
Aral Sea
Altai Mts.
Kurile Is
Bay of Biscay
Black Sea
L. Balkhash
Manchurian Plain
Tien Shan
Gobi
Caspian Sea
Sea of Japan
Hokkaidō
Iberia
Mediterranean Sea
Anatolia
Hindu Kush
Plateau of Tibet
Yellow R.
Yellow Sea
Honshū
Madeira
Atlas Mts.
Zagros Mts.
Iranian Plateau
Himalayas
Yangtze
East China Sea
Kyūshū
Canary Is.
Ganges
Thar Desert
Sahara
Arabian Peninsula
Taiwan
Cape Verde Is.
AFRICA
Red Sea
Deccan
Philippine Sea
Arabian Sea
Bay of Bengal
Mekong
South China Sea
Sahel
L. Chad
Ethiopian Highlands
Horn of Africa
Philippine Islands
Niger
Great Rift Valley
Sri Lanka
Nile
Somali Basin
Borneo
Melanesia
Gulf of Guinea
Congo
East Indies
New Guinea
Mid-Atlantic Ridge
L. Victoria
Congo Basin
Sumatra
L. Tanganyika
Java Sea
Timor
Seychelles
Java
Angola Basin
Timor Sea
L. Nyasa
Mozambique Channel
INDIAN
Great Barrier Reef
Arnhem Land
Zambezi
Mauritius
Réunion
Kalahari Desert
Namib Desert
AUSTRALIA
Madagascar
OCEAN
Great Victoria Desert
Cape Basin
Darling
Drakensberg
Cape of Good Hope
Southwest Indian Ridge
Bass Strait
Tasmania
Kerguelen
South Sandwich Is.
Dronning Maud Land
ANTARCTICA
Wilkes Land

ARCTIC OCEAN
Ellesmere I.
Queen Elizabeth Islands
Greenland
Limit of permanent pack ice
Baffin Bay
Chukchi Sea
Beaufort Sea
Baffin I.
Brooks Range
Great Bear Lake
Davis Strait
Arctic Circle
Bering Strait
Yukon
Mackenzie
Great Slave Lake
Iceland
Hudson Bay
Bering Sea
Rocky Mountains
Gulf of Alaska
Labrador Sea
Labrador
Mid-Atlantic Ridge
Aleutian Islands
Vancouver I.
NORTH AMERICA
Missouri
Great Lakes
Grand Banks
St Lawrence
Emperor Seamounts
North American Basin
Mississippi
Baja California
Sierra Madre
Gulf of Mexico
ATLANTIC
Tropic of Cancer
Hawaiian Is.
West Indies
PACIFIC
Caribbean Sea
OCEAN
Polynesia
OCEAN
Guiana Highlands
Amazon
Amazon Basin
Equator
Galápagos Is.
Micronesia
Andes
SOUTH AMERICA
Brazil Basin
Fiji
Tahiti
Mato Grosso
New Caledonia
Peru Basin
Tropic of Capricorn
Kermadec Trench
Paraná
Pampas
Southwest Pacific Basin
North I.
Argentine Basin
New Zealand
Patagonia
South I.
Falkland Is.
Tierra del Fuego
South Georgia
Cape Horn
Southeast Pacific Basin
Drake Passage
Antarctic Peninsula
Antarctic Circle
Ross Sea
ANTARCTICA
Weddell Sea

POLITICAL WORLD

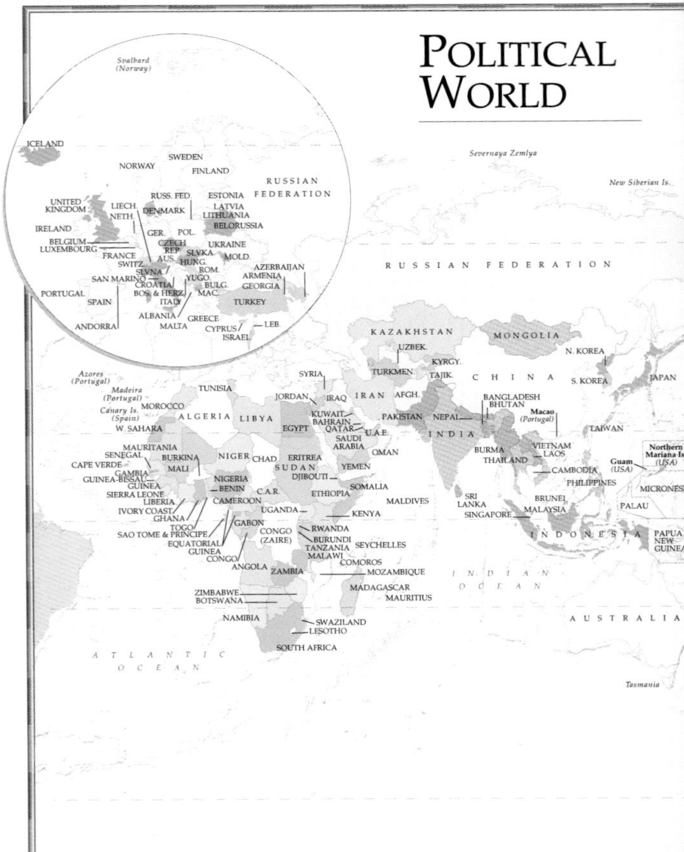

Svalbard (Norway)
ICELAND
NORWAY
SWEDEN
FINLAND
RUSSIAN FEDERATION
UNITED KINGDOM
LIECH.
NETH.
RUSS. FED.
DENMARK
ESTONIA
LATVIA
LITHUANIA
BELORUSSIA
IRELAND
GER.
POL.
BELGIUM
LUXEMBOURG
CZECH REP.
UKRAINE
FRANCE
AUS.
SLVKA.
MOLD.
SWITZ.
HUNG.
SLVNA.
ROM.
AZERBAIJAN
SAN MARINO
YUGO.
ARMENIA
CROATIA
BULG.
GEORGIA
PORTUGAL
BOS. & HERZ.
MAC.
SPAIN
ITALY
TURKEY
ALBANIA
GREECE
ANDORRA
MALTA
CYPRUS
LEB.
ISRAEL
Severnaya Zemlya
New Siberian Is.
RUSSIAN FEDERATION
KAZAKHSTAN
MONGOLIA
UZBEK.
KYRGY.
N. KOREA
TURKMEN.
TAJIK.
CHINA
JAPAN
S. KOREA
Azores (Portugal)
Madeira (Portugal)
Canary Is. (Spain)
MOROCCO
TUNISIA
SYRIA
JORDAN
IRAQ
IRAN
AFGH.
BANGLADESH
BHUTAN
ALGERIA
LIBYA
KUWAIT
BAHRAIN
QATAR
PAKISTAN
NEPAL
Macao (Portugal)
W. SAHARA
EGYPT
U.A.E.
TAIWAN
SAUDI ARABIA
INDIA
MAURITANIA
OMAN
VIETNAM
SENEGAL
BURKINA
NIGER
CHAD
ERITREA
BURMA
LAOS
Northern Mariana Is (USA)
CAPE VERDE
MALI
SUDAN
YEMEN
THAILAND
Guam (USA)
GAMBIA
GUINEA-BISSAU
NIGERIA
DJIBOUTI
CAMBODIA
GUINEA
BENIN
SOMALIA
PHILIPPINES
MICRONES
SIERRA LEONE
C.A.R.
ETHIOPIA
SRI LANKA
BRUNEI
LIBERIA
CAMEROON
MALDIVES
MALAYSIA
PALAU
IVORY COAST
UGANDA
KENYA
SINGAPORE
GHANA
GABON
TOGO
CONGO (ZAIRE)
RWANDA
INDONESIA
PAPUA NEW GUINEA
SAO TOME & PRINCIPE
BURUNDI
EQUATORIAL GUINEA
TANZANIA
SEYCHELLES
CONGO
MALAWI
COMOROS
ANGOLA
ZAMBIA
MOZAMBIQUE
INDIAN OCEAN
MADAGASCAR
ZIMBABWE
MAURITIUS
BOTSWANA
NAMIBIA
AUSTRALIA
SWAZILAND
LESOTHO
SOUTH AFRICA
ATLANTIC OCEAN
Tasmania

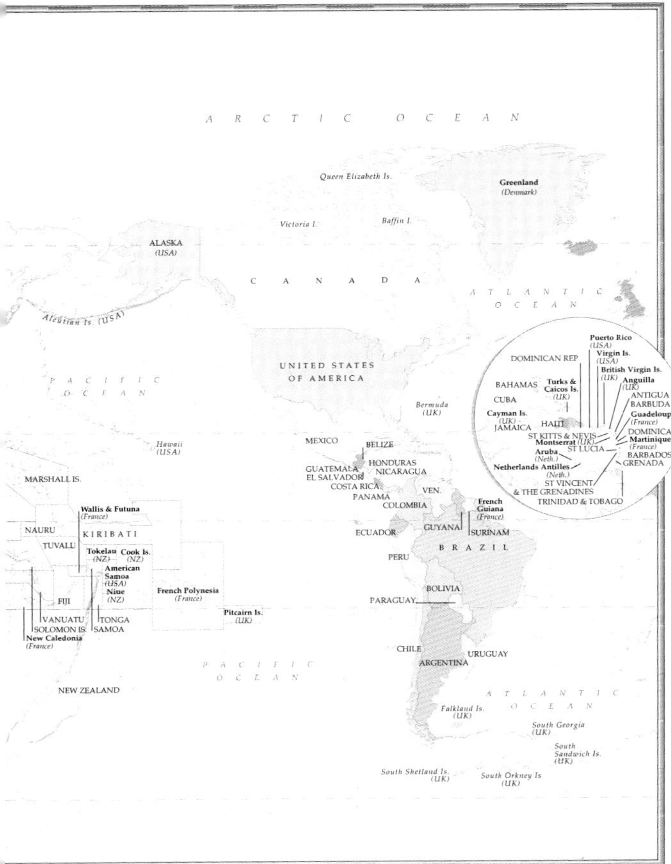
ARCTIC OCEAN
Queen Elizabeth Is.
Greenland
(Denmark)
Victoria I.
Baffin I.
ALASKA
(USA)
CANADA
ATLANTIC OCEAN
Aleutian Is. (USA)
UNITED STATES OF AMERICA
PACIFIC OCEAN
Bermuda
(UK)
Hawaii
(USA)
MEXICO
BELIZE
HONDURAS
GUATEMALA
EL SALVADOR
NICARAGUA
COSTA RICA
PANAMA
VEN.
COLOMBIA
MARSHALL IS.
Wallis & Futuna
(France)
NAURU
KIRIBATI
TUVALU
Tokelau
(NZ)
Cook Is.
(NZ)
American Samoa
(USA)
Niue
(NZ)
FIJI
VANUATU
TONGA
SOLOMON IS.
SAMOA
New Caledonia
(France)
French Polynesia
(France)
Pitcairn Is.
(UK)
ECUADOR
GUYANA
SURINAM
French Guiana
(France)
BRAZIL
PERU
BOLIVIA
PARAGUAY
CHILE
URUGUAY
ARGENTINA
PACIFIC OCEAN
NEW ZEALAND
ATLANTIC OCEAN
Falkland Is.
(UK)
South Georgia
(UK)
South Sandwich Is.
(UK)
South Shetland Is.
(UK)
South Orkney Is
(UK)
Puerto Rico
(USA)
DOMINICAN REP
Virgin Is.
(USA)
British Virgin Is.
(UK)
BAHAMAS
Turks & Caicos Is.
(UK)
Anguilla
(UK)
CUBA
ANTIGUA & BARBUDA
Cayman Is.
(UK)
Guadeloupe
(France)
JAMAICA
HAITI
DOMINICA
ST KITTS & NEVIS
Montserrat (UK)
Martinique
(France)
Aruba
(Neth.)
ST LUCIA
BARBADOS
GRENADA
Netherlands Antilles
(Neth.)
ST VINCENT
& THE GRENADINES
TRINIDAD & TOBAGO

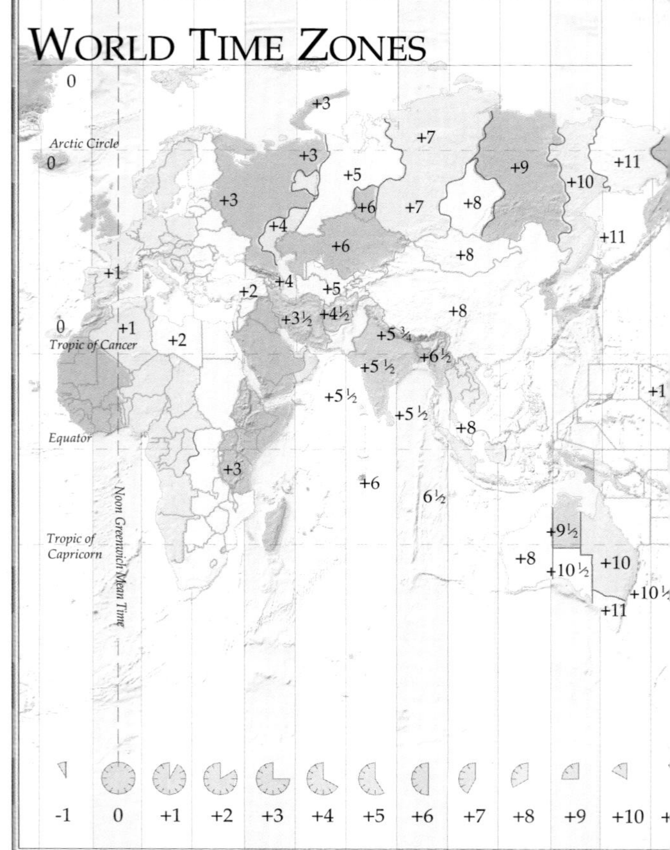
WORLD TIME ZONES
0
Arctic Circle
0
+3
+3
+3
+5
+7
+9
+11
+10
+6
+7
+8
+4
+6
+8
+11
+1
+4
+2
+5
+3½
+4½
+8
0
+1
Tropic of Cancer
+2
+5 ¾
+6½
+5 ½
+1
+5 ½
+5 ½
Equator
+8
+3
+6
6½
Noon Greenwich Mean Time
Tropic of Capricorn
+9½
+8
+10½
+10
+10½
+11
-1
0
+1
+2
+3
+4
+5
+6
+7
+8
+9
+10

Numbers on the map show the number of hours ahead of, or behind, GMT (Greenwich Mean Time).

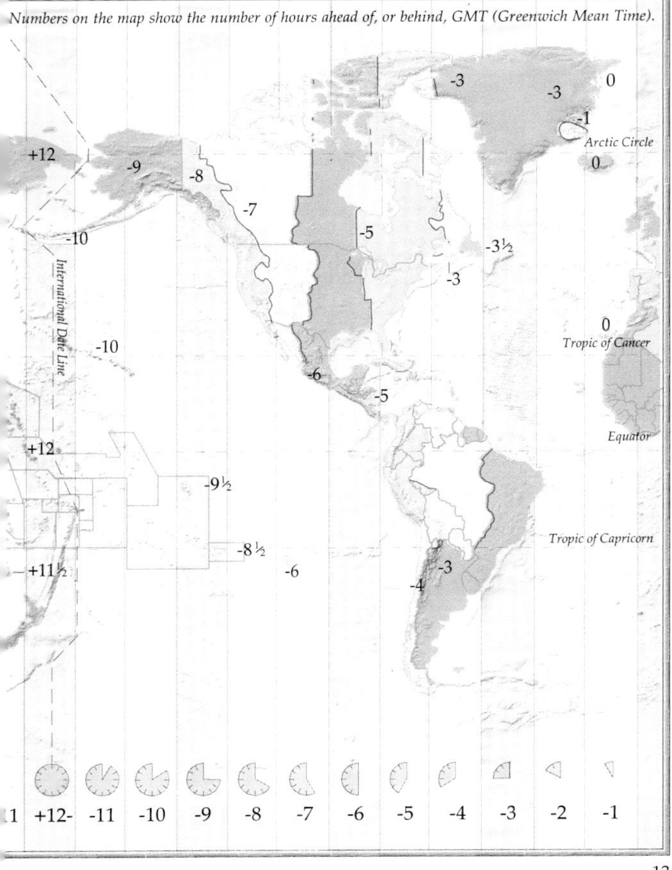

-3
0
-3
-1
Arctic Circle
+12
-9
-8
0
-7
-5
-10
-3½
International Date Line
-3
0
-10
Tropic of Cancer
-6
-5
Equator
+12
-9½
Tropic of Capricorn
-8½
+11½
-6
-3
-4
11
+12-
-11
-10
-9
-8
-7
-6
-5
-4
-3
-2
-1

RUSSIAN FEDERATION
North Pole
Svalbard
NORWAY
ARCTIC OCEAN
Bering Sea
Aleutian Islands
Ellesmere I.
Arctic Circle
UNITED STATES OF AMERICA (ALASKA)
Brooks Range
Beaufort Sea
Queen Elizabeth Islands
Greenland
(to Denmark)
Alaska Range
Alaska Peninsula
Mt. McKinley (Denali) 6194m
Denmark Strait
ICELAND
Kodiak I.
Victoria I.
Baffin Bay
Gulf of Alaska
Mt. Logan 6050m
Mackenzie Mts.
Baffin I.
Great Bear Lake
Davis Strait
Coast Mountains
Great Slave Lake
Queen Charlotte Is.
Rocky Mountains
C A N A D A
Peace
Athabasca
Péninsule d'Ungava
Labrador Sea
PACIFIC OCEAN
Hudson Bay
Vancouver I.
Nelson
Labrador
Mt. Rainier 4392m
Mt. St. Helens 2550m
Columbia
Lake Winnipeg
Great Plains
Newfoundland
Coast Ranges
Missouri
Lake Superior
Great Salt Lake
Great Basin
Great Lakes
St Lawrence
Sierra Nevada
Mt. Whitney 4417m
Death Valley -86m
Colorado
Lake Huron
Lake Michigan
Lake Ontario
Lake Erie
Mountains
Cape Cod
UNITED STATES OF AMERICA
180°
170°
160°
150°
140°
50°
40°
30°
20°
60°

ATLANTIC OCEAN
Tropic of Cancer
4000m/13124ft
3000m/9843ft
2000m/6562ft
1000m/3281ft
200m/656ft
Sea Level
Below Sea Level
1000 km
1000 miles
Baja California
Golfo de California
Sierra Madre Occidental
Sierra Madre Oriental
Rio Grande
Red River
Mississippi
Ohio
Appalachia
Cape Hatteras
Bermuda (to UK)
Mississippi Delta
The Everglades
Gulf of Mexico
MEXICO
Colima 4330m
Popocatepetl 5448m
Citlaltépetl 5700m
Peninsula de Yucatan
BAHAMAS
Turks & Caicos Is. (to UK)
Puerto Rico (to US)
British Virgin Is. (to UK)
Anguilla (to UK)
ANTIGUA & BARBUDA
Guadeloupe (to Fr.)
DOMINICA
Martinique (to Fr.)
ST LUCIA
BARBADOS
GRENADA
TRINIDAD & TOBAGO
CUBA
Cayman Is. (to UK)
Greater Antilles
HAITI
DOMINICAN REP.
Virgin Is. (to US)
ST KITTS & NEVIS
Montserrat (to UK)
ST VINCENT & THE GRENADINES
Aruba (to Neth.)
Netherland Antilles (to Neth.)
Lesser Antilles
BELIZE
JAMAICA
Caribbean Sea
GUATEMALA
HONDURAS
EL SALVADOR
NICARAGUA
COSTA RICA
Panama Canal
PANAMA
VENEZUELA
GUYANA
COLOMBIA
Equator

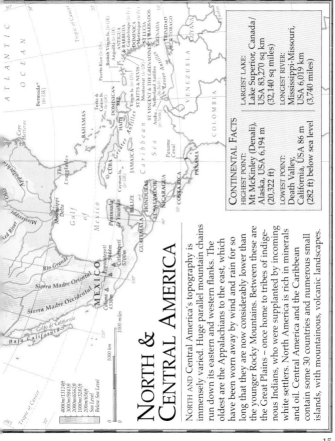

NORTH & CENTRAL AMERICA

NORTH AND Central America's topography is immensely varied. Huge parallel mountain chains run down its eastern and western flanks. The oldest are the Appalachians to the east, which have been worn away by wind and rain for so long that they are now considerably lower than the younger Rocky Mountains. Between these are the Great Plains – once home to tribes of indigenous Indians, who were supplanted by incoming white settlers. North America is rich in minerals and oil. Central America and the Caribbean contain some 30 countries and numerous small islands, with mountainous, volcanic landscapes.

CONTINENTAL FACTS

HIGHEST POINT:
Mt McKinley (Denali), Alaska, USA 6,194 m (20,322 ft)

LOWEST POINT:
Death Valley, California, USA 86 m (282 ft) below sea level

LARGEST LAKE:
Lake Superior, Canada/USA 83,270 sq km (32,140 sq miles)

LONGEST RIVER:
Mississippi-Missouri, USA 6,019 km (3,740 miles)

CANADA

Greenland
USA
CANADA
USA

CANADA EXTENDS from its long border with the US northwards to the Arctic Ocean. In recent years, the continued political relationship of French-speaking Québec with the rest of the country has been the key constitutional issue.

GEOGRAPHY

Arctic tundra and islands give way southwards to forests, interspersed with lakes and rivers, and then central plains, with vast prairies. Rocky Mountains in west, beyond which are the Coast Mountains, islands and fiords. Fertile lowlands in the east.

CLIMATE

Ranges from polar and sub-polar in the north, to cool in the south. Winters in the interior are colder and longer than on the coast, with temperatures well below freezing and deep snow; summers are hotter. Pacific coast has the warmest winters.

PEOPLE AND SOCIETY

Most people live along narrow strip near US border, fostering shared cultural values. Social differences, however, include wider welfare provision and Commonwealth membership. Government welcomes ethnic diversity among immigrants. Land claims by indigenous peoples settled in recent years.

THE ECONOMY

Wide-ranging resources, providing cheap energy and raw materials for manufactures, underpin high standard of living. Better productivity and rise of high-tech industries have increased unemployment. Concern over primary export prices.

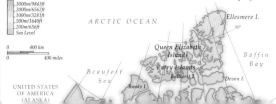

3000m/9843ft
2000m/6562ft
1000m/3281ft
500m/1640ft
200m/656ft
Sea Level

0 400 km
0 400 miles

ARCTIC OCEAN
Ellesmere I.
80°
Queen Elizabeth Islands
Parry Islands
Bathurst I.
Baffin Bay
Devon I.
Beaufort Sea
Banks I.
UNITED STATES OF AMERICA (ALASKA)
70°

◆ *INSIGHT: The magnetic north pole, where the dipping needle of a compass stands still, is located just off Bathurst Island in northern Canada*

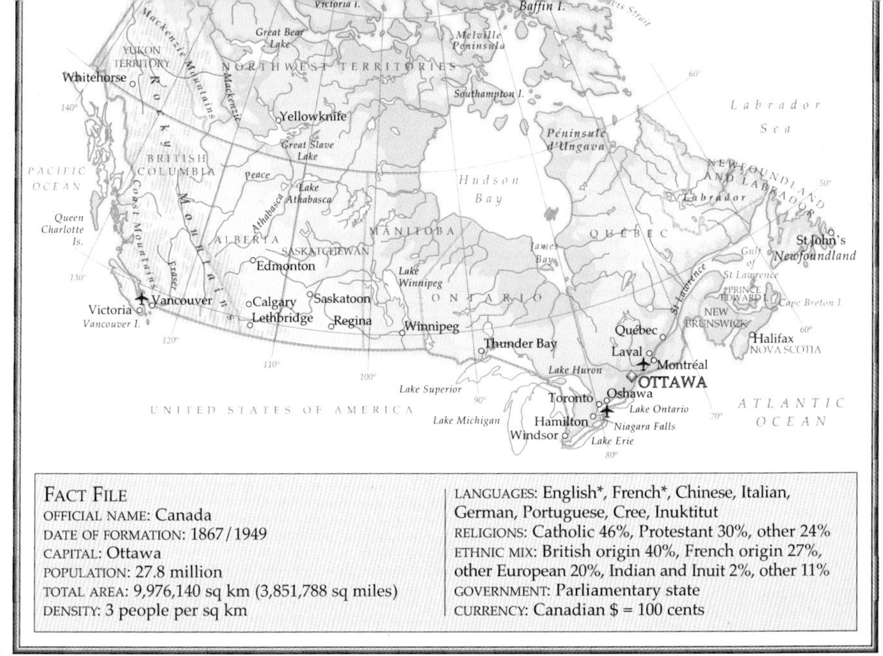
Victoria I.
Baffin I.
Melville Peninsula
Great Bear Lake
YUKON TERRITORY
Whitehorse
Mackenzie Mountains
Mackenzie
NORTHWEST TERRITORIES
Southampton I.
Rocky Mountains
Yellowknife
Great Slave Lake
Labrador Sea
Péninsule d'Ungava
BRITISH COLUMBIA
PACIFIC OCEAN
Peace
Lake Athabasca
Athabasca
Hudson Bay
NEWFOUNDLAND AND LABRADOR
Labrador
Coast Mountains
Queen Charlotte Is.
ALBERTA
MANITOBA
SASKATCHEWAN
QUÉBEC
St John's
Newfoundland
Gulf of St Lawrence
James Bay
Edmonton
Lake Winnipeg
Fraser
St Lawrence
PRINCE EDWARD I.
Cape Breton I.
Vancouver
Victoria
Vancouver I.
Calgary
Saskatoon
Lethbridge
Regina
ONTARIO
Winnipeg
NEW BRUNSWICK
Québec
Halifax
NOVA SCOTIA
Thunder Bay
Laval
Montréal
Lake Huron
OTTAWA
Lake Superior
Toronto
Oshawa
UNITED STATES OF AMERICA
Lake Ontario
ATLANTIC OCEAN
Lake Michigan
Hamilton
Niagara Falls
Windsor
Lake Erie
140°
130°
120°
110°
100°
90°
80°
70°
60°
50°

FACT FILE

OFFICIAL NAME: Canada
DATE OF FORMATION: 1867/1949
CAPITAL: Ottawa
POPULATION: 27.8 million
TOTAL AREA: 9,976,140 sq km (3,851,788 sq miles)
DENSITY: 3 people per sq km

LANGUAGES: English*, French*, Chinese, Italian, German, Portuguese, Cree, Inuktitut
RELIGIONS: Catholic 46%, Protestant 30%, other 24%
ETHNIC MIX: British origin 40%, French origin 27%, other European 20%, Indian and Inuit 2%, other 11%
GOVERNMENT: Parliamentary state
CURRENCY: Canadian $ = 100 cents

UNITED STATES OF AMERICA

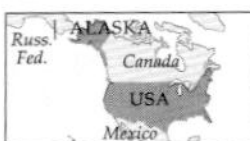
Russ. Fed.
ALASKA
Canada
USA
Mexico

STRETCHING ACROSS the most temperate part of North America, and with many natural resources, the USA is the world's leading economic power.

GEOGRAPHY

Central plain, mountains in west, hills and low mountains in east. Forested north and east, south-western deserts. Volcanic islands in Hawaii. Forest, tundra in Alaska.

CLIMATE

Wide variety. Continental in north, hot summers and mild winters in southeast, desert climate in southwest. Arctic climate in Alaska; Florida and Hawaii tropical.

PEOPLE AND SOCIETY

Multiracial population, established through successive waves of immigration, initially from Europe and Africa, with more recent influxes from Latin America and Asia. Strong sense of nationhood, despite cultural diversity. Conservative, usually Christian consensus, is increasingly challenged by liberal, secular values of US popular culture.

CANADA
Seattle
WASHINGTON
Spokane
Portland
PACIFIC OCEAN
Coast Ranges
OREGON
IDAHO
Boise
Great Salt Lake
Reno
Great Basin
NEVADA
Salt Lake City
Sacramento
Oakland
San Francisco
Sierra Nevada
UTAH
Fresno
CALIFORNIA
Death Valley
Bakersfield
Las Vegas
Grand Canyon
Los Angeles
Colorado
ARIZONA
San Diego
Phoenix
Tucson
MEXICO
PACIFIC OCEAN
Kauai
Oahu
Honolulu
HAWAII
Hawai'i
0 200 km
0 200 miles

FACT FILE

OFFICIAL NAME: United States of America
DATE OF FORMATION: 1787/1959
CAPITAL: Washington DC
POPULATION: 265.8 million
TOTAL AREA: 9,372,610 sq km (3,681,760 sq miles)
DENSITY: 28 people per sq km
LANGUAGES: English*, Spanish, other
RELIGIONS: Protestant 56%, Catholic 28%, Jewish 2%, other 14%
ETHNIC MIX: White (inc. Hispanic) 83%, Black 13%, other 4%
GOVERNMENT: Multiparty republic
CURRENCY: US $ = 100 cents

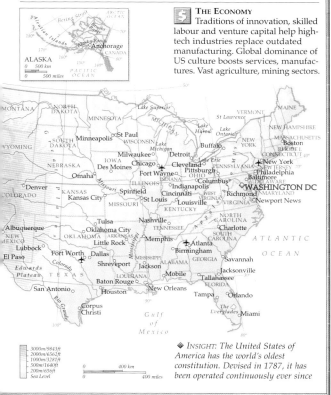

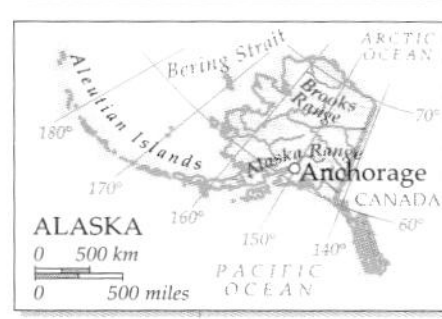
Bering Strait
ARCTIC OCEAN
Aleutian Islands
Brooks Range
Alaska Range
Anchorage
CANADA
180°
170°
160°
150°
140°
70°
60°
ALASKA
0 500 km
0 500 miles
PACIFIC OCEAN

THE ECONOMY

Traditions of innovation, skilled labour and venture capital help high-tech industries replace outdated manufacturing. Global dominance of US culture boosts services, manufactures. Vast agriculture, mining sectors.

MONTANA
NORTH DAKOTA
MINNESOTA
Lake Superior
VERMONT
MAINE
St Lawrence
Lake Huron
Lake Ontario
NEW HAMPSHIRE
MICHIGAN
SOUTH DAKOTA
Minneapolis
St Paul
WISCONSIN
Lake Michigan
NEW YORK
MASSACHUSETTS
Boston
WYOMING
Buffalo
RHODE I.
Milwaukee
Detroit
CONNECTICUT
IOWA
Lake Erie
New York
NEBRASKA
Des Moines
Chicago
Cleveland
PENNSYLVANIA
NEW JERSEY
Omaha
Fort Wayne
Pittsburgh
Philadelphia
OHIO
Baltimore
INDIANA
DELAWARE
Denver
ILLINOIS
Columbus
WASHINGTON DC
COLORADO
KANSAS
Missouri
Spinfield
Indianapolis
Kansas City
Cincinnati
WEST VIRGINIA
Richmond
MARYLAND
St Louis
MISSOURI
Louisville
VIRGINIA
Newport News
KENTUCKY
NORTH CAROLINA
Tulsa
Nashville
Albuquerque
Oklahoma City
TENNESSEE
Charlotte
NEW MEXICO
OKLAHOMA
ARKANSAS
Memphis
SOUTH CAROLINA
ATLANTIC OCEAN
Little Rock
Atlanta
Lubbock
Birmingham
El Paso
Fort Worth
Dallas
Mississippi
MISSISSIPPI
GEORGIA
Savannah
Colorado
Shreveport
Jackson
ALABAMA
Edwards Plateau
TEXAS
LOUISIANA
Mobile
Jacksonville
Tallahassee
Baton Rouge
FLORIDA
San Antonio
Houston
New Orleans
Tampa
Orlando
Rio Grande
Corpus Christi
The Everglades
Miami
Gulf of Mexico
3000m/9843ft
2000m/6562ft
1000m/3281ft
500m/1640ft
200m/656ft
Sea Level
0 400 km
0 400 miles

◆ *INSIGHT: The United States of America has the world's oldest constitution. Devised in 1787, it has been operated continuously ever since*

Mexico

USA
MEXICO
Belize
Guatemala

LOCATED BETWEEN the southern end of North America and the Central American states, Mexico was a Spanish colony for 300 years until 1836.

Geography

Coastal plains along Pacific and Atlantic seaboards rise to a high arid central plateau. To the east and west are Sierra Madre mountain ranges. Limestone lowlands in the Yucatan peninsula.

Climate

Plateau and high mountains are warm for much of year. Pacific coast is tropical: storms occur mostly March–December. Northwest is dry.

The Economy

One of the world's largest oil producers, with large reserves. Tropical fruits, vegetables grown as cash crops. Population growth outstripping job creation. North American Free Trade Agreement, signed with US and Canada, came into force in 1994. US companies poised to move into Mexico and enter competition with Mexican industry.

Tijuana
Mexicali
Ensenada
UNITED STATES O
Nogales
Ciudad Juáre
30°
Baja California
Hermosillo
Río Yaqui
Golfo de California
115°
Ciudad Obregón
Los Mochi
Guasav
25°
Culiacán
La Paz
Mazatlá
110°
Islas Tres Marías
20°
3000m/9843ft
2000m/6562ft
1000m/3281ft
500m/1640ft
200m/656ft
Sea Level
0 200 km
0 200 miles

Fact File

OFFICIAL NAME: United Mexican State
DATE OF FORMATION: 1836/1867
CAPITAL: Mexico City
POPULATION: 95.5 million
TOTAL AREA: 1,958,200 sq km (756,061 sq miles)
DENSITY: 49 people per sq km
LANGUAGES: Spanish*, Mayan dialects
RELIGIONS: Roman Catholic 89%, Protestant 6%, other 5%
ETHNIC MIX: *mestizo* 55%, Indian 30%, White 6%, other 9%
GOVERNMENT: Multiparty republic
CURRENCY: Peso = 100 centavos

◆ *Insight: More people emigrate from Mexico than any other state in the world. Hundreds of thousands of Mexicans cross into the US each year, many of them staying as illegal immigrants*

People and Society

Most Mexicans are *mestizos* of mixed Spanish and Indian descent. Rural Indians are largely segregated from Hispanic society and most live in poverty. The situation leads to intermittent rebellions by landless Indians. Men remain dominant in business and few women take part in the political process. Mexico is a multiparty democracy in name; in practice, the PRI (Institutional Revolutionary Party) has retained power since 1929. Rural depopulation and high unemployment are major problems. Mexico has a faster-growing population than any other large country. Between 1960 and 1980, its population doubled.

Rio Grande
Chihuahua
Nuevo Laredo
Monclova
Reynosa
Sierra Madre Occidental
Torreón
Monterrey
Saltillo
Matamoros
Durango
Sierra Madre Oriental
Ciudad Victoria
Caribbean Sea
Zacatecas
Ciudad de Valles
Tampico
San Luis Potosí
Yucatan Channel
Aguascalientes
León
Tepic
Mérida
Gulf of Mexico
Península de Yucatán
Irapuato
Querétaro
Poza Rica
Guadalajara
Salamanca
Pachuca
MEXICO CITY
Bahía de Campeche
Colima
Morelia
Toluca
Puebla
Orizaba
Veracruz
Chetumal
Río Balsas
Villahermosa
Coatzacoalcos
BELIZE
Sierra Madre del Sur
Oaxaca
Istmo de Tehuantepec
Tuxtla Gutiérrez
Acapulco
Sierra Madre
GUATEMALA
Tapachula
105°
100°
95°
90°
PACIFIC OCEAN

GUATEMALA

Mexico
Belize
GUATEMALA
Honduras
El Salvador

THE LARGEST state on the Central American isthmus, Guatemala returned to civilian rule in 1986, after 32 years of repressive military rule.

GEOGRAPHY

Narrow Pacific coastal plain. Central highlands with volcanoes. Short, swampy Caribbean coast. Tropical rainforests in the north.

CLIMATE

Tropical, hot and humid in coastal regions and north. More temperate in central highlands.

PEOPLE AND SOCIETY

Indians form a majority, but power, wealth and land controlled by *ladino* elite. Highland Indians were main victims of the military's indiscriminate campaign against guerrilla groups 1978–84. Since civilian rule, the level of violence has diminished, but extreme poverty is still widespread.

◆ INSIGHT: *Guatemala, which means 'land of trees', was the centre of the ancient Maya civilization*

THE ECONOMY

Agriculture is key sector. Sugar, coffee, beef, bananas and cardamom top exports. Political stability has revived tourism.

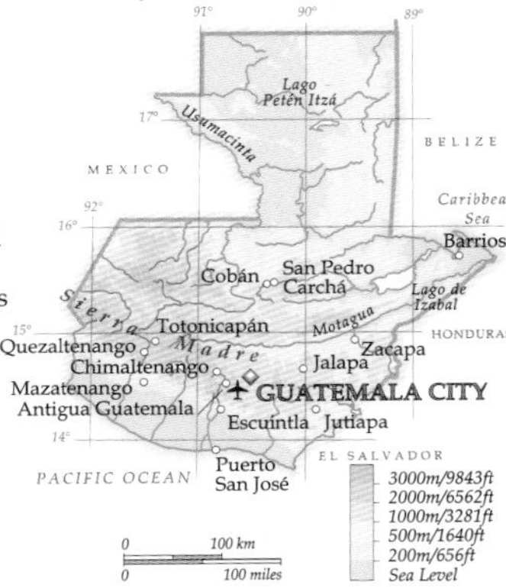
91°
90°
89°
Lago Petén Itzá
17°
Usumacinta
BELIZE
MEXICO
Caribbean Sea
92°
16°
Barrios
Cobán
San Pedro Carchá
Lago de Izabal
Sierra Madre
Totonicapán
Motagua
15°
Quezaltenango
HONDURAS
Zacapa
Chimaltenango
Jalapa
Mazatenango
GUATEMALA CITY
Antigua Guatemala
Escuintla
Jutiapa
14°
EL SALVADOR
PACIFIC OCEAN
Puerto San José
3000m/9843ft
2000m/6562ft
1000m/3281ft
500m/1640ft
200m/656ft
Sea Level
0
100 km
0
100 miles

FACT FILE

OFFICIAL NAME: Republic of Guatemala
DATE OF FORMATION: 1838
CAPITAL: Guatemala City
POPULATION: 10 million
TOTAL AREA: 108,890 sq km (42,043 sq miles)
DENSITY: 89 people per sq km
LANGUAGES: Spanish*, Quiché, Mam, Kekchí, Cakchiquel
RELIGIONS: Christian 99%, other 1%
ETHNIC MIX: Maya Indian 55%, *ladino* (Euro-Indian, White) 45%
GOVERNMENT: Multiparty republic
CURRENCY: Quetzal = 100 centavos

BELIZE

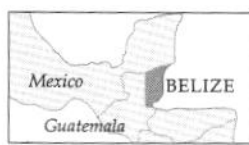
Mexico
BELIZE
Guatemala

BELIZE LIES on the eastern shore of the Yucatan Peninsula in Central America. A former British colony, it became fully independent in 1981.

GEOGRAPHY

Almost half the land area is forested. Low mountains in south-east. Flat swampy coastal plains.

CLIMATE

Tropical. Very hot and humid, with May–December rainy season.

PEOPLE AND SOCIETY

Spanish-speaking *mestizos* now outnumber black Creoles for the first time. Huge influx of migrants from other states in the region in the past decade. This has caused some tension. Newcomers provide manpower for agriculture, but have put pressure on social services. Creoles have traditionally dominated society. Emigration to US has weakened their influence.

THE ECONOMY

Agriculture, tourism and remittances from Belizeans living abroad are economic mainstays. Citrus fruit concentrates, lobsters, shrimps and textiles are exported.

Corozal
Louisville
MEXICO
Hondo
Orange Walk
New River
Maskall
Crooked Tree
Belize City
Belize
BELMOPAN
San Ignacio
Reef
Dangriga
GUATEMALA
Maya Mts.
Barrier
Monkey River Town
San Antonio
Punta Gorda
Caribbean Sea
Sarstoon
1000m/3281ft
500m/1640ft
200m/656ft
Sea Level
50 km
50 miles

◆ *INSIGHT: Belize's barrier reef is the second largest in the world*

FACT FILE

OFFICIAL NAME: Belize
DATE OF FORMATION: 1981
CAPITAL: Belmopan
POPULATION: 200,000
TOTAL AREA: 22,960 sq km (8,865 sq miles)
DENSITY: 9 people per sq km
LANGUAGES: English*, English Creole, Spanish, Maya, Garifuna
RELIGIONS: Christian 87%, other 13%
ETHNIC MIX: *Mestizo* 44%, Creole 30%, Indian 11%, Garifuna 8%, other 7%
GOVERNMENT: Parliamentary democracy
CURRENCY: Belizean $ =100 cents

EL SALVADOR

Guatemala
Honduras
EL SALVADOR

EL SALVADOR IS Central America's smallest state. A 12-year war between US-backed government troops and left-wing guerrillas ended in 1992.

GEOGRAPHY

Narrow coastal belt backed by mountain ranges with over 20 volcanic peaks. Central plateau.

CLIMATE

Tropical coastal belt is very hot, with seasonal rains. Cooler, temperate climate in highlands.

PEOPLE AND SOCIETY

Population is largely *mestizo*; ethnic tensions are few. The civil war was fought over economic disparities, which still exist, despite some reform. 75,000 people died during the war, many were unarmed civilians. Around 500,000 more were displaced – mainly rural peasant families. In 1992, left-wing movement gave up its arms and joined formal political process.

THE ECONOMY

Civil war caused $2 billion-worth of damage. Huge amounts of foreign aid needed for survival. Over-dependence on coffee, which accounts for 90% of exports.

◆ *INSIGHT: Named for the Saviour, Jesus Christ, El Salvador is the most densely populated state in the region*

Metapán
GUATEMALA
HONDURAS
Santa Ana
Chalchuapa
Chalatenango
Lempa
Embalse Cerrón Grande
Ahuachapán
SAN SALVADOR
Sensuntepeque
Sonsonate
Cojutepeque
San Francisco
San Vicente
Zacatecoluca
San Miguel
Usulután
La Unión
Jiquilisco
PACIFIC OCEAN
89°
90°
88°
14°
13°
0 25 km
0 25 miles
2000m/6562ft
1000m/3281ft
500m/1640ft
200m/656ft
Sea Level

FACT FILE

OFFICIAL NAME: Republic of El Salvador
DATE OF FORMATION: 1856/1838
CAPITAL: San Salvador
POPULATION: 5.4 million
TOTAL AREA: 21,040 sq km (8,124 sq miles)
DENSITY: 261 people per sq km
LANGUAGES: Spanish*, Nahua
RELIGIONS: Roman Catholic 75%, other (including Protestant) 25%
ETHNIC MIX: *Mestizo* (Euro-Indian) 89%, Indian 10%, White 1%
GOVERNMENT: Multiparty republic
CURRENCY: Colón = 100 centavos

Honduras

Guatemala
HONDURAS
El Salvador
Nicaragua

STRADDLING THE Central American isthmus, Honduras returned to democratic civilian rule in 1981, after a succession of military regimes.

Geography

Narrow plains along both coasts. Mountainous interior, cut by river valleys. Tropical forests, swamps and lagoons in the east.

Climate

Tropical coastal lowlands are hot and humid, with May–October rains. Interior is cooler and drier.

People and Society

Majority of population is *mestizo.* Garifunas on Caribbean coast maintain their own language and culture. Indians inhabit the east, and remote mountain areas; their land rights are often violated. Most of the rural population live in poverty. Land reform, and high unemployment are main issues facing the government.

The Economy

Second poorest country in the region. Bananas are traditional cash crop – production dominated by two US companies. Coffee, timber and livestock are also exported.

◈ INSIGHT: *Honduran currency is named after a Lenca Indian chief who was the main leader of resistance to the Spanish conquest in the 16th century*

Caribbean Sea
Puerto Cortés
Tela
La Ceiba
GUATEMALA
San Pedro Sula
Esparta
Olanchito
Laguna de Caratasca
Macuelizo
El Progreso
Florida
Villanueva
Santa Rosa de Copán
Siguatepeque
Juticalpa
Coco
Comayagua
TEGUCIGALPA
Danlí
Coco
EL SALVADOR
NICARAGUA
PACIFIC OCEAN
Choluteca
2000m/6562ft
1000m/3281ft
500m/1640ft
200m/656ft
Sea Level
0 100 km
0 100 miles

Fact File

OFFICIAL NAME: Republic of Honduras
DATE OF FORMATION: 1838
CAPITAL: Tegucigalpa
POPULATION: 5.6 million
TOTAL AREA: 112,090 sq km (43,278 sq miles)
DENSITY: 49 people per sq km
LANGUAGES: Spanish*, English Creole, Garifuna, Indian languages
RELIGIONS: Catholic 97%, other 3%
ETHNIC MIX: *Mestizo* 90%, Indian 7%, Garifuna (Black Carib) 2%, White 1%
GOVERNMENT: Multiparty republic
CURRENCY: Lempira = 100 centavos

NICARAGUA

Honduras
El Salvador
NICARAGUA
Costa Rica

NICARAGUA LIES at the heart of Central America. An 11-year war between left-wing Sandinistas and right-wing US-backed Contras ended in 1989.

GEOGRAPHY

Extensive forested plains in the east. Central mountain region with many active volcanoes. Pacific coastlands are dominated by lakes.

CLIMATE

Tropical. Hot all year round in the lowlands. Cooler in the mountains. Occasional hurricanes.

PEOPLE AND SOCIETY

The isolated Atlantic regions, populated by Miskito Indians and blacks, gained limited independence in 1987. Elections in 1990 brought a right-wing pro-US party to power, but the Sandinistas remain a major political force in a country where poverty and unrest are rising.

◆ INSIGHT: *Lake Nicaragua is the only freshwater lake to contain ocean animals*

THE ECONOMY

Coffee, sugar and cotton are the main exports. All are affected by low world prices. Economy dependent on foreign aid; the US is the largest donor.

1000m/3281ft
500m/1640ft
200m/656ft
Sea Level
HONDURAS
Coco
La Mosquitia
Caribbean Sea
Ocotal
Jinotega
Estelí
Matagalpa
Chinandega
Corinto
Telica
Matiguas
León
Nagarote
MANAGUA
Juigalpa
Bluefields
San Rafael del Sur
Granada
Nandaime
Diriamba
Jinotepe
Rivas
Lago de Nicaragua
COSTA RICA
San Juan
100 km
100 miles

FACT FILE

OFFICIAL NAME: Republic of Nicaragua
DATE OF FORMATION: 1838
CAPITAL: Managua
POPULATION: 4.1 million
TOTAL AREA: 130,000 sq km (50,193 sq miles)
DENSITY: 34 people per sq km
LANGUAGES: Spanish*, English Creole, Miskito
RELIGIONS: Catholic 95%, other 5%
ETHNIC MIX: *Mestizo* 69%, White 17%, Black 9%, Indian 5%
GOVERNMENT: Multiparty republic
CURRENCY: Córdoba = 100 pence

COSTA RICA

Nicaragua
COSTA RICA
Panama

COSTA RICA is the most stable country in Central America. Its neutrality in foreign affairs is long-standing, but it has very strong ties with the US.

GEOGRAPHY

Coastal plains of swamp and savannah rise to a fertile central plateau, which leads to a mountain range with active volcanic peaks.

CLIMATE

Hot and humid in coastal regions. Temperate uplands. High annual rainfall.

PEOPLE AND SOCIETY

Population has a mixture of Spanish, African and native Indian ancestry. Costa Rica's long democratic tradition, developed public health system and high literacy rates are unrivalled in the region. Plantation-owning families and the US are influential in politics.

◆ *INSIGHT: Costa Rica's constitution is the only one in the world to forbid national armies*

THE ECONOMY

Traditionally agricultural, but mining and manufacturing are developing rapidly. Bananas, beef and coffee are the leading exports. Tourist numbers have increased considerably in recent years.

NICARAGUA
San Juan
Caribbean Sea
Liberia
Cañas
Quesada
Alajuela
Heredia
San Ramón
Puntarenas
SAN JOSÉ
Turrialba
Limón
Cartago
San Isidro
Cordillera de Talamanca
PACIFIC OCEAN
PANAMA
Peninsula de Osa
3000m/9843ft
2000m/6562ft
1000m/3281ft
500m/1640ft
200m/656ft
Sea Level
0 50 km
0 50 miles

FACT FILE

OFFICIAL NAME: Republic of Costa Rica
DATE OF FORMATION: 1821 / 1838
CAPITAL: San José
POPULATION: 3.3 million
TOTAL AREA: 51,100 sq km (19,730 miles)
DENSITY: 64 people per sq km
LANGUAGES: Spanish*, English Creole, Bribri, Cabecar
RELIGIONS: Catholic 95%, other 5%
ETHNIC MIX: White / *mestizo* (Euro-Indian) 96%, Black 2%, Indian 2%
GOVERNMENT: Multiparty republic
CURRENCY: Colón = 100 centimos

PANAMA

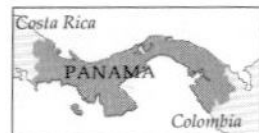
Costa Rica
PANAMA
Colombia

PANAMA IS the southernmost country in Central America. The Panama Canal (under US-control until 2000) links the Pacific and Atlantic oceans.

GEOGRAPHY

Lowlands along both coasts, with savannah-covered plains and rolling hills. Mountainous interior. Swamps and rainforests in the east.

CLIMATE

Hot and humid, with heavy rainfall in May–December wet season. Cooler at high altitudes.

PEOPLE AND SOCIETY

Multi-ethnic society, dominated by people of Spanish origin. Indians live in remote areas. The Canal, and US military bases, have given society a cosmopolitan outlook, but the Catholic extended family remains strong. In 1989, US troops invaded to arrest its dictator General Noriega, on drugs charges, and to restore civilian rule.

THE ECONOMY

Important banking sector, plus related financial and insurance services. Earnings from merchant ships sailing under Panamanian flag. Banana and shrimp exports.

◆ *INSIGHT: The Panama Canal extends for 80 km (50 miles). Around 12,000 ships pass through it each year*

Caribbean Sea
Colón
Cristóbal
Panama Canal
San Miguelito
Arraiján
PANAMA CITY
La Chorrera
Balboa
COSTA RICA
La Concepción
Serranía de Tabasará
David
Santiago
Archipiélago de las Perlas
La Palma
Golfo de Chiriquí
Chitré
Las Tablas
Golfo de Panamá
Isla de Coiba
COLOMBIA
PACIFIC OCEAN
80°
79°
78°
9°
8°
83°
82°
81°
0
100 km
0
100 miles
2000m/6562ft
1000m/3281ft
500m/1640ft
200m/656ft
Sea Level

FACT FILE

OFFICIAL NAME: Republic of Panama
DATE OF FORMATION: 1903/1914
CAPITAL: Panama City
POPULATION: 2.6 million
TOTAL AREA: 77,080 sq km (29,761 sq miles)
DENSITY: 33 people per sq km
LANGUAGES: Spanish*, English Creole, Indian languages
RELIGIONS: Catholic 93%, other 7%
ETHNIC MIX: *Mestizo* 70%, Black 14%, White 10%, Indian 6%
GOVERNMENT: Multiparty republic
CURRENCY: Balboa = 100 centesimos

JAMAICA

Haiti
Cuba
JAMAICA
Dominican Rep.

FIRST COLONIZED by the Spanish and then, from 1655, by the English, the Caribbean island of Jamaica achieved independence in 1962.

GEOGRAPHY

Mainly mountainous, with lush tropical vegetation. Inaccessible limestone area in the northwest. Low, irregular coastal plains are broken by hills and plateaux.

CLIMATE

Tropical. Hot and humid, with temperate interior. Hurricanes are likely June–November.

PEOPLE AND SOCIETY

Ethnically diverse, but tensions result from the gulf between rich and poor, rather than race. Economic and political life dominated by a few wealthy, long-established families. Armed crime, much of it drugs-related, is a problem. Large areas of Kingston are ruled by *Dons*, gang leaders who administer their own violent justice.

THE ECONOMY

Major producer of bauxite (aluminium ore). Tourism well developed. Light industry and data processing for US companies. Sugar, coffee and rum are exported.

◆ INSIGHT: *Jamaica's Rastafarians look to the late emperor of Ethiopia, Haile Selassie, as their spiritual leader, and Africa as their spiritual home*

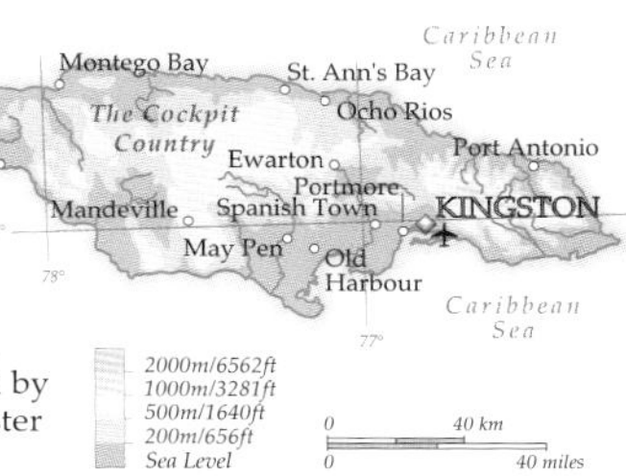
Caribbean Sea
Montego Bay
St. Ann's Bay
Ocho Rios
The Cockpit Country
Savanna -la-Mar
Ewarton
Port Antonio
Portmore
Mandeville
Spanish Town
KINGSTON
May Pen
Old Harbour
18°
78°
77°
Caribbean Sea
2000m/6562ft
1000m/3281ft
500m/1640ft
200m/656ft
Sea Level
0
40 km
0
40 miles

FACT FILE

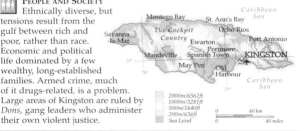

OFFICIAL NAME: Jamaica
DATE OF FORMATION: 1962
CAPITAL: Kingston
POPULATION: 2.5 million
TOTAL AREA: 10,990 sq km (4,243 sq miles)
DENSITY: 227 people per sq km
LANGUAGES: English*, English Creole, Hindi, Spanish, Chinese
RELIGIONS: Christian 60%, other 40%
ETHNIC MIX: Black 75%, mixed 15%, South Asian 5%, other 5%
GOVERNMENT: Parliamentary democracy
CURRENCY: Jamaican $ = 100 cents

CUBA

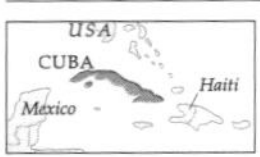
USA
CUBA
Haiti
Mexico

CUBA IS the largest island in the Caribbean and the only Communist country in the Americas. It has been led by Fidel Castro since 1959.

GEOGRAPHY

Mostly fertile plains and basins. Three mountainous areas. Forests of pine and mahogany cover one quarter of the country.

CLIMATE

Subtropical. Hot all year round, and very hot in summer. Heaviest rainfall in the mountains. Hurricanes can strike in autumn.

PEOPLE AND SOCIETY

Castro's regime has reduced once extreme wealth disparities, given education a high priority and established an efficient health service. Political dissent, however, is not tolerated. Dramatic fall in living standards in recent years has led 30,000 Cubans to flee by boat to the US, to seek asylum.

HAVANA (La Habana)
Straits of Florida
Marianao
Matanzas
Colón
Pinar del Río
Cienfuegos
Santa Clara
ATLANTIC OCEAN
Ciego de Avila
Camagüey
Archipiélago de los Canarreos
Las Tunas
Holguín
Bayamo
Guantánamo
Santiago de Cuba
GUANTÁNAMO BAY (to USA)
Caribbean Sea
84°
82°
80°
78°
76°
22°
20°
1000m/3281ft
500m/1640ft
200m/656ft
Sea Level
0 100 km
0 100 miles

THE ECONOMY

Main product is sugar. Cuba's economy is in crisis following the loss of its patron and supplier, the former USSR. Recent reforms have allowed small-scale enterprise and use of US dollar. The 30-year-old US trade embargo continues.

◆ *INSIGHT: To combat fuel shortages, over half a million traditional black bicycles have been imported from China*

FACT FILE

OFFICIAL NAME: Republic of Cuba
DATE OF FORMATION: 1902
CAPITAL: Havana
POPULATION: 10.9 million
TOTAL AREA: 110,860 sq km (42,803 sq miles)
DENSITY: 98 people per sq km
LANGUAGES: Spanish*, English, French, Chinese
RELIGIONS: Roman Catholic 85%, other 15%
ETHNIC MIX: White 66%, Afro-European 22%, other 12%
GOVERNMENT: Socialist republic
CURRENCY: Peso = 100 centavos

BAHAMAS

USA
BAHAMAS
Cuba

LOCATED IN the western Atlantic, off the Florida coast, the Bahamas comprises some 700 islands and 2,400 cays, 30 of which are inhabited.

GEOGRAPHY
Long, mainly flat coral formations with a few low hills. Some islands have pine forests, lagoons and mangrove swamps.

THE ECONOMY
Tourism accounts for half of all revenues. Major international financial services sector, including banking and insurance.

CLIMATE
Subtropical. Hot summers, and mild winters. Heavy rainfall, especially in summer. Hurricanes can strike from July–December.

PEOPLE AND SOCIETY
Over half the population live on New Providence. Tourist industry employs 40% of the work force. Remainder are engaged in traditional fishing and agriculture, or in administration. Close ties with US were strained in 1980s, with senior government members implicated in narcotics corruption. In 1993, tough policies instituted to deter settling of Haitian refugees.

◆ *INSIGHT: Six tourists per inhabitant visit the Bahamas every year*

Straits of Florida
Grand Bahama I.
Freeport
Great Abaco
Berry Is
New Providence
Eleuthera I.
Nicholls Town
NASSAU
Andros Town
Andros I.
ATLANTIC OCEAN
Exuma Sound
Cat I.
San Salvador
Exuma Cays
Rum Cay
Long I.
Crooked I.
Mayaguana
Acklins I.
Caicos Passage
Great Inagua
Sea Level
0 100 km
0 100 miles

FACT FILE	
OFFICIAL NAME: The Commonwealth of the Bahamas	DENSITY: 21 people per sq km
DATE OF FORMATION: 1973	LANGUAGES: English*, English Creole
CAPITAL: Nassau	RELIGIONS: Protestant 76%, Roman Catholic 19%, other 5%
POPULATION: 300,000	ETHNIC MIX: Black 85%, White 15%
TOTAL AREA: 13,880 sq km (5,359 sq miles)	GOVERNMENT: Parliamentary democracy
	CURRENCY: Bahamian $ = 100 cents

HAITI

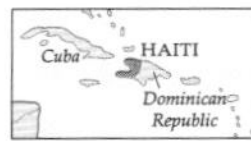
Cuba
HAITI
Dominican Republic

SHARES the Caribbean island of Hispaniola with the Dominican Republic. At independence in 1804, it became the world's first black republic.

GEOGRAPHY

Predominantly mountainous, with forests and fertile plains.

CLIMATE

Tropical, with rain throughout the year. Humid in coastal areas, much cooler in the mountains.

PEOPLE AND SOCIETY

Majority of population is of African descent. A few have European roots, primarily French. Rigid class structure maintains vast disparities of wealth. Most Haitians live in extreme poverty. In recent years, political oppression and a collapsing economy led thousands to seek asylum in the USA. In 1994, US-led troops reinstated the elected president, who was ousted by the military in 1991.

THE ECONOMY

Few natural resources. In 1994, after 3 years of UN sanctions, the country's economic links were restored and foreign aid resumed.

◆ *INSIGHT: Haiti's independence was achieved after Toussaint l'Ouverture led a slave rebellion in 1791*

Île de la Tortue
ATLANTIC OCEAN
20°
Port-de-Paix
Limbé
Cap-Haïtien
Fort-Liberté
Massif du Nord
Gonaïves
Golfe de la Gonâve
Desdunes
St-Marc
Hinche
Petite-Rivière-de-l'Artibonite
DOMINICAN REP.
19°
Île de la Gonâve
Jérémie
PORT-AU-PRINCE
Pétionville
Massif de la Hotte
Les Cayes
Jacmel
18°
Caribbean Sea
74°
72°

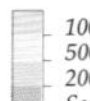
1000m/3281ft
500m/1640ft
200m/656ft
Sea Level

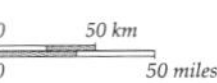
0
50 km
0
50 miles

FACT FILE

OFFICIAL NAME: Republic of Haiti
DATE OF FORMATION: 1804
CAPITAL: Port-au-Prince
POPULATION: 6.9 million
TOTAL AREA: 27,750 sq km (10,714 sq miles)
DENSITY: 234 people per sq km
LANGUAGES: French*, French Creole*, English
RELIGIONS: Roman Catholic 80%, Protestant 16%, Voodoo 4%
ETHNIC MIX: Black 95%, Afro-European 5%
GOVERNMENT: Multiparty republic
CURRENCY: Gourde = 100 centimes

DOMINICAN REPUBLIC

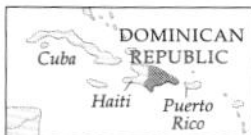
DOMINICAN
REPUBLIC
Cuba
Haiti
Puerto
Rico

OCCUPIES THE eastern two-thirds of the island of Hispaniola in the Caribbean. Frequent coups and a strong US influence mark its recent past.

GEOGRAPHY

Highlands and rainforested mountains – including highest peak in Caribbean, Pico Duarte – interspersed with fertile valleys. Extensive coastal plain in the east.

CLIMATE

Hot and humid close to sea level, cooler at altitude. Heavy rainfall, especially in the northeast.

PEOPLE AND SOCIETY

White landowners and the military hold political power. Mixed-race majority control commerce and form bulk of middle classes. Many of the poor are black. White and mixed-race women are starting to enter the professions. Widespread poverty and high unemployment have led some Dominicans to emigrate to the USA, or become drug-traffickers.

THE ECONOMY

Mining – mainly of nickel and gold – and sugar are major sectors. Hidden economy based on trans-shipment of narcotics to the US. Recent dramatic growth in tourism.

◆ *INSIGHT: Santo Domingo is the oldest city in the Americas. It was founded in 1496 by the brother of Christopher Columbus*

Monte Cristi
Puerto Plata
Mao
Santiago
ATLANTIC OCEAN
San Francisco de Macorís
La Vega
Cordillera Central
Pico Duarte 3088m
HAITI
San Juan
Lago Enriquillo
SANTO DOMINGO
El Seibo
San Pedro de Macorís
San Cristóbal
La Romana
Barahona
Caribbean Sea
0 50 km
0 50 miles
2000m/6562ft
1000m/3281ft
500m/1640ft
200m/656ft
Sea Level

FACT FILE

OFFICIAL NAME: Dominican Republic
DATE OF FORMATION: 1865
CAPITAL: Santo Domingo
POPULATION: 7.6 million
TOTAL AREA: 48,730 sq km (18,815 sq miles)
DENSITY: 149 people per sq km
LANGUAGES: Spanish*, French Creole
RELIGIONS: Roman Catholic 95%, other (Protestant, Jewish) 5%
ETHNIC MIX: Afro-European 73%, White 16%, Black 11%
GOVERNMENT: Multiparty republic
CURRENCY: Peso = 100 centavos

ST KITTS & NEVIS

Puerto Rico
Antigua & Barbuda
ST KITTS & NEVIS
Dominica

ST KITTS and Nevis lies in the northern part of the Leeward Islands chain in the Caribbean. Nevis is the less developed of the two islands.

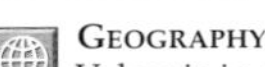

GEOGRAPHY
Volcanic in origin, with forested, mountainous interiors. Nevis has hot and cold springs.

CLIMATE
Tropical, tempered by trade winds. Little seasonal variation in temperature. Moderate rainfall.

PEOPLE AND SOCIETY
Majority of the population is of African descent. Intermarriage has blurred other racial lines and eliminated ethnic tensions. For most people, the extended family is the norm. Wealth disparities are not great, but urban professionals enjoy a higher standard of living than rural sugar cane farmers. Politics is based on the British system; funds are provided by professionals and the trade unions. The proposed Leeward Islands union is the main political issue.

THE ECONOMY
Sugar industry, currently UK-managed, has preferential access to EU and US markets. Successful and still expanding tourist industry.

◆ *INSIGHT: Nevis has been renowned as a spa since the 18th century, and is known as the 'Queen of the Caribbean'*

Dieppe Bay Town
St. Paul's
St Kitts
Cayon
ATLANTIC OCEAN
17°20'
62°50'
Old Road Town
Golden Rock Airport
BASSETERRE
62°45'
62°35'
17°15'
Caribbean Sea
The Narrows
Newcastle
62°40'
Nevis
17°10'
Charlestown
Zion
Bath
1000m/3281ft
500m/1640ft
200m/656ft
Sea Level
0 5 km
0 5 miles

FACT FILE

OFFICIAL NAME: Federation of Saint Christopher and Nevis
DATE OF FORMATION: 1983
CAPITAL: Basseterre
POPULATION: 44,000
TOTAL AREA: 360 sq km (139 sq miles)
DENSITY: 122.2 people per sq km
LANGUAGES: English*, English Creole
RELIGIONS: Protestant 85%, Roman Catholic 10%, other Christian 5%
ETHNIC MIX: Black 95%, mixed 5%
GOVERNMENT: Parliamentary democracy
CURRENCY: E. Caribbean $ = 100 cents

ANTIGUA & BARBUDA

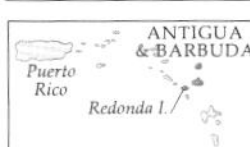
ANTIGUA
& BARBUDA
Puerto
Rico
Redonda I.

LYING AT the outer edge of the Leeward Islands group in the Caribbean, Antigua and Barbuda's area includes the uninhabited islet of Redonda.

GEOGRAPHY

Mainly low-lying limestone and coral islands with some higher volcanic areas. Antigua's coast is indented with bays and harbours.

CLIMATE

Tropical, moderated by trade winds and sea breezes. Humidity and rainfall are low for the region.

PEOPLE AND SOCIETY

Population almost entirely of African origin, with small communities of Europeans and South Asians. Women's status has risen as a result of greater access to education. Wealth disparities are small and unemployment is low. Politics dominated for past 30 years by the Bird family.

◆ *INSIGHT: In 1865, Redonda was 'claimed' by an eccentric Englishman as a kingdom for his son*

THE ECONOMY

Tourism is the main source of revenue and the biggest provider of jobs. Fishing and sea-island cotton industries are expanding.

ATLANTIC
OCEAN
200m/656ft
Sea Level
0 5 km
0 5 miles
Codrington
Codrington
Lagoon
The Highlands
Barbuda
V.C. Bird
Intl. Airport
Long I.
Palmetto
Point
ST JOHN'S
Guiana I.
Spanish
Point
Antigua
Bolans
Freetown
Green I.
Falmouth
Guadeloupe Passage
Caribbean Sea

FACT FILE

OFFICIAL NAME: Antigua and Barbuda
DATE OF FORMATION: 1981
CAPITAL: St John's
POPULATION: 65,000
TOTAL AREA: 440 sq km (170 sq miles)
DENSITY: 148 people per sq km
LANGUAGES: English*, English Creole
RELIGIONS: Protestant 87%, Roman Catholic 10%, other 3%
ETHNIC MIX: Black 98%, other 2%
GOVERNMENT: Parliamentary democracy
CURRENCY: E. Caribbean $ = 100 cents

DOMINICA

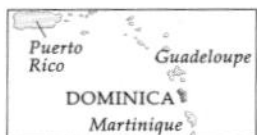
Puerto Rico
Guadeloupe
DOMINICA
Martinique

DOMINICA RESISTED European colonization until the 18th century, when it was controlled first by the French, and then, until 1978, by the British.

GEOGRAPHY

Mountainous and densely forested. Volcanic activity has given it very fertile soils, hot springs, geysers and black sand beaches.

CLIMATE

Tropical, cooled by constant trade winds. Heavy annual rainfall. Tropical depressions and hurricanes are likely June–November.

PEOPLE AND SOCIETY

Population mainly of African origin. Small community of Carib Indians – the last remaining in the Caribbean – on the east coast. Most people live in extended families. Electoral system based on British model; politicians tend to come from professional classes, usually doctors or lawyers. For 15 years until 1995, Dominica was governed by Eugenia Charles, the first female prime minister in the Caribbean.

THE ECONOMY

Bananas and tourism are the economic mainstays. Current preferential access to EU and US markets now threatened by moves to deregulate the banana trade.

◆ *INSIGHT: Dominica is known as the 'Nature Island' due to its spectacular flora and fauna*

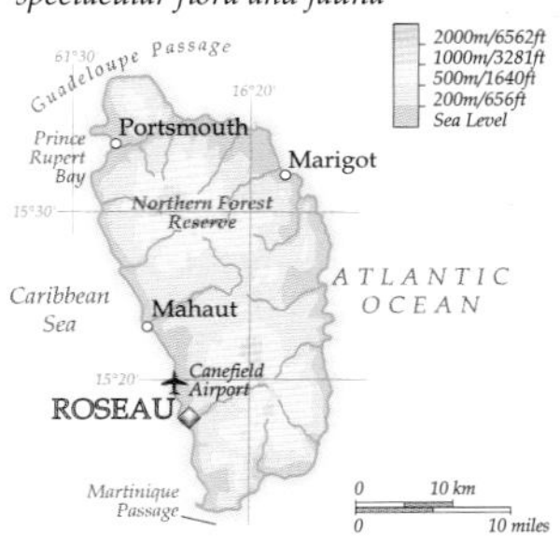
Guadeloupe Passage
Portsmouth
Prince Rupert Bay
Marigot
Northern Forest Reserve
ATLANTIC OCEAN
Caribbean Sea
Mahaut
Canefield Airport
ROSEAU
Martinique Passage
2000m/6562ft
1000m/3281ft
500m/1640ft
200m/656ft
Sea Level
0 10 km
0 10 miles

FACT FILE

OFFICIAL NAME: Commonwealth of Dominica
DATE OF FORMATION: 1978
CAPITAL: Roseau
POPULATION: 72,000
TOTAL AREA: 750 sq km (290 sq miles)
DENSITY: 96 people per sq km
LANGUAGES: English*, French Creole, Carib, Cocoy
RELIGIONS: Roman Catholic 77%, Protestant 15%, other 8%
ETHNIC MIX: Black 98%, Indian 2%
GOVERNMENT: Multiparty republic
CURRENCY: E. Caribbean $ = 100 cents

ST LUCIA

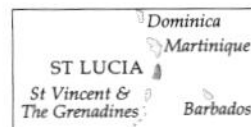
Dominica
Martinique
ST LUCIA
St Vincent & The Grenadines
Barbados

AMONG THE most beautiful of the Caribbean Windward Islands, St Lucia retains both French and British influences from its colonial history.

GEOGRAPHY

Volcanic and mountainous, with some broad fertile valleys. The Pitons, ancient lava cones, rise from the sea on the forested west coast.

CLIMATE

Tropical, moderated by trade winds. May–October wet season brings daily warm showers. Rainfall is highest in the mountains.

PEOPLE AND SOCIETY

Population is a tension-free mixture of descendants of Africans, Europeans and South Asians. Family life and the Church are important to most St Lucians. In rural areas women often head the households, and run much of the farming. There is growing local resistance to over-development of the island by tourism. A proposed union with the other Windward Islands is the main political issue.

THE ECONOMY

Mainly agricultural, with some light industry. Bananas are biggest export. Successful tourist industry, but most resorts are foreign-owned.

◆ *INSIGHT: St Lucia has the most Nobel laureates per capita in the world*

500m/1640ft
200m/656ft
Sea Level
0 5 km
0 5 miles
Saint Lucia Channel
14°05'
Gros Islet
CASTRIES
14°00'
13°55'
Canaries
Soufrière
13°50'
Praslin
ATLANTIC OCEAN
Micoud
Caribbean Sea
13°45'
Vieux Fort
61°00'
60°55'

FACT FILE

OFFICIAL NAME: Saint Lucia
DATE OF FORMATION: 1979
CAPITAL: Castries
POPULATION: 156,000
TOTAL AREA: 620 sq km (239 sq miles)
DENSITY: 251 people per sq km
LANGUAGES: English*, French Creole, Hindi, Urdu
RELIGIONS: Catholic 90%, other 10%
ETHNIC MIX: Black 90%, Afro-European 6%, South Asian 4%
GOVERNMENT: Parliamentary democracy
CURRENCY: E. Caribbean $ = 100 cents

ST VINCENT & THE GRENADINES

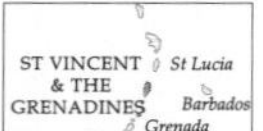
ST VINCENT & THE GRENADINES
St Lucia
Barbados
Grenada

INDEPENDENT FROM Britain in 1979, the volcanic islands of St Vincent and the Grenadines form part of the Windward group in the Caribbean.

GEOGRAPHY

St Vincent is mountainous and forested, with one of two active volcanoes in the Caribbean, La Soufrière. The Grenadines are 32 islands and cays fringed by beaches.

CLIMATE

Tropical, with constant trade winds. Hurricanes are likely during July–November wet season.

PEOPLE AND SOCIETY

Population is racially diverse, but intermarriage has reduced tensions. Society is informal and relaxed, but family life is strongly influenced by the Anglican Church. Locals fear that their traditional lifestyle is being threatened by the expanding tourist industry.

◆ *INSIGHT: The islands' pre-colonial inhabitants, the Carib Indians, named them 'Harioun' – home of the blessed*

THE ECONOMY

Dependent on agriculture and tourism. Bananas are the main cash crop. Tourism, targeted at the jet-set and cruise-ship markets, is concentrated on the Grenadines.

La Soufrière 1234m
Chateaubelair
13°20'
1000m/3281ft
500m/1640ft
200m/656ft
Sea Level
Georgetown
St Vincent
KINGSTOWN
Amos Vale Airport
13°10'
0 10 km
0 10 miles
Bequia
Caribbean Sea
13°00'
Isle à Quatre
Baliceaux
Mustique
The Grenadines
12°50'
Canouan
61°10'
Mayreau
12°40'
Union I.
ATLANTIC OCEAN
61°20'

FACT FILE

OFFICIAL NAME: St Vincent and the Grenadines
DATE OF FORMATION: 1979
CAPITAL: Kingstown
POPULATION: 109,000
TOTAL AREA: 340 sq km (131 sq miles)
DENSITY: 320 people per sq km
LANGUAGES: English*, English Creole
RELIGIONS: Protestant 62% Roman Catholic 19%, other 19%
ETHNIC MIX: Black 82%, mixed 14%, White 3%, South Asian 1%
GOVERNMENT: Parliamentary democracy
CURRENCY: E. Caribbean $ = 100 cents

BARBADOS

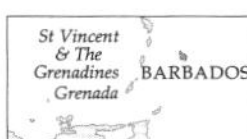
St Vincent & The Grenadines
BARBADOS
Grenada

BARBADOS IS the most easterly of the Caribbean Windward Islands. Under British rule for 339 years, it became fully independent in 1966.

GEOGRAPHY

Encircled by coral reefs. Fertile and predominantly flat, with a few gentle hills to the north.

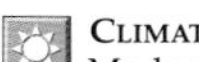

CLIMATE

Moderate tropical climate. Sunnier and drier than its more mountainous neighbours.

PEOPLE AND SOCIETY

Some latent tension between white community, who control politics and much of the economy, and majority black population, but violence is rare. Increasing social mobility has enabled black Bajans to enter the professions. Despite political stability and good welfare and education services, emigration is high, notably to the US and UK.

◆ *INSIGHT: Barbados retains a strong British influence and is referred to by its neighbours as 'Little England'*

THE ECONOMY

Sugar is the traditional cash crop. Well-developed tourist industry employs almost 40% of the work force. Financial services and information processing are important new growth sectors.

200m/656ft
Sea Level
0 5 km
0 5 miles
Speightstown
13°15'
ATLANTIC OCEAN
Bathsheba
Holetown
13°10'
Marchfield
BRIDGETOWN
13°05'
Hastings
Oistins
Grantley Adams Intl. Airport
59°35'
59°30'
ATLANTIC OCEAN

FACT FILE

OFFICIAL NAME: Barbados
DATE OF FORMATION: 1966
CAPITAL: Bridgetown
POPULATION: 260,000
TOTAL AREA: 430 sq km (166 sq miles)
DENSITY: 605 people per sq km
LANGUAGES: English*, English Creole
RELIGIONS: Protestant 94%, Roman Catholic 5%, other 1%
ETHNIC MIX: Black 80%, mixed 15%, White 4%, other 1%
GOVERNMENT: Parliamentary democracy
CURRENCY: Barbados $ = 100 cents

GRENADA

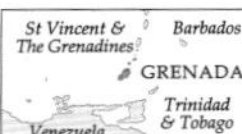
St Vincent & The Grenadines
Barbados
GRENADA
Trinidad & Tobago
Venezuela

THE WINDWARD island of Grenada became a focus of attention in 1983, when the US mounted an invasion to sever the growing links with Cuba.

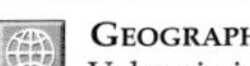

GEOGRAPHY

Volcanic in origin, with densely forested central mountains. Its territory includes the islands of Carriacou and Petite Martinique.

CLIMATE

Tropical, tempered by trade winds. Hurricanes are a hazard in the July–November wet season.

PEOPLE AND SOCIETY

Grenadians are mainly of African origin; their traditions remain strong, especially on Carriacou. Inter-ethnic marriage has reduced tensions between the groups. Extended families, often headed by women, are the norm. The invasion ousted the Marxist regime and restored democracy.

◆ *INSIGHT: Known as 'the spice island of the Caribbean', it is the world's second largest nutmeg producer*

THE ECONOMY

Nutmeg, the most important crop, is currently affected by low world prices. Mace, cocoa, saffron and cloves are also grown. Tourism has developed in the past decade.

Petite Martinique
Hillsborough
Carriacou
500m/1640ft
200m/656ft
Sea Level
0 8 km
0 8 miles
Diamond I.
Ronde I.
Caribbean Sea
ATLANTIC OCEAN
Victoria
Grand Roy
Grenada
Grenville
ST. GEORGE'S
Point Salines Airport
12°30'
12°25'
12°20'
12°15'
12°10'
12°05'
12°00'
61°25'
61°30'
61°35'
61°40'
61°45'

FACT FILE

OFFICIAL NAME: Grenada
DATE OF FORMATION: 1974
CAPITAL: St George's
POPULATION: 91,000
TOTAL AREA: 340 sq km (131 sq miles)
DENSITY: 268 people per sq km
LANGUAGES: English*, English Creole
RELIGIONS: Roman Catholic 68%, Protestant 32%
ETHNIC MIX: Black 84%, Afro-European 13%, South Asian 3%
GOVERNMENT: Parliamentary democracy
CURRENCY: E. Caribbean $ = 100 cents

TRINIDAD & TOBAGO

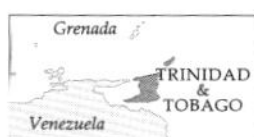
Grenada
TRINIDAD
&
TOBAGO
Venezuela

THE FORMER British colony of Trinidad and Tobago is the most southerly of the West Indies, lying just 15 km (9 miles) off the coast of Venezuela.

GEOGRAPHY

Both islands are hilly and wooded. Trinidad has a rugged mountain range in the north, and swamps on its east and west coasts.

CLIMATE

Tropical, with July–December wet season. Escapes the region's hurricanes, which pass to the north.

PEOPLE AND SOCIETY

Blacks and South Asians are the biggest groups. Minorities of Chinese and Europeans. Politics has recently become fragmented, and dominated by the race issue. An attempted coup by a Muslim sect in 1990 strengthened black opposition to the possibility of a South Asian prime minister.

◆ *INSIGHT: Trinidad and Tobago is the birthplace of steel bands and Calpyso*

THE ECONOMY

Oil accounts for 70% of export earnings. Gas is increasingly being exploited to support new industries. Tourism, particularly on Tobago, is being developed.

500m/1640ft
200m/656ft
Sea Level
0
30 km
0
30 miles
Little Tobago
Tobago
Scarborough
Caribbean Sea
PORT-OF-SPAIN
Arima
Caroni
Guaico
ATLANTIC OCEAN
Gulf of Paria
Trinidad
Rio Claro
San Fernando
Siparia
Columbus Channel

FACT FILE

OFFICIAL NAME: Republic of Trinidad and Tobago
DATE OF FORMATION: 1962
CAPITAL: Port-of-Spain
POPULATION: 1.3 million
TOTAL AREA: 5,130 sq km (1,981 sq miles)
DENSITY: 241 people per sq km
LANGUAGES: English*, other
RELIGIONS: Christian 58%, Hindu 30%, Muslim 8%, other 4%
ETHNIC MIX: Black 43%, South Asian 40%, mixed 14%, other 3%
GOVERNMENT: Multiparty republic
CURRENCY: Trin. & Tob. $ = 100 cents

Caribbean Sea
Gulf of Darien
PANAMA
Llanos
Orinoco
VENEZUELA
Angel Falls 980m
GUYANA
French Guiana (to France)
SURINAM
ATLANTIC
OCEAN
Magdalena
Ruiz 5400m
Andes
COLOMBIA
Guiana Highlands
Equator
Caquetá
Rio Negro
ECUADOR
Japurá
Amazon Delta
Ilha de Marajó
Amazon
Marañón
Amazonia
PERU
BRAZIL
Fernando de Noronha (to Brazil)
Huascarán 6768m
Cabo de Sao Roque
Tapajós
Xingu
Araguaia
Tocantins
Represa de Sobradinho
São Francisco
Lake Titicaca
BOLIVIA
Guallatiri 6060m
Sajama 6520m
Lago Poopó
Planalto de Mato Grosso
Brazilian Highlands
Gran Chaco
Pantanal
Paraguay
Atacama Desert
Tropic of Capricorn
Islas de los Desventurados (to Chile)
Paraná
Serra do Mar
PARAGUAY
PACIFIC

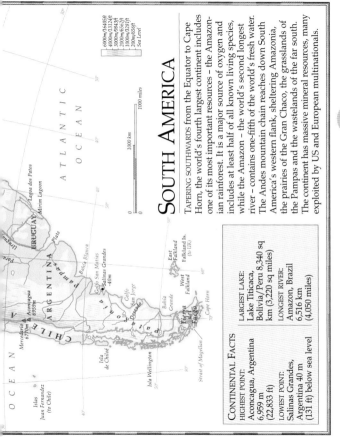

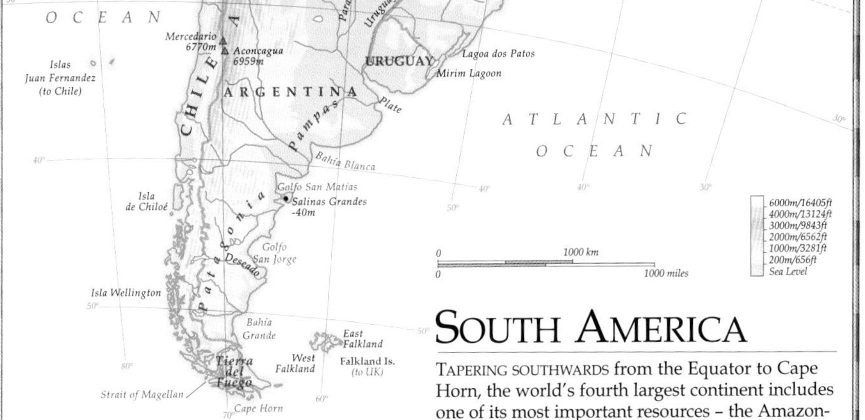
OCEAN
Mercedario 6770m
Aconcagua 6959m
Islas Juan Fernandez (to Chile)
CHILE
ARGENTINA
URUGUAY
Lagoa dos Patos
Mirim Lagoon
Plate
Pampas
Bahía Blanca
ATLANTIC OCEAN
Isla de Chiloé
Golfo San Matías
Salinas Grandes -40m
Patagonia
Golfo San Jorge
Deseado
Isla Wellington
Bahía Grande
East Falkland
West Falkland
Falkland Is. (to UK)
Tierra del Fuego
Strait of Magellan
Cape Horn
1000 km
1000 miles
6000m/16405ft
4000m/13124ft
3000m/9843ft
2000m/6562ft
1000m/3281ft
200m/656ft
Sea Level

SOUTH AMERICA

TAPERING SOUTHWARDS from the Equator to Cape Horn, the world's fourth largest continent includes one of its most important resources – the Amazonian rainforest. It is a major source of oxygen and includes at least half of all known living species, while the Amazon – the world's second longest river – contains one-fifth of the world's fresh water. The Andes mountain chain reaches down South America's western flank, sheltering Amazonia, the prairies of the Gran Chaco, the grasslands of the Pampas and the wastelands of the far south. The continent has massive mineral resources, many exploited by US and European multinationals.

CONTINENTAL FACTS

HIGHEST POINT:
Aconcagua, Argentina 6,959 m (22,833 ft)

LOWEST POINT:
Salinas Grandes, Argentina 40 m (131 ft) below sea level

LARGEST LAKE:
Lake Titicaca, Bolivia/Peru 8,340 sq km (3,220 sq miles)

LONGEST RIVER:
Amazon, Brazil 6,516 km (4,050 miles)

COLOMBIA

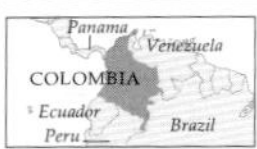
Panama
Venezuela
COLOMBIA
Ecuador
Peru
Brazil

LYING IN northwest South America, Colombia is one of the world's most violent countries, with powerful drugs cartels and guerrilla activity.

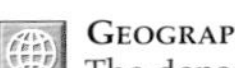

GEOGRAPHY

The densely forested and almost uninhabited east is separated from the western coastal plains by the Andes, which divide into three ranges with intervening valleys.

CLIMATE

Coastal plains are hot and wet. The highlands are cooler. The equatorial east has two wet seasons.

PEOPLE AND SOCIETY

Most Colombians are of mixed blood. Native Indians are concentrated in the southwest and Amazonia. Recent constitutional reform has given them a greater political voice. Blacks are the least represented group.The government, with US help, is engaged in an all-out war against the drugs barons.

◆ *INSIGHT: Colombia is the world's leading producer of emeralds*

THE ECONOMY

Healthy and diversified export sector – especially coffee and coal. Considerable growth potential, but drugs-related violence and corruption deter foreign investors.

Caribbean Sea
Santa Marta
Barranquilla
Valledupar
Cartagena
Sincelejo
Montería
0 200 km
0 200 miles
PANAMA
Cúcuta
VENEZUELA
Bucaramanga
Villa Rosario
Bello
Medellín
Meta
Orinoco
PACIFIC OCEAN
Manizales
Armenia
BOGOTÁ
Villavicencio
Cali
Palmira
Neiva
Amazonia
Negro
Popayán
Pasto
Equator
ECUADOR
BRAZIL
Putumayo
Caquetá
PERU
3000m/9843ft
2000m/6562ft
1000m/3281ft
500m/1640ft
Sea Level

FACT FILE

OFFICIAL NAME: Republic of Colombia
DATE OF FORMATION: 1819/1922
CAPITAL: Bogotá
POPULATION: 34 million
TOTAL AREA: 1,138,910 sq km (439,733 sq miles)
DENSITY: 30 people per sq km
LANGUAGES: Spanish*, Indian languages, English Creole
RELIGIONS: Catholic 95%, other 5%
ETHNIC MIX: *mestizo* 58%, White 20%, mixed 14%, other 8%
GOVERNMENT: Multiparty republic
CURRENCY: Peso = 100 centavos

VENEZUELA

VENEZUELA
Guyana
Colombia
Brazil

LOCATED ON the north coast of South America, Venezuela has the continent's most urbanized society. Most people live in the northern cities.

GEOGRAPHY

Andes mountains and the Maracaibo lowlands in the northwest. Central grassy plains drained by Orinoco river system. Forested Guiana Highlands in the southeast.

CLIMATE

Tropical. Hot and humid. Uplands are cooler. Orinoco plains are alternately parched or flooded.

PEOPLE AND SOCIETY

Latin America's 'melting pot' with immigrants from Europe and all over South America. The few indigenous Indians live in remote areas and maintain their traditional lifestyle. Oil wealth has brought prosperity, but many people still live in poverty. 1991 food riots forced government to initiate poverty programmes. Corruption is a feature of Venezuelan political life.

THE ECONOMY

In addition to oil, Venezuela has vast reserves of coal, bauxite, iron and gold. Government revenues dented by over-manned and often inefficient state sector, plus widespread tax evasion.

◆ INSIGHT: *Venezuela's Angel Falls (979 m) is the world's highest waterfall*

Maracay
Caribbean Sea
Maracaibo
Valencia
CARACAS
Cabimas
ATLANTIC OCEAN
Lago de Maracaibo
Petare
Cumaná
Maturín
Barquisimeto
Valera
Barcelona
Barinas
Llanos
Ciudad Guayana
San Cristóbal
Orinoco
Ciudad Bolívar
Meta
Angel Falls
GUYANA
COLOMBIA
Guiana Highlands
Orinoco
BRAZIL
2000m/6562ft
1000m/3281ft
500m/1640ft
200m/656ft
Sea Level
0 200 km
0 200 miles
Equator

FACT FILE

OFFICIAL NAME: Republic of Venezuela
DATE OF FORMATION: 1830/1929
CAPITAL: Caracas
POPULATION: 20.6 million
TOTAL AREA: 912,050 sq km (352,143 sq miles)
DENSITY: 22 people per sq km
LANGUAGES: Spanish*, Indian languages
RELIGIONS: Roman Catholic 96%, Protestant 2%, other 2%
ETHNIC MIX: *mestizo* 67%, White 21%, Black 10%, Indian 2%
GOVERNMENT: Multiparty republic
CURRENCY: Bolívar = 100 centimos

GUYANA

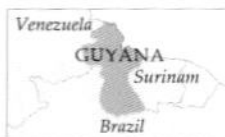
Venezuela
GUYANA
Surinam
Brazil

THE ONLY English-speaking country in South America, Guyana gained independence from Britain in 1966, and became a republic in 1970.

GEOGRAPHY

Mainly artificial coast, reclaimed by dykes and dams from swamps and tidal marshes. Forests cover 85% of the interior, rising to savannah uplands and mountains.

CLIMATE

Tropical. Coast cooled by sea breezes. Lowlands are hot, wet and humid. Highlands are a little cooler.

PEOPLE AND SOCIETY

Population largely descended from Africans brought over during slave trade, or from South Asian labourers who arrived after slavery was abolished. Racial rivalry exists between the two groups. Small numbers of Chinese and native Indians. Government was once characterized by favouritism towards Afro-Guyanese. This was reversed with the election in 1992 of a South Asian-dominated party.

THE ECONOMY

Free-market economics have improved prospects. Bauxite, gold, rice and diamonds are produced.

◈ *INSIGHT: Guyana means 'land of many waters' – it has 1,600 km of rivers*

ATLANTIC OCEAN
Suddie
GEORGETOWN
Bartica
New Amsterdam
Linden
Corriverton
VENEZUELA
Guiana Highlands
Courantyne
Essequibo
BRAZIL
SURINAM
1000m/3281ft
500m/1640ft
200m/656ft
Sea Level
0 100 km
0 100 miles

FACT FILE

OFFICIAL NAME: Republic of Guyana
DATE OF FORMATION: 1966
CAPITAL: Georgetown
POPULATION: 800,000
TOTAL AREA: 214,970 sq km (83,000 sq miles)
DENSITY: 4 people per sq km
LANGUAGES: English*, English Creole, Hindi, Urdu, Indian languages
RELIGIONS: Christian 57%, Hindu 33%, Muslim 9%, other 1%
ETHNIC MIX: South Asian 51%, Black and mixed 43%, other 6%
GOVERNMENT: Multiparty republic
CURRENCY: Guyana $ =100 cents

SURINAM

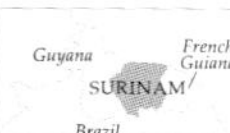
Guyana
French Guiana
SURINAM
Brazil

A FORMER Dutch colony on the north coast of South America. Democracy was restored in 1991, after almost 11 years of military rule.

GEOGRAPHY
Mostly covered by tropical rainforest. Coastal plain, central plateaux and the Guiana Highlands.

CLIMATE
Tropical. Hot and humid, cooled by trade winds. High rainfall, especially in the interior.

PEOPLE AND SOCIETY
About 200,000 people have emigrated to the Netherlands since independence. Of those left, 90% live near the coast, the rest live in scattered rainforest communities. Around 7,000 are indigenous Indians. Also *bosnegers* – descendants of runaway African slaves. They fought the Creole-dominated government in the 1980s. Many South Asians and Javanese work in farming. Since return to civilian rule, each group has a political party representing its interests.

THE ECONOMY
Aluminium and bauxite are the leading exports. Rice and fruit are main cash crops. Oil reserves.

◈ *INSIGHT: Surinam was ceded to Holland by the British, in exchange for New Amsterdam (New York), in 1667*

ATLANTIC OCEAN
PARAMARIBO
Boskamp
Nieuw Amsterdam
Nieuw Nickerie
Onverwacht
Moengo
Kwakoegron
Brokopondo
Corantijn
Marowijne
W.J. van Blommesteinmeer
FRENCH GUIANA
GUYANA
Guiana Highlands
BRAZIL
0 200 km
0 200 miles
1000m/3281ft
500m/1640ft
200m/656ft
Sea Level

FACT FILE

OFFICIAL NAME: Republic of Surinam
DATE OF FORMATION: 1975
CAPITAL: Paramaribo
POPULATION: 400,000
TOTAL AREA: 163,270 sq km (63,039 sq miles)
DENSITY: 3 people per sq km
LANGUAGES: Dutch*, Pidgin English (Taki-Taki), Hindi, Javanese, Carib
RELIGIONS: Christian 48%, Hindu 27%, Muslim 20%, other 5%
ETHNIC MIX: South Asian 37%, Creole 31%, Javanese 15%, other 17%
GOVERNMENT: Multiparty republic
CURRENCY: Guilder = 100 cents

ECUADOR

ECUADOR
Galápagos Islands
Colombia
Peru
Brazil

ECUADOR SITS high on South America's western coast. Its territory includes the Galápagos Islands, 970 km (610 miles) to the west.

GEOGRAPHY

Broad coastal plain, inter-Andean central highlands, dense jungle in upper Amazon basin.

CLIMATE

Hot and moist on the coast, cool in the Andes, and hot equatorial in the Amazon basin.

PEOPLE AND SOCIETY

Most people live in coastal lowlands or Andean highlands. Many have migrated from over-farmed Andean valleys to main port and commercial centre, Guayaquil. Strong and unified Indian movement backed by Catholic Church. Amazonian Indians are successfully pressing for recognition of land rights.

◆ *INSIGHT: Darwin's study on the Galápagos Islands in 1856 played a major part in his theory of evolution*

THE ECONOMY

World's biggest banana producer. Net oil exporter. Commercial agriculture is main employer. Fishing industry. Eco-tourism on Galápagos Islands.

PACIFIC OCEAN
COLOMBIA
Esmeraldas
Ibarra
San Miguel
Equator
Santo Domingo de los Colorados
QUITO
Napo
Manta
Portoviejo
Ambato
Riobamba
Milagro
Guayaquil
Gulf of Guayaquil
Cuenca
Machala
Loja
PERU
4000m/13124ft
2000m/6562ft
500m/1640ft
Sea Level
100 km
100 miles

FACT FILE

OFFICIAL NAME: Republic of Ecuador
DATE OF FORMATION: 1830/1942
CAPITAL: Quito
POPULATION: 11.3 million
TOTAL AREA: 283,560 sq km (109,483 sq miles)
DENSITY: 40 people per sq km

LANGUAGES: Spanish*, Quechua* and eight other Indian languages
RELIGIONS: Catholic 95%, other 5%
ETHNIC MIX: *mestizo* (Euro-Indian) 55%, Indian 25%, Black 10%, White 10%
GOVERNMENT: Multiparty republic
CURRENCY: Sucre = 100 centavos

PERU

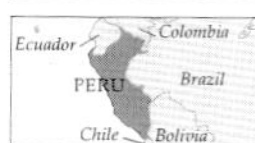
Ecuador
Colombia
PERU
Brazil
Chile
Bolivia

ONCE THE heart of the Inca empire, before the Spanish conquest in the 16th century, Peru lies on the Pacific coast of South America.

GEOGRAPHY

Coastal plain rises to Andes mountains. Uplands, dissected by fertile valleys, lie east of Andes. Tropical forest in extreme east.

CLIMATE

Coast is mainly arid. Middle slopes of Andes are temperate; higher peaks are snow-covered. East is hot, humid and very wet.

PEOPLE AND SOCIETY

Populated mainly by Indians or mixed-race *mestizos*, but society is dominated by a small group of Spanish descendants. Indians, together with the small black community, suffer discrimination in the towns. In 1980, *Sendero Luminoso* (Shining Path) guerrillas began armed struggle against the government. Since then, over 25,000 people have died as a result of guerrilla, and army, violence.

THE ECONOMY

Abundant mineral resources. Rich fish stocks. Illegal export of coca leaves for cocaine production.

◆ *INSIGHT: Lake Titicaca is the world's highest navigable lake*

0 200 km
0 200 miles
Equator
COLOMBIA
ECUADOR
Putumayo
Amazon
Iquitos
Marañón
Piura
Chiclayo
Ucayali
BRAZIL
Trujillo
Pucallpa
Chimbote
Huánuco
LIMA
Huancayo
Callao
Huancavelica
Cusco
PACIFIC OCEAN
Ayacucho
Ica
Puno
Lake Titicaca
Arequipa
BOLIVIA
Tacna
CHILE
4000m/13124ft
2000m/6562ft
500m/1640ft
Sea Level

FACT FILE

OFFICIAL NAME: Republic of Peru
DATE OF FORMATION: 1824 / 1942
CAPITAL: Lima
POPULATION: 22.9 million
TOTAL AREA: 1,285,220 sq km (496,223 sq miles)
DENSITY: 18 people per sq km
LANGUAGES: Spanish*, Quechua*, Aymará*, other Indian languages
RELIGIONS: Catholic 95%, other 5%
ETHNIC MIX: Indian 45%, *mestizo* 37%, White 15%, Black, Japanese, Chinese and other 3%
GOVERNMENT: Multiparty republic
CURRENCY: New sol = 100 centimos

BRAZIL

Venezuela
Colombia
Peru
BRAZIL
Bolivia
Paraguay

COVERING ALMOST half of South America, Brazil is the site of the world's largest and ecologically most important rainforest. The country has immense natural and economic resources, but many of its people still live in poverty.

GEOGRAPHY

Vast, heavily wooded Amazon Basin covers northern half of the country. Semi-arid scrubland in northeast mountains, fertile highlands in the south. Coastal plain with swampy areas in the southeast. Atlantic coastline is 2,000 km (1,240 miles) long.

CLIMATE

Constantly hot and humid in Amazon Basin. Frequent droughts in northeast. Greater range of temperature and rainfall on plateau. Hot summers and cool winters in south.

PEOPLE AND SOCIETY

Diverse population includes native Indians, blacks, and people of mixed race. Shanty towns in the cities attract poor migrants from the northeast. Urban crime, violent land disputes and unchecked Amazonia development tarnish image as a modern nation. Catholicism and the family remain strong.

THE ECONOMY

Hyperinflation, poor planning and corruption frustrate efforts to harness undoubted potential: vast mineral reserves, diverse industry and agriculture.

VENEZUELA
French Guiana (France)
SURINAM
GUYANA
Boa Vista
Branco
Guiana Highlands
Macapá
ATLANTIC
OCEAN
Equator
COLOMBIA
Japurá
Rio Negro
Amazon
Ilha de Marajó
Belém
Manaus
Santarém
Tocantins
São Luís
Juruá
Madeira
Tapajós
Parnaíba
Fortaleza
Amazonia
Iriri
Xingu
Imperatriz
Teresina
Fernando de Noronha
Purus

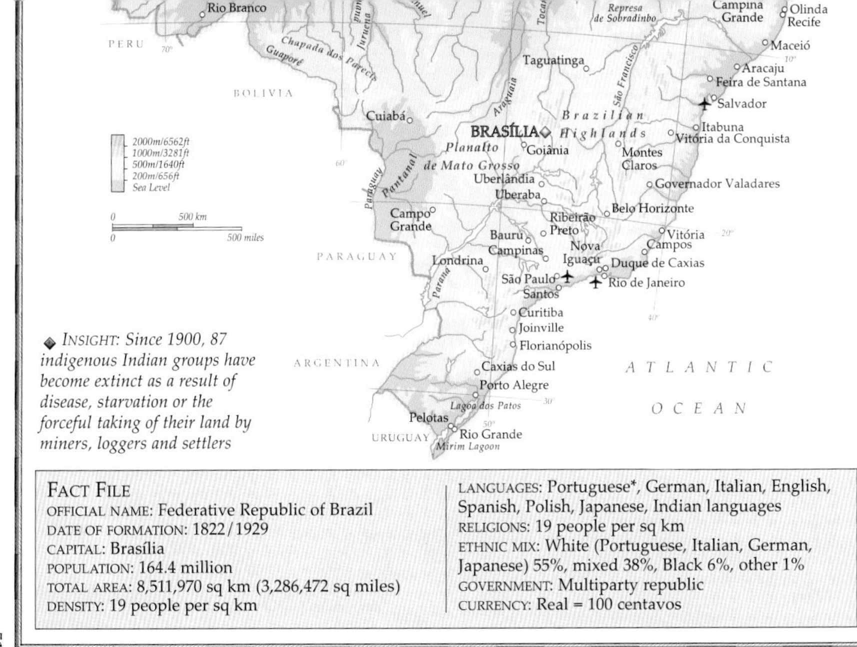
Rio Branco
PERU
BOLIVIA
Chapada dos Parecis
Guaporé
Juruena
Cuiabá
Represa de Sobradinho
Campina Grande
Olinda
Recife
Maceió
Aracaju
Feira de Santana
Salvador
Taguatinga
Tocantins
São Francisco
Araguaia
Brazilian Highlands
BRASÍLIA
Planalto de Mato Grosso
Goiânia
Itabuna
Vitória da Conquista
Montes Claros
Governador Valadares
Uberlândia
Uberaba
Pantanal
Paraguay
Campo Grande
Belo Horizonte
Ribeirão Preto
Bauru
Campinas
Vitória
Campos
Nova Iguaçu
Duque de Caxias
Rio de Janeiro
São Paulo
Santos
Londrina
Paraná
PARAGUAY
Curitiba
Joinville
Florianópolis
ARGENTINA
Caxias do Sul
Porto Alegre
Lagoa dos Patos
Pelotas
Rio Grande
Mirim Lagoon
URUGUAY
ATLANTIC OCEAN
2000m/6562ft
1000m/3281ft
500m/1640ft
200m/656ft
Sea Level
0 500 km
0 500 miles
70°
60°
50°
40°
10°
20°
30°

◆ INSIGHT: *Since 1900, 87 indigenous Indian groups have become extinct as a result of disease, starvation or the forceful taking of their land by miners, loggers and settlers*

FACT FILE

OFFICIAL NAME: Federative Republic of Brazil
DATE OF FORMATION: 1822 / 1929
CAPITAL: Brasília
POPULATION: 164.4 million
TOTAL AREA: 8,511,970 sq km (3,286,472 sq miles)
DENSITY: 19 people per sq km
LANGUAGES: Portuguese*, German, Italian, English, Spanish, Polish, Japanese, Indian languages
RELIGIONS: 19 people per sq km
ETHNIC MIX: White (Portuguese, Italian, German, Japanese) 55%, mixed 38%, Black 6%, other 1%
GOVERNMENT: Multiparty republic
CURRENCY: Real = 100 centavos

CHILE

Bolivia
CHILE
Paraguay
Uruguay
Argentina

EXTENDS IN a ribbon down the west coast of South America. It returned to democracy in 1989 after a referendum rejected its military dictator.

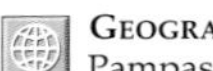

GEOGRAPHY

Pampas (broad grassy plains) between coastal uplands and Andes. Atacama Desert in north. Deep sea channels, lakes and fiords in south.

CLIMATE

Arid in the north. Hot, dry summers and mild winters in the centre. Higher Andean peaks have glaciers and year-round snow. Very wet and stormy in the south.

PEOPLE AND SOCIETY

Most people are of European stock, and are highly urbanized. Indigenous Indians live almost exclusively in the south. Poor housing, water and air pollution are problems in Santiago. General Pinochet's dictatorship was brutally repressive, but the business and middle classes prospered. Growth has continued under civilian rule, but many Chileans live in poverty.

THE ECONOMY

World's biggest copper producer. Growth in foreign investment due to political stability. Wine, fishmeal, fruits and salmon are exported.

◆ *INSIGHT: Chile's Atacama Desert is the driest place on Earth*

PERU
BOLIVIA
Arica
Iquique
Antofagasta
Atacama Desert
Andes
PACIFIC OCEAN
Valparaíso
Viña del Mar
SANTIAGO
Rancagua
Talca
Talcahuano
Concepción
Chillán
Temuco
Valdivia
Puerto Montt
Isla de Chiloé
ARGENTINA
Punta Arenas
Strait of Magellan
Cape Horn

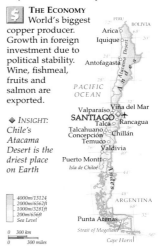

4000m/13124
2000m/6562ft
1000m/3281ft
200m/656ft
Sea Level

0 300 km
0 300 miles

FACT FILE

OFFICIAL NAME: Republic of Chile
DATE OF FORMATION: 1818 / 1929
CAPITAL: Santiago
POPULATION: 13.8 million
TOTAL AREA: 756,950 sq km (292,258 sq miles)
DENSITY: 18 people per sq km

LANGUAGES: Spanish*, Indian languages
RELIGIONS: Roman Catholic 89%, Protestant 11%
ETHNIC MIX: White and *mestizo* 92%, Indian 6%, other 2%
GOVERNMENT: Multiparty republic
CURRENCY: Peso = 100 centavos

BOLIVIA

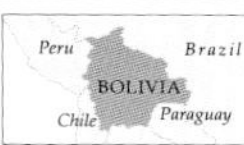
Peru
Brazil
BOLIVIA
Chile
Paraguay

BOLIVIA LIES land-locked high in central South America. Mineral riches once made it the region's wealthiest state. Today, it is the poorest.

GEOGRAPHY

A high windswept plateau, the *altiplano,* lies between two Andean mountain ranges. Semi-arid grasslands to the southeast; dense tropical forests to the north.

CLIMATE

Altiplano has extreme tropical climate, with night frost in winter. North and east are hot and humid.

PEOPLE AND SOCIETY

Indigenous majority is discriminated against at most levels of society. Political process and economy remain under the control of a few wealthy families of Spanish descent. Most Bolivians are poor subsistence farmers or miners. Women have low status.

◈ *INSIGHT: La Paz is the world's highest capital city, at 3,631 metres (13,385 feet) above sea level*

THE ECONOMY

Gold, silver, zinc and tin are mined. Recently discovered oil and natural gas deposits. Overseas investors remain deterred by social problems of extreme poverty, and the influence of cocaine barons.

3000m/9843ft
2000m/6562ft
1000m/3281ft
500m/1640ft
200m/656ft
Sea Level
Guayaramerín
Riberalta
PERU
Beni
Guaporé
Trinidad
Lake Titicaca
BRAZIL
LA PAZ
Cochabamba
Montero
Santa Cruz
Oruro
SUCRE
Puerto Suárez
Potosí
Gran Chaco
CHILE
Tupiza
Tarija
PARAGUAY
ARGENTINA
0 200 km
0 200 miles

FACT FILE

OFFICIAL NAME: Republic of Bolivia
DATE OF FORMATION: 1825 / 1938
CAPITALS: La Paz, Sucre
POPULATION: 7.8 million
TOTAL AREA: 1,098,580 sq km (424,162 sq miles)
DENSITY: 7 people per sq km
LANGUAGES: Spanish*, Quechua*, Aymará*, Tupi-Guaraní
RELIGIONS: Catholic 95%, other 5%
ETHNIC MIX: Indian 55%, *mestizo* 27%, White 10%, other 8%
GOVERNMENT: Multiparty republic
CURRENCY: Boliviano = 100 centavos

PARAGUAY

Bolivia
Brazil
PARAGUAY
Argentina

LAND-LOCKED in central South America. Its post-independence history has included periods of military rule. Free elections were held in 1993.

GEOGRAPHY

The River Paraguay divides hilly and forested east from a flat alluvial plain with marsh and semi-desert scrubland in the west.

CLIMATE

Subtropical. Gran Chaco is generally hotter and drier. All areas experience floods and droughts.

PEOPLE AND SOCIETY

Population mainly of mixed Spanish and native Indian origin. Most are bilingual, but Guaraní is spoken by preference outside the capital. Gran Chaco is home to small groups of pure Guaraní Indians, cattle-ranchers and Mennonites, a sect of German origin, who live by a co-operative farming system.

◆ *INSIGHT: The joint Paraguay-Brazil hydroelectric power project at Itaipú is the largest in the world*

THE ECONOMY

Agriculture employs 45% of the work force. Soybeans and cotton are main exports. Electricity exporter – earnings cover oil imports. Growth is slow due to remote, land-locked position.

BOLIVIA
60°
20°
Paraguay
BRAZIL
Gran Chaco
Pedro Juan Caballero
Concepción
ARGENTINA
25°
Represa de Itaipú
ASUNCIÓN
Coronel Oviedo
Caaguazú
Lambaré
Villarrica
1000m/3281ft
500m/1640ft
200m/656ft
Sea Level
Pilar
Paraná
0 100 km
0 100 miles
Encarnación
55°

FACT FILE

OFFICIAL NAME: Republic of Paraguay
DATE OF FORMATION: 1811/1938
CAPITAL: Asunción
POPULATION: 4.5 million
TOTAL AREA: 406,750 sq km (157,046 sq miles)
DENSITY: 11 people per sq km
LANGUAGES: Spanish*, Guaraní*, Plattdeutsch (Low German)
RELIGIONS: Catholic 90%, other 10%
ETHNIC MIX: *mestizo* (Euro-Indian) 95%, White 3%, Indian 2%
GOVERNMENT: Multiparty republic
CURRENCY: Guaraní = 100 centimos

URUGUAY

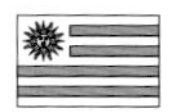

Brazil
URUGUAY
Argentina

URUGUAY IS situated in southeastern South America. It returned to civilian government in 1985, after 12 years of military dictatorship.

GEOGRAPHY

Low, rolling grasslands cover 80% of the country. Narrow coastal plain. Alluvial flood plain in southwest. Five rivers flow westwards and drain into the River Uruguay.

CLIMATE

Temperate throughout the country. Warm summers, mild winters and moderate rainfall.

PEOPLE AND SOCIETY

Uruguayans are largely second or third generation Italians or Spaniards. Wealth derived from cattle ranching enabled the country to become the first welfare state in South America. Economic decline since 1960s, but a large, if less prosperous, middle class remains. Although a Roman Catholic country, Uruguay is liberal in its attitude to religion and all forms are tolerated. Divorce is legal.

THE ECONOMY

Most land given over to crops and livestock. Wool, meat and hides are exported. Earnings as offshore banking centre. Buoyant tourism.

◆ *INSIGHT: Uruguay's literacy rates and life expectancy are the region's highest*

200m/656ft
Sea Level
0 100 km
0 100 miles
Uruguay
Rivera
BRAZIL
Salto
Tacuarembó
ARGENTINA
Embalse del Río Negro
Melo
Paysandú
Mirim Lagoon
Fray Bentos
Paso de los Toros
Mercedes
Treinta y Tres
Trinidad
Colonia del Sacramento
San José de Mayo
Las Piedras
Rocha
La Plata
Punta del Este
MONTEVIDEO
ATLANTIC OCEAN

FACT FILE

OFFICIAL NAME: Republic of Uruguay
DATE OF FORMATION: 1828 / 1909
CAPITAL: Montevideo
POPULATION: 3.1 million
TOTAL AREA: 177,410 sq km (68,498 sq miles)
DENSITY: 18 people per sq km
LANGUAGES: Spanish*, other
RELIGIONS: Roman Catholic 77%, Protestant 3%, Jewish 2%, other 18%
ETHNIC MIX: White 88%, *mestizo* (Euro-Indian) 8%, Black 4%
GOVERNMENT: Multiparty republic
CURRENCY: Peso = 100 centesimos

ARGENTINA

Bolivia
Brazil
Paraguay
Uruguay
ARGENTINA
Chile

OCCUPYING MOST of the southern half of South America, Argentina extends 3,460 km (2,145 miles) from Bolivia to Tierra del Fuego. It is beginning to realize its potential after decades of political and economic instability.

GEOGRAPHY

Andes Mountains in the west run north–south, forming a natural border with Chile. East of the Andes are heavily wooded plains (Gran Chaco) in the north, treeless but fertile Pampas plains in the centre. Bleak and arid Patagonia in the far south.

CLIMATE

Northeast is sub-tropical. Andes are semi-arid in the north and snowy in the south. Western lowlands are arid. Pampas have a mild climate with summer rains.

THE ECONOMY

Harsh economic recovery programme and new stable currency have offset worst excesses of hyperinflation and inefficient nationalized industries. Rich and varied agricultural base. Powerful agribusiness – Argentina is among the world's leading exporters of beef, wheat and fruit. Important known oil and gas reserves are still under-exploited. Skilled labour force.

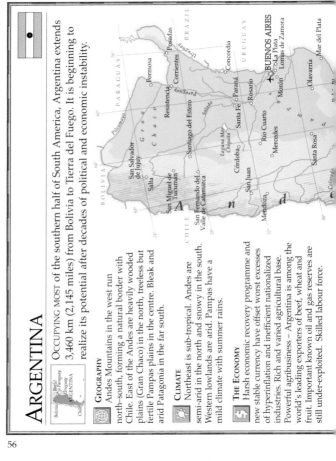

BOLIVIA
PARAGUAY
CHILE
BRAZIL
URUGUAY
Pilcomayo
Paraguay
Uruguay
Salado
Colorado
Gran Chaco
San Salvador de Jujuy
Salta
Formosa
San Miguel de Tucumán
Resistencia
Corrientes
Posadas
Santiago del Estero
San Fernando del Valle de Catamarca
Laguna Mar Chiquita
Concordia
Córdoba
Santa Fe
Paraná
San Juan
Rosario
Mendoza
Río Cuarto
BUENOS AIRES
Mercedes
Morón
La Plata
Lomas de Zamora
Olavarría
Santa Rosa
Mar del Plata
64°
60°
56°
68°
24°
28°
32°
36°

PEOPLE AND SOCIETY

People are largely of European descent, mostly from recent 20th-century migrations; over one-third are of Italian origin. Indigenous peoples are now in a minority, living mainly in Andean regions or in the Gran Chaco. Over 85% of Argentinians are urban dwellers, with 40% living in the capital. Paraguayan and Bolivian immigrants are the poorest groups. Catholicism and the extended family remain strong. Social and religious reunions are common. The family also forms the backbone of many successful businesses. Women have a higher profile than in most Latin American states. Many enter professional fields. Claim to the Falkland Islands remains an emotive issue.

◆ *Insight: The Tango originated in the poorer quarters of Buenos Aires at the end of the 19th century. The name 'Tango' predates the dance – it was given to the carnivals (and dances) of the country's black inhabitants in the early 1800s*

FACT FILE

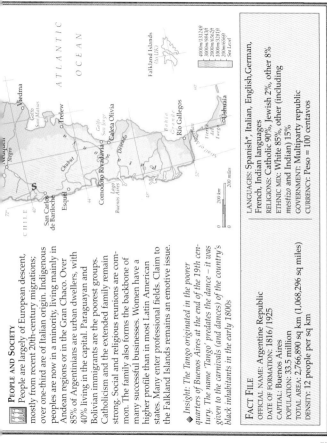

OFFICIAL NAME: Argentine Republic
DATE OF FORMATION: 1816 / 1925
CAPITAL: Buenos Aires
POPULATION: 33.5 million
TOTAL AREA: 2,766,890 sq km (1,068,296 sq miles)
DENSITY: 12 people per sq km
LANGUAGES: Spanish*, Italian, English, German, French, Indian languages
RELIGIONS: Catholic 90%, Jewish 2%, other 8%
ETHNIC MIX: White 85%, other (including *mestizo* and Indian) 15%
GOVERNMENT: Multiparty republic
CURRENCY: Peso = 100 centavos

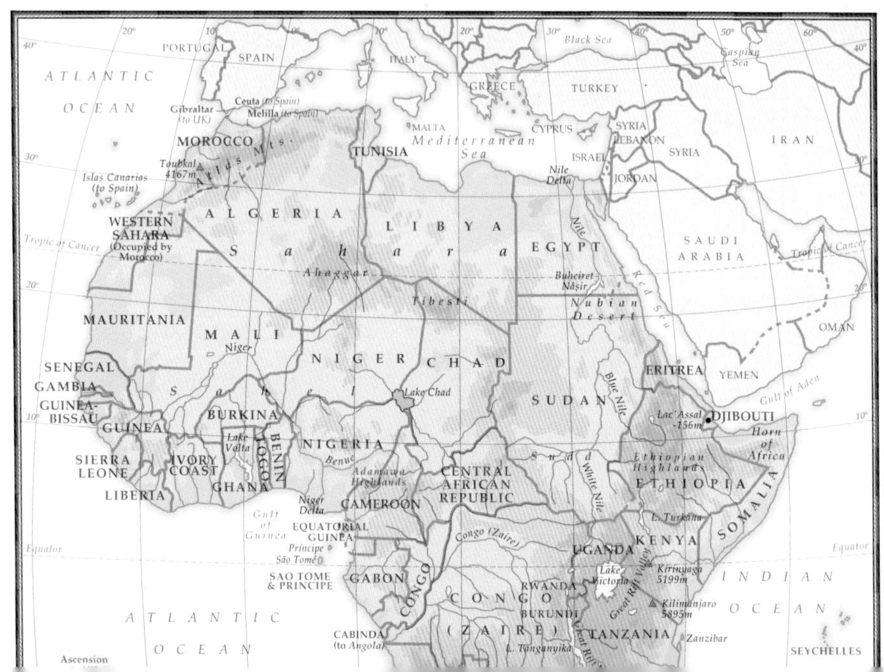

PORTUGAL
SPAIN
ITALY
GREECE
TURKEY
Black Sea
Caspian Sea
IRAN
ATLANTIC OCEAN
Ceuta (to Spain)
Melilla (to Spain)
Gibraltar (to UK)
MALTA
CYPRUS
SYRIA
LEBANON
SYRIA
MOROCCO
Atlas Mts.
Toubkal 4167m
TUNISIA
Mediterranean Sea
ISRAEL
JORDAN
Nile Delta
Islas Canarias (to Spain)
ALGERIA
LIBYA
Nile
EGYPT
SAUDI ARABIA
WESTERN SAHARA (Occupied by Morocco)
Tropic of Cancer
Sahara
Ahaggar
Buheiret Nâşir
Red Sea
Tibesti
Nubian Desert
MAURITANIA
MALI
Niger
OMAN
NIGER
CHAD
ERITREA
YEMEN
SENEGAL
GAMBIA
Lake Chad
Blue Nile
Gulf of Aden
GUINEA-BISSAU
Sahel
SUDAN
BURKINA
Lac'Assal -156m
DJIBOUTI
GUINEA
Horn of Africa
NIGERIA
Lake Volta
BENIN
TOGO
Sudd
Ethiopian Highlands
SIERRA LEONE
IVORY COAST
Benue
Adamawa Highlands
CENTRAL AFRICAN REPUBLIC
White Nile
ETHIOPIA
GHANA
LIBERIA
Niger Delta
CAMEROON
SOMALIA
L. Turkana
Gulf of Guinea
EQUATORIAL GUINEA
Congo (Zaire)
KENYA
Equator
Príncipe
UGANDA
São Tomé
Great Rift Valley
Lake Victoria
Kirinyaga 5199m
INDIAN OCEAN
SAO TOME & PRINCIPE
GABON
CONGO
RWANDA
CONGO (ZAIRE)
Kilimanjaro 5895m
BURUNDI
TANZANIA
Zanzibar
CABINDA (to Angola)
L. Tanganyika
Ascension
SEYCHELLES

ANGOLA
ZAMBIA
Lake Nyasa
MALAWI
Zambezi
MOZAMBIQUE
Mozambique Channel
COMOROS
Mayotte
(to France)
MADAGASCAR
MAURITIUS
Réunion
(to France)
Tropic of Capricorn
St Helena
(to UK)
Okavango
ZIMBABWE
NAMIBIA
Okavango
Delta
Limpopo
BOTSWANA
Kalahari
Desert
SWAZILAND
Orange
LESOTHO
SOUTH
AFRICA
Drakensberg
Cape of
Good Hope
0
1000 km
1000 miles
4000m/13124ft
3000m/9843ft
2000m/6562ft
1000m/3281ft
200m/656ft
Sea Level
Below Sea Level

AFRICA

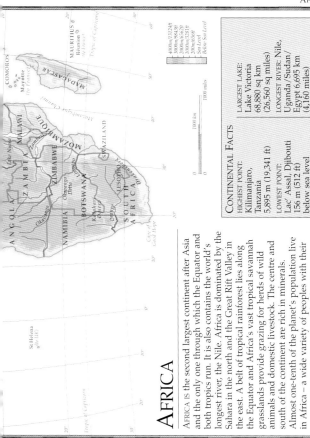

AFRICA IS the second largest continent after Asia and the only one through which the Equator and both tropics run. It is also contains the world's longest river, the Nile. Africa is dominated by the Sahara in the north and the Great Rift Valley in the east. A belt of tropical rainforest lies along the Equator and Africa's vast tropical savannah grasslands provide grazing for herds of wild animals and domestic livestock. The centre and south of the continent are rich in minerals. Almost one-tenth of the planet's population live in Africa – a wide variety of peoples with their own distinctive languages and cultures.

CONTINENTAL FACTS

HIGHEST POINT:
Kilimanjaro, Tanzania
5,895 m (19,341 ft)

LOWEST POINT:
Lac' Assal, Djibouti
156 m (512 ft) below sea level

LARGEST LAKE:
Lake Victoria
68,880 sq km
(26,560 sq miles)

LONGEST RIVER: Nile, Uganda/Sudan/ Egypt 6,695 km
(4,160 miles)

MOROCCO

Spain
MOROCCO
Western Sahara
Algeria
Mauritania
Mali

A FORMER French colony in northwest Africa, independent in 1956. Morocco has occupied the disputed territory of Western Sahara since 1975.

GEOGRAPHY

Fertile coastal plain is interrupted in the east by the Rif Mountains. Atlas Mountain ranges to the south. Beyond lies the outer fringe of the Sahara.

CLIMATE

Ranges from temperate and warm in the north, to semi-arid in the south. Cooler in the mountains.

PEOPLE AND SOCIETY

About 35% are descendants of original Berber inhabitants of northwest Africa, and live mainly in mountain villages. Arab majority inhabit lowlands. Large rural-urban gap in wealth. High birth rate. King Hassan heads a powerful monarchy. Government threatened by Islamic militants who fear country is losing its Islamic, Arab identity and becoming too influenced by Europe.

THE ECONOMY

World's main exporter of phosphates. Tourism and agriculture have great potential. Production of cannabis complicates closer EU links.

◆ *INSIGHT: Fès's Karueein University, founded in AD 859, is the world's oldest existing educational institution*

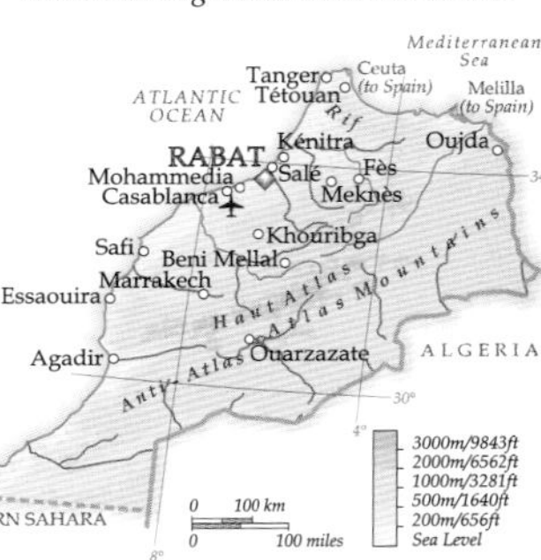
Mediterranean Sea
Tanger
Ceuta (to Spain)
Melilla (to Spain)
Tétouan
ATLANTIC OCEAN
Rif
Kénitra
Oujda
RABAT
Salé
Fès
Mohammedia
Casablanca
Meknès
Khouribga
Safi
Beni Mellal
Marrakech
Essaouira
Haut Atlas
Atlas Mountains
Agadir
Ouarzazate
Anti-Atlas
ALGERIA
WESTERN SAHARA
34°
30°
12°
8°
4°
0 100 km
0 100 miles
3000m/9843ft
2000m/6562ft
1000m/3281ft
500m/1640ft
200m/656ft
Sea Level

FACT FILE

OFFICIAL NAME: Kingdom of Morocco
DATE OF FORMATION: 1956
CAPITAL: Rabat
POPULATION: 27 million
TOTAL AREA: 698,670 sq km (269,757 sq miles)
DENSITY: 39 people per sq km
LANGUAGES: Arabic*, Berber, French
RELIGIONS: Muslim 99%, other 1%
ETHNIC MIX: Arab and Berber 99%, European 1%
GOVERNMENT: Constitutional monarchy
CURRENCY: Dirham = 100 centimes

ALGERIA

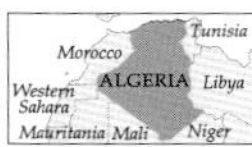
Tunisia
Morocco
ALGERIA
Libya
Western Sahara
Mauritania
Mali
Niger

ALGERIA ACHIEVED independence from France in 1962. Today, its military-dominated government faces a severe challenge from Islamic extremists.

GEOGRAPHY

85% of the country lies within the Sahara. Fertile coastal region with plains and hills rises in the southeast to the Atlas Mountains.

CLIMATE

Coastal areas are warm and temperate, with most rainfall during the mild winters. The south is very hot, with negligible rainfall.

PEOPLE AND SOCIETY

Algerians are predominantly Arab, under 30 years of age and urban. Most indigenous Berbers consider the mountainous Kabylia region in the northeast to be their homeland. The Sahara sustains just 500,000 people, mainly oil workers and Tuareg nomads with goat and camel herds, who move between the irrigated oases. In recent years, political violence has claimed the lives of 3,000 people.

THE ECONOMY

Oil and gas exports. Political turmoil has led to exodus of skilled foreign labour. Limited agriculture.

◆ INSIGHT: *The world's highest sand dunes are found in east central Algeria*

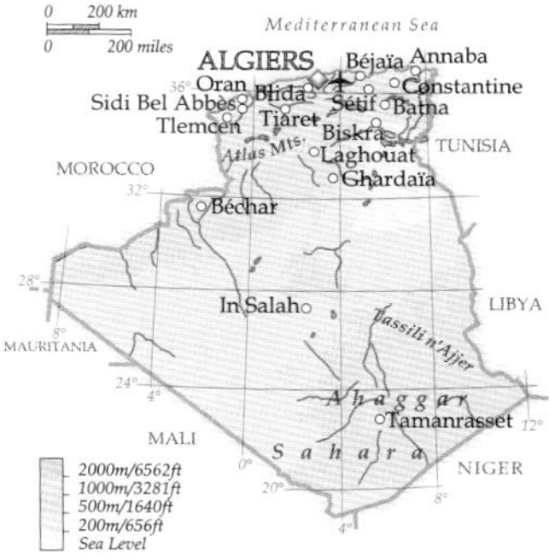
0 200 km
0 200 miles
Mediterranean Sea
ALGIERS
Béjaïa
Annaba
Constantine
Oran
Blida
Sidi Bel Abbès
Sétif
Batna
Tlemcen
Tiaret
Biskra
Atlas Mts.
Laghouat
Ghardaïa
TUNISIA
MOROCCO
Béchar
In Salah
LIBYA
Tassili n'Ajjer
MAURITANIA
Ahaggar
Tamanrasset
MALI
Sahara
NIGER
2000m/6562ft
1000m/3281ft
500m/1640ft
200m/656ft
Sea Level

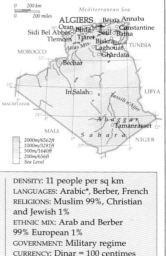

FACT FILE

OFFICIAL NAME: Democratic and Popular Republic of Algeria
DATE OF FORMATION: 1962
CAPITAL: Algiers
POPULATION: 27.1 million
TOTAL AREA: 2,381,740 sq km (919,590 sq miles)
DENSITY: 11 people per sq km
LANGUAGES: Arabic*, Berber, French
RELIGIONS: Muslim 99%, Christian and Jewish 1%
ETHNIC MIX: Arab and Berber 99% European 1%
GOVERNMENT: Military regime
CURRENCY: Dinar = 100 centimes

TUNISIA

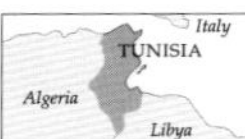
Italy
TUNISIA
Algeria
Libya

TUNISIA HAS traditionally been one of the more liberal Arab states, but its government is now facing a challenge from Islamic fundamentalists.

GEOGRAPHY

Mountains in the north are surrounded by plains. Vast, low-lying salt pans in the centre. To the south lies the Sahara.

CLIMATE

Summer temperatures are high. The north is often wet and windy in winter. Far south is arid.

PEOPLE AND SOCIETY

Population almost entirely of Arab-Berber descent, with Jewish and Christian minorities. Many still live in extended families. Women have better rights than in any other Arab country and make up 25% of the total work force. Politics, however, remains a male preserve. Low birth rate is a result of a long-standing family planning policy.

◆ *INSIGHT: Matmata – a Berber village – appeared in the film 'Star Wars'*

THE ECONOMY

Well-diversified, despite limited resources. Oil and gas exports. Expanding manufacturing. Tourism. European investment.

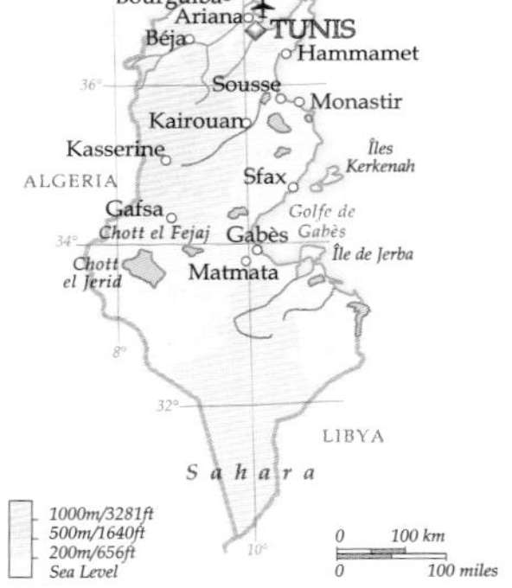
Mediterranean Sea
Menzel Bourguiba
Bizerte
Ariana
TUNIS
Béja
Hammamet
Sousse
Monastir
Kairouan
Kasserine
Îles Kerkenah
ALGERIA
Sfax
Gafsa
Golfe de Gabès
Chott el Fejaj
Gabès
Île de Jerba
Chott el Jerid
Matmata
LIBYA
Sahara
1000m/3281ft
500m/1640ft
200m/656ft
Sea Level
0 100 km
0 100 miles

FACT FILE

OFFICIAL NAME: Republic of Tunisia
DATE OF FORMATION: 1956
CAPITAL: Tunis
POPULATION: 8.6 million
TOTAL AREA: 163,610 sq km (63,170 sq miles)
DENSITY: 54 people per sq km
LANGUAGES: Arabic*, French
RELIGIONS: Muslim 98%, Christian 1%, other 1%
ETHNIC MIX: Arab and Berber 98%, European 1%, other 1%
GOVERNMENT: Multiparty republic
CURRENCY: Dinar = 1,000 millimes

LIBYA

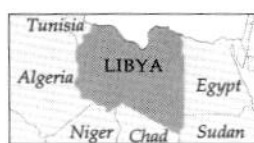
Tunisia
LIBYA
Algeria
Egypt
Niger
Chad
Sudan

SITUATED ON the Mediterranean coast of North Africa, Libya is a Muslim dictatorship, politically marginalized by the West for its terrorist links.

GEOGRAPHY

Apart from the coastal strip and a mountain range in the south, Libya is desert or semi-desert. Oases provide agricultural land.

CLIMATE

Hot and arid. Coastal area has temperate climate, with mild, wet winters and hot, dry summers.

PEOPLE AND SOCIETY

Most Libyans are of Arab and Berber origin. 1969 revolution brought Colonel Gadaffi to power. He represents independence, Islamic faith, belief in communal lifestyle and hatred of urban rich. Revolution wiped out private enterprise and middle classes. Jews and European settlers were banished. Since then, Libya has changed from being largely a nation of nomads and livestock herders to 70% city-dwellers.

THE ECONOMY

90% of export earnings come from oil. Subject to fluctuating world prices. Dates, olives, peaches and grapes are grown in the oases.

◆ *INSIGHT: Libya's sulphur-free oil gives out little pollution when burned*

Mediterranean Sea
Az Zāwiyah
TRIPOLI
TUNISIA
Al Khums
Mişrātah
Al Baydā'
Tubruq
Gharyān
Khalīj Surt
Surt
Banghāzī
Ghadāmis
ALGERIA
EGYPT
Sabhā
Libyan Desert
Ghāt
Fazzān
Al Kufrah
Sahara
NIGER
CHAD
SUDAN
2000m/6562ft
1000m/3281ft
500m/1640ft
200m/656ft
Sea Level
Below Sea Level
0 200 km
0 200 miles

FACT FILE

OFFICIAL NAME: The Great Socialist People's Libyan Arab *Jamahiriya*
DATE OF FORMATION: 1951
CAPITAL: Tripoli
POPULATION: 5.5 million
TOTAL AREA: 1,759,540 sq km (679,358 sq miles)
DENSITY: 3 people per sq km
LANGUAGES: Arabic*, Tuareg
RELIGIONS: Muslim 97%, other 3%
ETHNIC MIX: Arab and Berber 97%, other 3%
GOVERNMENT: Socialist *jamahiriya* (state of the masses)
CURRENCY: Dinar = 1,000 dirhams

EGYPT

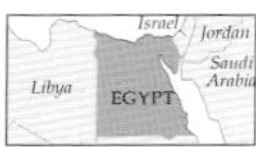
Israel
Jordan
Saudi
Libya
EGYPT

EGYPT OCCUPIES the northeast corner of Africa. Its essentially pro-Western, military-backed regime is being challenged by Islamic fundamentalists.

GEOGRAPHY

Fertile Nile valley separates arid Libyan Desert from smaller semiarid eastern desert. Sinai peninsula has mountains in south.

CLIMATE

Summers are very hot, but winters are cooler. Rainfall is negligible, except on the coast.

PEOPLE AND SOCIETY

Continuously inhabited for over 8,000 years, with a tradition of religious and ethnic tolerance. Egyptianare mostly Arabs, Bedouins, and Nubians. Women play full part in education system, politics, and economy. Government is fighting Islamic terrorist groups, whose acts of violence have included attacks on politicians, police, and tourists.

◆ *INSIGHT: Egypt has been a major tourist destination since the 1880s*

THE ECONOMY

Oil and gas are main sources of revenue. Tolls from the Suez Canal. Successful tourist industry is threatened by security fears.

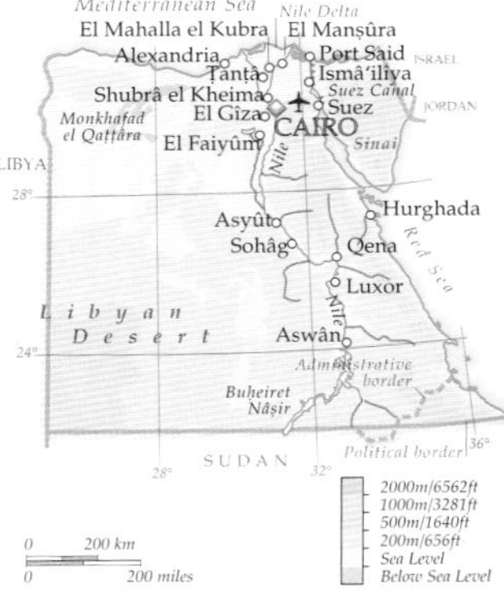
Mediterranean Sea
Nile Delta
El Mahalla el Kubra
El Manṣûra
Alexandria
Ṭanṭâ
Port Said
ISRAEL
Ismâ'iliya
Suez Canal
Shubrâ el Kheima
JORDAN
El Gîza
Suez
Monkhafad el Qaṭṭâra
CAIRO
El Faiyûm
Sinai
LIBYA
Nile
28°
Hurghada
Asyût
Sohâg
Qena
Red Sea
Luxor
Libyan Desert
Nile
Aswân
24°
Administrative border
Buheiret Nâṣir
Political border
36°
SUDAN
28°
32°
2000m/6562ft
1000m/3281ft
500m/1640ft
200m/656ft
Sea Level
Below Sea Level
0
200 km
0
200 miles

FACT FILE

OFFICIAL NAME: Arab Republic of Egypt
DATE OF FORMATION: 1936/1982
CAPITAL: Cairo
POPULATION: 64.2 million
TOTAL AREA: 1,001,450 sq km (386,660 sq miles)
DENSITY: 64 people per sq km
LANGUAGES: Arabic*, French, English, Berber, Greek, Armenian
RELIGIONS: Muslim 94%, other 6%
ETHNIC MIX: Eastern Hamitic 90%, other (inc. Greek, Armenian) 10%
GOVERNMENT: Multiparty republic
CURRENCY: Pound = 100 piastres

SUDAN

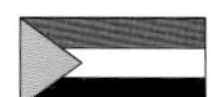

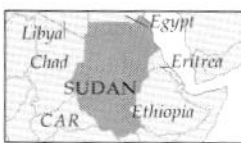
Libya
Egypt
Chad
Eritrea
SUDAN
Ethiopia
CAR

THE LARGEST country in Africa, Sudan borders the Red Sea. In 1989, an army coup installed a military Islamic fundamentalist regime.

GEOGRAPHY

Lies within the upper Nile basin. Mostly arid plains, with marshes in the south. Highlands border the Red Sea in the northeast.

CLIMATE

North is hot, arid desert with constant dry winds. Rainy season ranging from two months in the centre, to eight in the south.

PEOPLE AND SOCIETY

Large number of ethnic and linguistic groups. Two million people are nomads, moving over ancient tribal areas in the south. Major social division is between Arabized Muslims in north, and mostly African, largely Christian or animist peoples in south. Attempts to impose Arab and Islamic values throughout Sudan have been the root cause of the civil war that has ravaged the south since 1983.

THE ECONOMY

Sudan is affected by drought and food shortages. Sesame seeds, cotton, gum arabic are cash crops.

◆*INSIGHT: Sudan's Sudd plain contains the world's largest swamp*

EGYPT
LIBYA
Nubian Desert
Red Sea
Nile
Port Sudan
Atbara
CHAD
ERITREA
Omdurman
Khartoum North
KHARTOUM
Kassala
Geneina
Sodiri
Wad Medani
Gedaref
El Fasher
El Obeid
Kosti
White Nile
Blue Nile
ETHIOPIA
CENTRAL AFRICAN REPUBLIC
Jonglei Canal
Sudd
Elemi Triangle
Juba
CONGO (ZAIRE)
UGANDA
KENYA
2000m/6562ft
1000m/3281ft
500m/1640ft
200m/656ft
Sea Level
0 400 km
0 400 miles

FACT FILE

OFFICIAL NAME: Republic of Sudan
DATE OF FORMATION: 1956
CAPITAL: Khartoum
POPULATION: 27.4 million
TOTAL AREA: 2,505,815 sq km (967,493 sq miles)
DENSITY: 11 people per sq km
LANGUAGES: Arabic*, other
RELIGIONS: Muslim 70%, traditional beliefs 20%, Christian 5%, other 5%
ETHNIC MIX: Arab 51%, Dinka 13%, Nuba 9%, Beja 7%, other 20%
GOVERNMENT: Military regime
CURRENCY: Pound = 100 piastres

ERITREA

Sudan
Saudi Arabia
ERITREA
Yemen
Ethiopia

LYING ON the shores of the Red Sea, Eritrea effectively seceded from Ethiopia in 1991, following a 30-year war for independence.

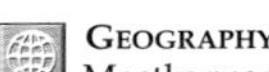

GEOGRAPHY

Mostly rugged mountains, bush, and the Danakil Desert, which falls below sea level.

CLIMATE

Warm in the mountains; desert areas are hot. Droughts from July onwards are common.

PEOPLE AND SOCIETY

Nine main ethnic groups. Tigrinya-speakers are the largest in number. Strong sense of nationhood forged by the war. Women played important role in the war, fighting alongside men. Over 80% of people are subsistence farmers. Few live beyond the age of 45. Transitional government will hold multiparty elections in 1997.

◆ *INSIGHT: 75% of Eritreans are dependent upon aid for all, or part, of their annual food supply*

THE ECONOMY

Legacy of disruption and destruction from war. Susceptible to drought and famine. Most of the population live at subsistence level. Potential for mining of gold, copper, silver and zinc. Possible foreign earnings from oil exports.

SUDAN
Kerora
Red Sea
40°
Dahlak Archipelago
16°
Keren
Massawa
Akordat
Barentu
ASMARA
Adi Ugri
Teseney
ETHIOPIA
Suwa
Red Sea
Danakil
Assab
DJIBOUTI
2000m/6562ft
1000m/3281ft
500m/1640ft
200m/656ft
Sea Level
Below Sea Level
0 100 km
0 100 miles

FACT FILE

OFFICIAL NAME: State of Eritrea
DATE OF FORMATION: 1993
CAPITAL: Asmara
POPULATION: 3.5 million
TOTAL AREA: 93,680 sq km (36,170 sq miles)
DENSITY: 37 people per sq km
LANGUAGES: Tigrinya*, Arabic*, Tigre, Afar, Bilen, Kunama, Nara
RELIGIONS: Coptic Christian 45%, Muslim 45%, other 10%
ETHNIC MIX: Nine main ethnic groups
GOVERNMENT: Provisional military government
CURRENCY: Ethiopian birr = 100 cents

DJIBOUTI

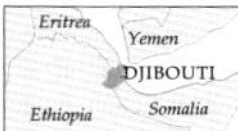
Eritrea
Yemen
DJIBOUTI
Ethiopia
Somalia

A CITY state with a desert hinterland, Djibouti lies in northeast Africa. Once known as French Somaliland, it became independent in 1977.

GEOGRAPHY

Mainly low-lying desert and semi-desert, with a volcanic mountain range in the north.

CLIMATE

Hot all year round, with June–August temperatures reaching 45°C (109°F). Very low rainfall.

PEOPLE AND SOCIETY

Dominant ethnic groups are the Issas in the south, and the mainly nomadic Afars in the north. Tensions between them developed into a guerrilla war in 1991. Smaller tribal groups make up the rest of the population, together with French and other European expatriates, and Arabs. Population was swelled by 20,000 Somali refugees in 1992. France still exerts considerable influence in Djibouti, supporting it financially and maintaining a naval base and a military garrison.

THE ECONOMY

Djibouti's major asset is its port in a key Red Sea location.

◆ INSIGHT: *Chewing the leaves of the mildly narcotic Qat shrub is an age-old social ritual in Djibouti*

1000m/3281ft
500m/1640ft
200m/656ft
Sea Level
Below Sea Level
0 30 km
0 30 miles
ERITREA
Red Sea
Bab el Mandeb
ETHIOPIA
Dadda'to
Obock
Gulf of Aden
Tadjoura
Gâlâfi
Lac 'Assal
Golfe de Tadjoura
DJIBOUTI
Goubétto
Damêrdjôg
Lake Abhe
Mouloud
Guélîlé
SOMALIA
ETHIOPIA

FACT FILE

OFFICIAL NAME: Republic of Djibouti
DATE OF FORMATION: 1977
CAPITAL: Djibouti
POPULATION: 500,000
TOTAL AREA: 23,200 sq km (8,958 sq miles)
DENSITY: 21 people per sq km
LANGUAGES: Arabic*, French*, Somali, Afar, other
RELIGIONS: Christian 87%, other 13%
ETHNIC MIX: Issa 35%, Afar 20%, Gadaboursis and Isaaks 28%, other (inc. Arab, European) 17%
GOVERNMENT: Single-party republic
CURRENCY: Franc = 100 centimes

ETHIOPIA

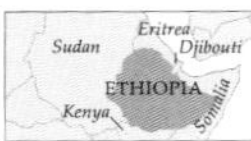
Sudan
Eritrea
Djibouti
ETHIOPIA
Kenya
Somalia

LOCATED IN northeast Africa, Ethiopia was a Marxist regime from 1974–91. It has suffered a series of economic, civil and natural crises.

GEOGRAPHY

Great Rift Valley divides mountainous northwest region from desert lowlands in northeast and southeast. Ethiopian Plateau is drained mainly by the Blue Nile.

CLIMATE

Generally moderate with summer rains. Highlands are warm, with night frost and snowfalls on the mountains.

PEOPLE AND SOCIETY

76 Ethiopian nationalities speak 286 languages. Oromo are largest group. In 1995, the first multiparty elections were held, ending four years of rule by transitional government, and beginning a new nine-state federation.

◆ *INSIGHT: Solomon and the Queen of Sheba are said to have founded the Kingdom of Abyssinia (Ethiopia) c. 1000 BC*

THE ECONOMY

World's second poorest nation. Most people are subsistence farmers. Despite war-damaged infrastructure and periodic serious droughts, agricultural and industrial output are growing as it moves towards a market economy.

0 200 km
0 200 miles
4000m/13124ft
3000m/9843ft
2000m/6562ft
1000m/3281ft
500m/1640ft
200m/656ft
Sea Level
Below Sea Level
ERITREA
Red Sea
Mek'elē
Gonder
T'ana Hāyk'
Bahir Dar
Gulf of Aden
DJIBOUTI
Desē
Blue Nile
Ethiopian
SUDAN
ADDIS ABABA
Debre Zeyit
Dirē Dawa
Hārer
SOMALIA
Plateau
Nazrēt
Jīma
Great Rift Valley
Ogaden
L. Turkana
SOMALIA
KENYA

FACT FILE

OFFICIAL NAME: *Undetermined*
DATE OF FORMATION: 1903 / 1993
CAPITAL: Addis Ababa
POPULATION: 56.7 million
TOTAL AREA: 1,128,221 sq km (435,605 sq miles)
DENSITY: 50 people per sq km
LANGUAGES: Amharic*, English, Arabic, Tigrinya, Orominga
RELIGIONS: Muslim 43%, Christian 37%, traditional beliefs, other 20%,
ETHNIC MIX: Oromo 40%, Amhara and Tigrean 32%, other 28%
GOVERNMENT: Multiparty republic
CURRENCY: Birr = 100 cents

SOMALIA

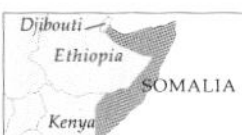
Djibouti
Ethiopia
SOMALIA
Kenya

A SEMI-ARID state occupying the horn of Africa. Italian Somaliland and British Somaliland were united in 1960 to form an independent Somalia.

GEOGRAPHY

Highlands in the north, flatter scrub-covered land to the south. Coastal areas are more fertile.

CLIMATE

Very dry, except for the north coast, which is hot and humid. Interior has among world's highest average yearly temperatures.

PEOPLE AND SOCIETY

Clan system forms the basis of all commercial, political and social activities. Most people are herders (Samaal) while the rest are farmers (Sab). Years of clan-based civil war have resulted in collapse of central government. US-led UN peacekeeping force was deployed, but it was withdrawn in 1994.

◈ *INSIGHT: Present-day Somalia was known to the Egyptians, Phoenicians and Greeks as 'the land of incense'*

THE ECONOMY

Somalia is heavily reliant on foreign aid, since all commodities, except arms, are in short supply. Formal economy has collapsed due to civil war and drought.

DJIBOUTI
Gulf of Aden
Raas Caseyr
Berbera
Hargeysa
Burco
Garoowe
ETHIOPIA
Gaalkacyo
Beledweyne
INDIAN OCEAN
KENYA
Baydhabo
MOGADISHU
Marka
Jilib
Equator
Kismaayo
1000m/3281ft
500m/1640ft
200m/656ft
Sea Level
Below Sea Level
0 200 km
0 200 miles

FACT FILE

OFFICIAL NAME: Somali Democratic Republic
DATE OF FORMATION: 1960
CAPITAL: Mogadishu
POPULATION: 9.5 million
TOTAL AREA: 637,660 sq km (246,200 sq miles)
DENSITY: 15 people per sq km
LANGUAGES: Somali*, Arabic*, other
RELIGIONS: Sunni Muslim 99%, other (inc. Christian) 1%
ETHNIC MIX: Somali 98%, Bantu, Arab 1.5%, European, other 0.5%
GOVERNMENT: Transitional
CURRENCY: Shilling = 100 cents

UGANDA

Sudan
Congo (Zaire)
UGANDA
Kenya
Rwanda

UGANDA LIES land-locked in East Africa. It was ruled by one of Africa's more eccentric leaders, the dictator Idi Amin Dada, from 1971–1980.

GEOGRAPHY

Predominantly a large plateau with Ruwenzori mountain range and Great Rift Valley in the west. Lake Victoria in the southeast. Vegetation is of savannah type.

CLIMATE

Altitude and the influence of the lakes modify the equatorial climate. Rain falls throughout the year; spring is the wettest period.

PEOPLE AND SOCIETY

Predominantly rural population comprises 13 main ethnic groups. Since 1986, President Museveni has worked hard to break down traditional animosities. In 1993, he allowed the restoration of Uganda's four historical monarchies. New constitution will use a federal system with boundaries based on those of the old kingdoms.

THE ECONOMY

Coffee earns 93% of export income. Hydroelectric power is to be developed to replace 50% of oil imports. Reopening of mines should improve the economy.

◆ *INSIGHT: Lake Victoria is the world's third largest lake*

3000m/9843ft
2000m/6562ft
1000m/3281ft
500m/1640ft
SUDAN
KENYA
Arua
Gulu
Albert Nile
Lake Albert
CONGO (ZAIRE)
Great Rift Valley
Lake Kyoga
Victoria Nile
Mbale
Tororo
Ruwenzori
Kabarole
Iganga
Jinja
Mubende
Kasese
KAMPALA
Entebbe
Equator
Lake Edward
Masaka
Sese Is.
Mbarara
Lake Victoria
Rukungiri
Kabale
TANZANIA
RWANDA
2°
32°
0 100 km
0 100 miles

FACT FILE

OFFICIAL NAME: Republic of Uganda
DATE OF FORMATION: 1962
CAPITAL: Kampala
POPULATION: 19.2 million
TOTAL AREA: 235,880 sq km (91,073 sq miles)
DENSITY: 94 people per sq km
LANGUAGES: English*, Luganda, Nkole, Chiga, Lango, Acholi, Teso
RELIGIONS: Catholic/Protestant 66%, traditional beliefs 18%, Muslim 16%
ETHNIC MIX: Buganda 18%, Banyoro 14%, Teso 9%, other 59%
GOVERNMENT: Multiparty republic
CURRENCY: Shilling = 100 cents

KENYA

Sudan
Ethiopia
Uganda
KENYA
Somalia
Tanzania

KENYA STRADDLES the Equator on Africa's east coast. It became a multiparty democracy in 1992 and has been led by President Moi since 1978.

GEOGRAPHY

Central plateau divided by Great Rift Valley. North of the Equator is mainly semi-desert. To the east lies a fertile coastal belt.

CLIMATE

Coast and Great Rift Valley are hot and humid. Plateau interior is temperate. Northeastern desert is hot and dry. Rain generally falls April–May and October–November.

PEOPLE AND SOCIETY

Kenya's 70 ethnic groups share about 40 languages. Rural majority has strong clan and family links. One of the world's highest population growth rates, together with poverty, has exacerbated the recent surge in ethnic violence.

◆ *INSIGHT: Kenya has more than 40 game reserves and national parks, and two marine parks in the Indian Ocean*

THE ECONOMY

Tourism is the leading foreign exchange earner. Tea and coffee grown as cash crops. Large and diversified manufacturing sector.

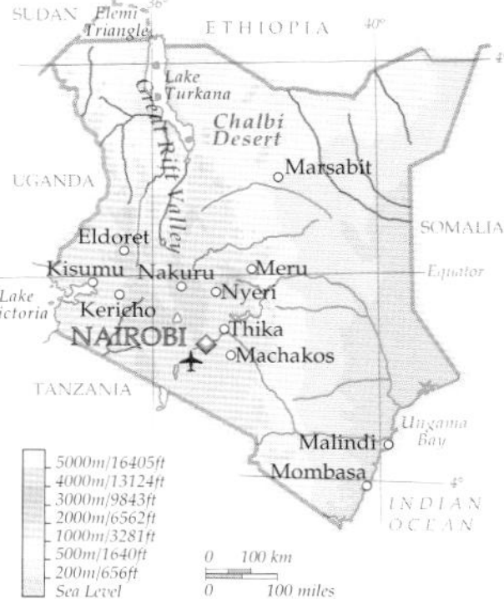
SUDAN
Ilemi Triangle
ETHIOPIA
Lake Turkana
Great Rift Valley
Chalbi Desert
Marsabit
UGANDA
SOMALIA
Eldoret
Kisumu
Nakuru
Meru
Equator
Nyeri
Lake Victoria
Kericho
NAIROBI
Thika
Machakos
TANZANIA
Ungama Bay
Malindi
Mombasa
INDIAN OCEAN
5000m/16405ft
4000m/13124ft
3000m/9843ft
2000m/6562ft
1000m/3281ft
500m/1640ft
200m/656ft
Sea Level
0 100 km
0 100 miles

FACT FILE

OFFICIAL NAME: Republic of Kenya
DATE OF FORMATION: 1963
CAPITAL: Nairobi
POPULATION: 29.1 million
TOTAL AREA: 580,370 sq km (224,081 sq miles)
DENSITY: 50 people per sq km
LANGUAGES: Swahili*, English, Kikuyu, Luo, Kamba, other
RELIGIONS: Catholic/Protestant 66%, animist 26%, Muslim 6%, other 2%
ETHNIC MIX: Kikuyu 21%, Luhya 14%, Kamba 11%, other 54%
GOVERNMENT: Multiparty republic
CURRENCY: Shilling = 100 cents

RWANDA

R

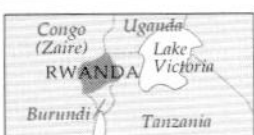
Congo (Zaire)
Uganda
Lake Victoria
RWANDA
Burundi
Tanzania

RWANDA LIES just south of the Equator in east central Africa. Since independence from France in 1962, ethnic tensions have dominated politics.

GEOGRAPHY

Series of plateaux descend from ridge of volcanic peaks in the west to Akagera River on eastern border. Great Rift Valley also passes through this region.

CLIMATE

Tropical, tempered by the altitude. Two wet seasons are separated by a dry season, June–August. Heaviest rain in the west.

PEOPLE AND SOCIETY

Rwandans live a subsistence existence. Traditional family and clan structures are strong. For over 500 years the cattle-owning Tutsi were politically dominant over the land-owning Hutu. In 1959, violent revolt led to a reversal of the roles. The two groups have since been waging a spasmodic war. In the most recent outbreak of violence, in 1994, over 200,000 people died.

THE ECONOMY

All economic activity has been suspended due to ethnic conflict. Rwanda has few resources, but assuming peace, it produces coffee. Possible oil and gas reserves.

◆ *INSIGHT: Rwanda is Africa's most densely populated country*

3000m/9843ft
2000m/6562ft
1000m/3281ft
UGANDA
TANZANIA
CONGO (ZAIRE)
Ruhengeri
Byumba
Gisenyi
Lake Kivu
KIGALI
2°
Kibuye
Gitarama
Kibungo
Cyangugu
Butare
30°
29°
BURUNDI
0
50 km
0
50 miles

FACT FILE

OFFICIAL NAME: Rwandese Republic
DATE OF FORMATION: 1962
CAPITAL: Kigali
POPULATION: 7.5 million
TOTAL AREA: 26,340 sq km (10,170 sq miles)
DENSITY: 285 people per sq km
LANGUAGES: Kinyarwanda*, French*, Kiswahili
RELIGIONS: Catholic 65%, Protestant 9%, traditional beliefs 25%, other 1%
ETHNIC MIX: Hutu 90%, Tutsi 9%, Twa pygmy 1%
GOVERNMENT: Multiparty republic
CURRENCY: Franc = 100 centimes

BURUNDI

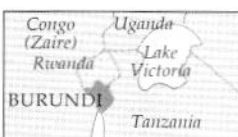
Congo (Zaire)
Uganda
Lake Victoria
Rwanda
BURUNDI
Tanzania

SMALL, DENSELY populated and land-locked, Burundi lies just south of the Equator, on the Nile–Congo watershed in Central Africa.

GEOGRAPHY

Hilly with high plateaux in centre and savannah in the east. Great Rift Valley on western side.

CLIMATE

Temperate, with high humidity. Heavy and frequent rainfall, mostly October–May.

PEOPLE AND SOCIETY

Burundi's post-independence history has been dominated by ethnic conflict – with repeated large-scale massacres – between majority Hutu and the Tutsi, who control the army. Over 120,000 people, mostly Hutu, have been killed since 1992. Twa pygmies are not involved in the conflict. Most people are subsistence farmers.

◆ *INSIGHT: Burundi's birth rate is one of the highest in Africa. On average women have seven children*

THE ECONOMY

Overwhelmingly agricultural economy. Small quantities of gold and tungsten. Potential of oil in Lake Tanganyika. Burundi has 5% of the world's nickel reserves.

RWANDA
Kirundo
Ngozi
Muyinga
Kayanza
Bubanza
Cankuzo
Karuzi
BUJUMBURA
Ruyigi
Gitega
CONGO (ZAIRE)
TANZANIA
Bururi
Rutana
Lake Tanganyika
Makamba
Nyanza-Lac
3°
4°
29°
30°
0 50 km
0 50 miles
2000m/6562ft
1000m/3281ft
500m/1640ft

FACT FILE

OFFICIAL NAME: Republic of Burundi
DATE OF FORMATION: 1962
CAPITAL: Bujumbura
POPULATION: 5.8 million
TOTAL AREA: 27,830 sq km (10,750 sq miles)
DENSITY: 198 people per sq km
LANGUAGES: Kirundi*, French*, Swahili, other
RELIGIONS: Catholic 62%, traditional beliefs 32%, Protestant 6%
ETHNIC MIX: Hutu 85%, Tutsi 13%, Twa pygmy 1%, other 1%
GOVERNMENT: Multiparty republic
CURRENCY: Franc = 100 centimes

CENTRAL AFRICAN REPUBLIC

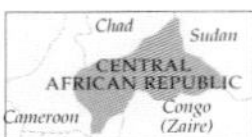
Chad
Sudan
CENTRAL AFRICAN REPUBLIC
Cameroon
Congo (Zaire)

A LAND-LOCKED country lying between the basins of the Chad and Congo rivers. Its arid north sustains less than 2% of the population.

GEOGRAPHY

Comprises a low plateau, covered by scrub or savannah. Rainforests in the south. One of Africa's great rivers, the Ubangi, forms the border with Congo (Zaire).

CLIMATE

The south is equatorial; the north is hot and dry. Rain occurs all year round, with heaviest falls between July and October.

PEOPLE AND SOCIETY

Baya and Banda are largest ethnic groups, but Sango, spoken by minority river peoples in the south, is the *lingua franca*. Most political leaders since independence have come from the south. Women, as in other non-Muslim African countries, have considerable power. Large number of ethnic groups helps limit disputes.

THE ECONOMY

Dominated by subsistence farming. Exports include gold, diamonds, cotton and timber. Country is self-sufficient in food production. Poor infrastructure.

◆ INSIGHT: *The country was severely depopulated in previous centuries by the Arab and European slave trades*

1000m/3281ft
500m/1640ft
200m/656ft
Birao
SUDAN
Ouanda Djallé
CHAD
Ndélé
Batangafo
Kaga Bandoro
Bozoum
Bouar
Sibut
Bambari
Carnot
BANGUI
Bangassou
Berbérati
Mobaye
Ubangi
CAMEROON
CONGO
CONGO (ZAIRE)
0
200 km
0
200 miles

FACT FILE

OFFICIAL NAME: Central African Republic
DATE OF FORMATION: 1960
CAPITAL: Bangui
POPULATION: 3.3 million
TOTAL AREA: 622,980 sq km (240,530 sq miles)
DENSITY: 5 people per sq km
LANGUAGES: French*, Sangho, Banda
RELIGIONS: Christian 50%, traditional beliefs 27%, Muslim 15%, other 8%
ETHNIC MIX: Baya 34%, Banda 27%, Mandjia 21%, Sara 10%, other 8%
GOVERNMENT: Multiparty republic
CURRENCY: CFA franc = 100 centimes

CONGO (ZAIRE)

C.A.R.
Sudan
Uganda
CONGO (ZAIRE)
Congo
Tanzania
Angola
Zambia

STRADDLING THE Equator in east central Africa, this is one of Africa's largest countries. It achieved independence from Belgium in 1960.

GEOGRAPHY

Rainforested basin of River Congo occupies 60% of the land. High mountain ranges stretch down the eastern border.

CLIMATE

Tropical and humid. Distinct wet and dry seasons south of the Equator. The north is mainly wet.

PEOPLE AND SOCIETY

12 main groups and around 190 smaller ones. Original inhabitants, Forest Pygmies, are now a marginalized group. Ethnic tensions inherited from colonial period were contained until 1990, since when outbreaks of ethnic violence have occurred.

◆ *INSIGHT: The rainforests comprise almost 6% of the world's, and 50% of Africa's, remaining woodlands*

THE ECONOMY

25 years of mismanagement have brought economy near to collapse. Hyperinflation. Minerals, including copper and diamonds, provide 85% of export earnings.

CENTRAL AFRICAN REPUBLIC
SUDAN
Ubangi
Buta
Bumba
Isiro
Lake Albert
Mbandaka
Kisangani
UGANDA
Lake Edward
Goma
CONGO
Congo (Zaire)
Lualaba
RWANDA
Bukavu
BURUNDI
KINSHASA
Ilebo
CABINDA (to Angola)
Great Rift Valley
Kikwit
Kananga
Kalemie
TANZANIA
Matadi
Mbuji-Mayi
Lake Tanganyika
Kamina
Lake Mweru
ANGOLA
Kasai
Likasi
ZAMBIA
Lubumbashi
ZAMBIA
2000m/6562ft
1000m/3281ft
500m/1640ft
200m/656ft
Sea Level
0 200 km
0 200 miles

FACT FILE

OFFICIAL NAME: Democratic Republic of the Congo
DATE OF FORMATION: 1960
CAPITAL: Kinshasa
POPULATION: 41.2 million
TOTAL AREA: 2,345,410 sq km (905,563 sq miles)
DENSITY: 18 people per sq km
LANGUAGES: French*, Kiswahili, Tshiluba, Kikongo, Lingala
RELIGIONS: Christian 70%, traditional beliefs 20%, Muslim 10%
ETHNIC MIX: Bantu 23%, Hamitic 23%, other (inc. Pygmy) 54%
GOVERNMENT: Transitional
CURRENCY: Congolese Franc

NIGER

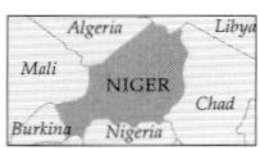
Algeria
Libya
Mali
NIGER
Chad
Burkina
Nigeria

NIGER LIES land-locked in West Africa, but it is linked to the sea by its one permanent river, the Niger. It became independent of France in 1960.

GEOGRAPHY

North and northeast regions are part of Sahara and Sahel. Aïr mountains in centre rise high above the desert. Savannah in the south.

CLIMATE

High temperatures for most of the year – around 35°C (95°F). The north is virtually rainless.

PEOPLE AND SOCIETY

A largely Islamic society. Women have limited rights, and restricted access to education. Considerable tensions exist between Tuareg nomads in the north and groups in the south. Tuaregs have felt alienated from mainstream politics. They mounted a low-key revolt in 1990. Sense of community and egalitarianism among southern peoples helps to combat economic difficulties.

THE ECONOMY

Vast uranium deposits. Frequent droughts and southwest expansion of Sahara are problems.

◆ *INSIGHT: Niger's name is derived from the Tuareg word* n'eghirren, *meaning 'flowing water'*

LIBYA
ALGERIA
Sahara
Aïr
Agadez
MALI
Niger
Tahoua
Sahel
Tillabéri
BURKINA
NIAMEY
Dosso
Birni-Nkonni
Zinder
Maradi
Dogondoutchi
Diffa
CHAD
Lake Chad
BENIN
NIGERIA
20°
16°
12°
4°
8°
12°
0 200 km
0 200 miles
1000m/3281ft
500m/1640ft
200m/656ft
Sea Level

FACT FILE

OFFICIAL NAME: Republic of Niger
DATE OF FORMATION: 1960
CAPITAL: Niamey
POPULATION: 8.5 million
TOTAL AREA: 1,267,000 sq km (489,188 sq miles)
DENSITY: 7 people per sq km
LANGUAGES: French*, Hausa, Djerma, Fulani, Tuareg, Teda
RELIGIONS: Muslim 85%, traditional beliefs 14%, Christian 1%
ETHNIC MIX: Hausa 56%, Djerma 22%, Fulani 9%, other 13%
GOVERNMENT: Multiparty republic
CURRENCY: CFA franc = 100 centimes

CHAD

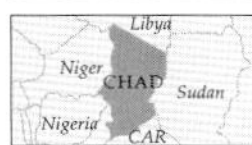
Libya
Niger
CHAD
Sudan
Nigeria
CAR

LAND-LOCKED IN north central Africa, Chad has been torn by intermittent periods of civil war since independence from France in 1960.

GEOGRAPHY

Mostly plateaux sloping westwards to Lake Chad. Northern third is Sahara. Tibesti Mountains in north rise to 3,300 m (10,826 ft).

CLIMATE

Three distinct zones: desert in north, semi-arid region in centre and tropics in south.

PEOPLE AND SOCIETY

Half the population live in southern fifth of the country. Northern third has only 100,000 people, mainly Muslim Toubeu nomads. Political strife between Muslims in north and Christians in south. Recent attempts to introduce multiparty system, after 30 years of military and one-party rule.

◆ *INSIGHT: Lake Chad is progressively drying up – it is now estimated to be just 20% of its size in 1970*

THE ECONOMY

One of Africa's poorest states. Vast majority of people involved in subsistence agriculture, notably cotton and cattle herding. Recent discovery of large oil deposits.

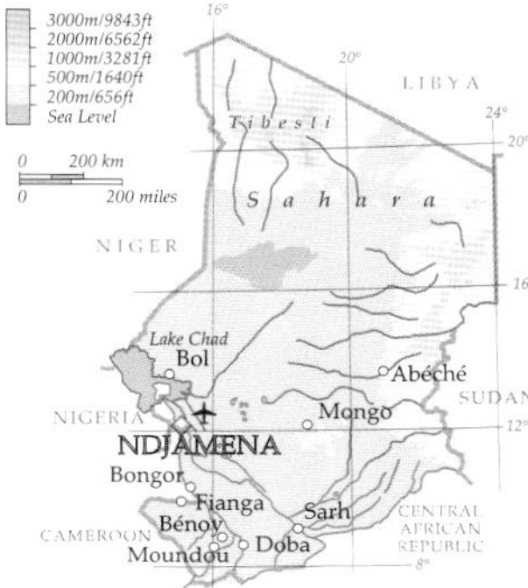
3000m/9843ft
2000m/6562ft
1000m/3281ft
500m/1640ft
200m/656ft
Sea Level
0 200 km
0 200 miles
LIBYA
Tibesti
Sahara
NIGER
Lake Chad
Bol
Abéché
SUDAN
NIGERIA
Mongo
NDJAMENA
Bongor
Fianga
Bénoy
Sarh
CAMEROON
Doba
Moundou
CENTRAL AFRICAN REPUBLIC

FACT FILE

OFFICIAL NAME: Republic of Chad
DATE OF FORMATION: 1960
CAPITAL: Ndjamena
POPULATION: 6 million
TOTAL AREA: 1,284,000 sq km (495,752 sq miles)
DENSITY: 5 people per sq km
LANGUAGES: French*, Sara, Maba
RELIGIONS: Muslim 44%, Christian 33%, traditional beliefs 23%
ETHNIC MIX: Bagirmi, Sara and Kreish 31%, Sudanic Arab 26%, Teda 7%, other 36%
GOVERNMENT: Transitional
CURRENCY: CFA franc = 100 centimes

MAURITANIA

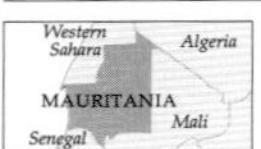
Western Sahara
Algeria
MAURITANIA
Mali
Senegal

SITUATED IN northwest Africa, two-thirds of Mauritania's territory is desert. A former French colony, it achieved independence in 1960.

GEOGRAPHY

The Sahara, barren with scattered oases, covers the north. Savannah lands to the south.

CLIMATE

Generally hot and dry, aggravated by dusty *harmattan* wind. Summer rain in the south, virtually none in the north.

PEOPLE AND SOCIETY

The Maures control political life and dominate the minority black population. Ethnic tension centres on the oppression of blacks by Maures. Tens of thousands of blacks are estimated to be in slavery. Family solidarity among nomadic peoples is particularly strong.

◆ *INSIGHT: Slavery officially became illegal in Mauritania in 1980, but* de facto *slavery still persists*

THE ECONOMY

Agriculture and herding. Iron and copper mining. World's largest gypsum deposits. Rich fishing grounds. Large foreign debt.

500m/1640ft
200m/656ft
Sea Level
ALGERIA
WESTERN SAHARA
Zouérat
Sahara
MALI
Nouâdhibou
Atâr
ATLANTIC OCEAN
Tidjikja
NOUAKCHOTT
Rosso
Kaédi
Kiffa
Néma
Senegal
SENEGAL
MALI
24°
20°
16°
4°
8°
12°
16°
0 200 km
0 200 miles

FACT FILE

OFFICIAL NAME: Islamic Republic of Mauritania
DATE OF FORMATION: 1960
CAPITAL: Nouakchott
POPULATION: 2.2 million
TOTAL AREA: 1,025,520 sq km (395,953 sq miles)
DENSITY: 2 people per sq km
LANGUAGES: French*, Hassaniyah Arabic, Wolof
RELIGIONS: Muslim 100%
ETHNIC MIX: Maure 80%, Wolof 7%, Tukulor 5%, other 8%
GOVERNMENT: Multiparty republic
CURRENCY: Ouguiya = 5 khoums

MALI

Algeria
Mauritania
MALI
Niger
Senegal
Burkina
Guinea

LAND-LOCKED in the heart of West Africa, Mali held its first free elections in 1992, more than 30 years after it gained independence from France.

GEOGRAPHY
Northern half lies in the Sahara. Inland delta of River Niger flows through grassy savannah region in the south.

CLIMATE
In the south, intensely hot, dry weather precedes the westerly rains. The north is almost rainless.

PEOPLE AND SOCIETY
Most people live in southern savannah region. Bambara are politically dominant. A few nomadic Fulani and Tuareg herders travel northern plains. Extended family provides social security. Tension between peoples of the south and Tuaregs in north.

◆ *INSIGHT: Tombouctou was the centre of the huge Malinke empire during the 14th century*

THE ECONOMY
One of the poorest countries in the world. Less than 2% of land can be cultivated. Most people are farmers, herders or river fishermen. Gold deposits now being mined.

500m/1640ft
200m/656ft
Sea Level
ALGERIA
MAURITANIA
Sahara
Adrar des Iforas
Niger
Tombouctou
Gao
Senegal
Kayes
Mopti
NIGER
SENEGAL
Ségou
Koulikoro
BAMAKO
BURKINA
Sikasso
GUINEA
IVORY COAST
0 200 km
0 200 miles

FACT FILE

OFFICIAL NAME: Republic of Mali
DATE OF FORMATION: 1960
CAPITAL: Bamako
POPULATION: 10.1 million
TOTAL AREA: 1,240,190 sq km (478,837 sq miles)
DENSITY: 8 people per sq km
LANGUAGES: French*, Bambara, Fulani, Senufo, Soninké
RELIGIONS: Muslim 80%, traditional beliefs 18%, Christian 2%
ETHNIC MIX: Bambara 31%, Fulani 13%, Senufo 12%, other 44%
GOVERNMENT: Multiparty republic
CURRENCY: CFA franc = 100 centimes

SENEGAL

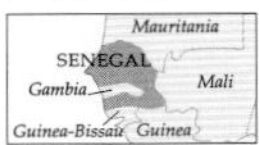
Mauritania
SENEGAL
Gambia
Mali
Guinea-Bissau
Guinea

A FORMER French colony, Senegal achieved independence in 1960. Its capital, Dakar, stands on the westernmost cape of Africa.

GEOGRAPHY

Arid semi-desert in the north. The south is mainly savannah bushland. Plains in the southeast.

CLIMATE

Tropical, with humid rainy conditions June–October, and drier season December–May. Coast is cooled by northern trade winds.

PEOPLE AND SOCIETY

Very little ethnic tension, due to considerable amount of inter-ethnic marriage. Groups can be identified regionally. Dakar is a Wolof area, the Senegal River is dominated by the Toucouleur, and the Malinke mostly live in the east. The Diola in Casamance have felt politically excluded and this has led to unrest. A French-influenced class system is still prevalent and has become more apparent in recent years.

THE ECONOMY

70% of people are farmers – groundnuts are main export crop. Phosphate is mined. More industry than most West African countries.

◆ *INSIGHT: Senegal's name derives from the Zenega Berbers who invaded in the 1300s, bringing Islam with them*

Senegal
Saint-Louis
MAURITANIA
Louga
Matam
Senegal
Pikine
Thiès
Diourbel
DAKAR
Mbour
Kaolack
Kaffrine
ATLANTIC OCEAN
Tambacounda
MALI
THE GAMBIA
Casamance
Kolda
Ziguinchor
Gambie
GUINEA-BISSAU
GUINEA
16°
12°
200m/656ft
Sea Level
0
100 km
0
100 miles

FACT FILE

OFFICIAL NAME: Republic of Senegal
DATE OF FORMATION: 1960
CAPITAL: Dakar
POPULATION: 7.9 million
TOTAL AREA: 196,720 sq km (75,950 sq miles)
DENSITY: 39 people per sq km
LANGUAGES: French*, Wolof, Fulani, Serer, Diola, Malinke, Soninke
RELIGIONS: Muslim 92%, traditional beliefs 6%, Christian 2%
ETHNIC MIX: Wolof 46%, Fulani 25%, Serer 16%, Diola 7%, Malinke 6%
GOVERNMENT: Multiparty republic
CURRENCY: CFA franc = 100 centimes

THE GAMBIA

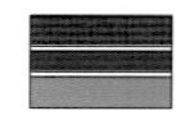

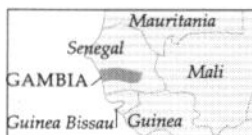
Mauritania
Senegal
GAMBIA
Mali
Guinea Bissau
Guinea

A NARROW state on the west coast of Africa, The Gambia was renowned for its stability until its government was overthrown in a coup in 1994.

GEOGRAPHY

Narrow strip of land which borders River Gambia. Long, sandy beaches backed by mangrove swamps along river. Savannah and tropical forests higher up.

CLIMATE

Sub-tropical, with wet, humid months July–October and warm, dry season November–May.

PEOPLE AND SOCIETY

Little tension between various ethnic groups. Creole community, known as the Aku, is small but socially prominent. People are increasingly leaving rural areas for the towns, where average incomes are four times higher. Each year seasonal immigrants from neighbouring states come to farm groundnuts. Women are active as traders.

THE ECONOMY

80% of the labour force is involved in agriculture. Groundnuts are the principal crop. The fisheries sector is being improved. Growth in tourism now halted by political instability. Most donor aid has been suspended until civilian rule is restored.

◆ *INSIGHT: Banjul's airport was upgraded by NASA in 1989, for US space shuttle emergency landings*

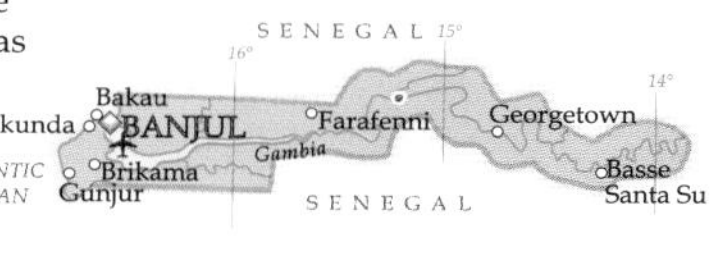
SENEGAL
15°
16°
14°
Bakau
Serekunda
BANJUL
Farafenni
Georgetown
Gambia
ATLANTIC OCEAN
Brikama
Gunjur
SENEGAL
Basse Santa Su
200m/656ft
Sea Level
0
50 km
0
50 miles

FACT FILE

OFFICIAL NAME: Republic of The Gambia
DATE OF FORMATION: 1965
CAPITAL: Banjul
POPULATION: 900,000
TOTAL AREA: 11,300 sq km (4,363 sq miles)
DENSITY: 90 people per sq km
LANGUAGES: English*, other
RELIGIONS: Muslim 85%, Christian 9%, traditional beliefs 6%
ETHNIC MIX: Mandinka 41%, Fulani 14%, Wolof 13%, other 32%
GOVERNMENT: Military regime
CURRENCY: Dalasi = 100 butut

CAPE VERDE

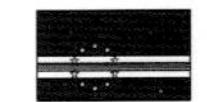

CAPE VERDE
Senegal
Gambia

OFF THE west coast of Africa, in the Atlantic Ocean, lies the group of islands that make up Cape Verde, a Portuguese colony until 1975.

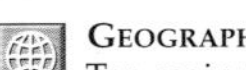

GEOGRAPHY
Ten main islands and eight smaller islets, all of volcanic origin. Mostly mountainous, with steep cliffs and rocky headlands.

CLIMATE
Warm, and very dry. Subject to droughts that may last for years at a time.

PEOPLE AND SOCIETY
Most people are of mixed Portuguese-African origin; rest are largely African, descended from slaves or from more recent immigrants from the mainland. 50% of the population live on Santiago. Roman Catholicism and the extended family are strong. Some ethnic tension between islands.

◆ *INSIGHT: Poor soils and lack of surface water mean that Cape Verde needs to import 90% of its food*

THE ECONOMY
Most people are subsistence farmers. Fish is the main export. Only minerals produced are salt, and volcanic rock for cement.

Santo Antão
17°
Mindelo
Santa Luzia
São Vicente
Sal
São Nicolau
Boa Vista
25°
Sal Rei
Ilhas de Barlavento
16°
ATLANTIC
OCEAN
Ilhas de Sotavento
Maio
Tarrafil
15°
São Filipe
PRAIA
Brava
Santiago (São Tiago)
23°
Fogo
24°
2000m/6562ft
1000m/3281ft
500m/1640ft
200m/656ft
Sea Level
0
50 km
0
50 miles

FACT FILE

OFFICIAL NAME: Republic of Cape Verde
DATE OF FORMATION: 1975
CAPITAL: Praia
POPULATION: 400,000
TOTAL AREA: 4,030 sq km (1,556 sq miles)
DENSITY: 99 people per sq km
LANGUAGES: Portuguese*, Creole
RELIGIONS: Roman Catholic 98%, Protestant 2%
ETHNIC MIX: Creole (*mestiço*) 71%, Black 28%, White 1%
GOVERNMENT: Multiparty republic
CURRENCY: Escudo = 100 centavos

GUINEA-BISSAU

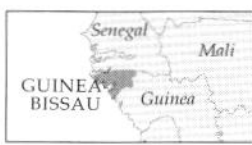
Senegal
Mali
GUINEA-BISSAU
Guinea

KNOWN AS Portuguese Guinea during its days as a colony, Guinea-Bissau is situated on Africa's west coast, bordered by Senegal and Guinea.

GEOGRAPHY

Low-lying, apart from savannah highlands in northeast. Rainforests and swamps are found along coastal areas.

CLIMATE

Tropical, with wet season May–November and dry season December–April. Hot *harmattan* wind blows during dry season.

PEOPLE AND SOCIETY

Largest ethnic group is Balante, who live in the south. Though less than 2% of the population, the mixed Portuguese-African *mestiços* dominate top ranks of government and bureaucracy. Most people live on small family farms in self-contained villages. After 20 years of single-party rule, the first multiparty elections were held in 1994.

THE ECONOMY

Mostly subsistence farming – maize, sweet potatoes, cassava. Main cash crops are cashews, groundnuts and palm kernels. Offshore oil as yet untapped.

◆ *INSIGHT: In 1974, Guinea-Bissau became the first Portuguese colony to gain independence*

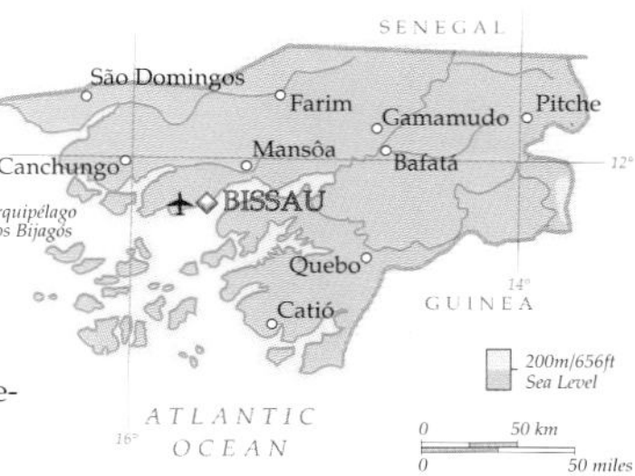
SENEGAL
São Domingos
Farim
Gamamudo
Pitche
Mansôa
Canchungo
Bafatá
12°
BISSAU
Arquipélago dos Bijagós
Quebo
14°
GUINEA
Catió
200m/656ft
Sea Level
ATLANTIC OCEAN
16°
0 50 km
0 50 miles

FACT FILE

OFFICIAL NAME: Republic of Guinea-Bissau
DATE OF FORMATION: 1974
CAPITAL: Bissau
POPULATION: 1 million
TOTAL AREA: 36,120 sq km (13,940 sq miles)
DENSITY: 35 people per sq km
LANGUAGES: Portuguese*, other
RELIGIONS: Traditional beliefs 54%, Muslim 38%, Christian 8%
ETHNIC MIX: Balante 27%, Fulani 22%, Malinke 12%, other 39%
GOVERNMENT: Multiparty republic
CURRENCY: Peso = 100 centavos

GUINEA

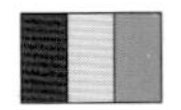

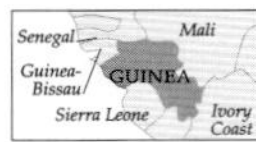
Senegal
Mali
Guinea-Bissau
GUINEA
Sierra Leone
Ivory Coast

FACING THE Atlantic Ocean, on the west coast of Africa, Guinea became the first French colony in Africa to gain independence, in 1958.

GEOGRAPHY

Coastal plains and mangrove swamps in west rise to forested or savannah highlands in the south. Semi-desert in the north.

CLIMATE

Tropical, with wet season April–October. Heavy annual rainfall. Hot *harmattan* wind blows from Sahara during dry season.

PEOPLE AND SOCIETY

Malinke and Fulani make up most of the population, but traditional rivalries between them have allowed coastal peoples such as the Susu to dominate politics. Daily life revolves around the extended family. Women gained influence under Marxist party rule from 1958–84, but Muslim revival since then has reversed the trend. First multiparty elections held in 1995.

THE ECONOMY

Two-thirds of people are farmers. Cash crops are palm oil, bananas, pineapples and rice. Gold, diamond and bauxite reserves.

◆ *INSIGHT: The colours of Guinea's flag represent the three words of the country's motto: work (red), justice (yellow) and solidarity (green)*

SENEGAL
MALI
GUINEA-BISSAU
Labé
Siguiri
Niger
Boké
Niger
Kindia
Kankan
CONAKRY
ATLANTIC OCEAN
SIERRA LEONE
Kissidougou
IVORY COAST
Nzérékoré
LIBERIA
1000m/3281ft
500m/1640ft
200m/656ft
Sea Level
0 100 km
0 100 miles

FACT FILE

OFFICIAL NAME: Republic of Guinea
DATE OF FORMATION: 1958
CAPITAL: Conakry
POPULATION: 6.3 million
TOTAL AREA: 245,860 sq km (94,926 sq miles)
DENSITY: 25 people per sq km
LANGUAGES: French*, Fulani, Malinke, Susu, Kissi, other
RELIGIONS: Muslim 85%, Christian 8%, traditional beliefs 7%
ETHNIC MIX: Fulani 40%, Malinke 25%, Susu 12%, Kissi 7%, other 16%
GOVERNMENT: Multiparty republic
CURRENCY: Franc = 100 centimes

SIERRA LEONE

Guinea
SIERRA LEONE
Ivory Coast
Liberia

THE WEST African state of Sierra Leone achieved independence from the British in 1961. Today, it is one of the world's poorest nations.

GEOGRAPHY

Flat plain, running the length of the coast, stretches inland for 133 km (83 miles). Beyond, forests rise to highlands near neighbouring Guinea in the northeast.

CLIMATE

Hot tropical weather, with very high rainfall and humidity. Dusty, northeastern *harmattan* wind blows November–April.

PEOPLE AND SOCIETY

Mende and Temne are major ethnic groups. Freetown's citizens are largely descended from slaves freed from Britain and the US, resulting in a strongly anglicized Creole culture. A military coup in 1992 halted plans to turn the government into a multiparty democracy. Rebel forces have been fighting the government since 1991; thousands have died in clashes.

THE ECONOMY

Vast majority of people are subsistance farmers. Cash crops include palm kernels, cocoa beans, and kola. Main export is diamonds.

◆ *INSIGHT: The British philanthropist Granville Sharp set up a settlement for freed slaves in Sierra Leone in 1787*

10°
GUINEA
Kabala
Makeni
Lunsar
Njaiama
FREETOWN
Boajibu
8°
Bo
Kenema
Sherbro I.
LIBERIA
Zimmi
ATLANTIC OCEAN
12°
0
50 km
0
50 miles
1000m/3281ft
500m/1640ft
200m/656ft
Sea Level

FACT FILE

OFFICIAL NAME: Republic of Sierra Leone
DATE OF FORMATION: 1961
CAPITAL: Freetown
POPULATION: 4.5 million
TOTAL AREA: 71,740 sq km (27,699 sq miles)
DENSITY: 61 people per sq km
LANGUAGES: English*, Krio (Creole)
RELIGIONS: Traditional beliefs 52%, Muslim 40%, Christian 8%
ETHNIC MIX: Mende 34%, Temne 31%, Limba 9%, Kono 5%, other 21%
GOVERNMENT: Military regime
CURRENCY: Leone = 100 cents

LIBERIA

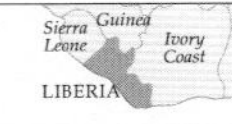
Sierra Leone
Guinea
Ivory Coast
LIBERIA

LIBERIA FACES the Atlantic Ocean in equatorial West Africa. Africa's oldest republic, it was established in 1847. Today it is torn by civil war.

GEOGRAPHY

Coastline of beaches and mangrove swamps rises to forested plateaux and highlands inland.

CLIMATE

High temperatures. Except in extreme southeast, there is only one wet season, May–October.

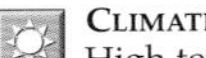

PEOPLE AND SOCIETY

Key social distinction has been between Americo-Liberians – descendants of freed slaves – and the indigenous tribal peoples. However, political assimilation and intermarriage have eased tensions. Inter-tribal tension is now a problem. A civil war has ravaged the country since 1990, with private armies competing for power.

◆ *INSIGHT: Liberia is named after the people liberated from slavery who arrived from the US in the 1800s*

THE ECONOMY

Civil war has led to collapse of economy – little commercial activity. Only 1% of land is arable. Estimated one billion tonnes of iron-ore reserves at Mount Nimba.

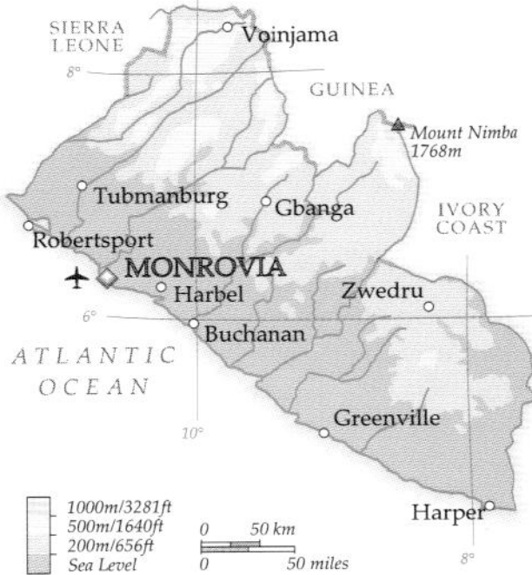
SIERRA LEONE
Voinjama
8°
GUINEA
Mount Nimba 1768m
Tubmanburg
Gbanga
IVORY COAST
Robertsport
MONROVIA
Harbel
Zwedru
6°
Buchanan
ATLANTIC OCEAN
Greenville
10°
Harper
8°
1000m/3281ft
500m/1640ft
200m/656ft
Sea Level
0 50 km
0 50 miles

FACT FILE

OFFICIAL NAME: Republic of Liberia
DATE OF FORMATION: 1847 / 1907
CAPITAL: Monrovia
POPULATION: 2.8 million
TOTAL AREA: 111,370 sq km (43,000 sq miles)
DENSITY: 29 people per sq km
LANGUAGES: English*, Kpelle, Bassa Vai, Grebo, Kru, Kissi, Gola
RELIGIONS: Traditional beliefs 70%, Muslim 20%, Christian 10%
ETHNIC MIX: Kpelle 20%, Bassa 14%, Americo-Liberians 5%, other 61%
GOVERNMENT: Transitional
CURRENCY: Liberian $ = 100 cents

IVORY COAST

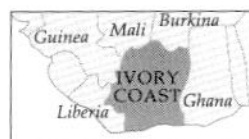
Guinea
Mali
Burkina
IVORY COAST
Ghana
Liberia

ONE OF the larger nations along the coast of West Africa, the Ivory Coast remains under the influence of its former colonial ruler, France.

GEOGRAPHY

Sandy coastal strip backed by a largely rainforested interior, and a savannah plateaux in the north.

CLIMATE

High temperatures all year round. South has two wet seasons; north has one, with lower rainfall.

PEOPLE AND SOCIETY

More than 60 ethnic groups. President Houphouët-Boigny, who ruled from independence until 1993, promoted his own group, the Baoule. Succession of Konan Bedic, another Baoule, has annoyed other tribes. The extended family keeps labourers who migrate to the cities in contact with their villages.

◆ *INSIGHT: The Basilica of Our Lady of the Peace in Yamoussoukro is the second largest church in the world. It holds up to 100,000 people*

THE ECONOMY

Cash crops include cocoa, coffee, palm oil, bananas and rubber. Teak, mahogany and ebony in rainforests. Oil reserves.

MALI
BURKINA
GUINEA
GHANA
LIBERIA
Odienné
Korhogo
Bandama Blanc
Bouaké
Man
Daloa
Abengourou
Dimbokro
Guiglo
YAMOUSSOUKRO
Gagnoa
Divo
Abidjan
Port-Bouët
San Pedro
Ivory Coast
Gulf of Guinea
ATLANTIC OCEAN
1000m/3281ft
500m/1640ft
200m/656ft
Sea Level
0 100 km
0 100 miles

FACT FILE

OFFICIAL NAME: Republic of the Ivory Coast
DATE OF FORMATION: 1960
CAPITAL: Yamoussoukro
POPULATION: 13.4 million
TOTAL AREA: 322,463 sq km (124,503 sq miles)
DENSITY: 41 people per sq km
LANGUAGES: French*, Akran, other
RELIGIONS: Traditional beliefs 63%, Muslim 25%, Christian 12%
ETHNIC MIX: Baoule 23%, Bété 18%, Kru 17%, Malinke 15%, other 27%
GOVERNMENT: Multiparty republic
CURRENCY: CFA franc = 100 centimes

BURKINA

Mali
Niger
BURKINA
Ivory Coast
Ghana
Togo
Benin

KNOWN AS Upper Volta until 1984, the West African state of Burkina has been under military rule for most of its post-independence history.

GEOGRAPHY

North of country is covered by the Sahara. South is largely savannah. Three main rivers are Black, White and Red Voltas.

CLIMATE

Tropical. Dry, cool weather November–February. Erratic rain March–April, mostly in southeast.

PEOPLE AND SOCIETY

No ethnic group is dominant, but the Mossi have always played an important part in government. Extreme poverty has led to a strong sense of egalitarianism. The extended family is important, and reaches from villages into towns and cities. Women wield considerable power and influence within this system, but most are still denied access to education.

THE ECONOMY

Based on agriculture – cotton is most valuable cash crop – but not self-sufficient in food. Gold is the leading non-agricultural export.

◆ *INSIGHT: Poor soils and droughts mean that many men have to migrate seasonally to Ghana and the Ivory Coast for work*

MALI
NIGER
Ouahigouya
Kaya
Koudougou
OUAGADOUGOU
12°
Black Volta
White Volta
Red Volta
Fada-Ngourma
Tenkodogo
Bobo-Dioulasso
Léo
BENIN
TOGO
Banfora
GHANA
Black Volta
0°
IVORY COAST
4°
0 100 km
0 100 miles
500m/1640ft
200m/656ft
Sea Level

FACT FILE

OFFICIAL NAME: Burkina
DATE OF FORMATION: 1960
CAPITAL: Ouagadougou
POPULATION: 9.8 million
TOTAL AREA: 274,200 sq km (105,870 sq miles)
DENSITY: 35 people per sq km
LANGUAGES: French*, Mossi, Fulani, Tuareg, Dyula, Songhai
RELIGIONS: Traditional beliefs 65%, Muslim 25%, Christian 10%
ETHNIC MIX: Mossi 45%, Mande 10%, Fulani 10%, others 35%
GOVERNMENT: Multiparty republic
CURRENCY: CFA franc = 100 centimes

GHANA

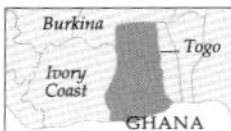
Burkina
Togo
Ivory Coast
GHANA

ONCE KNOWN as the Gold Coast, Ghana in West Africa has experienced intermittent periods of military rule since independence in 1957.

GEOGRAPHY

Mostly low-lying. West is covered by rainforest. Lake Volta – the world's third largest artificial lake – was created by damming the White Volta River.

CLIMATE

Tropical. Two wet seasons in the south; one in the north.

PEOPLE AND SOCIETY

Around 75 ethnic groups. The largest is the Akan. Over 100 languages and dialects are spoken. Southern peoples are richer and more urban than those of the north. In recent years, tension between groups in the north has erupted into violence. Multiparty elections in 1992 confirmed former military leader Jerry Rawlings in power.

◆ *INSIGHT: Ghana was the first British colony in Africa to gain independence*

THE ECONOMY

Produces 15% of the world's cocoa. Hardwood trees such as maple and sapele are exploited. Gold, diamonds, bauxite and manganese are major exports.

BURKINA
0 100 km
0 100 miles
Bolgatanga
Wa
White Volta
Black Volta
Tamale
IVORY COAST
Lake Volta
Sunyani
TOGO
Kumasi
Koforidua
Volta
Asamankese
Nsawam
Tema
Cape Coast
ACCRA
Sekondi-Takoradi
Gold Coast
Gulf of Guinea
ATLANTIC OCEAN
500m/1640ft
200m/656ft
Sea Level

FACT FILE

OFFICIAL NAME: Republic of Ghana
DATE OF FORMATION: 1957
CAPITAL: Accra
POPULATION: 16.4 million
TOTAL AREA: 238,540 sq km (92,100 sq miles)
DENSITY: 69 people per sq km
LANGUAGES: English*, Akan, Mossi, Ewe, Ga, Twi, Fanti, Gurma, other
RELIGIONS: Traditional beliefs 38%, Muslim 30%, Christian 24%, other 8%
ETHNIC MIX: Akan 52%, Mossi 15%, Ewe 12%, Ga 8%, other 13%
GOVERNMENT: Multiparty republic
CURRENCY: Cedi = 100 pesewas

TOGO

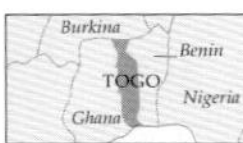
Burkina
Benin
TOGO
Nigeria
Ghana

TOGO LIES sandwiched between Ghana and Benin in West Africa. The 1993–94 elections were the first since its independence in 1960.

GEOGRAPHY

Central forested region bounded by savannah lands to the north and south. Mountain range stretches southwest to northeast.

CLIMATE

Coast hot and humid; drier inland. Rainy season March–July, with heaviest falls in the west.

PEOPLE AND SOCIETY

Harsh resentment between Ewe in the south and Kabye in the north. Kabye control military, but are far less developed than people of the south. Extended family is important. Tribalism and nepotism are key factors in everyday life. Some ethnic groups, such as the Mina, have matriarchal societies.

◆ *INSIGHT: The 'Nana Benz', the market-women of Lomé market, control Togo's retail trade*

THE ECONOMY

Most people are farmers. Self-sufficient in basic foodstuffs. Main export crops are coffee, cocoa and cotton. Half of all export revenues come from phosphate deposits with the world's highest mineral content.

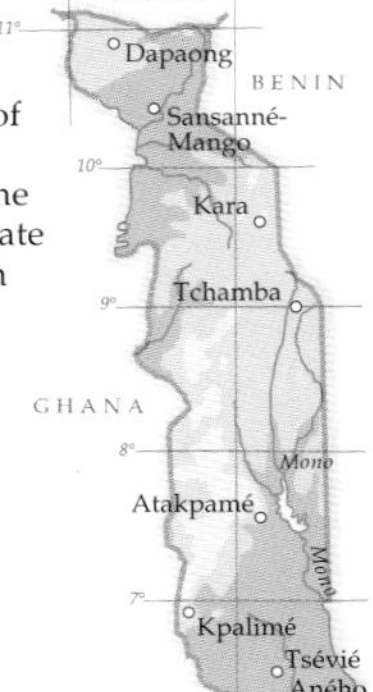
BURKINA
Dapaong
BENIN
Sansanné-Mango
Kara
Tchamba
GHANA
Mono
Atakpamé
Mono
Kpalimé
Tsévié
Aného
LOMÉ
ATLANTIC OCEAN
0°
1°
11°
10°
9°
8°
7°
6°

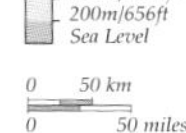
500m/1640ft
200m/656ft
Sea Level
0 50 km
0 50 miles

FACT FILE

OFFICIAL NAME: Togolese Republic
DATE OF FORMATION: 1960
CAPITAL: Lomé
POPULATION: 3.9 million
TOTAL AREA: 56,790 sq km (21,927 sq miles)
DENSITY: 70 people per sq km
LANGUAGES: French*, Ewe, Kabye, Gurma, other
RELIGIONS: Traditional beliefs 70%, Christian 20%, Muslim 10%
ETHNIC MIX: Ewe 43%, Kabye 26%, Gurma 16%, other 15%
GOVERNMENT: Multiparty republic
CURRENCY: CFA franc = 100 centimes

BENIN

Burkina
Nigeria
Togo
BENIN

STRETCHES NORTH from the West African coast. In 1990, it became one of the pioneers of African democratization, ending years of military rule.

GEOGRAPHY

Long, sandy coastal region. Numerous lagoons lie just behind the shoreline. Forested plateaux inland. Mountains in the northwest.

CLIMATE

Hot and humid in the south. Two rainy seasons. Hot, dusty *harmattan* winds blow during December–February dry season.

PEOPLE AND SOCIETY

Around 50 ethnic groups. Fon people in the south dominate politics. Other major groups are Adja and Yoruba. In the far north, Fulani follow a nomadic lifestyle. Tension between north and south, partly reflecting Muslim–Christian divide, and partly because south is more developed. Women hold positions of power in retail trade. Substantial differences in wealth reflect strongly hierarchical society.

THE ECONOMY

Mostly subsistence farming. Cash crops include cotton, cocoa beans and coffee. Some oil and limestone are produced. France is the main aid donor.

◆ *INSIGHT: Benin trains many doctors, but more of them work in France than in Benin*

NIGER
Niger
BURKINA
Malanville
Kandi
Natitingou
Djougou
Ndali
Parakou
TOGO
NIGERIA
Savè
Ouémé
Lokossa
PORTO-NOVO
Ouidah
Cotonou
ATLANTIC OCEAN
500m/1640ft
200m/656ft
Sea Level
0 100 km
0 100 miles

FACT FILE

OFFICIAL NAME: Republic of Benin
DATE OF FORMATION: 1960
CAPITAL: Porto-Novo
POPULATION: 5.1 million
TOTAL AREA: 112,620 sq km (43,480 sq miles)
DENSITY: 44 people per sq km
LANGUAGES: French*, Fon, Bariba, Yoruba, Adja, Houeda, Fulani
RELIGIONS: Traditional beliefs 70%, Muslim 15%, Christian 15%
ETHNIC MIX: Fon 39%, Yoruba 12%, Adja 10%, other 39%
GOVERNMENT: Multiparty republic
CURRENCY: CFA franc = 100 centimes

NIGERIA

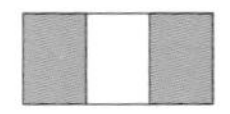

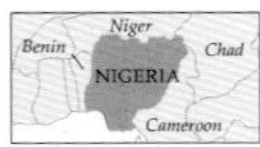
Niger
Benin
Chad
NIGERIA
Cameroon

FOUR TIMES the size of the United Kingdom, from which it gained independence in 1960, Nigeria in West Africa is a federation of 30 states.

GEOGRAPHY

Coastal area of beaches, swamps and lagoons gives way to rainforest, and then to savannah on high plateaux. Semi-desert in north.

CLIMATE

South is hot, rainy and humid for most of the year. Arid north has one very humid wet season. Jos plateau and highlands are cooler.

PEOPLE AND SOCIETY

Some 250 ethnic groups: the largest are Hausa, Yoruba, Ibo and Fulani. Tensions between groups constantly threaten national unity, although they have largely been contained in recent years. Members of one group tend to blame those of another for their problems, rather than the political system. Except in the Islamic north, women are allowed economic independence.

THE ECONOMY

Oil has been the economic mainstay since 1970s, accounting for 90% of export earnings.

◆ *INSIGHT: Nigeria is Africa's most populous state – one in every six Africans is Nigerian*

CHAD
NIGER
Lake Chad
Sokoto
Katsina
Kano
Maiduguri
Niger
BENIN
Kaduna
Jos Plateau
Benue
ABUJA
Ilorin
Ogbomosho
Oshogbo
Abeokuta
Ibadan
Makurdi
Lagos
Niger
Enugu
Benin City
Bight of Benin
Aba
Uyo
CAMEROON
ATLANTIC OCEAN
Port Harcourt
0 200 km
0 200 miles
1000m/3281ft
500m/1640ft
200m/656ft
Sea Level

FACT FILE

OFFICIAL NAME: Federal Republic of Nigeria
DATE OF FORMATION: 1960
CAPITAL: Abuja
POPULATION: 115 million
TOTAL AREA: 923,770 sq km (356,668 sq miles)
DENSITY: 124 people per sq km
LANGUAGES: English*, Hausa, Yoruba
RELIGIONS: Muslim 50%, Christian 40%, traditional beliefs 10%
ETHNIC MIX: Hausa 21%, Yoruba 20%, Ibo 17%, Fulani 9%, other 33%
GOVERNMENT: Military regime
CURRENCY: Naira = 100 kobo

CAMEROON

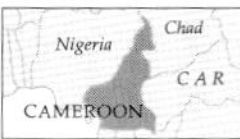
Chad
Nigeria
CAR
CAMEROON

SITUATED ON the central West African coast, Cameroon was effectively a one-party state for 30 years. Multiparty elections were held in 1992.

GEOGRAPHY

Over half the land is forested: equatorial rainforest in north, evergreen forest and wooded savannah in south. Mountains in the west.

CLIMATE

South is equatorial, with plentiful rainfall, declining inland. Far north is beset by drought.

PEOPLE AND SOCIETY

Around 230 ethnic groups; no single group is dominant. Bamileke is the largest, but it has neverheld political power. Some tension between more affluent south and poorer north, albeit diminished by the ethnic diversity. Also rivalry between majority French-speakers and minority English-speakers.

◆ *INSIGHT: Cameroon's name derives from the Portuguese* camarões *– after the prawns fished by the early explorers*

THE ECONOMY

Moderate oil reserves. Very diversified agricultural economy – timber, cocoa, coffee, rubber. Self-sufficient in food. Growing national debt owing to failure to adjust to falling oil revenues.

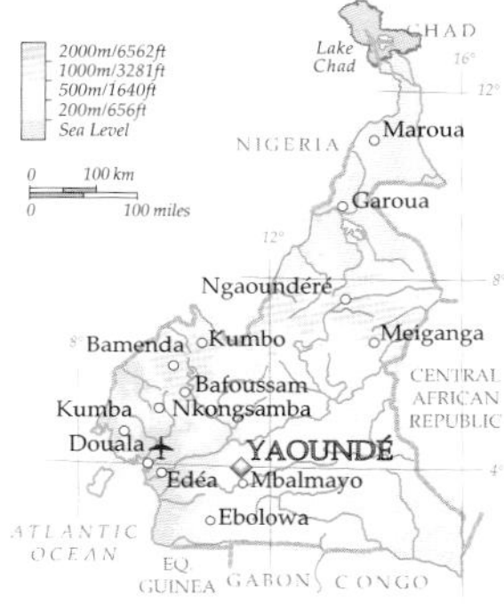
2000m/6562ft
1000m/3281ft
500m/1640ft
200m/656ft
Sea Level
0 100 km
0 100 miles
Lake Chad
CHAD
NIGERIA
Maroua
Garoua
Ngaoundéré
Bamenda
Kumbo
Meiganga
Bafoussam
CENTRAL AFRICAN REPUBLIC
Kumba
Nkongsamba
Douala
YAOUNDÉ
Edéa
Mbalmayo
Ebolowa
ATLANTIC OCEAN
EQ. GUINEA
GABON
CONGO

FACT FILE

OFFICIAL NAME: Republic of Cameroon
DATE OF FORMATION: 1960
CAPITAL: Yaoundé
POPULATION: 13.6 million
TOTAL AREA: 475,440 sq km (183,570 miles)
DENSITY: 29 people per sq km
LANGUAGES: English*, French*, Fang, Bulu, Yaunde, Duala, Mbum
RELIGIONS: Traditional beliefs 51%, Christian 33%, Muslim 16%
ETHNIC MIX: Bamileke and Manum 20%, Fang 19%, other 61%
GOVERNMENT: Multiparty republic
CURRENCY: CFA franc = 100 centimes

EQUATORIAL GUINEA

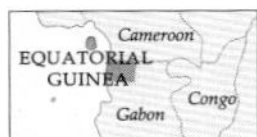
Cameroon
EQUATORIAL GUINEA
Gabon
Congo

COMPRISES THE mainland territory of Rio Muni and five islands on the west coast of central Africa. In 1993, the first free elections were held.

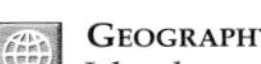

GEOGRAPHY

Islands are mountainous and volcanic. Mainland is lower, with mangrove swamps along coast.

CLIMATE

Bioko is extremely wet and humid. The mainland is only marginally drier and cooler.

PEOPLE AND SOCIETY

The mainland is sparsely populated. Most people are Fang, who dominate politics. Ruling Mongomo clan have most of the wealth. Bioko populated mostly by Bubi and minority of Creoles known as *Fernandinos*. Extended family ties have remained strong despite disruptive social pressure during the years of dictatorship.

◆ *INSIGHT: Some 100,000 Equatorial Guineans now live outside the country, having fled its dictatorial regimes*

THE ECONOMY

Bioko generates the most income. Main exports are tropical timber and cocoa. Oil and gas reserves yet to be fully exploited.

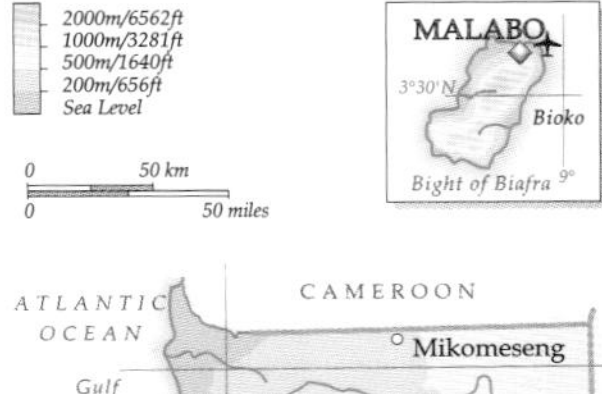
2000m/6562ft
1000m/3281ft
500m/1640ft
200m/656ft
Sea Level
0
50 km
0
50 miles
MALABO
3°30'N
Bioko
Bight of Biafra
9°

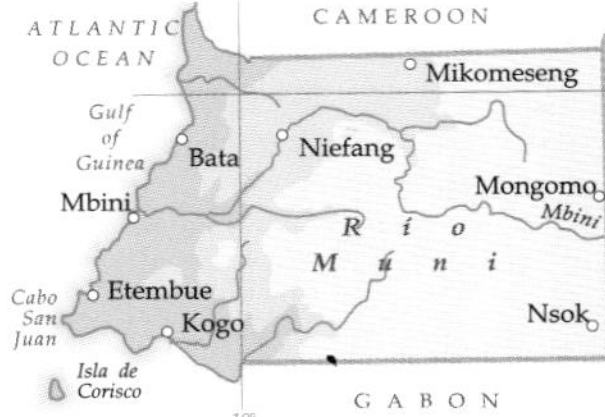
ATLANTIC OCEAN
CAMEROON
Mikomeseng
2°
Gulf of Guinea
Bata
Niefang
Mongomo
Mbini
Mbini
Rio Muni
Cabo San Juan
Etembue
Kogo
Nsok
Isla de Corisco
GABON
10°

FACT FILE

OFFICIAL NAME: Republic of Equatorial Guinea
DATE OF FORMATION: 1968
CAPITAL: Malabo
POPULATION: 400,000
TOTAL AREA: 28,050 sq km (10,830 sq miles)
DENSITY: 14 people per sq km
LANGUAGES: Spanish*, Fang, other
RELIGIONS: Christian (mainly Roman Catholic) 89%, other 11%
ETHNIC MIX: Fang 72%, Bubi 14%, Duala 3%, Ibibio 2%, other 9%
GOVERNMENT: Multiparty republic
CURRENCY: CFA franc = 100 centimes

SAO TOME & PRINCIPE

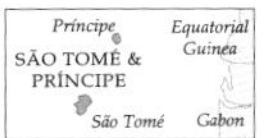
Príncipe
Equatorial Guinea
SÃO TOMÉ & PRÍNCIPE
São Tomé
Gabon

A FORMER Portuguese colony off Africa's west coast, comprising two main islands and smaller islets. 1991 elections ended 15 years of Marxism.

GEOGRAPHY

Islands are scattered across Equator. São Tomé and Príncipe are heavily forested and mountainous.

CLIMATE

Hot and humid, slightly cooled by Benguela Current. Plentiful rainfall, but dry July–August.

PEOPLE AND SOCIETY

Population is mostly black, although Portuguese culture predominates. Blacks run the political parties. Society is well integrated and free of racial prejudice. Wealth disparities are not great, although there is a growing business class. Extended family offers main form of social security. Príncipe assumed autonomous status in April 1995.

◆ *INSIGHT: The population is entirely of immigrant descent: the islands were uninhabited when colonized in 1470*

THE ECONOMY

Cocoa provides 90% of export earnings. Palm oil, pepper and coffee are farmed. One of Africa's highest aid-to-population ratios.

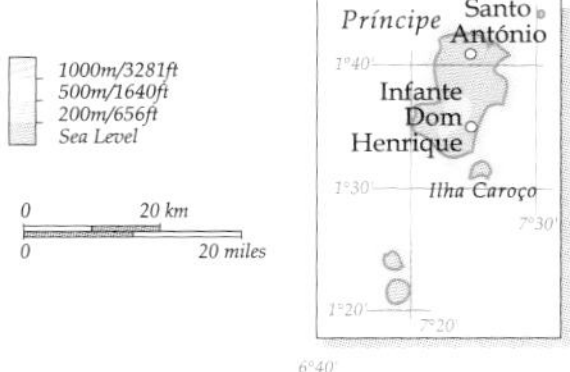
1000m/3281ft
500m/1640ft
200m/656ft
Sea Level
0
20 km
0
20 miles
Príncipe
Santo António
Infante Dom Henrique
Ilha Caroço

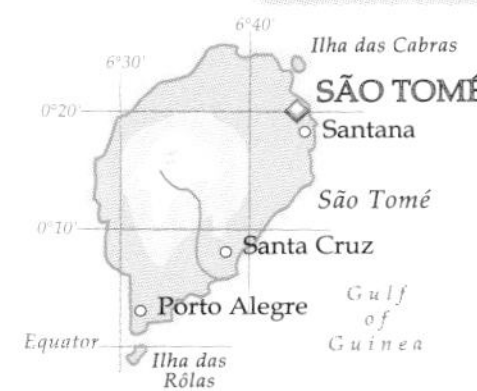
Ilha das Cabras
SÃO TOMÉ
Santana
São Tomé
Santa Cruz
Porto Alegre
Gulf of Guinea
Equator
Ilha das Rôlas

FACT FILE

OFFICIAL NAME: Democratic Republic of Sao Tome and Principe
DATE OF FORMATION: 1975
CAPITAL: São Tomé
POPULATION: 121,000
TOTAL AREA: 964 sq km (372 sq miles)
DENSITY: 129 people per sq km
LANGUAGES: Portuguese*, Portuguese Creole, other
RELIGIONS: Roman Catholic 90%, other Christian 10%
ETHNIC MIX: Black 90%, Portuguese and Creole 10%
GOVERNMENT: Multiparty republic
CURRENCY: Dobra = 100 centimos

GABON

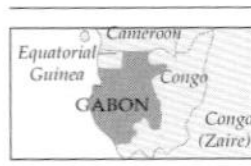
Cameroon
Equatorial Guinea
Congo
GABON
Congo (Zaire)

A FORMER French colony straddling the Equator on Africa's west coast. It returned to multiparty politics in 1990, after 22 years of one-party rule.

GEOGRAPHY

Low plateaux and mountains lie beyond the coastal strip. Two-thirds of the land is rainforested.

CLIMATE

Hot and tropical, with little distinction between seasons. Cold Benguela Current cools the coast.

PEOPLE AND SOCIETY

Some 40 different languages are spoken. The Fang, who live mainly in the north, are the largest ethnic group, but have yet to gain control of the government. Oil wealth has led to growth of an affluent middle class. Menial jobs are done by immigrant workers. Education follows the French system. With almost half its population living in towns, Gabon is one of Africa's most urbanized countries. The government is encouraging population growth.

THE ECONOMY

Oil is the main source of revenue. Tropical hardwoods are being exploited. Cocoa beans, coffee and rice grown for export.

◆ *INSIGHT: Libreville was founded as a settlement for freed French slaves in 1849*

0 100 km
0 100 miles
CAMEROON
EQUATORIAL GUINEA
Oyem
CONGO
Makokou
LIBREVILLE
Equator
Port-Gentil
Ogooué
Lambaréné
Koulamoutou
Moanda
Massoukou
Mouila
Tchibanga
CONGO
ATLANTIC OCEAN
12°
500m/1640ft
200m/656ft
Sea Level

FACT FILE

OFFICIAL NAME: The Gabonese Republic
DATE OF FORMATION: 1960
CAPITAL: Libreville
POPULATION: 1.3 million
TOTAL AREA: 267,670 sq km (103,347 sq miles)
DENSITY: 5 people per sq km
LANGUAGES: French*, Fang, other
RELIGIONS: Catholic, other Christian 96%, Muslim 2%, other 2%
ETHNIC MIX: Fang 36%, Mpongwe 15%, Mbete 14%, other 35%
GOVERNMENT: Multiparty republic
CURRENCY: CFA franc = 100 centimes

CONGO

Cameroon
CAR
Gabon
CONGO
Congo (Zaire)

ASTRIDE THE Equator in west central Africa, this former French colony emerged from 20 years of Marxist-Leninist rule in 1990.

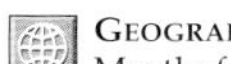

GEOGRAPHY

Mostly forest- or savannah-covered plateaux, drained by Ubangi and Congo River systems. Narrow coastal plain is lined with sand dunes and lagoons.

CLIMATE

Hot, tropical. Temperatures rarely fall below 30°C (86°F). Two wet and two dry seasons. Rainfall is heaviest south of the Equator.

PEOPLE AND SOCIETY

One of the most tribally conscious nations in Africa. Four main ethnic groups: Bakongo, Sangha, Teke and Mboshi. Main tensions between Bakongo in the north and Mboshi in the south. Middle class is sustained by oil wealth. Schools are run according to the French system and are still subject to inspection from Paris. Multiparty elections held in 1992.

THE ECONOMY

Oil is main source of revenue. Cash crops include sugar, coffee, cocoa and palm oil. Substantial industrial base. Large foreign debt.

◆ *INSIGHT: In 1970, Congo became Africa's first declared communist state*

0
200 km
0
200 miles
500m/1640ft
200m/656ft
Sea Level
CAR
CAMEROON
Ouésso
Sangha
Ubangi
Equator
Owando
GABON
Congo (Zaire)
Djambala
Mossendjo
CONGO (ZAIRE)
Loubomo
ATLANTIC OCEAN
Nkayi
BRAZZAVILLE
Kinkala
Pointe-Noire
CABINDA (Angola)
12°
16°
4°

FACT FILE

OFFICIAL NAME: The Republic of the Congo
DATE OF FORMATION: 1960
CAPITAL: Brazzaville
POPULATION: 2.4 million
TOTAL AREA: 342,000 sq km (132,040 sq miles)
DENSITY: 7 people per sq km
LANGUAGES: French*, Kongo, other
RELIGIONS: Catholic 50%, traditional beliefs 48%, other (inc. Muslim) 2%
ETHNIC MIX: Bakongo 48%, Teke 17%, Mboshi 17%, Sangha 5%, other 13%
GOVERNMENT: Multiparty republic
CURRENCY: CFA franc = 100 centimes

ANGOLA

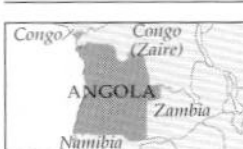
Congo
Congo (Zaire)
ANGOLA
Zambia
Namibia

LOCATED IN southwest Africa, Angola was in an almost continuous state of civil war from 1975–94, following independence from Portugal.

GEOGRAPHY
Most of the land is hilly and grass-covered. Desert in the south. Mountains in the centre and north.

CLIMATE
Varies from temperate to tropical. Rainfall decreases north to south. Coast is cooler and dry.

PEOPLE AND SOCIETY
Civil war was fought by two groups. UNITA cast itself as sole representative of the Ovimbundu, in order to attack ruling Kimbundu-dominated MPLA. In 1991–92, MPLA abandoned Marxist rule and held free elections. UNITA lost, and resumed civil war. Up to 500,000 people died as a result. In 1995, UN troops were deployed to begin a phased de-militarization operation.

◆ *INSIGHT: Angola has some of the world's richest alluvial diamond deposits*

THE ECONOMY
Potentially one of Africa's richest countries, but civil war has hampered economic development. Oil and diamonds are exported.

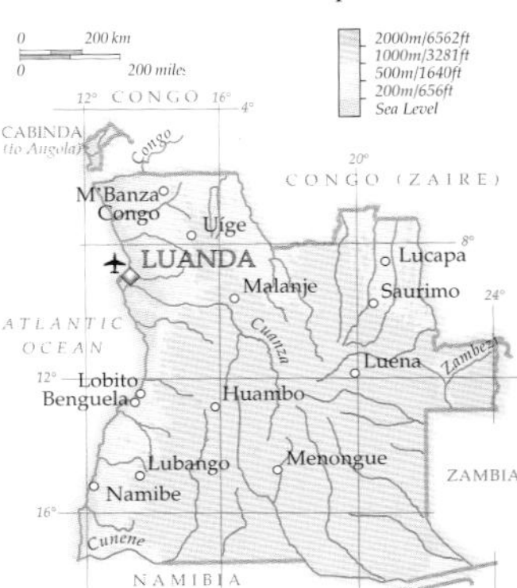
0 200 km
0 200 miles
2000m/6562ft
1000m/3281ft
500m/1640ft
200m/656ft
Sea Level
CONGO
CABINDA (to Angola)
Congo
CONGO (ZAIRE)
M'Banza Congo
Uíge
LUANDA
Lucapa
Malanje
Saurimo
ATLANTIC OCEAN
Cuanza
Luena
Zambezi
Lobito
Benguela
Huambo
Lubango
Menongue
ZAMBIA
Namibe
Cunene
NAMIBIA
BOTSWANA

FACT FILE

OFFICIAL NAME: Republic of Angola
DATE OF FORMATION: 1975
CAPITAL: Luanda
POPULATION: 10.3 million
TOTAL AREA: 1,246,700 sq km (481,551 sq miles)
DENSITY: 8 people per sq km
LANGUAGES: Portuguese*, other
RELIGIONS: Catholic/Protestant 64%, traditional beliefs 34%, other 2%
ETHNIC MIX: Ovimbundu 37%, Kimbundu 25%, Bakongo 13%, mixed 1%, other 24%
GOVERNMENT: Multiparty republic
CURRENCY: Kwanza = 100 lwei

ZAMBIA

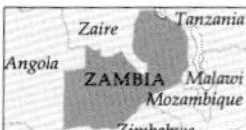
Zaire
Tanzania
Angola
ZAMBIA
Malawi
Mozambique
Zimbabwe

ZAMBIA LIES land-locked at the heart of southern Africa. In 1991, it made a peaceful transition from single-party rule to multiparty democracy.

GEOGRAPHY

A high savannah plateau, broken by mountains in northeast. Vegetation mainly trees and scrub.

CLIMATE

Tropical, with three seasons: cool and dry, hot and dry, and wet. Southwest is prone to drought.

PEOPLE AND SOCIETY

One of the continent's most urbanized countries. More than 70 different ethnic groups, but it has been less affected by ethnic tensions than many African states. Largest group is Bemba in northeast. Other major groups are Tonga in the south, and Lozi in the west. Urban life has done little to change the traditionally subordinate role of women in the family and politics. Rural population live by subsistence farming.

THE ECONOMY

Copper mining is the main industry – exports bring in 80% of foreign income. However, domestic reserves are declining rapidly.

◆ *INSIGHT: Zambia's Victoria Falls is known to Africans as* Musi-o-Tunyi *(The Smoke That Thunders)*

1000m/1640ft
500m/1640ft
200m/656ft
L. Tanganyika
TANZANIA
L. Mweru
Kasama
ZAIRE
Mansa
MALAWI
Chingola
Mufulira
Kitwe
Ndola
Luanshya
Chipata
ANGOLA
Kabwe
Mongu
LUSAKA
Kafue
MOZAMBIQUE
Zambezi
Monze
Choma
Lake Kariba
ZIMBABWE
NAMIBIA
Livingstone
Victoria Falls
BOTSWANA
0 200 km
0 200 miles

FACT FILE

OFFICIAL NAME: Republic of Zambia
DATE OF FORMATION: 1964
CAPITAL: Lusaka
POPULATION: 8.9 million
TOTAL AREA: 752,610 sq km (290,563 sq miles)
DENSITY: 12 people per sq km
LANGUAGES: English*, Bemba, Tonga, Nyanja, Lozi, Lunda
RELIGIONS: Christian 63%, traditional beliefs 35%, other 2%
ETHNIC MIX: Bemba 36%, Maravi 18%, Tonga 15%, other 31%
GOVERNMENT: Multiparty republic
CURRENCY: Kwacha = 100 ngwee

TANZANIA

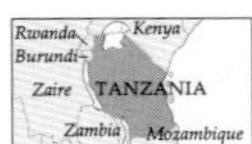
Rwanda
Kenya
Burundi
Zaire
TANZANIA
Zambia
Mozambique

THE EAST African state of Tanzania was formed in 1964 by the union of Tanganyika and Zanzibar. A third of its area is game reserve or national park.

GEOGRAPHY

Mainland is mostly a high plateau lying to the east of the Great Rift Valley. Forested coastal plain. Highlands in the north and south.

CLIMATE

Tropical on the coast and Zanzibar. Semi-arid on central plateau, semi-temperate in the highlands. March–May rains.

PEOPLE AND SOCIETY

99% of people belong to one of 120 small ethnic Bantu groups. Arabs, Asians and Europeans make up remaining population. Use of Swahili as *lingua franca* has eliminated ethnic rivalries. Politics is moving towards democracy.

◆ *INSIGHT: At 5,895 m (19,340 ft), Kilimanjaro in northeast Tanzania is Africa's highest mountain*

THE ECONOMY

Reliant on agriculture, including forestry and livestock. Cotton, coffee, tea and cloves are cash crops. Diamonds are mined.

0 200 km
0 200 miles
3000m/9843ft
2000m/6562ft
1000m/3281ft
500m/1640ft
200m/656ft
Sea Level
Equator
UGANDA
Lake Victoria
KENYA
Musoma
RWANDA
Mwanza
Kilimanjaro 5895m
BURUNDI
Shinyanga
Serengeti Plain
Arusha
Moshi
Masai Steppe
Kigoma
L. Tanganyika
Tabora
Tanga
Zanzibar
DODOMA
Dar es Salaam
Great Rift Valley
Morogoro
ZAIRE
Iringa
Mbeya
INDIAN OCEAN
ZAMBIA
Lindi
Songea
Mtwara
L. Nyasa
MALAWI
Ruvuma
MOZAMBIQUE

FACT FILE

OFFICIAL NAME: United Republic of Tanzania
DATE OF FORMATION: 1964
CAPITAL: Dodoma
POPULATION: 28.8 million
TOTAL AREA: 945,090 sq km (364,900 sq miles)
DENSITY: 31 people per sq km
LANGUAGES: English*, Swahili*
RELIGIONS: Traditional beliefs 42%, Muslim 31%, Christian 27%
ETHNIC MIX: 120 ethnic Bantu groups 99%, other 1%
GOVERNMENT: Single-party republic
CURRENCY: Shilling = 100 cents

MALAWI

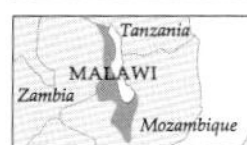
Tanzania
MALAWI
Zambia
Mozambique

A FORMER British colony, Malawi lies land-locked in southeast Africa. Its name means 'the land where the sun is reflected in the water like fire'.

GEOGRAPHY

Lake Malawi takes up one fifth of the country. Highlands lie west of the lake. Much of the land is covered by forests and savannah.

CLIMATE

Mainly sub-tropical. South is hot and humid. Highlands are cooler. May–October dry season.

PEOPLE AND SOCIETY

Few ethnic tensions as most people share common Bantu origin. However, tensions between north and south have arisen in recent years. Northerners are increasingly disaffected by their lack of political representation. Many Asians are involved in the retail trade. Multi-party politics introduced in 1993.

◆ *INSIGHT: Lake Malawi is 568 km (353 miles) in length and contains at least 500 species of fish*

THE ECONOMY

Tobacco accounts for 76% of export earnings. Tea and sugar production. Coal, bauxite reserves.

34°
Karonga
10°
TANZANIA
Mzuzu
Euthini
12°
ZAMBIA
Great Rift Valley
Chisumulti Likoma
(to Malawi)
MOZAMBIQUE
Lake
Nyasa
LILONGWE
Salima
36°
14°
Dedza
Mangochi
MOZAMBIQUE
Zomba
2000m/6562ft
1000m/3281ft
500m/1640ft
200m/656ft
Sea Level
Blantyre
16°
Nsanje
0 100 km
0 100 miles

FACT FILE

OFFICIAL NAME: Republic of Malawi
DATE OF FORMATION: 1964
CAPITAL: Lilongwe
POPULATION: 10.7 million
TOTAL AREA: 118,480 sq km (45,745 sq miles)
DENSITY: 110 people per sq km
LANGUAGES: English*, Chewa*, other
RELIGIONS: Protestant/Catholic 66%, traditional beliefs 18%, other 16%
ETHNIC MIX: Maravi 55%, Lomwe 17%, Yao 13%, Ngoni 7%, other (including Asian) 8%
GOVERNMENT: Multiparty republic
CURRENCY: Kwacha = 100 tambala

ZIMBABWE

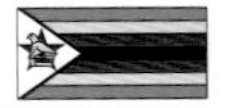

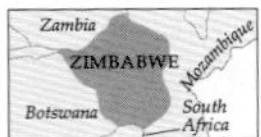
Zambia
ZIMBABWE
Mozambique
Botswana
South Africa

THE FORMER British colony of Southern Rhodesia became fully independent as Zimbabwe in 1980, after 15 years of troubled white minority rule.

GEOGRAPHY

High plateaux in centre bordered by Zambezi River in the north and Limpopo in the south. Rivers criss-cross central area.

CLIMATE

Tropical, though moderated by the altitude. Wet season November–March. Drought is common in eastern highlands.

PEOPLE AND SOCIETY

Two main ethnic groups, Ndebele in the north, and Shona in the south. Shona outnumber Ndebele by four to one. Whites make up just 1% of the population. Because of past colonial rule, whites are generally far more affluent than blacks. This imbalance has been somewhat redressed by government policies to increase black education and employment. Families are large and 45% of people are under 15.

THE ECONOMY

Most broadly based African economy after South Africa. Virtually self-sufficient in food and energy. Tobacco is main cash crop.

◆ INSIGHT: *The city of Great Zimbabwe, after which the country is named, was built in the 8th century. Its ruins are found near Masvingo*

0 100 km
0 100 miles
Zambezi
MOZAMBIQUE
16°
32°
28°
Kariba
Kariba Dam
ZAMBIA
Lake Kariba
HARARE
Chitungwiza
Marondera
NAMIBIA
Zambezi
Victoria Falls
Victoria Falls
Kadoma
Hwange
Kwekwe
Mutare
Gweru
Bulawayo
Masvingo
20°
Matopos
BOTSWANA
2000m/6562ft
1000m/3281ft
500m/1640ft
200m/656ft
Sea Level
Limpopo
SOUTH AFRICA

FACT FILE

OFFICIAL NAME: Republic of Zimbabwe
DATE OF FORMATION: 1980
CAPITAL: Harare
POPULATION: 10.9 million
TOTAL AREA: 390,580 sq km (150,800 sq miles)
DENSITY: 27 people per sq km
LANGUAGES: English*, Shona, Ndebele
RELIGIONS: Syncretic (Christian and traditional beliefs) 50%, Christian 26%, traditional beliefs 24%
ETHNIC MIX: Shona 71%, Ndebele 16%, other 11%, White, Asian 2%
GOVERNMENT: Multiparty republic
CURRENCY: Zimbabwe $ = 100 cents

MOZAMBIQUE

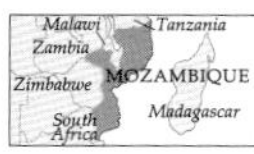
Malawi
Tanzania
Zambia
Zimbabwe
MOZAMBIQUE
Madagascar
South Africa

MOZAMBIQUE LIES on the southeast African coast. It was torn by a civil war between the Marxist government and a rebel group from 1977–1992.

GEOGRAPHY

Largely a savannah-covered plateau. Coast is fringed by coral reefs and lagoons. Zambezi River bisects country from east to west.

CLIMATE

Tropical. Hottest along the coast. Wet season usually March–October, but rains frequently fail.

PEOPLE AND SOCIETY

Racially diverse, but tensions in society are between northerners and southerners, rather than ethnic groups. Life is based around the extended family, which in some regions is matriarchal. Polygamy is fairly common. Government has faced huge task of re-settling the one million war refugees. 90% of the population live in poverty.

◆ *INSIGHT: Maputo, the capital has Africa's second largest harbour*

THE ECONOMY

Almost entirely dependent on foreign aid. 85% of the population is engaged in agriculture.

TANZANIA
Ruvuma
12°
Lake Nyasa
MALAWI
Lichinga
Pemba
Lúrio
ZAMBIA
Nacala
Lumbo
Lago de Cahora Bassa
Nampula
16°
Tete
Zambezi
Quelimane
36°
ZIMBABWE
Beira
Mozambique Channel
20°
INDIAN OCEAN
Limpopo
Funhalouro
Inhambane
24°
SOUTH AFRICA
Xai-Xai
32°
MAPUTO
SWAZILAND
SOUTH AFRICA
28°
2000m/6562ft
1000m/3281ft
500m/1640ft
200m/656ft
Sea Level
0
200 km
0
200 miles

FACT FILE

OFFICIAL NAME: Republic of Mozambique
DATE OF FORMATION: 1975
CAPITAL: Maputo
POPULATION: 15.3 million
TOTAL AREA: 801,590 sq km (309,493 sq miles)
DENSITY: 19 people per sq km
LANGUAGES: Portuguese*, other
RELIGIONS: Traditional beliefs 60%, Christian 30%, Muslim 10%
ETHNIC MIX: Makua-Lomwe 47%, Tsonga 23%, Malawi 12%, other 18%
GOVERNMENT: Multiparty republic
CURRENCY: Metical = 100 centavos

NAMIBIA

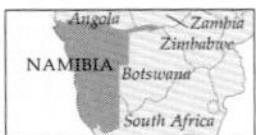
Angola
Zambia
Zimbabwe
NAMIBIA
Botswana
South Africa

LOCATED IN southwestern Africa, Namibia became free of South African control in 1990, after years of uncertainty and guerrilla activity.

GEOGRAPHY
Namib Desert stretches along coastal strip. Inland, a ridge of mountains rises to 2,500 m (8,200 ft). Kalahari Desert lies in the east.

CLIMATE
Almost rainless. Coast usually shrouded in thick fog, unless hot dry *berg* wind blows.

PEOPLE AND SOCIETY
Largest ethnic group, the Ovambo, live mainly in the north. Whites, including a large German community, are centred around Windhoek. Ethnic strife predicted at time of independence has not materialized. High illiteracy among blacks due to legacy of apartheid. Whites still control the economy.

◆ *INSIGHT: The Namib is the Earth's oldest, and one of its driest deserts*

THE ECONOMY
Third wealthiest country in sub-Saharan Africa. Varied mineral resources, including uranium and diamonds. Rich offshore fishing grounds. Lack of skilled labour.

ANGOLA
ZAMBIA
Zambezi
Rundu
Tsumeb
Grootfontein
Otjiwarongo
Swakopmund
WINDHOEK
Walvis Bay
Rehoboth
ATLANTIC OCEAN
BOTSWANA
Namib Desert
Kalahari Desert
Keetmanshoop
Lüderitz
Orange River
SOUTH AFRICA
2000m/6562ft
1000m/3281ft
500m/1640ft
200m/656ft
Sea Level
200 km
200 miles

FACT FILE

OFFICIAL NAME: Republic of Namibia
DATE OF FORMATION: 1990 / 1994
CAPITAL: Windhoek
POPULATION: 1.6 million
TOTAL AREA: 824,290 sq km (318,260 sq miles)
DENSITY: 2 people per sq km
LANGUAGES: English*, Afrikaans, Ovambo, Kavango, German, other
RELIGIONS: Christian 90%, other 10%
ETHNIC MIX: Ovambo 50%, Kavango 9%, Herero 7%, Damara 7%, White 6%, other 21%
GOVERNMENT: Multiparty republic
CURRENCY: Rand = 100 cents

BOTSWANA

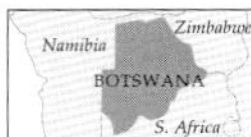
Namibia
Zimbabwe
BOTSWANA
S. Africa

ONCE THE British protectorate of Bechuanaland, Botswana lies land-locked in southern Africa. Diamonds provide it with a prosperous economy.

GEOGRAPHY

Lies on vast plateau, high above sea-level. Hills in the east. Kalahari Desert in centre and southwest. Swamps and salt-pans elsewhere and in Okavango Basin.

CLIMATE

Dry and prone to drought. Summer wet season, April–October. Winters are warm, with cold nights.

PEOPLE AND SOCIETY

Tswana make up 75% of the population. San, or Kalahari Bushmen, the first inhabitants, have been marginalized. 72% of people live in rural areas. Traditional forms of authority such as the village *kgotla*, or parliament, remain important.

◆ *INSIGHT: Water, Botswana's most precious resource, is honoured in the name of the currency – pula*

THE ECONOMY

Diamonds are the leading export. Also deposits of copper, nickel, coal, salt, soda ash. Beef is exported to Europe. Tourism aimed at wealthy wildlife enthusiasts.

ZAMBIA
200m/656ft
Sea Level
Kwando
Kasane
Okavango Delta
ZIMBABWE
NAMIBIA
Maun
Makgadikgadi
Francistown
Ghanzi
Selebi Phikwe
Serowe
Kalahari Desert
Mahalapye
Limpopo
Mochudi
GABORONE
Kanye
Lobatse
SOUTH AFRICA
0
200 km
0
200 miles

FACT FILE

OFFICIAL NAME: Republic of Botswana
DATE OF FORMATION: 1966
CAPITAL: Gaborone
POPULATION: 1.4 million
TOTAL AREA: 581,730 sq km (224,600 sq miles)
DENSITY: 2 people per sq km
LANGUAGES: English*, Tswana, Shona, San, Khoikhoi, Ndebele
RELIGIONS: Traditional beliefs 50%, Christian (mostly Anglican) 50%
ETHNIC MIX: Tswana 75%, Shona 12%, San 3%, White 1%, other 9%
GOVERNMENT: Multiparty republic
CURRENCY: Pula = 100 thebe

LESOTHO

LESOTHO
South Africa

THE LAND-LOCKED kingdom of Lesotho is entirely surrounded by South Africa, which provides all its land transport links with the outside world.

GEOGRAPHY
High mountainous plateau, cut by valleys and ravines. Maluti range in centre. Drakensberg range in the east. Lowlands in the west.

CLIMATE
Temperate. Summers are hot and wet. Snow is frequent in the mountains in winter.

PEOPLE AND SOCIETY
Almost everyone is Basotho, although there are some South Asians, Europeans and Taiwanese. Strong sense of national identity has tended to minimize ethnic tensions. Many men work as migrant labourers in South Africa, leaving 72% of households, and most of the farms, run by women.

◆ *INSIGHT: Lesotho has one of the highest literacy rates in Africa, and the highest female literacy rate – 84%*

THE ECONOMY
Few natural resources. Heavy reliance on incomes of its migrant workers. Subsistence farming is the main activity. Exports include livestock, wool, mohair.

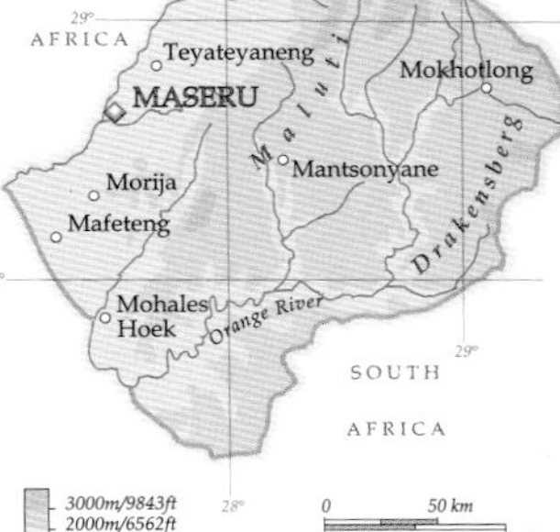
Caledon
SOUTH AFRICA
Hlotse
Teyateyaneng
Maluti
Mokhotlong
MASERU
Mantsonyane
Morija
Mafeteng
Drakensberg
Mohales Hoek
Orange River
SOUTH AFRICA
29°
30°
28°
3000m/9843ft
2000m/6562ft
1000m/328ft
0 50 km
0 50 miles

FACT FILE

OFFICIAL NAME: Kingdom of Lesotho
DATE OF FORMATION: 1966
CAPITAL: Maseru
POPULATION: 1.9 million
TOTAL AREA: 30,350 sq km (11,718 sq miles)
DENSITY: 59 people per sq km
LANGUAGES: English*, Sesotho*, Zulu
RELIGIONS: Roman Catholic and other Christian 93%, other 7%
ETHNIC MIX: Basotho 99%, other 1%
GOVERNMENT: Constitutional monarchy
CURRENCY: Loti = 100 lisente

SWAZILAND

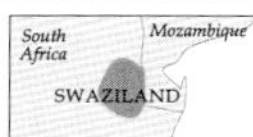
South Africa
Mozambique
SWAZILAND

THE SOUTHERN African kingdom of Swaziland gained independence from Britain in 1968. It is economically dependent on South Africa.

GEOGRAPHY
Mainly high plateaux and mountains. Rolling grasslands and low scrub plains to the east. Pine forests on western border.

CLIMATE
Temperatures rise and rainfall declines as land descends eastward, from high to low *veld*.

PEOPLE AND SOCIETY
One of Africa's most homogenous states. Also among its most conservative, although it is now coming under pressure from urban-based modernizers. Political system promotes Swazi tradition and is dominated by a powerful monarchy. Society is patriarchal and focused around clans and chiefs.

◆ *INSIGHT: Polygamy is practised in Swaziland. When King Sobhuza died in 1982, he left 100 wives and 600 children*

THE ECONOMY
Sugar-cane is the main cash crop. Others are pineapples, cotton, rice and tobacco. Asbestos, coal and wood pulp are also exported.

31°
32°
26°
27°
Piggs Peak
Tshaneni
SOUTH AFRICA
MBABANE
Siteki
Manzini
Bhunya
Sidvokodvo
Hlathikulu
Nhlangano
MOZAMBIQUE
SOUTH AFRICA
1000m/3281ft
500m/1640ft
200m/656ft
Sea Level
0
25 km
0
25 miles

FACT FILE

OFFICIAL NAME: Kingdom of Swaziland
DATE OF FORMATION: 1968
CAPITAL: Mbabane
POPULATION: 800,000
TOTAL AREA: 17,360 sq km (6,703 sq miles)
DENSITY: 46 people per sq km
LANGUAGES: Siswati*, English*, Zulu
RELIGIONS: Protestant and other Christian 60%, traditional beliefs 40%
ETHNIC MIX: Swazi 95%, other 5%
GOVERNMENT: Executive monarchy
CURRENCY: Lilangeni = 100 cents

SOUTH AFRICA

Namibia
Botswana
Swaziland
SOUTH AFRICA
Lesotho

SOUTH AFRICA is the southernmost nation on the African continent. After 80 years of white minority rule, and racial segregation under apartheid from 1948, the country's first multiracial, multiparty elections were held in 1994.

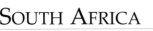

GEOGRAPHY

Much of the country is grassland plateaux, drained in the west by the Orange River system and in the east by the Limpopo and its tributaries. Mountain ridges stretch across south. Drakensberg range overshadows eastern coastal lowlands.

CLIMATE

Warm, temperate and dry. Interior of country gets most of its rain in summer. Coast around Cape Town has Mediterranean climate, with winter rains.

◆ *INSIGHT: South Africa dominates the world market in gold and diamonds. Over the past century, it has produced almost half of the world's gold*

PEOPLE AND SOCIETY

Since dismantling of apartheid in early 1990s, racial segregation has ended, but tensions remain. Some Zulus and whites have made demands for independent homelands. Government aims to redress social and economic imbalance between blacks and whites, focusing on education, housing, land reform.

THE ECONOMY

Africa's largest economy; highly diversified, with modern infrastructure. Growing manufacturing sector. Varied agriculture. Diamonds, gold, platinum, coal, silver, uranium, copper and asbestos mined.

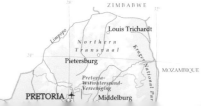

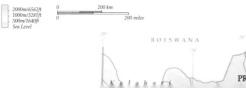

2000m/6562ft
1000m/3281ft
500m/1640ft
Sea Level

0 200 km
0 200 miles

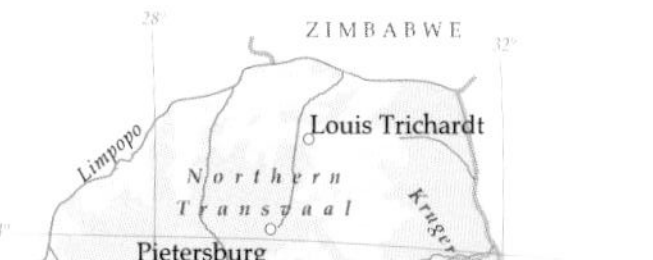
ZIMBABWE
BOTSWANA
MOZAMBIQUE
Limpopo
Louis Trichardt
Northern Transvaal
Pietersburg
Kruger National Par
Pretoria-Witwatersrand-Vereeniging
PRETORIA
Middelburg
Kalahari

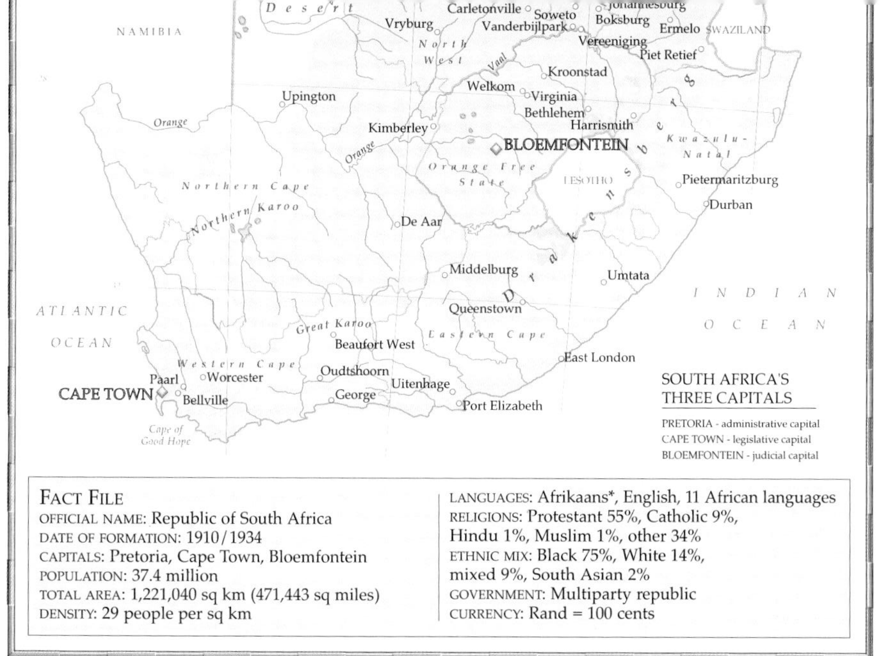
Desert
NAMIBIA
Vryburg
Carletonville
Soweto
Vanderbijlpark
Boksburg
Ermelo
SWAZILAND
Vereeniging
Piet Retief
North West
Vaal
Kroonstad
Welkom
Virginia
Bethlehem
Harrismith
Upington
Orange
Kimberley
Orange
BLOEMFONTEIN
Orange Free State
LESOTHO
Drakensberg
Kwazulu-Natal
Pietermaritzburg
Durban
Northern Cape
Northern Karoo
De Aar
Middelburg
Umtata
Queenstown
ATLANTIC OCEAN
INDIAN OCEAN
Great Karoo
Beaufort West
Eastern Cape
East London
Western Cape
Oudtshoorn
Paarl
Worcester
Uitenhage
CAPE TOWN
Bellville
George
Port Elizabeth
Cape of Good Hope
SOUTH AFRICA'S THREE CAPITALS
PRETORIA - administrative capital
CAPE TOWN - legislative capital
BLOEMFONTEIN - judicial capital

FACT FILE

OFFICIAL NAME: Republic of South Africa
DATE OF FORMATION: 1910/1934
CAPITALS: Pretoria, Cape Town, Bloemfontein
POPULATION: 37.4 million
TOTAL AREA: 1,221,040 sq km (471,443 sq miles)
DENSITY: 29 people per sq km
LANGUAGES: Afrikaans*, English, 11 African languages
RELIGIONS: Protestant 55%, Catholic 9%, Hindu 1%, Muslim 1%, other 34%
ETHNIC MIX: Black 75%, White 14%, mixed 9%, South Asian 2%
GOVERNMENT: Multiparty republic
CURRENCY: Rand = 100 cents

SEYCHELLES

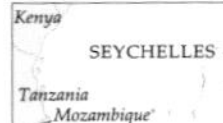
Kenya
SEYCHELLES
Tanzania
Mozambique

A FORMER British colony, comprising 115 islands in the Indian Ocean. Under one-party rule for 16 years, it became a multiparty democracy in 1993.

GEOGRAPHY

Mostly low-lying coral atolls, but 40 islands, including the largest, Mahé, are mountainous and are the only granitic islands in the world.

CLIMATE

Tropical oceanic climate. Hot and humid all year round. Rainy season December–May.

PEOPLE AND SOCIETY

The islands were uninhabited when French settlers arrived in the 18th century. Today, the population is homogeneous – a result of intermarriage between ethnic groups. Almost 90% of people live on Mahé. Living standards are among Africa's highest. Poverty is rare and the welfare system caters for all.

◆*INSIGHT: Host to unique flora and fauna – it is the only country to have two natural World Heritage sites*

THE ECONOMY

Tourism is main source of income, based on appeal of beaches and exotic plants and animals. Tuna fished and canned for export. Virtually no mineral resources. All domestic requirements imported.

VICTORIA
Mahé
0 5 km
0 5 miles
Inner Islands
Grand'Anse
Praslin
Mahé
Amirante Islands
INDIAN OCEAN
Outer Islands
Farquhar Group
Aldabra Group
500m/1640ft
200m/656ft
Sea Level
0 50 km
0 50 miles

FACT FILE

OFFICIAL NAME: Republic of the Seychelles
DATE OF FORMATION: 1976
CAPITAL: Victoria
POPULATION: 69,000
TOTAL AREA: 280 sq km (108 sq miles)
DENSITY: 252 people per sq km
LANGUAGES: Creole*, French, English
RELIGIONS: Catholic 90%, other 10%
ETHNIC MIX: Seychellois (mixed African, South Asian and European) 95%, Chinese and South Asian 5%
GOVERNMENT: Multiparty republic
CURRENCY: Rupee = 100 cents

COMOROS

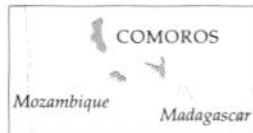
COMOROS
Mozambique
Madagascar

IN THE Indian Ocean between Mozambique and Madagascar lie the Comoros, comprising three main islands and a number of smaller islets.

GEOGRAPHY

Main islands are of volcanic origin and are heavily forested. The remainder are coral atolls.

CLIMATE

Hot and humid all year round. November–May is hottest and wettest period.

PEOPLE AND SOCIETY

Country has absorbed a diversity of people over the years: Africans, Arabs Polynesians and Persians. Also Portuguese, Dutch, French and Indian immigrants. Ethnic tension is rare. Wealth concentrated among political and business elite. Schools equipped to teach only basic literacy, hygiene and agricultural skills. Politically unstable – frequent coup attempts have been made during 1990s.

THE ECONOMY

One of the world's poorest countries. 80% of people are farmers Vanilla and cloves are main cash crops. Lack of basic infrastructure.

◆ *INSIGHT: The Comoros is the world's largest producer of ylang-ylang – an extract from trees used in manufacturing perfumes*

Grande Comore (Njazidja)
Koimbani
MORONI
Foumbouni
Dembéni
INDIAN OCEAN
Mohéli (Mwali)
Fomboni
Mozambique Channel
Ouani
Mutsamudu
Moya
Anjouan (Nzwani)
1000m/3281ft
500m/1640ft
200m/656ft
Sea Level
0 20 km
0 20 miles

FACT FILE

OFFICIAL NAME: Federal Islamic Republic of the Comoros
DATE OF FORMATION: 1975
CAPITAL: Moroni
POPULATION: 600,000
TOTAL AREA: 2,230 sq km (861 sq miles)
DENSITY: 269 people per sq km
LANGUAGES: Arabic*, French*, other
RELIGIONS: Muslim 86%, Roman Catholic 14%
ETHNIC MIX: Comorian 96%, Makua 2%, other (inc. French) 2%
GOVERNMENT: Islamic republic
CURRENCY: Franc = 100 centimes

MADAGASCAR

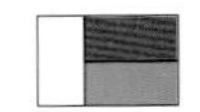

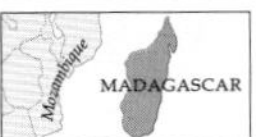
Mozambique
MADAGASCAR

LYING IN the Indian Ocean, Madagascar is the world's fourth largest island. Free elections in 1993 ended 18 years of socialist government.

GEOGRAPHY

More than two thirds of country is a savannah-covered plateau, which drops sharply to narrow coastal belt in the east.

CLIMATE

Tropical, and often hit by cyclones. Monsoons affect the east coast. Southwest is much drier.

PEOPLE AND SOCIETY

People are Malay-Indonesian in origin, intermixed with later migrants from African mainland. Main ethnic division is between Merina of the central plateau and the poorer *côtier* (coastal) peoples. Merina were the country's historic rulers. They remain the social elite, and largely run the government.

◆ *INSIGHT: 80% of Madagascar's plants, and many of its animal species, such as the lemur, are found nowhere else*

THE ECONOMY

Over 80% of people are farmers. Coffee is the most important cash crop. World's largest producer of vanilla. Prawns are a valuable export commodity.

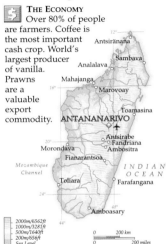

FACT FILE

OFFICIAL NAME: Democratic Republic of Madagascar
DATE OF FORMATION: 1960
CAPITAL: Antananarivo
POPULATION: 13.3 million
TOTAL AREA: 587,040 sq km (226,660 sq miles)
DENSITY: 22 people per sq km
LANGUAGES: Malagasy*, French*
RELIGIONS: Traditional beliefs 52%, Catholic/Protestant 41%, Muslim 7%
ETHNIC MIX: Merina 26%, Betsimisaraka 15%, Betsileo 12%, other 47%
GOVERNMENT: Multiparty republic
CURRENCY: Franc = 100 centimes

MAURITIUS

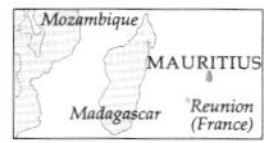
Mozambique
MAURITIUS
Madagascar
Reunion (France)

LOCATED TO the east of Madagascar in the Indian Ocean. Independent in 1968, as part of the Commonwealth, it became a republic in 1993.

GEOGRAPHY

Main island, of volcanic origin, is ringed by coral reefs. Rises from coast to fertile central plateau. Outer islands lie some 500 km (311 miles) to the north.

CLIMATE

Warm and humid. March–December are hottest and wettest months, with tropical storms.

PEOPLE AND SOCIETY

Most people are descendants of labourers brought over from India in the 19th century. Small minority of French descent are the wealthiest group. Literacy rate for under-30s is 95%. Crime rates on the main island are fairly low; outer islands are virtually crime free.

◆ *INSIGHT: The islands lie on what was once a land bridge between Asia and Africa – the Mascarene Archipelago*

THE ECONOMY

Sugar, tourism and clothing manufacture are main sources of income. Sugar accounts for 30% of exports. Potential as offshore financial centre is being developed.

Ile Plate
57°30'
Rodrigues
Port Mathurin
19°45'
63°25'
20°
Triolet
Grand Baie
Pamplemousses
PORT LOUIS
INDIAN OCEAN
Curepipe
Mahébourg
500m/1640ft
200m/656ft
Sea Level
Bel Ombre
20°30'
Souillac
0
10 km
0
10 miles

FACT FILE

OFFICIAL NAME: Mauritius
DATE OF FORMATION: 1968
CAPITAL: Port Louis
POPULATION: 1.1 million
TOTAL AREA: 1,860 sq km (718 sq miles)
DENSITY: 594 people per sq km
LANGUAGES: English*, French Creole, Hindi, Bhojpuri, Chinese
RELIGIONS: Hindu 52%, Catholic 26%, Muslim 17%, other 5%
ETHNIC MIX: Creole 55%, South Asian 40%, Chinese 3%, other 2%
GOVERNMENT: Multiparty republic
CURRENCY: Rupee = 100 cents

Arctic Circle
CANADA
Greenland
(to Denmark)
Svalbard
(to Norway)
Jan Mayen
(to Norway)
ICELAND
Norwegian Sea
Faeroe Is.
(to Denmark)
ATLANTIC OCEAN
Shetland Is.
NORWAY
Orkney Is.
Outer Hebrides
UNITED KINGDOM
North Sea
REP. OF IRELAND
Elbe
Thames
NETH.
English Channel
BELGIUM
Rhine
Seine
LUX.
Loire
LIECH.
FRANCE
Bay of Biscay
Mont Blanc 4807m
SWITZ.
Alps
Massif Central
C. Finisterre
ANDORRA
MONACO
ITALY
PORTUGAL
Pyrenees
SPAIN
Corsica
VATICAN CITY
Balearic Is.
Sardinia
Sicily
Gibraltar
(to UK)
MOROCCO
ALGERIA
TUNISIA
60°
70°
50°
10°
0°

EUROPE

EUROPE IS the smallest continent after Australia, yet it has a wide variety of climates, landforms and types of vegetation. The tundra of the far north gives way to a cool, wet, heavily forested region. The North European Plain is well-drained, fertile, and rich in natural resources. The shores of the Mediterranean are generally warm, dry and hilly. A great curve of mountain ranges, including the Pyrenees, Alps and Carpathians, roughly divide the continent from north to south. To the east are the rolling plains of European Russia and the Ukraine.

3000m/9843ft
2000m/6562ft
1000m/3281ft
200m/656ft
Sea Level
Below Sea Level
0 500 km
0 500 miles
Arctic Circle
Novaya Zemlya
Asiatic Russia
Barents Sea
North Cape
Ural Mountains
RUSSIAN FEDERATION
Irtysh
Kola Peninsula
Lapland
Lake Balkhash
Lake Onega
FINLAND
Lake Ladoga
ESTONIA
European Russia
KAZAKHSTAN
Baltic Sea
LATVIA
Volga
Aral Sea
LITHUANIA
RUSS. FED. (Kaliningrad)
North European Plain
BELORUSSIA
Don
UZBEKISTAN
POLAND
Dnieper
Volga Delta -28m
UKRAINE
Caspian Sea
TURKMENISTAN
SLOVAKIA
Carpathian Mts
MOLDAVIA
Crimea
El'brus 5642m
Caucasus
HUNGARY
SLVNA.
CROATIA
ROMANIA
GEOR.
AZ.
ARM.
Black Sea
BOS. & HERZ.
Danube
YUGO.
BULGARIA
TURKEY
IRAN
Adriatic Sea
MAC.
ALBANIA
GREECE
Ionian Sea
Aegean Sea
Etna 3369m
MALTA
Crete
Mediterranean Sea
LIBYA

CONTINENTAL FACTS

HIGHEST POINT:
El'Brus, Caucasus Mts, European Russia 5,642 m (18,510 ft)

LOWEST POINT: Volga Delta, Caspian Sea, European Russia 28 m (92 ft) below sea level

LARGEST LAKE:
Ladoga, European Russia 18,390 sq km (7,100 sq miles)

LONGEST RIVER:
Volga, European Russia 3,699 km (2,290 miles)

ICELAND

Greenland
ICELAND

EUROPE'S WESTERNMOST country, Iceland lies in the north Atlantic, straddling the mid-Atlantic ridge. Its spectacular landscape is largely uninhabited.

GEOGRAPHY

Grassy coastal lowlands, with fiords in the north. Central plateau of cold lava desert, glaciers and geothermal springs. Around 200 volcanoes.

CLIMATE

Location in middle of Gulf Stream moderates climate. Mild winters and brief, cool summers.

PEOPLE AND SOCIETY

Prosperous and homogeneous society includes only 4,000 foreign residents. High social mobility, free health care and heating (using geothermal power). Longevity rates are among the highest in the world. Equivocal attitude towards Europe accompanies increasing US influence. Strong emphasis on education and reading. Low crime rate, but concerns of alcohol abuse.

THE ECONOMY

Fish or fish products make up 80% of exports. Developing light industry produces knitwear, textiles, paint. Eco-tourism potential.

◆ *INSIGHT: Iceland has the world's oldest parliament, founded in AD 930*

1000m/3281ft
500m/1640ft
200m/656ft
Sea Level
Ice Cap
Denmark Strait
Arctic Circle
Norwegian Sea
Akureyri
Húsavík
Akranes
Keflavík
REYKJAVÍK
Hafnarfjördhur
Kópavogur
Selfoss
Egilsstadhir
Vestmannaeyjar
Vatnajökull
24°
22°
20°
18°
16°
14°
64°
66°
ATLANTIC OCEAN
0 50 km
0 50 miles

FACT FILE

OFFICIAL NAME: Republic of Iceland
DATE OF FORMATION: 1944
CAPITAL: Reykjavik
POPULATION: 300,000
TOTAL AREA: 103,000 sq km (39,770 sq miles)
DENSITY: 3 people per sq km
LANGUAGES: Icelandic*, other
RELIGIONS: Evangelical Lutheran 96%, other Christian 3%, other 1%
ETHNIC MIX: Icelandic (Norwegian-Celtic descent) 98%, other 2%
GOVERNMENT: Constitutional republic
CURRENCY: Krona = 100 aurar

NORWAY

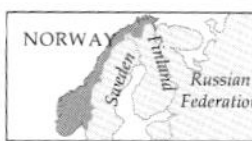
NORWAY
Sweden
Finland
Russian
Federatio

THE KINGDOM of Norway traces the rugged western coast of Scandinavia. Settlements are largely restricted to southern and coastal areas.

GEOGRAPHY

Highly indented coast with fiords and tens of thousands of islands. Mountains and plateaux cover most of the country.

CLIMATE

Mild coastal climate. Inland east is more extreme, with warm summers, and cold, snowy winters.

PEOPLE AND SOCIETY

Homogeneous, with some recent refugees from Bosnian conflict. Strong family tradition despite high divorce rate. Fair-minded consensus promotes female equality, boosted by generous childcare provision. Wealth more evenly distributed than in most developed countries.

◆ *INSIGHT: At a point near Narvik, mainland Norway is only 7 km (4 miles) wide*

THE ECONOMY

Europe's largest producer and exporter of oil and gas. Engineering, chemical and metal industries.

FACT FILE

OFFICIAL NAME: Kingdom of Norway
DATE OF FORMATION: 1905 / 1930
CAPITAL: Oslo
POPULATION: 4.3 million
TOTAL AREA: 323,900 sq km (125,060 sq miles)
DENSITY: 14 people per sq km
LANGUAGES: Norwegian* (*Bokmal* and *Nynorsk*), Lappish
RELIGIONS: Evangelical Lutheran 88%, other Christian 12%
ETHNIC MIX: Norwegian 95%, Lapp 1%, other 4%
GOVERNMENT: Constitutional monarchy
CURRENCY: Krone = 100 øre

see also Overseas Territories pp 230–236

DENMARK

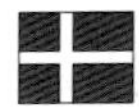

Sweden
DENMARK
Germany
Poland

OCCUPIES THE Jutland peninsula and over 400 islands in Scandinavia. Greenland and the Faeroe islands are self-governing associated territories.

GEOGRAPHY

Fertile farmland covers two-thirds of the terrain, which is among the flattest in the world. About 100 islands are inhabited.

CLIMATE

Damp, temperate climate with mild summers and cold, wet winters. Rainfall is moderate.

PEOPLE AND SOCIETY

Prosperous population maintains traditions of tolerance and welfare provision. High rates of divorce and cohabiting mean that almost 40% of children are brought up by unmarried couples or single parents. Over 75% of women work, due to generous state-funded childcare.

◆*INSIGHT: Denmark is Europe's oldest kingdom – the monarchy dates back to the 10th century*

THE ECONOMY

Few natural resources but a diverse manufacturing base. Skilled work force a key to high-tech industrial success. Bacon, ham and dairy products are exported.

200m/656ft
Sea Level
Skagerrak
Ålborg
Kattegat
Jylland
Viborg
Randers
Silkeborg
Århus
Herning
56°
Horsens
Vejle
COPENHAGEN
Helsingør
Roskilde
Kolding
Odense
Esbjerg
Fyn
Sjælland
North Sea
Svendborg
Næstved
Baltic Sea
Sønderborg
8°
GERMANY
Lolland
10°
Nykøbing-Falster
Falster
12°
Bornholm
15°
Rønne
55°
0 50 km
0 50 miles

FACT FILE

OFFICIAL NAME: Kingdom of Denmark
DATE OF FORMATION: AD 960/1953
CAPITAL: Copenhagen
POPULATION: 5.2 million
TOTAL AREA: 43,069 sq km (16,629 sq miles)
DENSITY: 123 people per sq km
LANGUAGES: Danish*, other
RELIGIONS: Evangelical Lutheran 91% other Protestant and Catholic 9%
ETHNIC MIX: Danish 96%, Faeroese and Inuit 1%, other 3%
GOVERNMENT: Constitutional monarchy
CURRENCY: Krone = 100 øre

see also Overseas Territories pp 230–236

SWEDEN

SWEDEN
Norway
Finland
Denmark

THE LARGEST Scandinavian country in both population and area, Sweden's strong industrial base helps to fund its extensive welfare system.

GEOGRAPHY

Heavily forested, with many lakes. Northern plateau extends beyond the Arctic Circle. Southern lowlands are widely cultivated.

CLIMATE

Southern coasts warmed by Gulf Stream. Northern areas have more extreme continental climate.

PEOPLE AND SOCIETY

Traditions of hard work and economic success are balanced by permissiveness and egalitarianism. High taxes pay for extensive child-care provision, medical protection and state education. Most industries and the bulk of the population are based in and around the southern cities. A 15,000-strong minority of Sami (Lapps) live in the north.

◆ *INSIGHT: Sweden has maintained a position of armed neutrality since 1815*

THE ECONOMY

Companies of global importance, including Volvo, Saab, SFK, Ericsson. Highly developed infrastructure. Up-to-date technology Skilled labour force.

FINLAND
20°
24°
16°
68°
Arctic Circle
Lapland
66°
Luleå
NORWAY
12°
64°
Umeå
Gulf of Bothnia
Östersund
Sundsvall
62°
1000m/3281ft
500m/1640ft
200m/656ft
Sea Level
0 100 km
0 100 miles
Uppsala
60°
Västerås
Örebro
Vänern
STOCKHOLM
Trollhättan
Vättern
Norrköping
Linköping
58°
Göteborg
Jönköping
Borås
Gotland
Kattegat
Öland
Helsingborg
Karlskrona
56°
Malmö
Baltic Sea

FACT FILE

OFFICIAL NAME: Kingdom of Sweden
DATE OF FORMATION: 1809 / 1905
CAPITAL: Stockholm
POPULATION: 8.7 million
TOTAL AREA: 449,960 sq km (173,730 sq miles)
DENSITY: 21 people per sq km
LANGUAGES: Swedish*, Finnish, Lappish, other
RELIGIONS: Evangelical Lutheran 94%, Catholic 2%, other 4%
ETHNIC MIX: Swedish 87%, Finnish and Lapp 1%, other European 12%
GOVERNMENT: Constitutional monarchy
CURRENCY: Krona = 100 öre

FINLAND

Norway
Sweden
FINLAND
Russian Federation

FINLAND'S DISTINCTIVE language and national identity have been influenced by both its Scandinavian and its Russian neighbours.

GEOGRAPHY

South and centre are flat, with low hills and many lakes. Uplands and low mountains in the north. 60% of the land area is forested.

CLIMATE

Long, harsh winters with frequent snowfalls. Short, warmer summers. Rainfall is low, and decreases northwards.

PEOPLE AND SOCIETY

More than half the population live in the five districts around Helsinki. The Swedish minority live mainly in the Åland Islands in the southwest. The Sami (Lapps) lead a semi-nomadic existence in the north. Over 50% of women go out to work, continuing a tradition of equality between the sexes.

◆ *INSIGHT: Finland has Europe's largest inland waterway system*

THE ECONOMY

Wood-based industries account for 40% of exports. Strong engineering and electronics sectors.

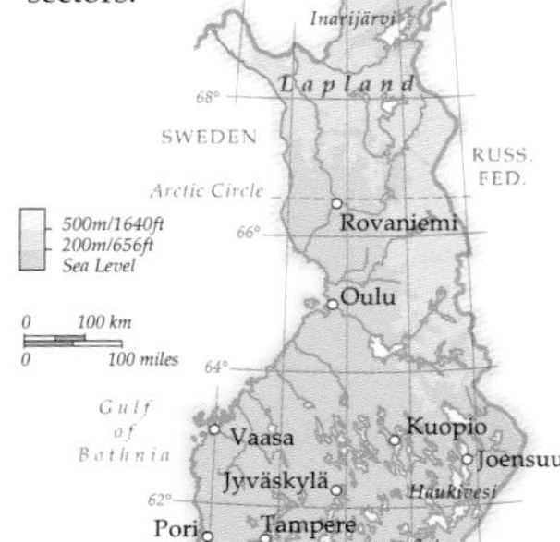
26°
28°
70°
NORWAY
Inarijärvi
Lapland
68°
SWEDEN
RUSS. FED.
Arctic Circle
500m/1640ft
200m/656ft
Sea Level
66°
Rovaniemi
Oulu
0
100 km
0
100 miles
64°
Gulf of Bothnia
Vaasa
Kuopio
Joensuu
Jyväskylä
Haukivesi
62°
Pori
Tampere
Saimaa
Lahti
30°
Åland
Turku
Vantaa
Kotka
60°
Espoo
HELSINKI
20°
22°
24°
Baltic Sea

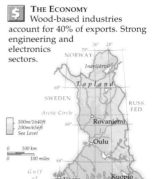

FACT FILE

OFFICIAL NAME: Republic of Finland
DATE OF FORMATION: 1917/1920
CAPITAL: Helsinki
POPULATION: 5 million
TOTAL AREA: 338,130 sq km (130,552 sq miles)
DENSITY: 16 people per sq km
LANGUAGES: Finnish*, Swedish, Lappish
RELIGIONS: Evangelical Lutheran 89%, Greek Orthodox 1%, other 10%
ETHNIC MIX: Finnish 93%, Swedish 6%, other (inc. Sami) 1%
GOVERNMENT: Multiparty republic
CURRENCY: Markka = 100 pennia

ESTONIA

Finland
ESTONIA
Russian Federation
Latvia

ESTONIA IS the smallest and most developed of the three Baltic states and has the highest standard of living of any former Soviet republic.

GEOGRAPHY

Flat, boggy and partly forested, with over 1,500 islands. Lake Peipus forms much of the eastern border with Russia.

CLIMATE

Maritime, with some continental extremes. Harsh winters, cool summers and damp springs.

PEOPLE AND SOCIETY

The Estonians are related linguistically and ethnically to the Finns. Friction between ethnic Estonians and the large Russian minority has led to reassertion of Estonian culture and language, as well as job discrimination. Some post-independence political upheaval reflects disenchantment with free-market economics. Families are small; divorce rates are high.

THE ECONOMY

Agricultural machinery, electric motors and ships are the leading manufactures. Strong timber industry. Increased trade links with Finland and Germany.

◆ *INSIGHT: Estonia is still pressing for the return of territories ceded to Russia during the Soviet period*

Gulf of Finland
TALLINN
Rakvere
Kohtla-Järve
Narva
Baltic Sea
Tapa
Haapsalu
Paide
Hiiumaa
Lake Peipus
RUSS. FED.
Saaremaa
Pärnu
Viljandi
Tartu
Võrtsjärv
Gulf of Riga
Lake Pskov
Valga
Võru
LATVIA
200m/656ft
Sea Level
0 50 km
0 50 miles

FACT FILE

OFFICIAL NAME: Republic of Estonia
DATE OF FORMATION: 1991
CAPITAL: Tallinn
POPULATION: 1.6 million
TOTAL AREA: 45,125 sq km (17,423 sq miles)
DENSITY: 36 people per sq km
LANGUAGES: Estonian*, Russian
RELIGIONS: Evangelical Lutheran 98%, Eastern Orthodox, Baptist 2%
ETHNIC MIX: Estonian 62%, Russian 30%, Ukrainian 3%, other 5%
GOVERNMENT: Multiparty republic
CURRENCY: Kroon = 100 cents

LATVIA

Estonia
Russ. Fed.
LATVIA
Lithuania
Belorussia

SITUATED ON the east coast of the Baltic Sea. Like its Baltic neighbours, it became independent in 1991. It retains a large Russian population.

GEOGRAPHY

Flat coastal plain deeply indented by the Gulf of Riga. Poor drainage creates many bogs and swamps in the forested interior.

CLIMATE

Temperate: warm summers and cold winters. Steady rainfall throughout the year.

PEOPLE AND SOCIETY

Latvia is the most urbanized of the three Baltic states, with more than 70% of the population living in cities and towns. Delicate relations with Russia are dictated by a large Russian minority, and energy and infrastructure investment dating from the Soviet period. The status of women is on a par with that in western Europe. The divorce rate is high.

THE ECONOMY

Transport and defence equipment lead strong industrial sector. Developed paper-making industry. Good ports. Russia remains main trading partner.

◆ *INSIGHT: Latvia's flag is said to represent a sheet stained with the blood of a 13th-century Latvian hero*

ESTONIA
Baltic Sea
Gulf of Riga
RUSS. FED.
Valmiera
Ventspils
Cēsis
Tukums
RIGA
Jūrmala
Saldus
Western Dvina
Jēkabpils
Dobele
Jelgava
Liepāja
Daugavpils
LITHUANIA
BELORUSSIA
58°
56°
22°
24°
26°
28°
200m/656ft
Sea Level
0 50 km
0 50 miles

FACT FILE

OFFICIAL NAME: Republic of Latvia
DATE OF FORMATION: 1991
CAPITAL: Riga
POPULATION: 2.7 million
TOTAL AREA: 64,589 sq km (24,938 sq miles)
DENSITY: 42 people per sq km
LANGUAGES: Latvian*, Russian
RELIGIONS: Evangelical Lutheran 85%, other Christian 15%
ETHNIC MIX: Latvian 52%, Russian 34%, Belorussian 5%, Ukrainian 4%, Polish 3%, other 2%
GOVERNMENT: Multiparty republic
CURRENCY: Lats = 100 santimi

LITHUANIA

Russ. Fed.
Latvia
LITHUANIA
Poland
Belorussia

THE LARGEST and most powerful of the Baltic states, Lithuania was the first Soviet republic to declare independence from Moscow, in 1991.

GEOGRAPHY

Mostly flat with moors, bogs and an intensively farmed central lowland. Numerous lakes, and forested sandy ridges in the east.

CLIMATE

Coastal location moderates continental extremes. Cold winters, cool summers and steady rainfall.

PEOPLE AND SOCIETY

Homogeneous population, with Lithuanians forming a large majority. Strong Roman Catholic tradition and historical links with Poland. Better relations among ethnic groups than in other Baltic states and inter-ethnic marriages are fairly common. However, some ethnic Russians and Poles see a threat of 'Lithuanianization'. Russian army presence until 1993, when all troops were withdrawn.

THE ECONOMY

Wide range of high-tech and heavy industries, includes textiles, engineering, shipbuilding and food processing. Agricultural surpluses.

◆ *INSIGHT: The Baltic states produce two-thirds of the world's amber – the fossilized sap of ancient trees. Most is found along Lithuania's 'amber coast'*

22°
24°
LATVIA
26°
56°
Viekšniai
Telšiai
Kuršėnai
Šiauliai
Plungė
Panevėžys
Baltic Sea
Klaipėda
Radviliškis
Ukmergė
Neman
Kaunas
RUSSIAN FEDERATION
VILNIUS
BELORUSSIA
Alytus
POLAND
Druskininkai
54°
200m/656ft
Sea Level
0 50 km
0 50 miles

FACT FILE

OFFICIAL NAME: Republic of Lithuania
DATE OF FORMATION: 1991
CAPITAL: Vilnius
POPULATION: 3.8 million
TOTAL AREA: 65,200 sq km (25,174 sq miles)
DENSITY: 58 people per sq km
LANGUAGES: Lithuanian*, Russian
RELIGIONS: Roman Catholic 87%, Russian Orthodox 10%, other 3%
ETHNIC MIX: Lithuanian 80%, Russian 9%, Polish 8%, other 3%
GOVERNMENT: Multiparty republic
CURRENCY: Litas = 100 centas

POLAND

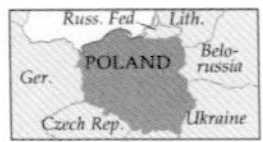
Russ. Fed.
Lith.
POLAND
Belo-russia
Ger.
Czech Rep.
Ukraine

WITH ITS seven international borders and strategic location, Poland has always played an important role in European affairs.

GEOGRAPHY

Lowlands, part of the North European plain, cover most of the country. Carpathian Mountains run along the southern borders.

CLIMATE

Peak rainfall during hot summers. Cold winters with snow, especially in mountains.

PEOPLE AND SOCIETY

Ethnic homogeneity masks a number of tensions. Secular liberals criticize semi-official status of Catholic Church; emerging wealth disparities resented by those unaffected by free-market reforms. German minority presses for action on Green issues. Many women hold policy-making posts.

◆ *INSIGHT: Poland's eastern forests are home to Europe's largest remaining herds of European bison*

THE ECONOMY

High growth, with foreign investment linked to government privatization programme. Heavy industries still dominate, but service sector is quickly emerging.

Baltic Sea
14°
16°
18°
20°
22°
24°
54°
52°
50°
RUSSIAN FEDERATION
LITHUANIA
GERMANY
BELORUSSIA
CZECH REP.
SLOVAKIA
UKRAINE
Gdynia
Gdańsk
Olsztyn
Szczecin
Bydgoszcz
Białystok
Oder
Włocławek
Poznań
WARSAW
Zielona Góra
Łódź
Wisła
Radom
Lublin
Wrocław
Częstochowa
Katowice
Gliwice
Sosnowiec
Zabrze
Rzeszów
Kraków
Carpathian Mts.
1000m/3281ft
500m/1640ft
200m/656ft
Sea Level
0
100 km
0
100 miles

FACT FILE

OFFICIAL NAME: Republic of Poland
DATE OF FORMATION: 1918/1945
CAPITAL: Warsaw
POPULATION: 38.5 million
TOTAL AREA: 312,680 sq km (120,720 sq miles)
DENSITY: 123 people per sq km
LANGUAGES: Polish*, German, other
RELIGIONS: Roman Catholic 95%, other (inc. Protestant and Eastern Orthodox) 5%
ETHNIC MIX: Polish 98%, other 2%
GOVERNMENT: Multiparty republic
CURRENCY: Zloty = 100 groszy

GERMANY

Neth.
Denmark
Belgium
GERMANY
Poland
Czech Rep.
Lux.
France
Switz
Austria

EUROPE'S STRONGEST economic power, Germany's democratic west and communist east were re-unified in 1990, after the fall of the east's regime.

GEOGRAPHY

Coastal plains in the north, rising to rolling hills of central region. Alpine region in the south.

CLIMATE

Damp, temperate in northern and central regions. Continental extremes in mountainous south.

PEOPLE AND SOCIETY

Social and economic differences reflect former divisions. Some prosperous Western Germans resent added taxes since re-unification. Far-right political groups have emerged. Immigrant 'guest workers' – mainly Turks – face citizenship problems and occasional racial attacks. Strong feminist and Green movements.

◆ *INSIGHT: Germany's rivers and canals carry as much freight as its roads*

THE ECONOMY

Massive exports of cars, heavy engineering, electronics and chemicals. Post-war 'miracle' powered by efficiency and good labour relations.

2000m/6562ft
1000m/3281ft
500m/1640ft
200m/656ft
Sea Level
DENMARK
Baltic Sea
Kiel
Lübeck
Rostock
North Sea
Hamburg
POLAND
Bremen
Elbe
Oder
NETHERLANDS
Hannover
BERLIN
Magdeburg
Dortmund
Duisburg
Essen
Kassel
Leipzig
Düsseldorf
Köln
Erfut
Dresden
Bonn
Chemnitz
Rhine
BELGIUM
Frankfurt am Main
CZECH REPUBLIC
LUX
Mannheim
Nürnberg
Danube
FRANCE
Stuttgart
Rhine
München
SWITZ.
Bavarian Alps
AUSTRIA
0 100 km
0 100 m.

FACT FILE

OFFICIAL NAME: Federal Republic of Germany
DATE OF FORMATION: 1871 / 1990
CAPITAL: Berlin
POPULATION: 80.6 million
TOTAL AREA: 356,910 sq km (137,800 sq miles)
DENSITY: 230 people per sq km
LANGUAGES: German*, Sorbian, other
RELIGIONS: Protestant 45%, Roman Catholic 37%, other 18%
ETHNIC MIX: German 92%, other 8%
GOVERNMENT: Multiparty republic
CURRENCY: Deutsche Mark = 100 pfennigs

NETHERLANDS

NETHERLANDS
Germany
Belgium

ASTRIDE THE delta of five major rivers in northwest Europe, the Netherlands has a long trading tradition. Rotterdam is the world's largest port.

GEOGRAPHY
Mainly flat, with 27% of the land below sea level and protected by dunes, dykes and canals. Low hills in the south and east.

CLIMATE
Mild, rainy winters and cool summers. Gales from the North Sea are common in autumn and winter.

PEOPLE AND SOCIETY
The Dutch see their country as the most tolerant in Europe. This reflects a long history of welcoming refugees and immigrants. Large urban concentration (89%) accounts for high population density. Laws concerning issues such as sexuality, euthanasia, and drug-taking are among the world's most liberal.

◆ *INSIGHT: A century ago there were 10,000 windmills in the Netherlands, compared with only 1,000 today*

THE ECONOMY
Diverse industrial sector exports metals, machinery, chemicals and electronics. Many high-profile multinationals.

Sea Level
Below Sea Level
Waddeneilanden
Waddenzee
Groningen
North Sea
IJsselmeer
AMSTERDAM
Haarlem
'S-GRAVENHAGE
(THE HAGUE)
Leiden
Utrecht
Apeldoorn
Enschede
Delft
Neder Rijn
Arnhem
Rotterdam
Nijmegen
Maas
GERMANY
Breda
Tilburg
Eindhoven
BELGIUM
Maastricht
0 40 km
0 40 miles

FACT FILE

OFFICIAL NAME: Kingdom of the Netherlands
DATE OF FORMATION: 1815/1890
CAPITALS: Amsterdam, The Hague
POPULATION: 15.3 million
TOTAL AREA: 37,330 sq km (14,410 sq miles)
DENSITY: 448 people per sq km
LANGUAGES: Dutch*, Frisian, other
RELIGIONS: Catholic 36%, Protestant 27%, other (inc. unaffiliated) 37%
ETHNIC MIX: Dutch 96%, other 4%
GOVERNMENT: Constitutional monarchy
CURRENCY: Guilder = 100 cents

see also Overseas Territories pp 230–236

BELGIUM

United Kingdom
Netherlands
Ger.
BELGIUM
France
Lux.

BELGIUM LIES in northwestern Europe. Its history has been marked by the division between its Flemish- and French-speaking communities.

GEOGRAPHY

Low-lying coastal plain covers two-thirds of the country. Land becomes hilly and forested in the southeast (Ardennes) region.

CLIMATE

Maritime climate with Gulf stream influences. Temperatures are mild, with heavy cloud cover and rain. More rainfall and weather fluctuations on coast.

PEOPLE AND SOCIETY

Since 1970, Flemish-speaking regions have become more prosperous than those of the minority French-speakers (Walloons), overturning the traditional roles and increasing friction. In order to contain tensions, Belgium began to move towards federalism in 1980. Both groups now have their own governments and control most of their own affairs.

THE ECONOMY

Variety of industrial exports, including steel, glassware, cut diamonds and textiles. Many foreign multinationals.

◆ *INSIGHT: The motorway network is extensive and so well lit that, along with the Great Wall of China, it is the most visible sight from space*

North Sea
NETHERLANDS
Oostende
Brugge
Antwerpen
Gent
Mechelen
Kortrijk
Aalst
Leuven
Meuse
BRUSSELS
Tournai
Liège
La Louvière
GER.
Mons
Namur
Charleroi
FRANCE
Ardennes
LUX.
500m/1640ft
200m/656ft
Sea Level
0 40 km
0 40 miles

FACT FILE

OFFICIAL NAME: Kingdom of Belgium
DATE OF FORMATION: 1830
CAPITAL: Brussels
POPULATION: 10 million
TOTAL AREA: 33,100 sq km (12,780 sq miles)
DENSITY: 305 people per sq km
LANGUAGES: French*, Dutch*, Flemish
RELIGIONS: Catholic 75%, other 25%
ETHNIC MIX: Flemish 58%, Walloon 32%, other European 6%, other 4%
GOVERNMENT: Constitutional monarchy
CURRENCY: Franc = 100 centimes

IRELAND

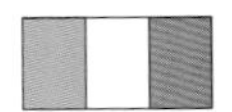

REP. OF IRELAND
United Kingdom

THE REPUBLIC of Ireland occupies 85% of the island of Ireland, with the remainder (Northern Ireland) being part of the United Kingdom.

GEOGRAPHY

Low mountain ranges along an irregular coastline surround an inland plain punctuated by lakes, undulating hills and peat bogs.

CLIMATE

The Gulf Stream accounts for the mild and wet climate. Snow is rare, except in the mountains.

PEOPLE AND SOCIETY

Although homogeneous in ethnicity and Catholic religion, the population show signs of change. Younger Irish question Vatican teachings on birth control, divorce, abortion. Many people still emigrate to find jobs. 1994 terrorist ceasefire in Northern Ireland tempered the traditional aim of reunification.

◆ *INSIGHT: About 20,000 people, in areas collectively known as the* Gaeltacht, *use Irish Gaelic as an everyday language*

THE ECONOMY

High unemployment tarnishes high-tech export successes and trade surplus. Highly educated work force. Efficient agriculture and food-processing industries.

1000m/3281ft
500m/1640ft
200m/656ft
Sea Level
Donegal
Donegal Bay
NORTHERN IRELAND
Sligo
Dundalk
54°
Irish Sea
Westport
Mullingar
Athlone
Galway
DUBLIN
Dún Laoghaire
Shannon
Lough Derg
Wicklow Mts.
ATLANTIC OCEAN
Limerick
Kilkenny
Shannon Airport
Tipperary
Wexford
Tralee
Clonmel
Waterford
Killarney
52°
Cork
Celtic Sea
6°
8°
10°
0 50 km
0 50 miles

FACT FILE

OFFICIAL NAME: Republic of Ireland
DATE OF FORMATION: 1921 / 1922
CAPITAL: Dublin
POPULATION: 3.5 million
TOTAL AREA: 70,280 sq km (27,155 sq miles)
DENSITY: 51 people per sq km
LANGUAGES: English*, Irish Gaelic*
RELIGIONS: Catholic 93%, Protestant (mainly Anglican) 5%, other 2%
ETHNIC MIX: Irish 95%, other (mainly British) 5%
GOVERNMENT: Multiparty republic
CURRENCY: Irish pound = 100 pence

UNITED KINGDOM

UNITED KINGDOM
Rep. of Ireland
Neth.
Belgium
France

SEPARATED FROM continental Europe by the North Sea and the English Channel, the UK comprises England, Wales, Scotland and Northern Ireland.

GEOGRAPHY

Mountainous in the north and west, undulating hills and lowlands in the south and east.

CLIMATE

Generally mild and temperate. Rainfall is heaviest in the west. Winter snow in mountainous areas.

PEOPLE AND SOCIETY

Although of mixed stock themselves, the British have an insular and ambivalent attitude towards Europe. The Welsh and Scottish are ethnically and culturally distinct. Asian and West Indian minorities in most cities. Class, the traditional source of division, is fading in the face of popular culture.

◆ *INSIGHT: The UK has produced 90 nobel laureates – more than any other nation in the world, apart from the US*

THE ECONOMY

World leader in financial services, pharmaceuticals and defence industries. Exports of steel, vehicles, aircraft, high-tech goods.

Orkney Is.
Outer Hebrides
Stornoway
Shetlands Is.
Lerwick
Inverness
Aberdeen
Scotland
Inner Hebrides
Oban
Dundee
Glasgow
Edinburgh
1000m/3281ft
500m/1640ft
200m/656ft
Sea Level
100 km
100 miles
Londonderry
Newcastle upon Tyne
Northern Ireland
Belfast
Isle of Man
Carlisle
Blackburn
Blackpool
Leeds
North Sea
REPUBLIC OF IRELAND
Liverpool
Manchester
Sheffield
Wales
Derby
Norwich
Birmingham
Leicester
England
Cambridge
Swansea
Oxford
LONDON
Celtic Sea
Cardiff
Reading
Dover
Thames
ATLANTIC OCEAN
Bristol
Southampton
Plymouth
Exeter
English Channel

FACT FILE

OFFICIAL NAME: United Kingdom of Great Britain and Northern Ireland
DATE OF FORMATION: 1801 / 1922
CAPITAL: London
POPULATION: 57.8 million
TOTAL AREA: 244,880 sq km (94,550 sq miles)
DENSITY: 239 people per sq km
LANGUAGES: English*, other
RELIGIONS: Protestant 52%, Catholic 9%, Muslim 3%, other 36%
ETHNIC MIX: English 81%, Scottish 10%, Welsh 2%, other 7%
GOVERNMENT: Constitutional monarchy
CURRENCY: Pound sterling = 100 pence

see also Overseas Territories pp 230–236

FRANCE

UK
Belgium
Germany
FRANCE
Switz.
Andorra
Italy
Spain

STRADDLING WESTERN Europe from the English Channel to the Mediterranean Sea, France is one of the world's leading industrial powers.

GEOGRAPHY

Broad plain covers northern half of the country. Tall mountain ranges in the east and southwest. Mountainous plateau in the centre.

CLIMATE

Three main climates: temperate and damp northwest; continental east; and Mediterranean south.

PEOPLE AND SOCIETY

Strong French national identity co-exists with pronounced regional differences, including local languages. Long tradition of absorbing immigrants (European Jews, North African Muslims, economic migrants from Southern Europe). Catholic Church is no longer central to daily life.

◆ *INSIGHT: The French wine industry dates back to around 600 BC*

THE ECONOMY

Steel, chemicals, electronics, heavy engineering, wine and aircraft typify a strong and diversified export sector.

Calais
Lille
English Channel
BELGIUM
Le Havre
Amiens
Channel Is. (to UK)
Rouen
Reims
GERMANY
Caen
PARIS
Strasbourg
Brest
Versailles
Le Mans
Nancy
Rennes
Orléans
Mulhouse
Rhine
Loire
Tours
Dijon
Nantes
Besançon
SWITZ.
L. Geneva
Bay of Biscay
Clermont-Ferrand
Mâcon
Limoges
Lyon
Cognac
Massif Central
St-Étienne
Grenoble
Rhône
Alps
ITALY
Bordeaux
Avignon
Aix-en-Provence
Biarritz
Montpellier
MONACO
Nice
Toulouse
Marseille
Cannes
Pyrenees
Toulon
SPAIN
ANDORRA
Perpignan
Corse (Corsica)
Mediterranean Sea
3000m/9843ft
2000m/6562ft
1000m/3281ft
500m/1640ft
200m/656ft
Sea Level
0 100 km
0 100 miles

FACT FILE

OFFICIAL NAME: The French Republic
DATE OF FORMATION: 1685/1920
CAPITAL: Paris
POPULATION: 57.4 million
TOTAL AREA: 551,500 sq km (212,930 sq miles)
DENSITY: 104 people per sq km
LANGUAGES: French*, Provençal, German, Breton, Catalan, Basque
RELIGIONS: Catholic 90%, Protestant 2%, Jewish 1%, Muslim 1%, other 6%
ETHNIC MIX: French 92%, North African 3%, German 2%, other 3%
GOVERNMENT: Multiparty republic
CURRENCY: Franc = 100 centimes

see also Overseas Territories pp 230–236

LUXEMBOURG

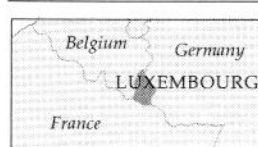
Belgium
Germany
LUXEMBOURG
France

MAKING UP part of the plateau of the Ardennes in Western Europe, Luxembourg is Europe's last independent duchy and one of its richest states.

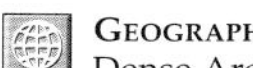

GEOGRAPHY

Dense Ardennes forests in the north, low, open southern plateau. Undulating terrain throughout.

CLIMATE

Moist climate with warm summers and mild winters. Snow is common only in the Ardennes.

PEOPLE AND SOCIETY

Society is peaceable, despite large proportion of foreigners (half the work force and one third of the residents). Integration has been straightforward; most are fellow Western Europeans and Catholics, mainly from Italy and Portugal. High salaries and very low unemployment promote stability.

◆ *INSIGHT: Luxembourg's capital, Luxembourg, is home to over 980 investment funds and 192 banks – more than any other city in the world*

THE ECONOMY

Traditional industries such as steel-making have given way in recent years to a thriving banking and service sector. Tax-haven status attracts foreign companies.

500m/1640ft
200m/656ft
Sea Level
0 10 km
0 10 miles
Clervaux
Ardennes
50°
GERMANY
Ettelbrück
Echternach
Mersch
Moselle
BELGIUM
LUXEMBOURG
Pétange
Differdange
Esch-sur-Alzette
Dudelange
49°30'
6°
FRANCE
6°30'

FACT FILE

OFFICIAL NAME: Grand Duchy of Luxembourg
DATE OF FORMATION: 1890
CAPITAL: Luxembourg
POPULATION: 400,000
TOTAL AREA: 2,586 sq km (998 sq miles)
DENSITY: 155 people per sq km
LANGUAGES: Letzeburgish*, French*, German*, Italian, Portuguese, other
RELIGIONS: Catholic 97%, other 3%
ETHNIC MIX: Luxemburger 72%, Portuguese 9%, Italian 5%, other 14%
GOVERNMENT: Constitutional monarchy
CURRENCY: Franc = 100 centimes

MONACO

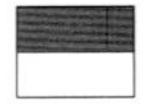

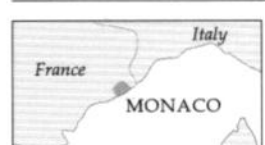
Italy
France
MONACO

A JET-SET image and a thriving service sector define the modern identity of this tiny enclave on the Côte d'Azur in southeastern France.

GEOGRAPHY

A rocky promontory overlooking a narrow coastal strip that has been enlarged through land reclamation.

CLIMATE

Mediterranean. Summers are hot and dry; days with 12 hours of sunshine are not uncommon. Winters are mild and sunny.

PEOPLE AND SOCIETY

Less than 20% of residents are Monégasques. The rest are Europeans – mainly French – attracted by the tax-haven, up-market lifestyle. Nationals enjoy considerable privileges, including housing benefits to protect them from high housing prices, and the right of first refusal before foreigners can take a job. Women have equal status but only acquired the vote in 1962.

THE ECONOMY

Tourism and gambling are the mainstays. Banking secrecy laws and tax-haven conditions attract foreign investment. Almost totally dependent on imports due to lack of natural resources.

◆ INSIGHT: *The Grimaldi princes (Rainier since 1949) have been Monaco's hereditary rulers for 700 years*

Lycée l'Annonciade
F R A N C E
43°45'
Musée Nation
Larvotto
Centre de la Culture et d'Expositions
Monte-Carlo Sporting Club d'Été
La Condamine
Hospitalier Grace
Grand Prix Circuit
Casino
Centre de Congrès
Monte-Carlo
Railway Station
Port de Monaco
Palais du Prince
Stade Louis II
Ministère d'Etat
Cathédrale
Côte d'Azur
Fontvieille
Musée Océanographique
Mediterranean Sea
7°25'
0
1000 m
0
1500 yds

FACT FILE

OFFICIAL NAME: Principality of Monaco
DATE OF FORMATION: 1861
CAPITAL: Monaco
POPULATION: 28,000
TOTAL AREA: 1.95 sq km (0.75 sq miles)
DENSITY: 14,359 people per sq km
LANGUAGES: French*, Italian, other
RELIGIONS: Catholic 95%, other 5%
ETHNIC MIX: French 47%, Monégasque 17%, Italian 16%, other 20%
GOVERNMENT: Constitutional monarchy
CURRENCY: French franc = 100 centimes

ANDORRA

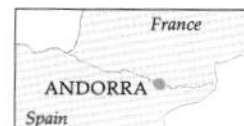
France
ANDORRA
Spain

A TINY land-locked principality, Andorra lies high in the eastern Pyrenees between France and Spain. It held its first full elections in 1993.

GEOGRAPHY

High mountains, and six deep, glaciated valleys that drain into the River Valira as it flows into Spain.

CLIMATE

Cool, wet springs followed by dry, warm summers. Mountain snows linger until March.

PEOPLE AND SOCIETY

Immigration is strictly monitored and restricted by quota to French and Spanish nationals seeking employment. A referendum in 1993 ended 715 years of semi-feudal status but society remains conservative. Divorce is illegal.

◆ *INSIGHT: Andorra is a co-principality whose status dates back to the 13th century, the 'princes' being the President of France and the Bishop of Urgel in Spain*

THE ECONOMY

Tourism and duty-free sales dominate the economy. Banking secrecy laws and low consumer taxes promote investment and commerce. Dependence on imported food and raw materials.

FRANCE
Pyrenees
Arinsal
Soldeu
Ordino
Canillo
Port d'Envalira
Encamp
Escaldes
Valira
ANDORRA LA VELLA
Sant Julià de Lòria
SPAIN
2000m/6562ft
1000m/3281ft
500m/1640ft
0 5 km
0 5 miles

FACT FILE

OFFICIAL NAME: Principality of Andorra
DATE OF FORMATION: 1278
CAPITAL: Andorra la Vella
POPULATION: 58,000
TOTAL AREA: 468 sq km (181 sq miles)
DENSITY: 125 people per sq km
LANGUAGES: Catalan*, Spanish, other
RELIGIONS: Catholic 86%, other 14%
ETHNIC MIX: Catalan 61%, Spanish Castilian 30%, other 9%
GOVERNMENT: Parliamentary democracy
CURRENCY: French franc, Spanish peseta

PORTUGAL

France
PORTUGAL
Spain

FACING THE Atlantic on the western side of the Iberian peninsula, Portugal is the most westerly country on the European mainland.

GEOGRAPHY

The River Tagus bisects the country roughly east to west, dividing mountainous north from lower and more undulating south.

THE ECONOMY

Agricultural exports include grain, vegetables, fruits and wine, but farming methods are outdated. Strong banking and tourism sectors.

CLIMATE

North is cool and moist. South is warmer with dry, mild winters.

PEOPLE AND SOCIETY

Homogeneous and stable society, losing some of its conservative traditions. Small, well-assimilated immigrant population, mainly from former colonies. Urban areas and south are more socially progressive. North is more responsive to traditional Catholic values. Family ties remain all-important.

◆ *INSIGHT: Portugal is the world's leading producer of cork, which comes from the bark of the cork oak*

Viana do Castelo
Braga
Póvoa de Varzim
Vila Real
Douro
Porto
Vila Nova de Gaia
ATLANTIC OCEAN
Coimbra
Santarém
SPAIN
Amadora
Estoril
LISBON
Barreiro
Évora
Setúbal
Beja
Algarve
Portimão
Faro
1000m/3281ft
500m/1640ft
200m/656ft
Sea Level
100 km
100 miles
Madeira
Madeira Is.
50 km
50 miles
São Miguel
Azores
200 km
200 miles

FACT FILE

OFFICIAL NAME: Republic of Portugal
DATE OF FORMATION: 1140/1640
CAPITAL: Lisbon
POPULATION: 9.9 million
TOTAL AREA: 92,390 sq km (35,670 sq miles)
DENSITY: 108 people per sq km
LANGUAGES: Portuguese*
RELIGIONS: Catholic 97%, Protestant 1%, other 2%
ETHNIC MIX: Portuguese 98%, African 1%, other 1%
GOVERNMENT: Multiparty republic
CURRENCY: Escudo = 100 centavos

 see also Overseas Territories pp 230–236

SPAIN

France
SPAIN
Andorra
Portugal
Morocco

LODGED BETWEEN Europe and Africa, the Atlantic and the Mediterranean, Spain has occupied a pivotal position since it was united in 1492.

GEOGRAPHY

Mountain ranges in north, centre and south. Huge central plateau. Verdant valleys in north-west, Mediterranean lowlands.

CLIMATE

Maritime in north. Hotter and drier in south. Central plateau has an extreme climate.

PEOPLE AND SOCIETY

Ethnic regionalism, suppressed under General Franco's regime (1936–75), is increasing. 17 regions are now autonomous. People remain church-going, although Catholic teachings on social issues are often flouted. Status of women rising quickly, with strong political representation.

THE ECONOMY

Outdated labour practices and low investment hinder growth. Heavy industry, textiles and food-processing lead exports. Tourism and agriculture are important.

0 100 km
0 100 miles
2000m/6562ft
1000m/3281ft
500m/1640ft
200m/656ft
Sea Level
Bay of Biscay
Gijón
Santander
Bilbao
San Sebastián
A Coruña
Vigo
León
Burgos
Vitoria
Ourense
Palencia
Soria
Logroño
Pyrenees
FRANCE
ANDORRA
Valladolid
Lleida
Zaragoza
Barcelona
Tarragona
PORTUGAL
Ávila
Tagus
MADRID
Leganés
Getafe
Fuenlabrada
Menorca
Mallorca
Palma
Valencia
Islas Baleares
Eivissa
Badajoz
Albacete
Alicante
Córdoba
Murcia
Huelva
Cartagena
Sevilla
Granada
Almería
Jerez de la Frontera
Málaga
Cádiz
Mediterranean Sea
Islas Canarias
Lanzarote
Tenerife
Fuerteventura
Gran Canaria

◆ *INSIGHT: Over 3,000 festivals and feasts take place each year in Spain*

FACT FILE

OFFICIAL NAME: Kingdom of Spain
DATE OF FORMATION: 1492/1713
CAPITAL: Madrid
POPULATION: 39.2 million
TOTAL AREA: 504,780 sq km (194,900 sq miles)
DENSITY: 78 people per sq km
LANGUAGES: Castilian Spanish*, Catalan*, Galician*, Basque*, other
RELIGIONS: Catholic 99%, other 1%
ETHNIC MIX: Castilian Spanish 72%, Catalan 16%, Galician 7%, Basque 2%, Gypsy 1%, other 2%
GOVERNMENT: Constitutional monarchy
CURRENCY: Peseta = 100 céntimos

ITALY

Switz.
Austria
France
ITALY
Tunisia
Greece

PROJECTING INTO the Mediterranean Sea in Southern Europe, Italy is an ancient land but also one of the continent's newest unified states.

GEOGRAPHY

Appennino form the backbone of a rugged peninsula, extending from the Alps into the Mediterranean Sea. Alluvial plain in the north.

CLIMATE

Mediterranean in the south. Seasonal extremes in mountains and on northern plain.

PEOPLE AND SOCIETY

Ethnically homogeneous, but gulf between prosperous, industrial north and poorer, agricultural south. Strong regional identities, especially on islands of Sicily and Sardinia. State institutions viewed as inefficient and corrupt. Allegiance to the family survives lessened influence of the Church.

◆ *INSIGHT: Italy was a collection of city states, dukedoms and monarchies before it became a unified nation in 1871*

THE ECONOMY

World leader in industrial and product design and textiles. Strong tourism and agriculture sectors. Weak currency. Large public sector debt.

SWITZERLAND
AUSTRIA
Lago di Como
Alps
Bolzano
SLVNA.
Milano
Monza
Trieste
Novara
Verona
Torino
Po
Venezia
FRANCE
Piacenza
Parma
Golfo di Venezia
Genova
Bologna
Rimini
Pisa
SAN MARINO
San Remo
Livorno
Firenze
Ancona
Perugia
Appennino
Adriatic Sea
ROME
VATICAN CITY
Sassari
Napoli
Bari
Taranto
Lecce
Alghero
Salerno
Sardegna (Sardinia)
Tyrrhenian Sea
Ionian Sea
Cagliari
Cosenza
Messina
Reggio di Calabria
Mediterranean Sea
Palermo
Catania
Siracusa
Sicilia (Sicily)
0 100 km
0 100 miles
3000m/9843ft
2000m/6562ft
1000m/3281ft
500m/1640ft
200m/656ft
Sea Level

FACT FILE

OFFICIAL NAME: Italian Republic
DATE OF FORMATION: 1871 / 1954
CAPITAL: Rome
POPULATION: 57.8 million
TOTAL AREA: 301,270 sq km (116,320 sq miles)
DENSITY: 197 people per sq km
LANGUAGES: Italian*, German, French, Rhaeto-Romanic, Sardinian
RELIGIONS: Catholic 99%, other 1%
ETHNIC MIX: Italian 98%, other (inc. German, French, Greek, Slovenian, Albanian) 2%
GOVERNMENT: Multiparty republic
CURRENCY: Lira = 100 centesimi

MALTA

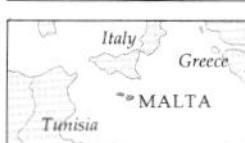
Italy
Greece
MALTA
Tunisia

THE MALTESE archipelago lies off southern Sicily, midway between Europe and Africa. The only inhabited islands are Malta, Gozo and Kemmuna.

GEOGRAPHY

The main island of Malta has low hills and a ragged coastline with numerous harbours, bays, sandy beaches and rocky coves. Gozo is more densely vegetated.

CLIMATE

Mediterranean climate. Many hours of sunshine throughout the year but very low rainfall.

PEOPLE AND SOCIETY

Over the centuries, the Maltese have been subject to Arab, Sicilian, Spanish, French and English influences. Today, the population is socially conservative and devoutly Roman Catholic. Divorce is illegal. Many young Maltese go abroad to find work – notably to the US and Australia – as opportunities for them on the islands are few.

THE ECONOMY

Tourism is the chief source of income. Offshore banking potential. Schemes to attract foreign high-tech industry. Almost all requirements have to be imported.

◆ *INSIGHT: The Maltese language has Phoenician origins but features Arabic etymology and intonation*

200m/656ft
Sea Level
0 5 km
0 5 miles
Ghawdex
(Gozo)
Victoria
Kemmuna
Mediterranean
Sea
36°
Buġibba
Mellieħa
St Julian's
Sliema
Mosta
Msida
VALLETTA
Malta
Qormi
Ħamrun
Mdina
Rabat
Luqa
Marsaxlokk
Birżebbuġa
Mediterranean
Sea
14°30'

FACT FILE

OFFICIAL NAME: Republic of Malta
DATE OF FORMATION: 1964
CAPITAL: Valletta
POPULATION: 400,000
TOTAL AREA: 320 sq km (124 sq miles)
DENSITY: 1,250 people per sq km
LANGUAGES: Maltese*, English
RELIGIONS: Catholic 98%, other (mostly Anglican) 2%
ETHNIC MIX: Maltese (mixed Arab, Sicilian, Norman, Spanish, Italian, English) 98%, other 2%
GOVERNMENT: Multiparty republic
CURRENCY: Lira = 100 cents

VATICAN CITY

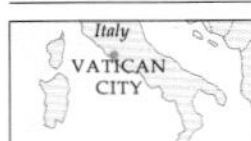
Italy
VATICAN
CITY

THE VATICAN City, the seat of the Roman Catholic Church, is a walled enclave in the city of Rome. It is the world's smallest fully independent state.

GEOGRAPHY

Territory includes ten other buildings in Rome, plus the papal residence. The Vatican Gardens cover half the City's area.

CLIMATE

Mild winters with regular rainfall. Hot, dry summers with occasional thunderstorms.

PEOPLE AND SOCIETY

The Vatican has about 1,000 permanent inhabitants, including several hundred lay persons, and employs a further 3,400 lay staff. Citizenship can be acquired through stable residence and holding an office or job within the City. Reigning Pope has supreme legislative and judicial powers, and holds office for life. State maintains a neutral stance in world affairs and has observer status in many international organizations.

THE ECONOMY

Investments and voluntary contributions by Catholics worldwide (known as Peter's Pence), backed up by tourist revenue and issue of Vatican stamps and coins.

◆ *INSIGHT: The Vatican City is the only state to have Latin as an official language*

Main Entrance
ROME
Pigna Courtyard
Vatican Museums
Vatican
Belvedere Courtyard
Monte Vaticano
Radio Vatican
Raphael Stanza
Papal apartments
Sistine Chapel
Gardens
Papal Heliport
Saint Peter's Basilica
St Peter's Square
Vatican Railway Station
0
200 m
0
250 yds
ROME

FACT FILE

OFFICIAL NAME: State of the Vatican City
DATE OF FORMATION: 1929
CAPITAL: Not applicable
POPULATION: 1,000
TOTAL AREA: 0.44 sq km (0.17 sq miles)
DENSITY: 2,273 people per sq km
LANGUAGES: Italian*, Latin*, other
RELIGIONS: Catholic 100%
ETHNIC MIX: Italian 90%, Swiss 10% (including the Swiss Guard, which is responsible for papal security)
GOVERNMENT: Papal Commission
CURRENCY: Italian lira = 100 centesimi

SAN MARINO

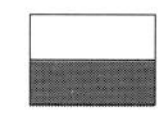

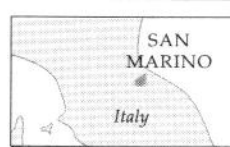
SAN
MARINO
Italy

PERCHED ON the slopes of Monte Titano in the Italian Appennino, San Marino has maintained its independence since the 4th century AD.

GEOGRAPHY

Distinctive limestone out-crop of Monte Titano dominates wooded hills and pastures near Italy's Adriatic coast.

CLIMATE

Altitude and sea breezes moderate Mediterranean climate. Hot summers and cool, wet winters.

PEOPLE AND SOCIETY

Territory is divided into nine 'castles', or districts. Tightly knit society, with 16 centuries of tradition. Strict immigration rules require 30-year residence before applying for citizenship. Catholic Church remains a more powerful influence than in neighbouring Italy. Living standards are similar to those in northern Italy.

◆ *INSIGHT: Sales of postage stamps contribute 10% of the national income*

THE ECONOMY

Tourism provides 60% of government income. Light industries – led by mechanical engineering and high-quality clothing – generate export revenue. Italian infrastructure is a boon.

0
4 km
0
4 miles
44°
500m/1640ft
200m/656ft
Sea Level
Dogana
Serravalle
Fiorina
Cailungo
Gualdicciolo
Borgo
Maggiore
SAN MARINO
ITALY
Monte Titano
739m
Faetano
Murata
ITALY
Appennino
Chiesanuova
Montegiardino
12°30'

FACT FILE

OFFICIAL NAME: Republic of San Marino
DATE OF FORMATION: AD 301 / 1862
CAPITAL: San Marino
POPULATION: 23,000
TOTAL AREA: 61 sq km (24 sq miles)
DENSITY: 377 people per sq km
LANGUAGES: Italian*, other
RELIGIONS: Catholic 96%, Protestant 2%, other 2%
ETHNIC MIX: Sammarinese 95%, Italian 4%, other 1%
GOVERNMENT: Multiparty republic
CURRENCY: Italian lira = 100 centesimi

SWITZERLAND

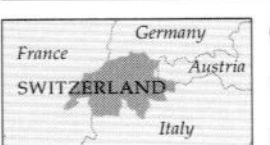
Germany
France
Austria
SWITZERLAND
Italy

ONE OF the world's most prosperous countries, with a long tradition of neutrality in foreign affairs, it lies at the centre of Western Europe.

GEOGRAPHY

Mostly mountainous, with river valleys. Alps cover 60% of its area; Jura in west cover 10%. Lowlands lie along east-west axis.

CLIMATE

Most rain falls in the warm summer months. Snowy winters, but milder and foggy away from the mountains.

PEOPLE AND SOCIETY

Composed of distinct Swiss-German, Swiss-French and Swiss-Italian linguistic groups, but national identity is strong. Country divided into 26 autonomous cantons (states), each with control over housing and economic policy. Tensions over membership of EU, drug abuse, and role of guest workers in economy. Some young see society as regimented and conformist.

THE ECONOMY

Diversified economy relies on services – with strong tourism and banking sectors – and specialized industries (engineering, watches).

◆ *INSIGHT: Genève is the headquarters of many UN agencies, although Switzerland itself is not a UN member*

GERMANY
Schaffhausen
Rhine
Lake Constance
Basel
Winterthur
Sankt Gallen
FRANCE
Jura
Biel
Zürich
AUSTRIA
LIECHTENSTEIN
Neuchâtel
Luzern
BERN
47°
Lac de Neuchâtel
Rhine
Chur
Interlaken
Davos
Lausanne
Alps
Lake Geneva
Montreux
Rhône
Sion
Brig
Locarno
Genève
ITALY
46°
6°
FRANCE
ITALY
8°
Lake Maggiore
Lugano
10°
3000m/9843ft
2000m/6562ft
1000m/3281ft
500m/1640ft
200m/656ft
0
50 km
0
50 miles

FACT FILE

OFFICIAL NAME: Swiss Confederation
DATE OF FORMATION: 1815
CAPITAL: Bern
POPULATION: 6.9 million
TOTAL AREA: 41,290 sq km (15,940 sq miles)
DENSITY: 171 people per sq km
LANGUAGES: German*, French*, Italian*, Romansch*, other
RELIGIONS: Catholic 48%, Protestant 44%, other 8%
ETHNIC MIX: German 65%, French 18%, Italian 10%, other 7%
GOVERNMENT: Federal republic
CURRENCY: Franc = 100 centimes

LIECHTENSTEIN

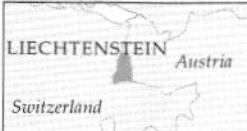
LIECHTENSTEIN
Austria
Switzerland

TUCKED IN the Alps between Switzerland and Austria, Liechtenstein became an independent principality of the Holy Roman Empire in 1719.

GEOGRAPHY

Upper Rhine valley covers western third. Mountains and narrow valleys of the eastern Alps make up the remainder.

CLIMATE

Warm, dry summers. Cold winters, with heavy snow in mountains December–March.

PEOPLE AND SOCIETY

Country's role as a financial centre accounts for its many foreign residents (over 35% of the population), of whom half are Swiss and the rest mostly German. High standard of living results in few social tensions. Sovereignty cherished, despite close alliance with Switzerland, which handles its foreign relations and defence.

◆ *INSIGHT: Women in Liechtenstein only received the vote in 1984*

THE ECONOMY

Banking secrecy and low taxes attract foreign investment. Well-diversified exports include dental products, furniture and chemicals.

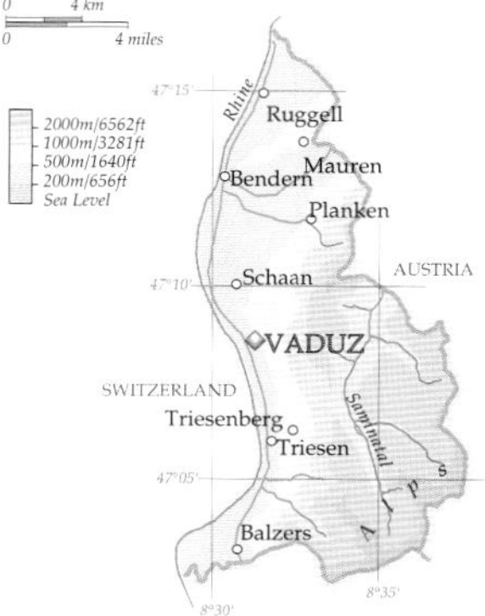
0 4 km
0 4 miles
2000m/6562ft
1000m/3281ft
500m/1640ft
200m/656ft
Sea Level
47°15'
47°10'
47°05'
8°30'
8°35'
Rhine
Ruggell
Mauren
Bendern
Planken
Schaan
AUSTRIA
VADUZ
SWITZERLAND
Triesenberg
Triesen
Samina
Balzers

FACT FILE	
OFFICIAL NAME: Principality of Liechtenstein	DENSITY: 184 people per sq km
DATE OF FORMATION: 1719	LANGUAGES: German*, Alemannish
CAPITAL: Vaduz	RELIGIONS: Catholic 87%, Protestant 8%, other 5%
POPULATION: 29,000	ETHNIC MIX: Liechtensteiner 63%, Swiss 15%, German 9%, other 13%
TOTAL AREA: 160 sq km (62 sq miles)	GOVERNMENT: Constitutional monarchy
	CURRENCY: Swiss franc = 100 centimes

AUSTRIA

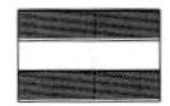

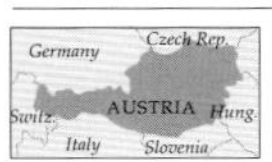
Germany
Czech Rep.
AUSTRIA
Switz.
Hung.
Italy
Slovenia

BORDERING EIGHT countries in the heart of Europe, Austria was created in 1920 after the collapse of the Austro-Hungarian Empire the previous year.

GEOGRAPHY

Mainly mountainous. Alps and foothills cover the west and south. Lowlands in the east are part of the Danube River basin.

CLIMATE

Temperate continental climate. Western Alpine regions have colder winters and more rainfall.

PEOPLE AND SOCIETY

Although all are German-speaking, Austrians consider themselves ethnically distinct from Germans. Minorities are few; there are a small number of Hungarians, Slovenes and Croats, plus refugees from conflict in former Yugoslavia. Some Austrians are beginning to challenge patriarchal and class-conscious social values. Legislation reflects strong environmental concerns.

THE ECONOMY

Large manufacturing base, despite lack of energy resources. Skilled labour force the key to high-tech exports. Strong tourism sector.

◆ *INSIGHT: Many of the world's great composers were Austrian, including Mozart, Haydn, Schubert and Strauss*

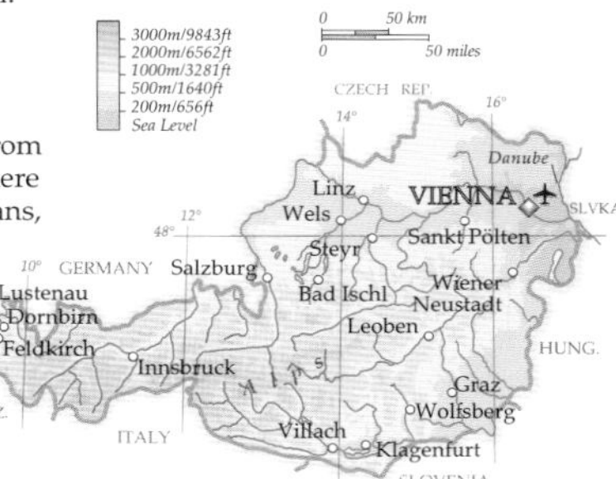
3000m/9843ft
2000m/6562ft
1000m/3281ft
500m/1640ft
200m/656ft
Sea Level
0 50 km
0 50 miles
CZECH REP.
14°
16°
Danube
Linz
Wels
VIENNA
SLVKA.
12°
48°
Steyr
Sankt Pölten
10°
GERMANY
Salzburg
Bad Ischl
Wiener Neustadt
Lustenau
Dornbirn
Feldkirch
Leoben
HUNG.
LIECH.
Innsbruck
Graz
SWITZ.
Wolfsberg
ITALY
Villach
Klagenfurt
SLOVENIA

FACT FILE

OFFICIAL NAME: Republic of Austria
DATE OF FORMATION: 1918/1945
CAPITAL: Vienna
POPULATION: 7.8 million
TOTAL AREA: 83,850 sq km (32,375 sq miles)
DENSITY: 94 people per sq km
LANGUAGES: German*, Croatian, Slovene, Hungarian (Magyar)
RELIGIONS: Catholic 85%, Protestant 6%, other 9%
ETHNIC MIX: German 99%, other (inc. Hungarian, Slovene, Croat) 1%
GOVERNMENT: Multiparty republic
CURRENCY: Schilling = 100 groschen

HUNGARY

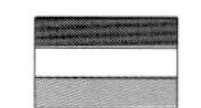

Slovakia
Ukr.
Austria
HUNGARY
Romania
Croatia
Yugo.

HUNGARY IS bordered by seven states in Central Europe. It has changed its economic and political policies to develop closer ties with the EU.

GEOGRAPHY

Fertile plains in east and northwest; west and north are hilly. River Danube bisects the country from north to south.

CLIMATE

Continental. Wet springs; late, but very hot summers, and cold, cloudy winters.

PEOPLE AND SOCIETY

Ethnically homogenous and stable society, showing signs of stress since change to market economy. Most homes are overcrowded, due to a severe housing shortage. Since 1989, a middle class has emerged, but life for the unemployed and unskilled is harder than under communism. Concern over treatment of Hungarian nationals in neighbouring states.

THE ECONOMY

Weak banking sector and unemployment hamper moves to open economy. Heavy industries and agriculture remain strong. Growing tourism and services.

◆ *INSIGHT: The Hungarian language is Asian in origin and has features not found in any other Western language*

0 50 km
0 50 miles
SLOVAKIA
UKRAINE
Miskolc
Nyíregyháza
Debrecen
Danube
Győr
AUSTRIA
Tatabánya
BUDAPEST
Szombathely
Szolnok
Székesfehérvár
Kecskemét
Balaton
Békéscsaba
SLOVENIA
Nagykanizsa
Danube
ROMANIA
Szeged
Pécs
CROATIA
YUGOSLAVIA
500m/1640ft
200m/656ft
Sea Level

FACT FILE

OFFICIAL NAME: Republic of Hungary
DATE OF FORMATION: 1918/1945
CAPITAL: Budapest
POPULATION: 10.5 million
TOTAL AREA: 93,030 sq km (35,919 sq miles)
DENSITY: 114 people per sq km

LANGUAGES: Hungarian (Magyar)*, German, Slovak, other
RELIGIONS: Catholic 68%, Protestant 25%, other 7%
ETHNIC MIX: Hungarian (Magyar) 90%, German 2%, other 8%
GOVERNMENT: Multiparty republic
CURRENCY: Forint = 100 filler

CZECH REPUBLIC

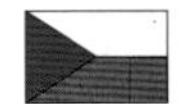

Ger.
Poland
CZECH REPUBLIC
Ger.
Austria
Slovakia

ONCE PART of Czechoslovakia in Central Europe, it became independent in 1993, after peacefully dissolving its federal union with Slovakia.

GEOGRAPHY

Western territory of Bohemia is a plateau surrounded by mountains. Moravia, in the east, has hills and lowlands.

CLIMATE

Cool, sometimes cold winters, and warm summer months, which bring most of the annual rainfall.

PEOPLE AND SOCIETY

Secular and urban society, with high divorce rates. Czechs make up the vast majority of the population. The 300,000 Slovaks left after partition now form largest ethnic minority. Ethnic tensions are few, but there is some hostility towards the Gypsy community. A new commercial elite is emerging alongside ex-communist entrepreneurs.

THE ECONOMY

Traditional heavy industries (machinery, iron, car-making) have been successfully privatized. Large tourism revenues. Skilled labour force. Rising unemployment.

◆ *INSIGHT: The Czech Republic is the most polluted country in Europe. Acid rain has devastated many of its forests*

1000m/3281ft
500m/1640ft
200m/656ft
Sea Level
0
50 km
0
50 miles
GERMANY
POLAND
AUSTRIA
SLOVAKIA
Liberec
Ústí nad Labem
Karlovy Vary
Elbe
PRAGUE
Kladno
Hradec Králové
Pardubice
Plzeň
Bohemia
Ostrava
Havířov
Olomouc
Moravia
Zlín
České Budějovice
Brno
Carpathians
50°
14°
16°
18°

FACT FILE

OFFICIAL NAME: Czech Republic
DATE OF FORMATION: 1993
CAPITAL: Prague
POPULATION: 10.4 million
TOTAL AREA: 78,370 sq km (30,260 sq miles)
DENSITY: 131 people per sq km
LANGUAGES: Czech*, Slovak, Romany, other
RELIGIONS: Catholic 44%, Protestant 6%, other Christian 12%, other 38%
ETHNIC MIX: Czech 85%, Moravian 13%, other (inc. Slovak, Gypsy) 2%
GOVERNMENT: Multiparty republic
CURRENCY: Koruna = 100 halura

SLOVAKIA

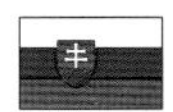

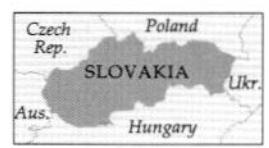

Czech Rep.
Poland
SLOVAKIA
Ukr.
Aus.
Hungary

LAND-LOCKED in Central Europe, Slovakia has been independent since 1993. It is the less-developed half of the former Czechoslovakia.

GEOGRAPHY

Carpathian Mountains stretch along northern border with Poland. Southern lowlands include the fertile Danube plain.

CLIMATE

Continental. Moderately warm summers and steady rainfall. Cold winters with heavy snowfalls.

PEOPLE AND SOCIETY

Slovaks are largest and most dominant group. Tension between them and the Hungarian minority has increased, particularly over directive that Hungarians should adopt Slovak name endings. Before partition, many skilled Slovaks took jobs in Prague, but few have returned to help structure the new Slovakia. Catholic Church remains influential.

THE ECONOMY

Narrow emphasis on heavy industry, with poor record on innovation and capital investment. High inflation and unemployment. Growing tourism sector.

◆ INSIGHT: *Separation from the Czech Republic gave Slovakia full independence for the first time in over 1,000 years*

POLAND
Carpathians
Bardejov
Žilina
Prešov
CZECH REPUBLIC
Martin
Košice
Trenčín
Banská Bystrica
UKRAINE
AUS.
Trnava
Nitra
Lučenec
BRATISLAVA
Danube
HUNGARY
2000m/6562ft
1000m/3281ft
500m/1640ft
200m/656ft
Sea Level
0 50 km
0 50 miles

FACT FILE

OFFICIAL NAME: Slovak Republic
DATE OF FORMATION: 1993
CAPITAL: Bratislava
POPULATION: 5.3 million
TOTAL AREA: 49,500 sq km (19,100 sq miles)
DENSITY: 108 people per sq km
LANGUAGES: Slovak*, Hungarian (Magyar), Romany, Czech, other
RELIGIONS: Catholic 80%, Protestant 12%, other 8%
ETHNIC MIX: Slovak 85%, Hungarian 9%, Czech 1%, other (inc. Gypsy) 5%
GOVERNMENT: Multiparty republic
CURRENCY: Koruna = 100 halura

SLOVENIA

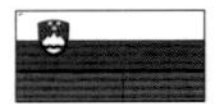

Austria
Italy
SLOVENIA
Croatia

NORTHERNMOST OF the former Yugoslav republics, it has the closest links with Western Europe. In 1991, it gained independence with little violence.

GEOGRAPHY

Alpine terrain with hills and mountains. Forests cover almost half the country's area. Short Adriatic coastline.

CLIMATE

Mediterranean climate on small coastal strip. Alpine interior has continental extremes.

PEOPLE AND SOCIETY

Homogeneous population accounts for relatively peaceful transition to independence. Traditional links with Austria and Italy, each with Slovene populations, account for the 'Alpine' rather than 'Balkan' outlook. Wages are the highest in Central Europe, but unemployment is rising. Institutional change is proceeding slowly.

THE ECONOMY

Competitive manufacturing industry. Prospects for growth in electronics industry. Well-developed tourist sector.

◆ *INSIGHT: Slovenia is a major producer of mercury, which is used in thermometers, barometers and batteries*

AUSTRIA
HUNGARY
Murska Sobota
Mura
Maribor
Drava
Ptuj
Jesenice
Kranj
Celje
LJUBLJANA
Sava
ITALY
16°
46°
Nova Gorica
Krško
Brežice
Postojna
Adriatic Sea
CROATIA
Kupa
14°
0 25 km
0 25 miles
1000m/3281ft
500m/1640ft
200m/656ft
Sea Level

FACT FILE

OFFICIAL NAME: Republic of Slovenia
DATE OF FORMATION: 1991
CAPITAL: Ljubljana
POPULATION: 2 million
TOTAL AREA: 20,250 sq km (7,820 sq miles)
DENSITY: 94 people per sq km
LANGUAGES: Slovene*, Serbo-Croatian
RELIGIONS: Roman Catholic 96%, Muslim 1%, other 3%
ETHNIC MIX: Slovene 92%, Croat 3%, Serb 1%, other 4%
GOVERNMENT: Multiparty republic
CURRENCY: Tolar = 100 stotins

CROATIA

Slovenia
Hungary
CROATIA
Bosnia & Herzegovina
Yugoslavia

A FORMER Yugoslav republic. Post-independence fighting thwarted its plans to capitalize on its prime location along the east Adriatic coast.

GEOGRAPHY

Rocky, mountainous Adriatic coastline is dotted with islands. Interior is a mixture of wooded mountains and broad valleys.

CLIMATE

The interior has a temperate continental climate. Mediterranean climate along the Adriatic coast.

PEOPLE AND SOCIETY

Turbulence was triggered by long-held ethnic hostilities. Open warfare between Croats and Serbs began in 1990. Some areas with local Serb majorities achieved *de facto* autonomy, after fierce fighting in 1992. Destruction was widespread; thousands of people were made homeless.

◈ *INSIGHT: The Croatian language uses the Roman alphabet, while Serbian employs Cyrillic (Russian) script*

THE ECONOMY

Economy was severely strained by fighting and influx of refugees. Potential for renewed success in manufacturing, tourism. Exports to the West have grown, despite conflict.

Čakovec
Varaždin
Koprivnica
HUNGARY
SLOVENIA
Drava
ZAGREB
Virovitica
Danube
Karlovac
Osijek
Rijeka
Kupa
Vukovar
Sava
Slavonski Brod
YUGO
Pula
BOSNIA & HERZEGOVINA
Zadar
Dinaric Alps
Dalmacija
Split
Adriatic Sea
Dubrovnik
YUGO
1000m/3281ft
500m/1640ft
200m/656ft
Sea Level
0 50 km
0 50 miles

FACT FILE

OFFICIAL NAME: Republic of Croatia
DATE OF FORMATION: 1991
CAPITAL: Zagreb
POPULATION: 4.9 million
TOTAL AREA: 56,540 sq km (21,830 sq miles)
DENSITY: 81 people per sq km
LANGUAGES: Croatian*, Serbian
RELIGIONS: Roman Catholic 77%, Orthodox Catholic 11%, Protestant 1%, Muslim 1%, other 10%
ETHNIC MIX: Croat 80%, Serb 12%, Hungarian, Slovenian, other 8%
GOVERNMENT: Multiparty republic
CURRENCY: Kuna = 100 para

BOSNIA & HERZEGOVINA

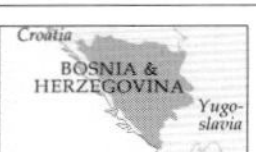
Croatia
BOSNIA & HERZEGOVINA
Yugo-slavia

DOMINATING THE western Balkans, Bosnia and Herzegovina was the focus of the bitter conflict surrounding the break-up of former Yugoslavia.

GEOGRAPHY

Hills and mountains, with narrow river valleys. Lowlands in the north. Mainly deciduous forest covers about half of the total area.

CLIMATE

Continental. Hot summers and cold, often snowy winters.

PEOPLE AND SOCIETY

Civil war between rival ethnic groups. Ethnic Bosnians (mainly Muslim) form the largest group, with large minorities of Serbs and Croats. Communities have been destroyed or uprooted ('ethnic cleansing') as Serbs and Croats established separate ethnic areas. The UN and Nato have been involved as peacekeepers.

◆ *INSIGHT: By 1995, over two million people had been made homeless and a further million had fled the country*

THE ECONOMY

Before 1991, Bosnia was home to five of former Yugoslavia's largest companies. It has the potential to become a thriving market economy with a strong manufacturing base.

CROATIA
Sava
Prijedor
Modriča
Bihać
Banja Luka
Doboj
Tuzla
Bosna
Zvornik
Dinaric Alps
Travnik
Zenica
Drina
Bugojno
Srebrenica
44°
16°
SARAJEVO
CROATIA
Mostar
2000m/6562ft
1000m/3281ft
500m/1640ft
200m/656ft
Sea Level
YUGOSLAVIA
0
50 km
18°
0
50 miles

FACT FILE

OFFICIAL NAME: The Republic of Bosnia and Herzegovina
DATE OF FORMATION: 1992
CAPITAL: Sarajevo
POPULATION: 3.5 million
TOTAL AREA: 51,130 sq km (19,741 sq miles)
DENSITY: 68 people per sq km
LANGUAGES: Serbo-Croatian*, other
RELIGIONS: Muslim 40%, Orthodox Catholic 31%, other 29%
ETHNIC MIX: Bosnian 44%, Serb 31%, Croat 17%, other 8%
GOVERNMENT: Multiparty republic
CURRENCY: Dinar = 100 para

YUGOSLAVIA (SERBIA & MONTENEGRO)

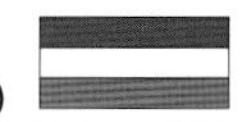

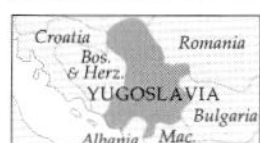
Croatia
Romania
Bos. & Herz.
YUGOSLAVIA
Bulgaria
Albania
Mac.

THE FEDERAL Republic of Yugoslavia, comprising Serbia and Montenegro, is the successor state to the former Yugoslavia.

GEOGRAPHY

Fertile Danube plain in north, rolling uplands in centre. Mountains in south, and behind narrow Adriatic coastal plain.

CLIMATE

Mediterranean along coast, continental inland. Hot summers and cold winters, with heavy snow.

PEOPLE AND SOCIETY

Social order has disintegrated since dissolution of the former Yugoslavia. Serbia was vilified in the international community for its role in the conflict in the region. Serbian concerns over Bosnia and Croatia have masked domestic tensions, particularly unrest among the Albanian population in the southern province of Kosovo.

◆ *INSIGHT: Belgrade means 'White City'. Its site has been settled for 7,000 years*

THE ECONOMY

Bosnian war and UN trade sanctions crippled the economy. Fuel and food shortages. Hyper-inflation created a barter economy.

2000m/6562ft
1000m/3281ft
500m/1640ft
200m/656ft
Sea Level
0 50 km
0 50 miles
HUNGARY
Subotica
Vojvodina
CROATIA
Zrenjanin
Danube
Novi Sad
Šabac
Pančevo
ROMANIA
BELGRADE
Smederevo
Serbia
Danube
BOSNIA & HERZEGOVINA
Kragujevac
Čačak
Kraljevo
Kruševac
Niš
Leskovac
Montenegro
Kosovska Mitrovica
Nikšić
Kosovo
BULG.
Podgorica
Peć
Priština
Uroševac
Adriatic Sea
Lake Scutari
Prizren
ALBANIA
MACEDONIA

FACT FILE

OFFICIAL NAME: Federal Republic of Yugoslavia
DATE OF FORMATION: 1992
CAPITAL: Belgrade
POPULATION: 10.6 million
TOTAL AREA: 25,715 sq km (9,929 sq miles)
DENSITY: 104 people per sq km
LANGUAGES: Serbo-Croatian*, other
RELIGIONS: Orthodox Catholic 65%, Muslim 19%, other 16%
ETHNIC MIX: Serb 63%, Albanian 14%, Montenegrin 6%, other 17%
GOVERNMENT: Multiparty republic
CURRENCY: Dinar = 100 para

ALBANIA

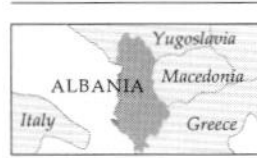
Yugoslavia
ALBANIA
Macedonia
Italy
Greece

LYING AT the southeastern end of the Adriatic Sea, Albania held its first multiparty elections in 1991, after nearly five decades of communism.

GEOGRAPHY

Narrow coastal plain. Interior is mostly hills and mountains. Forest and scrub cover over 40% of the land. Large lakes in the east.

CLIMATE

Mediterranean coastal climate, with warm summers and cool winters. Mountains receive heavy rains or snows in winter.

PEOPLE AND SOCIETY

Last eastern European country to move towards Western economic liberalism – pace of change remains a sensitive issue. Mosques and churches have reopened in what was once the world's only officially atheist state. Greek minority in the south suffers much discrimination.

◆ *INSIGHT: The Albanians' name for their nation,* Shqipërisë, *means 'Land of the Eagle'*

THE ECONOMY

Oil and gas reserves plus high growth rate have potential to offset rudimentary infrastructure and lack of foreign investment.

YUGOSLAVIA
Lake Scutari
Shkodër
Kukës
Adriatic Sea
MACEDONIA
Durrës
TIRANA
Elbasan
Lake Ohrid
Lushnjë
Lake Prespa
Fier
Berat
Korçë
Vlorë
2000m/6562ft
1000m/3281ft
500m/1640ft
200m/656ft
Sea Level
Ionian Sea
Delvinë
GREECE
0 50 km
0 50 miles

FACT FILE

OFFICIAL NAME: Republic of Albania
DATE OF FORMATION: 1912/1913
CAPITAL: Tirana
POPULATION: 3.3 million
TOTAL AREA: 28,750 sq km (11,100 sq miles)
DENSITY: 120 people per sq km
LANGUAGES: Albanian*, Greek
RELIGIONS: Muslim 70%, Greek Orthodox 20%, Roman Catholic 10%
ETHNIC MIX: Albanian 96%, Greek 2%, other (inc. Macedonian) 2%
GOVERNMENT: Multiparty republic
CURRENCY: Lek = 100 qindars

MACEDONIA

Yugoslavia
Bulgaria
MACEDONIA
Albania
Greece

LAND-LOCKED in the southern Balkans, Macedonia is affected by sanctions imposed on its northern trading partners and by Greek antagonism.

GEOGRAPHY

Mainly mountainous or hilly, with deep river basins in centre. Plains in northeast and southwest.

CLIMATE

Continental climate with wet springs and dry autumns. Heavy snowfalls in northern mountains.

PEOPLE AND SOCIETY

Slav Macedonians comprise two-thirds of the population. Officially 20% are Albanian, although Albanians claim they account for 40%. Tensions between the two groups have so far been restrained. Greek government is hostile towards the state because it suspects it may try to absorb northern Greece – also called Macedonia – in a 'Greater Macedonia'. Social structures remain essentially socialist.

THE ECONOMY

Serbian sanctions paralyze exports, but foreign aid and grants boost foreign exchange reserves. Growing private sector. Thriving black market in the capital.

◆ *INSIGHT: Lake Ohrid is the deepest lake in Europe at 294 m (964 ft)*

YUGOSLAVIA
BULGARIA
Kumanovo
Tetovo
SKOPJE
Kočani
Štip
Gostivar
Titov Veles
Kičevo
Strumica
ALBANIA
Vardar
Prilep
Ohrid
Bitola
Lake Ohrid
Lake Prespa
GREECE
42°
41°
22°
1000m/3281ft
500m/1640ft
200m/656ft
Sea Level
0
50 km
0
50 miles

FACT FILE

OFFICIAL NAME: Former Yugoslav Republic of Macedonia
DATE OF FORMATION: 1991
CAPITAL: Skopje
POPULATION: 1.9 million
TOTAL AREA: 25,715 sq km (9,929 sq miles)
DENSITY: 74 people per sq km
LANGUAGES: Macedonian, Serbo-Croatian (no official language)
RELIGIONS: Christian 80%, Muslim 20%
ETHNIC MIX: Macedonian 67%, Albanian 20%, Turkish 4%, other 9%
GOVERNMENT: Multiparty republic
CURRENCY: Denar = 100 deni

BULGARIA

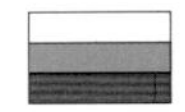

Romania
Yugo.
BULGARIA
Mac.
Greece
Turkey

LOCATED IN southeastern Europe, Bulgaria has made slow progress towards democracy since the fall of its communist regime in 1990.

GEOGRAPHY

Mountains run east–west across centre and along southern border. Danube plain in north, Thracian plain in southeast.

CLIMATE

Warm summers and snowy winters, especially in mountains. East winds bring seasonal extremes.

PEOPLE AND SOCIETY

Government has sought to assimilate separate ethnic groups, thereby suppressing cultural identities. Large exodus of Bulgarian Turks in 1989. Recent privatization programme has left many Turks landless and prompted further emigration. Gypsies suffer much discrimination. Female equality exists only in theory. Ruling party, mainly ex-communists, have resisted change.

THE ECONOMY

Political and technical delays hinder privatization programme. Good agricultural production, including grapes for well-developed wine industry, and tobacco.

◆ *INSIGHT: Shaking one's head implies 'yes' in Bulgaria while a nod means 'no'*

ROMANIA
44°
Danube
Ruse
Dobrich
Pleven
Vratsa
Varna
YUGO.
Veliko Tŭrnovo
Shumen
Balkan Mountains
SOFIA
Sliven
Burgas
Pernik
Kazanlŭk
Stara Zagora
Yambol
Black Sea
Pazardzhik
Plovdiv
42°
Khaskovo
MAC.
TURKEY
28°
24°
GREECE
26°
0 50 km
0 50 miles
2000m/6562ft
1000m/3281ft
500m/1640ft
200m/656ft
Sea Level

FACT FILE

OFFICIAL NAME: Republic of Bulgaria
DATE OF FORMATION: 1908 / 1923
CAPITAL: Sofia
POPULATION: 8.9 million
TOTAL AREA: 110,910 sq km (42,822 sq miles)
DENSITY: 81 people per sq km

LANGUAGES: Bulgarian*, Turkish, Macedonian, Romany, Armenian
RELIGIONS: Christian 85%, Muslim 13%, Jewish 1%, other 1%
ETHNIC MIX: Bulgarian 85%, Turkish 9%, Macedonian 3%, Gypsy 3%
GOVERNMENT: Multiparty republic
CURRENCY: Lev = 100 stotinki

GREECE

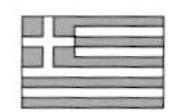

Mac.
Bulgaria
Albania
Turkey
GREECE

GREECE IS the southernmost Balkan nation. Surrounded by the Mediterranean, Aegean and Ionian seas, it has a strong seafaring tradition.

GEOGRAPHY
Mountainous peninsula with over 2,000 islands. Large central plain along the Aegean coast.

CLIMATE
Mainly Mediterranean with dry, hot summers. Alpine climate in northern mountain areas.

PEOPLE AND SOCIETY
Post-war industrial development altered the dominance of agriculture and seafaring. Rural exodus to industrial cities has been stemmed but over half the population now live in the two largest cities. Age-old culture and Greek Orthodox Church balance social mobility.

◆ *INSIGHT: The Parthenon in Athens has suffered more erosion in the last 20 years than in the previous 2,000*

THE ECONOMY
High inflation and poor investment work against strong economic sectors: tourism, shipping, agriculture. Thriving black economy.

BULGARIA
MACEDONIA
Dráma
Sérres
Xánthi
TURKEY
Thessaloníki
Alexandroúpoli
ALBANIA
Kateríni
Thracian Sea
Límnos
Ioánnina
Lárisa
Kérkyra (Corfu)
Kérkyra
Vólos
Voreioi Sporades
Lésvos
Lamía
Aegean Sea
Kefallonía
Chíos
Pátra
Peiraías
Kórinthos
ATHENS
Sámos
Zákynthos
Pelopónnisos
Isthmos Korinthou
Ionian Sea
Náxos
Kos
Kalámata
Sea of Crete
Ródos
Mediterranean Sea
Chaniá
Irákleio
Kárpathos
Kríti (Crete)
2000m/6562ft
1000m/3281ft
500m/1640ft
200m/656ft
Sea Level
0 100 km
0 100 miles

FACT FILE

OFFICIAL NAME: Hellenic Republic
DATE OF FORMATION: 1830 / 1947
CAPITAL: Athens
POPULATION: 10.2 million
TOTAL AREA: 131,990 sq km (50,961 sq miles)
DENSITY: 78 people per sq km
LANGUAGES: Greek*, Turkish, Albanian, Macedonian
RELIGIONS: Greek Orthodox 98%, Muslim 1%, other (mainly Roman Catholic and Jewish) 1%
ETHNIC MIX: Greek 98%, other 2%
GOVERNMENT: Multiparty republic
CURRENCY: Drachma = 100 lepta

ROMANIA

Hungary
Moldavia
ROMANIA
Yugoslavia
Bulgaria

ROMANIA LIES on the Black Sea coast. Since the overthrow of its communist regime in 1989, it has been slowly converting to a free-market economy.

GEOGRAPHY

Carpathian Mountains encircle Transylvanian plateau. Wide plains to the south and east. River Danube on southern border.

CLIMATE

Continental. Hot, humid summers and cold, snowy winters. Very heavy spring rains.

PEOPLE AND SOCIETY

Since 1989, there has been a rise in Romanian nationalism, aggravated by the hardships brought by economic reform. Incidence of ethnic violence has also risen, particularly towards Hungarians and Gypsies. Decrease in population in recent years due to emigration and falling birth rate.

◆ *INSIGHT: Romania is the only nation with a Romance language that does not have a Roman Catholic background*

THE ECONOMY

Outdated, polluting heavy industries and unmechanized agricultural sector. Wages have fallen since demise of communism. High number of small-scale foreign joint ventures. Tourism potential.

UKRAINE
Prut
Satu Mare
Baia Mare
Carpathian Mountains
Suceava
Botoşani
HUNGARY
Iaşi
Oradea
Cluj-Napoca
Bacău
MOLD.
Transylvania
Târgu Mureş
Arad
Timişoara
Sibiu
Focşani
UKRAINE
Reşiţa
Braşov
Carpaţii Meridionali
Brăila
Galaţi
Drobeta-Turnu Severin
Piteşti
Buzău
Danube Delta
Ploieşti
YUGO.
BUCHAREST
Constanţa
Black Sea
Craiova
Danube
Mangalia
BULGARIA
2000m/6562ft
1000m/3281ft
500m/1640ft
200m/656ft
Sea Level
0 50 km
0 50 miles

FACT FILE

OFFICIAL NAME: Romania
DATE OF FORMATION: 1947
CAPITAL: Bucharest
POPULATION: 23.4 million
TOTAL AREA: 237,500 sq km (91,700 sq miles)
DENSITY: 101 people per sq km
LANGUAGES: Romanian*, Hungarian
RELIGIONS: Romanian Orthodox 70%, Roman Catholic 6%, Protestant 6%, Greek Catholic 3%, other 15%
ETHNIC MIX: Romanian 89%, Hungarian 8%, other (inc. Gypsy) 3%
GOVERNMENT: Multiparty republic
CURRENCY: Leu = 100 bani

MOLDAVIA (MOLDOVA)

Ukraine
MOLDAVIA
Romania

SMALLEST AND most densely populated of the ex-Soviet republics, Moldavia has strong linguistic and cultural links with Romania to the west.

GEOGRAPHY

Steppes and hilly plains, drained by Dniester and Prut rivers.

CLIMATE

Warm summers and relatively mild winters. Moderate rainfall, evenly spread throughout the year.

PEOPLE AND SOCIETY

Shared heritage with Romania defines national identity, although in 1994 Moldavians voted against possible unification with Romania. Most of the population is engaged in intensive agriculture. The 1994 constitution granted special autonomous status to the Gagauz people in the south (Orthodox Christian Turks), and to the Slav peoples on the east bank of the River Dniester.

◆ *INSIGHT: Moldavia's vast underground wine vaults contain entire 'streets' of bottles built into rock quarries*

THE ECONOMY

Well-developed agricultural sector: wine, tobacco, cotton, food processing. Light manufacturing. Progress in establishing markets for exports. High unemployment.

Dniester
UKRAINE
Edinet
Soroki
Rîşcani
Floreşti
Rîbniţa
Bălţi
Prut
Dubăsari Reservoir
Orhei
Dniester
CHIŞINĂU
Tiraspol
Tighina
ROMANIA
Comrat
Cahul
200m/656ft
Sea Level
0 50 km
0 50 miles

FACT FILE

OFFICIAL NAME: Republic of Moldova
DATE OF FORMATION: 1991
CAPITAL: Chişinău
POPULATION: 4.4 million
TOTAL AREA: 33,700 sq km (13,000 sq miles)
DENSITY: 130 people per sq km
LANGUAGES: Moldavian*, Russian
RELIGIONS: Romanian Orthodox 98%, Jewish 1%, other 1%
ETHNIC MIX: Moldavian (Romanian) 65%, Ukrainian 14%, Russian 13%, Gagauz 4%, other 4%
GOVERNMENT: Multiparty republic
CURRENCY: Leu = 100 bani

BELORUSSIA (BELARUS)

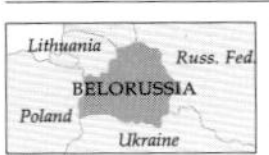
Lithuania
Russ. Fed
BELORUSSIA
Poland
Ukraine

FORMERLY KNOWN as White Russia, Belorussia lies land-locked in eastern Europe. It reluctantly became independent of the USSR in 1991.

GEOGRAPHY

Mainly plains and low hills. Dnieper and Dvina rivers drain eastern lowlands. Vast Pripet Marshes in the southwest.

CLIMATE

Extreme continental climate. Long, sub-freezing, but mainly dry winters, and hot summers.

PEOPLE AND SOCIETY

Only 2% of people are non-Slav, ethnic tension is minimal. Entire population have right to Belorussian citizenship, although only 11% are fluent in Belorussian. Slowest of the ex-Soviet states to implement political reform, a post-Soviet constitution was not adopted until 1994. Wealth is held by a small ex-communist elite. Fallout from 1986 Chornobil' nuclear disaster in Ukraine seriously affected Belorussians' health and environment.

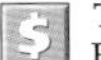

THE ECONOMY

Food processing and heavy industries stagnate while politicians argue over market reforms. Low unemployment but high inflation.

◆ *INSIGHT: The number of cancer and leukaemia cases is 10,000 above the pre-Chornobil' annual average*

0 100 km
0 100 miles
200m/656ft
Sea Level
LAT.
56°
Western Dvina
Vitsyebsk
RUSS. FED.
LITHUANIA
Orsha
Barysaw
54°
Lida
MINSK
Mahilyow
POLAND
Hrodna
Baranavichy
Slutsk
Babruysk
Dnieper
Homyel'
Brest
Pinsk
Rechytsa
52°
Pripet Marshes
Mazyr
32°
26°
UKRAINE
24°
UKRAINE
28°
30°

FACT FILE

OFFICIAL NAME: Republic of Belarus
DATE OF FORMATION: 1991
CAPITAL: Minsk
POPULATION: 10.3 million
TOTAL AREA: 207,600 sq km (80,154 sq miles)
DENSITY: 49 people per sq km
LANGUAGES: Belorussian*, Russian
RELIGIONS: Russian Orthodox 60%, Catholic 8%, other (including Uniate, Protestant, Muslim, Jewish) 32%
ETHNIC MIX: Belorussian 78%, Russian 13%, Polish 4%, other 5%
GOVERNMENT: Multiparty republic
CURRENCY: Rouble = 100 kopeks

UKRAINE

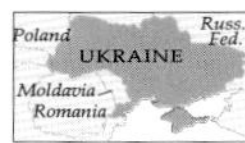
Poland
Russ. Fed.
UKRAINE
Moldavia
Romania

THE FORMER 'breadbasket of the Soviet Union', Ukraine balances assertive nationalism with concerns over its relations with Russia.

GEOGRAPHY

Mainly fertile steppes and forests. Carpathian Mountains in southwest, Crimean chain in south. Pripet Marshes in northwest.

CLIMATE

Mainly continental climate, with distinct seasons. Southern Crimea has Mediterranean climate.

PEOPLE AND SOCIETY

Over 90% of the population in western Ukraine is Ukrainian. However, in several cities in the east and south, Russians form a majority. In the Crimea, the Tartars comprise around 10% of the population. At independence in 1991, most Russians accepted Ukrainian sovereignty. However, tensions are now rising as both groups adopt more extremist nationalist policies.

THE ECONOMY

Hyperinflation, corruption, and hostility from economic elite stifle any reforms. Heavy industries and agriculture largely unchanged since independence.

◆ *INSIGHT: The name Ukraine means 'frontier', a reference to the country's position along the Russian border*

2000m/6562ft
1000m/3281ft
500m/1640ft
200m/656ft
Sea Level
BELORUSSIA
Pripet Marshes
Chernihiv
Luts'k
Chornobil'
KIEV
RUSS. FED.
POLAND
L'viv
Zhytomyr
Kremenchuts'ke Vdskh.
Kharkiv
Poltava
Vinnytsya
Cherkasy
Dnipropetrovs'k
Luhans'k
Mukacheve
Carpathian Mountains
Kirovohrad
Horlivka
Chernivtsi
Donets'k
Makiyivka
HUNGARY
MOLDAVIA
Zaporizhzhya
Mykolayiv
Mariupol'
ROMANIA
Odesa
Dnieper
Sea of Azov
Danube
Crimea
0 100 km
0 100 miles
Sevastopol'
Black Sea

FACT FILE

OFFICIAL NAME: Ukraine
DATE OF FORMATION: 1991
CAPITAL: Kiev
POPULATION: 52.2 million
TOTAL AREA: 603,700 sq km (223,090 sq miles)
DENSITY: 86 people per sq km
LANGUAGES: Ukrainian*, Russian, Tartar
RELIGIONS: Mostly Ukrainian Orthodox, with Roman Catholic, Protestant and Jewish minorities
ETHNIC MIX: Ukrainian 73%, Russian 22%, other (inc. Tartar) 5%
GOVERNMENT: Multiparty republic
CURRENCY: Karbovanets (coupons)

RUSSIAN FEDERATION

RUSSIAN FEDERATION

STILL THE world's largest state, despite the break-up of the USSR in 1991, the Russian Federation is struggling to capitalize on its diversity.

GEOGRAPHY

Ural Mountains divide European steppes and forests from tundra and forests of Siberia. South-central deserts and mountains.

CLIMATE

Continental in European Russia. Elsewhere from sub-arctic to Mediterranean and hot desert.

PEOPLE AND SOCIETY

Ethnic Russians now make up 80% of the population, but there are many minority groups. 57 nationalities have territorial status, a further 95 lack their own territory. 1994 war with Chechnya indicated potential for ethnic crisis. Wealth disparities, rising crime and black market activities have accompanied reforms. Extremist politicians have exploited standard-of-living and ethnic concerns. Strong resurgence of religious practice since late 1980s.

◆ *INSIGHT: The Trans-Siberian railway, which runs 9,335 km (5,800 miles) from Moscow to Vladivostok, is the world's longest. It crosses seven time zones*

FACT FILE

OFFICIAL NAME: Russian Federation
DATE OF FORMATION: 1991
CAPITAL: Moscow
POPULATION: 149.2 million
TOTAL AREA: 17,075,400 sq km (6,592,800 sq miles)
DENSITY: 2 people per sq km
LANGUAGES: Russian*, other
RELIGIONS: Russian Orthodox 80%, other (inc. Jewish, Muslim) 20%
ETHNIC MIX: Russian 80%, Tatar 4%, Ukrainian 3%, other 13%
GOVERNMENT: Multiparty republic
CURRENCY: Rouble = 100 kopeks

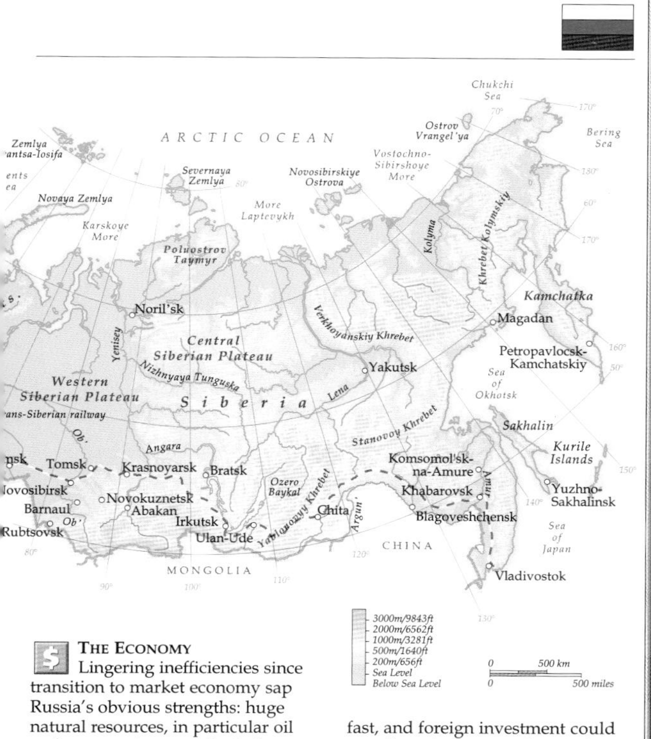
Chukchi Sea
ARCTIC OCEAN
Ostrov Vrangel'ya
Bering Sea
Zemlya Frantsa-Iosifa
Vostochno-Sibirskoye More
Severnaya Zemlya
Novosibirskiye Ostrova
Novaya Zemlya
More Laptevykh
Karskoye More
Kolyma
Khrebet Kolymskiy
Poluostrov Taymyr
Kamchatka
Noril'sk
Magadan
Verkhoyanskiy Khrebet
Yenisey
Central Siberian Plateau
Petropavlovsk-Kamchatskiy
Yakutsk
Nizhnyaya Tunguska
Sea of Okhotsk
Western Siberian Plateau
Siberia
Lena
Trans-Siberian railway
Ob'
Stanovoy Khrebet
Sakhalin
Angara
Kurile Islands
Tomsk
Krasnoyarsk
Bratsk
Komsomol'sk-na-Amure
Novosibirsk
Ozero Baykal
Khabarovsk
Amur
Yuzhno-Sakhalinsk
Novokuznetsk
Abakan
Yablonovyy Khrebet
Chita
Barnaul
Argun'
Blagoveshchensk
Irkutsk
Ulan-Ude
Rubtsovsk
CHINA
Sea of Japan
MONGOLIA
Vladivostok
3000m/9843ft
2000m/6562ft
1000m/3281ft
500m/1640ft
200m/656ft
Sea Level
Below Sea Level
0 500 km
0 500 miles

THE ECONOMY

Lingering inefficiencies since transition to market economy sap Russia's obvious strengths: huge natural resources, in particular oil and gas, precious metals, timber and hydrocarbons. Enormous engineering and scientific base. Privatization, which is proceeding fast, and foreign investment could transform industry and agriculture. Many of the skills developed under communism are not relevant in a competitive economy.

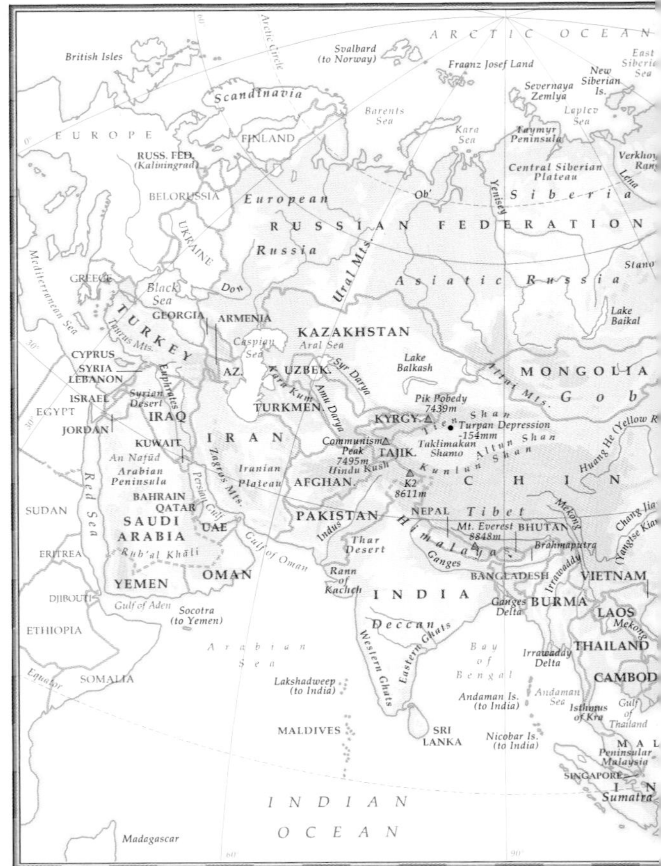

ARCTIC OCEAN
British Isles
Svalbard (to Norway)
Fraanz Josef Land
East Siberian Sea
New Siberian Is.
Severnaya Zemlya
Scandinavia
Barents Sea
Laptev Sea
Kara Sea
Taymyr Peninsula
EUROPE
FINLAND
RUSS. FED. (Kaliningrad)
Central Siberian Plateau
Verkhoyansk Range
Lena
BELORUSSIA
European
Ob'
Yenisey
Siberia
RUSSIAN FEDERATION
UKRAINE
Russia
Ural Mts.
Mediterranean Sea
GREECE
Black Sea
Don
Asiatic Russia
Stanovoy
TURKEY
GEORGIA
ARMENIA
Lake Baikal
Taurus Mts.
Caspian Sea
KAZAKHSTAN
Aral Sea
CYPRUS
SYRIA
LEBANON
AZ.
UZBEK.
Syr Darya
Lake Balkash
Altai Mts.
MONGOLIA
ISRAEL
Syrian Desert
Euphrates
Kara Kum
Amu Darya
Gobi
EGYPT
IRAQ
TURKMEN.
Pik Pobedy 7439m
JORDAN
KYRGY.
Tien Shan
Turpan Depression -154mm
Huang He (Yellow River)
KUWAIT
IRAN
Communism Peak 7495m
Taklimakan Shamo
Altun Shan
An Nafūd
Zagros Mts.
TAJIK.
Arabian Peninsula
Red Sea
Persian Gulf
Iranian Plateau
Hindu Kush
Kunlun Shan
CHINA
AFGHAN.
K2 8611m
BAHRAIN
QATAR
Mekong
SUDAN
PAKISTAN
NEPAL
Tibet
SAUDI ARABIA
UAE
Indus
Himalaya
Mt. Everest 8848m
BHUTAN
Chang Jiang (Yangtze Kiang)
Gulf of Oman
Thar Desert
Brahmaputra
ERITREA
Rub' al Khāli
Ganges
OMAN
YEMEN
Rann of Kachch
BANGLADESH
Irrawaddy
VIETNAM
DJIBOUTI
INDIA
Gulf of Aden
Socotra (to Yemen)
Ganges Delta
BURMA
LAOS
ETHIOPIA
Deccan
Eastern Ghats
Mekong
Arabian Sea
Western Ghats
Bay of Bengal
Irrawaddy Delta
THAILAND
Equator
SOMALIA
Lakshadweep (to India)
CAMBODIA
Andaman Is. (to India)
Andaman Sea
Isthmus of Kra
Gulf of Thailand
MALDIVES
SRI LANKA
Nicobar Is. (to India)
Peninsular Malaysia
SINGAPORE
Sumatra
INDIAN OCEAN
Madagascar

ASIA

The largest, highest, and most populous continent in the world, Asia is separated from Africa by the Red Sea and bounded in the north by the Arctic Ocean. In the extreme north, both land and sea are frozen for most of the year. Asia's great central mass of mountains and plateaux, including the highest in the world – the Himalayas – forms a barrier between North and South Asia. Vast alluvial plains border its major rivers: the Ganges, Ob, Mekong, Chang Jiang (Yangtze) and Yellow Rivers. Asia has important mineral resources, particularly the oil and natural gas deposits of the Arab states.

CONTINENTAL FACTS

HIGHEST POINT:
Mt Everest, Nepal
8,848 m (29,030 ft)

LOWEST POINT:
Dead Sea
About half of Bangladesh lies between sea level and 8 m (25 ft)

LARGEST LAKE:
Caspian Sea
371,000 sq km
(143,205 sq miles)

LONGEST RIVER:
Chang Jiang (Yangtze), China 6,380 km
(3,965 miles)

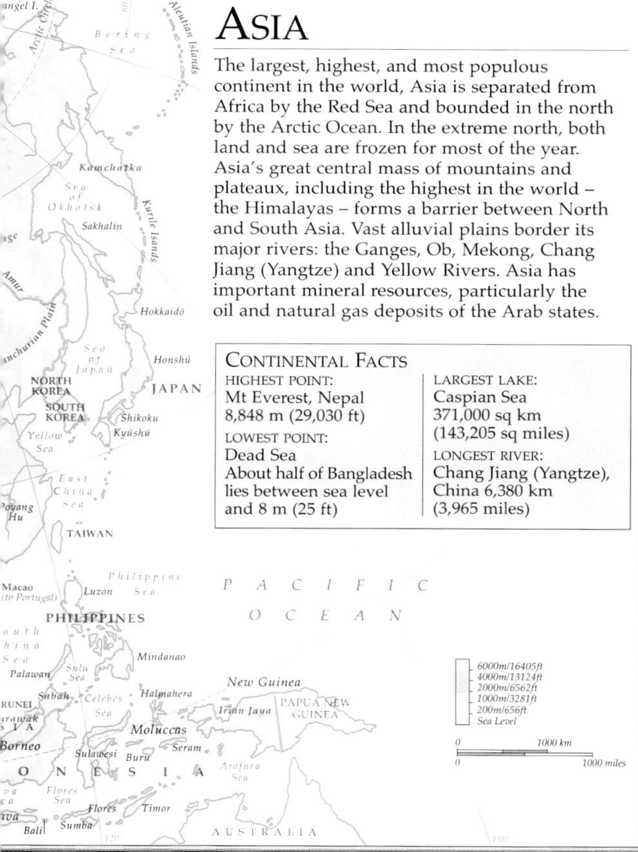

Bering Sea
Aleutian Islands
Arctic Circle
Kamchatka
Sea of Okhotsk
Sakhalin
Kurile Islands
Amur
Hokkaidō
Sea of Japan
Honshū
NORTH KOREA
SOUTH KOREA
JAPAN
Shikoku
Kyūshū
Yellow Sea
East China Sea
TAIWAN
Philippine Sea
Macao (to Portugal)
Luzon
PHILIPPINES
PACIFIC OCEAN
Mindanao
Palawan
Sulu Sea
Sabah
Celebes Sea
Halmahera
New Guinea
Irian Jaya
PAPUA NEW GUINEA
Moluccas
Seram
Borneo
Sulawesi
Buru
Arafura Sea
Flores Sea
Flores
Timor
Bali
Sumba
AUSTRALIA
6000m/16405ft
4000m/13124ft
2000m/6562ft
1000m/3281ft
200m/656ft
Sea Level
0
1000 km
0
1000 miles

Azerbaijan

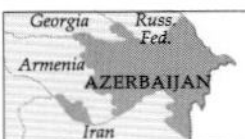
Georgia
Russ. Fed.
Armenia
AZERBAIJAN
Iran

Situated on the western coast of the Caspian Sea, Azerbaijan was the first Soviet republic to declare independence from Moscow in 1991.

Geography

Caucasus Mountains in west, including Naxçivan enclave in south of Armenia. Flat, low-lying terrain on the coast of the Caspian Sea.

Climate

Continental with pronounced seasonal extremes. Low rainfall, with peak months during summer.

People and Society

Azerbaijanis now form a large majority. Thousands of Armenians, Russians and Jews have left as a result of rising nationalism among Azerbaijanis. Racial hostility against those who remain is increasing. Influx of half a million Azerbaijani refugees fleeing war with Armenia over the disputed enclave of Nagorno Karabakh. Once effective social security system has collapsed.

The Economy

Oil and gas have considerable potential. War is a major drain on state resources. Market reforms attract foreign interest.

◆ *Insight: The fire-worshipping Zoroastrian faith originated in Azerbaijan in the 6th century* BC

GEORGIA
RUSS. FED.
Caspian Sea
Quba
Caucasus
Şäki
Kura
Gäncä
Mingäçevir
Sumqayıt
BAKU
Lesser Caucasus
ARMENIA
Nagorno-Karabakh
Kura
Xankändi
Äli-Bayramı
Aras
Naxçıvan
Länkäran
IRAN
42°
40°
46°
48°
50°
0 100 km
0 100 miles
4000m/13124ft
3000m/9843ft
2000m/6562ft
1000m/3281ft
500m/1640ft
200m/656ft
Sea Level

Fact File

OFFICIAL NAME: Republic of Azerbaijan
DATE OF FORMATION: 1991
CAPITAL: Baku
POPULATION: 7.3 million
TOTAL AREA: 86,600 sq km (33,436 sq miles)
DENSITY: 84 people per sq km
LANGUAGES: Azerbaijani*, Russian, Armenian, other
RELIGIONS: Muslim 83%, Armenian Apostolic, Russian Orthodox 17%
ETHNIC MIX: Azerbaijani 83%, Russian 6%, Armenian 6%, other 5%
GOVERNMENT: Multiparty republic
CURRENCY: Manat = 100 gopik

ARMENIA

Georgia
Azerbaijan
ARMENIA
Turkey
Iran

SMALLEST OF the former USSR's republics, Armenia lies in the Lesser Caucasus Mountains. Since 1988, it has been at war with Azerbaijan.

GEOGRAPHY

Rugged and mountainous, with expanses of semi-desert and a large lake in the east, Sevana Lich.

CLIMATE

Continental climate, little rainfall in the lowlands. Winters are often bitterly cold.

PEOPLE AND SOCIETY

Strong commitment to Christianity, and to Armenian culture. Minority groups are well integrated. War with Azerbaijan over the enclave of Nagorno Karabakh has meant 100,000 Armenians living in Azerbaijan forced to return home to live in poverty. In 1988, 25,000 people died in an earthquake in the west.

◆ *INSIGHT: In the 4th century, Armenia became the first country to adopt Christianity as its state religion*

THE ECONOMY

Few natural resources, though lead, copper and zinc are mined. Main agricultural products are wine, tobacco, olives and rice. Well-developed machine-building and manufacturing – includes textiles, and bottling of mineral water.

GEORGIA
Alaverdi
Vanadzor
Gyumri
Lesser Caucasus
AZERBAIJAN
Sevan
TURKEY
Hrazdan
Ashtarak
Sevana Lich
Ejmiadzin
Hoktemberyan
YEREVAN
Ararat
Aras
3000m/9843ft
2000m/6562ft
1000m/3281ft
500m/1640ft
AZERBAIJAN
Kapan
Aras
0
50 km
0
50 miles
IRAN

FACT FILE

OFFICIAL NAME: Republic of Armenia
DATE OF FORMATION: 1991
CAPITAL: Yerevan
POPULATION: 3.6 million
TOTAL AREA: 29,000 sq km (11,505 sq miles)
DENSITY: 117 people per sq km
LANGUAGES: Armenian*, Azerbaijani, Russian, Kurdish
RELIGIONS: Armenian Apostolic 90%, other Christian and Muslim 10%
ETHNIC MIX: Armenian 93%, Azerbaijani 3%, Russian, Kurdish 4%
GOVERNMENT: Multiparty republic
CURRENCY: Dram = 100 louma

TURKEY

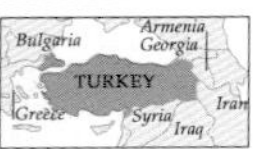
Bulgaria
Armenia
Georgia
TURKEY
Greece
Syria
Iran
Iraq

LYING PARTLY in Europe, but mostly in Asia, Turkey's position gives it significant influence in the Mediterranean, Black Sea and Middle East.

GEOGRAPHY

Asian Turkey (Anatolia) is dominated by two mountain ranges, separated by a high, semi-desert plateau. Coastal regions are fertile.

CLIMATE

Coast has a Mediterranean climate. Interior has cold, snowy winters and hot, dry summers.

PEOPLE AND SOCIETY

The Turks are racially diverse. Many are refugees or descendants of refugees, often from the Balkans or other territories once under Russian rule. However, the sense of national identity is strong. Since 1984, southeastern region has been the scene of a civil war waged by the Kurdish minority, demanding their rights within the country.

BULGARIA
GREECE
Kâğıthane
İstanbul Boğazi
İstanbul
Bursa
Dardanelles
Eskişehir
ANKARA
Manisa
İzmir
Aegean Sea
Ephesus
Bodrum
Antalya
Konya
Taurus Mountains
Adana
Black Sea
Samsun
Trabzon
GEORGIA
ARMENIA
Erzurum
Euphrates
Kayseri
Malatya
Van Gölü
Van
Diyarbakir
IRAN
Tigris
Kahramanmaraş
Şanlıurfa
Gaziantep
İskenderun
IRAQ
SYRIA
Mediterranean Sea
28°
32°
36°
40°
44°
0 200 km
0 200 miles
3000m/9843ft
2000m/6562ft
1000m/3281ft
500m/1640ft
200m/656ft
Sea Level

THE ECONOMY

Since the early 1980s, textiles, manufacturing and construction sectors all booming. Tourism is also a major foreign currency earner.

◆ *INSIGHT: Turkey had two of the seven wonders of the ancient world: the tomb of King Mausolus at Halicarnassus (now Bodrum), and the temple of Artemis at Ephesus*

FACT FILE

OFFICIAL NAME: Republic of Turkey
DATE OF FORMATION: 1923/1939
CAPITAL: Ankara
POPULATION: 63.1 million
TOTAL AREA: 779,450 sq km (300,950 sq miles)
DENSITY: 81 people per sq km
LANGUAGES: Turkish*, Kurdish, Arabic, Circassian, Armenian
RELIGIONS: Muslim 99%, other 1%
ETHNIC MIX: Turkish 80%, Kurdish 17%, other 3%
GOVERNMENT: Multiparty republic
CURRENCY: Turkish lira = 100 krural

GEORGIA

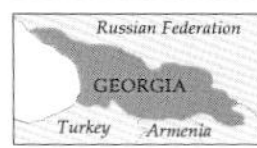
Russian Federation
GEORGIA
Turkey
Armenia

LOCATED ON the eastern shore of the Black Sea, Georgia has been torn by civil war since achieving independence from the USSR in 1991.

GEOGRAPHY

Kura valley lies between Caucasus Mountains in the north and Lesser Caucasus range in south. Lowlands along the Black Sea coast.

CLIMATE

Sub-tropical along the coast, changing to continental extremes at high altitudes. Rainfall is moderate.

PEOPLE AND SOCIETY

Paternalistic society, with strong family, cultural and literary traditions. Georgians are the majority group. An uneasy truce has followed the 1990–93 civil war, and the political scene remains volatile. In 1994, another civil war was fought, as ethnic Abkhazians attempted to secede from Georgia. Around one in five Georgians live in poverty, but a small, wealthy elite is found in the capital.

THE ECONOMY

Food processing and wine production are the main industries. Economy has broken down due to war and severance of links with other former Soviet republics.

◆ *INSIGHT: Western Georgia was the land of the legendary Golden Fleece of Greek mythology*

RUSSIAN FEDERATION
Caucasus
Sokhumi
Zugdidi
Black Sea
P'ot'i
K'ut'aisi
Samtredia
Tskhinvali
Gori
T'elavi
Bat'umi
Kura
Akhalts'ikhe
TBILISI
Rust'avi
Lesser Caucasus
TURKEY
ARMENIA
AZERBAIJAN
3000m/9843ft
2000m/6562ft
1000m/3281ft
500m/1640ft
200m/656ft
Sea Level
0
100 km
0
100 miles

FACT FILE

OFFICIAL NAME: Republic of Georgia
DATE OF FORMATION: 1991
CAPITAL: Tbilisi
POPULATION: 5.5 million
TOTAL AREA: 69,700 sq km (26,911 sq miles)
DENSITY: 79 people per sq km
LANGUAGES: Georgian*, Russian, other
RELIGIONS: Georgian Orthodox 70%, Russian Orthodox 10%, other 20%
ETHNIC MIX: Georgian 69%, Armenian 9%, Russian 6%, Azerbaijani 5%, other 11%
GOVERNMENT: Republic
CURRENCY: Coupons

LEBANON

Cyprus
Syria
LEBANON
Israel
Jordan

LEBANON IS dwarfed by its two powerful neighbours, Syria and Israel. The state is rebuilding after 14 years of civil war.

GEOGRAPHY

Behind a narrow coastal plain, two parallel mountain ranges run the length of the country, separated by the fertile El Beqaa valley.

CLIMATE

Hot summers, with high humidity on the coast. Mild winters.

PEOPLE AND SOCIETY

Population is split between Christians and Muslims. Although in the minority, Christians have been the traditional rulers. In 1975, civil war broke out between the two groups. A settlement, which gave the Muslims more power, was reached in 1989. Elections in 1992 brought hope of greater stability. A huge gulf exists between the poor and a small, immensely rich elite.

◆ *INSIGHT: The Cedar of Lebanon has been the nation's symbol for 2,000 years*

THE ECONOMY

Infrastructure wrecked by civil war. Post-war opportunity to regain position as Arab centre for banking and services. Potentially a major producer of wine and fruit.

Mediterranean Sea
SYRIA
Tripoli
Zgharta
Anti-Lebanon Mts.
Joûnié
BEIRUT
Baabda
Baalbek
Zahlé
El Beqaa
SYRIA
Saïda
Nabatîyé
Soûr
Golan Heights
ISRAEL
34°
36°
33°
3000m/9843ft
2000m/6562ft
1000m/3281ft
500m/1640ft
200m/656ft
Sea Level
0 20 km
0 20 miles

FACT FILE

OFFICIAL NAME: Republic of Lebanon
DATE OF FORMATION: 1944
CAPITAL: Beirut
POPULATION: 2.9 million
TOTAL AREA: 10,400 sq km (4,015 sq miles)
DENSITY: 274 people per sq km
LANGUAGES: Arabic*, French, Armenian, English
RELIGIONS: Muslim (mainly Shi'a) 57%, Christian (mainly Maronite) 43%
ETHNIC MIX: Arab 93% (Lebanese 83%, Palestinian 10%), other 7%
GOVERNMENT: Multiparty republic
CURRENCY: Pound = 100 piastres

SYRIA

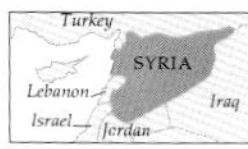
Turkey
SYRIA
Lebanon
Iraq
Israel
Jordan

STRETCHING FROM the eastern Mediterranean to the River Tigris, Syria's borders were created on its independence from France in 1946.

GEOGRAPHY

Northern coastal plain is backed by a low range of hills. The River Euphrates cuts through a vast interior desert plateau.

CLIMATE

Mediterranean coastal climate. Inland areas are arid. In winter, snow is common on the mountains.

PEOPLE AND SOCIETY

Most Syrians live near the coast, where the biggest cities are sited. 90% are Muslim, including the politically dominant Alawis. In the north and west are groups of Kurds, Armenians and Turkish-speaking peoples. Some 300,000 Palestinian refugees have also settled in Syria. They, together with the urban unemployed, make up the poorest groups in a growing gulf between rich and poor.

THE ECONOMY

High defence spending is major drain on economy. Exporter of crude oil. Agriculture is thriving: crops include cotton, wheat, olives.

◆ *INSIGHT: Aramaic, the language of the Bible, is still spoken in two villages in Syria*

TURKEY
Al Qāmishlī
Al Ḩasakah
Idlib
Ḩalab (Aleppo)
Ar Raqqah
Al Lādhiqīyah (Latakia)
Buḩayrat al Asad
Ḩamāh
Euphrates
Ţarţūs
Ḩimş
IRAQ
LEBANON
Anti-Lebanon
Syrian Desert
Dūmā
DAMASCUS
Golan Heights
ISRAEL
Dar'ā
JORDAN
36°
38°
40°
42°
34°
0 100 km
0 100 miles
2000m/6562ft
1000m/3281ft
500m/1640ft
200m/656ft
Sea Level

FACT FILE

OFFICIAL NAME: Syrian Arab Republic
DATE OF FORMATION: 1946
CAPITAL: Damascus
POPULATION: 13.8 million
TOTAL AREA: 185,180 sq km (71,500 sq miles)
DENSITY: 72 people per sq km
LANGUAGES: Arabic*, French, Kurdish, Armenian, Circassian, Aramaic
RELIGIONS: Sunni Muslim 74%, other Muslim 16%, Christian 10%
ETHNIC MIX: Arab 90%, other 10%
GOVERNMENT: Single-party republic
CURRENCY: Pound = 100 piastres

CYPRUS

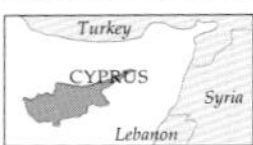
Turkey
CYPRUS
Syria
Lebanon

CYPRUS LIES in the eastern Mediterranean. Since 1974, it has been partitioned between the Turkish-occupied north and the Greek south.

GEOGRAPHY

Mountains in the centre-west give way to a fertile plain in the east, flanked by hills to the northeast.

CLIMATE

Mediterranean. Summers are hot and dry. Winters are mild, with snow in the mountains.

PEOPLE AND SOCIETY

Majority of the population is Greek Christian. Since the 16th century, a minority community of Turkish Muslims has lived in the north of the island. In 1974 Turkish troops occupied the north, which was proclaimed the Turkish Republic of Northern Cyprus, but is recognized only by Turkey. The north remains poor, while the south, where the tourist industry is booming, is richer.

THE ECONOMY

In the south, tourism is the key industry. Shipping and light manufacturing also important. In the north, the main exports are citrus fruits and live animals.

◆ *INSIGHT: The buffer zone that divides Cyprus is manned by UN forces, at an estimated cost of $100m a year*

Mediterranean Sea
Dipkarpaz (Rizokarpaso)
Lapta (Lapithos)
Girne (Kyrenia)
Çayirova (Ayios)
Değirmenlik (Kythrea)
Famagusta Bay
Güzelyurt (Morphou)
NICOSIA
Gazimağusa (Famagusta)
Ayia Napa
Troodos Mts.
Larnaca
Paphos
Limassol
Akrotiri
35°
34°
33°
Ceasefire line
0 25 km
0 25 miles
1000m/3281ft
500m/1640ft
200m/656ft
Sea Level

FACT FILE

OFFICIAL NAME: Republic of Cyprus
DATE OF FORMATION: 1960/1983
CAPITAL: Nicosia
POPULATION: 700,000
TOTAL AREA: 9,251 sq km (3,572 sq miles)
DENSITY: 76 people per sq km
LANGUAGES: Greek*, Turkish, other
RELIGIONS: Greek Orthodox 77%, Muslim 18%, other 5%
ETHNIC MIX: Greek 77%, Turkish 18%, other (mainly British) 5%
GOVERNMENT: Multiparty republic
CURRENCY: Cypriot £/Turkish lira

ISRAEL

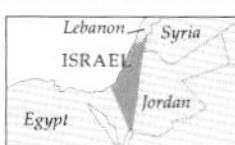
Lebanon
Syria
ISRAEL
Jordan
Egypt

CREATED AS a new state in 1948, on the east coast of the Mediterranean. Following wars with its Arab neighbours, it has extended its boundaries.

GEOGRAPHY

Coastal plain. Desert in the south. In the east lie the Great Rift valley and the Dead Sea – the lowest point on the Earth's surface.

CLIMATE

Summers are hot and dry. Wet season, March–November, is mild.

PEOPLE AND SOCIETY

Large numbers of Jews settled in Palestine before Israel was founded. After World War II there was a huge increase in immigration. Sephardi Jews from the Middle East and Mediterranean are now in the majority, but Ashkenazi Jews from Central Europe still dominate business and politics. Palestinians in Gaza and Jericho gained limited autonomy in 1994.

◆ *INSIGHT: All Jews worldwide have the right of Israeli citizenship*

THE ECONOMY

Huge potential of industrial, agricultural and manufacturing products. Major exporter of mineral salts. Important banking sector.

LEBANON
SYRIA
Golan Heights
Hefa
Teverya
Lake Tiberias
Nazerat
Mediterranean Sea
Jordan
Netanya
West Bank
Tel Aviv-Yafo
Petah Tiqwa
Holon
Ramat Gan
Ashdod
Jericho
Bethlehem
JERUSALEM
Gaza
Hebron
Gaza Strip
Dead Sea
Be'ér Sheva'
The West Bank, Gaza Strip and Golan Heights have been occupied by Israel since the Six Day War in 1967
Hanegev
Palestinians gained limited home rule of the Gaza Strip and Jericho in 1994
EGYPT
1000m/3281ft
500m/1640ft
200m/656ft
Sea Level
Below Sea Level
JORDAN
Elat
Gulf of Aqaba
0 50 km
0 50 miles

FACT FILE

OFFICIAL NAME: State of Israel
DATE OF FORMATION: 1948 / 1982
CAPITAL: Jerusalem
POPULATION: 5.4 million
TOTAL AREA: 20,700 sq km (7,992 sq miles)
DENSITY: 251 people per sq km
LANGUAGES: Hebrew*, Arabic, Yiddish, German, Russian, Polish, Romanian, Persian, English
RELIGIONS: Jewish 83%, Muslim 13%, Christian 2%, other 2%
ETHNIC MIX: Jewish 83%, Arab 17%
GOVERNMENT: Multiparty republic
CURRENCY: New shekel = 100 agorat

JORDAN

Lebanon
Syria
Iraq
Israel
JORDAN
Egypt
Saudi Arabia

THE KINGDOM of Jordan lies east of Israel. In 1993, King Hussein responded to calls for greater democracy by agreeing to multiparty elections.

GEOGRAPHY

Mostly desert plateaux, with occasional salt pans. Lowest parts lie along eastern shore of Dead Sea and East Bank of the River Jordan.

CLIMATE

Hot, dry summers. Cool, wet winters. Areas below sea level very hot in summer, and warm in winter.

PEOPLE AND SOCIETY

A predominantly Muslim country with a strong national identity, Jordan's population has Bedouin roots. There is a Christian minority and a large Palestinian population who have moved to Jordan from Israeli-occupied territory. Jordan gave up its claim to the West Bank to the PLO in 1988. The monarchy's power base lies among the rural tribes, which also provide the backbone of the military.

THE ECONOMY

Phosphates, chemicals and fertilizers are principal exports. Skilled, educated work force.

◆ INSIGHT: *King Hussein, who succeeded to the throne in 1952, is the longest-reigning Arab ruler*

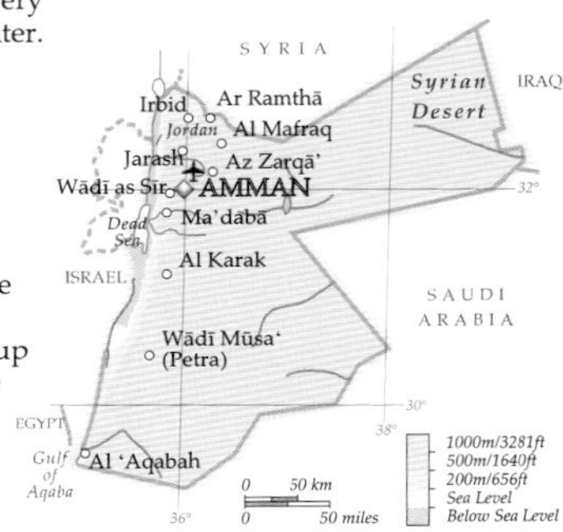
SYRIA
Syrian Desert
IRAQ
Irbid
Ar Ramthā
Jordan
Al Mafraq
Jarash
Az Zarqā'
Wādī as Sīr
AMMAN
32°
Ma'dabā
Dead Sea
Al Karak
ISRAEL
SAUDI ARABIA
Wādī Mūsa'
(Petra)
30°
EGYPT
38°
Gulf of Aqaba
Al 'Aqabah
36°
0 50 km
0 50 miles
1000m/3281ft
500m/1640ft
200m/656ft
Sea Level
Below Sea Level

FACT FILE

OFFICIAL NAME: Hashemite Kingdom of Jordan
DATE OF FORMATION: 1946/1976
CAPITAL: Amman
POPULATION: 4.4 million
TOTAL AREA: 89,210 sq km (34,440 sq miles)
DENSITY: 48 people per sq km
LANGUAGES: Arabic*, other
RELIGIONS: Muslim 95%, Christian 5%
ETHNIC MIX: Arab 98% (Palestinian 49%), Armenian 1%, Circassian 1%
GOVERNMENT: Constitutional monarchy
CURRENCY: Dinar = 1,000 fils

SAUDI ARABIA

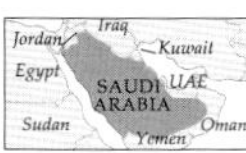
Iraq
Jordan
Kuwait
Egypt
SAUDI ARABIA
UAE
Sudan
Oman
Yemen

OCCUPYING MOST of the Arabian peninsula, the oil- and gas-rich kingdom of Saudi Arabia covers an area the size of Western Europe.

GEOGRAPHY

Mostly desert or semi-desert plateau. Mountain ranges in the west run parallel to the Red Sea and drop steeply to a coastal plain.

CLIMATE

In summer, temperatures often soar above 48°C (118°F), but in winter they may fall below freezing. Rainfall is rare.

PEOPLE AND SOCIETY

Most Saudis are Sunni Muslims who follow the strictly orthodox *wahabi* interpretation of Islam and embrace *sharia* (Islamic law) in their daily lives. Women are obliged to wear the veil, cannot hold driving licences, and have no role in public life. The Al-Saud family have been absolutist rulers since 1932. With the support of the religious establishment, they control all political life.

THE ECONOMY

Vast oil and gas reserves. Other minerals include coal, iron and gold. Most food is imported.

◆ INSIGHT: *Over two million Muslims a year make the* haj – *the pilgrimage to the holy city of Mecca*

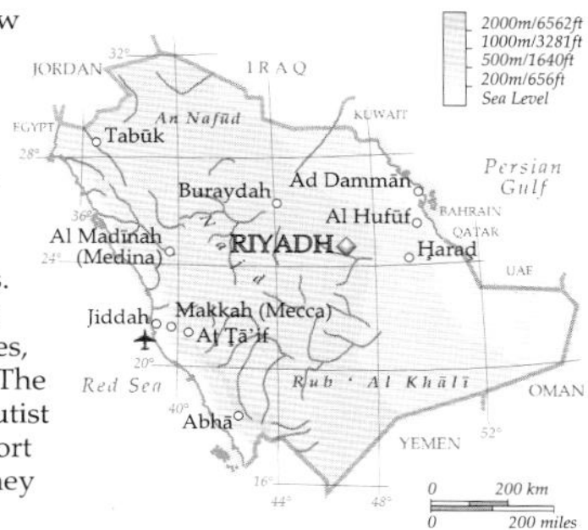
2000m/6562ft
1000m/3281ft
500m/1640ft
200m/656ft
Sea Level
JORDAN
IRAQ
KUWAIT
EGYPT
An Nafūd
Tabūk
Persian Gulf
Buraydah
Ad Dammān
BAHRAIN
Al Hufūf
QATAR
Al Madīnah (Medina)
RIYADH
Ḩaraḑ
UAE
Jiddah
Makkah (Mecca)
Aṭ Ṭā'if
Red Sea
Rub ' Al Khālī
OMAN
Abhā
YEMEN
0 200 km
0 200 miles

FACT FILE

OFFICIAL NAME: Kingdom of Saudi Arabia
DATE OF FORMATION: 1932 / 1981
CAPITAL: Riyadh
POPULATION: 16.5 million
TOTAL AREA: 2,149,690 sq km (829,995 sq miles)
DENSITY: 7 people per sq km
LANGUAGES: Arabic*, other
RELIGIONS: Sunni Muslim 85%, Shi'a Muslim 14%, Christian 1%
ETHNIC MIX: Arab 90%, Yemeni 8%, other Arab 1%, other 1%
GOVERNMENT: Absolute monarchy
CURRENCY: Riyal = 100 malalah

YEMEN

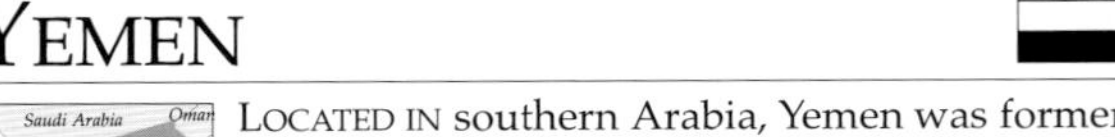

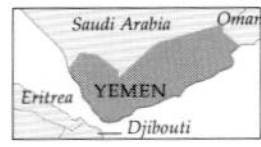
Saudi Arabia
Oman
Eritrea
YEMEN
Djibouti

LOCATED IN southern Arabia, Yemen was formerly two countries: a socialist regime in the south, and a republic in the north, which united in 1990.

GEOGRAPHY

Mountainous north with fertile strip along the Red Sea. Arid desert and mountains in south and east.

CLIMATE

Desert climate, modified by altitude, which affects temperatures by as much as 12°C (54°F).

PEOPLE AND SOCIETY

Yemenis are almost entirely of Arab and Bedouin descent. The majority are Sunni Muslims, of the Shafi sect. In rural areas and in the north, Islamic orthodoxy is strong and most women wear the veil. Tension continues to exist between the south, led by the cosmopolitan city of ‘Adan, and the more conservative north. Clashes between their former armies escalated into a brief civil war in 1994.

THE ECONOMY

Poor economic development due to political instability. Large oil and gas reserves discovered in 1984. Agriculture is the largest employer.

◆ *INSIGHT: Al Mukha (Mokha) on the Red Sea gave its name to the first coffee beans to be exported to Europe in the 17th and 18th centuries*

3000m/9843ft
2000m/6562ft
1000m/3281ft
500m/1640ft
200m/656ft
Sea Level
0 100 km
0 100 miles
OMAN
SAUDI ARABIA
Rub' Al Khali
Say'ūn
SANA
Sayhūt
Red Sea
Al Ḩudaydah
Ash Shiḩr
Dhamār
Al Mukallā
Bayt al Faqīh
Ta'izz
Al Mukhā (Mokha)
'Adan
Gulf of Aden
Abd-Al-Kuri
Suquṭrá

FACT FILE

OFFICIAL NAME: Republic of Yemen
DATE OF FORMATION: 1990
CAPITAL: Sana
POPULATION: 13 million
TOTAL AREA: 527,970 sq km (203,849 sq miles)
DENSITY: 24 people per sq km
LANGUAGES: Arabic*, other
RELIGIONS: Sunni Muslim 55%, Shi'a Muslim 42%, other 3%
ETHNIC MIX: Arab 95%, Afro-Arab 3%, South Asian, African, European 2%
GOVERNMENT: Multiparty republic
CURRENCY: Rial (North), Dinar (South) – both are legal currency

OMAN

Saudi Arabia
UAE
OMAN
Yemen

SITUATED ON the eastern coast of the Arabian peninsula, Oman is the least developed of the Gulf states, despite modest oil exports.

GEOGRAPHY

Mostly gravelly desert, with mountains in the north and south. Some narrow fertile coastal strips.

CLIMATE

Blistering heat in the north. Summer temperatures often climb above 45°C (113°F). Southern uplands receive rains June–September.

PEOPLE AND SOCIETY

Most Omanis still live on the land, especially in the south. The majority are Ibadi Muslims who follow an appointed leader, the Imam. Ibadism is not opposed to freedom for women, and a few women hold positions of authority. Baluchis from Pakistan are the largest group of foreign workers.

◆ *INSIGHT: Until the late 1980s, Oman was closed to all but business or official visitors*

THE ECONOMY

Oil accounts for most export revenue. Gas is set to eventually supplant oil. Other exports include fish, dates, limes and coconuts.

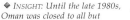

2000m/6562ft
1000m/3281ft
500m/1640ft
200m/656ft
Sea Level
Strait of Hormuz
Al Khaşab
Musandam Peninsula
Gulf of Oman
UAE
Şuḩār
Maţrah
MUSCAT
Al Khabūrah
Al Qābil
Ar Rustāq
Al Hadd
Bahlah
Samā'il
Şūr
Nazwá
SAUDI ARABIA
Arabian Sea
Rub' Al Khālī
INDIAN OCEAN
YEMEN
Şalahah
100 km
100 miles

FACT FILE

OFFICIAL NAME: Sultanate of Oman
DATE OF FORMATION: 1650 / 1951
CAPITAL: Muscat
POPULATION: 1.7 million
TOTAL AREA: 212,460 sq km (82,030 sq miles)
DENSITY: 8 people per sq km
LANGUAGES: Arabic*, Baluchi, other
RELIGIONS: Ibadi Muslim 75%, other Muslim 11%, Hindu 14%
ETHNIC MIX: Arab 75%, Baluchi 15%, other (mainly South Asian) 10%
GOVERNMENT: Monarchy with Consultative Council
CURRENCY: Rial = 1,000 baizas

UNITED ARAB EMIRATES

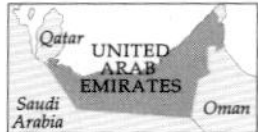
Qatar
UNITED ARAB EMIRATES
Saudi Arabia
Oman

BORDERING THE Persian Gulf on the northern coast of the Arabian peninsula is the United Arab Emirates, a federation of seven states.

GEOGRAPHY
Mostly flat, semi-arid desert with sand dunes, salt pans and occasional oases. Cities are watered by extensive irrigation systems.

CLIMATE
Summers are humid, despite minimal rainfall. Sand-laden *shamal* winds blow in winter and spring.

PEOPLE AND SOCIETY
People are mostly Sunni Muslims of Bedouin descent, and largely city-dwellers. In theory, women enjoy equal rights with men. Poverty is rare. Emirians make up only one fifth of the population. They are outnumbered by immigrants who arrived during 1970s oil boom. Western expatriates are permitted a virtually unrestricted lifestyle. Islamic fundamentalism, however, is a growing force among the young.

THE ECONOMY
Major exporter of oil and natural gas. Fish and shellfish are caught in the Persian Gulf, as well as oysters for their pearls. Most food and raw materials are imported.

◆ INSIGHT: *At present levels of production the country's crude oil reserves should last for over 100 years*

500m/1640ft
200m/656ft
Sea Level
0 50 km
0 50 miles
Persian Gulf
OMAN
Ras al Khaimah
Sharjah
Dubai
Fujairah
QATAR
ABU DHABI
Al Maqta'
Ghuwayfāt
Ţarīf
Al 'Ayn
Ḩabshān
OMAN
SAUDI ARABIA

FACT FILE

OFFICIAL NAME: United Arab Emirates
DATE OF FORMATION: 1971
CAPITAL: Abu Dhabi
POPULATION: 1.7 million
TOTAL AREA: 83,600 sq km (32,278 sq miles)
DENSITY: 20 people per sq km
LANGUAGES: Arabic*, Farsi (Persian), Urdu, Hindi, English
RELIGIONS: Sunni Muslim 77%, Shi'a Muslim 19% other 4%
ETHNIC MIX: South Asian 50%, Emirian 19%, other Arab 23%, other 8%
GOVERNMENT: Federation of monarchs
CURRENCY: Dirham = 100 fils

QATAR

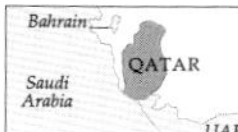
Bahrain
QATAR
Saudi Arabia
UAE

PROJECTING NORTH from the Arabian peninsula into the Persian Gulf, Qatar's reserves of oil and gas make it one of the region's wealthiest states.

GEOGRAPHY

Flat, semi-arid desert with sand dunes and salt pans. Vegetation limited to small patches of scrub.

CLIMATE

Hot and humid. Summer temperatures soar to over 40°C (104°F). Rainfall is rare.

PEOPLE AND SOCIETY

Only one in five Qataris is native-born. Most of the population are guest workers from the Indian subcontinent, Iran and North Africa. Qataris were once nomadic Bedouins, but since advent of oil wealth, have become city-dwellers. As a result, the north is dotted with abandoned villages. Political and religious life is dominated by the ruling Al-Thani family.

◆ *INSIGHT: There are over 700 mosques in the capital, Doha*

THE ECONOMY

Steady supply of crude oil and huge gas reserves, plus related industries. Economy is heavily dependent on foreign work force. All raw materials and most foods, except vegetables, are imported.

Ar Ru'ays
Al Khuwayr
Gulf of Bahrain
Madīnat al Ka'bān
Al Khawr
200m/656ft
Sea Level
Ash Shaḩanīyah
Madīnat Khalīfa
Al Gharrāfah
DOHA
Ar Rayyān
Umm Bāb
Al Wakrah
As Salwá
Persian Gulf
SAUDI ARABIA
UAE
0 30 km
0 30 miles

FACT FILE

OFFICIAL NAME: State of Qatar
DATE OF FORMATION: 1971
CAPITAL: Doha
POPULATION: 500,000
TOTAL AREA: 11,000 sq km (4,247 sq miles)
DENSITY: 45 people per sq km)
LANGUAGES: Arabic*, Farsi (Persian), Urdu, Hindi, English
RELIGIONS: Sunni Muslim 86%, Hindu 10%, Christian 4%
ETHNIC MIX: Arab 40%, South Asian 35%, Persian 12%, other 13%
GOVERNMENT: Absolute monarchy
CURRENCY: Riyal = 100 dirhams

BAHRAIN

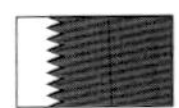

Iran
BAHRAIN
Qatar
Saudi Arabia

BAHRAIN IS an archipelago of 33 islands between the Qatar peninsula and the Saudi Arabian mainland. Only three islands are inhabited.

GEOGRAPHY

All islands are low-lying. The largest, Bahrain Island, is mainly sandy plains and salt marshes.

CLIMATE

Summers are hot and humid. Winters are mild. Low rainfall.

PEOPLE AND SOCIETY

Largely Muslim population is divided between Shi'a majority and Sunni minority. Tensions between the two groups. Ruling Sunni class hold the best jobs in bureaucracy and business. Shi'ites tend to do menial work. Al-Khalifa family has ruled since 1783. Regime is autocratic and political dissent is not tolerated. Bahrain is the most liberal of the Gulf States. Women have access to education and jobs.

◆ *INSIGHT: Bahrain was the first Gulf emirate to export oil, in the 1930s*

THE ECONOMY

Main exports are refined petroleum and aluminium products. As oil reserves run out, gas is of increasing importance. Bahrain is also the Arab world's major offshore banking centre.

Persian Gulf
Jazīrat al Muḩarraq
Al Busaytīn
Al Muḩarraq
Jidd Ḩafş
MANAMA
To mainland (Saudi Arabia)
Madīnat 'Īsá
Sitrah
26°10'
Ar Rifā' al Gharbī
Ar Rifā' ash Sharqī
Umm an Na'sān
Gulf of Bahrain
Bahrain
26°
Gulf of Bahrain
200m/656ft
Sea Level
50°30'
25°50'
50°40'
0
10 km
0
10 miles

FACT FILE

OFFICIAL NAME: State of Bahrain
DATE OF FORMATION: 1971
CAPITAL: Manama
POPULATION: 500,000
TOTAL AREA: 680 sq km (263 sq miles)
DENSITY: 735 people per sq km
LANGUAGES: Arabic*, English, Urdu
RELIGIONS: Muslim (Shi'a majority) 85%, Christian 7%, other 8%
ETHNIC MIX: Arab 73%, South Asian 14%, Persian 8%, other 5%
GOVERNMENT: Absolute monarchy (emirate)
CURRENCY: Dinar = 1,000 fils

KUWAIT

Iraq
KUWAIT
Saudi Arabia

KUWAIT LIES on the north of the Persian Gulf. The state was a British protectorate from 1914 until 1961, when full independence was granted.

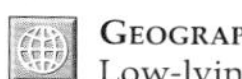

GEOGRAPHY

Low-lying desert. Lowest land in the north. Cultivation is only possible along the coast.

CLIMATE

Summers are very hot and dry. Winters are cooler, with some rain and occasional frost.

PEOPLE AND SOCIETY

Oil-rich monarchy, ruled by the Al-Sabah family. Oil wealth has attracted workers from India, Pakistan and other Arab states. In 1990, Iraq invaded Kuwait, claiming it as a province. A US-led alliance, backed by the UN, ousted Iraqi forces following a short war in 1991. Many foreign workers expelled after the war, in attempt to ensure Kuwaiti majority.

◆ *INSIGHT: During the Gulf War, 800 of Kuwait's 950 oil wells were damaged*

THE ECONOMY

Oil and gas production has been restored to pre-invasion levels. Skilled labour, raw materials and food have to be imported. Vulnerability to Iraqi attack deters Western industrial investment.

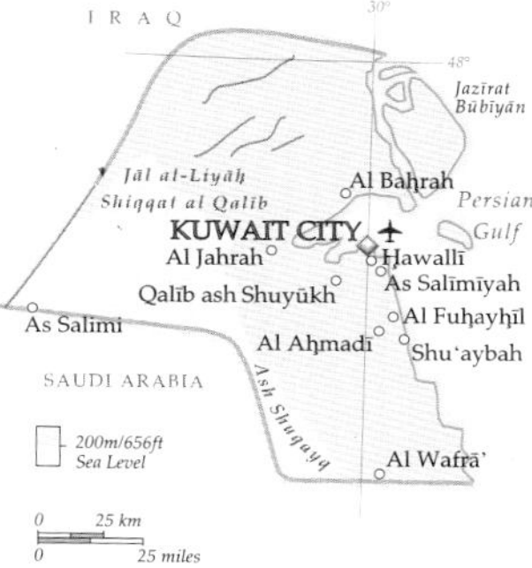
IRAQ
30°
48°
Jazīrat Būbiyān
Jāl al-Liyāḥ
Shiqqat al Qalīb
Al Baḥrah
Persian Gulf
KUWAIT CITY
Al Jahrah
Ḩawallī
As Salimiyah
Qalīb ash Shuyūkh
Al Fuḥayḥīl
As Salimi
Al Aḥmadī
Shu'aybah
SAUDI ARABIA
Ash Shuqayq
200m/656ft
Sea Level
Al Wafrā'
0 25 km
0 25 miles

FACT FILE

OFFICIAL NAME: State of Kuwait
DATE OF FORMATION: 1961 / 1981
CAPITAL: Kuwait City
POPULATION: 1.8 million
TOTAL AREA: 17,820 sq km (6,880 sq miles)
DENSITY: 112 people per sq km
LANGUAGES: Arabic*, English, other
RELIGIONS: Muslim 92%, Christian 6%, other 2%
ETHNIC MIX: Arab 85%, South Asian 9%, Persian 4%, other 2%
GOVERNMENT: Constitutional monarchy
CURRENCY: Dinar = 1,000 fils

IRAQ

Turkey
Syria
Iran
IRAQ
Jordan
Kuwait
Saudi Arabia

IRAQ IS situated in the central Middle East. Since the removal of the monarchy in 1958, it has experienced considerable political turmoil.

GEOGRAPHY

Mainly desert. Rivers Tigris and Euphrates water fertile regions and create southern marshland. Mountains along northeast border.

CLIMATE

South has hot, dry summers and mild winters. North has dry summers, but winters can be harsh in the mountains. Rainfall is low.

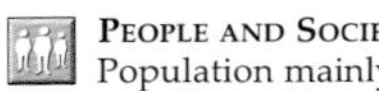

PEOPLE AND SOCIETY

Population mainly Arab and Kurdish. Small minorities of Turks and Persians. After coming to power in 1979, President Saddam Hussein led the country into an inconclusive war with Iran (1980–88). In 1990, invasion of Kuwait precipitated the Gulf War against UN forces. In recent years, drainage schemes in the southern marshlands have threatened the ancient and unique lifestyle of the Marsh Arabs.

THE ECONOMY

Gulf War and resulting UN sanctions had a devastating effect. Iraq is unable to sell its oil on the international market.

◆ *INSIGHT: As Mesopotamia, Iraq was the site where the Sumerians established the world's first civilization c. 4,000 BC*

0 100 km
0 100 miles
TURKEY
Al Mawşil
Arbīl
As Sulaymānīyah
36°
SYRIA
Tigris
Kirkūk
IRAN
40°
Euphrates
Buhayrat ath Tharthār
Ba'qūbah
Ar Ramādī
Syrian Desert
BAGHDAD
JORDAN
Karbalā
32°
Al 'Amārah
SAUDI ARABIA
An Najaf
Euphrates
An Nāsirīyah
Tigris
Al Başrah
3000m/9843ft
2000m/6562ft
1000m/3281ft
500m/1640ft
200m/656ft
Sea Level
30°
KUWAIT
44°
48°

FACT FILE

OFFICIAL NAME: Republic of Iraq
DATE OF FORMATION: 1932/1981
CAPITAL: Baghdad
POPULATION: 21 million
TOTAL AREA: 438,320 sq km (169,235 sq miles)
DENSITY: 48 people per sq km
LANGUAGES: Arabic*, Kurdish, Turkish, Farsi (Persian)
RELIGIONS: Shi'a Muslim 63%, Sunni Muslim 34%, other 3%
ETHNIC MIX: Arab 79%, Kurdish 16%, Persian 3%, Turkish 2%
GOVERNMENT: Single-party republic
CURRENCY: Dinar = 1,000 fils

IRAN

Turkmenistan
Iraq
IRAN
Afghanistan
Saudi Arabia
Pakistan

SINCE THE 1979 revolution led by Ayatollah Khomeini, the Middle Eastern country of Iran has become the world's largest theocracy.

GEOGRAPHY

High desert plateau with large salt pans in the east. West and north are mountainous. Fertile coastal land borders Caspian Sea.

CLIMATE

Mostly desert climate. Hot summers, and bitterly cold winters. Area around the Caspian Sea is more temperate.

PEOPLE AND SOCIETY

Many ethnic groups, including Persians, Azerbaijanis and Kurds. Large number of refugees, mainly from Afghanistan. Since 1979 Islamic revolution, political life has been dominated by militant Islamic idealism. Mullahs' belief that adherence to religious values is more important than economic welfare has resulted in declining living standards. The role of women in public life is restricted.

THE ECONOMY

One of the world's biggest oil producers. Government restricts contact with the West, blocking acquisition of vital technology. High unemployment and inflation.

◆ *INSIGHT: In Iran, a total of 109 offences carry the death penalty*

AZERBAIJAN
TURKEY
TURKMENISTAN
Ardabīl
Tabrīz
Orūmīyeh
Caspian Sea
Mashhad
TEHRĀN
Qom
Bākhtarān
Arāk
Eşfahān
Plateau of Iran
AFGHANISTAN
IRAQ
Ahvāz
Khorramshahr
Ābādān
Kermān
Zāhedān
PAKISTAN
KUWAIT
Shīrāz
Persian Gulf
Bandar-e 'Abbās
3000m/9843ft
2000m/6562ft
1000m/3281ft
500m/1640ft
200m/656ft
Sea Level
0 200 km
0 200 miles

FACT FILE

OFFICIAL NAME: Islamic Republic of Iran
DATE OF FORMATION: 1906
CAPITAL: Tehran
POPULATION: 68.7 million
TOTAL AREA: 1,648,000 sq km (636,293 sq miles)
DENSITY: 42 people per sq km
LANGUAGES: Farsi (Persian)*, other
RELIGIONS: Shi'a Muslim 95%, Sunni Muslim 4%, other 1%
ETHNIC MIX: Persian 52%, Azerbaijani 24%, Kurdish 9%, other 15%
GOVERNMENT: Islamic republic
CURRENCY: Rial = 100 dinars

TURKMENISTAN

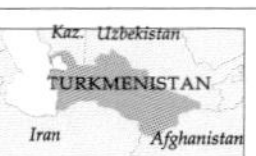
Kaz.
Uzbekistan
TURKMENISTAN
Iran
Afghanistan

STRETCHING FROM the Caspian Sea into the deserts of Central Asia, the ex-Soviet state of Turkmenistan has adjusted better than most to independence.

GEOGRAPHY

Low Karakumy desert covers 80% of the country. Mountains on southern border with Iran. Fertile Amu Darya valley in north.

CLIMATE

Arid desert climate with extreme summer heat, but sub-freezing winter temperatures.

PEOPLE AND SOCIETY

Before Tsarist Russia annexed the country in 1884, the Turkmen were a largely nomadic tribal people. Today, the tribal unit remains strong, with most of the population clustered around desert oases. Generally peaceful relations between Turkmen and Uzbek and Russian minorities. Resurgence of Islam fosters ties with its Muslim neighbours to the south.

THE ECONOMY

Abundant reserves of natural gas. Least industrialized of the ex-Soviet states. Large cotton crop, but most food has to be imported.

◆ *INSIGHT: Ashgabat is a breeding centre for the Akhal-Teke, a prized racehorse able to maintain its speed in the desert*

KAZAKHSTAN
Zaliv Kara-Bogaz-Gol
Këneurgench
Dashkhovuz
UZBEKISTAN
Krasnovodsk
Nebitdag
Amu Darya
Gumdag
Gyzylarbat
Caspian Sea
Karakumy
Chardzhev
ASHGABAT
IRAN
Tedzhen
Mary
Kerki
Karakumskiy Kanal
1000m/3281ft
500m/1640ft
200m/656ft
Sea Level
Below Sea Level
Gushgy
AFGHANISTAN
0 200 km
0 200 miles

FACT FILE

OFFICIAL NAME: Republic of Turkmenistan
DATE OF FORMATION: 1991
CAPITAL: Ashgabat
POPULATION: 4 million
TOTAL AREA: 488,100 sq km (188,455 sq miles)
DENSITY: 8 people per sq km
LANGUAGES: Turkmen*, Uzbek, other
RELIGIONS: Muslim 85%, Eastern Orthodox 10%, other 5%
ETHNIC MIX: Turkmen 72%, Russian 9%, Uzbek 9%, other 10%
GOVERNMENT: Single-party republic
CURRENCY: Manat = 100 tenge

UZBEKISTAN

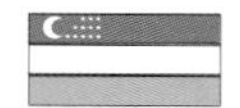

Kazakhstan
UZBEKISTAN
Turkmenistan
Tajiki.
Afghanistan

SHARING THE Aral Sea coastline with its northern neighbour, Kazakhstan, Uzbekistan lies on the ancient Silk Road between Asia and Europe.

GEOGRAPHY

Arid and semi-arid plains in much of the west. Fertile, irrigated eastern farmland below peaks of the western Pamirs.

CLIMATE

Harsh continental climate. Summers can be extremely hot and dry, winters are cold.

PEOPLE AND SOCIETY

Complex ethnic make-up, with potential for racial and regional conflict. Ex-communists are in firm control, but traditional social patterns based on family, religion, clan and region have re-emerged. Population is concentrated in the fertile east. High birth rates, continued low status of women. Constitutional measures aim to control influence of Islam.

THE ECONOMY

Strong agricultural sector, led by cotton production. Large unexploited deposits of oil and natural gas, gold and uranium. Very limited economic reform.

◆ INSIGHT: *The Aral Sea has shrunk to half of the area it covered in 1960, due to diversion of rivers for irrigation*

3000m/9843ft
2000m/6562ft
1000m/3281ft
500m/1640ft
200m/656ft
Sea Level
Aral Sea
KAZAKHSTAN
Nukus
Kyzyl Kum
Khodzheyli
Turan Lowland
Urgench
Amu Darya
KYRGY.
Chirchik
TASHKENT
Angren
Ozero Aydarkul'
Almalyk
Andizhan
Navoi
Fergana
Bukhara
KYRGY.
Samarkand
TURKMENISTAN
Karshi
TAJIKISTAN
0 100 km
0 100 miles
AFGHANISTAN

FACT FILE

OFFICIAL NAME: Republic of Uzbekistan
DATE OF FORMATION: 1991
CAPITAL: Tashkent
POPULATION: 21.9 million
TOTAL AREA: 1,138,910 sq km (439,733 sq miles)
DENSITY: 47 people per sq km
LANGUAGES: Uzbek*, Russian, other
RELIGIONS: Muslim 88%, other (mostly Eastern Orthodox) 12%
ETHNIC MIX: Uzbek 71%, Russian 8%, Tajik 5%, Kazakh 4%, other 12%
GOVERNMENT: Single-party republic
CURRENCY: Sum = 100 teen

KAZAKHSTAN

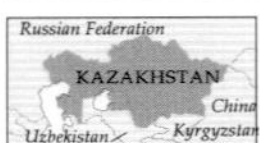
Russian Federation
KAZAKHSTAN
China
Uzbekistan
Kyrgyzstan

LARGEST OF the former Soviet republics, mineral-rich Kazakhstan has the potential to become the major Central Asian economic power.

GEOGRAPHY

Mainly steppe. Volga delta and Caspian Sea in the west. Central plateau. Mountains in the east. Semi-desert in the south.

CLIMATE

Dry continental. Hottest summers in desert south, coldest winters in northern steppes.

PEOPLE AND SOCIETY

Kazakhs only just outnumber Russians in a multi-ethnic society. Stable relations with Russia, plus increased international profile, preserve relative harmony. Few Kazakhs maintain a nomadic lifestyle, but Islam and loyalty to the three Hordes (clan federations) remain strong. Wealth is concentrated among former communists in the capital.

THE ECONOMY

Vast mineral resources, notably gas, oil, coal, uranium and gold. Increasing foreign investment, but living standards have fallen with market reforms to date.

◆ *INSIGHT: Russia's space programme was based at Baykonur, in the south*

FACT FILE

OFFICIAL NAME: Republic of Kazakhstan
DATE OF FORMATION: 1991
CAPITAL: Alma-Ata
POPULATION: 17.2 million
TOTAL AREA: 2,717,300 sq km (1,049,150 sq miles)
DENSITY: 6 people per sq km
LANGUAGES: Kazakh*, Russian, other
RELIGIONS: Muslim 47%, other 53% (mostly Russian Orthodox, Lutheran)
ETHNIC MIX: Kazakh 40%, Russian 38%, Ukrainian 6%, other 16%
GOVERNMENT: Multiparty republic
CURRENCY: Tenge = 100 tein

MONGOLIA

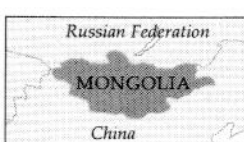
Russian Federation
MONGOLIA
China

LYING BETWEEN Russia and China, Mongolia is a vast and isolated country with a tiny population. Over two-thirds of the country is desert.

GEOGRAPHY

High steppe plateau, with mountains in the north. Lakes in the north and west. Desert region of the Gobi dominates the south.

CLIMATE

Continental. Mild summers, and long, dry, very cold winters, with heavy snowfall. Temperatures can drop to −30°C (−22°F).

PEOPLE AND SOCIETY

Mongolia was unified by Genghis Khan in 1206 and was later absorbed into Manchu China. It became a communist People's Republic in 1924, and after 66 years of Soviet-style communist rule, introduced democracy in 1990. Most Mongolians still follow a traditional nomadic way of life, living in circular felt tents called *gers*. Others live on state-run farms.

THE ECONOMY

Rich in oil, coal, copper and other minerals, which were barely exploited under communism. In 1990s, some shift in agriculture away from traditional herding and towards a market economy.

◆ *INSIGHT: Horse-racing, wrestling and archery are the national sports. During the* Nadam *festival each July, competitions are held all over Mongolia*

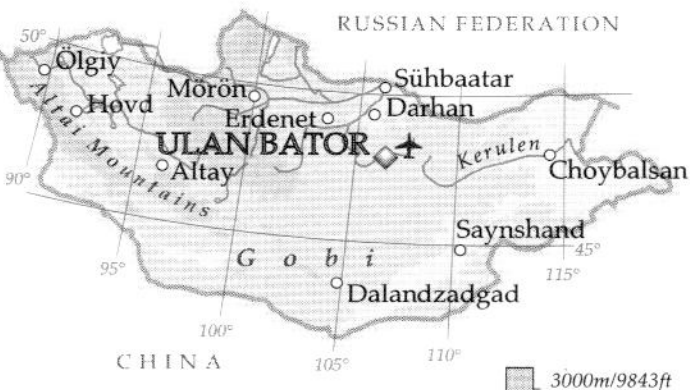
RUSSIAN FEDERATION
Ölgiy
Hovd
Altai Mountains
Mörön
Erdenet
Sühbaatar
Darhan
ULAN BATOR
Kerulen
Choybalsan
Altay
Saynshand
G o b i
Dalandzadgad
CHINA
50°
90°
95°
100°
105°
110°
115°
45°
0 400 km
0 400 miles
3000m/9843ft
2000m/6562ft
1000m/3281ft
500m/1640ft

FACT FILE

OFFICIAL NAME: Mongolia
DATE OF FORMATION: 1924
CAPITAL: Ulan Bator
POPULATION: 2.4 million
TOTAL AREA: 1,565,000 sq km (604,247 sq miles)
DENSITY: 1.4 people per sq km
LANGUAGES: Khalkha Mongol*, Turkic, Russian, Chinese
RELIGIONS: Predominantly Tibetan Buddhist, with a Muslim minority
ETHNIC MIX: Khalkha Mongol 90%, Kazakh 4%, Chinese 2%, other 4%
GOVERNMENT: Multiparty republic
CURRENCY: Tughrik = 100 möngös

KYRGYZSTAN

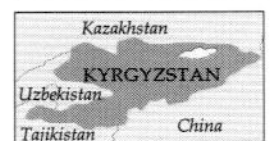
Kazakhstan
KYRGYZSTAN
Uzbekistan
China
Tajikistan

A MOUNTAINOUS, land-locked state in Central Asia. The most rural of the ex-Soviet republics, it only gradually developed its own cultural nationalism.

GEOGRAPHY

Mountainous spurs of Tien Shan range have glaciers, alpine meadows, forests and narrow valleys. Semi-desert in the west.

CLIMATE

Varies from permanent snow and cold deserts at altitude, to hot deserts in low regions.

PEOPLE AND SOCIETY

Ethnic Kyrgyz majority status dates only from the late 1980s, and is due to their higher birth rate. Considerable tension between Kyrgyz and other groups, particularly Uzbeks. Large Russian community no longer wields power, but is seen as necessary for transfer of skills. Concerns over rising crime rate and opium poppy cultivation accompany political reforms.

THE ECONOMY

Still dominated by the state, and tradition of collective farming. Small quantities of commercially exploitable coal, oil and gas. Great hydroelectric power potential.

◆ *INSIGHT: Kyrgyz folklore is based around the 1,000-year-old epic poem,* Manas, *which takes a week to recite*

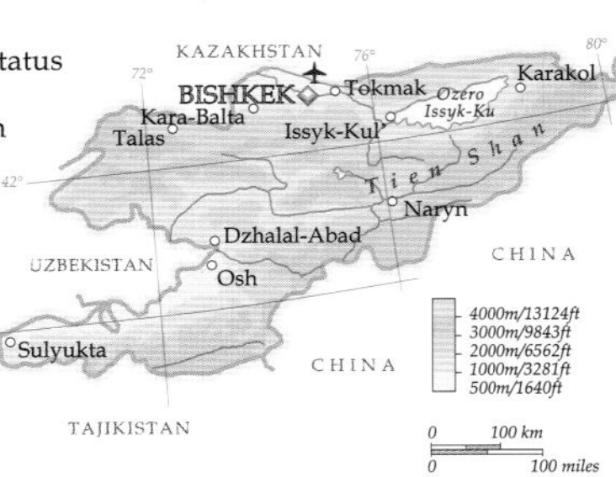
KAZAKHSTAN
BISHKEK
Tokmak
Karakol
Ozero Issyk-Ku
Kara-Balta
Talas
Issyk-Kul
Tien Shan
Naryn
Dzhalal-Abad
UZBEKISTAN
Osh
CHINA
Sulyukta
CHINA
TAJIKISTAN
72°
76°
80°
42°
40°
4000m/13124ft
3000m/9843ft
2000m/6562ft
1000m/3281ft
500m/1640ft
0 100 km
0 100 miles

FACT FILE

OFFICIAL NAME: Kyrgyz Republic
DATE OF FORMATION: 1991
CAPITAL: Bishkek
POPULATION: 4.6 million
TOTAL AREA: 198,500 sq km (76,640 sq miles)
DENSITY: 23 people per sq km
LANGUAGES: Kyrgyz*, Russian, Uzbek
RELIGIONS: Muslim 65%, other (mostly Russian Orthodox) 35%
ETHNIC MIX: Kyrgyz 52%, Russian 21%, Uzbek 13%, other (mostly Kazakh and Tajik) 14%
GOVERNMENT: Mutiparty republic
CURRENCY: Som = 100 teen

TAJIKISTAN

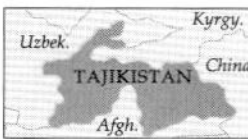
Kyrgy.
Uzbek.
TAJIKISTAN
China
Afgh.

LIES LAND-LOCKED on the western slopes of the Pamirs in Central Asia. The Tajiks' language and traditions are similiar to those of Iran.

GEOGRAPHY

Mainly mountainous: bare slopes of Pamir ranges cover most of the country. Small, but fertile Fergana Valley in northwest.

CLIMATE

Continental extremes in valleys. Bitterly cold winters in mountains. Low rainfall.

PEOPLE AND SOCIETY

Conflict between Tajiks, a Persian people, and minority Uzbeks (of Turkic origin), coupled with civil war between supporters of the government and Tajik Islamic rebels. Despite a ceasefire in late 1994, clashes continued in 1995. Already low living standards have been worsened by the conflict. Many Russians have left, to escape discrimination.

THE ECONOMY

Formal economy crippled by conflict. All sectors in decline, barter economy is widespread. Uranium potential and hydro-electric schemes depend on peace.

◆ *INSIGHT: Carpet-making, an ancient tradition learned from Persia, was a major source of revenue before the war*

0 100 km
0 100 miles
4000m/13124ft
3000m/9843ft
2000m/6562ft
1000m/3281ft
500m/1640ft
200m/656ft
UZBEKISTAN
Fergana Valley
Khudzhand
Isfara
KYRGYZSTAN
Ura-Tyube
CHINA
Pendzhikent
DUSHANBE
Pamirs
Nurek
Kurgan-Tyube
Kulyab
Khorog
Amu Darya
Parkhar
AFGHANISTAN
PAKISTAN

FACT FILE

OFFICIAL NAME: Republic of Tajikistan
DATE OF FORMATION: 1991
CAPITAL: Dushanbe
POPULATION: 5.7 million
TOTAL AREA: 143,100 sq km (55,251 sq miles)
DENSITY: 39 people per sq km
LANGUAGES: Tajik*, Uzbek, Russian
RELIGIONS: Sunni Muslim 85%, Shi'a Muslim 5%, other 10%
ETHNIC MIX: Tajik 62%, Uzbek 24%, Russian 4%, Tatar 2%, other 8%
GOVERNMENT: Single-party republic
CURRENCY: Tajik rouble = 100 kopeks

AFGHANISTAN

Turkmen.
Uzbek
Tajik
China
AFGHANISTAN
Iran
Pakistan

LAND-LOCKED IN southwestern Asia, about three-quarters of Afghanistan is inaccessible. Civil war means the country effectively has no government.

GEOGRAPHY

Predominantly mountainous. Highest range is the Hindu Kush. Mountains are bordered by fertile plains. Desert plateau in the south.

CLIMATE

Harsh continental. Hot, dry summers. Cold winters with heavy snow, especially in Hindu Kush.

PEOPLE AND SOCIETY

In 1979, Soviet forces invaded to support communist government against Islamic guerrillas. Last Soviet troops pulled out in 1989. Civil war continues between Pashtuns, the country's traditional rulers, and minority groups of Tajiks, Hazaras and Uzbeks. Health and education systems have collapsed. Many Afghans are nomadic sheep farmers and most live in extreme poverty.

THE ECONOMY

Economy has collapsed. The largest sector, agriculture, has been damaged. Illicit opium trade is the main currency earner.

◆ *INSIGHT: The UN estimates that it will take 100 years to remove the ten million land-mines laid in the country*

70°
65°
35°
30°
TAJIKISTAN
UZBEK
TURKMENISTAN
Feyzābād
Mazār-e Sharīf
Kunduz
Baghlan
Hindu Kush
Meymaneh
Charīkār
Herāt
KĀBUL
Jalālābād
Khyber Pass
Ghaznī
PAKISTAN
Gereshk
Kandahār
IRAN
3000m/9843ft
2000m/6562ft
1000m/3281ft
500m/1640ft
200m/656ft
0 100 km
0 100 miles

FACT FILE

OFFICIAL NAME: Islamic State of Afghanistan
DATE OF FORMATION: 1919
CAPITAL: Kābul
POPULATION: 20.5 million
TOTAL AREA: 652,090 sq km (251,770 sq miles)
DENSITY: 29 people per sq km
LANGUAGES: Persian*, Pashtu*, other
RELIGIONS: Sunni Muslim 84%, Shi'a Muslim 15%, other 1%
ETHNIC MIX: Pashtun 38%, Tajik 25%, Hazara 19%, Uzbek 6%, other 12%
GOVERNMENT: *Mujahideen* coalition
CURRENCY: Afghani = 100 puls

PAKISTAN

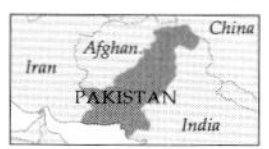
China
Afghan.
Iran
PAKISTAN
India

ONCE A part of British India, Pakistan was created in 1947 as an independent Muslim state. Today, it is divided into four provinces.

GEOGRAPHY

East and south is great flood plain drained by River Indus. Hindu Kush range in north. West is semi-desert plateau and mountains.

CLIMATE

Temperatures can soar to 50°C (122°F) in south and west, and fall to –20°C (–4°F) in the Hindu Kush.

PEOPLE AND SOCIETY

Majority Punjabis control bureaucracy and the army. Many tensions with minority groups. Vast gap between rich and poor. Bonded labourers, often recent converts to Islam, or Christians, form the underclass. Strong family ties, reflected in dynastic and nepotistic political system.

◆ *INSIGHT: In 1988, Pakistan elected the first female prime minister in the Muslim world*

THE ECONOMY

Leading producer of cotton and rice, but unpredictable weather conditions often affect the crop. Oil, gas reserves. Inefficient, haphazard government economic policies.

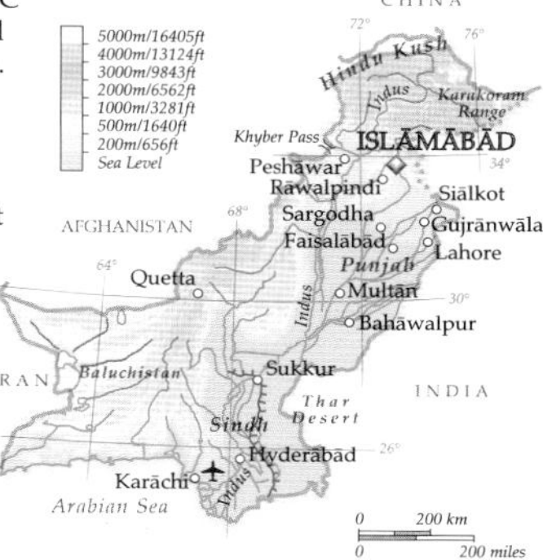
CHINA
5000m/16405ft
4000m/13124ft
3000m/9843ft
2000m/6562ft
1000m/3281ft
500m/1640ft
200m/656ft
Sea Level
Hindu Kush
Indus
Karakoram Range
Khyber Pass
ISLĀMĀBĀD
Peshāwar
Rāwalpindi
Siālkot
Sargodha
Gujrānwāla
AFGHANISTAN
Faisalābād
Lahore
Punjab
Quetta
Multān
Indus
Bahāwalpur
IRAN
Baluchistan
Sukkur
INDIA
Thar Desert
Sindh
Hyderābād
Karāchi
Indus
Arabian Sea
0 200 km
0 200 miles

FACT FILE

OFFICIAL NAME: Islamic Republic of Pakistan

DATE OF FORMATION: 1947 / 1972

CAPITAL: Islāmābād

POPULATION: 144.5 million

TOTAL AREA: 796,100 sq km (307,374 sq miles)

DENSITY: 182 people per sq km

LANGUAGES: Urdu*, Punjabi, other

RELIGIONS: Sunni Muslim 77%, Shi'a Muslim 20%, Hindu 2%, Christian 1%

ETHNIC MIX: Punjabi 56%, Sindhi 13%, Pashtun 8%, other 23%

GOVERNMENT: Multiparty republic

CURRENCY: Rupee = 100 paisa

NEPAL

China
NEPAL
India

NEPAL LIES between India and China, on the shoulder of the southern Himalayan mountains. It is one of the world's poorest countries.

GEOGRAPHY

Mainly mountainous. Includes some of the highest mountains in the world, such as Everest. Flat, fertile river plains in the south.

CLIMATE

July–October warm monsoon. Rest of year dry, sunny, mild. Valley temperatures in Himalayas may average −10°C (14°F).

PEOPLE AND SOCIETY

Few ethnic tensions, despite the variety of ethnic groups, including the Sherpas in the north, Terai peoples in the south, and the Newars, found mostly in the Kathmandu valley. Women's subordinate position enshrined in law. Hindu women are the most restricted. In 1991, first democratic elections for over 30 years ended period of absolute rule by the king.

THE ECONOMY

90% of the people work on the land. Crops include rice, maize and millet. Dependent on foreign aid. Tourism is growing. Great potential for hydroelectric power.

◆ *INSIGHT: Southern Nepal was the birthplace of Buddha (Prince Siddhartha Gautama), in 563 BC*

5000m/16405ft
4000m/13124ft
3000m/9843ft
2000m/6562ft
1000m/3281ft
500m/1640ft
200m/656ft
Sea Level
Dadeldhura
Jumla
Himalayas
CHINA
Baglung
Pokhara
Mt. Everest 8848m (Sagarmatha)
KATHMANDU
Bhaktapur
Lalitpur
Ilam
Janakpur
Biratnagar
INDIA
0 100 km
0 100 miles

FACT FILE

OFFICIAL NAME: Kingdom of Nepal
DATE OF FORMATION: 1769
CAPITAL: Kathmandu
POPULATION: 21.1 million
TOTAL AREA: 140,800 sq km (54,363 sq miles)
DENSITY: 151 people per sq km
LANGUAGES: Nepali*, Maithilli, other
RELIGIONS: Hindu 90%, Buddhist 5%, Muslim 3%, other 2%
ETHNIC MIX: Nepalese 58%, Bihari 19%, Tamang 6%, other 17%
GOVERNMENT: Constitutional monarchy
CURRENCY: Rupee = 100 paisa

BHUTAN

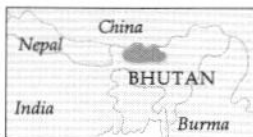
China
Nepal
BHUTAN
India
Burma

PERCHED IN the eastern Himalayas between India and China, the land-locked kingdom of Bhutan is largely closed to the outside world.

GEOGRAPHY

Low, tropical southern strip rising through fertile central valleys to high Himalayas in the north. Two-thirds of the land is forested.

CLIMATE

South is tropical, north is alpine, cold and harsh. Central valleys warmer in east than west.

PEOPLE AND SOCIETY

The king is absolute monarch, head of both state and government. Most people originate from Tibet, and are devoutly Buddhist. 25% are Hindu Nepalese, who settled in the south. Bhutan has 20 languages. In 1988, Dzongkha (a Tibetan dialect) was made the official language and Nepali was banned. Many southerners deported as illegal immigrants, creating fierce ethnic tensions.

THE ECONOMY

Reliant upon aid from, and trade with, India. 80% of people farm their own plots of land and herd cattle and yaks. Development of cash crops for Asian markets.

◆INSIGHT: TV is banned on the grounds that it might dilute Bhutanese values

0 50 km
0 50 miles
5000m/16405ft
4000m/13124ft
3000m/9843ft
2000m/6562ft
1000m/3281ft
500m/1640ft
200m/656ft
Sea Level
CHINA
Himalayas
THIMPHU
Paro International
Wangdi Phodrang
Shemgang
Tashigang
Chhukha
Phuntsholing
Samdrup Jonkhar
INDIA

FACT FILE

OFFICIAL NAME: Kingdom of Bhutan
DATE OF FORMATION: 1865
CAPITAL: Thimphu
POPULATION: 1.7 million
TOTAL AREA: 47,000 sq km (18,147 sq miles)
DENSITY: 34 people per sq km
LANGUAGES: Dzongkha*, Nepali, other
RELIGIONS: Mahayana Buddhist 70%, Hindu 24%, Muslim 5%, other 1%
ETHNIC MIX: Bhutia 61%, Gurung 15%, Assamese 13%, other 11%
GOVERNMENT: Constitutional monarchy
CURRENCY: Ngultrum = 100 chetrum

INDIA

Pakistan
Nepal
China
Bhutan
Bangladesh
INDIA

SEPARATED FROM the rest of Asia by the Himalayan mountain range, India forms a subcontinent. It is the world's second most populous country.

GEOGRAPHY

Three main regions: Himalayan mountains; northern plain between Himalayas and Vindhya Mountains; southern Deccan plateau. The Ghats are smaller mountain ranges on the east and west coasts.

CLIMATE

Varies greatly according to latitude, altitude and season. Most of India has three seasons: hot, wet and cool. In summer, the north is usually hotter than the south, with temperatures often over 40°C (104°F).

PEOPLE AND SOCIETY

Cultural and religious pressures encourage large families. Today, nationwide awareness campaigns aim to promote the idea of smaller families. Most Indians are Hindu. Each Hindu is born into one of thousands of castes and sub-castes, which determine their future status and occupation. Middle class enjoys a very comfortable lifestyle, but at least 30% of Indians live in extreme poverty. In Bombay alone, over 100,000 people live on the streets.

◆ *INSIGHT India's national animal, the tiger, was chosen by the Mohenjo-Daro civilization as their emblem, 4,000 years ago*

5000m/16405ft
4000m/13124ft
3000m/9843ft
2000m/6562ft
1000m/3281ft
500m/1640ft
200m/656ft
Sea Level

0 200 km
0 200 miles

PAKISTAN
Rann of Kachchh
Gulf of Kachchh
Ahmadābā
Jāmnagar
Rājkot
Gulf of Khambha
Arabian Sea

FACT FILE

OFFICIAL NAME: Republic of India
DATE OF FORMATION: 1947 / 1961
CAPITAL: New Delhi
POPULATION: 953 million
TOTAL AREA: 3,287,590 sq km (1,269,338 sq miles)
DENSITY: 290 people per sq km
LANGUAGES: Hindi*, English*, other
RELIGIONS: Hindu 83%, Muslim 11%, Christian 2%, Sikh 2%, other 2%
ETHNIC MIX: Indo-Aryan 72%, Dravidian 25%, Mongoloid and other 3%
GOVERNMENT: Multiparty republic
CURRENCY: Rupee = 100 paisa

THE ECONOMY

Undergoing radical changes from protectionist mixed economy to free market. Increasing foreign investment. New high-tech industries. Principal exports are clothing, jewellery, gems and engineering products.

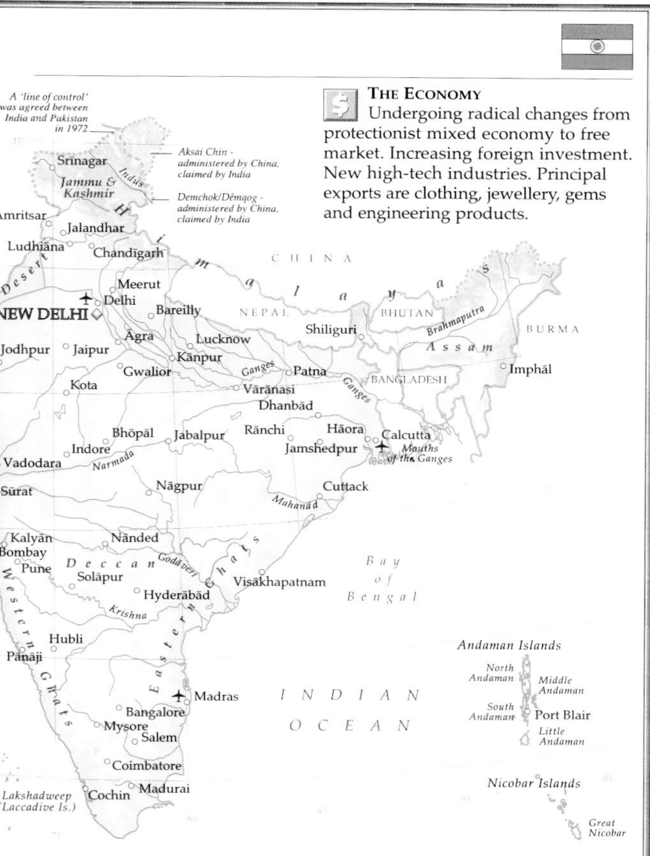

A 'line of control' was agreed between India and Pakistan in 1972
Aksai Chin - administered by China, claimed by India
Demchok/Dêmqog - administered by China, claimed by India
Srinagar
Jammu & Kashmir
Indus
Amritsar
Jalandhar
Ludhiāna
Chandīgarh
Desert
Himalayas
CHINA
Meerut
Delhi
NEW DELHI
Bareilly
NEPAL
BHUTAN
Brahmaputra
BURMA
Shiliguri
Assam
Āgra
Lucknow
Jodhpur
Jaipur
Kānpur
Gwalior
Ganges
Patna
Imphāl
BANGLADESH
Kota
Vārānasi
Dhanbād
Bhōpāl
Jabalpur
Rānchi
Hāora
Calcutta
Indore
Jamshedpur
Mouths of the Ganges
Vadodara
Narmada
Sūrat
Nāgpur
Cuttack
Mahanādi
Kalyān
Nānded
Bombay
Pune
Deccan
Godāvari
Solāpur
Eastern Ghats
Visākhapatnam
Bay of Bengal
Hyderābād
Krishna
Western Ghats
Hubli
Panāji
Andaman Islands
North Andaman
Middle Andaman
South Andaman
Port Blair
Little Andaman
Madras
INDIAN OCEAN
Bangalore
Mysore
Salem
Coimbatore
Nicobar Islands
Madurai
Cochin
Lakshadweep (Laccadive Is.)
Great Nicobar

MALDIVES

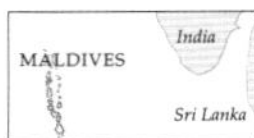
India
MALDIVES
Sri Lanka

THE MALDIVES is an archipelago of 1,190 small coral islands set in the Indian Ocean, southwest of Sri Lanka. Only 202 islands are inhabited.

GEOGRAPHY

Low-lying islands and coral atolls. The larger ones are covered in lush, tropical vegetation.

CLIMATE

Tropical. Rain in all months, but heaviest June–November, during monsoon. Violent storms occasionally hit northern islands.

PEOPLE AND SOCIETY

Maldivians are descended from Sinhalese, Dravidian, Arab and black ancestors. About 25% of the population, who are all Sunni Muslim, live on Male'. Tourism has grown in recent years, but resort islands are separate from settler islands. Politics is restricted to a small group of influential families, and is based around family and clan loyalties rather than formal parties. New young elite is pressing for a more liberal political system.

THE ECONOMY

Too dependent on fluctuating tourist industry, which is the economic mainstay. Fish, especially bonita and tuna, are the leading exports.

◆ *INSIGHT: Rising sea levels, brought about by global warming and climatic changes, are threatening to submerge the islands*

Ihavandippolhu Atoll
Faadhippolhu Atoll
Horsburgh Atoll
Male' Atoll
MALE'
Ari Atoll
Felidhu Atoll
Mulaku Atoll
Kolhumadulu Atoll
Hadhdhunmathi Atoll
One and Half Degree Channel
INDIAN OCEAN
North Huvadhu Atoll
South Huvadhu Atoll
Equator
200m/656ft
Sea Level
0 100 km
0 100 miles
Addu Atoll
Gan
73°

FACT FILE

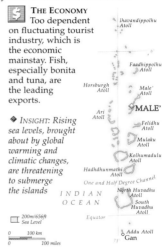

OFFICIAL NAME: Republic of Maldives
DATE OF FORMATION: 1965
CAPITAL: Male'
POPULATION: 200,000
TOTAL AREA: 300 sq km (116 sq miles)
DENSITY: 667 people per sq km
LANGUAGES: Dhivehi (Maldivian)*, Sinhala, Tamil
RELIGIONS: Sunni Muslim 100%
ETHNIC MIX: Maldivian 99%, Sinhalese and other South Asian 1%
GOVERNMENT: Republic
CURRENCY: Rufiyaa = 100 laari

SRI LANKA

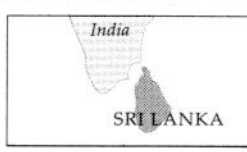
India
SRI LANKA

SEPARATED FROM India by the narrow Palk Strait, Sri Lanka comprises one large island and several coral islets to the northwest.

GEOGRAPHY

Main island is dominated by rugged central highlands. Fertile northern plains dissected by rivers. Much of the land is tropical jungle.

CLIMATE

Tropical, with breezes on the coast and cooler air in highlands. Northeast is driest and hottest.

PEOPLE AND SOCIETY

Majority Sinhalese are mostly Buddhist, minority Tamils are mostly Muslim or Hindu. Since independence from Britain in 1948, Tamils have felt sidelined, and support for secession has grown. Long-standing tensions between the groups erupted into civil war in 1983. Tamils demand an independent state in the north and east.

◆ *INSIGHT: Sri Lanka elected the world's first woman prime minister in 1960*

THE ECONOMY

World's largest tea exporter. Manufacturing now accounts for 60% of export earnings. Civil war is a drain on government funds and deters investors and tourists.

2000m/6562ft
1000m/3281ft
500m/1640ft
200m/656ft
Sea Level
0 50 km
0 50 miles
Palk Strait
Bay of Bengal
Gulf of Mannar
Jaffna
Trincomalee
Anuradhapura
Batticaloa
Negombo
Kandy
COLOMBO
Moratuwa
Sri Jayawardenapura
Ratnapura
INDIAN OCEAN
Galle
Matara

FACT FILE

OFFICIAL NAME: Democratic Socialist Republic of Sri Lanka
DATE OF FORMATION: 1948
CAPITAL: Colombo
POPULATION: 17.9 million
TOTAL AREA: 65,610 sq km (25,332 sq miles)
DENSITY: 273 people per sq km
LANGUAGES: Sinhala*, Tamil, English
RELIGIONS: Buddhist 70%, Hindu 15%, Christian 8%, Muslim 7%
ETHNIC MIX: Sinhalese 74%, Tamil 18%, Sri Lankan Moor 7%, other 1%
GOVERNMENT: Multiparty republic
CURRENCY: Rupee = 100 cents

BANGLADESH

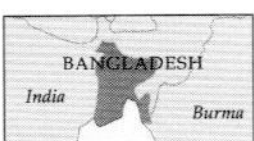
BANGLADESH
India
Burma

BANGLADESH LIES at the north of the Bay of Bengal. It seceded from Pakistan in 1971 and, after much political instability, returned to democracy in 1991.

GEOGRAPHY

Mostly flat alluvial plains and deltas of the Brahmaputra and Ganges rivers. Southeast coasts are fringed with mangrove forests.

CLIMATE

Hot and humid. During the monsoon, water level can rise six metres (20 feet) above sea level, flooding two-thirds of the country.

PEOPLE AND SOCIETY

Bangladesh has suffered from a cycle of floods, cyclones, famine, political corruption and military coups. Although 55% of people still live below the poverty line, living standards have improved in past decade. By providing independent income, textile trade is a factor in growing emancipation of women.

◆ *INSIGHT: Since 1960, there have been six cyclones with winds of over 200 kph*

THE ECONOMY

Heavily dependent on foreign aid. Agriculture is vulnerable to unpredictable climate. Bangladesh accounts for 80% of world jute fibre exports. Expanding textile industry.

Rangpur
Saidpur
Dinājpur
Brahmaputra
INDIA
Jamālpur
Sylhet
Mymensingh
Rājshāhi
Sirājganj
Brāhmanbāria
Pābna
Ganges (Padma)
DHAKA
INDIA
Comilla
Haringhat
Jessore
Khulna
Barisāl
Mouths of the Ganges
Chittagong
Bay of Bengal
BURMA
500m/1640ft
200m/656ft
Sea Level
100 km
100 miles

FACT FILE

OFFICIAL NAME: People's Republic of Bangladesh

DATE OF FORMATION: 1971

CAPITAL: Dhaka

POPULATION: 122.2 million

TOTAL AREA: 143,998 sq km (55,598 sq miles)

DENSITY: 891 people per sq km

LANGUAGES: Bangla*, Urdu, Chakma, Marma (Margh), other

RELIGIONS: Muslim 83%, Hindu 16%, other (Buddhist, Christian) 1%

ETHNIC MIX: Bengali 98%, other 2%

GOVERNMENT: Multiparty republic

CURRENCY: Taka = 100 paisa

BURMA (MYANMAR)

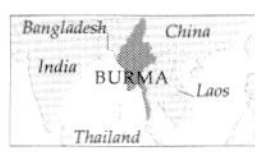
Bangladesh
China
India
BURMA
Laos
Thailand

BURMA FORMS the eastern shores of the Bay of Bengal and the Andaman Sea in Southeast Asia. It gained independence from Britain in 1948.

GEOGRAPHY

Fertile Irrawaddy basin in the centre. Mountains to the west, Shan plateau to the east. Tropical rainforest covers much of the land.

CLIMATE

Tropical. Hot summers, with high humidity, and warm winters.

PEOPLE AND SOCIETY

Under socialist military rule since 1962, Burma has suffered widespread political repression and ethnic conflict. Minority groups maintain low-level guerrilla activity against the state. 1990 election was won by opposition democratic party. Its leader, Aung San Suu Kyi, was placed under house arrest. She was released in 1995.

◆ *INSIGHT: Burma is the world's biggest teak exporter, although reserves are diminishing rapidly*

THE ECONOMY

Under socialism, Burma has plunged from prosperity to poverty. Nationwide black market, on which prices are soaring. Main products are teak, rice and gems.

INDIA
Myitkyina
CHINA
Irrawaddy
Monywa
Mandalay
Pakokku
Sagaing
Mekong
Sittwe
Taunggyi
Shan Plateau
LAOS
Toungoo
Sandoway
Prome
Bay of Bengal
Henzada
THAILAND
Insein
Pegu
Bassein
Thaton
RANGOON
Moulmein
Mouths of the Irrawaddy
Kyaikkami
4000m/13124ft
2000m/6562ft
1000m/3281ft
500m/1640ft
200m/656ft
Sea Level
Tavoy
Andaman Sea
Mergui
Mergui Archipelago
Isthmus of Kra
0 200 km
0 200 miles

FACT FILE

OFFICIAL NAME: Union of Myanmar
DATE OF FORMATION: 1948
CAPITAL: Rangoon (Yangon)
POPULATION: 47.5 million
TOTAL AREA: 676,550 sq km (261,200 sq miles)
DENSITY: 70 people per sq km
LANGUAGES: Burmese*, Karen, Shan, Chin, Kachin, Mon, Palaung, Wa
RELIGIONS: Buddhist 89%, Muslim 4%, Baptist 3%, other 4%
ETHNIC MIX: Burman 68%, Shan 9%, Karen 6%, Rakhine 4%, other 13%
GOVERNMENT: Military regime
CURRENCY: Kyat = 100 pyas

THAILAND

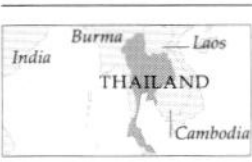
Burma
Laos
India
THAILAND
Cambodia

THAILAND LIES at the heart of mainland Southeast Asia. Continuing rapid industrialization has resulted in massive congestion in the capital.

GEOGRAPHY

One third is occupied by a low plateau, drained by tributaries of the Mekong River. Fertile central plain. Mountains in the north.

CLIMATE

Tropical. Hot, humid March–May, monsoon rains May–October, cooler season November–March.

PEOPLE AND SOCIETY

The king is head of state. Criticism of him is not tolerated. Buddhism is national binding force. North and northeast are home to about 600,000 hill tribespeople, with their own languages and culture. Sex tourism is a problem. Women from the poor northeast enter prostitution in Bangkok and Pattaya.

◆ *INSIGHT: Thailand, meaning 'land of the free', is the only Southeast Asian nation never to have been colonized*

THE ECONOMY

Rapid economic growth. Rise in manufacturing. Chief world exporter of rice and rubber. Gas reserves. Successful tourist industry.

BURMA
LAOS
Mekong
LAOS
Chiang Mai
Udon Thani
Salween
Khon Kaen
Phitsanulok
Nakhon Sawan
Ubon Ratchathani
Nakhon Ratchasima
BANGKOK
Thon Buri
Samut Prakan
CAMBODIA
Ratchaburi
Pattaya
Gulf of Thailand
Chumphon
Isthmus of Kra
Nakhon Si Thammarat
Phuket
Songkhla
Hat Yai
Malay Peninsula
Andaman Sea
MALAYSIA
2000m/6562ft
1000m/3281ft
500m/1640ft
200m/656ft
Sea Level
0 200 km
0 200 miles

FACT FILE

OFFICIAL NAME: Kingdom of Thailand
DATE OF FORMATION: 1822 / 1887
CAPITAL: Bangkok
POPULATION: 56.9 million
TOTAL AREA: 513,120 sq km (198,116 sq miles)
DENSITY: 110 people per sq km
LANGUAGES: Thai*, Chinese, Malay, Khmer, Mon, Karen, Miao, English
RELIGIONS: Buddhist 95%, Muslim 4%, other (inc. Hindu, Christian) 1%
ETHNIC MIX: Thai 75%, Chinese 14%, Malay 4%, Khmer 3%, other 4%
GOVERNMENT: Constitutional monarchy
CURRENCY: Baht = 100 stangs

LAOS

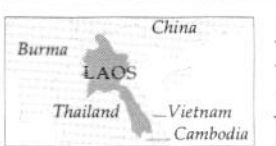
China
Burma
LAOS
Thailand
Vietnam
Cambodia

A FORMER French colony, independent in 1953, Laos lies land-locked in Southeast Asia. It has been under communist rule since 1975.

GEOGRAPHY

Largely forested mountains, broadening in the north to a plateau. Lowlands along Mekong valley.

CLIMATE

Monsoon rains September–May. Rest of the year is hot and dry.

PEOPLE AND SOCIETY

Over 60 ethnic groups. Lowland Laotians (*Lao Loum*), live along Mekong River and are wet-rice farmers. Upland Laotians (*Lao Theung*) and mountain-top Laotians (*Lao Soung*) practise slash-and-burn farming. Government efforts to halt this traditional farming method, which can destroy forests and watersheds, have been resisted.

◆ *INSIGHT: In the early 1990s, Laos and Thailand built a 'Friendship Bridge' across the Mekong at Vientiane*

THE ECONOMY

One of the world's 20 least-developed nations. Government began to introduce market-oriented reforms in 1986. Potential for timber, mining, garment manufacturing.

CHINA
BURMA
VIETNAM
THAILAND
CAMBODIA
Phôngsali
Ban Houayxay
Xam Nua
Mekong
Louangphrabang
Xiang Ngeun
Xiangkhoang
Muang Xaignabouri
Ban Naxon
Muang Pakxan
VIENTIANE
Muang Khammouar
Savannakhét
Muang Khôngxédôn
Saravan
Pakxé
2000m/6562ft
1000m/3281ft
500m/1640ft
Sea Level
0 100 km
0 100 miles

FACT FILE

OFFICIAL NAME: Lao People's Democratic Republic
DATE OF FORMATION: 1953
CAPITAL: Vientiane
POPULATION: 4.6 million
TOTAL AREA: 236,800 sq km (91,428 sq miles)
DENSITY: 20 people per sq km
LANGUAGES: Lao*, Miao, Yao, other
RELIGIONS: Buddhist 85%, Christian 2%, Muslim 1%, other 12%
ETHNIC MIX: Lao Loum 56%, Lao Theung 34%, Lao Soung 10%
GOVERNMENT: Single-party republic
CURRENCY: Kip = 100 cents

CAMBODIA

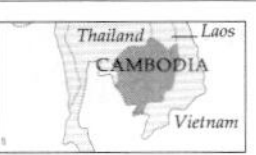
Thailand
Laos
CAMBODIA
Vietnam

LOCATED ON the Indochinese Peninsula in Southeast Asia, Cambodia has emerged from two decades of civil war and invasion from Vietnam.

GEOGRAPHY

Mostly low-lying basin. Tônlé Sap (Great Lake) drains into the Mekong River. Forested mountains and plateau east of the Mekong.

CLIMATE

Tropical. High temperatures throughout the year. Heavy rainfall during May–October monsoon.

PEOPLE AND SOCIETY

Under Pol Pot's Marxist Khmer Rouge regime between 1975 and 1979, over one million Cambodians died. Half a million more went into exile in Thailand. Effects of revolution and civil war are still felt and are reflected in the world's highest rate of orphans and widows. Free elections held under UN supervision in 1993 brought fragile stability, although the Khmer Rouge, still led by Pol Pot, continues its armed struggle.

THE ECONOMY

Economy is still recovering from civil war. Loss of skilled workers as result of Khmer Rouge anti-bourgeois atrocities in 1970s. Modest trade in rubber and timber.

◆ *INSIGHT: Cambodia has many impressive temples, dating from when it was the centre of the Khmer empire*

THAILAND
LAOS
Phumĭ Sâmraông
Chŏâm Khsant
Sisŏphŏn
Phumĭ Mlu Prey
Virôchey
14°
Bătdâmbâng
Phumĭ Kâmpóng Trâbék
Tônlé Sap
Mekong
Poŭthĭsăt
Kâmpóng Chhnăng
Krâchéh
Krŏng Kaôh Kŏng
Kâmpóng Cham
12°
PHNOM PENH
Prey Vêng
Gulf of Thailand
Kâmpóng Saôm
VIETNAM
104°
106°
1000m/3281ft
500m/1640ft
200m/656ft
Sea Level
0
100 km
0
100 miles

FACT FILE

OFFICIAL NAME: State of Cambodia
DATE OF FORMATION: 1953
CAPITAL: Phnom Penh
POPULATION: 9 million
TOTAL AREA: 181,040 sq km (69,000 sq miles)
DENSITY: 50 people per sq km
LANGUAGES: Khmer*, French, other
RELIGIONS: Buddhist 88%, Muslim 2%, Christian 1%, other 9%
ETHNIC MIX: Khmer 94%, Chinese 4%, Vietnamese 1%, other 1%
GOVERNMENT: Constitutional monarchy
CURRENCY: Riel = 100 sen

VIETNAM

China
Laos
VIETNAM
Cambodia

SITUATED ON the eastern coast of the Indochinese Peninsula, the country is still rebuilding after the devastating 1962–1975 Vietnam War.

GEOGRAPHY
Heavily forested mountain range separates northern Red River delta lowlands from southern Mekong delta in the south.

CLIMATE
Cool winters in north; south is tropical, with even temperatures.

PEOPLE AND SOCIETY
Partitioned in 1954, the communist north reunited the nation after the Vietnam War, in which two million people died. Women outnumber men, largely because of war deaths. Resettling of lowlanders in mountain regions has put pressure on farming and forest resources. Family life is based on kinship groups within village clans.

◆ *INSIGHT: A new mammal species, the* Vu Quang Ox, *was recently discovered in the forests of north Vietnam*

THE ECONOMY
After years of stagnation, the economy is recovering. Government seeking transfer to market economy. Growing steel, oil, gas, car industries.

CHINA
Red River
22°
LAOS
HANOI
Hông Gai
Nam Đinh
Hai Phong
Gulf of Tongking
Vinh
18°
2000m/6562ft
1000m/3281ft
500m/1640ft
200m/656ft
Sea Level
Huê
Đă Nâng
South China Sea
0 100 km
0 100 miles
14°
Quy Nhon
CAMBODIA
Nha Trang
Mekong
Đa Lat
Long Xuyên
Biên Hoa
Hô Chi Minh
Vung Tau
Gulf of Thailand
Cân Thơ
Mekong Delta
10°
104°
108°

FACT FILE

OFFICIAL NAME: Socialist Republic of Viet-Nam
DATE OF FORMATION: 1976
CAPITAL: Hanoi
POPULATION: 76.2 million
TOTAL AREA: 329,560 sq km (127,243 sq miles)
DENSITY: 231 people per sq km
LANGUAGES: Vietnamese*, other
RELIGIONS: Buddhist 55%, Catholic 7%, Muslim 1%, other 37%
ETHNIC MIX: Vietnamese 88%, Chinese 4%, Thai 2%, other 6%
GOVERNMENT: Single-party republic
CURRENCY: Dong = 10 hao = 100 xu

MALAYSIA

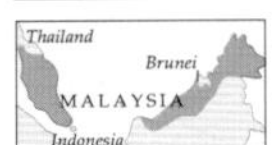
Thailand
Brunei
MALAYSIA
Indonesia

MALAYSIA'S THREE separate territories stretch over 2,000 km (1,240 miles) from the Malay Peninsula to the northeastern area of the island of Borneo.

GEOGRAPHY

Peninsular Malaysia (Malaya) has mountain ranges along its axis. Almost three-quarters of the land is tropical rainforest or swamp forest. Territories of Sabah and Sarawak in Borneo are rugged and forested.

CLIMATE

Equatorial. Warm, with year-round rainfall. Heaviest rain March–May and September–November.

◆ INSIGHT: *Malaysia accounts for almost half of world timber exports*

PEOPLE AND SOCIETY

Indigenous Malays are the largest ethnic group, but Chinese have traditionally controlled most economic activity. Malays favoured in education and jobs since 1970s, in order to address imbalance. Labour shortages attract many immigrants from other Southeast Asian states.

THE ECONOMY

Rapid growth since 1980s. Successful electronics, car industries. Leading producer of rubber, palm oil, pepper, tin, tropical hardwoods.

THAILAND
Kota Bharu
George Town
Malay
Peninsula
Kuala Terengganu
Taiping
Ipoh
Cameron Highlands
Kuantan
KUALA LUMPUR
Kelang
Seremban
Keluang
Johor Baharu
South China Sea
Kuching
Bandar Sri Aman
Sibu
Sarawak
Bintulu
Miri
BRUNEI
Borneo
Kota Kinabalu
Kudat
Sulu Sea
Sandakan
Sabah
INDONESIA
2000m/6562ft
1000m/3281ft
500m/1640ft
200m/656ft
Sea Level
0 100 km
0 100 miles

FACT FILE

OFFICIAL NAME: Malaysia
DATE OF FORMATION: 1957 / 1965
CAPITAL: Kuala Lumpur
POPULATION: 20.6 million
TOTAL AREA: 329,750 sq km (127,317 sq miles)
DENSITY: 62 people per sq km
LANGUAGES: Malay*, Chinese*, Tamil
RELIGIONS: Muslim 53%, Buddhist and Confucian 30%, other 17%
ETHNIC MIX: Malay and aborigine 60%, Chinese 30%, Indian 8%, other 2%
GOVERNMENT: Federal constitutional monarchy
CURRENCY: Ringgit = 100 cents

INDONESIA

Malaysia
INDONESIA
Australia

THE WORLD'S largest archipelago, Indonesia's 13,677 islands are scattered over 5,000 km (3,000 miles), from the Indian Ocean to the Pacific Ocean.

GEOGRAPHY

Mountains, tropical swamps, rainforests and over 200 volcanoes, many still active. Most larger islands have coastal lowlands.

CLIMATE

Predominantly tropical monsoon. Hilly areas are cooler. June–September dry season.

◆ *INSIGHT: Indonesia is the fifth most populous country in the world and 40% of its people are aged under 15*

PEOPLE AND SOCIETY

A mosaic of different cultures and languages. Islam, urbanization and national language, Bahasa Indonesia, are unifying factors. Papuans of Irian Jaya, East Timorese and Aceh of north Sumatra, denied autonomy, are all in conflict with government.

THE ECONOMY

Varied resources, especially energy. Timber, minerals, fishing, are all important. Rice is main cash crop for the rural population.

Kepulauan Natuna
MALAYSIA
BRUNEI
MALAYSIA
Celebes Sea
PACIFIC OCEAN
Medan
Pematangsiantar
Sumatra
Pakambaru
Pontianak
Padang
Jambi
Palembang
JAKARTA
Bandung
Semarang
Yogyakarta
Java
Surabaya
Denpasar
Bali
Borneo
Samarinda
Balikpapan
Banjarmasin
Palu
Sulawesi
Ujungpandang
Manado
Halmahera
Malaku (Moluccas)
Ambon
Seram
Equator
Jayapura
Irian Jaya
New Guinea
PAPUA NEW GUINEA
Java Sea
Flores
East Timor
Timor
Timor Sea
Arafura Sea
INDIAN OCEAN
4000m/13124ft
3000m/9843ft
2000m/6562ft
1000m/3281ft
500m/1640ft
Sea Level
0 500 km
0 500 miles

FACT FILE

OFFICIAL NAME: Republic of Indonesia
DATE OF FORMATION: 1949 / 1963
CAPITAL: Jakarta
POPULATION: 200.6 million
TOTAL AREA: 1,904,570 sq km (735,555 sq miles)
DENSITY: 105 people per sq km
LANGUAGES: Bahasa Indonesia*, 250 (est.) languages or dialects
RELIGIONS: Muslim 87%, Christian 10%, Hindu 2%, Buddhist 1%
ETHNIC MIX: Javanese 45%, Sundanese 14%, Madurese 8%, other 33%
GOVERNMENT: Multiparty republic
CURRENCY: Rupiah = 100 sen

SINGAPORE

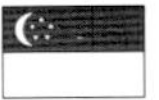

Malaysia
SINGAPORE

A CITY state linked to the southernmost tip of the Malay Peninsula by a causeway, Singapore is one of Asia's most important commercial centres.

GEOGRAPHY

Little remains of the original vegetation on Singapore island. The other 54 much smaller islands are swampy jungle.

CLIMATE

Equatorial. Hot and humid, with heavy rainfall all year round.

PEOPLE AND SOCIETY

Dominated by the Chinese, who make up three-quarters of the community. English-speaking Straits Chinese and newer Mandarin-speakers are now well integrated. There is a significant foreign work force. Society is highly regulated and government campaigns to improve public behaviour are frequent. Crime is limited and punishment can be severe.

THE ECONOMY

Highly successful financial, banking and manufacturing sectors. Produces 50% of the world's computer disk drives. All food and energy has to be imported.

◆ *INSIGHT: Singapore has full employment, and the world's highest rate of home ownership and national savings*

Causeway
Pulau Ubin
Lim Chu Kang
Bukit Panjang
Choa Chu Kang
Houngang New Town
Pulau Tekong
Changi International Airport
Jurong
Bukit Timah
Bedok New Town
Jurong Industrial Estate
Queenstown
City
Telok Blangah
South China Sea
Sedat Pandan
Sentosa
Pulau Brani
Urban areas
Open areas
Nature reserves
Strait of Singapore
0 5 km
0 5 miles

FACT FILE

OFFICIAL NAME: Republic of Singapore
DATE OF FORMATION: 1965
CAPITAL: Singapore City
POPULATION: 2.8 million
TOTAL AREA: 620 sq km (239 sq miles)
DENSITY: 4,590 people per sq km
LANGUAGES: Malay*, Chinese*, other
RELIGIONS: Buddhist 30%, Christian 20%, Muslim 17%, other 33%
ETHNIC MIX: Chinese 76%, Malay 15%, South Asian 7%, other 2%
GOVERNMENT: Multiparty republic
CURRENCY: Singapore $ = 100 cents

BRUNEI

Malaysia
BRUNEI
Malaysia
Indonesia

LYING ON the northwestern coast of the island of Borneo, Brunei is surrounded and divided in two by the Malaysian state of Sarawak.

GEOGRAPHY
Mostly dense lowland rainforest and mangrove swamps. Mountains in the southeast.

CLIMATE
Tropical. Six-month rainy season with very high humidity.

PEOPLE AND SOCIETY
Malays benefit from positive discrimination. Many in Chinese community are stateless. Independent from the UK since 1984, Brunei is ruled by decree of the Sultan. In 1990, 'Malay Muslim Monarchy' was introduced, promoting Islamic values as state ideology. Women less restricted than in some Muslim states.

◆ *INSIGHT: The Sultan spent US $450 million building the world's largest palace at Bandar Seri Begawan*

THE ECONOMY
Oil and natural gas reserves have brought one of the world's highest standards of living. Massive overseas investments. Major consumer of high-tech hi-fi, video recorders, Western designer clothes.

1000m/3281ft
500m/1640ft
200m/656ft
Sea Level
South China Sea
Pekan Muara
Kampong Bunut
BANDAR SERI BEGAWAN
Tutong
Bangar
Pekan Seria
Kuala Belait
Kampong Bukit Sawat
Kampong Batang Duri
Kampong Tanajor
Kampong Sukang
Kampong Teraja
MALAYSIA
Borneo
0 20 km
0 20 miles

FACT FILE

OFFICIAL NAME: The Sultanate of Brunei
DATE OF FORMATION: 1984
CAPITAL: Bandar Seri Begawan
POPULATION: 300,000
TOTAL AREA: 5,770 sq km (2,228 sq miles)
DENSITY: 57 people per sq km
LANGUAGES: Malay*, English, Chinese
RELIGIONS: Muslim 63%, Buddhist 14%, Christian 10%, other 13%
ETHNIC MIX: Malay 69%, Chinese 18%, other 13%
GOVERNMENT: Absolute monarchy
CURRENCY: Brunei $ = 100 cents

PHILIPPINES

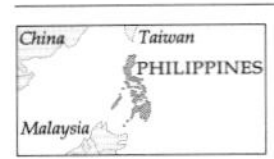
China
Taiwan
PHILIPPINES
Malaysia

AN ARCHIPELAGO of 7,107 islands between the South China Sea and the Pacific. After 21 years of dictatorship, democracy was restored in 1986.

GEOGRAPHY

Larger islands are forested and mountainous. Over 20 active volcanoes. Frequent earthquakes.

CLIMATE

Tropical. Warm and humid all year round. Typhoons occur in rainy season, June–October.

PEOPLE AND SOCIETY

Over 100 ethnic groups. Most Filipinos are of Malay origin, and Christian. Catholic Church is the dominant cultural force. It opposes state-sponsored family planning programmes designed to curb accelerating population growth. Women have traditionally played a prominent part in society. Many enter the professions. Half the population live on the poverty line.

◆ *INSIGHT: The Philippines is the only Christian state in Asia*

THE ECONOMY

Now open to outside investment. Agricultural productivity is rising. Power failures limit scope for expansion. Weak infrastructure.

2000m/6562ft
1000m/3281ft
500m/1640ft
200m/656ft
Sea Level
0 200 km
0 200 miles
Babuyan Is.
PACIFIC OCEAN
Philippine Sea
Luzon
Cabanatuan City
Angeles
MANILA
Batangas
Legaspi
South China Sea
Mindoro
Calbayog
Samar
Panay
Iloilo
Bacolod
Cebu
Palawan
Puerto Princesa
Negros
Butuan
Sulu Sea
Iligan
Balabac Strait
Davao
Zamboanga
General Santos
Sulu Archipelago
Mindanao
Celebes Sea

FACT FILE

OFFICIAL NAME: Republic of the Philippines
DATE OF FORMATION: 1946
CAPITAL: Manila
POPULATION: 66.5 million
TOTAL AREA: 300,000 sq km (115,831 sq miles)
DENSITY: 219 people per sq km
LANGUAGES: Pilipino*, English*, other
RELIGIONS: Catholic 83%, Protestant 9%, Muslim 5%, other 3%
ETHNIC MIX: Filipino 96%, Chinese 2%, other 2%
GOVERNMENT: Multiparty republic
CURRENCY: Peso = 100 centavos

TAIWAN

China
TAIWAN

THE ISLAND republic of Taiwan lies 130 km (80 miles) off the southeast coast of mainland China. China considers it to be one of its provinces.

GEOGRAPHY

Mountain region covers two-thirds of the island. Highly fertile lowlands and coastal plains.

CLIMATE

Tropical monsoon. Hot and humid. Typhoons July–September. Snow falls in mountains in winter.

PEOPLE AND SOCIETY

Most Taiwanese are Han Chinese, descendants of 17th-century settlers from the mainland. Taiwan came into existence in 1949, when the government was expelled from Beijing (then Peking) by the communists under Mao. 100,000 Nationalists arrived and established themselves as ruling class. Taiwan is diplomatically isolated and cannot gain representation at the UN.

◆ INSIGHT: *Taiwan has the world's second largest foreign currency reserves*

THE ECONOMY

One of the world's most successful economies, based on small, adaptable manufacturing companies. Goods include televisions calculators, footwear.

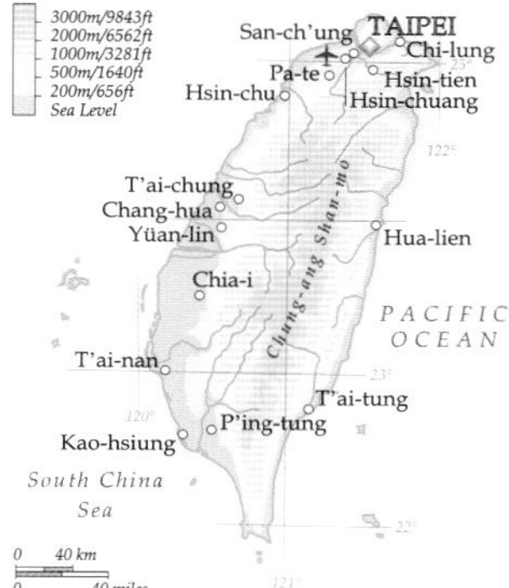
3000m/9843ft
2000m/6562ft
1000m/3281ft
500m/1640ft
200m/656ft
Sea Level
San-ch'ung
TAIPEI
Chi-lung
Pa-te
Hsin-tien
Hsin-chu
Hsin-chuang
T'ai-chung
Chang-hua
Yüan-lin
Hua-lien
Chia-i
Chung-ang Shan-mo
PACIFIC OCEAN
T'ai-nan
T'ai-tung
P'ing-tung
Kao-hsiung
South China Sea
0 40 km
0 40 miles

FACT FILE

OFFICIAL NAME: Republic of China (Taiwan)
DATE OF FORMATION: 1949
CAPITAL: Taipei
POPULATION: 20.8 million
TOTAL AREA: 36,179 sq km (13,969 sq miles)
DENSITY: 645 people per sq km
LANGUAGES: Mandarin*, other
RELIGIONS: Buddhist, Confucian and Taoist 93%, Christian 5%, other 2%
ETHNIC MIX: Taiwanese 84%, mainland Chinese 14%, other 2%
GOVERNMENT: Multiparty republic
CURRENCY: New Taiwan $ = 100 cents

CHINA

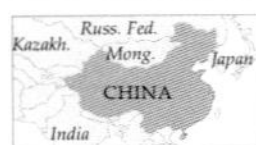
Russ. Fed.
Kazakh.
Mong.
Japan
CHINA
India

CHINA COVERS a vast area of East Asia. From the founding of Communist China in 1949, until his death in 1976, Mao Zedong dominated the nation.

GEOGRAPHY

Huge physical diversity. Great mountain chains and world's highest plateau in west. Arid basin in north and northeast. Deserts in northwest. South is mountainous. Rolling hills and plains in east.

CLIMATE

North and west are semi-arid or arid, with extreme temperature variations. South and east are warmer and more humid, with year-round rainfall. Winter temperatures vary with latitude. Summer temperatures are more uniform, rising above 21°C (70°F).

THE ECONOMY

Moving rapidly towards a market-oriented economy. Vast mineral reserves. Increasingly diversified industrial sector. Low wage costs. Self-sufficient in food.

◆ *INSIGHT: China has the world's oldest continuous civilization. Its recorded history began 4,000 years ago, with the Shang dynasty*

KAZAKHSTAN
Karamay
Yining
KYRGYZSTAN
XINJIANG
Korla
Kashi
TAJIKISTAN
Taklimakan Shamo
AFGHANISTAN
Altun Sha
PAKISTAN
Kunlun Sha
INDIA
XIZANG ZIZHIQU
(TIBET)
Himalaya
Lhasa
NEPAL
INDIA BHUTAN

FACT FILE

OFFICIAL NAME: People's Republic of China
DATE OF FORMATION: 1949/1950
CAPITAL: Beijing
POPULATION: 1,234.3 million
TOTAL AREA: 9,396,960 sq km (3,628,166 sq miles)
DENSITY: 131 people per sq km
LANGUAGES: Mandarin*, other
RELIGIONS: Confucianist 20%, Buddhist 6%, Taoist 2%, other 72%
ETHNIC MIX: Han 93%, Zhaung 1%, Hui 1%, other 5%
GOVERNMENT: Single-party republic
CURRENCY: Yuan = 10 jiao = 100 fen

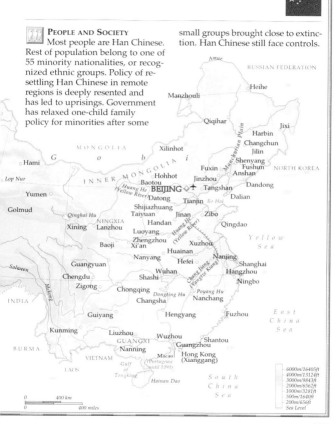

PEOPLE AND SOCIETY Most people are Han Chinese. Rest of population belong to one of 55 minority nationalities, or recognized ethnic groups. Policy of resettling Han Chinese in remote regions is deeply resented and has led to uprisings. Government has relaxed one-child family policy for minorities after some small groups brought close to extinction. Han Chinese still face controls.

Amur
RUSSIAN FEDERATION
Heihe
Manzhouli
Qiqihar
Manchurian Plain
Jixi
Harbin
Changchun
Jilin
MONGOLIA
Xilinhot
Gobi
Hami
Shenyang
Fushun
NORTH KOREA
Fuxin
Anshan
INNER MONGOLIA
Hohhot
Lop Nur
Jinzhou
Baotou
Dandong
Huang He (Yellow River)
BEIJING
Tangshan
Yumen
Datong
Dalian
Tianjin
Bo Hai
Golmud
Shijiazhuang
Taiyuan
Jinan
Zibo
Qinghai Hu
NINGXIA
Handan
Qingdao
Xining
Lanzhou
Huang He (Yellow River)
Luoyang
Yellow Sea
Zhengzhou
Baoji
Xi'an
Xuzhou
Huainan
Nanyang
Nanjing
Hefei
Shanghai
Salween
Guangyuan
Chang Jiang (Yangtze Kiang)
Wuhan
Hangzhou
Chengdu
Shashi
Ningbo
Mekong
Zigong
Chongqing
Dongting Hu
Poyang Hu
INDIA
Changsha
Nanchang
Guiyang
Hengyang
Fuzhou
East China Sea
Kunming
Liuzhou
Wuzhou
Shantou
GUANGXI
Guangzhou
BURMA
Nanning
Macao (Portuguese until 1999)
Hong Kong (Xianggang)
VIETNAM
Gulf of Tongking
LAOS
Hainan Dao
South China Sea
0 400 km
0 400 miles
6000m/16405ft
4000m/13124ft
3000m/9843ft
2000m/6562ft
1000m/3281ft
500m/1640ft
200m/656ft
Sea Level

NORTH KOREA

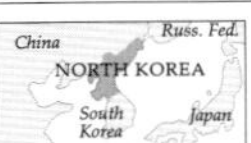
China
Russ. Fed.
NORTH KOREA
South Korea
Japan

NORTH KOREA comprises the northern half of the Korean peninsula. A communist state since 1948, it is largely isolated from the outside world.

GEOGRAPHY

Mostly mountainous, with fertile plains in the southwest.

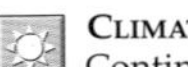

CLIMATE

Continental. Warm summers and cold winters, especially in the north, where snow is common.

PEOPLE AND SOCIETY

People live severely regulated lives. Divorce is non-existent and extra-marital sex highly frowned upon. Women form 57% of the work force, but are also expected to run the home. From an early age, children are looked after in state-run nurseries. Korean Workers' Party is only legal political party. Membership is essential for advancement. The political elite enjoy a privileged lifestyle.

◆ *INSIGHT: Private cars and telephones are forbidden in North Korea*

THE ECONOMY

Economy has suffered badly in 1990s, since end of aid from China and former Soviet Union. Manufacturing, agriculture and mining all in decline. Electricity shortage is a problem.

2000m/6562ft
1000m/3281ft
500m/1640ft
200m/656ft
Sea Level
0 50 km
0 50 miles
RUSS. FED.
CHINA
Ch'ŏngjin
Kanggye
Hŭich'ŏn
Kimch'aek
Sinŭiju
Hamhŭng
Iwŏn
Hŭngnam
Sea of Japan
Korea Bay
Wŏnsan
PYONGYANG
Namp'o
Haeju
Kaesŏng
SOUTH KOREA
Yellow Sea

FACT FILE

OFFICIAL NAME: Democratic People's Republic of Korea
DATE OF FORMATION: 1948
CAPITAL: Pyongyang
POPULATION: 23.1 million
TOTAL AREA: 120,540 sq km (46,540 sq miles)
DENSITY: 188 people per sq km
LANGUAGES: Korean*, Chinese
RELIGIONS: Traditional beliefs 16%, Ch'ondogyo 14%, Buddhist 2%, non-religious 68%
ETHNIC MIX: Korean 99%, other 1%
GOVERNMENT: Single-party republic
CURRENCY: Won = 100 chon

SOUTH KOREA

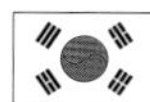

North Korea
SOUTH KOREA
Japan

SOUTH KOREA occupies the southern half of the Korean peninsula. Under US sponsorship, it was separated from the communist North in 1948.

GEOGRAPHY

Over 80% is mountainous and two-thirds is forested. Flattest and most populous parts lie along west coast and in the extreme south.

CLIMATE

Four distinct seasons. Winters are dry, and bitterly cold. Summers are hot and humid.

PEOPLE AND SOCIETY

Inhabited by a single ethnic group for the last 2,000 years. Tiny Chinese community. Family life is a central and clearly defined part of Korean society. Women's role is traditional; it is not respectable for those who are married to have jobs. Since the inconclusive Korean War (1950–53), North and South Korea have remained mutually hostile.

◆ *INSIGHT: Over 60% of Koreans are named Kim, Lee or Park*

THE ECONOMY

World's biggest ship-builder. High demand from China for Korean goods, especially cars. Electronics, household appliances also important.

NORTH KOREA
Sea of Japan
SEOUL
Inch'ŏn
Sŏngnam
Suwŏn
Kangnŭng
Tonghae
Taejŏn
Yellow Sea
Kunsan
Taegu
Ulsan
Kwangju
Masan
Mokp'o
Yŏsu
Pusan
Korea Strait
Cheju Strait
Cheju
Cheju-do
1000m/3281ft
500m/1640ft
200m/656ft
Sea Level
0 50 km
0 50 miles

FACT FILE

OFFICIAL NAME: Republic of Korea
DATE OF FORMATION: 1948
CAPITAL: Seoul
POPULATION: 44.5 million
TOTAL AREA: 99,020 sq km (38,232 sq miles)
DENSITY: 448 people per sq km
LANGUAGES: Korean*, Chinese
RELIGIONS: Mahayana Buddhist 47%, Protestant 38%, Catholic 11%, Confucian 3%, other 1%
ETHNIC MIX: Korean 99.9%, other (mainly Chinese) 0.1%
GOVERNMENT: Multiparty republic
CURRENCY: Won = 100 chon

JAPAN

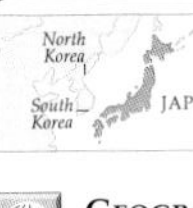
North Korea
South Korea
JAPAN

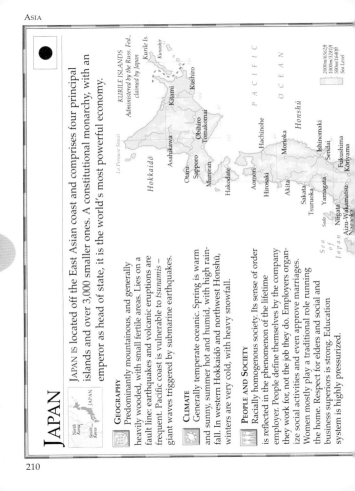

JAPAN IS located off the East Asian coast and comprises four principal islands and over 3,000 smaller ones. A constitutional monarchy, with an emperor as head of state, it is the world's most powerful economy.

GEOGRAPHY

Predominantly mountainous, and generally heavily wooded, with small fertile areas. Lies on a fault line: earthquakes and volcanic eruptions are frequent. Pacific coast is vulnerable to *tsunamis* – giant waves triggered by submarine earthquakes.

CLIMATE

Generally temperate oceanic. Spring is warm and sunny, summer hot and humid, with high rainfall. In western Hokkaidō and northwest Honshū, winters are very cold, with heavy snowfall.

PEOPLE AND SOCIETY

Racially homogenous society. Its sense of order is reflected in the phenomenon of the lifetime employer. People define themselves by the company they work for, not the job they do. Employers organize social activities and even approve marriages. Women mostly play a traditional role running the home. Respect for elders and social and business superiors is strong. Education system is highly pressurized.

La Perouse Strait
KURILE ISLANDS
Administered by the Russ. Fed., claimed by Japan
Kurile Is.
Kunashir
Hokkaidō
Asahikawa
Kitami
Otaru
Sapporo
Obihiro
Tomakomai
Kushiro
Muroran
Hakodate
Aomori
Hachinohe
Hirosaki
PACIFIC
OCEAN
Akita
Morioka
Honshū
Sakata
Tsuruoka
Ishinomaki
Sea of Japan
Sado
Yamagata
Sendai
Niigata
Fukushima
Aizu-Wakamatsu
Kōriyama
2000m/6562ft
1000m/3281ft
500m/1640ft
Sea Level

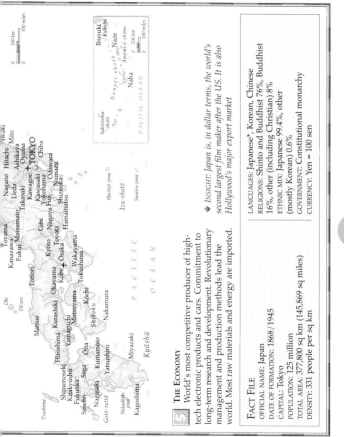

Oki
Dōzen
Toyama
Kanazawa
Fukui
Matsumato
Nagano
Ueda
Takasaki
Hitachi
Mito
Ashikaya
Oyama
Kawagoe
TOKYO
Chiba
Kawasaki
Yokohama
Fuji
Odawara
Numazu
Shizuoka
Hamamatsu
Gifu
Nagoya
Toyota
Kyōto
Ōsaka
Kōbe
Okayama
Kurashiki
Tottori
Matsue
Hiroshima
Yamaguchi
Matsuyama
Wakayama
Tokushima
Kōchi
Shikoku
Nakamura
Tsushima
Shimonoseki
Kitakyūshū
Fukuoka
Sasebo
Saga
Oita
Nagasaki
Kumamoto
Gotō-rettō
Yatsushiro
Nakadōri-jima
Miyazaki
Kagoshima
Kyūshū
PACIFIC OCEAN
Hachijō-jima
Izu-shotō
Sumisu-jima
0 100 km
0 100 miles
Sakishima-shotō
Nansei-shotō
Ibusuki
Kyūshū
Naze
Amami-ō-shima
Naha
PACIFIC OCEAN
0 100 km
0 100 miles

THE ECONOMY

World's most competitive producer of high-tech electronic products and cars. Commitment to long-term research and development. Revolutionary management and production methods lead the world. Most raw materials and energy are imported.

◆ INSIGHT: *Japan is, in dollar terms, the world's second largest film maker after the US. It is also Hollywood's major export market*

FACT FILE

OFFICIAL NAME: Japan
DATE OF FORMATION: 1868/1945
CAPITAL: Tokyo
POPULATION: 125 million
TOTAL AREA: 377,800 sq km (145,869 sq miles)
DENSITY: 331 people per sq km

LANGUAGES: Japanese*, Korean, Chinese
RELIGIONS: Shinto and Buddhist 76%, Buddhist 16%, other (including Christian) 8%
ETHNIC MIX: Japanese 99.4%, other (mostly Korean) 0.6%
GOVERNMENT: Constitutional monarchy
CURRENCY: Yen = 100 sen

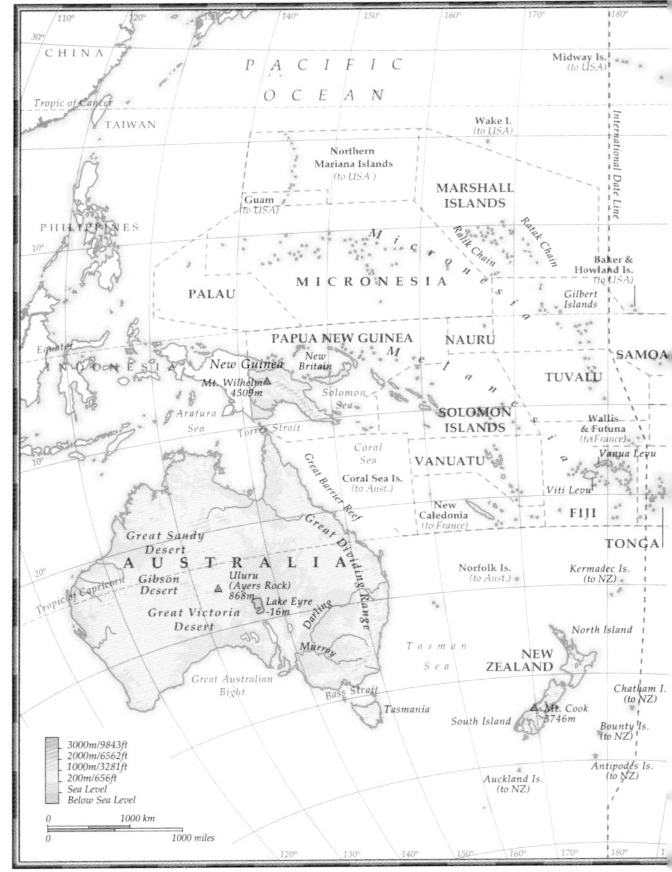
CHINA
PACIFIC OCEAN
Tropic of Cancer
TAIWAN
Midway Is. (to USA)
Wake I. (to USA)
International Date Line
Northern Mariana Islands (to USA)
Guam (to USA)
MARSHALL ISLANDS
Ratak Chain
Ralik Chain
PHILIPPINES
Micronesia
MICRONESIA
PALAU
Baker & Howland Is. (to USA)
Gilbert Islands
Equator
PAPUA NEW GUINEA
NAURU
Melanesia
SAMOA
INDONESIA
New Guinea
New Britain
Mt. Wilhelm 4509m
TUVALU
Solomon Sea
Arafura Sea
Torres Strait
SOLOMON ISLANDS
Wallis & Futuna (to France)
Coral Sea
VANUATU
Vanua Levu
Great Barrier Reef
Coral Sea Is. (to Aust.)
Viti Levu
New Caledonia (to France)
FIJI
Great Dividing Range
Great Sandy Desert
TONGA
AUSTRALIA
Norfolk Is. (to Aust.)
Kermadec Is. (to NZ)
Gibson Desert
Uluru (Ayers Rock) 868m
Tropic of Capricorn
Lake Eyre -16m
Great Victoria Desert
Darling
North Island
Murray
Tasman Sea
NEW ZEALAND
Great Australian Bight
Bass Strait
Chatham I. (to NZ)
Tasmania
Mt. Cook 3746m
South Island
Bounty Is. (to NZ)
3000m/9843ft
2000m/6562ft
1000m/3281ft
200m/656ft
Sea Level
Below Sea Level
Antipodes Is. (to NZ)
Auckland Is. (to NZ)
0 1000 km
0 1000 miles

AUSTRALASIA & OCEANIA

THIS REGION includes the world's smallest, flattest continent, Australia; large island groups such as New Zealand, Papua New Guinea and Fiji; and myriad volcanic and coral islands scattered across the Pacific Ocean, which comprise three main groups: Micronesia, Melanesia and Polynesia. The peoples of Oceania colonized the Pacific by AD 1500. Their insular farming and fishing communities have developed distinctive cultures. Owing to its isolation from other continents, Australia's flora and fauna have evolved many unique species.

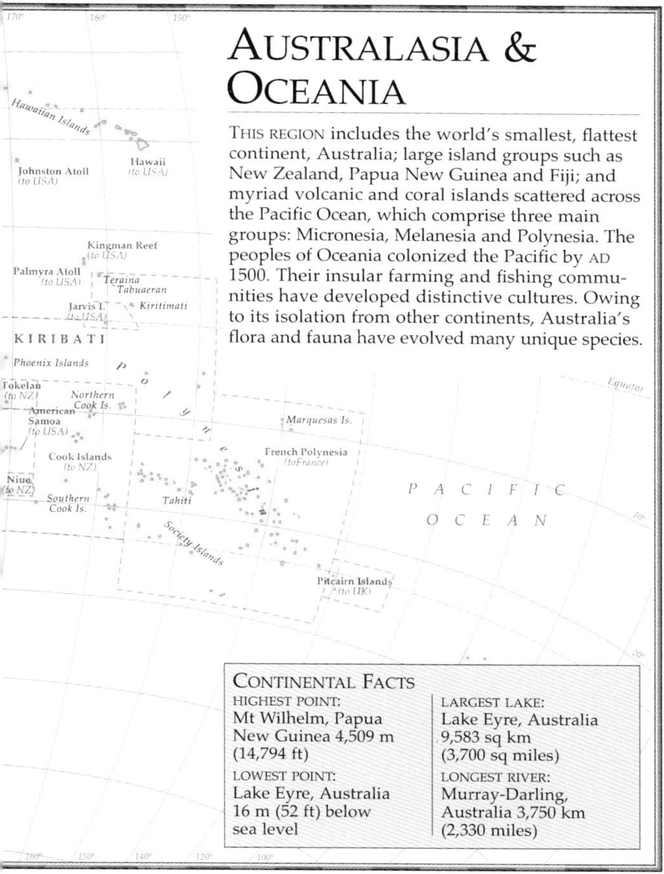

CONTINENTAL FACTS

HIGHEST POINT:
Mt Wilhelm, Papua New Guinea 4,509 m (14,794 ft)

LOWEST POINT:
Lake Eyre, Australia 16 m (52 ft) below sea level

LARGEST LAKE:
Lake Eyre, Australia 9,583 sq km (3,700 sq miles)

LONGEST RIVER:
Murray-Darling, Australia 3,750 km (2,330 miles)

AUSTRALIA

Indonesia
Papua New Guinea
AUSTRALIA
New Zealand

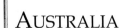

AN ISLAND continent located between the Indian and Pacific oceans. European settlement, mainly from Britain and Ireland, began 200 years ago. Today, Australia's international focus has shifted away from Europe towards Asia.

GEOGRAPHY

Western half is mostly arid plateaux, ridges and vast deserts. Central-eastern area comprises lowlands and river systems draining into Lake Eyre. To the east are the mountains of the Great Dividing Range. In the north are tropical rainforests.

CLIMATE

The interior, west and south are arid and very hot in summer. Central desert areas can reach 50°C (120°F). The north is hot throughout the year, and humid during the summer monsoon. East, southeast and southwest coastal areas are temperate.

PEOPLE AND SOCIETY

Immigration drives after 1945 brought many Europeans to Australia. Since 1970s, 50% of immigrants have been Asian. Aborigines, the first inhabitants, are sidelined economically and socially. They have made an increasingly organized stand over land rights in recent years. Wealth disparities are small, but 1990s recession increased gap between rich and poor.

THE ECONOMY

Efficient mining and agricultural industries. Successful tourist industry. Investor in booming Southeast Asian economies. High unemployment.

1000m/3281ft
500m/1640ft
200m/656ft
Sea Level
Below Sea Level
0 400 km
0 400 miles
INDIAN OCEAN
Timor Sea
Arafura Sea
Darwin
Arnhem Land
Kimberley Plateau
NORTHERN TERRITORY
Gulf of Carpentaria
Bamaga
Cape York
Great Barrier Reef
Cairns
Townsville
PACIFIC OCEAN
Coral Sea

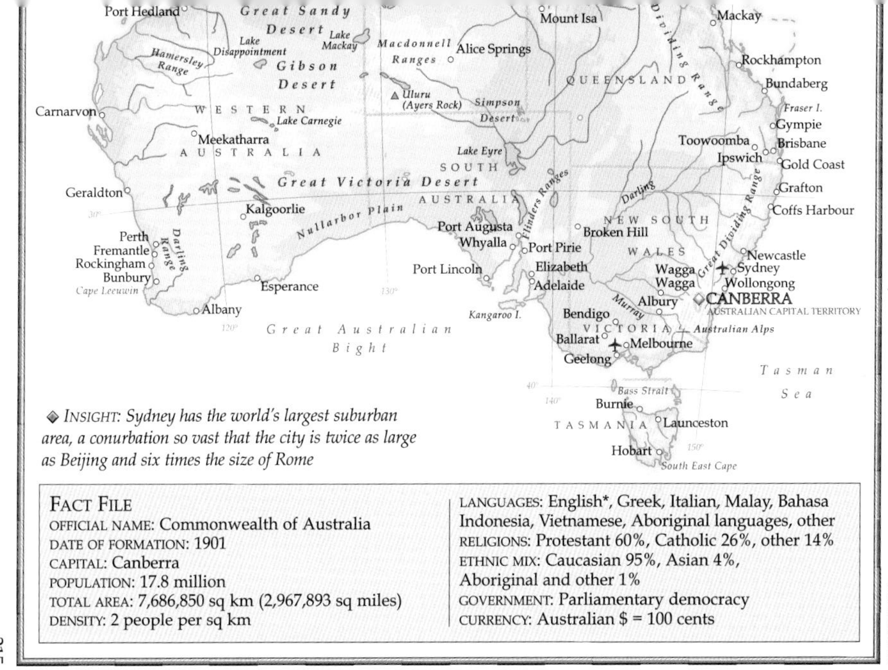
Port Hedland
Great Sandy Desert
Lake Disappointment
Lake Mackay
Macdonnell Ranges
Alice Springs
Mount Isa
Dividing Range
Mackay
Hamersley Range
Gibson Desert
Rockhampton
QUEENSLAND
Bundaberg
Uluru (Ayers Rock)
Simpson Desert
Fraser I.
Carnarvon
WESTERN AUSTRALIA
Lake Carnegie
Gympie
Meekatharra
Toowoomba
Brisbane
Ipswich
Gold Coast
Lake Eyre
SOUTH AUSTRALIA
Great Victoria Desert
Flinders Ranges
Darling
Grafton
Geraldton
Kalgoorlie
Nullarbor Plain
Great Dividing Range
Coffs Harbour
NEW SOUTH WALES
Port Augusta
Broken Hill
Perth
Fremantle
Rockingham
Bunbury
Cape Leeuwin
Darling Range
Whyalla
Port Pirie
Newcastle
Sydney
Port Lincoln
Elizabeth
Adelaide
Wagga Wagga
Wollongong
Esperance
Albury
CANBERRA
AUSTRALIAN CAPITAL TERRITORY
Albany
Murray
Kangaroo I.
Bendigo
VICTORIA
Australian Alps
Great Australian Bight
Ballarat
Melbourne
Geelong
Tasman Sea
Bass Strait
Burnie
TASMANIA
Launceston
Hobart
South East Cape

◆ *INSIGHT: Sydney has the world's largest suburban area, a conurbation so vast that the city is twice as large as Beijing and six times the size of Rome*

FACT FILE

OFFICIAL NAME: Commonwealth of Australia
DATE OF FORMATION: 1901
CAPITAL: Canberra
POPULATION: 17.8 million
TOTAL AREA: 7,686,850 sq km (2,967,893 sq miles)
DENSITY: 2 people per sq km
LANGUAGES: English*, Greek, Italian, Malay, Bahasa Indonesia, Vietnamese, Aboriginal languages, other
RELIGIONS: Protestant 60%, Catholic 26%, other 14%
ETHNIC MIX: Caucasian 95%, Asian 4%, Aboriginal and other 1%
GOVERNMENT: Parliamentary democracy
CURRENCY: Australian $ = 100 cents

VANUATU

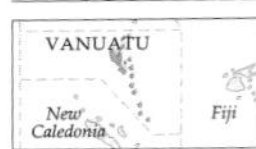
VANUATU
New Caledonia
Fiji

AN ARCHIPELAGO of 82 islands and islets in the Pacific Ocean, it was ruled jointly by Britain and France from 1906 until independence in 1980.

GEOGRAPHY

Mountainous and volcanic, with coral beaches and dense rainforest. Cultivated land along coasts.

CLIMATE

Tropical. Temperatures and rainfall decline from north to south.

PEOPLE AND SOCIETY

Indigenous Melanesians form a majority. 80% of the population live on 16 main islands. People are among the most traditional in the Pacific: local social and religious customs are strong, despite centuries of missionary influence. Subsistence farming and fishing are the main activities. Women have lower social status than men and payment of bride-price is common.

◆ INSIGHT: *With 105 indigenous languages, Vanuatu has the world's highest per capita density of languages*

THE ECONOMY

Copra and cocoa are the largest exports. Recent upsurge in tourist industry. Offshore financial services are also important.

Torres Islands
Banks Islands
PACIFIC OCEAN
Espiritu Santo
Luganville
Aoba
Maéwo
Pentecost
Norsup
Ambrym
Malekula
Épi
Coral Sea
Shepherd Islands
PORT-VILA
Éfaté
Erromango
Tanna
Isangel
Anatom
1000m/3281ft
500m/1640ft
200m/656ft
Sea Level
0 100 km
0 100 miles

FACT FILE

OFFICIAL NAME: Republic of Vanuatu
DATE OF FORMATION: 1980
CAPITAL: Port-Vila
POPULATION: 155,000
TOTAL AREA: 12,190 sq km (4,706 sq miles)
DENSITY: 13 people per sq km
LANGUAGES: Bislama (Melanesian pidgin)*, English*, French*, other
RELIGIONS: Protestant 77%, Catholic 15%, traditional beliefs 8%
ETHNIC MIX: Ni-Vanuatu 98%, European 1%, other 1%
GOVERNMENT: Multiparty republic
CURRENCY: Vatu = 100 centimes

FIJI

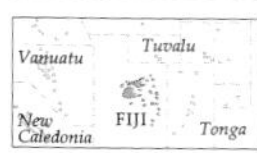
Vanuatu
Tuvalu
New Caledonia
FIJI
Tonga

A VOLCANIC archipelago in the southern Pacific Ocean, Fiji comprises 2 large islands and 880 islets. From 1874 to 1970, it was a British colony.

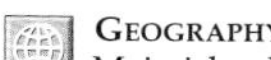

GEOGRAPHY

Main islands are mountainous, fringed by coral reefs. Remainder are limestone and coral formations.

CLIMATE

Tropical. High temperatures year round. Cyclones are a hazard.

PEOPLE AND SOCIETY

The British introduced workers from India in the late 19th century, and by 1946 their descendants outnumbered the Native Fijian population. In 1987, the Indian-dominated government was overthrown by Native Fijians. Many Indo-Fijians left the country. Civilian rule returned in 1990, and a new constitution discriminating against Indo-Fijians was introduced.

◆ *INSIGHT: Both Fijians and Indians practise fire-walking; Indians walk on hot embers, Fijians on heated stones*

THE ECONOMY

Well-diversified economy based on sugar production, gold mining, timber and commercial fishing. Tourists are returning after a drop in numbers after the coups.

PACIFIC OCEAN
Yasawa Group
Nabavatu
Labasa
Vanua Levu
Nabouwalu
Bligh Water
Taveuni
Koro
Rakiraki
Ovalau
Lautoka
Viti Levu
Sigatoka
Koro Sea
Gau
SUVA
Lakeba Passage
Lau Group
Moala
Kadavu Passage
Kadavu
PACIFIC OCEAN
1000m/3281ft
200m/656ft
Sea Level
0 100 km
0 100 miles

FACT FILE

OFFICIAL NAME: Republic of Fiji
DATE OF FORMATION: 1970
CAPITAL: Suva
POPULATION: 700,000
TOTAL AREA: 18,270 sq km (7,054 sq miles)
DENSITY: 38 people per sq km
LANGUAGES: English*, Fijian*, Hindi, Urdu, Tamil, Telugu
RELIGIONS: Christian 52%, Hindu 38%, Muslim 8%, other 2%
ETHNIC MIX: Native Fijian 49%, Indo-Fijian 46%, other 5%
GOVERNMENT: Multiparty republic
CURRENCY: Fiji $ = 100 cents

PAPUA NEW GUINEA

Indonesia
PAPUA
NEW GUINEA

ACHIEVING INDEPENDENCE from Australia in 1975, PNG occupies the eastern section of the island of New Guinea and several other island groups.

GEOGRAPHY

Mountainous and forested mainland, with broad, swampy river valleys. 40 active volcanoes in the north. Around 600 outer islands.

CLIMATE

Hot and humid in lowlands, cooling towards highlands, where snow can fall on highest peaks.

PEOPLE AND SOCIETY

Around 750 language groups – the highest number in the world – and even more tribes. Main social distinction is between lowlanders, who have frequent contact with the outside world, and the very isolated, but increasingly threatened, highlanders who live by hunter-gathering. Great tensions exist between highland tribes: anyone who is not a *wontok* (of one's tribe) is seen as potentially hostile.

THE ECONOMY

Significant quantities of gold, copper, silver. Oil and natural gas reserves. Secessionist violence on Bougainville deters investors.

◆ *INSIGHT: PNG is home to the only known poisonous birds; contact with the feathers produces skin blisters*

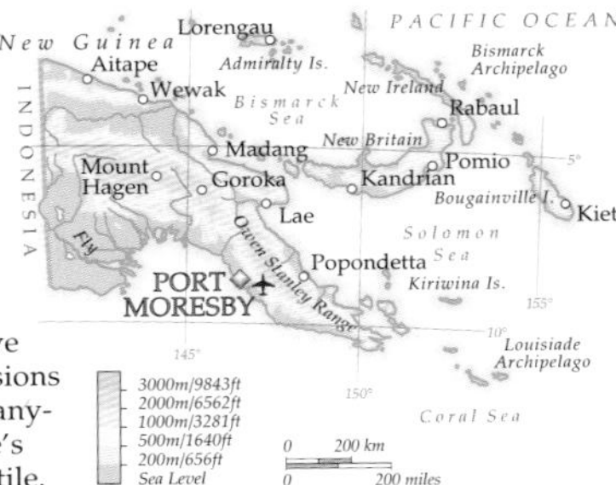
PACIFIC OCEAN
New Guinea
Lorengau
Admiralty Is.
Bismarck Archipelago
Aitape
Wewak
Bismarck Sea
New Ireland
Rabaul
INDONESIA
Madang
New Britain
Pomio
Mount Hagen
Goroka
Kandrian
Bougainville I.
Kieta
Lae
Solomon Sea
Fly
Owen Stanley Range
Popondetta
PORT MORESBY
Kiriwina Is.
Louisiade Archipelago
Coral Sea
145°
150°
155°
10°
5°
3000m/9843ft
2000m/6562ft
1000m/3281ft
500m/1640ft
200m/656ft
Sea Level
0 200 km
0 200 miles

FACT FILE

OFFICIAL NAME: The Independent State of Papua New Guinea
DATE OF FORMATION: 1975
CAPITAL: Port Moresby
POPULATION: 4.1 million
TOTAL AREA: 462,840 sq km (178,700 sq miles)
DENSITY: 9 people per sq km
LANGUAGES: Pidgin English*, Motu*, Papuan, 750 (est.) native languages
RELIGIONS: Christian 66%, other 34%
ETHNIC MIX: Papuan 85%, other 15%
GOVERNMENT: Parliamentary democracy
CURRENCY: Kina = 100 toea

SOLOMON ISLANDS

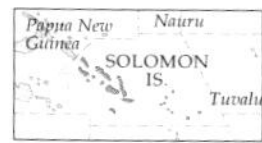
Papua New Guinea
Nauru
SOLOMON IS.
Tuvalu

THE SOLOMONS archipelago comprises several hundred islands scattered in the southwestern Pacific. Independence from Britain came in 1978.

GEOGRAPHY

The six largest islands are volcanic, mountainous and thickly forested. Flat coastal plains provide the only cultivable land.

CLIMATE

Northern islands are hot and humid all year round; further south a cool season develops. November–April wet season brings cyclones.

PEOPLE AND SOCIETY

Most Solomon Islanders are Melanesian. Around 87 native languages are spoken, but Pidgin English is used as a contact language between tribes. Most people live on shifting, subsistence agriculture in small rural villages. Villagers work collectively on community projects and there is much sharing among clans. Animist beliefs are maintained alongside Christianity.

THE ECONOMY

Main products are palm oil, copra, cocoa, fish and timber. Bauxite deposits found on Rennell Island, but islanders persuaded the government that exploiting them would destroy the island.

◆ *INSIGHT: The Solomons have no television service; the islanders oppose television as it might dilute their culture*

PACIFIC OCEAN
Choiseul
Santa Isabel
New Georgia
Gizo
Munda
Malaita
Santa Cruz Islands
HONIARA
Kirakira
Lata
New Georgia Is.
San Cristobal
Solomon Sea
Rennell
160°
165°
170°
500m/1640ft
Sea Level
0 200 km
0 200 miles

FACT FILE

OFFICIAL NAME: Solomon Islands
DATE OF FORMATION: 1978
CAPITAL: Honiara
POPULATION: 400,000
TOTAL AREA: 289,000 sq km (111,583 sq miles)
DENSITY: 11 people per sq km
LANGUAGES: English*, Pidgin English, 87 (est.) native languages
RELIGIONS: Christian 91%, other 9%
ETHNIC MIX: Melanesian 94%, other (Polynesian, Chinese, European) 6%
GOVERNMENT: Parliamentary democracy
CURRENCY: Solomon Is. $ = 100 cents

PALAU

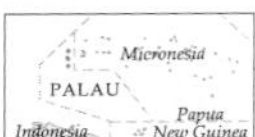
Micronesia
PALAU
Papua New Guinea
Indonesia

THE PALAU archipelago, a group of over 300 islands, lies in the western Pacific Ocean. In 1994, it became the world's newest independent state.

GEOGRAPHY

Terrain varies from thickly-forested mountains to limestone and coral reefs. Babelthuap, the largest island, is volcanic, with many rivers and waterfalls.

CLIMATE

Hot and wet. Little variation in daily and seasonal temperatures. February–April is the dry season.

PEOPLE AND SOCIETY

Palau was the last remaining US-administered UN Trust Territory of the Pacific Islands, until 1994. Only nine islands are inhabited and two-thirds of the population live in Koror. Society is matrilineal; women choose which males will be the clan chiefs. Local traditions remain strong, despite US influence.

◆ *INSIGHT: Palau's reefs contain 1,500 species of fish and 700 types of coral*

THE ECONOMY

Subsistence level. Main crops are coconuts and cassava. Revenue from fishing licences and tourism. Heavily reliant on US aid.

134°30'
Ngaruangl
Kayangel Islands
8°
200m/656ft
Sea Level
0
30 km
0
30 miles
Konrei
Ngardmau
Melekeiok
Babelthuap
PACIFIC OCEAN
OREOR
Airai
Oreor
Urukthapel
Eil Malk
Peleliu
7°
Angaur

FACT FILE

OFFICIAL NAME: Republic of Palau
DATE OF FORMATION: 1994
CAPITAL: Oreor
POPULATION: 16,000
TOTAL AREA: 497 sq km (192 sq miles)
DENSITY: 30 people per sq km
LANGUAGES: Palauan*, English*, Sonsorolese-Tobian, other
RELIGIONS: Christian (mainly Catholic) 70%, traditional beliefs 30%
ETHNIC MIX: Palaun 99%, other (mainly Filipino) 1%
GOVERNMENT: Multiparty republic
CURRENCY: US $ = 100 cents

MICRONESIA

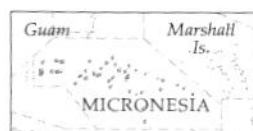
Guam
Marshall Is.
MICRONESIA

THE FEDERATED States of Micronesia, situated in the western Pacific, comprise 607 islands and atolls grouped into four main island states.

GEOGRAPHY

Mixture of high volcanic islands with forested interiors, and low-lying coral atolls. Some islands have coastal mangrove swamps.

CLIMATE

Tropical, with high humidity. Very heavy rainfall outside the January–March dry season.

◆ *INSIGHT: A major Japanese naval base during World War II, Chuuk's lagoon contains the sunken wrecks of over 100 Japanese ships and 270 planes*

PEOPLE AND SOCIETY

Part of the US-administered UN Trust Territory of the Pacific Islands, until independence in 1979, but it still relies on US aid, which funds food stamps, schools and hospitals. Most islanders live without electricity or running water. Society is traditionally matrilineal.

THE ECONOMY

Fishing and copra production are the mainstays. Construction industry is largest private-sector activity. High unemployment.

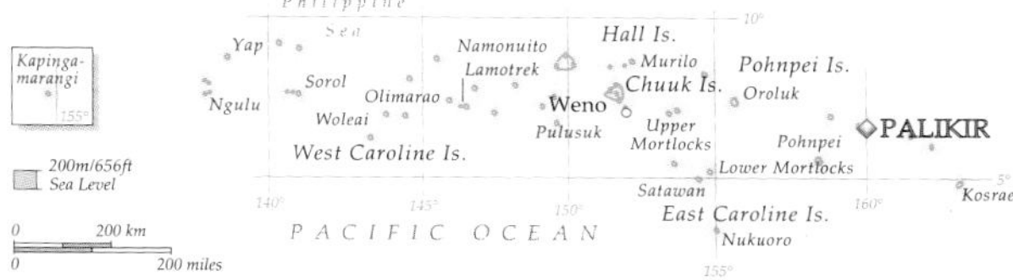
Philippine Sea
Kapingamarangi
Yap
Ngulu
Sorol
Woleai
Olimarao
Namonuito
Lamotrek
West Caroline Is.
Hall Is.
Murilo
Chuuk Is.
Weno
Pulusuk
Upper Mortlocks
Pohnpei Is.
Oroluk
Pohnpei
PALIKIR
Lower Mortlocks
Satawan
East Caroline Is.
Nukuoro
Kosrae
PACIFIC OCEAN
200m/656ft
Sea Level
0 200 km
0 200 miles

FACT FILE

OFFICIAL NAME: Federated States of Micronesia
DATE OF FORMATION: 1986
CAPITAL: Palikir
POPULATION: 101,000
TOTAL AREA: 2,900 sq km (1,120 sq miles)
DENSITY: 144 people per sq km
LANGUAGES: English*, Trukese, Pohnpeian, Mortlockese, other
RELIGIONS: Catholic 50%, Protestant 48%, other 2%
ETHNIC MIX: Micronesian 99%, other 1%
GOVERNMENT: Republic
CURRENCY: US $ = 100 cents

MARSHALL ISLANDS

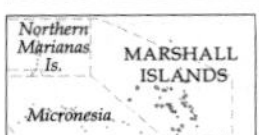
Northern Marianas Is.
MARSHALL ISLANDS
Micronesia

UNDER US rule as part of the UN Trust Territory of the Pacific Islands until independence in 1986, the Marshall Islands comprise a group of 34 atolls.

GEOGRAPHY

Narrow coral rings with sandy beaches enclosing lagoons. Those in the south have thicker vegetation. Kwajalein is the world's largest atoll.

CLIMATE

Tropical oceanic, cooled year-round by northeast trade winds.

PEOPLE AND SOCIETY

Majuro, the capital and commercial centre, is home to almost half the population. Tensions are high due to poor living conditions. Life on the outlying islands is still traditional, based around subsistence agriculture and fishing. Society is matrilineal: chiefly titles descend through the mother.

◆ *INSIGHT: In 1954, Bikini atoll was the site for the testing of the largest US H-bomb – the 18–22 megaton* Bravo

THE ECONOMY

Almost totally dependent on US aid and the rent paid by the US for its missile base on Kwajalein atoll. Revenue from Japan for use of Marshallese waters for tuna-fishing. Copra and coconut oil are the only significant agricultural exports.

Bokak
PACIFIC OCEAN
Enewetak
Bikini
Rongelap
Ratik Chain
10°
Likiep
Wotje
Ujelang
Kwajalein
Maloelap
164°
Ralik Chain
Jabat
MAJURO
Majuro
All land under 100m/328ft
Jaluit
Narikrik
0 200 km
0 200 miles
Ebon
170°

FACT FILE

OFFICIAL NAME: Republic of the Marshall Islands
DATE OF FORMATION: 1986
CAPITAL: Majuro
POPULATION: 48,000
TOTAL AREA: 181 sq km (70 sq miles)
DENSITY: 265 people per sq km
LANGUAGES: English*, Marshallese*
RELIGIONS: Protestant 80%, Catholic 15%, other 5%
ETHNIC MIX: Marshallese 90%, other Pacific islanders 10%
GOVERNMENT: Republic
CURRENCY: US $ = 100 cents

NAURU

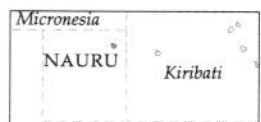
Micronesia
NAURU
Kiribati

NAURU LIES in the Pacific, 4,000 km (2,480 miles) northeast of Australia. Phosphate deposits have made its citizens among the richest in the world.

GEOGRAPHY

Low-lying coral atoll, with a fertile coastal belt. Coral cliffs encircle an elevated interior plateau.

CLIMATE

Equatorial, moderated by sea breezes. Occasional long droughts.

PEOPLE AND SOCIETY

Native Nauruans are of mixed Micronesian and Polynesian origin. Most live in simple, traditional houses and spend their money on luxury cars and consumer goods. Government provides free welfare and education. Diet of imported processed foods has caused widespread obesity and diabetes. Mining is left to an imported labour force, mainly from Kiribati. Many young attend boarding school in Australia.

◆ *INSIGHT: Phosphate mining has left 80% of the island uninhabitable*

THE ECONOMY

Phosphate, the only resource, is sold to Pacific Rim countries for use as a fertilizer. Deposits are near exhaustion. Huge investments in Australian and Hawaiian property. Possible future as a tax haven.

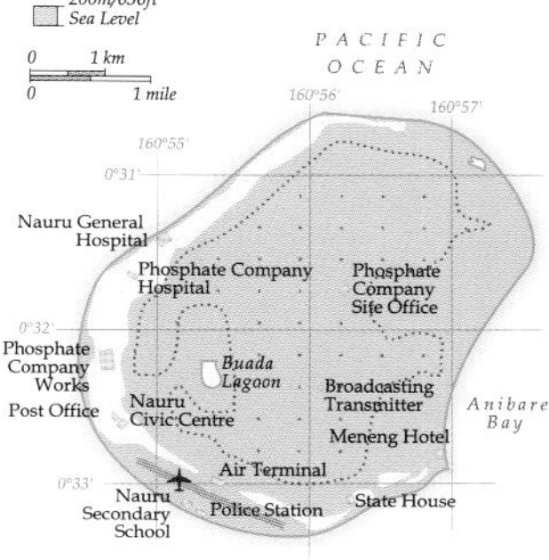
200m/656ft
Sea Level
0 1 km
0 1 mile
PACIFIC OCEAN
160°56'
160°57'
160°55'
0°31'
0°32'
0°33'
Nauru General Hospital
Phosphate Company Hospital
Phosphate Company Site Office
Phosphate Company Works
Post Office
Buada Lagoon
Nauru Civic Centre
Broadcasting Transmitter
Anibare Bay
Meneng Hotel
Air Terminal
Nauru Secondary School
Police Station
State House

FACT FILE

OFFICIAL NAME: Republic of Nauru
DATE OF FORMATION: 1968
CAPITAL: No official capital
POPULATION: 10,000
TOTAL AREA: 21.2 sq km (8.2 sq miles)
DENSITY: 428 people per sq km
LANGUAGES: Nauruan*, English, other
RELIGIONS: Christian 95%, other 5%
ETHNIC MIX: Nauruan 58%, other Pacific islanders 26%, Chinese 8%, European 8%
GOVERNMENT: Parliamentary democracy
CURRENCY: Australian $ = 100 cents

KIRIBATI

Marshall Is.
KIRIBATI
Tuvalu Tokelau
Cook Is.

PART OF the British colony of the Gilbert and Ellice Islands until independence in 1979, Kiribati comprises 33 islands in the mid-Pacific Ocean.

GEOGRAPHY

Three groups of tiny, very low-lying coral atolls scattered across 5 million sq km (1,930,000 sq miles) of ocean. Most have central lagoons.

CLIMATE

Central islands have maritime equatorial climate. Those to north and south are tropical, with constant high temperatures. Little rainfall.

PEOPLE AND SOCIETY

Locals still refer to themselves as Gilbertese. Apart from the inhabitants of Banaba, who employed anthropologists to establish their racial distinction, almost all people are Micronesian. Most are poor subsistence farmers. The islands are effectively ruled by traditional chiefs, though there is a party system based on the British model.

THE ECONOMY

Until 1980, when deposits ran out, phosphate from Banaba provided 80% of exports. Since then, coconuts, copra, fish, have become main exports, but the islands are heavily dependent on foreign aid.

◆ *INSIGHT: In 1981, the UK paid A$10 million in damages to Banabans for the destruction of their island by mining*

Tarawa
Bonriki
Betio
BAIRIKI

PACIFIC OCEAN
Gilbert Is.
Tarawa
Banaba (Ocean I.)
Phoenix Is.
Kiritimati
Line Islands
Equator
All land under 200m/656ft
0 600 km
0 600 miles

FACT FILE

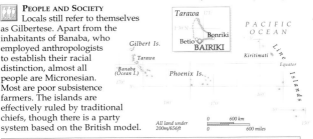

OFFICIAL NAME: Republic of Kiribati
DATE OF FORMATION: 1979
CAPITAL: Bairiki
POPULATION: 7,500
TOTAL AREA: 710 sq km (274 sq miles)
DENSITY: 93 people per sq km
LANGUAGES: English*, Kiribati, other
RELIGIONS: Catholic 53%, Protestant (mainly Congregational) 40%, other Christian 4%, other 3%
ETHNIC MIX: I-Kiribati 98%, other 2%,
GOVERNMENT: Multiparty republic
CURRENCY: Australian $ = 100 cents

TUVALU

Kiribati
TUVALU
Solomon Is.

A TINY isolated state, linked to the Gilbert Islands as a British colony until independence in 1978, Tuvalu's nine islands lie in the central Pacific.

GEOGRAPHY

Coral atolls, none more than 4.6 metres (15 feet) above sea level. Poor soils restrict vegetation to bush, coconut palms and breadfruit trees.

CLIMATE

Hot all year round. Heavy annual rainfall. Hurricane season brings many violent storms.

PEOPLE AND SOCIETY

People are mostly Polynesian, related to the Samoans and Tongans. Almost half the population live on Funafuti, where government jobs are centred. Life is communal and traditional. Most people live by subsistence farming, digging pits out of the coral to grow crops. Fresh water is precious due to frequent droughts.

◆ *INSIGHT: Tuvaluans have a reputation as excellent sailors. Many work overseas as merchant seamen on foreign ships*

THE ECONOMY

World's smallest economy. Fish stocks exploited mainly by foreign boats in return for licensing fees. Exports are few: copra, stamps and garments. Aid is crucial.

Nanumea
Niutao
Nanumaga
PACIFIC OCEAN
Nui
Vaitupu
Nukufetau
FONGAFALE
Funafuti
PACIFIC OCEAN
Nukulaelae
200m/656ft
Sea Level
0
100 km
0
100 miles
Niulakita

FACT FILE

OFFICIAL NAME: Tuvalu
DATE OF FORMATION: 1978
CAPITAL: Fongafale
POPULATION: 9,000
TOTAL AREA: 26 sq km (10 sq miles)
DENSITY: 346 people per sq km
LANGUAGES: Tuvaluan, Kiribati, other (no official language)
RELIGIONS: Protestant 97%, other 3%
ETHNIC MIX: Tuvaluan 95%, other (inc. Micronesian, I-Kiribati) 5%
GOVERNMENT: Constitutional monarchy
CURRENCY: Australian \$ = 100 cents

SAMOA

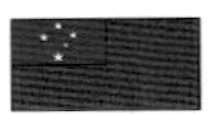

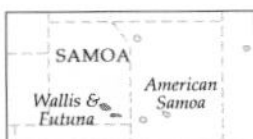
SAMOA
Wallis & Futuna
American Samoa

THE SOUTHERN Pacific islands of Samoa gained independence from New Zealand in 1962. Four of the nine islands are inhabited.

GEOGRAPHY

Comprises two large islands and seven smaller ones. Two largest islands have rainforested, mountainous interiors surrounded by coastal lowlands and coral reefs.

CLIMATE

Tropical, with high humidity. Cooler May–November. Hurricane season December–March.

PEOPLE AND SOCIETY

Ethnic Samoans are world's second largest Polynesian group, after the Maoris. Way of life is communal and formalized. Extended family groups own 80% of the land. Each family has an elected chief, who looks after its political and social interests. Large-scale migration to the US and New Zealand reflects lack of jobs and attractions of Western lifestyle.

THE ECONOMY

Agricultural products include taro, coconut cream, cocoa and copra. Growth of service sector since 1989 launch of offshore banking. Dependent on aid and expatriate remittances. Rainforests increasingly exploited for timber.

◆ *INSIGHT: Samoa was named for the sacred* (sa) *chickens* (moa) *of Lu, son of Tagaloa, the god of creation*

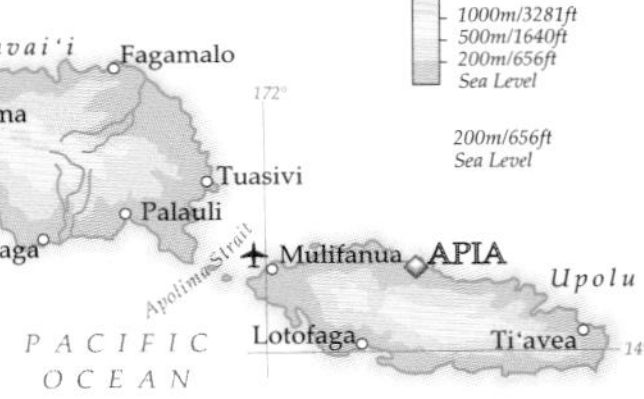
Savai'i
Fagamalo
Falelima
Tuasivi
Palauli
Taga
Apolima Strait
Mulifanua
APIA
Upolu
Lotofaga
Ti'avea
PACIFIC OCEAN
172°
14°
1000m/3281ft
500m/1640ft
200m/656ft
Sea Level
200m/656ft
Sea Level

FACT FILE

OFFICIAL NAME: Independent State of Samoa
DATE OF FORMATION: 1962
CAPITAL: Apia
POPULATION: 162,000
TOTAL AREA: 2,840 sq km (1,027 sq miles)
DENSITY: 60 people per sq km
LANGUAGES: Samoan*, English*
RELIGIONS: Protestant (mostly Congregational) 74%, Catholic 26%
ETHNIC MIX: Samoan 93%, mixed European and Polynesian 7%
GOVERNMENT: Parliamentary state
CURRENCY: Tala = 100 sene

TONGA

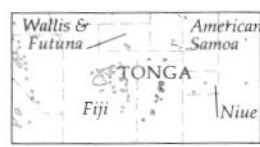
Wallis & Futuna
American Samoa
TONGA
Fiji
Niue

TONGA IS an archipelago of 170 islands, 45 of which are inhabited, in the South Pacific. Politics is effectively controlled by the king.

GEOGRAPHY

Easterly islands are generally low and fertile. Those in the west are higher and volcanic in origin.

CLIMATE

Tropical oceanic. Temperatures range between 20°C (68°F) and 30°C (86°F) all year round. Heavy rainfall, especially February–March.

PEOPLE AND SOCIETY

The last remaining Polynesian monarchy, and the only Pacific state never brought under foreign rule. All land is property of the crown, but is administered by nobles who allot it to the common people. Respect for traditional institutions and values remains high, although younger, Westernized Tongans are starting to question some attitudes.

◆ *INSIGHT: Tonga has the world's lowest annual death rate at one in 2,790*

THE ECONOMY

Most people are subsistence farmers. Commercial production of coconuts, cassava and passion fruit. Tourism is increasing slowly.

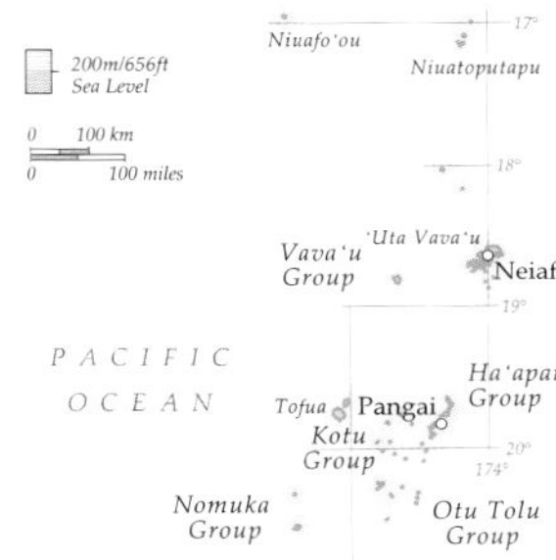
200m/656ft
Sea Level
0 100 km
0 100 miles
Niuafo'ou
Niuatoputapu
17°
18°
'Uta Vava'u
Vava'u Group
Neiafu
19°
PACIFIC OCEAN
Ha'apai Group
Tofua
Pangai
Kotu Group
20°
174°
Nomuka Group
Otu Tolu Group
21°
NUKU'ALOFA
Tongatapu
Tongatapu Group
'Eua
'Ohonua
175°

FACT FILE

OFFICIAL NAME: Kingdom of Tonga
DATE OF FORMATION: 1970
CAPITAL: Nuku'alofa
POPULATION: 101,000
TOTAL AREA: 750 sq km (290 sq miles)
DENSITY: 131 people per sq km
LANGUAGES: Tongan*, English
RELIGIONS: Protestant 82% (mainly Methodist), Catholic 18%
ETHNIC MIX: Tongan 98%, mixed European and Polynesian 2%
GOVERNMENT: Constitutional monarchy
CURRENCY: Pa'anga = 100 seniti

NEW ZEALAND

Australia
NEW ZEALAND

LYING SOUTHEAST of Australia, New Zealand comprises the North and South Islands, separated by the Cook Strait, and many smaller islands.

GEOGRAPHY

North Island has mountain ranges, valleys and volcanic central plateau. South Island is mostly mountainous, with eastern lowlands.

CLIMATE

Generally temperate and damp. Extreme north is almost sub-tropical; southern winters are cold.

PEOPLE AND SOCIETY

Maoris were the first settlers, 1,200 years ago. Today's majority European population is descended mainly from British migrants who settled after 1840. Maoris' living and education standards are generally lower than average. Tense relations beween the two groups in recent years. Government now negotiating settlement of Maori land claims.

◆ *INSIGHT: New Zealand women were the first in the world to get the vote*

THE ECONOMY

Modern agricultural sector; world's biggest exporter of wool, cheese, butter and meat. Growing manufacturing industry. Tourism.

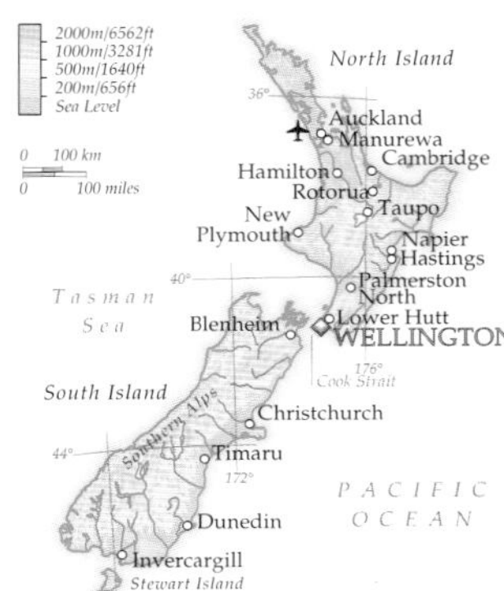
2000m/6562ft
1000m/3281ft
500m/1640ft
200m/656ft
Sea Level
0 100 km
0 100 miles
North Island
36°
Auckland
Manurewa
Hamilton
Cambridge
Rotorua
Taupo
New Plymouth
Napier
Hastings
40°
Palmerston North
Tasman Sea
Blenheim
Lower Hutt
WELLINGTON
176°
Cook Strait
South Island
Southern Alps
Christchurch
44°
Timaru
172°
PACIFIC OCEAN
Dunedin
Invercargill
Stewart Island
168°

FACT FILE

OFFICIAL NAME: The Dominion of New Zealand
DATE OF FORMATION: 1947
CAPITAL: Wellington
POPULATION: 3.5 million
TOTAL AREA: 268,680 sq km (103,730 sq miles)
DENSITY: 13 people per sq km
LANGUAGES: English*, Maori, other
RELIGIONS: Protestant 62%, Catholic 18%, other 20%
ETHNIC MIX: European 88%, Maori 9%, other (inc. Malay, Chinese) 3%
GOVERNMENT: Constitutional monarchy
CURRENCY: NZ $ = 100 cents

ANTARCTICA

Argentina
Chile
ANTARCTICA

THE CIRCUMPOLAR continent of Antarctica is almost entirely covered by ice over 2 km (1.2 miles) thick. It contains 90% of the Earth's fresh water reserves.

GEOGRAPHY & CLIMATE

The bulk of Antarctica's ice is contained in the Greater Antarctic Ice Sheet – a huge dome that rises steeply from the coast and flattens to a plateau in the interior. Powerful winds create a storm belt around the continent, which brings cloud, fog and blizzards. Winter temperatures can fall to –80°C (–112°F).

PEOPLE

No indigenous population. Scientists and logistical staff work at the 40 permanent, and as many as 100 temporary, research stations. A few Chilean settler families live on King George Island. Tourism is mostly by cruise ship to the Antarctic Peninsula. Tourist numbers increased by over 600% between 1985 and 1992.

TOTAL AREA:
13,900,000 sq km
(5,366,790 sq miles)

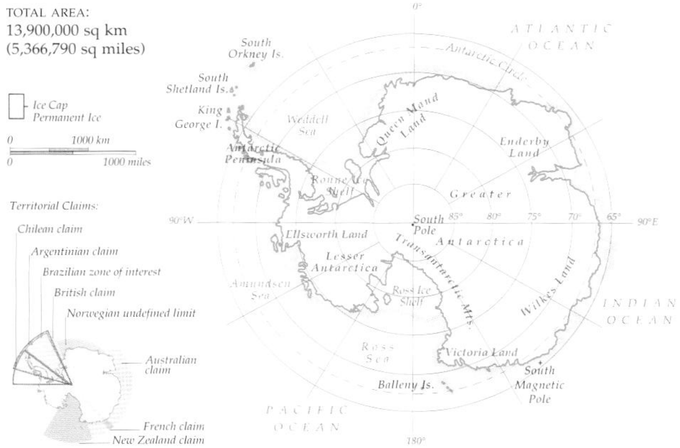
Ice Cap
Permanent Ice
0 1000 km
0 1000 miles
Territorial Claims:
Chilean claim
Argentinian claim
Brazilian zone of interest
British claim
Norwegian undefined limit
Australian claim
French claim
New Zealand claim
0°
ATLANTIC OCEAN
Antarctic Circle
South Orkney Is.
South Shetland Is.
King George I.
Weddell Sea
Antarctic Peninsula
Queen Maud Land
Enderby Land
Ronne Ice Shelf
Greater
90°W
South Pole
85° 80° 75° 70° 65°
90°E
Antarctica
Ellsworth Land
Transantarctic Mts.
Lesser Antarctica
Amundsen Sea
Ross Ice Shelf
Wilkes Land
INDIAN OCEAN
Ross Sea
Victoria Land
Balleny Is.
South Magnetic Pole
PACIFIC OCEAN
180°

The Antarctic Treaty of 1959 holds all territorial claims in abeyance in the interest of international co-operation

◆ *INSIGHT: If Antarctica's ice sheets were to melt, the world's oceans would rise by as much as 60–65 m (200–210 ft)*

OVERSEAS TERRITORIES

DESPITE THE rapid process of decolonization since World War II, around 10 million people in 59 territories around the world continue to live under the protection of either France, Australia, Denmark, Norway, Portugal, New Zealand, the UK, the USA, or the Netherlands. These territories are administered in a wide variety of ways.

AUSTRALIA

Australia's overseas territories have not been an issue since Papua New Guinea became independent in 1975. Consequently there is no over-riding policy towards them. Norfolk Island is inhabited by descendants of the *HMS Bounty* mutineers and more recent Australian migrants. Phosphate is mined on Christmas Island.

ASHMORE & CARTIER ISLANDS (Indian Ocean)

STATUS: External territory
CLAIMED: 1978
AREA: 5.2 sq km (2 sq miles)

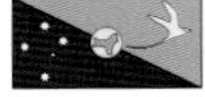

CHRISTMAS ISLAND (Indian Ocean)

STATUS: External territory
CLAIMED: 1958
CAPITAL: Flying Fish Cove
POPULATION: 1,275
AREA: 134.6 sq km (52 sq miles)

COCOS ISLANDS (Indian Ocean)

STATUS: External territory
CLAIMED: 1955
CAPITAL: West Island
POPULATION: 647
AREA: 14.24 sq km (5.5 sq miles)

CORAL SEA ISLANDS (S. Pacific)

STATUS: External territory
CLAIMED: 1969
POPULATION: 3 (meteorologists)
AREA: Less than 3 sq km (1.16 sq miles)

HEARD & MCDONALD ISLANDS (Indian Ocean)

STATUS: External territory
CLAIMED: 1947
AREA: 417 sq km (161 sq miles)

NORFOLK ISLAND (S. Pacific)

STATUS: External territory
CLAIMED: 1913
CAPITAL: Kingston
POPULATION: 2,665
AREA: 34.4 sq km (13.3 sq miles)

DENMARK

The Faeroe Islands have been under Danish administration since Queen Margrethe I of Denmark inherited Norway in 1380. The Home Rule Act of 1948 gave the Faeroese control over all their internal affairs. Greenland first came under Danish rule in 1380. Today, Denmark remains responsible for the island's foreign affairs and defence.

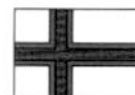

Faeroe Islands (N. Atlantic)

STATUS: External territory
CLAIMED: 1380
CAPITAL: Tórshavn
POPULATION: 48,065
AREA: 1,399 sq km (540 sq miles)

Strong sense of national identity. Voted against joining the EC with Denmark in 1973. Economy based on fishing, agriculture, Danish subsidies.

Greenland (N. Atlantic)

STATUS: External territory
CLAIMED: 1380
CAPITAL: Nuuk
POPULATION: 55,385
AREA: 2,175,516 sq km (840,000 sq miles)

World's largest island. Much of the land is permanently ice-covered. Self-governing since 1979. Left the EU in 1985. Population is a mixture of Inuit and European in origin.

France

France has developed economic ties with its *Territoires d'Outre-Mer,* thereby stressing interdependence over independence. Overseas *départements,* officially part of France, have their own governments. Territorial *collectivités* and overseas *territoires* have varying degrees of autonomy.

Clipperton Island (E. Pacific)

STATUS: Dependency of French Polynesia
CLAIMED: 1930
AREA: 7 sq km (2.7 sq miles)

French Guiana (S. America)

STATUS: Overseas department
CLAIMED: 1817
CAPITAL: Cayenne
POPULATION: 133,376
AREA: 90,996 sq km (35,135 sq miles)

The last colony in South America. Population is largely African and indigenous Indian. European Space Agency rocket launch facility.

French Polynesia (S. Pacific)

STATUS: Overseas territory
CLAIMED: 1843
CAPITAL: Papeete
POPULATION: 210,333
AREA: 4,165 sq km (1,608 sq miles)

Most people live on Tahiti. Economy dependent on tourism and French military. Recent calls for autonomy.

Guadeloupe (West Indies)

STATUS: Overseas department
CLAIMED: 1635
CAPITAL: Basse-Terre
POPULATION: 422,114
AREA: 1,780 sq km (687 sq miles)

Prospers from a strong infrastructure, plus French and EU aid. Indigenous population demands more autonomy.

Martinique (West Indies)

STATUS: Overseas department
CLAIMED: 1635
CAPITAL: Fort-de-France
POPULATION: 387,656
AREA: 1,100 sq km (425 sq miles)

Population largely of African origin. High living standards resulting from tourism and French subsidies.

MAYOTTE (Indian Ocean)

STATUS: Territorial collectivity
CLAIMED: 1843
CAPITAL: Mamoudzou
POPULATION: 89,938
AREA: 374 sq km (144 sq miles)

NEW CALEDONIA (S. Pacific)

STATUS: Overseas territory
CLAIMED: 1853
CAPITAL: Noumeá
POPULATION: 178,056
AREA: 19,103 sq km (7,374 sq miles)

Tensions between francophile expatriates and indigenous population over wealth inequalities and independence. Large nickel deposits.

RÉUNION (Indian Ocean)

STATUS: Overseas department
CLAIMED: 1638
CAPITAL: Saint-Denis
POPULATION: 639,622
AREA: 2,512 sq km (970 sq miles)

Wealth disparities between white and black communities. Ethnic tensions erupted into rioting in 1991. Large French military base.

ST PIERRE & MIQUELON (N. America)

STATUS: Territorial collectivity
CLAIMED: 1604
CAPITAL: Saint Pierre
POPULATION: 6,652
AREA: 242 sq km (93.4 sq miles)

WALLIS & FUTUNA (Pacific)

STATUS: Overseas territory
CLAIMED: 1842
CAPITAL: Mata-Utu
POPULATION: 14,175
AREA: 274 sq km (106 sq miles)

NETHERLANDS

The country's two remaining territories were formerly part of the Dutch West Indies. Both are now self-governing, but the Netherlands remains responsible for their defence.

ARUBA (West Indies)

STATUS: Autonomous part of the Netherlands
CLAIMED: 1643
CAPITAL: Oranjestad
POPULATION: 62,365
AREA: 194 sq kms (75 sq miles)

In 1990, Aruba requested and received from the Netherlands cancellation of the agreement to automatically give independence to the island in 1996.

NETHERLANDS ANTILLES (West Indies)

STATUS: Autonomous part of the Netherlands
CLAIMED: 1816
CAPITAL: Willemstad
POPULATION: 191,311
AREA: 800 sq km (308 sq miles)

Economy based on tourism, oil refining and offshore finance. Living standards are high. Political instability and allegations of drug-trafficking on smaller islands.

NEW ZEALAND

New Zealand's government has no desire to retain any overseas territories. However, the economic weakness of Tokelau, Niue and the Cook Islands has forced it to remain responsible for their foreign policy and defence.

Cook Islands (S. Pacific)

STATUS: Associated territory
CLAIMED: 1901
CAPITAL: Avarua
POPULATION: 18,903
AREA: 293 sq km (113 sq miles)

Niue (S. Pacific)

STATUS: Associated territory
CLAIMED: 1901
CAPITAL: Alofi
POPULATION: 1,977
AREA: 264 sq km (102 sq miles)

Tokelau (S. Pacific)

STATUS: Dependent territory
CLAIMED: 1926
POPULATION: 1,544
AREA: 10.4 sq km (4 sq miles)

Norway

In 1920, 41 nations signed the Spitsbergen treaty recognizing Norwegian sovereignty over Svalbard. There is a Nato base on Jan Mayen. Bouvet Island is a nature reserve.

Bouvet Island (S. Atlantic)

STATUS: Dependency
CLAIMED: 1928
AREA: 58 sq km (22 sq miles)

Jan Mayen (N. Atlantic)

STATUS: Dependency
CLAIMED: 1929
AREA: 381 sq km (147 sq miles)

Peter I Island (Southern Ocean)

STATUS: Dependency
CLAIMED: 1931
AREA: 180 sq km (69 sq miles)

Svalbard (Arctic Ocean)

STATUS: Dependency
CLAIMED: 1920
CAPITAL: Longyearbyen
POPULATION: 3,209
AREA: 62,906 sq km (24,289 sq miles)

In accordance with 1920 Spitsbergen Treaty, nationals of the treaty powers have equal rights to exploit Svalbard's coal deposits, subject to Norwegian regulation. The only companies still mining are Russian and Norwegian.

Portugal

After a coup in 1974, Portugal's overseas possessions were rapidly granted sovereignty. By 1976, Macao was the only one remaining.

Macao (S. China)

STATUS: Special territory
CLAIMED: 1557
CAPITAL: Macao
POPULATION: 477,850
AREA: 18 sq km (7 sq miles)

By agreement with Beijing in 1974, Macao is a Chinese territory under Portuguese administration. It is to become a Special Administrative Region of China in 1999. Macanese born before 1981 can claim a Portuguese passport.

United Kingdom

The UK has the largest number of overseas territories. Locally governed by a mixture of elected representatives and appointed officials, they all enjoy a large measure of internal self-government, but certain powers, such as foreign affairs and defence, are reserved for Governors of the British Crown.

ANGUILLA (West Indies)

STATUS: Dependent territory
CLAIMED: 1650
CAPITAL: The Valley
POPULATION: 8,960
AREA: 96 sq km (37 sq miles)

ASCENSION (Atlantic)

STATUS: Dependency of St Helena
CLAIMED: 1673
POPULATION: 1,099
AREA: 88 sq km (34 sq miles)

BERMUDA (N. Atlantic)

STATUS: Crown colony
CLAIMED: 1612
CAPITAL: Hamilton
POPULATION: 60,686
AREA: 53 sq km (20.5 sq miles)

Britain's oldest colony. People are of African or European descent. 74% voted against independence in 1995. One of the world's highest *per capita* incomes. Financial services and tourism are main currency earners.

BRITISH INDIAN OCEAN TERRITORY

STATUS: Dependent territory
CLAIMED: 1814
CAPITAL: Diego Garcia
POPULATION: 3,400
AREA: 60 sq km (23 sq miles)

BRITISH VIRGIN ISLANDS (West Indies)

STATUS: Dependent territory
CLAIMED: 1672
CAPITAL: Road Town
POPULATION: 16,644
AREA: 153 sq km (59 sq miles)

CAYMAN ISLANDS (West Indies)

STATUS: Dependent territory
CLAIMED: 1670
CAPITAL: George Town
POPULATION: 25,355
AREA: 259 sq km (100 sq km)

FALKLAND ISLANDS (S. Atlantic)

STATUS: Dependent territory
CLAIMED: 1832
CAPITAL: Stanley
POPULATION: 2,121
AREA: 12,173 sq km (4,699 sq miles)

British sovereignty not recognized by Argentina, despite Falklands War in 1982. Economy based on sheep farming, sale of fishing licenses. Large oil reserves have been discovered.

GIBRALTAR (S.W. Europe)

STATUS: Crown colony
CLAIMED: 1713
CAPITAL: Gibraltar
POPULATION: 28,074
AREA: 6.5 sq km (2.5 sq miles)

Disputes over sovereignty between UK and Spain. The colony has traditionally survived on military and marine revenues, but cuts in defence spending by the UK have led to the development of an offshore banking industry.

GUERNSEY (Channel Islands)

STATUS: Crown dependency
CLAIMED: 1066
CAPITAL: St Peter Port
POPULATION: 58,867
AREA: 65 sq km (25 sq miles)

ISLE OF MAN (British Isles)

STATUS: Crown dependency
CLAIMED: 1765
CAPITAL: Douglas
POPULATION: 69,788
AREA: 572 sq km (221 sq miles)

JERSEY (Channel Islands)

STATUS: Crown dependency
CLAIMED: 1066
CAPITAL: St Helier
POPULATION: 82,809
AREA: 116 sq km (45 sq miles)

MONTSERRAT (West Indies)

STATUS: Dependent territory
CLAIMED: 1632
CAPITAL: Plymouth
POPULATION: 11,852
AREA: 102 sq km (40 sq miles)

PITCAIRN ISLANDS (S. Pacific)

STATUS: Dependent territory
CLAIMED: 1887
CAPITAL: Adamstown
POPULATION: 52
AREA: 3.5 sq km (1.35 sq miles)

ST HELENA (Atlantic)

STATUS: Dependent territory
CLAIMED: 1673
CAPITAL: Jamestown
POPULATION: 6,720
AREA: 122 sq km (47 sq miles)

SOUTH GEORGIA & THE SANDWICH ISLANDS (S. Atlantic)

STATUS: Dependent territory
CLAIMED: 1775
POPULATION: No permanent residents
AREA: 3,592 sq km (1,387 sq miles)

TRISTAN DA CUNHA (S. Atlantic)

STATUS: Dependency of St Helena
CLAIMED: 1612
POPULATION: 297
AREA: 98 sq km (38 sq miles)

TURKS & CAICOS ISLANDS (West Indies)

STATUS: Dependent territory
CLAIMED: 1766
CAPITAL: Cockburn Town
POPULATION: 12,350
AREA: 430 sq km (166 sq miles)

UNITED STATES OF AMERICA

US Commonwealth territories are self-governing incorporated territories that are an integral part of the US. Unincorporated territories have varying degrees of autonomy.

AMERICAN SAMOA (S. Pacific)

STATUS: Unincorporated territory
CLAIMED: 1900
CAPITAL: Pago Pago
POPULATION: 50,923
AREA: 195 sq km (75 sq miles)

BAKER AND HOWLAND ISLANDS (S. Pacific)

STATUS: Unincorporated territory
CLAIMED: 1856
AREA: 1.4 sq km (0.54 sq miles)

GUAM (W. Pacific)

STATUS: Unincorporated territory
CLAIMED: 1898
CAPITAL: Agaña
POPULATION: 133,152
AREA: 549 sq km (212 sq miles)

JARVIS ISLAND (Pacific)

STATUS: Unincorporated territory
CLAIMED: 1856
AREA: 4.5 sq km (1.7 sq miles)

JOHNSTON ATOLL (Pacific)

STATUS: Unincorporated territory
CLAIMED: 1858
POPULATION: 1,375
AREA: 2.8 sq km (1 sq miles)

KINGMAN REEF (Pacific)

STATUS: Administered territory
CLAIMED: 1856
AREA: 1 sq km (0.4 sq miles)

MIDWAY ISLANDS (Pacific)

STATUS: Administered territory
CLAIMED: 1867
POPULATION: 453
AREA: 5.2 sq km (2 sq miles)

NAVASSA ISLAND (West Indies)

STATUS: Unincorporated territory
CLAIMED: 1856
AREA: 5.2 sq km (2 sq miles)

NORTHERN MARIANA IS. (Pacific)

STATUS: Commonwealth territory
CLAIMED: 1947
CAPITAL: Saipan
POPULATION: 48,581
AREA: 457 sq km (177 sq miles)

PALMYRA ATOLL (Pacific)

STATUS: Unincorporated territory
CLAIMED: 1898
AREA: 12 sq km (5 sq miles)

PUERTO RICO (West Indies)

STATUS: Commonwealth territory
CLAIMED: 1898
CAPITAL: San Juan
POPULATION: 3.6 million
AREA: 8,959 sq km (3,458 sq km)

Population voted in 1993 to maintain the current compromise between statehood and independence.

V
I

VIRGIN ISLANDS (West Indies)

STATUS: Unincorporated territory
CLAIMED: 1917
CAPITAL: Charlotte Amalie
POPULATION: 101,809
AREA: 355 sq km (137 sq miles)

WAKE ISLAND (Pacific)

STATUS: Unincorporated territory
CLAIMED: 1898
POPULATION: 302
AREA: 6.5 sq km (2.5 sq miles)

INTERNATIONAL ORGANIZATIONS

THIS LISTING provides acronym definitions for the main international organizations concerned with economics, trade and defence, plus an indication of membership.

ASEAN
Association of Southeast Asian Nations
ESTABLISHED: 1989 MEMBERS: Brunei, Indonesia, Malaysia, Singapore, Thailand

CIS
Commonwealth of Independent States
ESTABLISHED: 1991 MEMBERS: Armenia, Belorussia (Belarus), Kazakhstan, Kyrgyzstan, Moldavia (Moldova), Russia, Tajikistan, Turkmenistan, Ukraine, Uzbekistan

COMM
The Commonwealth
ESTABLISHED: 1931; evolved out of the British Empire. Formerly known as the British Commonwealth of Nations. MEMBERS: 53

EU
European Union
ESTABLISHED: 1965; formerly known as EEC (European Economic Community) and EC (Economic Community) MEMBERS: Belgium, Denmark, France, Germany, Greece, Ireland, Italy, Luxembourg, Netherlands, Portugal, Spain, UK, Austria, Finland and Sweden

GATT
General Agreement on Tariffs and Trade
ESTABLISHED: 1947 MEMBERS: 104

G7
Group of 7
ESTABLISHED: 1985 MEMBERS: Canada, France, Germany, Italy, Japan, UK, US

IMF
International Monetary Fund (UN agency)
ESTABLISHED: 1944 MEMBERS: 175

NAFTA
North American Free Trade Agreement
ESTABLISHED: 1994 MEMBERS: Canada, Mexico, US

NATO
North Atlantic Treaty Organization
ESTABLISHED: 1949 MEMBERS: Belgium, Canada, Denmark, France, Germany, Greece, Iceland, Italy, Luxembourg, Netherlands, Norway, Spain, Turkey, UK, US

OPEC
Organization of Petroleum Exporting Countries
ESTABLISHED: 1960 MEMBERS: Algeria, Gabon, Indonesia, Iran, Iraq, Kuwait, Libya, Nigeria, Qatar, Saudi Arabia, United Arab Emirates, Venezuela

UN
United Nations
ESTABLISHED: 1945 MEMBERS: 184; all nations are represented, except Palau, Kiribati, Nauru, Taiwan, Tonga and Tuvalu. Switzerland and Vatican City have 'observer status' only.

KEY

International border

Disputed border

Claimed border

Ceasefire line

State/Province border

River

Lake

Canal

Seasonal river

Seasonal lake

Waterfall

Capital city

Other towns

International airport

Spot height - feet

Spot depth - feet

The asterisk in the Fact File denotes the country's official language(s)

DATE OF FORMATION in the Fact File denotes the date of political origin or independence; the second date (if any) identifies when its current borders were established

ABBREVIATIONS

Abbreviations used throughout this book are listed below:

abbrev. abbreviation
Afgh. Afghanistan
Arm. Armenia
Aus. Austria
Aust. Australia
Az. Azerbaijan

Bel. Belorussia (Belarus)
Belg. Belgium
Bos. & Herz. Bosnia & Herzegovina
Bulg. Bulgaria

C. Central
C. Cape
Cam. Cambodia
CAR Central African Republic
Czech Rep. Czech Republic

D.C. District of Columbia
Dominican Rep. Dominican Republic

E. East
EQ. Equatorial
Est. Estonia
est. estimated

Fr. France
ft feet

Geo. Georgia
Ger. Germany

Hung. Hungary

I. Island
Is. Islands
inc. including

Kaz. Kazakhstan
km kilometres
Kyrgy. Kyrgyzstan

L. Lake, Lago
Lat. Latvia
Leb. Lebanon
Liech. Liechtenstein
Lith. Lithuania
Lux. Luxembourg

m metres
mi. miles
Mac. Macedonia
Med. Sea Mediterranean Sea
Mold. Moldavia (Moldova)
Mt. Mount / Mountain
Mts. Mountains

N. North
N. Korea North Korea
Neth. Netherlands
NZ New Zealand

Peg. Pegunungan (Indonesian / Malay for mountain range)
Pol. Poland

R. River, Rio, Río
Rep. Republic
Res. Reservoir
Rom. Romania
Russ. Fed. Russian Federation

S. South / Southern
S. Korea South Korea
SA South Africa
Slvka. Slovakia
Slvna. Slovenia
St/St. Saint
Str. Strait
Switz. Switzerland

Tajik. Tajikistan
Turkmen. Turkmenistan

UAE United Arab Emirates
UK United Kingdom
USA/US United States of America
Uzbek. Uzbekistan

Ven. Venezuela

W. West
W. Sahara Western Sahara

yds yards
Yugo. Yugoslavia

INDEX

KEY:
❍ = Country
❑ = Overseas territory

Afghanistan ❍ SW. Asia, 160, 186
Albania ❍ S. Europe, 114, 150
Algeria ❍ N. Africa, 58, 61
American Samoa ❑ Pacific , 235
Andorra ❍ SW. Europe, 114, 133
Angola ❍ C. Africa, 58, 98
Anguilla ❑ W. Indies, 234
Antarctica ❍ S. hemisphere, 212, 229
Antigua & Barbuda ❍ W. Indies, 14, 35
Argentina ❍ S. America, 42, 56
Armenia ❍ SW. Asia, 160, 163
Aruba ❑ W. Indies, 232
Ascension ❑ Atlantic, 234
Ashmore & Cartier Is. ❑ Indian Ocean, 230
Australia ❍ Indian Ocean/ Pacific, 212, 214
Austria ❍ C. Europe, 114, 142
Azerbaijan ❍ SW. Asia, 160, 162

Bahamas ❍ W. Indies, 14, 31
Bahrain ❍ SW. Asia, 160, 176
Baker & Howland Is. ❑ Pacific, 235
Bangladesh ❍ S. Asia, 160, 194
Barbados ❍ W. Indies, 14, 39
Belarus see Belorussia
Belgium ❍ W. Europe, 114, 127
Belize ❍ C. America, 14, 23
Belorussia ❍ E. Europe, 114, 156
Benin ❍ Africa, 58, 91
Bermuda ❑ Atlantic, 234
Bhutan ❍ S. Asia, 160, 189
Bolivia ❍ S. America, 42, 53
Bosnia & Herzegovina ❍ SE. Europe, 114, 148
Botswana ❍ S. Africa, 58, 105
Bouvet I. ❑ Atlantic 233
Brazil ❍ S. America, 42, 50
British Indian Ocean Territory ❑ Indian Ocean, 234
British Virgin Is. ❑ W. Indies, 234
Brunei ❍ E. Asia, 160, 203
Bulgaria ❍ E. Europe, 114, 152
Burkina ❍ W. Africa, 58, 88
Burma ❍ S. Asia, 160, 195
Burundi ❍ C. Africa, 58, 73

Cambodia ❍ SE. Asia, 160, 198
Cameroon ❍ W. Africa, 58, 93
Canada ❍ N. America, 14, 16
Cape Verde ❍ Atlantic, 58, 82
CAR see Central African Republic
Cayman Is. ❑ W. Indies, 234
Central African Republic ❍ C. Africa, 58, 74
Chad ❍ C. Africa, 58, 77
Chile ❍ S. America, 42, 52
China ❍ E. Asia, 160, 206
Christmas Island ❑ Indian Ocean, 230
Clipperton Island ❑ Pacific, 231
Cocos Is. ❑ Indian Ocean, 230
Colombia ❍ S. America, 42, 44
Comoros ❍ Indian Ocean, 58, 111
Congo ❍ C. Africa, 58, 97
Congo (Zaire) ❍ C. Africa, 58, 75
Cook Is. ❑ Pacific, 233
Coral Sea Is. ❑ Pacific, 230
Costa Rica ❍ C. America, 14, 27
Croatia ❍ SE. Europe, 114, 147
Cuba ❍ W. Indies, 14, 30
Cyprus ❍ Med Sea, 160, 168
Czech Republic ❍ C. Europe, 114, 144

Denmark ❍ NW. Europe, 114, 118
Djibouti ❍ NE. Africa, 58, 67
Dominica ❍ W. Indies, 14, 36
Dominican Republic ❍ W. Indies, 14, 33
Ecuador ❍ S. America, 42, 48
Egypt ❍ NE. Africa, 58, 64
El Salvador ❍ C. America, 14, 24
Equatorial Guinea ❍ W. Africa, 58, 94
Eritrea ❍ E. Africa, 58, 66
Estonia ❍ E. Europe, 114, 121
Ethiopia ❍ E. Africa, 58, 68

Faeroe Is. ❑ Atlantic, 231
Falkland Is. ❑ Atlantic, 234
Fiji ❍ Pacific, 212, 217
Finland ❍ N. Europe, 114, 120
France ❍ W. Europe, 114, 130
French Guiana ❑ S. America, 231
French Polynesia ❑ Pacific, 231

Gabon ❍ W. Africa, 58, 96
Gambia ❍ W. Africa, 58, 81
Georgia ❍ SW. Asia, 160, 165
Germany ❍ W. Europe, 114, 125
Ghana ❍ W. Africa, 58, 89
Gibraltar ❑ SW. Europe, 234
Greece ❍ SE. Europe, 114, 153
Greenland ❑ Atlantic, 231
Grenada ❍ W. Indies, 14, 40
Guadeloupe ❑ W. Indies, 231
Guam ❑ Pacfic, 236
Guatemala ❍ C. America, 14, 22
Guernsey ❑ W. Europe, 234
Guinea ❍ W. Africa, 58, 84
Guinea-Bissau ❍ W. Africa, 58, 83
Guyana ❍ S. America, 42, 46

Haiti ❍ W. Indies, 14, 32
Heard & McDonald Is. ❑ Indian Ocean, 230
Honduras ❍ C. America, 14, 25
Hungary ❍ C. Europe, 114, 143

Iceland ❍ Atlantic, 114, 116
India ❍ S. Asia, 160, 190
Indonesia ❍ SE. Asia, 160, 201
Iran ❍ SW. Asia, 160, 179
Iraq ❍ SW. Asia, 160, 178
Ireland, Republic of ❍ W. Europe, 114, 128
Israel ❍ SW. Asia, 160, 169
Italy ❍ S. Europe, 114, 136
Ivory Coast ❍ W. Africa, 58, 87

Jamaica ❍ W. Indies, 14, 29
Jan Mayen ❑ Atlantic, 233
Japan ❍ E. Asia, 160, 210
Jarvis I. ❑ Pacific, 236
Jersey ❑ W. Europe, 235
Johnston Atoll ❑ Pacific, 236
Jordan ❍ SW. Asia, 160, 170

Kazakhstan ❍ C. Asia, 160, 182
Kenya ❍ E. Africa , 58, 71
Kingman Reef ❑ Pacific, 236
Kiribati ❍ Pacific, 212, 224
Kuwait ❍ SW. Asia, 160, 177
Kyrgyzstan ❍ C. Asia, 160, 184

Laos ❍ SE. Asia, 160, 197
Latvia ❍ NE. Europe, 114, 122
Lebanon ❍ SW. Asia, 160, 166
Lesotho ❍ S. Africa, 58, 106
Liberia ❍ W. Africa, 58, 86
Libya ❍ N. Africa, 58, 63
Liechtenstein ❍, C. Europe, 114, 141
Lithuania ❍ E. Europe, 114, 123
Luxembourg ❍ W. Europe, 114, 131

Macao ❑ E. Asia, 233
Macedonia ❍ SE. Europe, 114, 151
Madagascar ❍ Indian Ocean, 58, 112

Malawi ❍ SE. Africa, 58, 101
Malaysia ❍ SE. Asia, 160, 200
Maldives ❍ Indian Ocean, 160, 192
Mali ❍ W. Africa, 58, 79
Malta ❍ Med. Sea, 114, 137
Man, Isle of ❑ W. Europe, 235
Marshall Is. ❍ Pacific, 212, 222
Martinique ❑ W. Indies, 231
Mauritania ❍ W. Africa, 58, 78
Mauritius ❍ Indian Ocean, 58, 113
Mayotte ❑ Indian Ocean, 232
Mexico ❍ C. America, 14, 20
Micronesia ❍ Pacific, 212, 222
Midway Is. ❑ Pacific, 236
Moldavia ❍ E. Europe, 114, 155
Moldova see Moldavia
Monaco ❍ W. Europe, 114, 132
Mongolia ❍ E. Asia, 160, 183
Montserrat ❑ W. Indies, 235
Morocco ❍ N. Africa, 58, 60
Mozambique ❍ SE Africa, 58, 103
Myanmar see Burma

Namibia ❍ S. Africa, 58, 104
Nauru ❍ Pacific, 212, 223
Navassa Island ❑ W. Indies, 236
Nepal ❍ S. Asia, 160, 188
Netherlands ❍ W. Europe, 114, 126
Netherlands Antilles ❑ W. Indies, 232
New Caledonia ❑ Pacific, 232
New Zealand ❍ Pacific, 212, 228
Nicaragua ❍ C. America, 14, 26
Niger ❍ W. Africa, 58, 76
Nigeria ❍ W. Africa, 58, 92
Niue ❑ Pacific, 233
Norfolk Island ❑ Pacific, 230
North Korea ❍ E. Asia, 160, 208
Northern Mariana Is. ❑ Pacific, 236
Norway ❍ N. Europe, 114, 11

Oman ❍ SW. Asia, 160, 173

Pakistan ❍ S. Asia, 160, 187
Palau ❍ Pacific, 212, 220
Palmyra Atoll ❑ Pacific, 236
Panama ❍ C. America, 14, 28
Papua New Guinea ❍ Indian Ocean/Pacific, 212, 218
Paraguay ❍ S. America, 42, 54
Peru ❍ S. America, 42, 49
Peter I Island ❑ Antarctica, 233
Philippines ❍ Asia, 160, 204
Pitcairn Is. ❑ Pacific, 235
PNG see Papua New Guinea
Poland ❍ E. Europe, 114, 124
Portugal ❍ W. Europe, 114, 134
Puerto Rico, ❑, W. Indies, 236

Qatar ❍ SW. Asia, 160, 175

Réunion ❑ Indian Ocean, 232
Romania ❍ SE. Europe, 114, 154
Russian Federation ❍ Asia/Europe, 158, 160
Rwanda ❍ C. Africa, 58, 72

Samoa ❍ Pacific, 212, 226
San Marino ❍ S. Europe, 114, 139
Sao Tome & Principe ❍ Atlantic, 58, 95
Saudi Arabia ❍ SW. Asia, 160, 171
Senegal ❍ W. Africa, 58, 80
Seychelles ❍ Indian Ocean, 58, 110
Sierra Leone ❍ W. Africa, 58, 85
Singapore ❍ SE. Asia, 160, 202
Slovakia ❍ C. Europe, 114, 145
Slovenia ❍ SE. Europe, 114, 146
Solomon Is. ❍ Pacific, 212, 219
Somalia ❍ E. Africa, 58, 69
South Africa ❍ S. Africa, 58, 108
South Georgia & the South Sandwich Is ❑ Atlantic, 235
South Korea ❍ E. Asia, 160, 209
Spain ❍ W. Europe, 114, 135
Sri Lanka ❍ S. Asia, 160, 193
St Helena ❑ Atlantic, 235
St Kitts & Nevis ❍ W. Indies, 14, 34
St Lucia ❍ W. Indies, 14, 37
St Pierre & Miquelon ❑ N. America, 232
St Vincent & the Grenadines ❍ W. Indies, 14, 38
Sudan ❍ NE. Africa, 58, 65
Surinam ❍ S. America, 42, 47
Svalbard ❑ Arctic Ocean, 233
Swaziland ❍ S. Africa, 58, 107
Sweden ❍ N. Europe, 114, 119
Switzerland ❍ C. Europe, 114, 140
Syria ❍ SW. Asia, 160, 167

Taiwan ❍ E. Asia, 160, 205
Tajikistan ❍ C. Asia, 160, 185
Tanzania ❍ E. Africa, 58, 100
Thailand ❍ SE. Asia, 160, 196
Togo ❍ W. Africa, 58, 90
Tokelau ❑ Pacific, 233
Tonga ❍ Pacific, 212, 227
Trinidad & Tobago ❍ W. Indies, 14, 41
Tristan da Cunha ❑. Atlantic, 235
Tunisia ❍ N. Africa, 58, 62
Turkey ❍ Europe/Asia, 160, 164
Turkmenistan ❍ C. Asia, 160, 180
Turks & Caicos Is. ❑ W. Indies, 235
Tuvalu ❍ Pacific, 212, 225

UAE see United Arab Emirates
Uganda ❍ C. Africa, 58, 71
Ukraine ❍ E. Europe, 114, 157
United Arab Emirates ❍ SW. Asia, 160, 174
United Kingdom (UK) ❍ NW. Europe, 114, 129
United States of America (USA) ❍ N. America, 14, 18
Uruguay ❍ S. America, 42, 55
Uzbekistan ❍ C. Asia, 160, 181

Vanuatu ❍ Pacific, 212, 216
Vatican City ❍ S. Europe, 114, 138
Venezuela ❍ S. America, 42, 45
Vietnam ❍ SE. Asia, 160, 199
Virgin Is. (US) ❑ W. Indies, 236

Wake I. ❑ Pacific, 236
Wallis & Futuna ❑ Pacific, 232

Yemen ❍ SW. Asia, 160, 172
Yugoslavia ❍ SE. Europe, 114, 149

Zambia ❍ S. Africa, 58, 99
Zimbabwe ❍ S. Africa, 58, 102